Global Islamic Politics

SECOND EDITION

Mir Zohair Husain

University of South Alabama

Longman

New York   San Francisco   Boston
London   Toronto   Sydney   Tokyo   Singapore   Madrid
Mexico City   Munich   Paris   Cape Town   Hong Kong   Montreal

On the cover:

Qubbat al-Sakhra (Dome of the Rock). Located in Jerusalem, for Muslims this commemorates Prophet Muhammad's ascension to heaven. Qubbat al-Sakhra is one of the oldest architectural monuments of Islamic civilization and metaphorically illustrates not only the connection between earth and heaven but between man and God as well. (See Box 7.4, page 187.)

Vice President and Publisher: Priscilla McGeehon
Executive Editor: Eric Stano
Marketing Manager: Megan Galvin-Fak
Senior Production Manager: Bob Ginsberg
Project Coordination, Text Design, and Electronic Page Makeup: Sunflower Publishing
    Services
Cover Designer/Manager: Wendy Ann Fredericks
Cover: PhotoLink/PhotoDisc/PictureQuest
Publishing Services Manager: Kara Frye
Printer and Binder: The Maple-Vail Book Manufacturing Group
Cover Printer: Phoenix Color Corporation

CIP data on file.

Please visit our website at http://www.ablongman.com

ISBN 0-321-12935-0

12345678910—MA—05040302

Contents

Preface

In the eight years since *Global Islamic Politics* (1995) was published, much has happened in the Muslim world and in international relations. I was, therefore, delighted and honored when Eric Stano, the executive editor at Longman Publishers, gave me permission to revise and update the book.

Islamism has consistently and dramatically caught the attention of the West in recent decades. With the end of the Cold War, dismemberment of the Soviet Union, and demise of communism in the former Soviet bloc, Islamism—also known as political Islam, Islamic fundamentalism, Islamic revivalism, or the Islamic revival—is now recognized as a potent force in international relations; and since the attacks on New York City and Washington, D.C., on September 11, 2001, it is now in the forefront of Western consciousness. Initiating both reform and revolution throughout the Muslim world, Islamism fueled Iran's 1979 Islamic Revolution and the concurrent "Islamization" campaign in Pakistan and Sudan. It contributed to turmoil in Lebanon, chased the well-equipped Soviets from Afghanistan, was responsible for the assassination of Egypt's President Muhammad Anwar al-Sadat, and has been an essential factor in the continuing Arab-Israeli dispute. Islamism has deep roots in Saudi Arabia, Algeria, Pakistan, Jordan, Tunisia, Morocco, and Egypt. Forms of Islamism run the gamut from moderate and modernist to reactionary and revolutionary.

Throughout the 1990s, and particularly during the period from the end of the Persian Gulf War until 2001, the West has not paid sufficient attention to the Muslim world. The tragic events of September 11, 2001, the ongoing cycle of violence in the Israeli-Palestinian dispute, and the United States' "war on terrorism" in several Muslim countries around the world have made it clear that a deeper understanding of Islamic politics and the major strains of Islamism in the Muslim world is needed.

The size and economic power of the Muslim world make the subject important for any student in world affairs. There are over 1.2 billion Muslims in the world, comprising one-fifth of humankind. They constitute a majority in at least fifty-five countries, a substantial minority in another seven countries, and a sizable minority in at least nine others. While present throughout the world, exhibiting numerous cultures, and speaking as many different languages, Muslims are most heavily concentrated in Asia, where they constitute more than two-thirds of the population. Africa comprises the second greatest concentration of Muslims, where they constitute more than a quarter of the population.

Muslim countries are active participants in a number of international organizations, the most prominent being the Organization of Arab Petroleum Exporting Countries (OAPEC), the Organization of Petroleum Exporting Countries (OPEC), the Arab League, the Organization of African Unity (OAU), the Association of Southeast Asian Nations (ASEAN), the Group of 77, the Organization of the Islamic Conference (OIC), the Non-Aligned Movement (NAM), and the United Nations.

A closer examination of global Islamic politics is further merited by the proximity of the Muslim world to seven strategically important sea routes, namely, the Mediterranean Sea, the Bosphorus, the Black Sea, the Suez Canal, the Red Sea, the Persian Gulf, and the Straits of Malacca. In addition, Muslim countries possess innumerable raw materials, produce nearly half the oil consumed in the West, and control two-thirds of the world's known oil reserves. Owning an exhaustible and vital international commodity—for which there are countless uses and no immediate substitutes—has greatly empowered the ten predominantly Muslim nations in the twelve-member Organization of Petroleum Exporting Countries (OPEC). Moreover, the Muslim world also possesses a substantial pool of inexpensive labor and is a lucrative market for goods and services.

In spite of the economic power and tremendous potential of the Muslim world, much of the region, stretching from Africa in the West to Asia in the East, suffers terrible poverty, inequality, and political oppression. The Muslim world endures all the political and economic ills of the Third World. Consequently, political changes in the Muslim world, as part of the interdependent international community, are inherently significant and deserve Western interest and concern. In recent years, the West has discouraged any political change that might threaten a "satisfactory" status quo in an area of such vital importance. Islamism represents just such a change.

The Middle East, which is an important part of the Muslim world, deserves particular attention. The region seems in perpetual crisis and is in the news every day of the week. The Middle East is the birthplace of three of the most prominent monotheistic religions in the world: Judaism, Christianity, and Islam. Founded in the Middle East, all three faiths have spread outside the Middle East. Today, the majority of their adherents live outside the region. This gives the Middle East a special significance to its inhabitants' coreligionists living around the world.

The Middle East is also known to possess many natural resources, such as petroleum, natural gas, iron ore, phosphate rock, and cotton, among others. In fact, over 55 percent of the world's known petroleum reserves are to be found in the Middle East. Petroleum and petroleum products are used in a myriad different ways all over the world, especially in highly industrialized, urbanized, and developed societies. Approximately 45 percent of the petroleum used in the United States is from the nation's own domestic oil wells, while 55 percent of U.S. petroleum comes from abroad—a significant portion of that coming from the Middle East. Approximately 60 percent of the world's phosphate rock (from which fertilizer, soap, and detergents are made) is found in Morocco and Morocco-controlled Western Sahara. Furthermore, with over 350 million people living in twenty-two countries, the Middle East provides a lucrative market for U.S. goods and services (including arms and technical military training).

In this age of globalization and global interdependence, an understanding of Islam and Muslims as well as the Muslim world and the Middle East is crucial. When there is an increase in tension between Israel and its Palestinian and Arab neighbors, the United States—which is Israel's most important strategic ally—sees an increase in anti-Americanism around the Muslim world. It is this conflict, as well as the stationing of U.S. troops in Saudi Arabia, that inspires anti-American anger and, among the most radicalized Islamists, support for terrorists like Osama bin Laden. However, anti-American sentiment should not be confused with support for terrorism. There are many negative stereotypes and misconceptions of Muslims and Islam. Many Muslims oppose U.S. policy in the Middle East; but they also oppose and denounce terrorism and believe that men like bin Laden have "hijacked" the true meaning of Islam. If bridges of understanding are not built between the West and the Muslim world, political scientist Samuel Huntington's thesis of a "clash of civilizations" will become a reality in the twenty-first century.

In the West today Revolutionary Islamism is as reviled an ideology as revolutionary Communism was before 1991. However, Western fear of Revolutionary Islamism is rooted less in reality than in misunderstanding. The Western mass media, focusing on the most sensational aspects of extremist Islamism, have contributed to its distortion by characterizing it as a monolithic, menacing, and inherently antimodern and anti-Western force; it is not. The primary intention of this book is, therefore, to explore, analyze, and explain global Islamic politics, its root causes, characteristics, consequences, and implications.

The single greatest barrier to an intelligent inquiry into political Islam is the ambiguity of related terminology. Terms like *Islamism, Islamic revival, Islamic fundamentalist, Islamic neofundamentalism, Islamic traditionalist, Islamic neotraditionalist, Islamic conservative, Islamic modernist*, and *Islamic* state are often vaguely and inconsistently approached. Definitions of Islamic terms and labels given to Muslims by the influential Western mass media are seldom satisfactory or comprehensive.

To help clarify Islamism, this book provides in-depth definitions of relevant terms. More than that, however, *Global Islamic Politics* is an attempt to present multilevel, multidisciplinary, and typological perspectives of the causes and manifestations of Islamism. This book also offers an examination of the historical precedents to modern Islamism, presents essential general information on the Muslim world through concise profiles of Muslim leaders and Islamists—Revolutionary Islamists, Traditionalist Islamists, and Modernist Islamists. Also included is a glossary of important concepts and Islamic terms, and a bibliography to assist those interested in further reading or research in the field. Finally, this work offers suggestions for ameliorating the relations between the Muslim World and the West in the hope that these recommendations may contribute to peace and understanding.

Major new features in this second edition include:

- Chapter One, "An Overview of Islam." This chapter contains twelve fascinating boxes that highlight vitally important facts and figures about Islam, Muslims, and the Muslim world; centrally important Islamic terms; and two key Islamic issues.

- One of Chapter One's most noteworthy features is Table 1.1, which succinctly and clearly compares and contrasts Islam, Judaism, and Christianity so that readers can learn about these three great monotheistic religions at a glance.

- Chapter Two, "Islamism and Islamic Revivals," has integrated and condensed Chapters One and Two of the first edition of *Global Islamic Politics*. There is a new box in Chapter Two: "Reasons for Anti-Western and Anti-American Sentiments in the Muslim World." The other two boxes, namely, *"Ikhwan al-Muslimeen"* and *"Jama'at-e-Islami,"* have been revised and shortened.

- The typology of Islamic Revivalists—including Muslim Fundamentalists, Muslim Traditionalists, Muslim Modernists, and Muslim pragmatists—discussed in four chapters in the first edition, has been thoroughly revised and updated for this second edition. Terms such as *Muslim Fundamentalist* and *Muslim Fundamentalism*, which most Muslims find objectionable, have been dropped and substituted with the terms *Revolutionary Islamist* and *Revolutionary Islamism,* which are far more value neutral. I have also substituted the terms *Muslim Traditionalists* and *Muslim Modernists* with *Traditionalist Islamists* and *Modernist Islamists.* In fact, throughout this second edition, the term *Islamists* (for both Islam-oriented individuals and organizations) and *Islamism* (Islamists promoting the Islamic worldview) have been used instead of *Islamic Revivalists* and *Islamic Revivalism.*

- The first edition's category of "Muslim Pragmatists" (secular Muslims who manipulate and/or exploit Islam, thereby contributing to Islamic revivals) has been excluded from the second edition. While the Muslim Pragmatists, along with the devout Islamic Revivalists or Islamists, contributed to Islamic Revivals, Muslim Pragmatists are for the most part Secularists rather than Islamists and thus cannot be included in the typology of Islamists. The typology is now discussed in three chapters of the second edition and ends with Table 5.1, "A Typology of Islamists," which concisely compares and contrasts the three types of Islamists—Revolutionary Islamists, Traditionalist Islamists, and Modernist Islamists. In fact, the first edition's chapter on "The Muslim Pragmatists" has been completely revamped, condensed, and incorporated into Box 6.1, "Who Are the Secularists?" which now appears in Chapter Six, "Failure of Muslim Secularists in the Postcolonial Muslim States."

- Chapter Six, "Failure of Muslim Secularists in the Postcolonial Muslim States," has been revised to include several new boxes, including ones about Turkey's Mustafa Kemal Ataturk, who tried not only to modernize but to Westernize Turkey; Ba'athism and Nasserism—two dominant ideologies in the Arab world till the late 1960s; and Sudan's Ja'afar al-Numeiri and Hasan al-Turabi. A boxed profile of the latter appears here because, although al-Turabi was an influential Revolutionary Islamist, Sudan and al-Turabi are briefly mentioned in Chapter Six.

- Chapter Seven, "Islamic Politics in the Arab-Israeli Conflict," has been expanded and significantly updated because much has happened in the region since the publication of the first edition eight years ago. In this chapter, three new boxes have been introduced: profiles of President Yasir Arafat of the Palestinian National Authority, Egyptian President Gamal Abdel Nasser, and Shaykh Ahmed Yassin, who is the spiritual leader of Harakat al-Muqawama al-Islamiyyah (HAMAS).

- Chapter Eight, "OPEC, OAPEC and the OIC," has been updated, expanded, and revised. It appears with three new boxes, concerning the Organization of Arab Petroleum Exporting Countries (OAPEC); Muammar al-Qaddafi of Libya, who started the oil price explosion in the early 1970s that was then continued by the Organization of Petroleum Exporting Countries (OPEC); and the Organization of the Islamic Conference (OIC), that represents the fifty-seven countries of the Islamic bloc.

- Chapter Nine, "The Islamic Revolution in Iran," has been updated and has a new timeline of major Iranian events at the end of the chapter. Also several new boxes have been added, including "The Pahlavi Dynasty," "Ayatollah," "A Comparison of Ayatollahs Khomeini and Shariatmadari," "Ayatollah Ali Khameini," "Abdol Karim Saroush," and "President Muhammad Khatami."

- Chapters Ten and Eleven are also new to this second edition.

- Chapter Ten, "Afghanistan: One Nation, Divisible" (with several boxed profiles of Afghan Islamists and an "Afghanistan Timeline").

- Chapter Eleven, "Perceiving Islam: The Causes and Consequences of Islamophobia in the Western Mass Media."

- The "Conclusion" (Chapter Twelve) has been significantly expanded, updated, and revised.

- Most of the profiles of Muslim leaders, Islamists, and Islamist organizations are much shorter and written in an interesting journalistic style rather than the longer and scholarly biographies written for the first edition.

- The Glossary has been significantly expanded and revised with many new terms that will prove helpful to readers in understanding Islam, Muslims, and global Islamic politics.

- The Bibliography, comprising articles and books, has been greatly expanded and updated. Students, teachers, professors, and scholars have also been provided with numerous Internet sites on Islam, Muslims, the Muslim world, and global Islamic politics.

Acknowledgments

Above all, I wish to express my immense gratitude to David M. Rosenbaum, with whom this manuscript was revised and without whom this manuscript would never have been completed on time. His invaluable assistance in editing, revising, and updating several chapters and boxes made it possible to meet an otherwise impossible deadline. His insightful suggestions and his expertise as a writer contributed significantly to this edition.

I would also like to express my deep appreciation to the following: Elena Loginova and Jana Tatum, our university's departmental research assistants, for downloading many articles from the World Wide Web; Omer Farooq, a graduate student in computer and information sciences, who navigated the World Wide Web, searching for good Web sites on the leaders, events, issues, and problems covered in the book; Ata Khan, my childhood friend and neighbor, who checked out all the Web sites, then advised me about the ones to include in the book and the ones to drop. I would also like to thank the following religious scholars for correcting inaccuracies in my table comparing Islam, Judaism, and Christianity: Dr. Timothy Carmody, professor of biblical studies in the Department of Theology at Springhill College in Mobile, Alabama; Steven Silberman, the officiating rabbi at the Conservative Ahavas Chesed Synagogue in Mobile; and Donald Konstadt, the officiating rabbi at the Springhill Avenue Temple–Reform.

Finally, I owe a profound debt of gratitude to my deceased father for the good values he instilled in me, my saintly mother for her prayers, and my wife for her patience. With their prayers and moral support they contributed more than they may realize.

Mir Zohair Husain

CHAPTER ONE

An Overview of Islam

Islam is the religion, the way of life, and the common thread that binds over 1.2 billion Muslims, one-fifth of the world's population, people of diverse nationalities and ethnic groups. Islam infuses the everyday lives of Muslims with existential meaning, spiritual strength, and inner peace. Therefore, an understanding of the elemental principles and precepts of Islam is a prerequisite to an understanding of global Islamic politics.

Islam, Salaam, and Muslim

The Arabic language is based on root words made up of consonants. For example, the Arabic terms *Islam, Salaam,* and *Muslim* are derived from the root consonants *s, l,* and *m*. The word **Islam** stems from the fourth verbal form of the root *slm: aslama*, which literally means "to submit" or "to surrender." Thus the word Islam has come to mean "submission," "surrender," "resignation," and "obedience" to God and His guidance.

Islam's emphasis on **tawhid** (the absolute oneness, unity, and uniqueness of God), though prevalent throughout the **Qur'an** (which Muslims believe is God's holy book, revealed to Prophet Muhammad) is concisely, cogently, and lucidly demonstrated in a Qur'anic chapter entitled *Al-Ikhlas* (Sincerity). *Al-Ikhlas* is so important and central to Islam that it is recited during each prayer performed by Muslims five times a day. *Al-Ikhlas* has been translated from the classical Arabic in the Qur'an to English as follows:

> In the name of the merciful and compassionate God.
> Say (O Muhammad): He is God, the One and Only!
> God is Eternal.
> He did not give birth (to anyone),
> Nor did anyone give birth to Him.
> And there is no one equal to (or similar to) Him [Qur'an: **Surah** 112, **Ayats** 1–4].[1]

---

[1]Hereafter citations to the Qur'an will give the Qur'anic *Surah* (Chapter) number, followed by a colon, and then the number of the specific Qur'anic *Ayah/Ayats* (Verse/Verses). Thus this first Qur'anic citation is (112:1–4).

BOX 1.1   Vital Facts about Islam and the Muslim World

1. Islam is the world's second-largest religion, with over 1.2 billion Muslims. Christianity is the largest religion in the world, with over 2 billion Christians.

2. Islam is one of the world's most widely diffused religions. Muslims comprise a majority in over fifty countries (i.e., in over one-fourth of the world's independent nation-states, each pursuing its own national interests), are a significant minority in over thirty countries, and are found in most of the world's nation-states. However, though Islam calls on the members of the global ***ummah*** (community of believers) to view each other as brothers and sisters and remain united, the Muslim world remains divided and weak.

3. The five largest Muslim countries are non-Arab: Indonesia (comprising 220 million Muslims), Pakistan (comprising 140 million Muslims), predominantly Hindu India (135 million Muslims), and Bangladesh (130 million Muslims).

4. There are approximately 300 million Arabs in the world, with 290 million in the Arab world. The overwhelming majority of Arabs are Muslims. However, at least 5 percent of Arabs are non-Muslims. Since 1948, many Jewish Arabs emigrated to Israel, and many Christian and Jewish Arabs emigrated to the West. Arab Muslims constitute less than 25 percent of all Muslims in the world. Indeed, nearly as many Muslims live in Pakistan (140 million) and Bangladesh (135 million) than in the entire Arab world!

5. **The Arab world** and **Middle East** are not synonymous. Although there are 290 million Arabs in most of the twenty-two Middle Eastern countries, only three non-Arab countries in the Middle East—Turkey (70 million), Iran (70 million), and Israel (6 million)—account for nearly half the population of the Middle East.

6. Christians and Jews of Arab descent and heritage have made significant contributions to Arab civilization through the ages. In the last three decades, a number of prominent Palestinian Christians in both the Middle East and the West have eloquently espoused the Palestinian cause and presented Arabs and the Arab world in a positive light.

7. The Western mass media have portrayed devout Muslims as hotheaded religious zealots or terrorists, who marry up to four wives because their religion gives them permission to do so. The truth is that only a very tiny fraction of the Muslim population is violent and an even tinier fraction of the Muslim adult male population can afford to, or does, marry more than one wife.

8. Sometimes the Western mass media give the erroneous impression that the Arab world is a region heavily populated with nomadic "bedouins" and dominated by numerous oil-rich shaykhs. They also give a false impression when they occasionally imply that the majority of Muslim countries have petroleum or "black liquid gold." In reality, only 2 percent of Arabs can be classified as bedouins, and there may be three thousand or so wealthy royal family members (mainly in the Arab kingdoms of the Persian Gulf) out of 300 million Arabs (and over 1.2 billion Muslims worldwide). In fact, petrodollars no more belong to the

Arabs than the enormous wealth of Wall Street belongs to New Yorkers and Hollywood's assets belong to Los Angelenos. The majority of Arab countries (and non-Arab Iran and Turkey) are agrarian societies, more than half of whose working population is engaged in agriculture. The majority of the 7.3 million Somalis, 35 million Sudanese, 68.5 million Egyptians, 5 million Jordanians, 16.3 million Syrians, 30 million Moroccans, 17.5 million Yemenis, 22.6 million Iraqis, 9.6 million Tunisians, 3.6 million Lebanese, and 31 million Algerians are poor rather than rich or even middle class. Furthermore, the majority of Muslim countries are poor in petroleum resources, and must import oil from the few oil-rich states like Saudi Arabia, Kuwait, Libya, the United Arab Emirates (U.A.E.), Qatar, Algeria, Iran, Nigeria, and Indonesia.

9. Around 1900, Captain Alfred T. Mahan (1840–1914), an American naval historian and strategist, coined the term **Middle East.** This term reflects the fact that Mahan must have been familiar with the European use of the terms *Near East* for the Ottoman Empire and *Far East* for the Orient. He saw the "Middle East" comprising the geographical area between the Near East and Far East. The term was adopted by European military strategists during World War I and by Europeans and Americans during World War II. Soon Mahan's **ethnocentric** term—ethnocentric because the region comprising North Africa and Southwest Asia can be considered in the Middle East only if someone is looking toward the East from the United States or Great Britain—was universally accepted and is still widely used.

10. The six most prominent Muslim empires in Islamic history were the Arab Umayyad Empire (661–750 CE) and the Arab Abbasid Empire (750–1258 CE); the Muslim civilization of Andalusia in southern Spain, which was the most advanced civilization in Medieval Europe (800–1400); the Turkish Ottoman Empire (1520–1920); the Mughal Empire in the Indian subcontinent (1526–1857); and the Safavid Empire of Persia/Iran (1501–1732).

11. Most Muslim countries cannot be classified as Islamic states, because they are governed on the basis of Western secular laws and secularism rather than the *shariah* (Islamic law) and Islamism. In fact, most Muslim regimes have strenuously tried to keep the domain of religion (and the mosque) separate from the domain of the state (government).

12. A significant number of the 1.2 billion Muslims in the world like naming their children "Muhammad" (as their first name, middle name, or surname) because it stands for Islam's last prophet and role model and because it literally means "the praised one." No wonder more people are called "Muhammad" than any other name!

13. In the non-Muslim world, **jihad** is often erroneously defined as "holy war." In Arabic, *jihad* literally means "to strive" and "to struggle." In Islam, *jihad-i-akbar* (the greatest *jihad*) is the nonviolent spiritual struggle to control and vanquish one's baser instincts and impulses; and *jihad-i-asghar* (the lesser *jihad*) is to actively defend oneself against tyrants, aggressors, and colonizers.

14. There are over 7 million Muslims in the United States. Most are immigrants or their descendants from Muslim countries in Asia, the Middle East, and Africa. About a third are African Americans, a quarter are Arabs, and a small number are whites. A significant number of them attend at least one of the 1,209

(Continued)

> **Vital Facts about Islam and the Muslim World**   *(Continued)*
>
> mosques spread all over the United States (U.S. News & World Report, October 29, 2001, p. 51).
>
> 15. More than three-quarters of the Arab Americans, whose fathers and forefathers hailed from the Arab world, were born in the United States. More than three-quarters of Arab Americans are Christian. Almost 60 percent of Arab Americans are of Lebanese descent (http://www.usinfo.state.gov/usa/islam.zogby.htm p. 31).
>
> http://www.islam.com
> http://www.sultan.org/
> http://www.understanding-islam.com
> http://www.beconvinced.com
> http://www.ubfellowship.org/archive/readers/601islam.htm

Salaam, which literally means "peace," is an integral part of Islam. According to the Qur'an, *As-Salam* is one of the ninety-nine attributes or names of God, as well as the name given to the blissful abode of Heaven/Paradise. A Muslim might expect heavenly reward provided that he or she totally submits to God, the Creator, by conforming to the code of Islamic ethics and guidance presented in the Qur'an and *sunnah* (Prophet Muhammad's sayings and deeds). This submission to the will of God means, on one hand, complete surrender to God but, on the other hand, the complete freedom from every other form of bondage known to humankind. Peace is such an important idea in Islam that Muslims often say, "*salaam alaykum*" (peace be upon/with you), when they meet and greet someone, and are given the response *wa' alaykum as-salaam* (peace be upon/with you too).[2] The definition of *Islam* as "peace" is an a priori definition, independent of the actions of Muslims. Thus their actions do not define Islam; rather their actions should be judged according to the dictates of the Islamic faith's message of peace and obedience.

It is incorrect to call the religion of Islam "**Muhammadanism**" and totally inappropriate to call Muslims "Muhammadans," for three major reasons: Prophet Muhammad did not create the religion of Islam; the Qur'an does not consider him divine; and Muslims do not worship him. In fact, to worship Muhammad would be regarded as **shirk** (associating someone with God), violating the central Islamic principle of **tawhid**, which is the axial or defining doctrine of Islam for all Islamists. Muslims acknowledge all the Old Testament prophets and revere

---

[2]The Qur'an states: "When those who believe in Our signs come to you, say: peace be upon you" (6:54); "When you are welcomed with a greeting, then answer back with something finer than it or (at least) return it. Truly Allah takes count of all things" (4:86); "When you enter houses greet one another with greetings from Allah, blessed and sweet . . ." (24:61).

Muhammad as the "seal of the Prophets" (the last in a long line of prophets sent by God to guide humankind on "the straight path"). The Qur'an labels the messages that God revealed to all His messengers—from Adam and all the biblical prophets (including Abraham, David, Moses, and Jesus) to Muhammad—as "Islam." Muslims view Prophet Muhammad as an exemplary human being and an ideal role model who ought to be emulated. However, Muslims believe that the creator of Islam and everything in the universe is God Himself. In fact, most Muslims invoke God's help by saying, **Bismillah-ir-Rahmanir Raheem** (In the name of God, the Most Beneficent, the Most merciful, when they start any major endeavor.

The word **Muslim**, which literally means "one who submits," is an active participle of *aslama* (to submit). Thus, Muslims are "those who submit to the will of God" and believe that only by totally submitting to God's will and by obeying His commands, as embodied in the Qur'an, can one achieve true happiness in this world and in the hereafter. Muslims also believe that Islam is God's final message to humankind, a reconfirmation and perfection of the messages that God has revealed through earlier prophets.

Muhammad: Islam's Last Prophet

The name *Muhammad* comes from the Arabic verb *hamada*, which literally means "to praise," "to laud," and "to glorify." Thus *Muhammad* means "the praised one" or "he who is glorified."

Muhammad was born in **Makkah** (in present-day Saudi Arabia) in 570 CE. His father, Abdullah, died before his birth. His mother, Aminah, died when he was six, and his grandfather, Abdul Muttalib, died when he was eight. Muhammad's upbringing was then taken over by his uncle (father's brother), Abu Talib, who remained his guardian for the next forty years.

Muhammad was deeply disturbed by the ignorance and primitive customs prevalent in Arabia. At the time, the practice of female infanticide was common; slavery, alcoholism, and gambling were widespread; wealthy and influential men kept large harems; widows and orphans suffered poverty and terrible indignities; and tribal wars were frequent. While Muhammad quietly sought spiritual answers to these social ills, he earned his living as a merchant-trader. By his mid-twenties, he had acquired a reputation in Mecca for his integrity and wisdom. People called him **Al-Ameen** (the trustworthy) and **As-Sadiq** (the honest), left their valuables with him for safekeeping, and often came to him to settle their disputes. Hearing of Muhammad's impeccable character and charismatic personality, **Khadijah bint Khuwaylid**, a wealthy and influential woman of one of Makkah's successful trading houses, employed him. Muhammad's exceptional character, personality, and work habits so impressed Khadijah that she proposed marriage.

In his thirties, Muhammad meditated regularly in the cave of Hira on the outskirts of Makkah. When he reached forty, in 610 CE, according to Muslims, Muhammad was visited in the cave by the Archangel Gabriel, who told him that he should announce his prophethood and preach the message of Islam. His wife, Khadijah, and a handful of relatives converted immediately to Islam.

So brutal was the persecution suffered by the first Muslims at the hands of the corrupt leaders of Makkah that in 622 CE Muhammad led his followers to the nearby city of **Madinah**, where a small band of converts had invited him. This migration, called the **Hijrah**, marks the beginning of the Islamic calendar.

In Madinah Muhammad established and governed the first Islamic state. The Makkans, however, gave the Prophet no peace, and a series of wars between the Makkans and the Muslims ensued for nine years. When Muhammad conquered

---

BOX 1.2   The Islamic Calendar

Muslims commemorate all their religious festivals and ceremonies based on the Islamic lunar calendar, not on the Gregorian calendar—a calendar instituted by Pope Gregory XIII in 1582 that is in use all over the world. The **Islamic calendar** dates from Prophet Muhammad's Hijrah (migration) from Makkah to Yathrib (renamed Madinah) in 622 CE. "Year One" of the Islamic calendar begins with the establishment of the first Islamic state in Madinah in 622 CE, following the Hijrah. This year is thus designated as 1st Hijri and all subsequent years are referred to as "After Hijrah" (abbreviated "A.H.").

The Islamic calendar was adopted during Umar ibn Khattab's caliphate, at the suggestion of Ali ibn Abu Talib in 16 A.H., before which there was no fixed calendar in the Arabian peninsula. Rather than starting with the birth of Muhammad or the first revelation that God's last prophet received in 610 CE, the Islamic calendar starts from the critically important Hijrah (as a result of which Islam survived) and the establishment of the first Islamic state in history, illustrating the centrality of the *ummah* and the fusion of religion and politics in Islam.

The Islamic calendar is based on the moon's orbit around the earth. It consists of twelve lunar months, each alternating between 29 and 30 days in length from one new moon to the next, for a total of 354 days that it takes the moon to complete its orbit. Hence the lunar year is approximately 11 days shorter than the 365-day solar year in the twelve months of the Western (Gregorian) calendar.

The names of the twelve lunar months of the Islamic calendar in proper sequence are: (1) Muharram, (2) Safar, (3) Rabi al-Awwal, (4) Rabi al-Thani, (5) Jamadi al-Awwal, (6) Jamadi al-Thani, (7) Rajab, (8) Shaban, (9) Ramadan, (10) Shawwal, (11) Dhul-Qadah, and (12) Dhul-Hijjah. Each lunar month lasts from one first sighting of the crescent moon to the next.

Most Muslim nation-states follow the Western (Gregorian) solar calendar, while a few, like Saudi Arabia, use the Islamic lunar calendar. In the countries that have retained the Islamic lunar calendar, the day goes from sunset to sunset rather than from midnight to midnight. Thus the first of Muharram (the first day in the Islamic new year) really begins on the night preceding the first of Muharram. Furthermore, the date of any Islamic holiday will advance eleven days from one year to the next.

Makkah, he accepted the conversion to Islam of his former enemies. In 632 CE, at the age of sixty-three, Muhammad died, leaving behind a young and dynamic faith and the foundations of an empire. Muslims admire him so much that they refer to him as *insan-i-kamil* (the perfect being) and when they mention his name, they often often add *"Allahumma Salli Ala Muhammadin Wa 'AAla Muhammad"* (O God, let Your blessing come upon Muhammad and his family).

The Qur'an

The Qur'an (sometimes spelled "Koran") literally means "recitation" in Arabic. According to Muslims, the Qur'an is a collection of God's revelations sent down to Prophet Muhammad through the agency of Archangel Gabriel. Most often these revelations, which started when Muhammad was forty years old (in 610 CE), and ended when he died, at the age of sixty-two (in 632 CE), were revealed to Muhammad in classical, eloquent, and powerful Arabic prose. Muhammad, in turn, recited these revelations to the **sahabah** (Companions) with him, who wrote them down, memorized them, and recited them to others. The name Qur'an was later given to the Holy Book containing all these revelations. The Qur'an provides guidance for almost every aspect of a believer's life.

According to Muslims, the Qur'an is the last of all Holy Books, those sacred books containing the authoritative "Word of God." The Qur'an comprises 114 **Surahs** (chapters). Each chapter is further divided into **Ayats** (verses); there are approximately 6,200 *Ayats* in the entire Qur'an. According to Phillip Hitti, there are approximately 77,934 words in the complete Qur'an. Muslims believe that it is God's final guidance to humankind everywhere and until the Day of Judgment.

Most Muslims all over the world learn to recite the Qur'an in Arabic, whatever their native language. They have to learn to recite at least some short *Surahs* in order to perform their *salah* (ritual prayers) in the correct manner. Many millions of Muslims memorize the entire Qur'an. They are called **hafiz-i-Qur'an**.[3]

Iman

Iman literally means "faith," "belief," or "spiritual convictions." The Qur'an refers to the five articles of faith, or the basic foundations of the Islamic belief system:

> O ye who believe! Believe in God and His Apostle and the scripture which He hath sent to His Apostle and the scripture which he sent to those before (him). Any who denieth God, His angels, His Books, His Apostles, and the day of Judgment, hath gone far, far astray [4:136].

---

[3]For more information on the Qur'an, see the following web sites: http://ourworld.compuserve.com/homepages/ABewley/tafsir.html; http://www.al-islam.org/quran/; http://www.iiu.edu.my/deed/quran/in the shade of quran/index.html; and www.islamicinterlink.com/subject/quran.html.

Thus the five articles are (a) belief in Allah (God); (b) belief in angels; (c) belief in God's prophets, with Adam as the first prophet and Muhammad as the last; (d) belief in the holy books revealed by God—the Torah, the Bible, and the Qur'an—and (e) belief in the Day of Judgment. Each article of faith can be further defined as follows:

- The first and most important foundational tenet on which Islam rests is the total belief in Allah. **Allah** is the Islamic term for the one omnipotent, omnipresent, omniscient, eternal, perfect, just, and merciful God or Supreme Being. Muslims believe that God is the sole Creator, Sustainer, Provider, and Controller of the universe; that He, and He alone, ought to be worshiped; and that He has neither feminine nor plural attributes. This last tenet, of paramount importance, is succinctly articulated in the *shahadah* (declaration or profession of the Islamic faith): *Ash hadu an La ilaha illa 'llah, Muhammad ar rasul Allah* (I bear witness that there is no God but Allah and Muhammad is His messenger). The *shahadah* marks a person's entry into Islam and the worldwide **ummah** (brotherhood of believers); it is the first statement that Muslim parents (often the father) utters into the ears of a newborn; and it is the last words a Muslim should utter before death.

- The second doctrine of Islam is belief in God's angels. Unlike human beings, these celestial creatures are made not of dust but of light; have no physical desires nor material needs of any kind; do not eat, drink, or sleep; have no capacity for reasoning; have no free will; are immortal; and obediently carry out God's orders during the day or night. Some of these angels have been assigned special duties. Archangel Gabriel is believed to have brought God's messages to all His prophets; two angels, one on each side, accompany every individual and record his or her deeds for the Day of Judgment; and some angels help true believers when the latter call out to God to help them.

- The third foundational principle of Islam is the belief in God's prophets. Muslims believe that every known nation has had a warner or messenger from God. God chose these messengers to teach humankind and deliver His divine messages. Although the Qur'an alludes to 124,000 prophets since the time of creation (with Adam as the very first prophet), it specifically mentions the name of only 25 of them. Among them, Muhammad stands as the last and most important of God's prophets.

- The fourth basic premise of Islam is to believe in God's Holy Books. Muslims believe that God revealed the *Suhuf* (Scrolls) to Ibrahim (Abraham), the *Zabur* (Psalms) to Dawud (David), the *Tawrah* (Torah) to Musa (Moses), the *Injil* (Gospels) to Isa (Jesus), and the Qur'an to Muhammad. Each of these Holy Books mentioned in the Qur'an showed their respective people the straight path that God wanted human beings to follow. However, according to Islam, the original scriptures given to prophets Abraham, David, Moses, Jesus, and others were lost or corrupted (tampered with by fallible human beings) over the centuries, while the only authentic and complete book with God's final message to humankind that is in existence today is embodied in the Qur'an.

- The fifth and final article of the Islamic faith is belief in **Yaum al-Akhira** (the Day of Judgment). The Qur'an clearly informs Muslims that the world will come to an end some day. On that Day of Judgment, the dead from the time of creation will be resurrected to be judged by an all-knowing, totally just, and immensely merciful God. Righteous human beings who have done good deeds in this world will be rewarded with an eternal life of happiness in Heaven/Paradise, while those who have refused to follow God's guidance, hurt their fellow human beings, and done evil deeds in this world will be sent to Hell to suffer.

Faraidh

Faraidh literally means "compulsory duties" or "obligations." Muslims believe that neglect of the five *faraidh,* also known as the five **arkan ad-din** or the "five pillars of the faith," will be punished in the next world, while their fulfillment will be rewarded. The five *faraidh* enjoined on all Muslims are the *shahadah, salat, zakat, sawm,* and *hajj.*

Shahadah is Arabic for witnessing, professing, or declaring. In Islam *Ash hadu an La ilaha illa 'llah, Muhammad ar rasul Allah* (I bear witness that there is no God but Allah, and Muhammad is His messenger) is the first and most important pillar of Islam. This declaration of faith in God and in Muhammad as His last prophet implies that there is none worthy of worship except God and that Muhammad is His messenger to all human beings till the Day of Judgment. Accepting Muhammad as God's last prophet obliges Muslims to see him as an ideal role model and to follow his wise *hadith* (sayings) and exemplary *sunnah* (deeds). More important, those who see Muhammad as a man of honesty and integrity are obliged to believe in the Qur'an as God's final and perfect message to humankind, revealed to Muhammad by Archangel Gabriel.

Salat, or *salah,* the ritual of daily prayers to worship God, is the second pillar of Islam. The Qur'an expects Muslims to establish a direct relationship with God and be conscious of His presence from the time they rise in the morning till the time they go to bed at night. However, although the Qur'an mentions prayer many times, the obligation for adult Muslims to pray five times a day derives from Prophet Muhammad's *hadith* rather than the Qur'an. Each prayer is offered in a fixed pattern of recitation of Qur'anic verses coupled with prostrations. The times of prayer, with their Arabic terms, are as follows: (1) the morning prayer before sunrise (*salat al-subh* or *salat al-fajr*); (2) the midday prayer (*salat al-zuhr*); (3) the afternoon prayer before sunset (*salat al-asr*); (4) the evening prayer after sunset (*salat al-maghrib*); and the night prayer before midnight (*salat al-ishah*), thereby mentioning God numerous times in their prayer rituals throughout the day.[4] The Qur'an instructs Muslims to offer their Friday prayers: "O ye who believe! When the call is proclaimed for prayer on Friday, hasten earnestly to the rememberance of God, and leave of business; that is best for you if you but knew" (62:9). Prophet Muhammad recommended that Muslims offer their Friday midday prayers along with their brethren at a mosque. These congregational prayer services often include a sermon by a respected Islamic cleric in the community called *Imam-i-Jum'ah wa Jama'at* (Friday congregational prayer leader).

Zakat, or *zakah*, almsgiving, is the third pillar of Islam. A Muslim's service to humanity (which includes non-Muslims) is considered an essential part of his or her service to God; the obligatory humanitarian duty of *zakat* epitomizes and illustrates this most vividly. Muslims with the financial means to do so are enjoined by the Qur'an and *sunnah* to donate at least 2.5 percent of their net worth—not just their annual income—to the welfare of the poor and needy, to charitable institutions, and/or to orphanages every year. *Zakat* literally means "purification" in Arabic. This is because, when a Muslim contributes a small portion of his or her wealth to the welfare of the poorest and neediest human beings, he or she pleases the beneficiaries of this generosity and earns their heartfelt prayers; plays a small role in reducing poverty and bridging the gap between the rich and poor; pleases God, who loves to see human beings helping one another; and feels a sense of emotional and psychological gratification by reaffirming his or her humanity and goodness.

Sawm is the fourth pillar of Islam. The Qur'an clearly states: "O ye who believe! Fasting is prescribed to you as it was prescribed to those before you, that ye may (learn) self-restraint" (11:183). *Sawm* represents the obligation of all adult Muslims to fast from dawn to dusk during the ninth Islamic calendar month of **Ramadan,** when the revelations of God started coming down to Prophet Muhammad to guide humankind to "the straight path." The word *Ramadan* is derived from the Arabic root *ramz,* which literally means "to burn." Ideally, fasting during Ramadan should metaphorically "burn away one's sins." During the month of Ramadan, adult Muslims are expected to abstain from food, liquids, and sexual intercourse from sunrise till sunset. When one fasts, all the sense organs—eyes, ears, nose, tongue, hands, and feet—ought to do the right thing. The eyes should see no evil; the ears should abstain from hearing music, lies, and gossip; the tongue should not tell lies or spread rumors; the hand should not physically hurt anyone or steal; and the feet should not walk toward forbidden places. Fasting was also enjoined to

---

[4]During the five ritual prayers, Muslims say the *Surah-i-Fatihah* (The Opening), the first chapter in the *Qur'an*, seventeen times. This is how it goes: "In the name of God, the Most Beneficent, the Most Merciful; Praise be to God, the Lord of the worlds; the Most Beneficent, the Most Merciful; Master of the Day of Judgment; You alone we worship, You alone we ask for help; Guide us along the straight path: The path of those upon whom You have bestowed Your grace, not (the path) of those with whom You are angry, nor of those who go astray." This prayer could just as easily be said by Jews and Christians.

build good character traits, such as a social conscience, patience, tolerance, will power, and altruism. Just before the end of Ramadan, Muslims are enjoined to donate *zakat al-fitr* (donations to the poor).

Hajj, the fifth pillar of Islam, is the obligation of all adult Muslims of sound mind and body to make a religious journey to Makkah at least once in their lifetime. The pilgrimage must take place between the seventh and tenth days of the Islamic month of Dhul-Hijjah, which is the twelfth and last month in the Islamic calendar. On the tenth and last day of the pilgrimage, Muslims (who can afford it) have been enjoined to slaughter an animal commemorating Prophet Abraham's obedience to God's command that he should sacrifice his son (Ishmael). Of course, when Abraham was about to carry out God's command, He sent a ram (through the agency of Archangel Gabriel) to be sacrificed instead of his son. Such total obedience to God vividly illustrates the very essence of true Islam, which entails a ***mu'min***, or true believer, surrendering his or her entire self to God (2:131). Indeed, most pilgrims at the *hajj* pay for an animal to be sacrificed to God, as do most Muslims all over the world who can afford it. The meat is frozen and sent to the poor throughout the Muslim world. Many Muslims also pay to send meat to needy Muslims in other countries. The pilgrim who completes the *hajj* during the annual *hajj* season is called a *hajji*.

Prophet Muhammad's Hadith

The sayings of Prophet Muhammad are known as the *hadith*. *Hadith* is an Arabic term for an eyewitness account, narrative, report, or record of a saying of Prophet Muhammad that has been passed through a chain of reliable oral transmitters. Prophet Muhammad's *hadith* are second in importance to the Qur'an as the major source of the *shariah* (Islamic law). Prophet Muhammad's advice to children is as follows:

- "He who wishes to enter Paradise must please his father and mother."
- "A man must be good to his parents, although they may have injured him."

Prophet Muhammad's advice to parents is as follows:

- "Respect your children and develop good habits in them."
- "Whosoever does good to daughters will be saved from the fires of hell."
- "Always fulfill the promises made with your children."

Prophet Muhammad emphasizes the acquisition of knowledge:

- "To acquire knowledge is binding on Muslims, whether male or female."
- "Seek after knowledge though it be in China" (which was a distant and pagan land with a glorious civilization; therefore, despite the long and arduous journey from Makkah or Madinah, it would give Muslims a first-hand experience of a great non-Islamic civilization).

■

BOX 1.3   The Ka'abah and the Story of the Hajj

K*a'abah* is an Arabic term that literally means "cube." The **Ka'abah** is a large black, majestic, cube-shaped shrine in Makkah, Saudi Arabia, that stands in the middle of the enormously expansive square enclosure of the colossal *al-Masjid al-Haram* (the Holy Mosque or Grand Mosque, which is the biggest in Islamdom. The "Black Stone," called **Hajar al-Aswad** in Arabic, lies imbedded in the southeastern corner of the Ka'abah's wall, near the monument's door. The Hajar al-Aswad is the most sacred stone in Islamdom because Muslims believe that it was given to Abraham by God and is imbedded in the holiest shrine in Islam. Pilgrims try to kiss the Hajar al-Aswad and start their seven circuits of the Ka'abah from the position of the Black Stone. The Grand Mosque's courtyard has been extended many times to accommodate the increasing number of pilgrims that come to perform the *hajj* each year. The *Ka'abah* contains an empty room (which is not entered except for ritual cleaning each year) and is covered with a black cloth, called a *kiswah*, that is embroidered in gold with the *shahadah* and Qur'anic verses.

According to Islamic tradition, Prophet Abraham left his second wife, Hagar, and their newborn son, **Ishmael,** in present-day Makkah at the command of God and then returned to his first wife, Sarah, in Jerusalem. When Hagar ran out of drinking water, she ran desperately between two hills in a narrow valley, pleading with God to provide her with drinking water to quench their thirst. Her prayers were answered when Archangel Gabriel, on God's orders, provided them with a spring of clean, cool, and sweet water from the Well of Zamzam—a source of holy water that pilgrims drink from and return home with to this day.

Abraham returned to Makkah years later with a vision from God commanding him to sacrifice his son Ishmael. When Abraham was about to carry out God's command, which actually was intended to test Abraham's faith, God asked Archangel Gabriel to let a ram be slaughtered instead. Muslims all over the world commemorate that event by sacrificing an animal at the conclusion of the *hajj* and distributing the meat of the slaughtered animal among the poor and needy.

It is also mentioned in the Qur'an that, to thank God for saving his son twice, Abraham and his son Ishmael built the first Bayt Allah (House of God) for the worship of one God nearly four thousand years ago (22:26–28). In fact, some legends say that Hagar was buried under a mound where the ruins of Adam's temple once stood and that is the hallowed ground Abraham chose to build the Ka'abah, which remains in the same place to this day.

With the passage of time, the Ka'abah became a house of idolatory, filled with pagan statues, and very few people remained true to the worship of one God. Among these few believers in the one true God, according to Muslims, was Prophet Muhammad. In 630 CE, when Muhammad conquered Makkah peacefully, he destroyed as many as 360 idols that had been placed in the Ka'abah and rededicated the shrine to the belief of one God. Since that time, Muslims all over the world have been enjoined to pray in the direction of the Ka'abah.

- "The worst of men is a poorly learned man, and a good learned man is the best."
- "The ink of the scholar is holier than the blood of the martyr."

Prophet Muhammad's Sunnah

Sunnah is an Arabic term that refers to a path, road, or way. In Islam, it is understood as the trodden path, way, custom, or tradition of the Prophet Muhammad (who is considered by all Muslims as an exemplary human being worthy of emulation). The *sunnah* comprises all the customs and examples of Prophet Muhammad's behavior, reliable reports about his sayings and deeds, as well as his *sirah* (stories about his life). The *sunnah* provides a valuable source of information and guidance for Muslims about what to do and how to behave; in this respect the *sunnah* complements the Qur'an as the major source of Islamic faith and practice.[5]

The Shariah

Shariah comes from the Arabic root *shara'a,* which literally means "to introduce," "enact," or "prescribe." The Qur'an and *sunnah* provide the framework for the *shariah*, which is the comprehensive, eternal, immutable, and divine law of Islam that governs all aspects of the public and private, social and economic, religious and political life of every Muslim. The *shariah*'s provisions were compiled by the **ulama** (Islamic scholars) during the Middle Ages using the discipline of *fiqh* (Islamic jurisprudence), *hadith* (Prophet Muhammad's sayings), *ijma* (consultation and consensus), and **qiyas** (analogy). Shi'ahs commonly substitute **ijtihad** (independent reasoning) for *qiyas*, and interpret *ijma* as the consensus of the Imams or the Grand Ayatollahs. For a Muslim country to be called an Islamic state, it must impose the *shariah* as the law of the land. No wonder all Islamists call for the imposition of the *shariah*.

Reign of the First Four Caliphs

Abu Bakr was one of the first converts to Islam and a close companion of Prophet Muhammad. The influential Muslim leaders of Makkah nominated the sixty-year-old Abu Bakr to succeed Muhammad as the first *khalifah* (caliph) over the *ummah*. During his brief reign (632–634 CE), the rebellious bedouins were suppressed, and Abu Bakr consolidated his rule over the Arabian peninsula. He also sent his armies to conquer Iraq and Syria.

---

[5]For more information on Prophet Muhammad's Hadith and Sunnah, see the following web site: http://aolsearch.aol.com/dirsearch.adp?knf=1&query=hadeeth.

BOX 1.4   Islam Condemns Terrorism and Suicide

The Qur'an, and thus Islam, clearly, categorically, and specifically condemns and prohibits terrorism and suicide. The taking of innocent people's lives, which is always the result of terrorism and suicide missions by misguided Muslim zealots, is considered a sin in Islam, because human life is considered sacrosanct and only God has the right to bestow it and take it away. In fact, Islam emphasizes peace, moderation, and tolerance and opposes all types of violent extremism, including hostage taking, hijacking, planting bombs in public places, and killing innocent noncombatants. Below are some Qur'anic verses that address this issue:

- "Take not life, which Allah hath made sacred, except by way of justice and law" (6:151).
- "Whoever kills a person not in retaliation for murder or to spread corruption in the land, it would be as if he murdered the whole of humankind. And (likewise) if anyone saved a life, it would be as if he saved the whole of humankind" (5:32).
- ". . . Nor kill (or destroy) yourselves. Surely, Allah is Most Merciful to you" (4:29).
- "Make not your hands contribute to (your) destruction; but do good; for God loveth those who do good" (2:194).
- "Let there be no hostility except to those who practice oppression" (2:193).
- "Let there be no compulsion in religion. The right direction is distinctly clear from error" (2:256).
- "And fight in the way of Allah those who fight you. But do not transgress the limits. Truly Allah loves not the transgressors" (2:190).
- "Those who spend (freely), whether in prosperity or adversity, who restrain their anger and pardon (all) human beings; For God loves those who do good" (3:134).
- "O mankind! We created you from a single (pair) of a male and female, and made you into nations and tribes, that ye may know each other (not that ye may despise each other). Verily the most honored in the sight of God is (the) most righteous of you. And God has full knowledge and is well acquainted (with all things)" (49:13).
- "O ye who believe! Enter into Islam wholeheartedly; And follow not the footsteps of the Evil one; For he is to you an avowed enemy" (11:208).
- "Say ye: 'We believe in God, and the revelation given to us, and to Abraham, Ishmael, Isaac, Jacob, and the Tribes, and that given to Moses and Jesus, and that given to all Prophets from their Lord: We make no difference between one and another of them: And we bow to God in Islam' " (2:136).

The Prophet Muhammad is believed to have made the following statements, which can be construed as condemning terrorism and suicide, and are to be found in Sahi Bukari and Sahi Muslim:

- "Indeed, whoever [intentionally] kills himself, then certainly he will be punished in the fire of hell, wherein he shall dwell forever."

- "God has no mercy on one who has no mercy for others."
- "None of you truly believes until you wish for others what you wish for yourself."
- "Powerful is not he who knocks the other down; indeed powerful is he who controls himself in a fit of anger."
- Before every battle, Prophet Muhammad gave standing orders to his soldiers not to kill noncombatants (innocent men, women, and children); not to kill animals, destroy trees, burn crops, pollute waters, nor destroy homes and houses of worship. Prophet Muhammad repeated these orders to his soldiers when he set out from Madinah to conquer Makkah in 630 CE.
- Burhanuddin Rabbani, the former president of Afghanistan (1992–1996), referred to how dangerous possessing only a little knowledge of medicine or religion can be when he said: "We have a proverb: half a *mullah* is a danger to your faith, half a doctor is a danger to your life. A person who is not a proper doctor can kill, and a person who is not a proper *mullah* can ruin the faith of Muslims" (Babak Dehghanpisheh's interview in *Newsweek,* January 28, 2002, p. 4).
- The Organization of the Islamic Conference (OIC), which represents fifty-seven Muslim countries strongly condemned the terrorist attacks in the United States one day after they occurred. On Wednesday, September 12, 2001, OIC secretary general Abdel Wahad Belkaziz said: "We condemn these savage and criminal acts which are anathema to all human conventions and values and the monotheist religions, led by Islam."
- The political leaders and Islamic clerics of many Muslim countries have also individually condemned the terrorist attacks in the United States, for the simple reasons that they are clearly forbidden in Islam and are a grotesque misrepresentation of the Islamic doctrine of *jihad.*

> http://www.islamdenouncesterrorism.com/islam_middleeast.html
> http://www.thetruereligion.org/usattack.htm
> http://www.religioustolerance.org/islam.htm

Umar ibn al-Khattab converted to Islam in the sixth year of Muhammad's Prophethood. Abu Bakr nominated Umar, who was then endorsed by the Makkan tribal leaders, to be the second caliph. He reigned for a decade (634–644 CE) and contributed significantly to the spread of Islam. Umar's armies conquered Mesopotamia, Egypt, Syria, Palestine, the greater part of Persia, Tabristan, Azerbaijan, Armenia, and even some parts of Turkey. He was also the first Muslim leader to assume the title of supreme commander of the faithful. As a competent public administrator, Umar created a number of new departments, including a police department, a welfare service to assist the needy, and an education department. Umar also organized a sound financial system, constructed several forts and new cities throughout the Islamic empire, and established a consultative body that deliberated on public policy and guided him in its implementation. Caliph Umar was assassinated by a disgruntled non-Muslim Persian slave.

Uthman ibn Affan was a wealthy merchant and among the first converts to Islam. Uthman married Prophet Muhammad's daughter Ruqayya and, after her death, her sister Umm Kulthum. Muslim tribal leaders chose Uthman to be Islam's third caliph, succeeding Umar. During Uthman's reign (644–656 CE), his armies conquered much of Persia and North Africa. Although Abu Bakr started the process of collating the Qur'an and the process continued under Caliph Umar, it was during Uthman's reign that Islamic experts completed the process of the Qur'an's collation and codification. Before Uthman was murdered, he oversaw the publication and distribution of the standard edition of the Qur'an throughout the empire. He also introduced the first organized news service in Islamic history.

ibn Ali Tahib was the cousin and son-in-law of Prophet Muhammad. He was also the first convert to Islam after Khadijah. He was raised by the Prophet and one year after the *Hijrah,* at the age of twenty-four, he married the Prophet's daughter Fatimah. She bore him two sons, Hasan and Hussein. Ali became the fourth and last of the four rightly guided caliphs and reigned from 656 to 661 CE. Shi'ahs believe that, on account of Ali's piety, knowledge, valor in the field of battle, and closeness to Prophet Muhammad, the Prophet nominated Ali to succeed him as the first *Imam* (religiopolitical leader) or *khalifah* of the Muslim world. The first major schism in the "House of Islam" owes its origins to this very matter of succession and has not been resolved to this day.

Islamic Sects

To understand sects in Islam, one needs first to understand the concept of *fiqh.* In Arabic the term *fiqh* literally means "intelligence," "understanding," or "knowledge." In Islam the term means "Islamic jurisprudence," which covers all aspects of religious, political, economic, and social life. While not being as comprehensive, divine, eternal, and immutable as the *shariah*, each *madhab* (sect) in Islam has its own *fiqh*, which is interpreted by a theologian and jurist known as a *faqih.*

The Muslim world is divided into two major *madhabs*, the **Sunnis** and the **Shi'ahs**. These two sects, in turn, comprise several minor **madhabs** (schools of Islamic jurisprudence) or subsects. Sunnis are the majority sect of Islam and comprise over 80 percent of the Muslim world. The term *sunni* in Arabic literally means "those who follow the *sunnah*" (Prophet Muhammad's way), comprising the Prophet's sayings and deeds. There are four main Sunni *madhabs*—the Hanafi, Maliki, Shafi'i, and the Hanbali—named after the four learned *ulama* who played a principal role in developing these four major schools of Islamic jurisprudence.

Hanifis follow the Islamic jurisprudence of the Iraqi-born *Imam* Abu Hanifah al-Nu'man ibn-Thabit (699–569 CE). In this case, two of Abu Hanifah's most illustrious pupils meticulously collected and presented many of their mentor's lectures and writings. The Hanafi sect was actively promoted by a number of Abbasid and Ottoman rulers and is widely prevalent in Turkey, Afghanistan, Egypt, Central Asia, China, and South Asia.

Malikis follow the Islamic jurisprudence of Imam Abu Abd Allah Malik ibn Anas (716–795 CE). He received part of his early Islamic education from Sahl ibn-Sa'ad, a companion of Prophet Muhammad. Imam Malik was one of the most learned Islamic scholars and a friend of Abu Hanifa, with whom he had a number of discussions on Islamic issues. Ash-Shafi'i—who later became famous for founding the Shafi'i sect of Sunni Islam—was one of his pupils. Among Imam Malik's writings is a treatise on the *hadith* entitled *Kitab-al-Muwatta (The Book of the Trodden Path)*, in which he codified Islamic common law. In his research, Imam Malik relied heavily on the *sunnah* and as far as possible refrained from resorting to inferences and deductions. The Maliki sect spread in Muslim Spain and Africa.

Shafi'is follow the instruction of Imam Muhammad ibn'Idris ash-Shafi'i (767–820 CE). He was brought up in Makkah, where he studied the Qur'an, *hadith,* and *fiqh* (Islamic jurisprudence). When he was twenty, he went to Madinah and studied under Malik ibn-Anas until the latter's death. He traveled in many parts of the Muslim Middle East and taught for some time in Baghdad, Egypt, and Makkah. He researched the Islamic legal material that was available, investigated the principles and methods of jurisprudence, and articulated specific rules for *qiyas* (analogical reasoning). Eventually his efforts made him the founder of the **Usul al-Fiqh** (Principles of Islamic Jurisprudence). He promoted a moderate and eclectic brand of Islam that stood for the continuity of tradition as well as change through *ijtihad* (independent reasoning). The Shafi'i sect spread in southwestern Asia and northern Egypt. Its decline began when the Ottoman government, comprising members mostly of the Hanafi sect, propagated their Hanafi *madhab* throughout the Ottoman Empire.

Hanbalis belong to the most puritanical and iconoclastic of the four Sunni schools of Islamic jurisprudence. The founder of the Hanbali sect was the Iraqi-born theologian and jurist Imam Ahmad ibn-Hanbal (780–855 CE). His puritanism brought him into a conflict with the **Mutazilite** school of rationalism and free will, which was at its zenith during the reigns of Abbasid caliphs al-Ma'mun, al-Mu'tasim, and al-Watiq (833–849 CE). He condemned *bid'a* (innovations in the purity of Islamic beliefs and practices), including the Mutazilite notion that the Qur'an was "created," not revealed, by Allah as well as Sufism (see Box 1.5). He was imprisoned and even subjected to corporal punishment for his convictions but regained his position under Abbasid caliph al-Mutawakkil. His knowledge of Islam, piety, and steadfastness won him many disciples and admirers. But the puritanism of the Hanbali *madhab,* combined with the promotion of the Hanafi *madhab* by the Ottoman rulers, who attempted to aggressively suppress Wahhabism (a religiopolitcal ideology within the Hanbali *madhab*), resulted in the Hanbalis being the smallest of the four established Sunni *madhabs.* Significant credit for the Hanbali *madhab* must also be given to Taqi al-Din ibn-Taimiyyah (1263–1328 CE) and Muhammad ibn Abd al-Wahhab (1703–1792 CE), who did more than anyone else in popularizing Imam ibn Hanbal's *fiqh* and worldview. In the last quarter century, Saudi Arabia and Qatar (where the Hanbali *madhab* is practiced)

BOX 1.5   Sufism

Sufism is that body of Islamic beliefs and practices that tends to promote a mystical communion between Muslims and God. Sufism is practiced by *sufis*, who have contributed significantly to the peaceful spread of Islam in many parts of the Muslim world.

Sufis are ascetic and pious Muslim mystics. The term *sufi* is derived from early Muslim ascetics and mystics who wore simple clothes made out of *suf* (coarse wool). The founders of the *sufi tariqahs* (fraternities or social organizations) were Islamic scholars and emphasized the *shariah* (Islamic law). Later, *sufis* became lax in their observance of the *shariah* and devoted their lives to meditation and proselytization. Their teachings are replete with a love for God and Prophet Muhammad, the esoteric rather than the literal interpretation of the Qur'an and the *sunnah* (Prophet Muhammad's sayings and deeds), and a search for eternal truth and goodness. Because *sufis* appeal to the practical religious attitudes of the masses, their "folk Islam" has been responsible for the conversion of large numbers to Islam.

The term *tariqah* is often associated with Sufism. Tariqah literally means "path" or "way" in Arabic. The term refers to the path or method of mysticism and spiritualism promoted by *sufi* teachers. It also refers to the social organization (like *sufi* fraternities, orders, or brotherhoods) formed by the followers of such *sufi* teachers. *Tariqahs* began as informal groups in which individuals interested in religious philosophy and sociocultural issues gathered around famous *sufi* instructors. By the twelfth century, these *tariqahs* became popular, large-scale, and formalized associations based on devotional traditions. While there is no centralized organization or headquarters for the numerous *tariqahs* around the world, they have provided a unifying force for Islam at the international level.

http://www.geocities.com/Athens/Olympus/5352/sufism.htm
http://www.geocities.com/Athens/Olympus/5352/
http://www.al-islam.org/beliefs/spirituality/suffism.html
http://www.digiserve.com/mystic/Muslim/
http://isfahan.anglia.ac.uk/glossary/sufi/sufism1.html
http://www.gss.org/articles/sufism/toc.html
http://www.geocities.com/Athens/5738/title.htm
http://www.sufismjournal.org/
http://www.arches.uga.edu/~godlas/Sufism.html
http://www.ias.org/featured.html
http://www.nimatullahi.org/us/WIS/WIS1.html
http://www.sufism.org/society/articles/women.html

---

have made a significant effort to promote the Hanbali *madhab* and Wahhabism to the four corners of the Muslim world.

The term **Shi'ah** literally means "party," "partisan," "follower," or "split." Members of this second major sect of Islam (after the majority Sunni sect), comprising 15 to 20 percent of the world's *ummah*, believe that Prophet Muhammad nominated Ali to be the first *Imam* of the *ummah* because he was best qualified for the job. The Arabic term *Shi'ah* is thus an abbreviation for *shi'at-i-Ali* (Ali's faction). Within the Shi'ah sect there are a number of subsects, namely, the Ithna Asharis, Bohris, Ismailis, and Alawites. The Ithna Ashari Shi'ah sect represents a majority in Iran, Iraq, Bahrain, and Lebanon. They are also approximately 15 to 20 percent of the Muslim population in India and Pakistan.[6]

Sunnis and Shi'ahs: A Comparison

In addition to the *shahadah* (profession of the faith), "I bear witness that there is no God but Allah, and Muhammad is His Messenger," Shi'ahs often add the phrase "Ali is the beloved of God." Although Ali did become Islam's fourth caliph, he was preceded by Abu Bakr, Umar, and Uthman. Therefore, while Sunnis revere the first four "rightly guided" or "pious" caliphs, many orthodox Shi'ahs usually reject the legitimacy of Ali's three predecessors and all his successors. This difference in belief is an obstacle to Shi'ah and Sunni reconciliation and reunification.

In addition, Sunnis insist that Prophet Muhammad was a mere human being through whom God revealed his message (as recorded in the Qur'an), whereas Shi'ahs contend that the Prophet was infallible and possessed some semidivine attributes because of the **Nur-i-Elahi** (Divine Light) shared by all of God's prophets. Moreover, Shi'ahs assert, elements of the Nur-i-Elahi were bestowed upon Muhammad's daughter, Fatimah, her husband, Imam Ali, and their descendants through their male progeny. While Sunnis respect Ali and his descendants, they do not revere them to the extent that Shi'ahs do. Indeed, the Sunnis reject the Shi'ah contention that Muhammad selected Ali to be the first *Imam* of the Islamic state and thus repudiate the Shi'ah institution of the **Imamate** (the divine right of Ali and his male descendants to lead the *ummah*). These differences in doctrine have contributed to Shi'ah-Sunni conflict.

Closely connected to the institution of the Imamate is the doctrine of the **Ithna Ashari** (Twelver) Shi'ah sect regarding the disappearance of the twelfth apostolic Imam in 873 CE and his expected reappearance as the **Mahdi** (the divinely guided one or messianic savior), who will usher in a golden age of Islamic justice, equality, and unity of the *ummah*. So powerful is the idea of the Mahdi in Islam that many Sunnis have accepted it, as well.

Another major difference between Shi'ahs and Sunnis is in the realm of *fiqh* (Islamic jurisprudence). While Sunnis recognize four schools or rites of *fiqh* (the Hanafi, Hanbali, Maliki, and Shafi'i sects), the Shi'ah have only one major *madhab* (sect), **Fiqh-i-Ja'fariyyah**, which was compiled and codified by the sixth Shi'ah *imam*, Ja'afar-i-Sadiq (died 765 CE). Shi'ahs promote the exercise of *ijtihad* (independent reasoning and judgment) by experienced *mujtahids* (*ulama*, entitled to exercise *ijtihad*) and reject the Sunni concept of *qiyas* (deduction by analogy) as the fourth source of Islamic law after the Qur'an, the *sunnah*, and *ijma* (consen-

[6]See the following web sites to learn more about Shi'ahs and Shi'ism: www.al.Islam.org; www.al-shia.com; and www.AskUs_AboutIslam.org.

sus). Furthermore, differences exist between Shi'ahs and Sunnis in the laws of marriage, divorce, and inheritance. Twelver Shi'ahs, for example, permit temporary marriage, or **mut'ah**. For Sunnis, any marriage contract that sets a limit to the duration of marriage is sinful. Shi'ahs, by contrast, place greater restrictions than do Sunnis on the husband's right to divorce his wife. In addition, in matters of inheritance, female heiresses often are treated far more generously in the Shi'ah Fiqh-i-Ja'fariyyah than under the Hanafi, Hanbali, Maliki, or Shafi'i schools of Sunni *fiqh*. Further differentiating Shi'ahs from Sunnis is the exclusively Shi'ah practice of **taqiyyah** (concealment), which permits an individual to conceal his true religious, ideological, or political beliefs to avoid persecution or death at the hands of enemies. This practice evolved in response to fifteen hundred years of persecution of Shi'ahs throughout the Muslim world.

The two major sects of Islam likewise differ with respect to religious tradition. The Shi'ahs engage in more rituals than do the Sunnis. Indeed, Sunni revolutionary Islamists (especially the Wahhabis) often denounce Shi'ahs for their adulation of saints, especially the most prominent members of the **Ahl al-Bayt** (Prophet Muhammad's extended family), and their pilgrimages to the mausoleums of saints in Iraq, Iran, and Syria. Portraits of Prophet Muhammad, Imam Ali, Imam Hussein, and the battle of Karbala are publicly displayed and sold in Iran. Such pictures would never be displayed in predominantly Sunni societies where there is a much greater concern that people would start venerating, idolizing, and even worshiping Prophet Muhammad and prominent members of his family.

The practice of daily liturgical prayers also differs between Sunnis and Shi'ahs. Shi'ahs are permitted to perform their five daily prayers three times a day (between dawn and sunrise, between midday and sunset, and between sunset and midnight) instead of the five times practiced by Sunnis (before sunrise, around midday, in the late afternoon, at dusk, and before midnight). The two sects' calls to prayer also differ, as do their manners of praying: Shi'ahs stand with their arms hanging straight down, whereas Sunnis fold their arms in front of themselves.

Shi'ahs and Sunnis differ greatly in their commemoration of **Muharram,** the first month in the Islamic lunar calendar and the month in 680 CE in which Prophet Muhammad's grandson **Hussein ibn Ali** and his male followers were martyred on the battlefield of **Karbala** by Umayyad caliph Yazid's army. While Sunnis revere Hussein and lament his martyrdom, the Ithna Ashari (Twelver) Shi'ahs attend **majlises** (meetings) where Islamic scholars deliver sermons recounting the lives, deeds, and sayings of the twelve *imams* as well as portraying vivid and powerful stories about the significance of Karbala. After all *majlises,* Shi'ahs engage in *ma'atam* (breast beating) and deeply mourn the massacre of Imam Hussein and his small band of followers and the deplorable treatment of the female members of the Ahl al-Bayt. Through these *majlises*, Shi'ahs educate the younger generation in the lessons of true Islam. Sunnis, however, feel that Shi'ahs have created an inappropriate cult around the personalities of Hussein and his father, Ali, and strongly criticize the manifest masochism of some Shi'ahs during Muharram.

Although Shi'ahs and Sunnis have their differences, as do adherents of the four Sunni sects, Muslims of both sects agree that they have much in common.

Not only do they share most fundamental religious beliefs, but the devout members of all Islamic sects express their conviction that Islam provides answers and guidance in all endeavors, even political. Thus, Muslims of all sects are sharing in the Islamic revival that is sweeping through the Muslim world.

The Status of Women in Islam

Many non-Muslims think that Islam is unfair to women. This misperception is based on the improper practice of Islam by some Muslims. The negative stereotype of Muslim women as uneducated, subjugated, and abused, with no rights and no opportunities, is a caricature born of ignorance or malevolence. In the following quotations from the Qur'an and Prophet Muhammad's *hadith*, it will be obvious that Islam actually raised the status of women and that it is the cultural traditions of male chauvinism in patriarchal Muslim societies that are holding women back.

- In the Qur'anic account of Creation, woman was *not* created from the rib of man as Judaism and Christianity suggest. Rather, the first person (indefinite gender) was created, and then that person's mate was created (4:1). Moreover, Eve was not considered the temptress and the cause of "original sin"; both Adam and Eve were equally responsible for disobeying and annoying God in the Garden of Eden (7:20–25; 20:21).

- The Qur'an prohibits the pagan Arab practice of female infanticide prevalent in pre-Islamic Arabia: "You shall not kill your children for fear of want; We will provide for them and for you. To kill them is a great sin" (17:31).

- In the Arabian peninsula of the sixth century CE, women who were lucky to survive to adulthood were treated like chattel, sold into marriage by their fathers, kidnapped, raped, and purchased both as concubines and as members of large harems. Some tribal chieftains had as many as fifty wives. Prophet Muhammad abhorred the practice of forced marriages made by a woman's guardian and instead converted marriage into a legal agreement or civil contract between two consenting individuals. Based on a Qur'anic revelation, Muhammad also limited the number of women any one man could marry to four, "provided they were treated equally" (4:3). As there were several tribal wars, resulting in numerous male fatalities and consequently an overabundance of widows and orphans, Muhammad felt that through marriage the warring tribes could be brought closer while providing care for widows and orphans. The Qur'an later added that it was impossible for a man to do justice to more than one wife (4:129).

- Islam gave women inheritance rights in the sixth century, long before the practice became common in the West. Although women were given half the amount assigned to corresponding males, this was still a big step forward in the Arabia of those days (4:11). This is in sharp contrast to many Western cultures, where until only a couple of centuries ago, daughters could not inherit anything if there were sons in the family. In fact, even in

BOX 1.6   The Nation of Islam

In 1930, Wallace Fard Muhammad—an itinerant peddler selling trinkets, silks, and rain-coats—began making the rounds in the predominantly black ghettoes of Detroit, Michigan, USA. He claimed to have been born in Makkah in the Arabian peninsula, enter-tained his customers by drawing on his travels in Africa, and eloquently spoke of the com-mon heritage of African-Americans. A year later, when Fard saw that his following had significantly expanded, he established the first "University of Islam" (with a primary, mid-dle, and high school) and Temple No. 1.

Drawing on claims previously made by Noble Drew Ali (1886–1929)—founder of the Moorish Holy Temple of Science in Newark, New Jersey, in 1913—Fard told blacks that their ancestors were from the ancient and distinguished Muslim tribe of Shabazz in Africa; that "racist whites" were "blue-eyed devils" who would continue to deprive blacks the fruits of their labor and the benefits of American life; that blacks in the United States could free themselves from white racist domination, as well as earn God's favor, only through self-knowledge, self-help, self-love, and solidarity in their own united Black Muslim Nation that was separate from the white race; that Allah had summoned him to redeem the original race of humankind—the black race; and that only through the "Lost-Found Nation of Islam," with belief in a black God, could they expect to realize their just economic, political, and social rights.

By 1934, Fard had converted several hundred blacks to the Nation of Islam; devel-oped a paramilitary organization, the "Fruit of Islam," trained in the use of firearms to pro-tect the Black Nation's members and institutions; trained a spiritual minister and a cadre of administrators to run the organization; and anointed Elijah Poole (1897–1975)—a for-mer member of the Moorish Temple of Science—as his successor. Then Fard disap-peared without a trace.

Elijah Poole assumed the name Elijah Muhammad, moved to Chicago to establish Temple No. 2, and gave the impression that he was God's prophet, while Fard, who had anointed him, was the divine savior of the black race, akin to the second coming of Jesus Christ, the long-awaited "Messiah" and "Mahdi." Elijah Muhammad claimed that God had originally created blacks to rule His kingdom and that whites were the product of a eugenics experiment that had gone terribly wrong and created the devil-ish white race that sought to enslave blacks. On another occasion, Elijah Muhammad said that an evil scientist called Yaqub created whites in a fit of anger, and the Nation of Islam's principal mission was to prepare blacks for the coming Battle of Armageddon, in which blacks would prevail over whites and regain their God-given right to control the world.

Besides Fard's divinity, his own prophethood, and the teachings of black supremacy and racial separation, Elijah Muhammad's pseudo-Islamic Nation of Islam was based on the following key ideas: the Qur'an and the scriptures of all the Old Testament prophets are equally valid (while Muslims believe the latter have been corrupted and only the Qur'an remains the authentic Word of God); on the Day of Judgment, only the souls of all human beings would be resurrected (while Muslims believe in the physical resurrection of all dead human beings from the time of Creation); adherents should pray to God every day (but not the five ritual Islamic prayers in Arabic that Muslims are expected to offer daily); adherents should fast during December, but fasting during the Islamic lunar month of Ramadan is optional; a "poor due" is required on income only, and this goes to support only black members of the Nation of Islam (not the 2.5 percent of wealth that Muslims are obligated to contribute annually to the needy irrespective of their religion, color, ethnicity, or nationality anywhere in the world); and there is no obligation to perform the *hajj* during the twelfth Islamic month of Dhul-Hijjah.

When Elijah Muhammad died in 1975, his autocratically run, highly disciplined, tightly knit, and enterprising organization had several hundred thousand African American members; over fifty universities of Islam and 150 temples in the United States and the Caribbean; thousands of acres of farmland; numerous schools, supermarkets, banks, newspapers, restaurants, and dry cleaning establishments. His organization had also established many social service programs (such as running drug and alcohol rehabilitation programs and sending missionaries to reform prisoners).

On Elijah Muhammad's death, his son, Wallace D. Muhammad, assumed the leadership of the Nation of Islam. He changed his name to Warith Deen Muhammad; called his father merely a teacher and not a divinely sent prophet; rejected the antiwhite racism of his father; encouraged nonblacks to join the Nation of Islam; did away with the rigid dress code (including the long garments that covered women from head to toe); encouraged members to participate in American politics and permitted them to join the U.S. armed forces; renamed the organization The "American Muslim Mission," then "World Community of Islam," and finally "Community of Al-Islam in the West"; and in 1985 asked his followers to join mainstream Sunni Islam.

In 1980, Louis Farrakhan, born Louis Eugene Walcott in 1933—the charismatic minister and spellbinding orator of the Nation of Islam's New York temple became the leader of a breakaway faction within the Nation of Islam that was committed to espousing much of Elijah Muhammad's ideology while tempering the message of "separatism." Farrakhan encouraged voter registration drives in black communities and tried to rebuild the poor African American ghettoes of the inner cities with the assistance of the United States government, churches, private corporations and banks, and other nongovernmental black organizations.

The crowning achievement of Farrakhan's controversial career as the leader of the Nation of Islam thus far was the October 1995 "Million Man March" in Washington, D.C. This much publicized event that his organization planned and organized with numerous African American churches for several months was intended to celebrate black pride, unity, and responsibility. In his keynote address to the massive gathering in America's capital, Farrakhan called on African American men to rededicate themselves to their families and their communities.

Source: Kwame Anthony Appiah and Henry Louis Gates, Jr., eds., *Africana: The Encyclopedia of the African and African American Experience* (New York: Basic Civitas Books, 1999); Columbus Alley, *The Black 100: A Ranking of the Most Influential African-Americans, Past and Present*, 3rd ed. (Secausus, NJ: Citadel Press, 1999); M. Amir Ali, "Comparison between Islam and Farrakhanism" (under Pseudo-Islamic Cults at <http://www.iiie.net>).

Great Britain, the so-called mother of democracies, women were granted the right to own property independent of their husbands only in 1870.

- The bridal gift was no longer payable to the guardian but to the woman directly. A woman was also given the right to own property, manage it herself, and bequeath it to whomsover she chose (4:11).

- A woman could earn her own living as an independent individual, without any obligation to contribute her income or wealth to her husband or her family (4:32).

- The Qur'an states: "O you who believe! You are forbidden to inherit Women against their will. Nor should you treat them with harshness, that you may take away part of the dower you have given them, except where they have been guilty of open lewdness; On the contrary, live with them on a footing of kindness and equity" (4:19).

- The Qur'an emphasizes that all people, men and women, are equal, and "the noblest among you in the sight of God is the most God-fearing and the best in conduct" (46:13). It also states that a woman on the Day of Judgment will be absolutely equal to a man (4:124).

- Prophet Muhammad's open-minded, progressive, and "feminist" attitudes toward women can best be illustrated in his first marriage to Khadijah. She was a confident and mature widow, and an enterprising and self-actualized businesswomen who ran a successful trading company herself; earned her living outside the home in a patriarchal, male chauvinist, and sexist society; was the Prophet's employer under whom he actively and happily worked; and was fifteen years older than him (she was forty and he was twenty-five) when she proposed a love marriage in an era when arranged marriages were common. For nearly fifteen years thereafter, Muhammad and Khadijah were partners in the international trading company—the first recorded male–female partnership in the region. She was the first person with whom he shared Archangel Gabriel's visit in the cave. Intimately knowing his impeccable character, she was the one who reassured him that God had anointed him as His Prophet and who became his first convert. She also decided to contribute her entire fortune, time, and support to the spread of Islam in the teeth of fierce Makkan persecution.

Below are some of Prophet Muhammad's most noteworthy *hadith* relating to the status of women in Islam. All of them can be found in two of the most reputable authentic sources, namely, Sahih Muslim and Sahih Bukhari.

- Prophet Muhammad often stated that "all people are equal, as equal as the teeth of a comb. There is no merit of an Arab over a non-Arab, or of a white over a black person, or of a male over a female. Only God-fearing people merit preference."

- Two famous *hadith* attributed to Prophet Muhammad are "Paradise lies at the feet of thy mother" and "He who wishes to enter Paradise must please his father and mother."

- A woman can retain her name and does not have to adopt her husband's surname after she gets married. Prophet Muhammad's daughter Fatimah remained Fatimah bint Muhammad ("bint" meaning "daughter of") even after she married Ali ibn Abu Talib.

- When several girls complained to Prophet Muhammad that the boys in their classes were surpassing them in learning the Qur'an and *hadith*, the Prophet assigned the girls special time for instruction so that they might catch up.

- It is nevertheless true that in Islam a woman is enjoined to dress modestly in public and give her full commitment to being a homemaker first and foremost. However, what is rarely mentioned by non-Muslims is that Islam enjoins men to dress modestly, too.

- Women in most Western countries—which have been developing democratic institutions over centuries instead of only a few decades, as in independent Muslim countries—did not gain the right to vote until the twentieth century. Great Britain enfranchised women in 1918, the United States in 1920, France in 1944, and Switzerland in 1971.

- While five Muslim women have governed Muslim countries (see Box 1.7), the United States, the preeminent power in the Western world, has yet to have a female vice president or president.[7]

The Heterogeneous Muslim World

The Muslim world is by no means monolithic. In fact, it is very heterogeneous and pluralistic. Were it not for Islam, the countries of the Muslim world would have little in common. Some Muslim countries are ancient in origin, like Iran, Iraq, Egypt, and Yemen, while others are recent creations of the colonial powers, like Nigeria and Pakistan, or are federations of formerly separate peoples, like Malaysia. By the same token, Muslim countries have different political histories. The impact of various colonialists powers has contributed to differentiation in political and economic development among the nation-states of the Muslim world. Many were colonized for decades before finally gaining independence, while a few, like Afghanistan, endured only a decade-long colonial era (1979–1989).

Muslim countries like Bangladesh, Egypt, Pakistan, Indonesia, Nigeria, Jordan, and Malaysia are dangerously overpopulated, while others, like Libya,

---

[7]Below are a few web sites that focus on women in Islam: http://answering-islam.org/Women/inislam.html; http://www.beconvinced.com/WOMENINDEX.htm; http://www.islamzine.com/women/; http://www.geocities.com/Athens/Academy/7368/w_comparison_full2.htm# Toc335566668; http://sultan.org/articles/women.html; http://www.usc.edu/dept/MSA/ humanrelations/womeninislam/; http://www.submission.org/women/; http://www.geocities .com/Athens/Agora/6526/CC5.htm; http://www.submission.org/women-comp.html; http://www.arches.uga.edu/~godlas/islamwomen.html; and http://www.mwlusa.org/welcome.html.

■

BOX 1.7   Five Women Who Have Governed Muslim Countries

In 1988 Pakistan became the first Muslim country with a woman head of government: Benazir Bhutto was sworn in as Pakistan's prime minister. Bhutto was born in Karachi in 1953 and educated abroad at Radcliffe College and Oxford University. She was the daughter of Zulfikar Ali Bhutto, the Pakistani prime minister who was overthrown by the military government of Zia al-Haq in 1977 and executed in 1979. Benazir and her mother were elected cochairs of her father's political party, the Pakistan People's Party. Benazir Bhutto was elected prime minister in 1988 but was dismissed by Pakistan's president in 1990. In 1993 she was reelected prime minister and served until dismissed from office again in 1996. During her second term, her government was accused of corruption and mismanagement, and Bhutto's husband was arrested and jailed. Despite attempts to return to power in 1997 and 1998, Benazir Bhutto now lives in exile abroad.

Turkey elected Tansu Ciller, its first female prime minister, in 1993. Ciller's leadership, however, was tarnished by accusations of graft and corruption. To protect her hold on power, she formed an alliance with an Islamist political party, a move that shocked and alienated her secular supporters. Although she lost her position as prime minister in 1996, she was appointed foreign minister. Ciller was to serve as prime minister again in 1997, but her coalition government lost its majority later that year.

Bangladesh can lay claim to two female prime ministers in the last ten years. Khaleda Zia became Bangladesh's first female prime minister in 1991. Her husband, Ziaur Rehman, was elected president in 1979. Khaleda Zia entered politics shortly after her husband's assassination in 1981, as head of the Bangladesh Nationalist Party (BNP). Khaleda Zia's party lost its majority in 1996, and Hasina Wajed, the daughter of Mujibur Rahman, Bangladesh's first prime minister, became the second female prime minister of Bangladesh. In October 2001 Wajed's party lost its majority and Khaleda Zia began another term as prime minister.

Indonesia, the most populous Muslim country, was thrown into constitutional turmoil in July 2001, when President Abdurrahman Wahid declared a state of emergency to prevent his impeachment by Indonesia's parliament. With military backing, the parliament reconvened, stripped Wahid of his office, and made his vice president, Megawati Sukarnoputri, the first female president of Indonesia. Sukarnoputri's road to the presidency began with her father, Indonesia's first president, Sukarno, who led his country to independence in 1949. In 1966 Sukarno was forced from power by Suharto. In 1993 Sukarno's daughter, Megawati, began her political career and benefited from her father's populist legacy. Nevertheless, Sukarnoputri has been successful in her own right, ably balancing her nation's support of U.S.-led war on terror against street demonstrations in Indonesia opposed to that support.

http://www.wic.org/bio/bbhutto.htm
http://europe.cnn.com/resources/newsmakers/world/asia/bhutto.html
http://www.defencejournal.com/2001/october/hasina.htm
http://www.benazir-bhutto.net/default.asp
http://www.virtualbangladesh.com/biography/khaleda.html
http://www.un.int/bangladesh/gen/pm-bio.htm
http://gos.sbc.edu/w/zia.html
http://csf.colorado.edu/bcas/sample/megawati.htm
http://www.hebatindo.com/infopages/mega_eng.htm

BOX 1.8   Crescent and Star: The Symbol of Islam

The term *crescent,* or **hilal** in Arabic, is used particularly for the new moon, or the moon's shape in the first quarter. It has also become the emblem or symbol of Islam and can be found on the flags of a number of Muslim countries, on the coins of many Muslim countries, and in jewelry and art.

One reason given for the crescent and star being the emblem or symbol of Islam is that it is mentioned in the Qur'an: "They ask you concerning the phases of the moon. Say (O Muhammad), these are appointed times for the people and the pilgrimage" (2:189). From this verse we understand that the moon, the stars, and the sun are natural signs that are connected with the commemoration of Islamic holy days. The Islamic calendar starts with Prophet Muhammad's Hijrah (migration) and the establishment of the first Islamic state in Madinah. Each Islamic calendar month starts with the sighting of the new moon.

Another reason given is that the crescent initially symbolized the horns of a ram and was placed by the Turkish tribal chieftains of Central Asia at the top of their flagstaffs and tent poles. It became identified with Islam when the Muslim Turks began using the crescent (as the equivalent of the Christian cross) on their military and naval standards as well as on top of their mosques and other religious buildings.

Today the white crescent may be seen along with one to five stars on the national flags of several Muslim countries. Moreover, the Red Crescent is the Muslim equivalent of the International Red Cross organization. The International Red Cross recognized these Red Crescent societies as members of its international humanitarian and welfare network—informally at first, but formally since 1949. In 1986 the League of Red Cross Societies was renamed the "League of Red Cross and Red Crescent Societies."

Zbigniew Brzezinski coined the term "crescent of crisis" back in the late 1970s, when he was President Jimmy Carter's national security advisor. The term covers the turbulent heartland of the Muslim world that lies in the Middle East and South Asia, forming an arc or crescent.

http://www.ummah.net/ildl/

Saudi Arabia, the United Arab Emirates, Qatar, and Quwait, are sparsely populated. Others, like Lebanon and Bahrain, are largely urbanized societies, while Sudan, Pakistan, Bangladesh, Jordan, Egypt, Morocco, Tunisia, Algeria, Malaysia, and Indonesia are predominantly agrarian societies.

Some Muslim nations are enormous in territorial size, like Saudi Arabia, Iran, Egypt, and Sudan, while others like Djibouti, Brunei, Kuwait, Bahrain, Qatar, Oman, and the Maldive Islands are mere specks on the world map. Muslim nations like Egypt have a population that is relatively homogeneous, while others, including Iran, Iraq, Pakistan, Malaysia, and the Sudan, have heterogeneous populations. Politically, many Muslim countries are governed by monarchs, others by military juntas, and still others by authoritarian one-party regimes; only a few can be considered democratic. Likewise, some Muslim countries are based on the socialist economic model, while others are capitalist.

TABLE 1.1   An Overview of Islam, Judaism, and Christianity

Key Subjects	Islam	Judaism	Christianity
Symbol of the Religion	Crescent and Star	Menorah; the Star of David	Cross
Holy City(ies)	Makkah, Madinah, and Jerusalem.	Jerusalem	Jerusalem (for all Christians) and Vatican City in Rome, Italy (for Roman Catholics)
House of Worship	*Masjid* (mosque)	Synagogue	Church
Use of Images in Worship	Forbidden		Eastern Orthodox Church and Catholicism condone it; Protestant churches don't.
Religious School(s)	*Madrassahs* (Islamic schools) often in *masjids* (mosques)	Synagogues and Jewish community centers have Sunday and day Jewish schools; and Jewish community programs for adult education.	Sunday schools at church; and parochial primary and secondary schools during week days.
Training for Religious Leadership	Islamic seminaries for aspiring teachers and *ulama* (Islamic scholars)	Yeshiva and/or rabbinical seminaries for the training of rabbis.	Christian seminaries and theological institutes for aspiring ministers, bishops, and priests
Spiritual Ministers/ Clerics (People of the Cloth)	*Mullahs, maulanas, moulvis, ulama* (Islamic scholars), *muftis* (authorities in Sunni Islam), and *ayatollahs* (authorities in Shi'ah Islam)	Rabbis	Ministers/reverends in Protestant denominations; bishops and priests in Catholicism.
Number of Believers Worldwide	There are over 1.2 billion Muslims (one-fifth of the world's population): approximately 57.6% in South and Southeast Asia; 28.1% in North and Sub-Saharan Africa; 8.9% in Southwest Asia; 4.4% in the former Soviet Republics and in present-day Russia; and 1% other. In fact, less than 25% of the Muslim world is made up of arab Muslims (over 24% of them living in the Middle East), and no more than 35% of the Muslim world reside in the Middle East (Southwest Asia and North Africa).	There are approximately 18 million Jews in the world: approximately 48% in North America (most in the U.S.); 27% in Israel; 18% in Europe, Russia, and former Soviet Republics; 4.5% in the Middle East (minus Israel); 1% in Africa; 0.5% in South America; 1% other.	There are over 2 billion Christians in the world. Thus, nearly one-third of the world's population is Christian: approximately 37% in North and South America; 22% in Europe; 18% in Africa; 16% in Asia; 7% other.

Key Subjects	Islam	Judaism	Christianity
Major Sects or Branches, and Subsects	Sunni and Shi'ah sects; several subsects within each	Orthodox (e.g., Hasidim), Conservative, Reform, and Reconstructionist	Three major sects: Orthodox, Catholic, and Protestant; several denominations in each of these three.
Greetings among the Faithful	*Salaam alaykum* (Peace be on/with you) and *Wa'alaykum as-Salaam* (peace be on/with you too)	*Shalom* (Peace)	No greeting of equivalence.
Concept of God	Believe in the one, transcendent, omnipotent, omnipresent, omniscient, eternal, just, and merciful God.		
Monotheism	• Believe that God is indivisible, has no equals, no partner, and no offspring. • Disagree with Christianity's belief in the Holy Trinity: God the Father, the Son (Jesus Christ), and Holy Spirit.		Believe in the Holy Trinity: God the Father, the Son (Jesus Christ), and Holy Spirit. These three persons coexist within one Godhead.
	• Muslims call God *Allah*. • Islam's uncompromising monotheism is present throughtout the Qur'an. *Al-Akhlas (the Purity of Faith)*, the briefest chapter in the Qur'an, states it best: "Say (O Muhammad): He is Allah, The One and Only! Allah, the Eternal, Absolute; He did not give birth (to anyone), Nor did anyone give birth to Him. And there is no one equal (similar) to Him" (112:1–4).	• Jews call God *Adonai*. • Judaism's uncompromising monotheism is present throughout the Hebrew Bible. For instance, the Hebrew *Shema*, "Hear O Israel, the Lord our God, the Lord is one," is often recited in synagogues.	
The Creation	All three religions believe that God created the universe at a definite point in time.		
Adam	All three religions believe that Adam was the first human that God created.		
	Regard Adam as the first of God's prophets.	Do not regard Adam as God's first prophet.	
Eve	• In the Qur'anic account of Creation, the first person (indefinite gender) was created, and then that person's mate was created. • In the Qur'an, Satan (in the guise of a serpent) persuaded Adam and Eve to eat the fruit from the Tree of Life at the same time. Thus, in Islam, Eve was not the temptress who persuaded Adam to disobey God's command.	• In the Torah and Old Testament, God first created Adam. Then, while Adam slept, He created Eve from the side of Adam's body or from his rib. • Believe that the serpent tempted Eve to disobey God and eat the fruit from the Tree of Life. Eve, in turn, tempted Adam to eat the fruit.	

(Continued)

TABLE 1.1   *(Continued)*

Key Subjects	Islam	Judaism	Christianity
"Original Sin"	• Both Islam and Judaism reject the concept of "original sin." If no one is responsible for another's sins, the whole human race could not be condemned by God because of Adam's sin. The Old Testament states: "The fathers shall not be put to death for the children, nor shall the children be put to death for the fathers; every man shall be put to death for his own sin" (Deuteronomy 24:16). The Qur'an states: "My behavior is my own concern, while your behavior is your own concern. You are innocent of anything I do, while I am innocent of what you are doing (10:41). Thus both Muslims and Jews believe that we cannot be blamed for the "sins" of Adam and Eve, who lived many centuries ago—we had nothing to do with their disobedience to God's command, nor could we prevent it. Since God is absolutely just, He would not condemn all of humankind for the "sins" of people we had no control over. Since God did not condemn the world to sin because of Adam and Eve, He did not have to send Jesus Christ to take away our sins. We have to overcome our own sins by believing in Him, following His guidance, living a righteous life, and doing noble deeds.		• The Christian scriptures contain various interpretations of the concept of "original sin."
	Both Islam and Judaism believe that human beings are born sinless and only by their disobedience of God's guidance do they become sinful.		Adam and Eve "sinned" when they disobeyed God and ate from the the fruit Tree of Life.
	Adam and Eve erred, but did not sin, when they disobeyed God and ate the fruit from the Tree of Life. Above all, "sin" cannot be passed on to succeeding generations.	Adam and Eve did sin when they disobeyed God and ate the fruit from the Tree of Life, but their sin cannot be passed on to succeeding generations.	Adam and Eve's "sin" in the Garden of Eden was passed on to succeeding generations.
Angels	Believe in angels who act as God's agents and operate throughout the universe to carry out God's divine scheme of things.		
Satan/the Devil	In the Qur'an, Satan became a fallen angel when he refused to obey God and bow to Adam. After that point in time, Satan resolved to turn human beings against God and His guidance of humankind.	In the Hebrew Bible, Satan wasn't the fallen angel but the "Adversary" in God's court. Most Jews do not have a strong belief in the individual power of evil.	Christian scriptures do mention Satan as the fallen angel. They also discuss the evil role that Satan/the Devil/the Evil One plays in the world. In the Old and New Testament, the Devil is regarded as the enemy of God and the source of all evil.
Abraham (lived after c. 1800 BCE)	Abraham is revered in all three religions as the first monotheist, the "father of the faith" (the patriarch), and the promoter of that monotheistic creed.		
	• In the Qur'an, there is no mention of God promising Abraham the Land of	• In the Hebrew Bible/Old Testament, God promised Abraham the Land of Canaan/biblical Israel to pass on to his son Isaac, by his first wife, Sara.	

Key Subjects	Islam	Judaism	Christianity
Abraham (lived after c. 1800 BCE)	Canaan/biblical Israel to pass on to his descendents from his first wife Sara.		
	• In the Qur'an, Abraham and his eldest son, Ishmael, built the first house of worship to pray to God. Muslims believe that this house of worship was located exactly where the Ka'abah, which Muhammad purified of idols in 630 CE, is currently located (in present-day Makkah, Saudi Arabia).	• In the Hebrew Bible/Old Testament, Abraham and his youngest son, Isaac, built altars at Bethel (north of Jerusalem) and at Shechem (Nablus) upon which to worship God.	
	• Abraham was going to sacrifice Ishmael because God commanded him to in a dream.	• In the Hebrew Bible/Old Testament, Abraham was going to sacrifice Isaac because God commanded him to.	
Moses (c. 1450–1300 BCE)	A great prophet in all three religions. Adherents of all three faiths believe that God gave Moses the Torah (the Five Books of Moses: Genesis, Exodus, Leviticus, Numbers, and Deuteronomy). These books include the Mosaic Law, which governed the conduct of the Jews in biblical times and which include the Ten Commandments/ Ten Statements, adhered to by the adherents of all three faiths: (1) I am the Lord, thy God, thou shall have no God before me; (2) Thou shalt not take the name of the Lord, thy God, in vain; (3) Thou shalt establish a holy day; (4) Honor thy Father and thy Mother; (5) Thou shalt not kill; (6) Thou shalt not commit adultery; (7) Thou shalt not steal; (8) Thou shalt not bear false witness against thy neighbor; (9) Thou shalt not covet thy neighbor's wife; (10) Thou shalt not covet thy neighbor's goods.		
David (died c. 970 BCE)	The Qur'an, Hebrew Bible, and Old Testament regard David as one of God's great prophets; a just, competent, and successful king of Biblical Israel; and the young man who, with God's help, killed Goliath, the Philistine giant.		
	God revealed the Psalms to David. In their original form, they were the Word of God. However, human revisions over three-thousand years, have corrupted them.	Many Jews believe that David wrote the Psalms.	The Book of Psalms in the Old Testament is attributed to David, but scholars of religion don't believe that he wrote all of them.
		In the Hebrew Bible/Old Testament, God makes the promise to David that his house and kingdom will endure forever. Once there is no Jewish kingdom, there develops the expectation of a future descendant of David, who will come to rule again. This person is known as the "Messiah."	
		For Jews, the Messiah has not yet come.	For Christians, Jesus is this Messiah.
Solomon (died c. 931 BCE)	• The Qur'an, Hebrew Bible, and Old Testament regard David's son, Solomon, to be one of God's great prophets, one of the greatest kings of Biblical Israel, and the one renowned for his wisdom and justice.		
	• All three faiths believe that Solomon had the temple in Jerusalem constructed, only one wall of which remains today.		

(Continued)

TABLE 1.1   *(Continued)*

Key Subjects	Islam	Judaism	Christianity
Solomon **(died c. 931 BCE)**		Jews called this the "Wailing Wall" till the creation of Israel on May 14, 1948. Since then, it is referred to as the "Western Wall."	
Mary, Mother of **Jesus (born c. 25 BCE)**	Maryam (Arabic name for Mary) is a revered figure in Islam. The Qur'an devotes one chapter comprising 98 verses to her (chapter 19).	An unimportant figure in Jewish theology and history.	A revered figure in Christian theology and history. The New Testament tells the story of the virginal conception of Jesus. Orthodox Christians and Catholic Christians give her the title "Mother of God." And Blessed Virgin Mary is a saintly figure in Catholicism.
Jesus Christ **(c. 6 BCE–30 CE)**	• The Qur'an mentions Jesus as one of God's great prophets. • The Qur'an states that Jesus performed several miracles: he spoke from the crib to silence those who doubted his mother's virginity, cured lepers and gave sight to the blind, fed the multitude that came to hear him talk with abundant food provided by God, put life into a bird of clay, and raised Lazarus from the dead. • The Qur'an states that Jesus was not crucified on the cross: "They did not really slay him, neither crucified him; only a likeness of that was shown unto them," (4:157) but someone who came to look like him was (Judas Iscariot, who betrayed Jesus, is mentioned); he ascended to Heaven alive; and he will return at the end of time.	• Do not believe that Jesus was the prophet or son of God. Consider him to be a rabbi and/or a teacher. • Question the many miracles that Jesus performed. • Believe that Jesus Christ was crucified because the Romans saw him as a threat to their rule and that Jews had absolutely nothing to do with his crucifixion.	• Believe that Jesus Christ was the Son of God; was the unique demonstration of God's love for humankind; and was sinless. • The New Testament recalls Jesus Christ performing many miracles: he cured lepers and gave sight to the blind, fed the multitude that came to hear him talk with abundant food provided by God, raised Lazarus from the dead, changed water into wine, exorcized demons from within people, and walked on water. • The New Testament states that Jewish leaders handed Jesus over to the Romans to be crucified. Denying Jesus Christ's crucifixion and bodily death is to deny the very means of atonement and salvation for which God sent Jesus into the world. • The New Testament also states that in the resurrection, God raises Jesus Christ to Heaven, only to return at the end of time.

Key Subjects	Islam	Judaism	Christianity
Paul (c. 4 BCE–64 CE)	Viewed negatively because Saul of Tarsus, who converted to Christianity, was responsible for the following ideas: Jesus was divine; Christ died for humankind's sins; his crucifixion and suffering on the cross can redeem us; and if you don't accept Jesus Christ as the Lord and Savior, you cannot be "saved" and go to Heaven.	He is not only viewed favorably but considered a saint because he played a critically important role in the development of Christian theology. His writings constitute a considerable portion of the New Testament, and he was the main proselytizing force for Christianity during the first century CE.	
Muhammad (570–632 CE)	Believe that Prophet Muhammad is God's last Prophet (the "Seal of the Prophets," according to the Qur'an); that Archangel Gabriel revealed God's final message to him; and that God's final message, embodied in the Qur'an, was the continuation of the same message that God sent to Abraham, David, Moses, and Jesus earlier in history.	Do not believe that Muhammad was God's prophet.	
Best Male Role Model(s)	Prophet Muhammad	Abraham, Moses, David, and Solomon	Jesus Christ
Best Female Role Model(s)	Maryam (mother of Jesus); Khadijah (Prophet Muhammad's first wife); Fatimah (Prophet Muhammad's daughter)	Sarah (Abraham's first wife); Rebbeca (Abraham's daughter-in-law/Isaac's wife); Leah and Rachel (Jacob's wives)	Mary (mother of Jesus Christ)
Sacred Texts	• Believe that the Qur'an is the Word of God; is the last Message of God to humankind; was revealed to Prophet Muhammad by Archangel Gabriel; that God's revelations came to Muhammad over a period of 22 years (610–622 CE); and that the Qur'an was Muhammad's greatest miracle. • Do not believe that the Psalms of David, the Hebrew Bible, Old Testament, and the Gospels of Jesus Christ are in their original form. Thus, do not believe that they contain the original Word of God.	Do not believe that the Qur'an was the Word of God. Believe in the Hebrew Bible, comprising the Torah (the Five Books Of Moses: Genesis, Exodus, Leviticus, Numbers, and Deuteronomy), the Prophets, and the Writings.	Believe that both the Old Testament and the New Testament (Bible) are the Word of God. The Old Testament comprises the Pentateuch (the Five Books of Moses), the Historical Books, the Wisdom Books, and the Prophets.

(Continued)

TABLE 1.1 (Continued)

Key Subjects	Islam	Judaism	Christianity
Original Language(s) of the Scriptures	Arabic	Mainly Hebrew (however, some Aramaic in the third section of the Hebrew Bible)	Aramaic, Hebrew, and Greek
Obligatory Duties	Belief in one God and His last prophet; ritual prayers (five times a day); fasting during the month of Ramadan; giving alms to the poor and needy; and pilgrimage to Makkah once in one's lifetime in the twelfth Islamic calendar month.	Believe in one God and in the Hebrew Bible prophets, observe the Sabbath and all Jewish holidays, pray thrice daily, and give alms to the poor and needy.	Belief in God, the Father, Jesus Christ as Lord and Savior, and the work of the Holy Spirit. Also attend church on Sundays and give alms to the poor and needy.
View of Humanity	Adherents of all three faiths regard human beings as the highest of God's creation.		
Sanctity of Life	• All three religions believe in the sanctity of life. The Qur'an states: "Whosoever killeth a human being for other than manslaughter or corruption on earth, it shall be as if he had killed all humankind, and whosoever saveth the life of one, it shall be as if he had saved the life of all mankind" (5:32). Judaism has a similar verse in the Sanhedrin (laws of jurisprudence) in Chapter 4, Mishnah 5. Christianity has a similar thought mentioned in Genesis: 9:5–6. • All three religions strongly condemn suicide and state that only God has the right to create and take life.		
The Golden Rule	All three religions enjoin their followers to pursue the "Golden Rule." Jesus Christ said: "Do unto others as you would want others to do unto you." Rabbi Hillel said: "Do not do to others what you would not have them do to you." Prophet Muhammad said: "None of you truly believes until he wishes for his brother what he wishes for himself."		
Humanity's Problem	Not following "the straight path" revealed in the Qur'an.	Not following the dictates of their faith (disobeying God's guidance as revealed in the Hebrew Bible).	Because of "Original Sin," the human race is born into sin. Not accepting Jesus Christ as "redeemer" is another reason for humanity's problem.
Solution for Humanity or Basis for Salvation	Follow "the straight path" as revealed in the Qur'an and found in Prophet Muhammad's *sunnah* (words and deeds). Good works and charitable deeds are also strongly recommended.	Follow the Torah and do good works in society to earn salvation.	To attain God's forgiveness and to be reconciled with Him, one needs to trust in the saving work of Jesus Christ. God has completed the work of salvation on humankind's behalf by allowing His son, Jesus Christ, to be crucified. Christ's blood has washed away the sins of those who believe in Him as Lord and Savior. Salvation cannot be earned by good works alone; one must accept Jesus Christ as Lord and Savior.

Key Subjects	Islam	Judaism	Christianity
Historical Religion	All three religions are "historical religions," i.e., God cares about history and expects people to be involved in shaping it. Many in all three faiths also believe that there is a beginning and an end to human history.		
Organic Religion	Islam and Judaism are "organic religions" because they have a comprehensive body of sacred laws governing every aspect of society.		• Catholicism and the Eastern Orthodox Church are "church religions," with a well-established and highly structured clerical organization having a separate identity from both government and society. • Protestantism is neither an "organic" nor a "church" religion.
Religion and Politics	Religion and politics do mix in Islam and Judaism. Many Muslim countries have Islamists actively lobbying for an Islamic system and some actively trying to come to power and establish an Islamic state. Likewise, in Israel many Jewish political parties are lobbying the Israeli government to make Israel a truly Jewish state.		Although Christian fundamentalists/evangelicals do believe that religion has an important role to play in politics, much of the Western Christian world has effectively separated religion and politics, or church and state.
	In Islam religion and politics are fused and inseparable.	In Judaism religion and politics are fused before the modern era, but they are much less so today.	
Proselytization	Islam encourages the propagation of the faith and proselytization.	Judaism does not encourage proselytization.	Christianity encourages missionary work and "saving souls."
Calendar	• Muslims and Jews follow lunar calendars to commemorate their holy days. • Both lunar calendars are twelve lunar months or 354 days long.		• Christians follow the Gregorian (solar) calendar. The Gregorian calendar is made up of twelve months or 365 days.
	• The Islamic lunar calendar began with Prophet Muhammad's Hijrah (migration) from Makkah to Madinah in 622 CE.	• The Jewish lunar calendar began at least 2,200 years ago.	• The Gregorian calendar was introduced in 1582 CE by Pope Gregory XIII. It is based on zero being the birth of Jesus Christ.
Sabbath Day	No sabbath day; the *ummah* (brotherhood of believers) has been encouraged to go to the *masjid* for noontime congregational prayers on Fridays.	Saturday	Sunday
Main Holy Days	Eid ul Fitr (Festival of the Fast Breaking) at the end	Rosh Hashanah (Jewish New Year); Yom Kippur	Christmas (celebrating the birth of Jesus on

(Continued)

TABLE 1.1 *(Continued)*

Key Subjects	Islam	Judaism	Christianity
Main Holy Days	of the ninth Islamic calendar month of Ramadan; Eid ul Azha (Festival of Sacrifice) at the close of the ritual of *hajj* in the twelfth Islamic calendar month of Dhul-Hijjah, commemorating Abraham's willingness to sacrifice his son Ishmael, as commanded by God in a dream to test his faith.	(Day of Atonement); Sakkot (commemorating 40 years of wandering); Passover (commemorates redemption from Egyptian slavery); Shavuoth (Anniversary of the Ten Commandments); Purim (Jews saved from Persian genocide); and Hanukkah (commemorates victory of Maccabees over Syrian armies of Antiochus Epiphanes)	December 25) is based on the solar calendar; and Easter (commemorating the death of Jesus on Good Friday and his resurrection on Easter Sunday) is calculated on the basis of the lunar calendar. Thus Easter does not come on the same day every year.
Circumcision and "Unclean" Foods	The Qur'an and the Hebrew Bible enjoin Muslims and Jews, respectively, to circumcise their baby boys, avoid consuming pork, and eat kosher meat.		The New Testament does not require Christians to circumcise their baby boys and has no food taboos.
	Muslims have also been commanded not to drink alcohol.	There is no taboo in the Hebrew Bible against alcohol.	
The Afterlife	Unlike Hinduism's and Buddhism's belief in reincarnation (rebirth of the soul in successive life forms in this world), Islam, Judaism, and Christianity hold that there is one life only in this finite world.		
	Believe that after death, individuals await Judgment Day, when all will be resurrected, judged, and sent to Paradise for doing good deeds or to Hell for doing evil deeds.	Diverse Jewish beliefs include judgment by God, eternal afterlife, messianic redemption for everyone, and individual death as lasting and complete.	The New Testament mentions the resurrection of the dead at the end of time and a final judgment made then. Most Christians also believe in an individual judgment that takes place at the time of death.
Most Misunderstood Aspect of the Religion	• Islam is not Muhammadanism and Muslims are not Muhammadans; • *Jihad* means "to struggle," primarily against one's baser instincts and secondly against invaders/aggressors. Islam never intended *jihad* to be an aggressive "holy war" against infidels.	Judaism and Zionism are not synonymous—the former is a 4,000-year-old religion, the latter is a century-old religiopolitical ideology.	"The Trinity" is the most misunderstood concept. Most non-Christians incorrectly think that Christians believe in three Gods: the Father; His Son, Jesus Christ; and the Holy Spirit.

Internet Sites

http://www.islamfortoday.com/akbar01.htm

http://www.dianedew.com/islam.htm

http://www.geocities.com/Athens/Agora/6526/ICmenu.html

http://www.islam101.com/religions/

http://www.jews-for-allah.org

http://www.answering-islam.org/Women/place.html

http://www.sultan.org/articles/women.html

http://www.interfaith-center.org/ (International Interfaith Centers)

http://www.mdx.ac.uk/www/religion/cifd.htm (Center for Interfaith Dialogue)

http://www.interfaith.org.uk/ (The interfaith network)

http://www.cpwr.org/ (Council for a Parliament of World's Religions)

http://www.uri.org/index.htm (United Religious Initiatives)

http://www.worldfaiths.org/ (World Congress of Faiths)

http://www.multifaithnet.org/ (Multi Faith Net)

http://www.interfaith-metrodc.org/ (Interfaith Conference; Washington DC)

CHAPTER TWO

Islamism and Islamic Revivals

Islam: A Vehicle of Political Action

In the West, the domain of religion, represented by the church, and the domain of politics, represented by the state, are separate and coexist with their own distinct laws and chains of authority. This concept of separating church and state in the West follows the Christian maxim "Render unto Caesar the things that are Caesar's, and unto God the things that are God's."[1] Separation of church and state was also discussed in the writings of Benedict de Spinoza, John Locke, and the philosophers of the European Enlightenment. The idea was implemented in the West only three hundred years ago, after much sectarianism and bloodshed.[2]

In Islam, however, religion and politics are inseparable. The domain of Caesar (civil/temporal authority) and the domain of God (the religion of Islam) are mutually inclusive. According to the famous Muslim philosopher Al-Ghazali (1058–1111), "religion and temporal power are twins." They are two sides of the same coin.

Islam is both "this-worldly" and "other-worldly." While the faithful are enjoined to be actively involved in this world and to enjoy the good things life has to offer, they are just as strongly commanded to lead virtuous and God-fearing lives in the hope of attaining paradise when they die. Islam is more than a set of obligatory rituals, like praying and alms giving. It is an integrated and holistic belief system governing all aspects of a Muslim's life, making no distinction between religious and political responsibilities. The Qur'an is the devout Muslim's

---

[1]Luke 20:25.

[2]Bernard Lewis, "The Roots of Muslim Rage," *The Atlantic*, Vol. 266, No. 3 (September 1990), p. 47.

ultimate authority in all matters, offering "Divine Guidance for all fields of human life, whether private or public, political or economic, social or cultural, moral or legal and judicial. Islam is an all-embracing social ideology."[3] Islam thus provides models for both individual and political action. Hence, when secular ideologies fail in the Muslim world, Muslims often turn to the Islamic alternative. An Islamic revival is the end result.

Islam is both a "historical" and an "organic" religion.[4] These concepts help explain why and how Islam becomes a vehicle for political change in the Muslim world.

Islam: A Historical Religion

Unlike "ahistorical" religions, like Hinduism and Buddhism,[5] Islam perceives history as divinely ordained. Muslims see the hand of God purposefully guiding history, presumably toward a "Kingdom of God" on Earth. As Wilfred Cantwell Smith wrote, "In essence, Islamic history, therefore, is the fulfilment, under divine guidance, of the purpose of human history."[6] The greater a religion's emphasis on history as divinely ordained, the greater the likelihood that religion will assume a significant role in the region's political life.[7] This is true in Islam. Within a "historical" religion, human history is, in general, a process of progressive revelation and promised fulfilment. Religion explains the beginning and end of human history and the direction it must take. But because "particular historical events are [considered] crucial acts of revelation,"[8] such events set specific precedents for establishing a social, economic, and political order that conforms to a divine design. In effect, what Muhammad did is as important to devout Muslims as what Muhammad said; and it is lost on no believer that Muhammad, escaping persecution in Makkah, established the first Islamic state in the neighboring city of Madinah.

Prophet Muhammad frowned upon celibacy and the renunciation of one's responsibilities to one's work, family, colleagues, and friends in this world for

---

[3]Sayyid Abul A'la Maududi, *Islamic Law and Constitution,* 6th ed., trans. and ed. Khurshid Ahmad (Lahore, Pakistan: Islamic Publications Ltd., 1977), p. 1.

[4]See Donald Eugene Smith, *Religion and Political Development* (Boston: Little, Brown, 1970), pp. 24–40, 248–249; Donald Eugene Smith, ed., *Religion and Political Modernization* (New Haven: Yale University Press, 1974), Ch. 1.

[5]According to Donald Eugene Smith, "ahistorical religions," like Hinduism and Buddhism, consider history irrelevant to the spiritual quest, although the guidance of religious leaders both past and present may be useful. Moreover, in these religions "history has no divine purpose, no beginning, no end, and may be cyclical in nature. Individual salvation or self-realization is the goal of the spiritual quest, and historical events bear no significant relationship to the process" (D. E. Smith, *Religion and Political Development,* p. 249; also see Smith, ed., *Religion and Political Modernization,* Ch. 1).

[6]Wilfred Cantwell Smith, *Islam in Modern History* (New York: Mentor Books, 1957), pp. 14, 24, 47, 11–47.

[7]D. E. Smith, *Religion and Political Development,* pp. 24–40, 248–249.

[8]Ibid., pp. 248–249.

"other-worldly" pursuits, such as praying and meditating. Indeed, Muhammad's life exemplifies the importance of adopting an active and assertive worldly orientation. Islam demands the building of a political, social, and economic order that, because the religion is historical, is based on divine principles laid down not only in Islamic theology and jurisprudence and the *shariah* but in specific historical precedents set by Muhammad and his first four "rightly guided caliphs."

In Islam today, Muhammad remains, to the devout believer, the most significant role model. The Prophet was a charismatic religious leader, a statesman with vision, a just judge, a competent administrator, a courageous military general, a loving husband and father, and a trustworthy friend. Hence, throughout the Muslim world, Muhammad has had a greater immediate impact on the course of history than any other religious leader and has been the most fully involved in the events of social and political life.[9] Islam, both at its inception, during the classical era, and for some, during the middle ages, is the blueprint by which today's Islamist, disillusioned by secular ideologies, seeks to build an Islamic state.

Although Muhammad is regarded as in san-i-kamil (perfect human being) to Muslims, other historical personalities and events provide models to emulate or interpret. For example, victory in battle has always been considered a sign of God's favor, and defeat as either punishment for deviation from Islam's "straight path" or a test of faith. Muhammad's victory in the Battle of Badr (624 CE) against the numerically superior Makkan forces signified that "God willed that He should cause the truth to triumph by His words, and cut the root of the disbelievers" (8:7–9).[10] Moreover, Muhammad's victory was purely God's doing: "Ye slew them not, but God slew them" (8:17).

Likewise, defeat in battle was also God's doing. Following the Battle of Badr, the Prophet's army was overwhelmed by the Makkans in the Battle of Uhud. The Qur'an provides two explanations for this defeat. The first suggests that God was testing the Muslims to distinguish the true believers from the hypocrites: "If you have suffered from a wound, so did the [disbelieving] people. We alternate these vicissitudes among mankind so that God may know the true believers and choose martyrs from among you" (3:140). The second explanation implies that a portion of Muhammad's army had incurred God's displeasure by disobeying the Prophet's orders and abandoning a strategic pass when the Makkans fled. These Muslims, who were gathering booty left behind by the retreating Makkans, were unprepared for the returning Makkan forces and were overcome.[11] The Qur'an explains:

---

[9]Newell S. Booth, "The Historical and Non-Historical in Islam," *Muslim World*, Vol. 60, No. 2 (April 1970), p. 109.

[10]Interpretations of most Qur'anic verses in this work are derived from three sources: *The Meaning of the Quran*, 5th ed., checked and revised by Mahmud Y. Zayid (Beirut, Lebanon: Dar al-Choura, 1980); Mohammed Marmaduke Pickthall, *The Meaning of the Glorious Koran* (New York: Mentor Books, 1953); and N. J. Dawood, *The Koran*, 4th ed. (Baltimore: Penguin Books, 1974). Often the Qur'anic interpretations appearing here are a synthesis of all three aforementioned sources.

[11]William Montgomery Watt, *Muhammad in Medina* (Oxford: Clarendon Press, 1968), pp. 26–27.

"God fulfilled His pledge to you when, by His leave, you went on killing them. But afterwards your courage failed you, and you disobeyed [the Apostle] after he had brought you within view of what you wished for" (3:152).

Therefore, according to devout Muslims, the outcome of the battles of Badr and Uhud, and by implication of all battles throughout Islamic history, depended on the favor of God. Moreover, Islam's conspicuous success and expansion in its first three centuries confirmed "divine support and power."[12] Such historical glory, in turn, provided the devout Muslim both failures to be avoided and successes to be emulated. And since Muslims believed historical success resulted from the establishment of a spiritually unified Islamic state, the conviction was reinforced that "true faith was indeed inseparable from social and political action in this world."[13]

Today's Muslims likewise interpret recent successes and failures in the Muslim world from a religious context. The establishment of the new nation-state of Pakistan, the economic empowerment of the Organization of Arab Petroleum Exporting Countries (OAPEC), the success of Khomeini in defiance of the United States, and the Afghan *mujahideen*'s expulsion of the Soviets from Afghanistan are events perceived by Muslims as God's vindication of the righteous. Meanwhile, the dismemberment of Pakistan and the defeat of the Arabs by Israel in the 1967 war are interpreted by many Muslims as divine punishment for the Muslim world becoming too secular and Western, thus straying from the "straight path."

As a historical religion, orthodox Islam, at least in theory, bridges the gulf between the sacred and the profane, the religious and the political.[14] In essence, "Islam has been inseparable from the political vicissitudes of the Islamic peoples to such an extent that the history of Islam turns out to be political history."[15] Moreover, for the Islamist, history serves as both model and warning for the future.

Islam: An Organic Religion

While "church" religions emphasize the role of a well-established and well-structured clerical organization that, in theory and in structure, has a separate identity from both government and society, an "organic" religion maintains no such church hierarchy or priestly class. In fact, within an organic religion, "sacral law and sacral social structure are of the essence. . . . Religion is largely equated with society, and distinct ecclesiastical organizations . . . are secondary."[16]

By the above definition, Islam is an organic religion possessing a comprehensive code of ethics, morals, instructions, and recommendations for individual

---

[12]Booth, "The Historical and Non-Historical in Islam," pp. 109–110.

[13]Ibid.

[14]Binnaz Toprak, *Islam and Political Development in Turkey* (Leiden, The Netherlands: E. J. Brill, 1981), pp. 22–23.

[15]Booth, "The Historical and Non-Historical in Islam," p. 109.

[16]D. E. Smith, *Religion and Political Development*, p. 249.

action and social interaction. It is also a legalistic religion whose rules and regulations form the basis of a divine law governing every aspect of the devout Muslim's life. Islam provides a political ideology that has mobilized, integrated, and governed all sects and all classes of believers.

In an organic religion the distinction between religious and social systems is obscured; the two systems merge.[17] In Islam, this merger is both prescribed and effected by the *shariah*, which Islamists throughout the Muslim world endow with the force of law. Drawn from the Qur'an and the *sunnah* (Prophet Muhammad's saying and deeds), the *shariah* has something to say about every aspect of life: manners and hygiene, marriage and divorce, crime and punishment, economics and politics, war and peace, and so forth. By strictly regulating a devout Muslim's life, the *shariah* binds the temporal to the eternal.

Acceptance of the divine origin of the *shariah* implies a concurrent acceptance of the divine basis of society. Thus, religious law becomes civil law as well as the principal means of social and political action. No social or political theory exists separately from what is prescribed in the *shariah*. Society is the *ummah*; the state is the political expression of God and the political organization of His *ummah*. The *ummah* in Islam has a dual character—it is a religious community and a political society. Theoretical distinctions drawn in Christianity between the realms of God and of the ruler are absent in Islam. The *shariah* incorporates the temporal within the spiritual realm. The divinity of the *shariah* presupposes that both the private and public lives of an entire community are subject to divine guidance. Islam is not only a belief system in the religious sense but a political doctrine that sets the limits of authority and obligation within the Muslim community. The Islamic community, based on God's revelation, is the Muslim's ideal political model, whose laws and institutions are comprehensive and infallible.[18]

Thus in Islam, political institutions are designed to defend and promote Islam, not the state. Such institutions are intended to establish and uphold an Islamic system based on the *shariah*.[19] The primary loyalty of Muslim citizens is to the *ummah*, rather than the state, and to the *shariah*, rather than the ruler, because "at the heart of Islamic political doctrine lies neither state, nor the individual, nor yet a social class, but the *ummah*, the Islamic community tied by bonds of faith alone."[20] When a ruler in a predominantly Muslim country is unjust or perceived as "un-Islamic" and imposes laws incompatible with the *shariah*, the devout Muslim is enjoined by the Qur'an to take political action. This has been the primary impetus driving periodic and cyclical Islamic political revivals today and throughout history.

As both a historical and organic religion, Islam clashes with conspicuous elements of Western-style modernization, including secularization and

---

[17]Toprak, *Islam*, p. 23.

[18]Ibid., p. 24.

[19]Ibid., pp. 24–25.

[20]Henry Siegman, "The State and the Individual in Sunni Islam," *Muslim World*, Vol. 54, No. 1 (January 1964), p. 14.

Westernization. The secularization process in those Muslim societies where the majority of Muslims are still steeped in the Islamic tradition (e.g., Pakistan, Afghanistan, Lebanon, Iran, Sudan, Algeria, and Tunisia) is punctuated with periodic reversals. This is because modernization, adopted wholesale from the West and implemented hastily, has not been adapted to the Muslim world. Conflicting with Islamic principles that emphatically discourage secularization and the complete separation of the religious realm from the political, social, and economic realms, the process of modernization perpetuates a political reaction in which Islam is the idiom of dissent.

Social and Economic Equity and Justice in Islam

The modernization process occurring throughout the Muslim world has not only caused secularization, which devout Muslims oppose and which most Islamists seek to reverse, but has also led to a concentration of wealth in fewer and fewer hands, a situation that the teachings of Islam oppose. Such economic polarization has contributed to social and political injustices, again inconsistent with Islam. It is this injustice and social and economic inequity in the secularizing Muslim world that today fuels the fires of Islamic politics.

The Qur'an and *hadith,* two of Islam's most revered textual sources, emphasize the importance of justice and social and economic equity. According to the

---

◼

BOX 2.1   Anti-Western Sentiments in the Muslim World

Anti-Western feelings in the Muslim world are due to the long shadow of history: two centuries of the Crusades (1095–1291 CE); over 700 years of Muslim rule in Spain (711–1492) that was gradually lost to Christian conquerors, who took it back over a period of 100 years and then ended the last vestiges of the Muslim civilization there with the Spanish Inquisition (1492); over 150 years of European Christian imperialism and colonialism (1800 to the mid-twentieth century); the West's creation of Israel in Palestine (1948), where over 90 percent of the inhabitants were Palestinian Muslim Arabs at the beginning of the twentieth century; the West's continued support of the Jewish state despite its continued occupation of Palestinian and Syrian lands; and the West's support of many corrupt, incompetent, autocratic, and secular Muslim regimes in the newly independent Muslim countries—a policy that continues to this day. Last but not least, strong anti-Western feelings are fueled by the spread of Western secular and liberal culture, which Muslims perceive as emphasizing excessive individualism, freedom, capitalism, materialism, consumerism, sexual permissiveness, and hedonism.

Four Types of Anti-Americanism

Alvin Z. Rubinstein and Donald E. Smith, two political science professors at the University of Pennsylvania, have studied the spreading and intensifying phenomenon of anti-

(Continued)

Anti-Western Sentiments in the Muslim World   *(Continued)*

Americanism in the developing countries of Asia, Africa, the Middle East, and Latin America. According to the two authors, "anti-Americanism can be defined as any hostile action or expression that becomes part and parcel of an undifferentiated attack on the foreign policy, society, culture, and values of the United States." They believe that there are four principal types of anti-Americanism in the developing world—each resulting from different motives and aims.

First and perhaps most prevalent is *issue-oriented anti-Americanism*. This involves a pattern of verbal and/or violent military attacks directed against policies and actions of the U.S. government with which a developing country disagrees. It results from policy disagreements that are caused by the conflicting national interests of nation-states. It is evident in the United States' aid to and strategic alliance with Israel despite the latter's occupation of Palestinian lands and flagrant abuse of Palestinian human rights; the heavy bombing of Iraq during the Persian Gulf War (1991) and sanctions that the United States has imposed on Iraq for over a decade, which have resulted in the deaths of over a million Iraqi infants; the presence of American troops in Saudi Arabia, considered the heartland of Islamdom because two of the holiest cities of Islam, Makkah and Madinah, are located there; and democratic India's constant complaint against the U.S. government for giving military aid to its arch rival Pakistan, which has had authoritarian rule for most of its existence.

A second variant, *ideological anti-Americanism*, derives from the belief that the United States is the principal villain in the world today and that American society epitomizes Godless secularization, greedy capitalism, excessive materialism, wasteful consumerism, decadent hedonism, and aggressive neoimperialism. This deep-rooted ideological animus accounts for the opposition from communists, socialists, and Islamists alike. To them and others of their ilk, the United States is the main obstacle to systemic and just transformational change.

Third, there is *instrumental anti-Americanism*, in which regimes in the developing world instigate and manipulate hostility toward the United States in order to mobilize domestic support and provide a plausible scapegoat for the regimes' own governmental failures, mismanagement, and corruption. It is easily generated and relatively cost free for the regimes that engage in it.

Finally, *revolutionary anti-Americanism* is found among anti-government opposition groups seeking to overthrow regimes that are closely identified with the United States. Attacking such regimes thus involves attacking the United States. After the overthrow of the pro-U.S. government, as in Iran, revolutionary anti-Americanism becomes a mass phenomenon and a force justifying the rule of the new leadership. In fact, in Iran, long after the fall of Muhammad Reza Shah Pahlavi, the United States continues to be denounced by the Revolutionary and Traditionalist Islamists as the "Great Satan" and deadliest enemy of the Islamic revolution and the theocratic regime.

Source: Alvin Z. Rubinstein and Donald E. Smith, "Anti-Americanism in the Third World," in Thomas Perry Thornton, ed., in *Anti-Americanism: Origins and Context*, Vol. 497 of *Annals of The American Academy of Political and Social Science*, May 1988, pp. 35–45.

Qur'an, "the creation of justice on earth is one of the basic goals for which God sent his prophets and provided their guidance" (57:25). Muhammad actively preached and propagated social justice. The powerful and wealthy Makkan elite did not see Muhammad as merely another religious preacher. They saw him as a revolutionary leader espousing an ideological message that threatened their social, economic, and political dominance.

In the Qur'an, general pronouncements about justice are linked to more specific injunctions: justice means a roughly equal distribution of wealth, and it means piety. "All human creatures have a right to everything that God made available, and for this reason God's gifts are to be distributed equally to all. The poor and needy have the right to share in the wealth of the rich" (51:19). To many Muslims this means more than simple charity, but the creation of a social and economic order that guarantees an equitable distribution of wealth. According to the Qur'an, the unreligious will not observe the principle of economic equality: "Signs of corruption also include the covetousness of the rich for the little that the weak and the poor possess" (38:21–24). And the Qur'an states: "Hast thou observed him who belieth religion? That is he who repelleth the orphan, and urgeth not the feeding of the needy" (107:1–3).

Islam also stresses the importance of justice and moderation in conflict resolution:

> Make peace between them, but then, if one of the two (groups) goes on acting wrongfully towards the other, fight against the one that acts aggressively until it reverts to God's commandment; and if they revert, make peace between them with justice, and deal equitably (with them); for verily, God loves those who act equitably! [49:9]

Muhammad repeatedly emphasizes the place of justice and equality in Islam. He says: "The anger of God against the unjust man is all the greater when the victim of injustice has no defense save in God."[21] Likewise, Muhammad enjoins the believer to act: "If you see evil being done, put it right with your hand. If you can't do that, use your tongue. If you can't do even that, correct it in your heart, but that last is the weakest."[22] As for criminal punishment, the Qur'an states: "life for life, eye for eye, nose for nose, ear for ear, tooth for tooth, and wounds equal for equal" (5:45). However, such an injunction is not the end of the matter: "But if the thief repents after his crime, and amends his conduct, God turneth to him in forgiveness for God is often forgiving and most merciful" (5:39).

On more than one occasion Muhammad said that a man enjoys no immunity when he transgresses divine law, whether he be a powerful king or a powerless slave, a wealthy aristocrat or a poor nomad. In one *hadith*, Muhammad declares:

> The nations that lived before you declined because they punished men of humble origins for their offenses and let those of noble origin go unpunished for their crimes; I

---

[21]Quoted in Abderrahman Cherif-Chergui, "Justice and Equality in Islam," *The Month*, Vol. 13, No. 2 (February 1980), p. 2.

[22]Ibid., p. 6.

swear by God who holds my life in His hand that even if (my daughter) committed a theft, I would have her hand amputated.[23]

Muhammad frequently stated that all are equal before God and His divine laws on earth, whatever their race, color, or creed, their social, economic, or political status. "All people are equal, as equal as the teeth of a comb. There is no merit of an Arab over a non-Arab, or of a white over a black person, or of a male over a female. Only God-fearing people merit preference."[24]

The spirit of Islamic equality and social, economic, and political justice continued to be the hallmark of Islam during the period of the "rightly guided caliphs." The first caliph, Abu Bakr, told his audience immediately after being elected caliph:

> You have made me your leader although I am in no way superior to you. Cooperate with me when I do right; correct me when I err; obey me so long as I follow the commandments of God and His Prophet; but turn away from me when I deviate.[25]

Rhetoric alone does not suffice in Islam; specific measures are recommended to establish social and economic equity. These distributive measures include (1) *zakat,* which requires Muslims to pay 2.5 percent of their wealth in alms to the poor or to charitable institutions;[26] (2) **ushr,** which requires Muslim farmers to pay a tenth of the wealth derived from their farms to the poor or to charitable institutions; (3) **khums,** which requires Shi'ah Muslims to pay a fifth of their savings to poor or needy **sayyids** (descendants of Prophet Muhammad's family); (4) **sadaqah,** which encourages Muslims to give money or food to the poor and needy; (5) contribution of the *zakat, ushr,* and *sadaqah* funds into the **auqaf,** which are charitable institutions operated by the government or private organizations that assist the *ummah* by supporting *masjids* (mosques), *madrassahs* (Islamic

---

[23]Quoted in A. G. Noorani, "Human Rights in Islam," *Illustrated Weekly of India,* May 3, 1981, p. 20; Mouloud Kassim Nait-Belkacem, "The Concept of Social Justice in Islam," in Altaf Gauhar, ed., *The Challenge of Islam* (London: Islamic Council of Europe, 1978), p. 135; also quoted in Yvonne Yazbeck Haddad, *Contemporary Islam and the Challenge of History* (Albany: State University of New York Press, 1982), p. 186. The Qur'anic verse that prescribes amputation for theft is followed by another that says: "But whoever repents after his crime and reforms, God will accept his repentence" (quoted in Noorani, "Human Rights," p. 20). Thus amputation in Islam is reserved for the habitual offender who has failed to reform himself. Likewise, the flogging or stoning of adulterers cannot be undertaken without the testimony of four adult males who personally witnessed the offense. Since the Qur'an explicitly forbids spying on individuals doing no one any harm, such testimony is likely only when the offence is blatantly public. Hence, the aim of harsh punishments for adultery is to deter a public display of such permissive behavior, which would otherwise lead to a decay of the social fabric (ibid., p. 20).

[24]A *hadith* of Prophet Muhammad quoted in Darlene May, "Women in Islam: Yesterday and Today," in Cyriac K. Pullipilly, ed., *Islam in the Contemporary World* (Notre Dame, Ind.: Cross Roads Books, 1980), p. 370.

[25]Quoted in Noorani, "Human Rights," p. 20.

[26]In fact, Islam stresses the principle of **haq** (legal rights or claims of an individual), especially for the poor and needy. According to the Qur'an, "In the wealth of the rich is a recognized right for the needy and the deprived" (70:24–25); "and woe unto those who ascribe divinity to aught beside him; those who do not pay *zakat*" (41:6–7).

schools), orphanages, health clinics, and other humanitarian concerns; (6) the abolition of **riba** (usury), the charging of excessive interest by lenders to borrowers; (7) government regulation of interest rates charged by financial institutions to lenders; (8) **mudarabah,** which encourages Muslim entrepreneurs (business owners and bankers) to engage in profit sharing with their employees; (9) **musharakah,** in which businessmen are encouraged to engage in profit and loss sharing with investors.

Islam's emphasis on justice and social and economic equity obliges the Islamic state—or Muslims governing a modern nation-state—to ensure a just distribution of the public revenues, "so that it (wealth) may not (merely) make a circuit between the wealthy among you" (41:7). Although Islam operates from within what economists would call a capitalist context, concepts like "just distribution" are espoused by twentieth-century "Islamic socialists," who quote the Qur'an and *hadith* to buttress their arguments for creating a "welfare state" in the "true spirit of Islam."

Socialists notwithstanding, the importance of social and economic equity and justice in Islam is particularly relevant to Islamists. It is central to their struggle to replace politically and economically unjust, hence "un-Islamic," regimes throughout the Muslim world with an Islamic state governed by the principles of equity and justice.

Jihad in Islam

Principal to an understanding of Islamic political action, particularly in nations that preclude the participation of Islamists in the political system, is the doctrine of *jihad*. In the West, *jihad* is a highly pejorative and much maligned term, commonly associated by the media with the most extreme Islamist factions and outrageous acts of political violence. By mistaking *jihad* for jingoism, war, kidnapping, and terrorism, the West judges Islam as a radical, militant, uncompromising, and intolerant faith.

For centuries, the Christian West has denigrated Islam as a faith that "never gained any Proselyte where the Sword, its most forcible, and strongest argument hath not prevailed."[27] Christians maintained that *jihad* is purely offensive war waged to spread the faith, thus confusing *jihad* with wars of aggression, imperialism, and forced conversion. Western scholars and mass media have contributed to these misconceptions by emphasizing the martial connotations of *jihad* and by narrowly defining it as "military 'effort' in the cause of Islam,"[28] usually involving the expansion of the *dar al-Islam* (the Muslim world) at the expense of the *dar al-harb* (variously defined as the non-Muslim world, the world of "unbelievers," or the

---

[27]Quoted in the preface of *The Koran Interpreted*, trans. Arthur J. Arberry (New York: Macmillan), 1955, p. 8.

[28]Gerard Endress, *An Introduction to Islam*, trans. Carole Hillenbrand (New York: Columbia University Press, 1988), p. 75.

world of conflict).[29] This definition, though accurate, is incomplete; it misleads the non-Muslim and fails to convey the rich meaning embodied in *jihad* as it applies to the daily lives of over a billion Muslims, the overwhelming majority of whom will never lift a weapon in anger.

The term *jihad* is derived from the Arabic root *jhd*, which means "to strive," "to exert oneself to the utmost," "to endeavor," or "to struggle in the way of God."[30] The term does not merely mean "holy war," as it has often been defined by non-Muslims. Ideally, *jihad* has three meanings: a battle against evils within oneself (personal *jihad*), a battle against evils within the Muslim community *(ummaic jihad)*, and a battle in defense of the faith and the *ummah* against pagan aggressors or authoritarian apostates and tyrants oppressing Muslims within a country.[31]

The personal *jihad*, or **jihad-i-akbar**, is the greatest *jihad*. It represents the perpetual struggle required of all Muslims to purge their baser instincts. Greed, racism, hedonism, jealousy, revenge, hypocrisy, lying, cheating, and calumny must each be driven from the soul by waging *jihad-i-akbar*, warring against one's lower nature and leading a virtuous life. Thus *jihad* in the daily life of a practicing Muslim is the constant struggle to "avoid evil and do good." This interpretation of the greater or greatest *jihad* is very similar to the Christian injunction to "fight temptation." Ummaic *jihad* addresses wrongs done by deeds within the ummah, by the written or spoken word. *Ummaic jihad* represents the nonviolent struggle for freedom and justice within the *dar al-Islam*. Thus the doctrine of *jihad* is not exclusive to Islam but is typical of religious faiths that demand personal discipline, moral and ethical deeds, and community justice and responsibility.

Martial or violent *jihad* is referred to in Islam as *jihad-i-asghar* (literally, the "smaller," "lower," or "lesser" *jihad*). Martial *jihad* ideally represents a struggle against aggressors who are not practicing Muslims. In Islamic theory, martial *jihad* should be undertaken in God's name and with pure and noble intentions, never for self-aggrandizement. Martial *jihad* should be used to protect and to promote the integrity of Islam and to defend the *ummah* against hostile unbelievers, whether they are invading armies or un-Islamic internal despots. In the latter case, the line between ummaic *jihad* and martial *jihad* becomes blurred.

---

[29]Revolutionary Islamists and Traditionalist Islamists alike perceive the world as divided into two regions: lands of those who believe in God and endeavor to do his bidding *(dar al-Islam)*, and those who do not *(dar al-harb)*. The **dar al-Islam** contains all lands ruled by Muslims, where ideally, Islamic laws are in effect. Within the *dar al-Islam*, non-Muslims are protected and live according to their own laws in matters relating to their religion and customs. Nevertheless, non-Muslims are not allowed to occupy strategic positions in the military or government. The **dar al-harb**, in contrast, contains lands ruled by non-Muslims. There, the laws, rules, and regulations are of a non-Islamic character. Moreover, in the *dar al-harb*, Muslim minorities suffer discrimination, prejudice, or intolerance. Thus, a constant state of suspicion, tension, and conflict prevails between the *dar al-harb* and *dar al-Islam*. If war does break out between the two antagonistic systems, it is for Muslims a martial *jihad*, in which the *mujahideen* (freedom fighters) who die are *shaheed* (martyrs) and are rewarded with paradise.

[30]Rafiq Zakaria, *Muhammad and the Quran* (New York: Penguin Books, 1991), p. 97.

[31]Arthur Goldschmidt, Jr., *A Concise History of the Middle East*, 4th ed. (Boulder, Colo.: Westview Press, 1991), p. 400.

Martial *jihad* is not the sixth pillar of Islam, as is often claimed, but is strictly circumscribed by Prophet Muhammad. The use of lethal force in martial *jihad* may be authorized and conducted only by the *ummah* or in the name of the *ummah*. Thus, martial *jihad* is strictly a corporate responsibility directed against the *dar al-harb* by the *dar al-Islam*. The individual Muslim cannot independently wage martial *jihad* on an unbelieving individual. Likewise, Islam forbids martial *jihad* of Muslims against Muslims; only nonviolent ummaic *jihad* is permissible within the *ummah* against practicing Muslims.

Muhammad said, "If you see those in authority doing something you disapprove of . . . then disapprove of the act [ummaic *jihad*], but do not resort to rebellion [martial *jihad*]."[32] When asked about fighting unjust rulers within the *ummah*, the Prophet answered, "No, not so long as they pray."[33] This reply, however, leaves the door open for martial *jihad* against nonpracticing Muslim rulers and governors who oppress the people. Otherwise, martial *jihad* against Muslim leaders is discouraged in order to avoid internecine or fratricidal bloodshed. According to Sahih Bakhari and Sahih Muslim, Muhammad said, "the highest (greatest) *jihad* is a word of justice addressed to an unjust ruler."[34] Thus in ummaic *jihad*, there is no mention of war.

Jihad is, in its ideal form, essentially nonviolent. Muhammad said, "the scholar's ink is more precious than the martyr's blood." However, martial *jihad* is often used as a last resort because "Islam's ultimate goals might be achieved by peaceful as well as violent means."[35] But even when martial *jihad* is authorized and carried out by the *ummah*, further Qur'anic injunctions apply. Believers engaging in martial *jihad* are cautioned to show mercy in victory just as Muhammad pardoned Abu Sufyan, his greatest persecutor. Oppressors should be given the opportunity to refrain from their actions:

> Say to the unbelievers that if they refrain, then whatever they have done before will be forgiven them, but if they turn back, then they know what happened to earlier nations. And fight against them until there is no oppression and the religion is wholly for God. But if they refrain, then God is watching over their actions. But if they do not then know that God is your Ally and He is your Helper [8:38].

This verse implies limits in the pursuit of justice. "Fight in the cause of God against those who attack you, but do not attack them first and be careful to maintain the limit since God does not love transgressors" (2:190). The force used in martial *jihad* must be restricted to the minimum sufficient to restrain attackers. Theoretically, martial *jihad* must be moderate and merciful; it is not to be used to exact revenge, engage in imperialism, or conquer for personal gain.

---

[32]Cited in Abdul Hamid A. Abu Sulayman, "The Quran and the Sunnah on Violence, Armed Struggle, and the Political Process," *American Journal of Islamic Social Sciences*, Vol. 8, No. 2 (1991), p. 19.

[33]Ibid.

[34]Ibid.

[35]Majid Khadduri, *The Islamic Conception of Justice* (Baltimore: Johns Hopkins University Press, 1984), p. 164.

The three carefully delimited categories of *jihad*—personal, ummaic, and martial—are not recommendations; they are commands. Within the *ummah*, ummaic *jihad* is enjoined on all believers who perceive wrongdoing. Ummaic *jihad* is the means for realizing the social and economic equity and justice promised by Islam. According to *Al-Tafsir al-Quran lil Tarikh (History of Qur'anic Commentary)*, many Qur'anic verses place the greatest responsibility for oppression, corruption, injustice, and vice on those in positions of power and influence.[36] One such Qur'anic verse states:

> There is no doubt that corruption in the system of government is one of the most important factors that lead to the collapse of nations. One of the signs of this corruption is the injustice inflicted on the weak by the oppressors [28:4].

However, according to Islam, the governing elite is not solely accountable for the deterioration of society. The ignorant, apathetic, apolitical, and cowardly people among the governed must also shoulder the blame. When despots deny freedom of thought, conscience, and choice to the people, devout Muslims are obliged by their faith to work to restore such freedoms, either through writing, speeches, or financial contributions, or if the oppressors and despots are unbelievers, by the sword.

The Qur'an teaches that "true" Muslims with **taqwa** (fear of God) must write and speak out against unjust regimes and must wage *jihad* to arouse public action. Nor will God deny the people the right to defend themselves; otherwise "corruption would surely overwhelm the earth" (2:251). All believers are enjoined to defend God and justice, even if it seems against their own interests:

> O you who believe, be firm in justice and as witnesses for God even though it be against yourselves, your parents, those close to you, and whether it concerns rich or poor. . . . So do not follow caprice, lest ye swerve from truth [4:135].

Thus, justice in Islam takes greater priority than personal well-being. The individual must strive, no matter how great the sacrifice, for the good of the community.

Martial *jihad* is required at times of crisis, and none is relieved of the duty to fight unbelieving oppressors and attackers. Even fighting in the sacred months is a lesser evil than oppression:

> They ask thee about fighting in the sacred months; Say: Fighting in them is a great sin, but to prevent people from the way of God, and to reject God, and to stop people from visiting the sacred mosque, and to expel people from their homes are a much greater sin and oppression is worse than killing [2:217].

The Qur'an warns Muslims of the terrible retribution they will suffer if they ignore their duty to fight oppression and, instead, support oppressors: "And incline not to those who do wrong and oppress others, or the Fire will seize you, and you have not protectors other than God, nor shall you be supported" (11:133).

---

[36]Haddad, *Contemporary Islam*, p. 186.

If the *ummah* is oppressed by a believer, then nonviolent ummaic *jihad* is required. If the oppressor is an "unbeliever," then martial *jihad* is permitted. The Qur'an specifically enjoins oppressed believers to act, not to stand idly by, in the face of oppression:

> Fight against them! God will chastise them by your hands, and will bring disgrace upon them, and will succor you against them; and He will soothe the bosoms [hearts] of those who believe [9:14].

In Islamic history, Muhammad and his first converts were persecuted; only by rising up against their adversaries did they ensure Islam's survival. Hence, *jihad* in the face of oppression is a duty of the devout Muslim.

Although enjoined in Islam, *jihad* is not without reward to the **mujahid** (one who engages in a *jihad*). Muslims believe that those who engage in *jihad* will be rewarded, if not in this world, then certainly in the next: "So let them fight in the way of God who sell the present life for the world to come; and whosoever fights in the way of God and is slain, or conquers, we shall bring him a mighty wage" (4:76). And for those who give their lives in martial *jihad*, God promises the greatest reward, Paradise. According to Islamists, an Islamic political movement cannot succeed without dedicated and unqualified commitment both to ummaic and martial *jihad*, and to the readiness to die in the way of God.

Examples of martyrdom from Islam's past are numerous. Muhammad's grandson Imam Hussein is renowned among Shi'ahs and Sunnis alike for his refusal in 680 CE to legitimize the caliphate of Yazid, whose credentials as a practicing Muslim were highly suspect. Imam Hussein rejected Yazid's bribes and chose instead, when cornered by the caliph's armies on the plain of Karbala, to defend himself and die a martyr in a martial *jihad*. The martyrdom of Imam Hussein and seventy-one male members of his extended family at Karbala, far from a defeat, made all Muslims aware of the Islamic ideals for which he stood. By upholding the revolutionary Islamic tradition of struggle and sacrifice, Imam Hussein became a role model for all Muslims.

The broad and rich meaning of *jihad* has, despite clear injunctions and proscriptions, been open more than any other Islamic doctrine to abuse. During Muhammad's life, God enjoined Muslims to wage martial *jihad* only during times of dire necessity, when the nascent community of believers was in peril. Under the first four "rightly guided caliphs," who succeeded Muhammad, Islam defeated its enemies and expanded its borders. Martial *jihad* was not frivolously waged, nor was it undertaken for the personal glory of any individual. During this period martial *jihad* was truly "just war," and those who were conquered by the Muslims were shown mercy and were not obliged to convert to Islam since the Qur'an clearly states that "there shall be no compulsion in religion" (2:256).

With the establishment of the Umayyad dynasty (661 CE), however, martial *jihad* was increasingly declared with little or no Qur'anic justification. Corrupt caliphs often perverted the practice of martial *jihad*. "Just wars" became instead naked wars of aggression. Although early Muslim scholars declared that martial *jihad* was permissible against unbelievers only after provocation from the *dar al-harb*, later scholars broadened this interpretation and declared that martial *jihad* was justified against unbelievers simply for their disbelief.[37] Thus, the imperatives of empire overcame the letter and spirit of Islam, and the practice of martial *jihad* was perverted by corrupt officials. War between the *dar al-Islam* and the *dar al-harb* became inherently "just," regardless of provocation. It is this corrupted tradition of *jihad* that has drawn the condemnation of the West and has unfairly maligned Islam.

Varying questionable interpretations and practices of martial *jihad* today, particularly in terror attacks against civilians, have likewise contributed to non-Muslims' fear of revolutionary political Islam and antipathy toward devout Muslims who peacefully practice their faith. Appropriate uses of martial *jihad* have become complicated, because the *ummah* has been divided and the *dar al-harb* is now within the *dar al-Islam.* Accordingly, martial *jihad* has, more than ever, been directed against adversaries within the Muslim world, not on its borders. With the universal *ummah* lacking a caliph, many Revolutionary Islamists have placed themselves in the vanguard of martial *jihad,* directing a "holy war" to rid the Muslim world of unbelievers and hypocrites while reestablishing a united Islamic bloc. The Ayatollah Khomeini declared: "In this holy *jihad* and serious duty, we must lead the other people by virtue of our mission and position."[38]

The question in the Muslim world is no longer whether political Islam is necessary for change, but whether its form will be nonviolent ummaic *jihad* or violent martial *jihad.* Since Muslims do not perceive the leaders of many Muslim nations as practicing Muslims, martial *jihad* is more probable. Naturally, foreigners as well as authoritarian leaders are distressed by a *jihad* that promises the blessings of Paradise in martyrdom. Today, numerous grassroots Islamic movements struggle to overthrow what they perceive as "un-Islamic" regimes throughout the Muslim world. Islamists in most Islamic movements are convinced that European imperialism succeeded because secular Muslim regimes failed to establish Islamic states and to live up to the promise and principle of pan-Islamism. By oppressing their people and depriving them of any participation in the political process, the Muslim Secularists governing Muslim nations today have made ummaic *jihad* impossible—and martial *jihad* inevitable.

Islam: An Idiom of Dissent

Islamism can be defined as the reawakening of interest in Islamic symbols, ideas, and ideals subsequent to a period of relative dormancy. It is the reemergence of Islam as a social and political force in the world. According to Ali E. Hillal Dessouki, Islamic resurgence refers to

> an increasing political activism in the name of Islam by governments and opposition groups alike. . . . Islamic groups have assumed a more assertive posture and projected themselves in many Arab and Islamic countries as contenders for public allegiance

---

[37]Khadduri, *The Islamic Conception of Justice,* pp. 165–166.

[38]Ayatollah Ruhollah Khomeini, *Islamic Government,* trans. Joint Publications Research Service (New York: Manor Books, 1979), p. 88.

and political loyalty. . . . Thus, Islamic resurgence refers to the increasing prominence and politicization of Islamic ideologies and symbols in Muslim societies and in the public life of Muslim individuals.[39]

Manifestations of the Islamic revival include (a) a groundswell or resurgence—involving a broad spectrum of Muslim society—of public sentiment for and interest in an Islamic system, which has been referred to both as an Islamic resurgence and as "populist Islam"; (b) grassroots or populist Islamic movements involving selected segments of Muslim society—for example, members of the working class or of a student community—who want to establish an Islamic system; and (c) government-sponsored Islamic programs that reassert religion as a primary ideological force (referred to as "governmental Islam" or "official Islam"). In the latter programs the leadership in power may resort to Islam for any number of reasons, including sincere religious beliefs, appeasement of an influential domestic religious pressure group, enhancement of governmental legitimacy, assistance in the integration of a fragmented society, and acquisition of funds from rich Muslim countries.

The Islamism of the past two decades encompasses at least five prominent features: First, the spread of Islam from homes, *masjids* (mosques), and *madrassahs* (Islamic schools) into the mainstream of not only the sociocultural life of Muslim societies but the legal, economic, and political spheres of the modern-day Muslim nation-states as well. Islamists stress the observance of the five *faraidh*, or five pillars of Islam: *shahadah, salat, sawm, zakat,* and *hajj.* They also emphasize modesty in dress for all, the **hijab** (veil) for women, and segregation of the sexes wherever possible. The Revolutionary Islamists, Traditionalist Islamists, and Modernist Islamists (to be defined shortly) within these movements exert considerable pressure on their respective governments to ban alcohol, gambling, nightclubs, prostitution, pornography, and a number of other corrupting influences. They further demand the formulation of an Islamic constitution and the implementation of the *shariah,* the comprehensive and divine Islamic law that includes severe penalties for a broad spectrum of crimes. Facing political ferment among Islamists, the governments of Muslim countries often display their Islamic credentials by stepping up mosque construction and increasing their funding of mosques and *madrassahs.* There is also an increased attendance of Muslims of all walks of life at Jum'ah (Friday) prayer services and during the annual *hajj* to Makkah in the Islamic calendar month of Dhul-Hijjah.

Second, Islamism engenders widespread discussion and debate of Islamic issues in the mass media, leading to a proliferation of books and articles on Islamic theology, history, jurisprudence, culture, and civilization. More important, Islamism produces efforts at the reformulation and revision of Islamic theory and practice in light of contemporary times. This has been achieved particularly by Modernist Islamists through *ijma* (consensus) and *ijtihad* (independent reasoning and judgment). *Ijma* requires dissemination of pertinent information by the *ulama* (Islamic scholars) and Islamic experts of various schools of thought, so that an

---

[39]Ali E. Hillal Dessouki, "The Islamic Resurgence: Sources, Dynamics, and Implications," in Ali E. H. Dessouki, ed., *Islamic Resurgence in the Arab World* (New York: Praeger, 1982), p. 4.

enlightened consensus can result from informed public opinion. *Ijtihad* demands that *mujtahids* (*ulama* who practice *ijtihad*) provide relevant solutions to contemporary problems.

Third, coming at a time of great disparity of wealth between the affluent elite and the impoverished majority, as well as a time of sociopolitical injustice in most Muslim societies, Islam's emphasis on social and economic equality and justice has significant populist appeal. In fact, this appeal is one of the most important features in political Islam.

Fourth, Islamists often reassert the relevance of the religious (Islamic) approach to solving contemporary problems, while at the same time presenting a critique of the dominant materialist values imported from the West or the socialist-communist world. For instance, Revolutionary Islamists and Traditionalist Islamists denounce secularization as "un-Islamic" because it implies that God and His guidance are relegated to the personal domain of an individual's life and that the larger political, economic, social, and cultural areas should be independent of His influence. Many contemporary Islamists are eager to accept modern scientific methods and technology from anywhere in the world. However, they are adamantly opposed to and totally reject whatever they perceive as "un-Islamic" and harmful to the *ummah*.

Last but not least, Islamist movements have strong anti-imperialist and anti-colonialist undercurrents. Islamists call for an end to international dependence on Western powers. They champion the development of a united Islamic bloc of fraternal Muslim nations, which in turn could become an influential force in international relations for the good of the *ummah*.

Although Islamism has been defined here in the most general terms, it must be understood that political Islam should not be seen as a monolithic force under a single leadership. Indeed, there is a different expression of Islamism for each self-proclaimed Islamist. In general, differing and sometimes contradictory views of Islamism prevail in the Muslim world.

The term *Islamist* refers generically to anyone who has contributed or is contributing significantly to the revival of Islam. In propagating their perception of "true" Islam, Islamists frequently, but not necessarily, promote the creation of an Islamic state by teaching, preaching, and/or writing and on rare occasions by resorting to force of arms. The individuals, groups, and movements that have fueled Islamism and Islamic revivals fall into three ideal-typical categories: Revolutionary Islamists, Traditionalist Islamists, and Modernist Islamists. Like any classification scheme, this typology imperfectly represents reality. However, it is far better to create these three ideal-typical categories of Islamists than lumping all Islamists together in one undifferentiated category. Many Islamist leaders may combine elements of two (or more) of these major categories, depending on specific issues and circumstances. But for the sake of clarity and simplicity, individual Islamists are categorized according to the principal thrust of their beliefs.

Revolutionary Islamists tend to be puritanical and radical in their religious and political orientation. They support *ijtihad*, independent reasoning, in matters of Islamic law and theology, while rejecting Western ideas and ideals. However, Revolutionary Islamists are not inherently opposed to the nations of the West, only to their influence in the Muslim world; nor do these Islamists always struggle through turbulent revolution. Many are willing, if given the opportunity, to participate in democratic elections and to abide by those elections. In general, however, Revolutionary Islamists desire to establish an "Islamic state" based on the comprehensive and rigorous application of the *shariah*.

Traditionalist Islamists are often Islamic scholars who want to conserve and preserve the Islamic laws, customs, and traditions practiced in the classical and medieval periods of Islam. In contrast to both Sunni and Shi'ah Revolutionary Islamists, Sunni Traditionalist Islamists reject *ijtihad* and believe instead in rigid and unquestioning adherence to certain legal rulings compiled during Islam's medieval period. Unlike Sunni Traditionalist Islamists, who generally rule out *ijtihad*, a minority of Shi'ah Traditionalist Islamists—who have gained the stature of *mujtahids* (learned theologians, or *ulama*) after much learning and scholarship— prefer to exercise *ijtihad*. However, most Shi'ah Traditionalist Islamists (the majority of whom are not *mujtahids*) closely and rigidly adhere to the Fiqh-i-Jafariyyah, just as Sunni Traditionalist Islamists rigidly adhere to one of their four schools of jurisprudence, the Hanafi, Maliki, Shafi'i, or Hanbali *fiqh*. While both Sunni and Shi'ah Traditionalist Islamists are often apolitical, passive, and status quo oriented, these scholarly custodians of Islam do get involved in politics when they perceive Islam and/or the *ummah* to be in imminent danger.

The **Modernist Islamists**, also called adaptationists, apologists, syncretists, and even revisionists, are religiously devout but unafraid of Western sciences and learning. Unlike conservative Traditionalist Islamists and puritanical Revolutionary Islamists, the pragmatic Modernist Islamists advocate the reconciliation of traditional religious doctrine with secular scientific rationalism. Predictably, Modernist Islamists are critics of *taqlid* (legal conformity) and proponents of *ijtihad*. They advocate the incorporation of many "modern-day" ideas and revisions of Islamic law. Revolutionary Islamists, in contrast, reject anything "modern" as un-Islamic.

Islamism: Past and Present

Historically, Islamism appeared in cycles followed by periods of relative dormancy. The modern form of Islamism, like previous forms, advocates simplicity, purity, and piety in a time of trouble and confusion. However, two major differences separate contemporary Islamism from its historical antecedents. First, modern Islamism is not a regional phenomenon; it is global in scope. Second, modern Islamism is not monolithic but polycentric, heterogenous, and multifaceted.

The universal application of modern Islamism can best be understood through such theoretical concepts in international relations as transnational relations, linkage politics, and global interdependence. These three phenomena have occurred in conjunction with revolutions in mass communications and mass transportation that have led to the shrinking of time and space. Joseph S. Nye and Robert O. Keohane have defined transnational relations as "the movements of tangible or intangible items across state boundaries when at least one actor is not an agent of a government or an intergovernmental organization."[40] For instance, due to the low cost and relative ease of modern mass transportation, as well as to the presence of Islamism in the Muslim world, the number of pilgrims annually performing the *hajj* has increased dramatically in the last fifteen years. In 1930, just over 230,000 Muslims performed the *hajj*; in 1940, the number was over 280,000. By 1950, the annual number of *hajjis* (those performing the *hajj*) had reached 895,000. Throughout the 1950s and 1960s approximately 1 million pilgrims performed the *hajj* annually. The 1970s witnessed a dramatic doubling of pilgrims to almost 2 million each year. In 1983, this number reached 2.25 million.[41] Since then 2 million to 2.5 million Muslims have performed the *hajj* annually.

Some of the many participants in transnational relations are the nongovernmental, religiopolitical organizations that operate across the international boundaries of a number of countries. The **Ikhwan al-Muslimun** (Muslim Brotherhood) is one such (see Box 2.2). The group was founded in Egypt in 1928 and established branches in several Arab countries, including Syria, Jordan, and Sudan. The Egyptian Ikhwan al-Muslimun maintains close contacts with its branch organizations and is reported to have received financial assistance from the regimes of Saudi Arabia and Libya during the 1970s. Another such organization is the **Jama'at-i-Islami** (Islamic Association) of Pakistan (see Box 2.3). Not only does it keep in regular touch with a number of friendly Muslim governments (such as Saudi Arabia) and global Islamic institutions (such as Al-Azhar in Cairo), but it also publishes numerous books and monographs that are translated from Urdu into many languages and distributed internationally. Libya's Muammar al-Qaddafi is also known to have funded the Moro Muslims of Southern Philippines, who are waging their *jihad* (holy struggle) for greater autonomy. The external support given to the Ikhwan al-Muslimun (particularly during the era of Gamal Abdel Nasser in Egypt), the Jamaat-i-Islami (during the era of Zulfikar Ali Bhutto in Pakistan), and the Moro rebels (during the 1970s) was strongly resented by the governments in whose territories these Islamic movements operate. Another transnational entity is the Organization of the Islamic Conference (OIC), whose many organs help promote its objectives in the Muslim world (see Box 8.3).

In Iran, Ayatollah Khomeini engaged in transnational relations when he brought about the first "cassette revolution." According to Anthony Sampson, Ayatollah Khomeini's revolutionary religiopolitical ideas and anti-government speeches on audio cassette tapes smuggled into Iran by his former students and supporters from Najaf, Iraq, where the exiled cleric lived, influenced numerous Iranians throughout the length and breadth of Muhammad Reza Shah Pahlavi's domain. These audio cassettes were widely disseminated and heard in numerous homes and mosques that had audio cassette recorders. In this way Khomeini

---

[40]Quoted in Walter S. Jones, *The Logic of International Relations*, 8th ed. (New York: Longman, 1997), p. 412; Joseph S. Nye and Robert O. Keohane, "Transnational Relations and World Politics: An Introduction," *International Organization*, Vol. 25 (1971), pp. 329–349.

[41]Ziauddin Sardar, "The Greatest Gathering of Mankind," *Inquiry*, Vol. 1, No. 4 (September 1984), p. 27; David Lamb, "Muslim Faithful Worldwide Preparing for Annual Pilgrimmage to Mecca," *Los Angeles Times*, August 19, 1984, Part I, p. 28.

BOX 2.2   Egypt's Ikhwan al-Muslimun

The Ikhwan al-Muslimun (Muslim Brotherhood) was founded by the Revolutionary Islamist Hasan al-Banna in the 1930s. A party dedicated to Islamic revivalism and social, economic, and political equity, the Ikhwan's membership swelled into a mass movement. Rapid industrialization and urbanization in Egypt spawned widespread dislocation and alienation. The Ikhwan's activist message of radical reform appealed to unemployed and underemployed Egyptians. In addition, the Ikhwan blamed Egypt's problems on Western colonial powers and Egypt's secular dictators who ruled under their influence.

In 1952 the Ikhwan supported the Free Officers Movement, led by Gamal Abdel Nasser, which toppled the government of Egypt's King Farouk. The Ikhwan assisted in the insurrection and cooperated with the Free Officers Movement to maintain law and order. The Free Officers were secular nationalists and were dedicated to Egyptian nationalism, pan-Arabism, and Arab socialism. Nasser excluded Ikhwan leaders from his government and rejected the Ikhwan's goals of an Islamic state and the promotion of pan-Islamism. Suspicious of the Ikhwan, Nasser ordered the arrest of *Ikhwan* activists. However, in the late 1960s the Ikhwan was revitalized, partially in reaction to the silence of the Traditionalist *ulama* to Nasser's socialism and dictatorship and to undue Soviet influence in Egypt.

After the terrible defeat suffered by the Arab armies in the 1967 Arab-Israeli War, President Nasser turned to Islamic themes and ritual observances to relieve Egypt's trauma. In 1970 Nasser died and was succeeded by his vice president, Muhammad Anwar al-Sadat, who, to counter the Nasserite threat to his power, unleashed the Ikhwan. He freed members of the Ikhwan from jail, encouraged their exiled leaders to return to Egypt, permitted the Ikhwan to recruit new members, and allowed the Ikhwan to obtain financing from abroad. However, the Ikhwan was incensed when Egypt signed a peace treaty with Israel in 1979. The Ikhwan declared that Sadat had sold out Islamic Palestinian land. In 1981 Sadat was assassinated by an Ikhwan splinter group called Islamic Jihad.

Since Sadat's death, Egypt's president Hosni Mubarak has pursued the Ikhwan and other Islamists aggressively. However, Egyptians continue to turn to the Ikhwan and its radical spin-offs as disillusionment with and alienation from the Egyptian government persists. The Ikhwan has been impeded, however, by its ideological inconsistency and incoherent organizational structure. Thus, it is impossible to talk about the methods or aspirations of a monlothic Ikhwan. This lack of organizational discipline has obstructed the Ikhwan's effectiveness as a political party.

http://www.ummah.org.uk/ikhwan/

---

totally bypassed the tightly controlled government mass media and reached Iranians directly. Iranians were free to listen to the tapes over and over again in the privacy of their homes and in the sanctuary of mosques, away from the prying eyes and ears of the Shah's secret police.[42]

---

[42]Anthony Sampson, *New York Times*, May 6, 1979, p. 27.

■

BOX 2.3   South Asia's Jama'at-i-Islami

The Jama'at-i-Islami (Islamic Association, or JI) was founded in 1941 in India by Sayyid Abul A'la Maududi. The tightly organized, highly disciplined, and revolutionary JI was founded to oppose British rule of India, to protect Muslims in India from the Hindu majority, and to transform India into the *dar al-Islam* (abode of Islam) again. Following the partition of India and the creation of Pakistan, the JI dedicated itself to fashioning Pakistan into an Islamic state. The JI's practice of selective recruitment has impeded its growth. The JI is no mass movement like Egypt's Ikhwan al-Muslimun, although the JI is better organized.

The JI serves not just as a political entity but also as an educational and social welfare organization in Pakistan. It operates schools and orphanages, provides financial support for widows, and runs health clinics. During the Soviet invasion of Afghanistan, the JI contributed money to Afghan *mujahideen* (Muslims fighting a *jihad*) groups.

Although the JI is influential politically, its success in elections has been limited. The organization's strict insistence on ideological purity, narrow interpretation of Islamic theory and practice, and zealous propagation of revolutionary Islamism have frightened away the support of Modernist Islamists and Muslim Secularists, who comprise the economic, social, and political elite. Moreover, the JI's promise to bring equity to the lord-serf relationship in Pakistan's countryside has earned them the vehement opposition of the *pirs* (spiritual guides), *zamindars* (large landlords), and *sardars* (tribal chieftains). Likewise, the Jama'at-i-Islami's plan to segregate women from men in Pakistani society has alienated many women. The JI has also been engaged in heated doctrinal disputes with the two other prominent Islamic political parties of Pakistan, the Jamiat-i-Ulama-i-Islam (Association of the Ulama of Islam) and Jamiat-i-Ulama-i-Pakistan (Association of the Ulama of Pakistan). The JI has other electoral liabilities: its leaders thus far have lacked charisma and political shrewdness; its original opposition to the Pakistan Movement put the JI's loyalty to Pakistan in doubt; and its religious appeal has been diminished by Muslim Secularists' use of the same Islamic symbols and imagery. Most important, however, the JI has forged no realistic developmental strategy for Pakistan in a modern and increasingly interdependent world. Yet although the JI has failed to capture power, it remains an effective interest group commanding considerable influence. Indeed, the JI collaborated, if briefly, with Zia's military government (1978–1983) and, later, with the government of Nawaz Sharif. But the unpopularity of both governments has tarnished the image of the JI, and it has had diminished success at the ballot box.

http://atheism.about.com/library/islam/blfaq_islam_jamaat1.htm
http://www.jamaat.org/
http://www.jamaat.org/news/pr052001.html

With the revolution in mass communications (which includes print media, radio, and television), news of any major adversity or victory experienced by Muslims anywhere in the world can be transmitted through the mass media and grieved or celebrated, respectively, by Muslims worldwide the very same day. Graphic images of

Israel's invasion of Lebanon in the summer of 1982; the massacre of Palestinians by the Lebanese Christian Phalangists in the Sabra and Shatila refugee camps in September 1982; the slaughter of Muslims by Hindus in Assam in February 1983, in Bombay in May 1984, and in Kashmir for most of the 1990s; the genocide of Bosnian Muslims by Serbs and Croats in the former Yugoslavia from February 1992 until the fall of 1995; and the civil war and starvation of Somalis for much of 1992–1993; the Russian government's genocide of Muslim Chechens in the Russia province of Chechnya from August 1998 to February 2000; the Serbian genocide of Muslim Kosovars in Yugoslavia's province of Kosovo in 1999; the U.S.-led war in Afghanistan in the fall and winter 2001; and Israel's war against the Palestinians in the West Bank and Gaza in spring 2002 were moments of terrible grief for the *ummah* worldwide. Conversely, moments of exhilaration and ecstasy were provided by Yassar Arafat's address to the United Nations in November 1974; the periodic summit meetings of Muslim leaders; Ayatollah Khomeini's triumphant return to Iran in February 1979; the takeover of the government in Afghanistan by the Afghan *mujahideen* in April 1992 in Kabul; and the annual congregation of Muslims from all over the world in Makkah to perform the *hajj*.

Modern forms of communication and transportation have helped maintain the momentum of modern Islamism. It has grown stronger and shows no sign of subsiding. The modern spread of Islamism is—again, unlike prior cycles of Islamism—a global phenomenon with worldwide repercussions. Its endurance may continue indefinitely insofar as the circumstances fueling Islamism show little sign of abating and the grievances of Islamists are global in scope.

Iran's Islamic Revolution (1978–1979) still exerts a powerful influence on people and events in the Muslim world. That the reverberations of this Islamic revolution have been sustained, despite Western enmity, represents a victory for Islamism that Revolutionary Islamists around the world hope to emulate. Again and again, Islamists (individuals and organizations) take their inspiration, and sometimes even the money and leadership, from Tehran. Organizations like Islamic Amal (Hope) and Hezbollah (Party of God) in Lebanon and Iraq's Dawa (the Call) are supported directly or indirectly by the Islamic Republic of Iran.

Other organizations that are Sunni rather than Shi'ah in orientation, like Algeria's Islamic Salvation Front (FIS) and Gama 'al-Islamiyyah (armed Islamic group or GIA); Tunisia's Ennahdah party; the Islamic Renaissance Party (IRP) of the Central Asian Republics and Azerbaijan; the Ikhwan al-Muslimun, al-Takfir w'al-Hijra, Islamic Jihad, and al-Gama'a al-Islamiyyah in Egypt; and the Jama 'at-i-Islami in Pakistan despite their ideological differences and notwithstanding severe governmental repression, have not only endured but are emboldened by the consolidation of Iran's Islamic government. Meanwhile, the Revolutionary Islamist Taliban in Afghanistan (1996-December 2001) and the Revolutionary Islamist military regime in Sudan, were also encouraged by the Iranian Revolution and Islamic state and hoped to build an even stronger Islamic state in their countries. In turn, Islamist organizations like Islamic Jihad, Hamas, Hezbollah, and the Islamic Amal, as well as governments like those of Afghanistan and Sudan perpetuate their own models for emulation, for which Iran was the catalyst. Consequently, Islamism is not only spreading but also becoming self-perpetuating.

The former Soviet Union's predominantly Muslim republics (Azerbaijan, Kazakhstan, Turkmenistan, Uzbekistan, Kyrgyzstan, and Tajikistan) are experiencing an Islamic revival after emerging from the seventy-four-year-old Soviet Communist shadow. Iran, Pakistan, Saudi Arabia, and Turkey are actively competing for influence in the region by sending money, building and renovating *masjids* (mosques) and *madrassahs* (Islamic schools), and sending clerics and Islamic literature. Iran and Afghanistan have already exerted considerable sway in neighboring Tajikistan. Before their fall, the Taliban smuggled arms to the Islamist IRP, which enjoys a powerful base of support in the mountain regions. Moreover, the Tajiks, unlike the other Central Asian Muslims and Azerbaijanis, have strong cultural and linguistic ties to neighboring Iran. Thus as the political situation in the republic degenerates into civil war, the Islamists are gaining new converts to their cause every day. The example provided by Tajikistan may, in turn, inspire Islamists throughout the other former Soviet Muslim republics. Already, neighboring Uzbekistan is feeling the linkages.

The revolution in mass communication and mass transportation has created global linkages and "global interdependence." Witness, for example, the far-reaching consequences of the OPEC oil-price increases (1976–1982), which have affected the economic, political, and social structures of many countries and dictated adjustments that in turn have begotten their own unique results. A pebble dropped in the pool of human endeavor makes ripples far away from the point of impact, and the pool is never the same again.

Modern Islamism is polycentric, heterogeneous, and multifaceted because of a number of factors. First, all three types of Islamists—Revolutionary, Traditionalist, and Modernist—are very active simultaneously, and each group believes that it is working for the greater good of the *ummah*. An example of struggles among well-meaning partisans of each of these three groups is illustrated in the short history of the Iranian Revolution. All three groups were very clearly delineated: Revolutionary Islamists typified by Ayatollah Ruhollah Khomeini, Ayatollah Hussein Ali Montazeri, and Ayatollah Sayyid Ali Khamanei; Traditionalists exemplified by Ayatollah Shariatmadari; and Modernist Islamists represented by Mehdi Bazargan, Abul Hassan Banisadr, Abdul Karim Saroush, and Muhammad Khatami.

Second, in this age of nation-states, the twin ideals of nationalism and national interest are motivating the present leaders of most Muslim countries far more than the utopian ideal of an integrated and unified Islamic empire, or even the more attainable vision of a unified Islamic bloc. This was vividly illustrated in Khomeini's failure to create a pan-Islamic bloc. Despite some conviction at the grassroots, the forces of nationalism overwhelmed any incipient movement in the pan-Islamic direction.

Third, because the leaders of nearly all Muslim states have different worldviews, they find it difficult to unite for any sustained period on more than a few issues. Some Muslim leaders are anti-Western Revolutionary Islamists, such as Iran's Ayatollahs Ruhollah Khomeini (1979–1989) and Ali Hussein Khamenei (1989–present); and Mullah Muhammad Omar of Afghanistan's Taliban regime (1996–2001). Other Muslim leaders are Modernist Islamists, such as Mehdi Bazargan (1979), Abul Hassan Banisadr (1980–1981), Ali Akbar Hashemi

Rafsanjani (1989–1997), and Muhammad Khatami (1997–present); Turkey's Necmettim Erbakan (1996–1997); and Indonesia's Abdurrahman Wahid (1999–2001). Many Muslim leaders are pro–Western capitalists, such as Iran's Muhammad Reza Shah Pahlavi (1941–1979), Jordan's King Hussein (1952–1999), Morocco's King Hassan II (1962–1999), Saudi Arabia's King Fahd (1982–present), Egypt's Muhammad Anwar al-Sadat (1970–1981), and Hosni Mubarak (1981–present). A few Muslim leaders are anti-Western socialists, such as Egypt's Gamal Abdel Nasser (1954–1970), Libya's Muammar Qaddafi (1969–present), and Pakistan's Zulfikar Ali Bhutto (1971–1977). And many Muslim leaders are Secularists, such as Turkey's Mustafa Kemal Ataturk (1922–1936) and Tansu Ciller (1993–1996); Pakistan's Benazir Bhutto (1988–1990, 1993–1996) and Pervez Musharraf (1999–present); Indonesia's General Suharto (1968–1998) and Megawati Sukarnoputri (2001–present); Malaysia's Prime Minister Mahathir bin Muhammad (1982–present); Syria's Hafiz al-Asad (1970–2000); Iraq's Saddam Hussein (1979–present); Jordan's King Abdullah bin Hussein (1999–present); Yassar Arafat (1994–present); and Bangladesh's Shaykh Hasina Wajid (1996–2001).

Martin Kramer probably best summed up the diversity of the Muslim world:

> There is [as yet] no prestigious center for the propagation of the true faith, no compelling leader to whom the faithful look for authoritative pronouncements, no model Islamic order to which all turn in emulation. An Islamic order is in truth many orders, many nostalgias, many visions of the future. There are those across Asia and Africa who do call for Islam, who proclaim in harmony that "the Quran is our constitution," but beyond the single slogan are countless ideals.[43]

The "multipolarization" of the global system that began in the early 1970s has continued to grow. Likewise at the level of the Muslim world a number of different power centers have also evolved, namely, Saudi Arabia, Iran, Egypt, Turkey, Indonesia, Libya, Syria, and Pakistan. Thus, the Muslim world is not experiencing the homogeneous and monolithic Islamic revival necessary to help make it an international power bloc.

Nevertheless, Islamism or political Islam, is a potent and significant global movement. Representing a potentially powerful political ideology that all Muslims can embrace and support, Islamism is growing rapidly as a popular idiom of protest against unjust and repressive "un-Islamic" regimes. A number of major questions remain, however: What shape will political Islam take? And, most important to Western policymakers, which of the three Islamist types will enjoy the greatest support in the Muslim world?

Internet Sites

http://www.witness-pioneer.org/vil/Articles/politics/politicalframeworkofislam.htm

http://www.witness-pioneer.org/vil/Articles/politics/understandingpoliticsinislam.htm

---

[43]Martin Kramer, "Political Islam," *The Washington Papers*, Vol. 8, No. 73 (Beverly Hills: Sage Publications, 1980), p. 39.

CHAPTER THREE

Revolutionary Islamists

Revolutionary Islamists constitute the first major category of Islamists. They are also variously referred to in both popular and scholarly literature as *funda-mentalists,* scripturalists, legalists, literalists, restorationists, restitutionists, puritans, militants, and radicals.[1]

Instead of the term *fundamentalists,* which is a favorite of the mass media, I am using the term *Revolutionary Islamist* in this book. **Fundamentalism** applied originally to a conservative Protestant movement of nineteenth century America; the word now signifies conservative movements among most major religions, including Christianity, Judaism, Hinduism, and Islam. Certain identifying traits prevail among fundamentalists whatever their faith: authoritarianism, a messianic spirit, subordination of secular politics to their religious beliefs, belief in the infallibility of holy scripture, belief in the supernatural, charismatic leadership, and enforced moralism. Taken together, these distinguishing characteristics represent a political vision fundamentalists hope to achieve through aggressive political action.[2]

For purposes of this chapter and throughout the book, these so-called "fundamentalists" will be referred to as Revolutionary Islamists. This is because

---

[1]The term *fundamentalism* has been taken from Christianity. Webster's defines it as "a movement in twentieth-century Protestantism emphasizing the literally interpreted Bible as fundamental to Christian life and teaching." The *Encyclopedia Britannica* defines *fundamentalism* as a "conservative movement in American Protestantism arising out of the millenarian movement in the nineteenth century and emphasizing as fundamental to Christianity the literal interpretation and absolute inerrancy of the Scriptures, the imminent and physical second coming of Jesus Christ, the Virgin Birth, Resurrection, and Atonement."

[2]Roy C. Macridis, *Contemporary Political Ideologies,* 5th ed. (New York: HarperCollins, 1992), pp. 231–234.

Muslims strongly object to the term *fundamentalist* on the following grounds: (1) Muslims believe that the term *fundamentalism* has its origins in Christianity and does not transfer well to Islam; (2) Muslims maintain that they all believe in the "fundamentals" of their faith and therefore all of them are fundamentalists; (3) the term *fundamentalists* has been much maligned and has come to mean "extremists," "zealots," and even "terrorists." No wonder even Christian fundamentalists would prefer to call themselves "evangelicals."

However, whatever the terminology, one fact is obvious. Revolutionary Islamists are no strangers to aggressive political action and occupy the vanguard in Islamism and Islamic revivals around the world. Most are revolutionary in temperament, particularly when rapidly secularizing and modernizing political environments undermine their religious convictions and perquisites. The Revolutionary Islamists advocate rigid adherence to the fundamentals of their faith, as literally interpreted from the Qur'an and the *sunnah*, and actively crusade to impose the *shariah* on society and purge those influences that they feel detract from or demean the fundamentals of Islam. In this regard, most Revolutionary Islamists crusade against prostitution, pornography, the sale or use of alcohol and drugs, gambling, Western music, singing, dancing, wearing ornaments of gold and silver, palm reading, astrology, fortune-telling, fatalism, and superstition. In Iran today prohibition of these "vices" is rigorously enforced.

Revolutionaries

One of the first movements of Revolutionary Islamism in Islamic history was that of the Kharijites. These misguided Islamic zealots were such extremists that they even engaged in what they claimed was a "*jihad*" against caliph Ali, who is recognized by all Muslims as one of the four rightly guided caliphs. The civil war that ensued caused unnecessary fratricide well beyond Ali's caliphate (see Box 3.1).

One of the most celebrated Revolutionary Islamists was Muhammad ibn Abd al-Wahhab (1703–1792; see Box 3.1). A rigid and revolutionary preacher and **qadhi** (Islamic judge) in the Arabian peninsula, Muhammad ibn Abd al-Wahhab established a puritanical Islamic state when he forged a "holy alliance" with tribal chieftain Muhammad ibn Saud, who founded the Saudi dynasty. Together, they launched the **Wahhabi** movement in the second half of the eighteenth century. Eventually, the Wahhabi movement, led by the Saudi dynasty, conquered much of the Arabian peninsula, giving the dynasty's name to Saudi Arabia that dominates the peninsula.

Another noteworthy Revolutionary Islamist was Sayyid Muhammad ibn Ali al-Sanusi (1787–1859). After studying in Makkah and Madinah for several years, this Algerian Islamist of the Bani Sanus tribe established the Sanusi movement in the late 1930s and spread his revolutionary Islamic message in North Africa (see Boxes 3.3 and 3.4).

On the Indian subcontinent, Sayyid Ahmad Barelvi (1786–1831), alias Sayyid Ahmad Shaheed, revered and emulated Muhammad ibn Abd al-Wahhab. Around 1817 Sayyid Ahmad launched his own revolutionary Islamist movement, the Tariqah-i-Muhammadiyah (The Way of Prophet Muhammad). In the 1820s

BOX 3.1   The Kharajites: The First Revolutionary Islamists

The term **Kharijite** has been derived from the Arabic words *kharij* and *khuruj*. *Kharij* literally means "to leave" or "to go out." *Khuruj* (plural, *khawarij*) literally means "to rebel," "to revolt," and "to secede." In Islamic history the Kharijites or Khawarij were the first group of Revolutionary Islamists that emerged after caliph Uthman's assassination and Ali's assumption as Islam's fourth righteous caliph.

Mu'awiyah, the ambitious governor of Syria, wanted to be caliph in place of Ali. He therefore dispatched an army to challenge Ali's Caliphate. In 657 CE, the Battle of Siffin was fought between the armies of Ali and Mu'awiyah. Ali, concerned about fratricide within the *ummah*, decided to let a few prominent Muslims acceptable to Mu'awiyah to arbitrate their dispute.

A segment of Muslims from the Tamim tribe were furious with Ali for permitting a group of fallible human beings to arbitrate an issue as sacred as who should govern the Caliphate. This segment consequently defected from Ali's army and camped outside Kufa (present-day Iraq), thereby earning the name Khariji or Khawarij. When arbitration failed to resolve the dispute between caliph Ali and Mu'awiyah, Kharijite ranks swelled.

The Kharijites objected to Islam's caliph being chosen only from the Quraysh tribe, and after Ali's assassination, they were opposed to the Umayyad dynasty's hereditary rule. While they were willing to follow a pious and just Muslim caliph of any race, color, or ethnic origin, they did expect a caliph that had sinned to confess publicly his sins, and to resign if the *ummah* did not forgive him. The Kharijites believed that a *jihad* against a caliph or Muslim ruler that had lost his legitimacy in the eyes of the *ummah* was fully justified.

The Kharijites interpreted the Qur'an literally and had rigid notions of piety, austerity, and equality. They were moral absolutists who believed that God expected righteousness; who perceived those Muslims who deviated from the "true" path to be apostates and who deserved to be expelled from the Islamic fold and, in some cases, even executed; who considered *jihad* to be the sixth pillar of the Islamic faith; and who believed that they were "God's holy warriors" committed to "Islamizing" society.

The so-called "*jihad*" that the Kharijites engaged in against Caliph Ali and the Umayyad dynasty that followed him were pursued with fanatical zeal. The caliphs responded by using their armies to capture, imprison, and/or kill these misguided Revolutionary Islamists in order to end the civil war that these **"jihadists"** had started. It took many years, though, to subdue these Islamic zealots and rid the Islamic empire of their destabilizing and destructive influence.

In retrospect, the Kharijites—like the **Gama'a al-Islamiyyah** and **al-Qaeda** in contemporary times—can be regarded as the extremist fringe of Revolutionary Islamist movements that have punctuated Islamic history.

■

BOX 3.2   Muhammad ibn Abd al-Wahhab

The Puritan-Intellectual and Founding Father of Wahhabism

Muhammad ibn Abd al-Wahhab (1703–1792) was a puritanical Muslim cleric who joined Muhammad ibn Saud, the tribal chieftain of the small town of Dariya in central Arabia, in a "holy alliance." Together they started the Wahhabi movement in the Arabian peninsula. The Revolutionary Islamist Wahhabi movement, allied with the fortunes of the House of Saud, exists today—institutionalized and less puritanical—as the official sect of modern Saudi Arabia.

When the young al-Wahhab traveled to Makkah in the late 1720s to perform the *hajj* and to study Islamic theology and law, he was angered by the adulterated brand of Islam that he witnessed. He became an influential Islamic judge and was known for his harsh judgments. He ordered the demolition of venerated shrines and tombs and once even condemned an adulterous woman to death. In 1745 al-Wahhab journeyed to nearby Dariya, where he converted its ruler, Muhammad ibn Saud, and many of its citizens to his brand of Revolutionary Islam, which the British labeled "Wahhabism."

The belief of the Wahhabis in *tawhid* (Allah's oneness) is so absolute and uncompromising that they denounce the practices of venerating Prophet Muhammad and the members of his extended family as heretical polytheism. They reject all the ceremonies, rituals, and customary traditions that were absent during the classical period of Islam, considering them to be un-Islamic accretions. Wahhabis work for a return to the simplicity, austerity, and piety of Islam's classical period. This includes praying five times daily, fasting during the holy month of Ramadan, and waging *jihad* against infidels, which to Wahhabis include not only non-Muslims but backsliding Muslims as well. Wahhabis support the implementation of the *shariah* in society. In related fashion, the Wahhabis demand strict and scrupulous adherence to its severe punishments for crimes and transgressions; they prohibit drinking alcohol, smoking, singing, listening to music, dancing, wearing silk, wearing ornaments of gold or silver, drawing and painting animate objects, palm reading, astrology, fortune-telling, and all forms of divination.

Encouraged by their initial successes, al-Wahhab and ibn Saud launched a *jihad* to convert those beyond their immediate domain to what they considered "true" Islam. In subsequent conquests, the Wahhabis gained dominion over much of the Arabian peninsula. Perhaps the greatest impact of al-Wahhab and his Wahhabi movement is that he not only reignited a revolutionary brand of Islamism in the Arabian peninsula but spread his influence to India, North Africa, and throughout the Muslim world. As all Muslims were obliged in the *hajj* to visit Makkah and Madinah, all were thus exposed to the Wahhabi movement.

In the last quarter-century, Saudi Arabia has spent billions of its petrodollars financing the building of *masjids*, paying for *masjid imams, madrassahs*, and Islamic literature with strong Wahhabi undertones. As a result, the Hanbali *madhab*, to which the Wahhabis belong and which used to be the smallest of the four Sunni sects, has grown markedly in numbers and in influence all over the Muslim world.

http://atheism.about.com/library/islam/blfaq_islam_wahhab.htm
http://lexicorient.com/e.o/abdu_l-wahhab.htm

■

BOX 3.3   Sayyid Muhammad ibn Ali al-Sanusi

Founder of the Sanusiyyah

Algerian Islamist Sayyid Muhammad ibn Ali al-Sanusi (1787–1859) left Algeria in his late teens and attended the Islamic university Al-Azhar in Cairo. In his journey across North Africa to Cairo, he stopped at many **zawiyas** (*sufi* lodges). While in Cairo, Sayyid Muhammad discussed the sad state of Islam and the *ummah* with the *shaykhs* (learned and wise clerics) at Al-Azhar. Disappointed with their responses and with their failure to address contemporary problems facing Muslims, Sayyid Muhammad left Al-Azhar for the Arabian peninsula.

In Hijaz, Sayyid Muhammad studied Islam with a number of learned *shaykhs*, particularly with Sayyid Ahmad ibn Iris al-Fasi, a *sufi* who had recently become fascinated with Wahhabism. Sayyid Muhammad also met Muslim pilgrims from many countries, with whom he discussed the conditions of the *ummah* and the state of Islam within their respective regions and countries. Following al-Fasi's death in 1837, Sayyid Muhammad founded the Sanusi brotherhood (Sanusiyyah) and established the first *zawiya* in the Hijaz. For three more years, he preached his revolutionary Islamist vision of Islam and established additional *zawiyas* between Makkah and Madinah. By 1840 Sayyid Muhammad's Sanusi brotherhood had grown popular enough to prompt the jealous enmity of Makkah's Traditionalist Islamist *shaykhs*, who pressured Sayyid Muhammad to leave the Arabian peninsula.

Sayyid Muhammad returned to North Africa and began to establish a network of *zawiyas*. These Sanusi centers provided a comprehensive religious education, trained the boarders in the use of firearms, taught them agricultural techniques, and instructed them in the conduct of trade and commerce. More generally, the Sanusi lodges built a semblance of unity among the scattered and often conflicting local tribes of Cyrenaica and Tripolitania, bridging present-day Algeria and Libya. Sayyid Muhammad also sent committed Sanusi missionaries to Central and West Africa to propagate his fundamentalist doctrine. Sayyid Muhammad denounced materialism and hedonism, exhorting his followers to eschew such sins as listening to music, dancing, and smoking. Moreover, he advocated *ijtihad* and rejected *taqlid*. But unlike many fellow Revolutionary Islamists, ibn Taimiyyah included, Sayyid Muhammad did not denounce Sufism.

The founder of the Sanusi movement came to be referred to as the "Grand Sanusi." His imposing personality, public speeches, organizing talents, depth of knowledge, and prolific scholarship won innumerable converts to his brand of Revolutionary Islamism. His influence continued even after his death. Until 1969 the Sanusi movement flourished, leading the fight in North Africa against the Italians and bringing spiritual and material improvement to the lives of the people.

http://www.hf.uib.no/smi/sa/6notices.html

Sayyid Ahmad became famous among Indian Muslims for launching a *jihad* against the Sikhs—the followers of Guru Nanak (1469–1538), who separated from

---

BOX 3.4   The Wahhabi and Sanusi Movements Compared

The first generation of Sanusis emulated the first generation of Wahhabis and consequently had much in common with them. Muhammad ibn Abd al-Wahhab, who founded the Wahhabi movement, and Sayyid Muhammad ibn Ali al-Sanusi, who established the Sanusi movement, were shocked to see Muslims not rigorously adhering to Islam's fundamentals. Both these Revolutionary Islamists reverted back to the Qur'an and *sunnah* to establish an Islamic state on the *shariah* and classical Islamic principles. Both drew on Taqi al-Din ibn Taimiyyah's puritanical writings. However, while al-Wahhab adhered scrupulously to ibn Taimiyyah's teachings, al-Sanusi moderated them with the more traditionalist and far less puritanical teachings of Abu Hamid al-Gazali.

Both al-Wahhab and al-Sanusi criticized the conservative and traditionalist *ulama* for failing to be competent, dynamic, and assertive standard-bearers of the Islamic faith and *ummah*. Both recommended discontinuing *taqlid* and exercising *ijtihad*, and both lived an ascetic and pious life, condemning ornamentation, music, dancing, and singing.

However, there were major differences between the two movements. While the Wahhabis denounced all accretions that had crept into Islam since the classical era, the Sanusis rejected only those accretions they considered reprehensible while tolerating those they considered helpful. In this regard, the Sanusis were tolerant of Sufism and even built tombs to honor sufi saints. Wahhabis, on the other hand, condemned such practices as *shirk* (polytheism) and made every effort to eliminate them.

Both the Wahhabis and Sanusis were so disgusted with the widespread corruption in the Ottoman empire that they launched an Islamic revival. However, their strategy and tactics were markedly different. While the Wahhabis aggressively confronted the armies of the Ottoman sultan in a war in the early nineteenth century (1811–1818) and suffered terribly as a result, the Sanusis paid nominal homage to the Ottoman sultan and, thereby, secured some privileges.

Finally, while the Sanusis generally adopted a peaceful missionary approach to win over converts and became militaristic only when attacked by the European colonialists, the Wahhabis engaged in a militaristic *jihad* as their principal means of winning converts and redirecting "wayward" Muslims to what they considered "the righteous path."

Hinduism–of Punjab, thereby avenging the persecution of Punjabi Muslims by Punjabi Sikhs.[3] Sayyid Ahmad also dreamed of creating an Islamic state based on scrupulous adherence to the *shariah* in the predominantly Muslim West Punjab

---

[3]Barbara Daly Metcalf, *Islamic Revival in British India: 1860–1900* (Princeton, N.J.: Princeton University Press, 1982), pp. 52–63; W. W. Hunter, *The Indian Musalmans* (Comrade, 1945; reprint of 1876 ed.), pp. 12–13; P. Hardy, *The Muslims of British India* (Cambridge: Cambridge University Press, 1972), p. 52; Ghulam Rasul Mehr, *Sayyid Ahmad Shahid* (Lahore: Kitab Manzil, 1956), pp. 251–252; Hafeez Malik, *Moslem Nationalism in India and Pakistan* (Washington, D.C.: Public Affairs Press, 1963), pp. 142–144.

and in the Indian subcontinent's northwest frontier. He eventually established an Islamic state in Peshawar; however, it was extremely short lived (1829–1830) because it alienated the freedom-loving Pathans, who were in a majority there and did not want to live by the rigors of the *shariah*. For instance, the Pathans resented payment of *zakat*, the severe Islamic punishments for various crimes, and the requirement for their widows to marry non-Pathan *mujahideen* from distant parts of northern India. Accordingly, the tribal Pathans declined to support the *mujahideen* in the 1831 Battle of Balakot in the Kaghan Valley, when the better-armed and numerically superior Sikh army defeated and killed Sayyid Ahmad Barelvi.[4]

Mir Nisar Ali (1782–1831), popularly known as Titu Mir, was an ardent follower of Sayyid Ahmad Barelvi. From 1827 to 1831, Titu Mir preached his Revolutionary Islamism among the Muslim peasants of predominantly Hindu West Bengal. In his sermons and lectures he encouraged the Bengali Muslims to treat each other as equals, to distinguish themselves from non-Muslims by growing beards as Prophet Muhammad had encouraged, and by tying their saronglike *dhotis*[5] in a distinctive manner, and to stand united against the Hindu landlords, who generally treated their peasants like slaves.[6]

To embarrass Titu Mir's bearded Muslim followers, some Hindu landlords imposed a tax on beards. Titu Mir and his followers sought justice for this and other grievances in the local court system and even sent a representative to Calcutta to seek help. Finding no legal support, in 1831 Titu Mir led his followers to slaughter a cow, sacred to Hindus, and to defile the village temple with its blood. This unleashed a storm of Hindu fury in which Titu Mir and his followers fought off vicious attacks by Hindu landlords, Hindu peasants, and the village police. Influential landlords summoned British troops to crush the poorly armed religious dissidents. Titu Mir and all those who fought with him were killed. The corpses of slain Muslim revolutionaries were burned in intentional violation of the Islamic practice of burial; their homes were looted, and relatives and sympathizers were jailed.[7]

Titu Mir's violent death in 1831 while fighting his *jihad* endeared him to the Bengali Muslim peasantry, inspiring them in their struggle against oppression at the hands of *zamindars* (wealthy landowners), indigo planters, and moneylenders.[8] Coincidentally, Titu Mir's revolt and death occurred in the same year that

---

[4]Hardy, *Muslims of British India*, pp. 52–53; Ishtiaq Hussain Qureshi, *The Muslim Community of the Indo-Pakistan Subcontinent (610–1947): A Brief Historical Analysis*, 2nd ed. (Karachi, Pakistan: Ma'aref, 1977), pp. 228–229; Mian Abdur Rashid, *Islam in the Indo-Pakistan Subcontinent: An Analytical Study of the Islamic Movements* (Lahore: National Book Foundation, 1977), pp. 38–40; K. A. Nizami, "Socio Religious Movements in Indian Islam (1763–1898)," *Islamic Culture*, Vol. 44, No. 3 (July 1970), pp. 137–139.

[5]A long, broad strip of cloth wrapped around the waist and covering the legs to the ankles.

[6]Metcalf, *Islamic Revival in British India*, p. 62.

[7]Ibid.

[8]Muinuddin Ahmad Khan, *Muslim Struggle for Freedom in Bengal: From Plassey to Pakistan 1757–1947 A.D.*, 2nd ed. (Dacca, Bangladesh: Islamic Foundation of Bangladesh, 1982), p. 25.

his mentor, Sayyid Ahmad Barelvi, died fighting in a *jihad* at the other end of India. However, the martyrdom of these two Revolutionary Islamists did not deter their followers from continuing the Islamic crusade in India. But in the 1860s, the British, recovering from the shock of the Indian Mutiny (1857), killed or imprisoned the remaining followers of Sayyid Ahmad Barelvi and Titu Mir.[9]

Titu Mir's revolutionary Islamism in predominantly Hindu West Bengal stirred up the weak and poor, formerly apathetic and apolitical Muslim peasants. Although the Muslim revolt against the exploitative and oppressive Hindu and British masters failed, Titu Mir's missionary efforts profoundly affected the Muslims of Bengal.

Another prominent Revolutionary Islamist was Mohsenuddin Ahmad (1819–1860), popularly known as Dadu Mian, who succeeded his father, Haji Shariatullah, to the leadership of the Faraidhiah movement, dedicated to the promotion of Islam's five obligatory duties. Dadu Mian received his early education under his father's supervision. At an early age he was sent for further studies to Makkah, where he was profoundly influenced by Wahhabism. After five years of intensive Islamic education in the Arabian peninsula, he returned home to support his father's missionary activities. When his father died in 1840, Dadu Mian assumed the leadership of the Faraidhiah movement and immediately distinguished himself.[10] Whereas his father had devoted himself to peaceful religious, moral, and cultural reform, Dadu Mian was an aggressive political agitator and an effective organizer and administrator. He created and trained a group of fearless, obedient, club-wielding volunteers to protect members of the Faraidhiah movement and, when possible, to punish those *zamindars* and indigo planters known for their oppression of peasants and laborers.[11] In 1841 and 1842 Dadu Mian led successful military campaigns against two Hindu *zamindars* who had mistreated their Faraidhi peasants. With these successes, ranks of the Faraidhiah movement increased.[12]

As a devout Muslim, Dadu Mian proclaimed the equality of all men before God. He campaigned vigorously against the levying by landlords of illegal taxes that were spent on polytheistic Hindu rites and shrines.[13] He also encouraged his followers to challenge the Hindu ban on cow slaughter and to eat beef against the wishes of Hindu *zamindars*.[14] As Muslim peasants exhibited a greater degree of

---

[9]Metcalf, *Islamic Revival in British India*, p. 62.

[10]S. Moinul Haq, *Islamic Thought and Movements in the Subcontinent: 711–1947* (Karachi: Pakistan Historical Society, 1979), p. 452; Mujib Ashraf, *Muslim Attitudes towards British Rule and Western Culture in India in the First Half of the Nineteenth Century* (Delhi: Idarah-i-Adabiyat-i-Delli, 1982), p. 149.

[11]Haq, *Islamic Thought and Movements*, p. 452; Hardy, *Muslims of British India*, pp. 56–57.

[12]Haq, *Islamic Thought and Movements*, pp. 453–454; Ashraf, *Muslim Attitudes*, pp. 149–150.

[13]A. S. Tritton, *Islam: Beliefs and Practices*, 2nd ed. (London: Hutchinson), 1954, p. 160; S. M. Ikram, *Muslim Civilization in India* (New York: Columbia University Press, 1964), p. 284; Haq, *Islamic Thought and Movements*, p. 453; Ashraf, *Muslim Attitudes*, p. 149; Qureshi, *Muslim Community*, p. 26.

[14]Haq, *Islamic Thought and Movements*, p. 453.

self-confidence and assertiveness, Hindu landlords, the village *banias* (Indian Hindu moneylenders), and British indigo planters stepped up their anti-Faraidhiah propaganda campaign. Moreover, the majority of poor and powerless Muslim peasants feared harassment, unemployment, imprisonment, and misery if they joined the Faraidhiah movement.

The British perceived Dadu Mian as an agitator, and when the Indian Mutiny broke out, in 1857, they jailed him, hoping to cripple his movement. But Dadu Mian had assiduously trained a number of Faraidhis in several Bengali districts to assume the leadership of the movement if something happened to him, and as a result, his two-year confinement did not adversely affect the Faraidhiah movement or the Islamic revival that it generated.[15]

Dadu Mian's greatest accomplishment was the creation of a close-knit hierarchical organization called the "Khilafat system." He established *halqahs* (circles) of his followers in villages, towns, and districts. Each circle had its own leader, called a *khalifah* (caliph). The caliphs at village, township, and district levels directly reported to Dadu Mian, who was the **ustad** (teacher) and supreme leader of the Faraidhis. Each caliph or deputy was responsible for protecting and promoting the interests of the Faraidhis by teaching, preaching, and proselytizing; collecting membership fees and/or donations; settling most disputes between members, instead of letting them go to British courts; and overseeing a spy network.[16] This institutionalization helped sustain the Islamic revival initiated by Dadu Mian in Bengal long after his death, despite the poor leadership qualities of his sons and successors.

Muhammad Ahmad Abdullah al-Mahdi (1843–1885; see Box 3.5), known as the Mahdi, also launched a revolutionary Islamic movement, known as the Mahdiyyah, in Sudan, with the aim of establishing a puritanical Islamic state based on the *shariah*. The Mahdi launched his military crusade in 1881 and, because of the religious zeal displayed by his followers, was able to win early military encounters with the government's larger and better-equipped forces. With each military victory the Mahdi's followers grew in number and in strength. In January 1885, with the fall of Khartoum and the overthrow of the unpopular Sudanese regime, the Mahdi could fashion the kind of Islamic state of which he dreamed. He had only just initiated the implementation of the *shariah* when he died in June 1885. The Mahdi was succeeded by his faithful lieutenant and protege, Khalifah Abdullahi al-Ta'ashi. Abdullahi ruled Sudan according to the *shariah* for the next thirteen years, until Anglo-Egyptian armies overwhelmed his forces and dismantled the Islamic state.[17]

---

[15]Qureishi, *The Muslim Community*, p. 238; Haq, *Islamic Thought and Movements*, p. 454; Ashraf, *Muslim Attitudes*, pp.150–151.

[16]Hardy, *Muslims of British India*, p. 57; Ashraf, *Muslim Attitudes*, p. 149; Metcalf, *Islamic Revival in British India*, pp. 69–70; Murray Titus, *Islam in India and Pakistan: A Religious History* (Calcutta: YMCA Publishing House, 1959), pp. 187–188.

[17]Leon Carl Brown, "The Sudanese Mahdiya," in Robert I. Rotberg, ed., *Rebellion in Black Africa* (Oxford: Oxford University Press, 1971), pp. 9–11; Richard H. Dekmejian and Margaret J. Wyszomirski, "Charismatic Leadership in Islam: The Mahdi of the Sudan," *Comparative Studies in Society and History*, Vol. 14 (1972), pp. 205–207; Peter M. Holt, *The Mahdist State in the Sudan, 1881–1898: A Study of Its Origins, Development and Overthrow*, 2nd ed. rev. (Oxford: Clarendon Press, 1970), p. 52.

■

BOX 3.5   Muhammad Ahmad Abdullah al-Mahdi

Crusader for a Puritanical Islamic State in the Sudan

Muhammad Ahmad Abdullah al-Mahdi (1843–1885) is famous in Islamic history for having launched the Revolutionary Islamist Mahdiyyah movement in Sudan. The Sudanese al-Mahdi founded his puritanical movement in response to social decay, political oppression, and economic decline, culminating in the establishment of a puritanical Islamic state.

The Mahdi, as al-Mahdi was known, had the appropriate credentials for charismatic leadership. A descendent of Prophet Muhammad, he had devoted a decade to community service and was perceived as a principled ***mujaddid*** (renewer of the faith). He openly accused the alien Turco-Egyptian regime in Sudan of injustice, hedonism, and disbelief. Like many Revolutionary Islamists, the Mahdi was strict and unbending in his judgments of others. He believed independent and permissive women were directly responsible for the decline of Sudanese society and, therefore, denied them their freedom. Furthermore, the Mahdi demanded scrupulous adherence to the *shariah* and exacted the harshest punishment permissible for violations. Like any puritan, the Mahdi also banned dancing, singing, and music. Unlike most Revolutionary Islamists, however, the Mahdi did not advocate *ijtihad*, although he himself exercised it. The Mahdi claimed direct inspiration from God and Muhammad in his interpretation of the Qur'an and the *sunnah*.

Initially, the Mahdi won a series of battles against better-trained and better-equipped government forces. These victories were the result of the crusading zeal of the Mahdi's followers and their willingness to be martyrs in a *jihad* and earn Paradise. The government forces lacked effective leadership and morale. With every military victory, the Mahdi's ranks swelled.

By the end of 1883, the Mahdi began to promote pan-Islamism, with himself at the head. But before spreading revolutionary Islamism beyond Sudanese borders, he first had to defeat British soldiers based in Khartoum. By January 1885, the Mahdi succeeded in routing the Egyptian forces of the Ottoman Empire, defeating the British, and becoming the undisputed ruler of Sudan. However, within a few months, the Mahdi himself was dead. His successor, Abdullahi al-Ta'ashi, ruled only a few years, until 1898, when Anglo-Egyptian armies returned and reconquered the Sudan.

Although Muslims in other parts of the world were generally unfamiliar with the writings of the Mahdi and the kind of Islamic state he briefly established, the fact that an Islamic movement had succeeded in expelling colonialists and setting up a sovereign Islamic state, however temporarily, inspired and emboldened anticolonialist Islamist movements around the world.

Egyptian revolutionary Hasan al-Banna (1906–1949; see Box 3.6), a twentieth-century Revolutionary Islamist, created the Ikhwan al-Muslimun, one of the first populist and essentially urban-oriented organizations dedicated to coping with the plight of Islam in the modern world. This organization became the first

BOX 3.6   Hasan al-Banna

The Founder of Egypt's Ikhwan al-Muslimun

Hasan al-Banna (1906–1949) was born in Egypt to a lower-middle-class family. He attended the Dar al-Ulum (House of Learning), an Islamic teacher-training college located in Cairo, and studied in the schools of Islamic jurisprudence, Sufism, and even Modernist Islamic ideology.

Al-Banna graduated and taught Arabic at a public elementary school near the Suez Canal. There, he and six colleagues became incensed by the inequity they witnessed between foreigners and exploited Egyptian workers. In response, al-Banna founded the Ikhwan al-Muslimun (the Muslim Brotherhood). As head of the Revolutionary Islamist Ikhwan (Brotherhood), al-Banna declared that Egyptian poverty and powerlessness resulted from Egypt's Western orientation. According to al-Banna, strict adherence to Islam was the answer.

Al-Banna and the Ikhwan promoted the establishment of an Islamic state in Egypt. He called for a constitution derived from the Qur'an, the *sunnah*, and the traditions of the first four rightly guided caliphs; for the imposition of the *shariah* as the law of the land; for the collection and distribution of *zakat* among the needy; for the prohibition of usury and monopolies; for the enforcement of daily prayers and fasting during Ramadan; for the segregation of the sexes; for the banning of prostitution, gambling, alcohol, and nightclubs; and for the proscription of all customs not conforming to Islamic principles.

Although al-Banna was interested in pan-Islamism, he did not oppose Egyptian nationalism and pan-Arabism, ideologies popular in Egypt during this period. Al-Banna and the Ikhwan endorsed Arab unity, but only as a first step toward Muslim unity. Moreover, al-Banna did not embrace Western democracy. The *shariah,* he insisted, answered all questions with regard to law and justice.

The secular government of Egypt's King Farouk, unsettled by the political activism and growing popularity of al-Banna and his Ikhwan, cracked down on the organization. At first, the Ikhwan operated as a legitimate political party working to change Egypt from within. However, government corruption, cheating at the polls, and persecution of the Ikhwan by Egyptian authorities convinced al-Banna that violent revolutionary struggle was necessary. Islamic militants took to urban guerrilla warfare. In 1948 Farouk banned the Ikhwan. The Ikhwan retaliated by assassinating Egypt's prime minister. Government agents, in turn, assassinated al-Banna in 1949. This, however, did not put an end to the Ikhwan's activities. Despite frequent government crackdowns, the Ikhwan, al-Banna's most lasting legacy, remains intact and is still a potent force for Islamism in Egypt.

http://www.al-banna.net/
http://i-cias.com/e.o/banna_h.htm

transnational religiopolitical party in the Muslim world.[18] Al-Banna called for a *jihad* against ignorance, disease, and poverty. His economic program called for equal employment opportunity for all, a guaranteed minimum wage, a fixed ceiling on incomes, prohibition of usury and monopolies, a progressive system of taxation that included *zakat* and *ushr*, and a system of social security.[19]

The Ikhwan al-Muslimun's chief ideologue and spiritual leader after Hasan al-Banna's assassination in 1949 was Syed Qutb (1906–1966; see Box 3.7). Qutb was well-versed in Islam, possessed an impeccable character, was a powerful writer, and was genuinely committed to Islam and the *ummah*. His writings were so popular among the masses that Egypt's president Gamal Abdel Nasser perceived him as a major threat to his secular military regime and had him arrested twice, once in the mid-1950s and the second time in the mid-1960s. Nasser had Qutb executed in 1966, but this Revolutionary Islamist's writings on Islam are still widely read all over the world.

The Revolutionary Islamist Sayyid Abul A'la Maududi (1903–1979; see Box 3.7) lobbied for over thirty years in Pakistan, with the help of his Jama'at-i-Islami (Islamic Association), not only for a constitution that was Islamic in letter and spirit but also for a comprehensive Islamic state based on the *shariah*. The Jama'at-i-Islami's revolutionary election manifesto of December 1969 clearly reflects Maududi's views. The party promised to "deliver a death blow to capitalism and feudalism" by breaking up the monopoly control that a few powerful families had over industries, banks, insurance companies, and large properties in the rural areas. They promised to redistribute land and help peasants, tenant farmers, and small landholders; to increase wages and fringe benefits and improve the working conditions of low-income laborers; to reduce the disparity between rich and poor and to abolish "un-Islamic" methods of acquiring wealth (including excessive interest charges by moneylenders, illegal hoarding, and fraudulent trading); and to assist the elderly, orphans, and the children of the poor by enforcing a *zakat* tax of 2.5 percent on income. In the socioeconomic realm, laws were to be passed to cleanse society of vices and to require educational institutions to focus more intensively on Islam. Teachers' salaries were to be increased, provided that they support the Islamic ideology and were "morally capable of teaching." In the area of foreign policy, Maududi's platform opposed the Western capitalist and socialist-communist power blocs and instead supported pan-Islamism and the establishment of an international Islamic court.[20]

The most prominent Revolutionary Islamist in the twentieth century was Ayatollah Ruhollah Khomeini (1900–1989) of Iran. The Shi'ah **alim** (Islamic scholar) became the symbolic leader of the Islamic Revolution in Iran (1978–1979) and went on to establish an Islamic state based on the *shariah* by placing many **mullahs**

---

[18]"The Autobiography of Hassan al-Banna," quoted in Richard Mitchell, *The Society of the Muslim Brothers,* Oxford: Oxford University Press, 1969, p. 235.

[19]Ishak Musa Husaini, *The Brethren: The Greatest Modern Islamic Movements*, Beirut: Khayat College Book Cooperative, 1956, p. 165.

[20]"Election Manifesto of the Jamaat-e-Islami," *The Criterion* (Karachi), January/February 1970.

BOX 3.7   Sayyid Qutb (1906–1966)

Sayyid Qutb was born in 1906 near the city of Asyut, in southern Egypt. He attended a traditional religious school in his village but moved on to a modern government school, from which he graduated in 1918. He graduated from a teacher's training college in 1928 and from Dar al-Ulum, a modern university on the Western model, in 1933. He began teaching and also joined Egypt's Ministry of Education. In 1948 the ministry sent him abroad to study teaching methods overseas. While in the United States, he was impressed by America's economic and scientific progress but was shocked by its racism and permissiveness. He considered the West to be spiritually bankrupt and felt that it stood inherently in opposition to Islam.

After his return to Egypt, Qutb became more involved in Egyptian political and social issues. He joined the Ikhwan al-Muslimun (Muslim Brotherhood) and became editor of its weekly paper. Qutb also served as a liaison between the Ikhwan and the Free Officers Movement of Gamal Abdel Nasser. With the Ikhwan's support, the Free Officers overthrew the Egyptian monarchy and seized power. Friendly relations between the Ikhwan and the new government did not last long. In 1954, Nasser accused the Ikhwan of plotting against him and arrested scores of *Ikhwan* members, including Qutb.

Qutb was sentenced to fifteen years in prison; he was tortured, and many of his colleagues were murdered while in prison. This treatment angered Qutb and inclined him to the view that violence against an oppressive government is appropriate if undertaken in self-defense. Later, his views became more radical, and he believed that committing violence against any unjust government, whatever the circumstances, was justified.

However, Qutb did not make his belief about armed revolt known to anyone but his colleagues in the Ikhwan. Qutb's writings stipulated only that an oppressive government should be resisted by creating social and legal institutions based on Islam at the community level. Muslims could then appeal to these institutions and not rely on the government. Ultimately these institutions would take the place of the government, and a true Islamic state would thus be founded. Qutb also believed that Islam provided answers to all social and political problems. Islam, in Qutb's view, required political activism. His writings are still a source of inspiration to Revolutionary Islamists like al-Jihad, Hamas, the Ikhwan, and even the revolutionaries who overthrew the Shah of Iran.

Qutb was released early from prison but was quickly rearrested. In 1965 he was tried for terrorism and attempts to overthrow the government. Evidence against Qutb was weak, but the trial was closed to the mass media, and Qutb was convicted and sentenced to death. He was executed by the Egyptian government in 1966.

http://www.icna.org/tm/greatmuslim3.htm
http://www.ahram.org.eg/weekly/1999/459/bk2_459.htm
http://www.muslimedia.com/archives/features99/qutb.htm
http://www.indyflicks.com/danielle/paper15.htm

BOX 3.8 Sayyid Abul A'la Maududi

Founder of South Asia's Jama'at-i-Islami

Sayyid Abul A'la Maududi (1903–1979) was born into a devout Hanafi Muslim middle-class family in the city of Aurangabad, India. Although Maududi originally pursued a religious education, he left school and became a journalist for an Islamic newspaper. While writing for the paper, Maududi improved his Urdu and learned English, Arabic, and Persian.

Following World War I, Maududi participated in the Khilafat Movement, dedicated to saving the Ottoman Empire and the Khilafat from Western influences, and in the Hijrat movement, which urged Muslims to migrate from the *dar al-harb* of India to the *dar al-Islam* of Afghanistan, which, unlike India, was governed by Muslims. Maududi wrote numerous scholarly books on the subject of Islam and founded a journal dedicated to reducing Western influence on India's Muslim intelligentsia. Maududi translated Islamic precepts for Indian Muslim readers and interpreted them in terms of contemporary applications.

Before 1947, Maududi opposed the Pakistan Movement's efforts to create an independent Muslim homeland in the Indian subcontinent. He denounced the leaders of the movement as Westernized secular nationalists. Once Pakistan was founded, however, Maududi settled there and hoped to transform the country into an Islamic state.

Maududi envisioned an Islamic world state in which racial prejudices and national interests would be erased and mankind would enjoy genuine civil rights. However, Maududi, like all Revolutionary Islamists, opposed Western democracy, in which sovereignty rests with the people. Maududi believed that sovereignty rested with God alone.

Maududi founded the Jama'at-i-Islami (the Islamic Association, or JI), which continues to support implementation of an Islamic system in Pakistan on Maududi's model. In 1956 Maududi and his JI played a role in the formulation of a Pakistani constitution that was Islamic in both letter and spirit. Moreover, Maududi and JI served as an Islamic interest group pressuring Pakistani regimes and contributing to the Islamic revival that swept Pakistan in the 1970s. In 1977, he supported the military coup that brought General Muhammad Zia-ul-Haq to power. Zia, who admired Maududi, promised to establish an Islamic state. However, before his death in 1979, Maududi expressed concern about Zia's increasingly unpopular military regime.

Maududi's publications and political activities provided Revolutionary Islamists around the world with an intellectual foundation and a clear understanding of the nature, meaning, and administration of an Islamic state. Moreover, Maududi's legacy has been perpetuated by the JI, an organization dedicated to the creation of an Islamic state after Maududi's model.

http://www.islam101.com/people/century20/maududi.htm
http://www.hidayatullah.com/2000/01/sejarah.htm
http://www.jamaat.org/overview/founder.html

(Islamic clerics) in influential governmental positions. In his book *Velayat-i-Faqih (The Guardianship of the Islamic Jurist)*, published in 1970, Khomeini advised Muslims to shun wicked governments. He recommended that clerics, educators, journalists, lawyers, and the rest of the intelligentsia be in the vanguard of nonviolent movements, enlightening, politicizing, and organizing the masses against their unjust and illegitimate governments. The passive civil disobedience that he recommended involved noncooperation with the unjust governments' institutions and laws. He suggested that this noncooperation could be achieved by establishing alternative judicial, economic, political, and cultural institutions. For instance, Khomeini wanted the masses to take their lawsuits to their own *qadhis* (Islamic judges) rather than to the state's civil law courts, to pay their taxes to their religious establishments rather than to the government, and to respect and obey religious leaders rather than civil and political leaders.[21] Khomeini also recognized the sacrifices involved in a revolutionary struggle; he repeatedly stated that fighting and dying for the Islamic cause was preferable to a life of humiliation in a state that violated Islamic principles and corrupted the *ummah*. Khomeini's rhetoric carried extra weight both because of his eminent position within the Shi'ah hierarchy and because of the Islamic belief that those who die fighting a *jihad* against unjust, corrupt, and tyrannical governments are not dead but *shaheed* (martyrs) who have earned their place in Heaven.[22]

Khomeini's vision of an Islamic revolution came to pass in Iran only a decade after his book was published. Within seven years of his ascent to de facto power in 1979, Khomeini brought about an Islamic political, social, judicial, and economic revolution in Iran and completely transformed Iran's foreign policy. Khomeini not only broke Iran's dependent relationship with the West but likewise avoided dependence on the Communist bloc for security or aid. As a result, Iran became genuinely nonaligned and truly independent, with a revolutionary Islamic foreign policy that denounces both the Western and Communist blocs. The price of such independence, however, has been high. Khomeini alienated the outside world. Iran could find no friends, no allies in the community of nations. Khomeini's Iran stood isolated in the world.

In Khomeini's revolutionary Islamic state, women were not only enjoined to dress "modestly" but to wear a *hijab* (head scarf) and not wear heavy makeup or jewelry. The **pasdaran** (Revolutionary guard) stopped and warned any woman caught violating this dress code. Repeat offenders were sent to prison, where they were lectured on the reasons for the dress code. Today, under the moderate and Modernist Islamist president Muhammad Khatami, the Iranian government has eased up on the rigorous enforcement of the dress code for women; however, the majority of the population still frowns on women who do not dress modestly or cover their hair.

The **Wahhabi** zealots that took over the Grand Mosque in Makkah in November 1979 (see Box 3.10) were similar in their aggressive, intolerant, and

---

[21]Shaul Bakhash, *The Reign of the Ayatollahs: Iran and the Islamic Revolution*, rev. ed. (New York: Basic Books, 1990), pp. 38–39.

[22]J. S. Ismael and T. Y. Ismael, "Social Change in Islamic Society: The Political Thought of Ayatollah Khomeini," *Social Problems*, Vol. 27, No. 5 (June 1980), pp. 612–613.

BOX 3.9   Ayatollah Ruhollah Khomeini

Symbolic Leader of the First Islamic Revolution in Modern Times

Sayyid Ruhollah al-Musavi al-Khomeini (1900–1989) was born in the town of Khomein, 180 miles south of Tehran. The young Khomeini's education, both formal and informal, was predominantly Islamic. In Qom, Khomeini became a teacher and made his political preferences known. Khomeini claimed that the *ulama* should not stand idly by in politics but should become actively involved, as Prophet Muhammad had been. Khomeini himself actively opposed the *shah* and his programs of secularization and westernization. As his stature grew, Khomeini was exiled by the *shah* in November 1964.

Khomeini spent his long exile in Turkey, Iraq, and then France, urging on his supporters in Iran and declaring that hereditary monarchical regimes were intrinsically un-Islamic; that Islam is a revolutionary political ideology enjoining Muslims to overthrow un-Islamic governments; that all foreign influences must be extirpated, and that a single learned and just religious leader should exercise supreme leadership in an Islamic state based on the Qur'an and the *sunnah*. Recordings of Khomeini's vitriolic anti-*shah* sermons were sold in Iran, and his writings were disseminated nationwide. As revolutionary ferment grew in the late seventies, Khomeini's name was the refrain of demonstrators, and his picture appeared all over Iran.

When the *shah* was deposed in 1979, Khomeini returned to Iran, was welcomed as a conquering hero, and acted as "guardian" of the Islamic Republic of Iran, enjoying supreme leadership of Iran for the next decade. During his "guardianship," however, Khomeini made several crucial errors. First, Khomeini embraced much of the repressive authoritarianism that had tarnished the *shah*'s regime. Also, Khomeini permitted and endorsed the seizure of the United States embassy and its staff, an act that earned Khomeini few friends outside Iran and introduced a devastating economic and diplomatic isolation. Khomeini was also responsible for alienating possible allies by denouncing all secular, monarchical, and pro-Western Arab leaders and by declaring his intention to export the Islamic Revolution. Finally, Khomeini prolonged the Iran-Iraq War, which Iraq had begun, by another six years in an effort to topple Iraq's president Saddam Hussein.

In spite of his failures, Khomeini led the first modern Islamic revolution, toppling the firmly entrenched fifty-seven-year-old Pahlavi dynasty, implementing the Islamic model of development, and making Iran genuinely nonaligned. His revolutionary brand of Islamism emboldened Islamists all over the world and thereby fortified global Islamism and the global Islamic revival.

http://www.time.com/time/special/moy/1979.html
http://www.asiasource.org/society/khomeini.cfm
http://www.time.com/time/time100/leaders/profile/khomeini.html

---

impulsive fanatical zeal to the **Kharijites** of the classical Islamic era. In some respects, they were not all that dissimilar to the austere, ascetic, pious, and puritanical Wahhabi warriors that were determined to "Islamize" the Arabian peninsula in the eighteenth and nineteenth centuries.

■

BOX 3.10   Seizure of the Grand Mosque

In November 1979, on the first day of Islam's fifteenth century, 350 Revolutionary Islamists, emboldened by the success of the Iranian Revolution and the seizure of the U.S. embassy in Tehran, seized the Grand Mosque and as many as fifty thousand pilgrims inside. The Grand Mosque in Makkah, Saudi Arabia, is the holiest mosque in Islam. Muslims all over the world turn toward the Ka'abah when they pray. Muslims are required by their faith to visit the Ka'abah once in their lifetime to perform the *hajj*.

The leader, Juhayman ibn Saif al-Utaybi, was a charismatic twenty-year-old cashiered corporal from the Saudi National Guard. In the weeks before the operation, the hostage takers had secretly hidden small arms and food inside the Grand Mosque. On the day of operation, the zealots brought heavy weapons, walkie-talkies, and food in coffins. The guards and pilgrims were not alarmed to see people carrying coffins because Makkans often bring relatives or friends who have died during the night to the Grand Mosque for a final blessing before burial. Juhayman began to denounce the Saudi Arabian government for impiety, injustice, corruption, and decadence. Juhayman also decried the presence of Westerners and alcohol in Saudi Arabia, demanded only Islamic programming on radio and television, voiced opposition to the higher education and employment of women, and generally advocated an Islamic purification of the Saudi kingdom.

The Saudi government acceded to none of these demands. Within two weeks, the Saudi government's security forces, with help from Western advisors, overpowered the Wahhabi zealots who had seized the Grand Mosque. The event was significant not only as an aftershock of militant political Islam in Iran but as a cause of further revolutionary Islamist militancy throughout the Muslim world. The seizure of the Grand Mosque in the holiest city of Islam, the point of Muslim adoration, shook the foundations of Saudi Arabia's government, sent shock waves through the secular governing elites of neighboring Muslim countries, and captivated audiences worldwide, bringing to their attention the powerful revival of militant politicized Islam. If Saudi Arabia, the geographic birthplace of Islam and Wahhabi Revolutionary Islamism, the site of two of Islam's holiest cities, one of the most religious Islamic states in the world, and a principal exponent of Islamism, was vulnerable to accusations of religious laxity, then what indictment would be made against those Muslim countries where the secularization process had progressed much further?

http://www.bglatzer.de/aga/funda.htm

Another extreme and violent fringe group of Revolutionary Islamists are members of the ***al-Qaeda*** (the base) organization (see Box 3.11). Al-Qaeda's goal has been to engage in a long and sustained guerrilla campaign, which they refer to as a *jihad*, against Muslim Secularist regimes, the Big Powers, and Israel. Just like Trotskyites wanted to see a permanent and worldwide proletarian revolution, the misguided Muslim *jihadists* of al-Qaeda want to see a permanent and worldwide Islamic revolution in Muslim countries all over the world.

President Muhammad Zia-ul-Haq of Pakistan (1924–1988; see Box 3.12) represented a more moderate and less confrontational brand of revolutionary Islamism. Thus, Pakistan never suffered the isolation endured by Iran.

BOX 3.11   Al-Qaeda

Al-Qaeda, which literally means "the base," was established in 1988, as Soviet troops began their withdrawal from Afghanistan. Members of the organization were drawn primarily from the Arab volunteers who had traveled to Afghanistan in order to take part in the *jihad* against the Soviet Union. These "Arab Afghans," with Osama bin Laden as one of their leaders, helped establish al-Qaeda "cells" in as many as fifty different countries throughout the world, including Europe and the United States. Training camps for al-Qaeda members are located either in lawless countries, like Somalia, or in countries whose governments provide tacit support, such as Sudan and, until recently, Afghanistan. Other countries likely to be hosting al-Qaeda's terrorist training camps are Yemen, Indonesia, and Pakistan.

Al-Qaeda's ideology, as expressed by Osama bin Laden, is to rid Muslim countries of Muslim Secularist regimes and to fight non-Muslim countries that support that Secularist leadership. Generally, this means engaging in a *jihad* against Israel and the United States. Al-Qaeda also supports Revolutionary Islamists in countries around the world.

Al-Qaeda's primary strength is its loose organization. Cells operate with considerable autonomy, raising their own money and planning and/or implementing activities locally. Al-Qaeda's international leadership, until recently headquartered in Afghanistan, provides general direction and sometimes financial support, however. The core of al-Qaeda includes Osama bin Laden as head, working closely with a consultative body of perhaps ten members. Administrative levels of the organization include military operations, religious education, commercial activity, and public relations. Networks below this are involved in any number of activities, including humanitarian work, recruiting, and training. Members know only what they need to know; the capture or elimination of any one member will not harm the organization as a whole. Control of specific activities is decentralized; some of those activities likely cannot be directly linked to al-Qaeda leadership.

In 1998 al-Qaeda merged with another known Revolutionary Islamist organization, the Egyptian group Islamic Jihad, headed by Ayman Zawahiri. Zawahiri, now the number two leader in al-Qaeda after bin Laden, is widely considered the "brains" of the operation and the mastermind of the U.S. embassy bombings in 1998 and the September 11, 2001, attacks on the United States. Other attacks by al-Qaeda or affiliated cells include the 1993 bombing of the World Trade Center, the 1995 assassination attempt on Egyptian president Hosni Mubarak, and the 1996 bombing of the Khobar towers that killed U.S. soldiers in Saudi Arabia.

Following the September 11 attacks, European and American authorities have frozen funds believed to belong to al-Qaeda and its members and is actively breaking up its numerous cells. The American-led attack on Afghanistan was motivated by the Taliban's refusal to turn over bin Laden and the leadership of al-Qaeda in Afghanistan. While al-Qaeda is finished in Afghanistan, the organization is resilient. Even without Osama bin Laden or Ayman Zawahiri, al-Qaeda cells will continue to operate for some time.

http://www.pbs.org/wgbh/pages/frontline/shows/binladen/who/alqaeda.html
http://web.nps.navy.mil/~library/tgp/qaida.htm
http://www.satp.org/satporgtp/usa/Al_Queda.htm
http://cns.miis.edu/research/wtc01/alqaida.htm
http://www.time.com/time/nation/article/0,8599,182746,00.html
http://www.terrorismfiles.org/organisations/al_qaida.html

BOX 3.12   Muhammad Zia-ul-Haq

Pakistan's "Soldier of Islam"

Muhammad Zia-ul-Haq (1924–1988) was born in Jullunder, a city that lies today in India. Zia attended Saint Stephen College, New Delhi's renowned elitist Anglican missionary school. After matriculating in 1943, Zia entered the Royal Indian Military Academy at Dehra-Dun. In 1947, Zia-ul-Haq, by then a captain, migrated to the newly created Muslim homeland of Pakistan. In Pakistan, Zia was repeatedly promoted. By 1969 he was made brigadier and was sent as a military advisor to the Hashemite kingdom of Jordan. In Jordan, Zia advised the Jordanian troops who quashed the Palestine Liberation Organization (PLO) guerrilla uprising of September 1970.

In 1975 Pakistan's President Zulfikar Ali Bhutto purged the army of senior officers whom he suspected of harboring "Bonapartic" ambitions and promoted the apolitical Zia to the position of major general for three major reasons. In 1973, Zia had served as the presiding judge at the Attock conspiracy case. At the end of the military court proceedings of the conspirators, Zia pleased Bhutto by dispensing harsh punishments to the two dozen junior military officers who had conspired to overthrow Bhutto's popularly elected constitutional government. Zia had also loyally carried out Bhutto's order to crush the Baluchi separatist movement in the province of Baluchistan (1973–1977). Zia's self-effacing loyalty to Bhutto and to the constitution earned him a promotion in 1975 to lieutenant general and armored corps commander. In 1976 Zia was made a four-star general and army chief of staff. After his promotion, many army officers felt Zia was nothing more than a sycophant and referred to the new army chief of staff as "Bhutto's butler."

Zia, however, did attempt to exert influence in his new position. He lectured recruits to observe the prayers and fasting obligatory in Islam and invited a prominent leader of the Jama'at-i-Islami to deliver lectures on the importance of Islam. But when Bhutto heard of Zia's activities, he ordered him to desist, and Zia, despite his strong faith and personal misgivings, submitted to the prime minister's demand.

Bhutto was accused of rigging the 1977 election, and a series of intense riots began. After four months of virtual civil war, Zia assumed power in July 1977 and placed Pakistan under martial law. Zia had Bhutto executed and initiated an Islamization campaign. A number of factors prompted his adoption of Islamic policies. The Muslim Secularist Bhutto had already utilized Islamic symbolism and rhetoric that, in turn, had engendered a political atmosphere of Islamic revivalism. The failure of capitalism under President Muhammad Ayub Khan and socialism under Prime Minister Z. A. Bhutto had resulted in demands for an Islamic alternative to address the country's chronic problems. Also, Zia faced pressure from Islamists to transform Pakistan into a genuinely Islamic state. Finally, Zia himself had strong Islamic predilections.

As a conduit for U.S. assistance to the Afghan *mujahideen* fighting the Soviets, Zia's regime fostered an Islamic resurgence in Afghanistan. Furthermore, Zia's domestic policies coupled with his enlightened foreign policy helped the country prosper and play a significant role in Southwest Asia.

Nevertheless, Zia's Islamist ardor was unqualified and the sincerity of his Revolutionary Islamist "Islamization" campaign was unquestionable. The Zia government established numerous agencies to study, plan, and implement the Islamic transformation of Pakistani society. The government arranged international, regional, national, and local conferences and seminars pertaining to Islam and ordered the mass media to cover them. It hosted national conventions of the *ulama* and *mashaykh* (spiritual leaders) and undertook a thorough revision of textbooks and course curricula to "prepare a new generation wedded to the ideology of Pakistan and Islam."[23] Islamiyat (Islamic studies) was made compulsory for all Muslims. A Shariat faculty to teach Islamic law was set up at Quaid-i-Azam University in 1979; a year later, the school became a separate institution and was renamed the Islamic University.[24] Radio and television productions were ordered to conform to strict Islamic standards of morality and ethics, as well as to reinforce the national identity of the citizenry. A law was introduced severely punishing those who defile the names of the Prophet Muhammad and the **Khulafah-i-Rashidun** (first four "rightly guided" caliphs), Abu Bakr, Umar, Uthman, and Ali.[25] In essence, Zia-ul-Haq proposed to enforce Islamic morality and piety in Pakistan.

Islamic revolutions and revolutionaries are of varying types. While the ultimate goals of various Revolutionary Islamists may be similar, the methods by which they achieve those goals often differ. For example, Iran's Ayatollah Khomeini, in his revolutionary Islamist zeal, rode the Islamic revolutionary wave to the zenith of absolute authority, established a theocratic Islamic state, and crusaded against the West, especially against America. In contrast, Pakistan's Zia-ul-Haq implemented his Revolutionary Islamist policies and programs at home, adopted a pan-Islamic foreign policy, while working closely with the West (especially the U.S.) in defeating the Soviet colonialists in Afghanistan. Consequently, while Khomeini isolated Iran from the rest of the world, Zia-ul-Haq, despite his Revolutionary Islamist baggage, obtained a significant amount of economic and military aid from the West without surrendering his nation's sovereignty or his Revolutionary Islamist domestic and foreign policy.

Puritanical Muslims

Tawhid, Allah's oneness, is the central premise of Islam, a doctrine all Muslims accept. However, Muslims differ in their interpretations of *tawhid*. Many Revolutionary Islamists are obsessed with its importance. Many Sunni

---

[23]Ibid., pp. 150, 155.

[24]Anita M. Weiss, "The Historical Debate on Islam and the State in South Asia," in Anita M. Weiss, ed., *Islamic Reassertion in Pakistan: The Application of Islamic Laws in a Modern State* (Syracuse, N.Y.: Syracuse University Press, 1986), p. 15; Lucy Carrol, "Nizam-i-Islam: Process and Conflicts in Pakistan's Programme of Islamisation, with Special Reference to the Position of Women," *Journal of Commonwealth and Comparative Politics*, No. 20 (1982), p. 74.

[25]William L. Richter, "Pakistan," in Mohammed Ayoob, ed., *The Politics of Islamic Reassertion* (New York: St. Martin's Press, 1981), p. 150.

Revolutionary Islamists, for instance, have such a literal interpretation of *tawhid* that they denounce any agent mediating between man and God as *shirk* (ascribing partners to God as sharers of His divinity) because in their eyes such an intermediary undermines and compromises the principle of *tawhid*. Therefore, these puritanical Muslims condemn such traditions as the veneration of Prophet Muhammad, *Imams*, saints, martyrs, and **pirs** (spiritual guides); the offering of prayers for assistance at their tombs or at shrines built in their honor; the sacrifice of animals, sanctification of water, lighting of candles, donation of money, or distribution of food in honor of those venerated with expectation of special favors; the wearing of *tawidhes* (amulets) with verses from the Qur'an to ward off evil or bring good luck; and excessive displays of mourning, such as weeping, *ma'atam* (breast-beating), and **taziyah** (mourning) processions during the Islamic calendar month of Muharram to commemorate the martyrdom of Imam Hussein.[26]

One of the most prominent Revolutionary Islamists to react to the undermining of *tawhid* in the Indian subcontinent was an East Punjabi Hanafi scholar named Shaykh Ahmad Sirhindi (1564–1624). Reverentially known by millions of Sunnis in the Indian subcontinent as Mujaddid Alf-i-Thani (the renewer of the faith in the second millennium of Islamic history) and Imam-i-Rabbani (pious leader of a thousand years), Sirhindi served for fourteen years in the Moghul court of Emperor Jalal-ud-Din Muhammad Akbar (r. 1556–1605 CE). There Sirhindi wrote *The Epistle on the Refutation of the Shi'ah*, which was a strong indictment of the religious rituals adopted by Shi'ahs, who enjoyed influential positions in Akbar's empire.[27]

Profoundly disturbed by the un-Islamic practices that he witnessed in the emperor's court and among the Moghul elite, Sirhindi left the city of Agra in 1600 and joined the puritanical Naqshbandi *tariqah* (sufi brotherhood), headquartered in Delhi, where he spent the rest of his life writing about the plight of Islam in India. In most of his writings he courageously denounced Moghul emperor Akbar, criticizing him for creating **Din-i-Elahi**, a liberal, eclectic, and syncretic religious ideology; for refusing to implement the *shariah*; for prohibiting the slaughter of cows, which are sacred to Hindus, but permitting the sale of pork, which is **haram** (forbidden) in Islam; for encouraging believers in Din-i-Elahi to wear the emperor's likeness on their turbans and to prostrate themselves before him; for marrying non Muslim (especially Hindu) women while prohibiting the practice of polygamy for Indian Muslims; for having many influential non-Muslim courtiers, civil servants, and officers in the armed forces; for permitting singing, dancing, gambling, and charging interest, and alcohol consumption and prostitution; for posing as Allah's vice regent on earth; for promoting Sanskritic Hindi instead of Arabic or Persian in schools; and for encouraging secular education and the study of the new syncretic faith instead of Islamic theology, jurisprudence, history, and civilization. Sirhindi's writings also condemned the Moghul elite for labeling

---

[26]Metcalf, *Islamic Revival in British India*, pp. 57–58.

[27]Yohanan Friedmann, *Shaykh Ahmad Sirhindi: An Outline of His Thought and a Study of His Image in the Eyes of Posterity* (Montreal: McGill-Queen's University Press, 1971), pp. xiii, 4, 51–53.

Islamic culture the product of illiterate and uncivilized Arabs living thirteen hundred years ago; for doubting that the Qur'an was the Word of God and that it could have been revealed to Prophet Muhammad by Allah; for questioning life after death, the Day of Judgment, the existence of the angels, and miracles (e.g., the ascension of the Prophet Muhammad); for criticizing Prophet Muhammad's polygamy and holy wars; and for slighting the importance of the five obligatory *faraidh* (duties). Finally, Sirhindi criticized a number of "worldly-minded" and "unrighteous" *ulama* who had, through their active support or passive silence, allowed Akbar and the Moghul elite to promote the aforementioned heresies.[28]

The Revolutionary Islamist Wahhabi movement is also fanatically dedicated to the concept of *tawhid*. During the movement's early years in the late eighteenth century in the Arabian peninsula, the Wahhabis strenuously objected to the name assigned them by their detractors. The term *Wahhabi* implied that they venerated Muhammad ibn Abd al-Wahhab, when actually they vehemently condemned the veneration of anyone but Allah. The Wahhabis preferred to be known as *al-Muwahhidun*, or "those affirming the notion of *tawhid*." However, since the two English interpretations of the word *al-Muwahhidun*—"Monotheists" or "Unitarians"—were considered by the group as either too broad (encompassing all Muslims and many non-Muslims) or too loaded with Christian overtones, the term *Wahhabi* stuck.[29]

In their absolute and obsessive dedication to *tawhid*, the Wahhabis demolished holy shrines and mausoleums, pressuring all Muslims to pray directly only to Almighty Allah. In 1802, for instance, the Wahhabis invaded the Shi'ah sect's holiest cities of Najaf and Karbala in Iraq, where they destroyed tombs, mausoleums, and shrines. They exhibited the same kind of iconoclasm in Islam's holiest cities of Makkah and Madinah in the following three to four years.[30]

Strongly influenced by the Wahhabi movement and equally dedicated to *tawhid*, Haji Shariatullah (1781–1840), the son of a petty *talukdar* (landowner) in East Bengal and a product of traditional Islamic education, spent nineteen years in Makkah studying Islam. While remaining a Hanafi, he returned to his village of Shamail in East Bengal (now in the Faridpur district of Bangladesh) in 1818 with the puritanical ideals of the Wahhabi doctrine in mind.[31] He was so agitated to see

[28]See S. Abul A'la Maududi, *A Short History of the Revivalist Movements in Islam*, 3rd ed., trans. Al-Ashari (Lahore, Pakistan: Islamic Publications, 1976), pp. 72–77; I. A. Arshad, "Mujaddid's Revivalist Movement," in Sardar Ali Ahmad Khan, ed., *The Naqshbandis* (Sharaqpur Sharif, Pakistan: Darul Muballeghin Hazrat, 1982), p. 93; Muhammad Yasin, "Mujaddid Alif-i-Sani," in Khan, ed., *Naqshbandis*, pp. 69–70, 75, 77–78.

[29]Robert Lacey, *The Kingdom: Arabia and the House of Saud* (New York: Avon Books, 1981), p. 56; John Obert Voll, *Islam: Continuity and Change in the Modern World* (Boulder, Colo.: Westview Press, 1982), p. 59.

[30]Edward Mortimer, *Faith and Power: The Politics of Islam* (New York: Vintage, 1982), p. 63; Julius Germanus, *Modern Movements in the World of Islam* (Lahore, Pakistan: Al-Biruni, reprinted 1978), p. 14.

[31]Metcalf, *Islamic Revival in British India*, p. 68; Qureishi, *The Muslim Community*, p. 237; Ikram, *Muslim Civilization in India*, pp. 283–284; Hardy, *The Muslims of British India*, pp. 55–56; Haq, *Islamic Thought and Movements*, pp. 448–449.

his village folk steeped in the polytheistic influences of Hinduism that in 1821, after performing the *hajj* for a second time, he launched the Faraidhiah movement. Shariatullah's mission was to "save" his village folk from the evil ways they had adopted and encourage them to perform Islam's five *faraidh*.[32] In addition, he recommended that Muslims repent their sins and vow to lead lives according to the Qur'an and the *sunnah*. He prohibited many of the Muslim practices that he felt had been permeated with non-Islamic influences in West Bengal. He forbade veneration of prophets and saints; condemned emotional displays of mourning in *taziyah* (mourning) processions; disapproved of certain rituals performed in birth and burial ceremonies; prohibited the practice of **bai'ya**, in which an aspiring *murid* (disciple) swore allegiance to his *pir* (spiritual mentor); and substituted the terms *ustad* (teacher) and **shagird** (pupil) for *pir* and *murid* to eliminate the implication of abject submission held by the terms.[33]

Haji Shariatullah abhorred both the oppressive and exploitative Hindu landlords and the British colonialist rulers, whose commercial monopoly seriously jeopardized Muslim interests in East Bengal. However, being a realist and a pacifist, he did not promote a martial *jihad* against them. Instead, he actively taught and preached to the downtrodden but responsive Muslim villagers. Some of his rulings were controversial and unpopular; for example, his prohibition of the customary Jum'ah (Friday) and *Eid* (festival) congressional prayers, because he felt India had become a *dar al-harb* (abode of conflict).[34] Nonetheless, Haji Shariatullah was revered by his Bengali coreligionists because they perceived him as a devout and learned Muslim who was genuinely concerned about their welfare and sincere about eradicating the Hindu beliefs and practices that had permeated the Islamic culture of the region. His ceaseless missionary efforts aroused the consciousness of his poor, formerly apathetic, and disenfranchised brethren.

The puritanical orientation of the Sudanese Muhammad Ahmad Abdullah al-Mahdi is evident in his proclamations and his letters, which repeatedly emphasized *tawhid*. He also strongly objected to the freedom enjoyed by Sudanese women and was appalled when once approached by a prostitute. Perceiving women as the major culprits in the increasing permissiveness of the Sudanese society, he dramatically restricted their civil rights and liberties and imposed stringent penalties against men and women who violated a strict code of behavior. For example, he ordained that women must stay in their homes and be veiled in front of all but their immediate family members. Any woman caught by the Mahdi's

---

[32]Metcalf, *Islamic Revival in British India*, pp. 68–69; Ikram, *Muslim Civilization in India*, p. 284; Qureishi, *The Muslim Community*, pp. 237–238; also see "Faraidiya" in H. A. R. Gibb amd J. H. Kramers, *The Shorter Encyclopedia of Islam* (Leiden, the Netherlands: E. J. Brill, 1974), pp. 99–100; Muinuddin Ahmad Khan, *History of the Faraidi Movement in Bengal (1818–1906)* (Karachi, Pakistan: Pakistan Historical Society, 1965).

[33]Haq, *Islamic Thought and Movements*, pp. 449–450; J. Takle, "Islam in Bengal," *Muslim World*, Vol. 4, No. 1 (January 1914), p. 15; also see Jagdish Narayan Sarkar, *Islam in Bengal: Thirteenth to Nineteenth Century* (Calcutta: Ratna Prakashan, 1972).

[34]Nizami, "Socio-Religious Movements," p. 139; Tritton, *Islam: Beliefs and Practices*, p. 160. The Friday and *eid* prayers were revived after 1947. Also see Metcalf, *Islamic Revival in British India*, p. 69.

secret informers with her head uncovered in public was to be beaten, and any man caught speaking to a female stranger was to receive one hundred lashes and be forced to fast for two months. Any woman caught wearing jewelry was to have her hair plucked out.[35] Like Muhammad ibn Abd al-Wahhab, the Sudanese Mahdi prohibited various forms of music, dancing, and singing.[36] He also banned the sale and consumption of alcohol and tobacco and imposed severe penalties against their use.[37]

Emulators of Prophet Muhammad and His Pious Companions

While all Muslims talk about emulating the good deeds of Prophet Muhammad and the ***aslaf*** (the pious Companions of Prophet Muhammad), the Revolutionary Islamists make a determined and dedicated effort to do so. As a rationale, the Revolutionary Islamists often quote a popular *hadith* in which Prophet Muhammad declares: "The best generation is mine [i.e., that of my companions]"[38] Most Revolutionary Islamists revere those Muslims who were closest to Prophet Muhammad as paragons of Islamic austerity, purity, and piety. For many Revolutionary Islamists, the classical period of Islamic history, in which the ideal Islamic state was established and governed by Prophet Muhammad and thereafter by the first four rightly guided caliphs, became the "classic" and normative period worthy of emulation and restoration.[39]

Sayyid Ahmad Barelvi tried to emulate the life of Prophet Muhammad in the 1820s by scrupulously adhering to the *shariah* himself and expecting his *mujahideen* to do the same. Like the Prophet Muhammad, Sayyid Ahmad Barelvi wrote letters to Muslim rulers in Central Asia. In these letters Sayyid Ahmad used the title *Amir al-Mu'minin* (Leader of the Faithful) and called on the Central Asian leaders to recognize his *khilafat*. In his letters he noted that, while India had fallen under the rule of the Christian colonialists, he was attempting to reestablish the *dar al-Islam* (abode of Islam), in which the *shariah* was supreme.[40]

Likewise, the Mahdi of Sudan read the life of Prophet Muhammad and tried his best to emulate him. He even imitated Prophet Muhammad's Hijrah (migration) by moving from Aba Island, where the government's forces could easily capture him, to the more inaccessible Mount Qadir in the Nuba Mountains, which he renamed "Masa," after the mountain on which Prophet Muhammad had meditated. Like the Prophet, the Mahdi called on his followers to undertake the *hijrah* to escape from the sinful environment controlled by the ***kafirs*** (infidels). Those who undertook the *hijrah* were called ***muhajirun*** (migrants). As the government's

---

[35]Mortimer, *Faith and Power*, p. 79; John Obert Voll, "The Sudanese Mahdi: Frontier Fundamentalist," *International Journal of Middle East Studies*, Vol. 10, No. 2 (May 1979), p. 156.

[36]F. R. Wingate, *Mahdism and the Egyptian Sudan*, 2nd ed. (London: Frank Cass, 1968), p. 59.

[37]Voll, "The Sudanese Mahdi," p. 156; Holt, *Mahdist State in the Sudan*, p. 131.

[38]Quoted in Fazlur Rahman, *Islam*, 2nd ed. (Chicago: University of Chicago Press, 1979), p. 236.

[39]W. C. Smith, *Islam in Modern History*, p. 43.

[40]Hardy, *Muslims of British India*, pp. 53–54.

military campaign against the Mahdi's forces began, he made *jihad* one of the most frequent themes of his speeches and writings.[41]

Abd al-Aziz ibn Abd al-Rahman al-Saud (1880–1953) alias Ibn Saud, the great grandson of the founder of the Saudi dynasty, also closely emulated Prophet Muhammad. He required that everyone in his movement—the Ikhwan (brotherhood)—treat each other as equals and call each other *akhi* (brother). Each settlement was known as a *hijrah*, a migration from a corrupted to a purifying existence, like Prophet Muhammad's flight from Makkah to Madinah.[42]

The Revolutionary Islamists' overwhelming desire to follow the *aslaf* is also evident in their writings, speeches, statements, and interviews and in the literature published by any Revolutionary Islamist organization. For instance, the December 1969 election manifesto of Pakistan's Jama'at-i-Islami, inspired by the writings and teachings of its founder and first *amir* (leader), Sayyid Abul A'la Maududi, promised to make "Pakistan a state where the laws of *Qur'an* and the *sunnah* would be in full force and which would take the Rashidun Caliphate [the caliphate of the first four pious caliphs after Prophet Muhammad] as a model."[43] Moreover, when Iran's Shi'ah Revolutionary Islamist Ayatollah Khomeini was asked what he meant by an Islamic state, he replied tersely, "The only reference point, in our view, is the time of the Prophet and Imam Ali."[44]

Crusaders for the *Shariah*'s Implementation

The Revolutionary Islamists entirely reject the church/state dichotomy that non-Muslims and nonpracticing Muslims encourage, and they aggressively crusade against such separation. Revolutionary Islamists believe that a government without the ethical foundation of Islam is unjust and easily corrupted.

Hasan al-Banna, the founder and first *amir* of the Ikhwan al-Muslimun in Egypt, expressed the Revolutionary Islamist view of Islam when he said,

> We believe the rules and teachings of Islam to be comprehensive, to include the people's affairs in the world and the hereafter. . . . Islam is an ideology and a faith, a home and a nationality, a religion and a state, a spirit and work, a book and a sword.[45]

---

[41]Leon Carl Brown, "The Role of Islam in Modern North Africa," in Leon Carl Brown, ed., *State and Society in Independent North Africa* (Washington, D.C.: Middle East Institute, 1966), pp. 9–10; Dekmejian and Wyszomirsky, "Charismatic Leadership in Islam," pp. 204–205.

[42]James P. Piscatori, "Ideological Politics in Saudi Arabia," in James P. Piscatori, ed., *Islam and the Political Process* (Cambridge: Cambridge University Press, 1983), p. 58; Christine Moss Helms, "The Ikhwan: Badu Answer the Wahhabi 'Call to Unity,' " in Christine Moss Helms, *The Cohesion of Saudi Arabia: Evolution of Political Identity* (Baltimore: Johns Hopkins University Press, 1981), pp. 127–150.

[43]"Election Manifesto of the *Jamaat-e-Islami*," p. 154.

[44]First published in *Le Monde* (Paris), May 6, 1978; later quoted in "The Start of a Gigantic Explosion: An Interview with Iranian Shi'ite Leader Ayatollah Khomenie," *Middle East Research and Information Project* (henceforth *Merip Reports*), Vol. 8, No. 6 (July–August 1978), p. 20.

[45]Abd al-Moneir Said Aly and Manfred W. Wenner, "Modern Islamic Reform Movements: The Muslim Brotherhood in Contemporary Egypt," *Middle East Journal*, Vol. 36, No. 3 (Summer 1982), p. 340.

Al-Banna also stated that, if he came to power in Egypt, he would use the numerous government mechanisms to replace most of the prevailing secular laws with the *shariah*. He used his party to crusade actively for the imposition of the *shariah* in Egypt. Similarly, in Pakistan the Revolutionary Islamist Maududi, formed the Jama'at-i-Islami to lobby actively for the establishment of a "Kingdom of God" run in accordance with the Qur'an, the *sunnah*, and the *shariah*.[46]

Like other Revolutionary Islamists, Ayatollah Khomeini publicly iterated the comprehensive and "organic" nature of Islam:

> Do not heed those who imagine that Islam is like present-day Christianity, that the mosque is no different than the church or that Islam is merely a relationship between the individual and his God. . . . Imperialist institutions instilled evil in the hearts of men, saying that religion does not mix with politics . . . most unfortunately some of us have given credence to those lies.[47]

On another occasion Khomeini more succinctly conveyed the holistic nature of Islam from the Revolutionary Islamist's point of view in the phrase "This world is political!"[48] This phrase could just as easily have been said by the Mahdi of Sudan, al-Banna of Egypt, or Maududi of Pakistan.

The Revolutionary Islamists believe that one of the most important functions of the Islamic state is to maintain and enforce the *shariah*. In fact, the Revolutionary Islamists consider it their Islamic duty to struggle actively and ceaselessly to implement the *shariah* in its entirety.[49] In this regard, Khomeini stated unequivocally that "government in Islam means obedience to the law [*shariah*] and its arbitration."[50] On another occasion Khomeini said:

> We do not say that the government must be composed of the clergy but that the government must be directed and organized according to the divine law, and this is only possible with the supervision of the clergy.[51]

Pakistan's chief martial-law administrator, General Muhammad Zia-ul-Haq, who had strong Islamic predilections of his own, believed that Pakistan had been created in 1947 to be an Islamic state. In his first speech after becoming president in 1977, Zia-ul-Haq stated that Pakistan was "created in the name of Islam" and would "survive only if it sticks to Islam."[52] Most of Zia-ul-Haq's press conferences and public

---

[46]Abul A'la Maududi, *Islamic Law and Constitution*, 6th ed., trans. and ed. Khurshid Ahmad (Lahore, Pakistan: Islamic Publications, 1977), pp. 119, 132–133, 211–232.

[47]Khomeini, *Islamic Government*, p. 7; also quoted in Martin Kramer, "The Ideals of an Islamic Order," *Washington Quarterly*, Vol. 3, No. 1 (Winter 1980), pp. 3–4.

[48]Quoted by Daniel Pipes, "This World is Political: The Islamic Revival of the Seventies," *Orbis*, Vol. 24, No. 1, Spring 1980, p. 9.

[49]H. A. R. Gibb, cited in Donna Robinson Divine, "Islamic Culture and Political Practice in British Mandated Palestine, 1918–1948," *The Review of Politics*, Vol. 45, No. 1, January 1983, p. 78.

[50]Cited in Kramer, "The Ideals of an Islamic Order," *Washington Quarterly*, Vol. 3, No. 1, Winter 1980, p. 7.

[51]Raymond H. Anderson, "Ayatollah Ruhollah Khomeini, 89, Relentless Founder of the Islamic Republic," *New York Times*, June 5, 1989, p. B-11.

[52]*Pakistan Times*, July 7, 1977, p. 1.

speeches were in Urdu and started with a recitation from the Qur'an. A few days after coming to power, Zia-ul-Haq introduced a number of *shariah*-based Islamic punishments, including public flogging for murder, rape, theft, alcohol consumption, fornication, prostitution, adultery, bearing false witness, and destroying government property in demonstrations and riots. These measures were implemented to intimidate the opposition and to instill the fear of God in the society's criminal and disruptive elements. Several months later, Zia-ul-Haq introduced other Islamic changes: women were told to dress modestly, cover their heads, and wear little or no makeup on television, in government offices, and in other public places;[53] entertainment in all educational institutions was strictly monitored to comply with Islamic standards of morality and ethics; walls of offices and educational institutions, calendars, and billboards were adorned with quotations from the Qur'an and the *hadith*;[54] and Friday was officially designated as the weekly holiday instead of Sunday.[55] Two years later even dancing and music were discouraged by the administration because they violated the Islamic sensibilities of the Revolutionary Islamists.

On December 2, 1978, Zia-ul-Haq committed himself to the Islamic transformation of Pakistan. He announced his intention to establish a legal system based on **Nizam-i-Islam** (the Islamic system). He founded a permanent law commission to simplify the legal system and bring all the existing laws into conformity with Islamic guidelines. His ultimate goal was to make the *shariah* the basis of all law in Pakistan. In February 1979 Zia-ul-Haq announced the establishment of special Shariat benches (courts that would decide cases on the basis of the *shariah*), to supplement the existing judicial system. These courts would review a limited range of laws and adjudicate cases brought under the *shariah*. Each Shariat bench consisted of five judges who were advised by competent *ulama* in matters of classical Islamic law. The main function of these Islamic legal bodies was to exercise a form of Islamic judicial review, whereby any citizen could request the judiciary to declare a law either wholly or partially un-Islamic. The addition of a Shariat bench to the supreme court allowed cases to be brought challenging the validity of any law. This was a big step toward granting the supremacy of the *shariah* over the secular Anglo-Saxon law inherited from the British.[56]

---

[53]Urdu is the national language of Pakistan. It is a hybrid of Arabic, Persian, and Sanskrit. It is written from right to left like Arabic and Persian. Spoken Urdu is similar to Hindi (the national language of India, which is written from left to right in the Devnagri script). Urdu was initiated in the army barracks during the Muslim-dominated Moghul Empire, which lasted from 1525 to 1857. Ironically, most of Pakistan's presidents before Zia were fluent in English but not in Urdu.

[54]Kemal A. Faruki, "Pakistan: Islamic Government and Society," in John Esposito, ed., *Islam in Asia: Religion, Politics, and Society* (Oxford: Oxford University Press, 1987), p. 59.

[55]Zulfikar Ali Bhutto first started the practice of making Friday a holiday instead of Sunday to allow Muslims to follow the command of Prophet Muhammad to go to the mosques on Friday at noon to pray with the congregation.

[56]Craig Baxter, "Restructuring the Pakistan Political System," in Shahid Javed Burki and Craig Baxter, *Pakistan under the Military: Eleven Years of Zia-ul-Haq* (Boulder, Colo.: Westview Press, 1991), p. 36; Mumtaz Ahmad, "Islamic Revival in Pakistan," in Cyriac Pullapilly, ed., *Islam in the Contemporary World* (Notre Dame, Ind.: Cross Roads Books, 1980), p. 266; Richter, "Pakistan," p. 146; also see Jan Mohammed, "Introducing Islamic Laws in Pakistan, I," *Dawn*, July 15, 1983, p. 15; Hakim Mohammed Said, "Enforcement of Islamic Laws in Pakistan," *Hamdard Islamicus*, Vol. 2, No. 2 (Summer 1979), pp. 71–80.

On February 10, 1979, President Zia-ul-Haq utilized the happy occasion of Eid-i-Milad-un-Nabi (Prophet Muhammad's birthday) to introduce a more comprehensive Islamic penal code. In that announcement, the government prescribed the **hadd** (Shariah-prescribed punishment) of eighty lashes for adult Muslims caught drinking alcohol. If evidence was insufficient, then the *ta'azir* (lesser) punishment of three years imprisonment and/or thirty lashes would be imposed. The *ta'azir* punishment also applied to non-Muslim Pakistani citizens found drinking alcohol (except as part of a religious ritual) and to non-Muslim foreigners found drinking alcohol in a public place. Furthermore, anyone who imported, transported, manufactured, processed, sold, or allowed consumption of an intoxicant on his or her premises was liable for a maximum of five years imprisonment, thirty lashes, and a fine. For simply possesssing an intoxicant, the punishment in Zia-ul-Haq's Pakistan was two years imprisonment or thirty lashes and a fine.[57] Under Zia-ul-Haq's penal code, many people were publicly flogged for a variety of crimes. There were also two cases in which habitual thieves had their hands amputated under medical supervision and one case in which a woman was stoned to death for adultery. Though far from the comprehensive Islamic system that Zia-ul-Haq had wanted to implement, these laws nevertheless constituted one additional step in his series of sociocultural, judicial, economic, and political reforms designed to incorporate Islam more fully into the nation's daily life.[58]

Zealous Promoters of the Five *Faraidh*

The Revolutionary Islamists believe in practicing the five *faraidh* expected of all Muslims—the *shahadah, salat, sawm, zakat*, and *hajj*. Yet unlike other Muslims, the Revolutionary Islamists crusade with missionary zeal for the obligatory practice of the five *faraidh*. The revolutionary Islamist movement launched by Haji Shariatullah in 1821 in East Bengal was called "the Faraidhiah" precisely because it attempted to "save" the "wayward" Bengali Muslims by encouraging them to perform the five *faraidh*. In the same way, all Revolutionary Islamist movements could well be called Faraidhiah movements because of their constant exhortation to perform the five *faraidh*. Pakistan's Zia-ul-Haq, like all Revolutionary Islamists, encouraged and obliged his citizens to fulfill the duties of Islam. Ramadan was seriously observed: fasting was glorified and heavily promoted in the mass media, and restaurants, shops, motels, and hotels were forbidden to serve food to Muslims from dawn to dusk. Government offices were ordered to set aside appropriate times for daily prayers during the workday, and tremendous governmental and peer-group pressure was applied toward prayer observation (especially the midday prayer) in offices and factories; civil and military officers were advised to lead or at least attend these prayers. The government publicized the annual *hajj*,

---

[57]Weiss, "The Historical Debate on Islam," p. 15; Richter, "Pakistan," p. 144; Baxter, "Restructuring the Pakistan Political System," pp. 36–37; also see Mohammad Suleman Siddiqi, "The Concept of Hudud and Its Significance," in Anwar Moazzam, ed., *Islam and the Contemporary Muslim World* (New Delhi: Light and Life, 1981), pp. 160–180; Said, "Enforcement of Islamic Laws," pp. 61–90.

[58]Said, "Enforcement of Islamic Laws," pp. 143–144.

with high government officials photographed and televised sending off and welcoming home pilgrims at the docks and airports.[59] Zia-ul-Haq himself was shown personally seeing off planeloads and shiploads of pilgrims going to perform the *hajj* or embracing *hajjis* on their return.[60]

During the holy month of Ramadan in 1979, Zia-ul-Haq's regime began collecting *zakat* and *ushr* with much fanfare. A central *zakat* fund was established to help the poor and needy (such as those who were widowed, orphaned, handicapped, or aged). In the Ramadan period of 1980, Zia-ul-Haq proudly inaugurated the distribution of *zakat* on national radio and television.

On August 14, 1984, Pakistan's Independence Day, Zia-ul-Haq announced the immediate appointment of a *nazim-i-salat* (organizer of prayers) for every village and urban precinct—an action that frightened and annoyed the Shi'ahs and liberal Muslims. These prayer organizers were not only to organize the midday prayers on Fridays but also to encourage Muslims to say all five prayers daily.[61] Zia-ul-Haq said:

> Only those persons are being appointed for this service of religion who have sound moral character and their piety is so exemplary that their words will have deep effect on the hearts of people. The procedure for this exercise for the time being is based on persuasion and motivation and not on compulsion. But we are determined to succeed in establishing the system of prayer at all cost.[62]

Opponents of *Taqlid* and Proponents of *Ijtihad*

Virtually all Revolutionary Islamists reject the dogma of *taqlid* and embrace its antithesis, the dynamic notion of *ijtihad*. *Taqlid* entails blind and unquestioning adherence to the legal rulings (in one or more schools of Islamic jurisprudence) of the learned, competent, and renowned theologian-jurists of the medieval Islamic era. *Ijtihad*, conversely, means to strive or exert oneself intellectually to the utmost, with the assistance of the Qur'an and the *sunnah*, to draw independent conclusions and judgments on legal or other issues. Taha J. al-Alwani—a member of the Fiqh Academy of the Organization of the Islamic Conference (OIC), chairman of the Fiqh Council of North America, and president of the International Institute of Islamic Thought in the United States—clearly summarized the Revolutionary Islamist point of view about *taqlid* and *ijtihad*:

> What has happened to the penetrating and enlightened mind inspired by Islam, the one which freed our ancestors from their idols and the obstacles blocking their progress? How did such a mind return to its former prison and fetters, robbed of any chance to renew and reform the *ummah* through *ijtihad?* In a word, the answer is *taqlid*, an illness which entered the Muslim mind and then fed on it until it returned to its prison.[63]

---

[59]Faruki, "Pakistan: Islamic Government and Society," p. 59.

[60]Richter, "Pakistan," pp. 150–151.

[61]Faruki, "Pakistan: Islamic Government and Society," p. 61.

[62]Ibid.; *Dawn*, August 16, 1984, p. 1.

[63]Taha J. al-Alwani, "Taqlid and the Stagnation of the Muslim Mind," *American Journal of Islamic Social Sciences*, Vol. 8, No. 3 (1991), pp. 513–514.

However, Revolutionary Islamists often limit the right of *ijtihad* to those knowledgeable and competent in Islamic theology and law.

Most Sunni Revolutionary Islamists applaud the Syrian-born Hanbali theologian-jurist Taqi al-Din ibn Taimiyyah (1263–1328 CE) for his courageous denunciations of *taqlid* and fearless practice of *ijtihad* at a time when such ideas were considered heretical by the conservative *ulama* because they were seen as sowing the seeds of division and discord in the *ummah*.[64] In fact, because of his systematic and forcefully argued stand in his scholarly writings, ibn Taimiyya is regarded by most Sunni Revolutionary Islamists as the father of revolutionary Islamism.[65]

The archetypical Sunni Revolutionary Islamist, Muhammad ibn Abd al-Wahhab, closely emulated ibn Taimiyyah in his bitter condemnation of *taqlid* and extensive use of *ijtihad* in eighteenth-century Arabia. His beliefs spread from Arabia when Muslim pilgrims who had come to Makkah for the *hajj* returned home espousing the popular ideas of the Wahhabis. For example, the East Bengali Haji Shariatullah was profoundly influenced by Wahhabism while a pilgrim and student in the Arabian peninsula in the nineteenth century; he returned home to found the Faraidhiah movement. On his return to North Africa from Arabia Sayyid Muhammad ibn Ali al-Sanusi advocated *ijtihad* for men who were pious and knowledgeable about the Qur'an and the *sunnah* and categorically rejected *taqlid*.[66]

Most Revolutionary Islamists and Modernist Islamists today wholeheartedly agree with Shah Waliullah (1702–1762), a Revolutionary Islamist and one of the greatest Islamic revivalists of the Indian subcontinent, that the major cause for the decline of Muslim rule in the world was the discontinuance of the spirit of *ijtihad* and the dominance of the dogma of *taqlid* among the Traditionalist Islamists.[67] As Waliullah said: "The *ulama* of today are like camels with strings in their noses. They are tightened by *taqlid* and do not think over problems afresh."[68]

Ardent Foes of Secular Nationalism

While all Traditionalist Islamists and many Modernist Islamists claim to oppose secular nationalism, they display less vehemence in their opposition than do the Revolutionary Islamists. The most extreme example of this Revolutionary Islamist opposition is that of Maududi and his Jama'at-i-Islami. Maududi's stubborn and aggressive opposition to the Pakistan Movement was rooted in his belief in

---

[64]Quoted in Maududi, *Short History of the Revivalist Movement*, pp. 57–70.

[65]The Shi'ahs are very critical of ibn Taimiyyah because of his condemnation of accretions in Shi'ah beliefs and practices.

[66]Nicola A. Ziadeh, *Sanusiyah: A Study of a Revivalist Movement in Islam* (Leiden, the Netherlands: E. J. Brill, 1958), pp. 36–40.

[67]A. D. Muztar, *Shah Waliullah: A Saint-Scholar of Muslim India* (Islamabad, Pakistan: National Commission on Historical and Cultural Research, 1979), p. 75; Freeland Abbott, "The Decline of the Moghul Empire and Shah Waliullah," *Muslim World*, Vol. 55, No. 2 (April 1965), p. 347.

[68]Quoted in Nizami, "Socio-Religious Movements in Indian Islam," p. 132.

"Islamic universalism," as mentioned in the Qur'an and *sunnah*, and in his bitter opposition to the alien, secular, and territorial nature of nationalism, which, he was convinced, would divide and weaken the *ummah* by allowing national interests to prevail over global Islamic interests. Maududi believed Islam and nationalism were totally incompatible. Writing in 1947, he stated, " 'Muslim Nationalist' and 'Muslim Communist' are as contradictory terms as 'Communist Fascist,' and 'Socialist Capitalist,' and 'Chaste Prostitute!' "[69] Maududi's view was clear:

> One ultimate goal of Islam is a world state in which the claims of racial and national prejudices would be dismantled and all mankind incorporated in a cultural and political system, with equal rights and equal opportunities for all.[70]

Maududi went on to elaborate how nationalism divides humanity and breeds localism and how it inculcates the love of a particular territory rather than the love of humanity in general. He felt nationalism was "the greatest curse in the world, . . . the greatest menace to human civilization; it makes man wolf to all other nations except his own."[71] To Maududi, Jinnah, Pakistan's founder, was a Westernized, secular nationalist who did not fulfill Islam's obligatory *faraidh* and who espoused the ideology of nationalism (which was *shirk*, i.e., ascribing partners to God as sharers of His divinity) instead of the religion of Islam. Maududi felt Jinnah was an inappropriate leader of the new Islamic state and that Jinnah's Pakistan would be pagan and its leaders pharaohs, nimrods, and infidel tyrants.[72] Maududi was so bitterly opposed to the creation of a Pakistan led by the secular Muslim elite that he wrote, "When I look at the [Muslim] League's resolution [demanding Pakistan] my soul laments."[73] He went on to write:

> Sad it is, that from the *Quaid-i-Azam* of the League to its lowliest followers there is not one who has an Islamic mentality and way of thinking or who looks at matters with an Islamic viewpoint.[74]

Later Maududi stated: "The result of it [Pakistan] will be a heretic government of Muslims."[75] And again:

> Why should we foolishly spend our time in waiting for, or in the struggle for the creation of, this so-called Muslim government, which we know will be not only disadvantageous for our objective but a substantial hindrance to it?[76]

The election of 1946 was crucial to the creation of Pakistan, yet Maududi told his supporters to ignore it:

---

[69]See Sayyid Abul A'la Maududi, *Nationalism and India*, 2nd ed. (Malihabad, India: Maktaba-e-Jamaat-e-Islami [Hind], 1948), pp. 9–10.

[70]Ibid., pp. 10–11.

[71]Ibid., p. 18.

[72]Cited in Aziz Ahmad, "Maudidi and Orthodox Fundamentalists in Pakistan," *Middle East Journal*, Vol. 21 (1967), p. 374.

[73]Abul A'la Maududi, *Musalman aur Maujuda Seyasi Kashmakash* [Muslims and the Present Political Conflict], in Urdu, Vol. 3 (Pathankot, India: n.p., 1942), p. 29.

[74]Ibid., p. 29.

[75]Ibid., p. 132.

[76]Ibid., p. 138.

As a principled organization, we cannot sacrifice our principles, in which we have faith, for temporary advantage; whatever the importance of the coming elections and whatever effect they may have on our nation and our country.[77]

Revolutionary Islamists have also spoken out and written against secular pan-Arabism. As one Revolutionary Islamist noted: "It [pan-Arabism] evolved into a surrogate for religious bonds under the impact of a set of ideas which had developed in Europe in a specifically Christian situation."[78] In Syria the Ikhwan al-Muslimun has accused President Hafiz al-Assad's regime of "apostasy" and "infidelity" for the promotion of Ba'athism, which has elements of Arab nationalism, pan-Arabism, Arab socialism, and secularism.[79]

Revolutionary Islamists in the Modern Period

Revolutionary Islamists in the late twentieth century, unlike their predecessors, are willing to embrace what they perceive as beneficial modern values that conform to the basic tenets of Islam. For example, although they wish to follow the revered body of *shariah* strictly, they are willing to interpret the letter of the law more broadly than in the past. Many, though certainly not all, Revolutionary Islamists in the modern period have come to accept Western notions of democracy, which entail periodic elections on the basis of secret balloting and one vote for every adult person, a multiparty political system, and a national assembly or parliament to pass laws for the entire nation. However, in order to ascertain that no legislation is passed or decisions made that are not in keeping with the Qur'an or *sunnah*, the Revolutionary Islamists still insist that competent Revolutionary Islamist *ulama* advise the democratically elected representatives of the people and ratify all legislation.

Maududi's Revolutionary Islamist critique of the Traditionalist Islamist *ulama* articulated the Revolutionary Islamist approach to the modern world:

> The conservatist approach, represented by the orthodox *ulama*, is unrealistic. It fails to take note of the fact that life is everchanging. . . . New situations are arising, new relationships are being formed and new problems are emerging. . . . The approach fails to grapple with the problems of the day [and] is bound to fail. It cannot but drive religion out of the flux of life and confine it to the sphere of private life. And when estrangement is effected between religion and life, then even the private life cannot remain religion's preserve. . . . Furthermore, the conservative elements had not the full understanding of the constitutional, political, economic and culture problems of the day. The result was that they could not talk the language of today and failed to impress the intelligentsia and the masses alike. . . .[80]

Maududi likewise critiqued Modernist Islamists, charging that they were attempting to modernize Islam by emulating Western ideas, values, institutions, and processes that were alien to Islam. Although he agreed with the necessity of

---

[77]Abul A'la Maududi, *Tarjuman al-Quran*, September-October 1945, p. 1.

[78]Quoted in Emmanuel Sivan, *Radical Islam: Medieval Theology and Modern Politics* (New Haven Conn.: Yale University Press, 1985), p. 49.

[79]Ibid., p. 49.

[80]Maududi, *Islamic Law and Constitution*, p. 18.

ijtihad and the use of reason to interpret God's commands, he insisted that *ijtihad* be undertaken according to, and not against, Islam's clear commands. While concurring that Islam contains nothing contrary to reason and the latest scientific knowledge, he disagreed with the Modernists' belief that the Qur'an and the *sunnah* should be interpreted by the standard of reason. Instead of starting with the proposition that "true reason is Islam," the Modernist Islamists believed that Islam was a truly rational and reasonable religion. Like the Mutazilite *ulama* of the eighth, ninth, and tenth centuries, the Modernist Islamists implicitly designated reason rather than the Qur'an and *sunnah* as the final authority.[81]

Summary

Revolutionary Islamists are radical and puritanical in their orientation. They are extremely critical of *taqlid* and scathing in their denunciation of Western ideas. They are obsessed with the notions of *tawhid*, the finality of Prophet Muhammad, and the five *faraidh* and try to closely emulate Prophet Muhammad and the pious *aslaf*. Above all, Revolutionary Islamists have the sincere and passionate desire to establish an Islamic state based on the comprehensive and rigorous application of the *shariah*.

Internet Sites

http://atheism.about.com/library/islam/blfaq_islam_mahdi.htm

http://atheism.about.com/library/islam/blfaq_islam_qutb.htm

http://atheism.about.com/library/islam/blfaq_islam_jamaat1.htm

http://philtar.ucsm.ac.uk/encyclopedia/islam/sufi/sanusi.html

http://africanhistory.about.com/library/glossary/bldef-muslim_brotherhood.htm

http://www.icna.org/tm/greatmuslim3.htm

---

[81]Mortimer, *Faith and Power*, pp. 203–204.

CHAPTER FOUR

Traditionalist Islamists

Traditionalist Islamists constitute the second category of Islamists or Islamic revivalists. The products of traditional Islamic education, Traditionalist Islamists are often drawn from the ranks of the devout and learned *ulama* and, hence, typically are Islamic scholars.

Non-Muslims, especially Westerners, have tended to equate "Fundamentalists" (called Revolutionary Islamists in this book) and Traditionalist Islamists because both are religiously conservative and disapproving of the West. But there the ideological affinity ends. To depict any general ideological consensus among devout Muslims or to portray Islam as a monolithic force is to completely misunderstand and misrepresent Islam, Islamism, and Islamic Revivalism. Even between strictly conservative Revolutionary Islamists and Traditionalist Islamist clerics, agreement is rarely reached on such intrinsic issues as *tawhid* and tradition, *taqlid* and *ijtihad*, or predestination and political activism. In fact, their conflicting stands on these issues are what differentiate Traditionalist Islamists from Revolutionary Islamists.

Preservers of Medieval Islamic Traditions Who Tolerate Local Customs

Among the most divisive issues separating Revolutionary Islamists from Traditionalist Islamists are their conflicting definitions of an appropriate normative period. The Revolutionary Islamists look to Islam's classical period for inspiration and emulation and denigrate the traditions and practices of subsequent historical periods as impure and fundamentally un-Islamic "accretions" and "innovations." Often Revolutionary Islamists' opposition to such "accretions" is based on their strict interpretation of *tawhid*. Many Muslim traditions, particularly those in which saints, holy men and women, or *Imams* are venerated as intermediaries between humans and God, violate *tawhid* by Revolutionary Sunni Islamist standards and thus must be extirpated. Indeed, Revolutionary Sunni Islamists are committed to eradicating all Muslim practices except those prevalent during the classical period of Islam. The Revolutionary Islamist Wahhabis, for example, strongly denounce the practice of venerating Prophet Muhammad and members of his extended family as *shirk* (polytheism) and, therefore, heresy. This is why Wahhabi holy warriors invaded Shi'ah Islam's holiest cities in 1801 and demolished a number of tombs, mausoleums, and shrines built in the memory of Islam's heroes.

In stark contrast, Traditionalist Islamists conserve and preserve not only the Islamic beliefs, customs, and traditions practiced in the classical period of Islam but also those of subsequent Islamic periods. They are tolerant of Sufism, mysticism, and numerous local and regional customs and traditions commonly referred to collectively as "folk Islam" or "popular Islam." Traditionalist Islamists believe that Islam is not merely a set of abstract and utopian principles but a comprehensive and living belief system that interacts with the historical and cultural traditions of devout Muslims. To suppress these traditions, therefore, would be to weaken the form of devotion popular among the Muslim majority. The Traditionalist Islamist Farangi Mahallis (Sunni *ulama* who lived in a *mahal*—Urdu for "mansion"—in late seventeenth-century Lucknow, India), for instance, revered a pantheon of saints, including their own ancestors, and visited their tombs often to offer prayers and express their gratitude for prayers that had been answered.[1] In fact, the *madrassahs* (Islamic schools) in which Farangi Mahallis taught were invariably closed on the birthdays or death anniversaries of prominent saints so that both teachers and pupils could partake in celebrations to commemorate the occasions.[2]

The Barelvis (see Box 4.1) also taught that Prophet Muhammad as well as *pirs* and *ulama* were effective intermediaries to God and the best interpreters of His divine message.[3] The Barelvis advocated spiritualism and *tasawwuf* (mysticism) and believed that the spirits of dead saints can be invoked for help. Visits to the tombs of saints, *pirs*, *ulama*, and *sufis* are characteristic Barelvi traditions, as is **urs**, the graveside celebration of the death anniversary of a prominent saint. The Barelvis also used the fatalism and superstition widely accepted by commoners to promote the power of the Qur'an in healing, warding off evil, and gaining success. This was done by using relevant Qur'anic verses in *taweezes* (amulets) and *imam-zamins* (armbands with Qur'anic verses).[4]

---

[1]Francis Robinson, "The Ulama of Farangi Mahall and their Adab," in Barbara Daly Metcalf, ed., *Moral Conduct and Authority: The Place of Adab in South Asian Islam* (Berkeley and Los Angeles: University of California Press, 1984), pp. 155–156, 160–161, 164–170.

[2]Francis Robinson, "The Veneration of Teachers in Islam by Their Pupils: Its Modern Significance," *History Today*, Vol. 30 (March 1980), p. 24.

[3]Metcalf, *Islamic Revival in British India 1860–1900* (Princeton, N.J.: Princeton University Press, 1982), p. 267.

[4]Mohammad Arif Ghayur and Asaf Hussain, "The Religio-Political Parties (JI, JUI, JUP): Role of the Ulema in Pakistan's Politics," paper presented at the New England Conference, Association for Asian Studies, University of Connecticut, Storrs, Connecticut, October 20–21, 1979, p. 16.

■

BOX 4.1   Ahmad Raza Khan Berelvi

A hmad Raza (1856–1921) was born in India. His photographic memory enabled him to memorize numerous books on Islamic jurisprudence in his youth, which helped him later to become one of the best scholars of the *fiqh* in his time.

Ahmad Raza wrote sixteen books and composed numerous verses in Urdu in praise of Prophet Muhammad. He also authored a commentary on the *hadith* and on the Prophet's family and companions. In common with other Traditionalists Islamists, Ahmad Raza invoked the Prophet Muhammad as an intercessor between humans and God, inasmuch as the Prophet enjoyed complete knowledge of spiritual matters, of the meaning of all metaphorical passages in the Qur'an, of the obscure past, and of the unknown future. Ahmad Raza also believed that saints were intermediaries between humanity and God, and he encouraged the practice of calling upon their assistance in all situations. He also urged Muslims to recite specified readings and to offer food at the graves of saints to hasten the answering of prayers.

As a fervent believer in folk Islam, Ahmad Raza condoned many other practices and rituals widely prevalent in India. A revered *shaykh* in the Qadiriyyah brotherhood—a major *sufi* order named after Abd al-Qadir al-Jilani—Ahmad Raza handled correspondence dealing with Sufism and was a master of *taksir* (the making of numerical charts to serve as amulets). He also provided recipes for formulas intended to secure blessings and approved the practice of kissing one's thumbs and placing them on one's eyes upon hearing the name of Prophet Muhammad in the call to prayer—a practice believed to help induce visions of the Prophet. Moreover, he condoned such folk rituals as keeping a white chicken, drawing blood on Saturdays, and praising the Prophet when plucking a flower. He justified the practice of "folk Islam" by declaring that unless a ritual was specifically prohibited by a *hadith*, it was legitimate.

Though a typically apolitical Traditionalist Islamist, Ahmad Raza did become politically involved near the end of his life in opposition to the Khilafat Movement. He discouraged Muslim cooperation with Mahatma Gandhi and with the Hindu-dominated All-India Congress Party. To this end, he even convened a conference of Indian *ulama* in 1921, the year he died.

Ahmad Raza was one of the most prominent scholars, teachers, and leaders of the Barelvi school. His charisma and his adherence to traditional Islamic beliefs and practices appealed to devout Indian Muslims throughout rural northern India. His promotion of folk Islam, therefore, left a deep and lasting imprint in the history of Traditionalist Islamism in the South Asian subcontinent.

The Deobandis derived their name from a devout Hanafi and practicing *sufi*, Haji Muhammad Abid of Deoband, founder of the Madrassah-i-Deoband in his hometown in 1866.[5] The Deobandis, like the Farangi Mahallis and Barelvis,

---

[5]S. M. Ikram, *Modern Muslim India and the Birth of Pakistan (1858–1951)*, rev. ed. (Lahore, Pakistan: Shaikh Muhammad Ashraf Publishers, 1965), pp. 124–125.

believed that the bodies and souls of prophets and saints were immortal, and therefore they regularly visited their tombs to pray and ask for help from God through them.[6] However, the Deobandis, unlike the Barelvis, strongly discouraged other aspects of folk or popular Islam.

In general, the practice of folk Islam is tolerated by Traditionalist Islamists as a healthy expression of the faith. The Revolutionary Islamists, in contrast, oppose "folk Islam" in all its manifestations and discourage its practice, sometimes by force, as essentially un-Islamic.

Generally Apolitical Pacifists But Occasionally Political Activists

Folk Islam is not the only issue that separates Revolutionary Islamists from Traditionalist Islamists. Their comparative approaches to political action likewise differ—a difference more essential than the question of *tawhid* versus tradition. When not at the apex of power, Revolutionary Islamists often play an aggressive political role. The Traditionalist Islamists, however, disdain political activism and are generally detached and apolitical scholars, teachers, and preachers. In fact, because of their nonviolent and apolitical orientation, Traditionalist Islamists are often easily coopted by Muslim regimes to support the status quo. There is no guarantee, however, of the silence of Traditionalist Islamists in times of political upheaval. Even after periods of relative dormancy, when Islam or the *ummah*—whether at local, regional, or global levels—appears to be in imminent danger, Traditionalist Islamists have vigorously asserted themselves politically.

Two decades ago, this political activism on the part of Traditionalist Islamists was obvious in the case of the Islamic Revolution in Iran (1978–1979), when the Traditionalist *ulama* joined the anti-*shah* opposition and toppled the Pahlavi monarchy. The most prominent Traditionalist *alim* involved in the Iranian Revolution was Ayatollah Sayyid Kazem Shariatmadari (1905–1986). Grand Ayatollah Shariatmadari was an erudite, passive, and apolitical gentleman whose final years in Ayatollah Khomeini's Islamic Republic read like a Greek tragedy (see Box 4.2).

The Farangi Mahalli school of Sunni Traditionalist Islamists, for instance, consisted of learned *ulama* and practicing *sufis* who, by virtue of their teaching and advisory roles, brought about a gradual Islamic revival in the Indian subcontinent during the eighteenth and nineteenth centuries. For most of those two centuries the Farangi Mahallis educated Sunnis and Shi'ahs for careers in religion and education and as advisors to local rulers. They also educated the sons of *pirs* and *sufis* and were heavily relied upon by both Sunni and Shi'ah princes.[7]

---

[6]Aziz Ahmad, *Islamic Modernism in India and Pakistan, 1857–1964* (Oxford: Oxford University Press, 1967), p. 107.

[7]Metcalf, *Islamic Revival in British India*, pp. 29–34; Ahmad, *Islamic Modernism in India and Pakistan*, pp. 103, 107, 113.

■

BOX 4.2   Ayatollah Sayyid Kazem Shariatmadari

Born into a religious household in 1905, Sayyid Kazem Shariatmadari pursued Islamic studies under the tutelage of erudite Shi'ah *ulama* (Islamic scholars) in Iran and Iraq. After concluding his advanced Islamic studies in Najaf, Iraq, he returned home to Tabriz, where he taught *fiqh* (Islamic jurisprudence) and then, at age forty-four went on to teach at *madrassahs* in Qom.

When the Grand Ayatollah Hussein ibn Ali Tabatabai Burujerdi died in 1961, no single clerical candidate proved learned enough to succeed him as the sole **marja-i-taqlid** (source of emulation). Ayatollah Shariatmadari became one of the three *marja-i-taqlids* chosen to succeed him. Shariatmadari's personal influence was greatest among the fourteen million Turkish-speaking Azerbaijani minority living in northwestern Iran and in Khorasan and among the **bazaaris** (businessmen) in Tehran.

Shariatmadari founded the Dar al-Tabligh Islami (House of Islamic Propagation) in 1963 at Qom to encourage traditional apolitical missionary activities, worldwide distribution of Shi'ah literature, and education through modern methods. He also served as administrator of the Madrassah-i-Fatimah in Qom and gave instruction in *akhlaq* (etiquette) and *fiqh* to students from around the Muslim world.

On the death of Grand Ayatollah Mohsen Hakim in 1970, the *shah* conveyed his condolences on Hakim's death in a personal letter to Shariatmadari in an effort to secure the apolitical Ayatollah's succession to Ayatollah Hakim's place as the supreme *marja-i-taqlid*. By favoring Shariatmadari, however, the *shah*—who was despised by the overwhelming majority of clerics—sabotaged Shariatmadari's prospects of rising to the top of the Shi'ah clerical hierarchy. Indeed, the clerics reacted to the *shah*'s support for Shariatmadari by turning instead to Ayatollah Khomeini, the *shah*'s most vocal and uncompromising critic.

As the Iranian revolution rapidly progressed, Shariatmadari, who opposed bloodshed and believed that the *ulama* should advise rulers and not become rulers themselves, accepted the *shah*'s nomination of Shahpour Bakhtiar as prime minister and the institution of constitutional monarchy. However, with the departure of the *shah*, the end of the monarchy, and even the abrupt resignation of Prime Minister Bakhtiar's short-lived administration, Khomeini became Iran's de facto leader. Shariatmadari disapproved of the dominant role played by Khomeini's Revolutionary Islamists in devising the Islamic constitution; the doctrine of **Velayat-i-Faqih** (Supreme Law Giver), which would make Khomeini the ultimate arbiter of Iran's destiny; the influential political role played by the Islamic Republican Party (IRP); and the suppression of dissent by Khomeini's regime.

In April 1979 Shariatmadari's supporters, who were predominantly Azerbaijani merchants, middle-class politicians, and clerics, founded the Islamic People's Republican Party (IPRP) to oppose the IRP's domination. IPRP supporters demonstrated in the streets, particularly in Iran's Azerbaijani province. As the demonstrations intensified, Shariatmadari defused the crisis by requesting millions of his supporters to end their demonstrations.

In April 1982, Ayatollah Khomeini's ruling Revolutionary Islamists found a pretext for neutralizing Shariatmadari's influence when a plot was uncovered to overthrow

(Continued)

Ayatollah Sayyid Kazem Shariatmadari   *(Continued)*

Khomeini. On the basis of rumors that Shariatmadari was conspiring to overthrow Khomeini, Ayatollah Khomeini and his Revolutionary Islamist clerical allies, in an unprecedented move, demoted Shariatmadari and confined him to his home. When Shariatmadari was formally stripped of his clerical rank and his allies were purged from senior positions in the Shi'ah clerical establishment, not one senior cleric came to their defense. These actions succeeded in silencing the dissident clerics as a political force and disabled them from supporting a grassroots opposition movement against the Revolutionary Islamists who controlled Khomeini's theocracy.

Shariatmadari had dreamed of a democratic Islamic republic in Iran; but he was profoundly disillusioned. After spending the last four years of his life in obscurity under virtual house arrest, Shariatmadari died brokenhearted in Qom in 1986; his services to Islam and the Iranian Revolution were limited to a brief obituary in the Iranian mass media.

However, between 1909 and 1926 the Farangi Mahallis, under the leadership of Qayam-ud-Din Muhammad Abdul Bari (1878–1926; see Box 4.3), became increasingly involved in politics because they believed that the *ummah* was in danger from external non-Muslim aggressors. In 1909 Abdul Bari agitated for separate electorates for Indian Muslims. A year later, he founded an organization to promote the cause of the Ottoman Empire in its war against Russia.[8] Concerned over the Balkan War, in which non-Muslim European powers were carving up the Ottoman Empire, and about possible British control of Islam's holiest shrines, in Makkah and Madinah, he helped initiate a major Islamic conference in Lucknow, India, in December 1913 to discuss ways to protect Islam, the holy shrines, and the *ummah* from European colonialism. After the conference, he helped to establish and became president of the Anjuman-i-Khuddam-i-Ka'abah (Organization to Protect the Ka'abah).[9]

Abdul Bari also played a significant role in launching the post–World War I **Khilafat Movement**. In December 1918, under the auspices of the All-India Muslim League, he convened a conference at which the leading *ulama* of India (except the Barelvi school *ulama*) participated. He then cultivated a friendly relationship with Mahatama Gandhi and urged that he involve himself in the Khilafat

---

[8]Francis Robinson, *Separatism among Indian Muslims: The Politics of the United Provinces' Muslims, 1860–1923* (Cambridge: Cambridge University Press, 1974), pp. 419–420; M. Naeem Qureshi, "The Ulama of British India and the Hijrat of 1920," *Modern Asian Studies*, Vol. 13, No. 1 (1979), p. 47.

[9]Pan Chopra, ed., *The Role of the Indian Muslims in the Struggle for Freedom* (New Delhi: Light and Life Publishers, 1979), p. 92.

BOX 4.3   Qayam-ud-Din Muhammad Abdul Bari

Qayam-ud-Din Muhammad Abdul Bari (1878–1926) received a traditional Islamic education and pursued his studies in Istanbul and in the Hijaz of Saudi Arabia. Abdul Bari began his political activity in the early twentieth century. In India, he became involved in the Muslim agitation for separate electorates. In following years, he became president of the newly founded Majlis-i-Mu'yad al-Islam (Association to Strengthen Islam), whose immediate aim was to help the Ottoman Empire in its war against czarist Russia.

Because of continued European encroachments on the territory of the ailing Ottoman Empire, Abdul Bari helped organize a major Islamic conference in Lucknow in December 1913 to discuss ways to protect Islam, the holy shrines in Makkah and Madinah, and the *ummah* (global brotherhood of Muslims) from European colonialism. At the end of World War I Abdul Bari was instrumental in starting up the Khilafat Movement to protest British attempts to divide the Ottoman Empire and undermine the influence of the sultan. In December 1918 he brought together the leading *ulama* of India for an All-India Muslim League conference. He also befriended Mahatama Gandhi and prodded him to join his Indian nationalist noncooperation movement with the Khilafat Movement. In September 1919 Abdul Bari was elected leader of an influential group of *ulama* at the Lucknow All-India Khilafat Conference, at which he produced a plan for the Central Khilafat Committee. Abdul Bari dominated the Delhi Khilafat conference of November 1919, where he was elected president of the Jami'at-i-Ulama-i-Hind (Association of Indian Ulama).

In 1924, when ibn Saud's puritanical Wahhabi warriors conquered Makkah and Medinah and began to destroy all the mausoleums and shrines of Islam's heroes, Maulana Bari formed yet another pan-Islamic organization, the Anjuman-i-Khuddam-i-Haramain (Guardians of Islam's Holiest Shrines) and led demonstrations against the conquest of Islam's holiest cities. Around the same time he also resisted the growing Hindu revival that Mahatma Gandhi had ushered in with his use of Hindu rhetoric and symbolism.

Despite his political and educational commitments, Abdul Bari found time to write about one hundred books. He founded and taught at the Madrassah-i-Nizamiyyah, executed his duties as a *pir* (spiritual teacher) to a large following of disciples, and served on the boards of the shrine of Muin-ud-Din Chishti (a famous *sufi* saint who has a large following in the South Asian subcontinent) at Ajmere and of the Nadwat-ul-Ulama (Islamic Scholars of Nadwa) seminary at Lucknow. He was the major catalyst responsible for the Islamic revival in India at the beginning of the twentieth century.

Movement. At the Lucknow All-India Khilafat Conference held in September 1919, Abdul Bari produced a plan for the Central Khilafat Committee and was elected the leader of the Khilafat Movement. In November 1919 he dominated the Delhi Khilafat conference; moreover, he was elected president of a newly created organization of Indian *ulama*, the Jami'at-i-Ulama-i-Hind (Ulama Association of India).[10]

In 1924, when ibn Saud and his Revolutionary Islamist Wahhabi warriors overran Makkah and Madinah, Abdul Bari perceived a new threat to the holy cities, coming for the first time not from European Christian colonialists but from fanatical coreligionists. In response, Abdul Bari founded yet another pan-Islamic organization, the Anjuman-i-Khuddam-i-Haramain (Guardians of Islam's Holiest Shrines). He also led peaceful demonstrations decrying the Wahhabi conquest of Makkah and Madinah. Meanwhile, colonialist threats receded further, and Abdul Bari turned to resisting the growing Hindu revival fueled by Gandhi.[11]

When the Khilafat Movement was at its peak, in the summer of 1920, a segment of the Traditionalist Islamist *ulama* began the Hijrat Movement, in which about fifty thousand devout Indian Muslims were persuaded by the *ulama* to abandon their homes and emigrate to the neighboring Muslim homeland of Afghanistan because India under British rule was no longer part of *dar al-Islam* (abode of Islam), whereas Afghanistan under the Muslim rule of Amir Amanullah was. Initially, the ruler, government, and people of Afghanistan warmly welcomed the refugees. Yet as the penniless refugees became a socioeconomic burden to Afghanistan, Amanullah's armed forces sealed the Afghan border. By autumn 1920 many of the Indian Muslim pilgrims had returned to India disillusioned, alienated, and angry.[12]

The Traditionalist Deobandis also displayed political activism in their support of the Khilafat Movement and opposition to the Pakistan Movement. Their actions, which truly represented a political reaction to specific imperialist, Revolutionary Islamist, and Hindu fundamentalist threats, were consistent with their otherwise apolitical Traditionalist Islamist orientation.[13] In fact, during the 1980 celebrations commemorating the fourteen-hundredth anniversary of Islam, Prime Minister Indira Gandhi and other eminent Hindu politicians paid glowing tribute to the Deobandi school for its world-renowned scholarship, exemplary patriotism, and

---

[10]Ibid., p. 92; Robinson, *Separatism among Indian Muslims*, p. 420; Robinson, "Ulama of Farangi Mahall," pp. 157–158; Leonard Binder, *Religion and Politics in Pakistan* (Berkeley and Los Angeles: University of California Press, 1961), p. 53; Qureishi, "The Ulama of British India," p. 41; The Khilafat Movement was a peaceful protest campaign started less than a year after the end of World War I (1914–1918) by a segment of the Muslim population in India attempting to influence the British government to preserve the authority of the Ottoman/Turkish sultan as caliph of Islam. The movement gained strength when it allied itself with Mahatma Gandhi's Indian nationalist non-cooperation movement in 1919. The movement declined and ended when Mustafa Kemal—a Turkish military hero who was later reverentially called "Ataturk" or "Father of the Turks" for laying the foundations of modern Turkey—assumed power in Turkey (1921) and formally ended the Ottoman Sultanate (1922), abolishing the Caliphate in 1924 (see Gail Minault, *The Khilafat Movement: Religious Symbolism and Political Mobilization in India* (Oxford: Oxford University Press, 1982)).

[11]Robinson, *Separatism among Indian Muslims*, p. 420.

[12]See Qureishi, "Ulama of British India," p. 41; Binder, *Religion and Politics in Pakistan*, pp. 52–57; Kramer, "Political Islam," p. 33; Stanley Wolpert, *Roots of Confrontation in South Asia* (Oxford: Oxford University Press, 1982), pp. 94–95.

[13]Ziya-ul-Hasan Faruqi, *The Deoband School and the Demand for Pakistan* (Bombay, India: Asia Publishing House, 1963).

significant contribution to the cultural mosaic of a pluralistic society. The Indian government also issued a thirty-paisa (three-cent) stamp in honor of the Dar al-Ulum of Deoband.[14] No Revolutionary Islamist organization crusading for a puritanical Islamic system could have been so honored by the Indian government.

The Traditionalist Islamists observed limits in their pursuit of goals and, conversely, their goals were limited. Even politicized, the Traditionalist Islamists at heart lacked the devastating and destabilizing political agenda of their crusading Revolutionary Islamist coreligionists.

Opponents of *Ijtihad,* Proponents of *Taqlid*

Most Sunni Traditionalist Islamists reject *ijtihad* (which encourages independent thought in legal matters) and accept the dogma of *taqlid* (unquestioning conformity to prior legal rulings). For the Traditionalist Islamist, *ijtihad* represents an attack on traditional values and practices and therefore undermines Islam. Author Leonard Binder voices the belief of many Traditionalist Islamists:

> To alter the decision that has been accepted for ages would be to deny the eternal immutability of God's law and to admit that earlier jurists erred would be to destroy the idea of the continuity of the divine guidance of the Muslim community.[15]

The Farangi Mahallis, the Barelvis, and the Deobandis of the Indian subcontinent all subscribed to *taqlid* and rejected *ijtihad*. For instance, it was their rigid adherence to the *fiqh* (Islamic jurisprudence) of Abu Hanifa (699–769 CE), the founder of the Hanafi sect of Sunni Islam, that made famous Deobandi theologians, like Muhammad Qasim Nanautawi (d. 1879), resent and attempt to undermine the efforts of Shah Waliullah to create an interjuristic discipline of Islamic theology and law.[16]

The Revolutionary Islamists and Shi'ah Traditionalist Islamists, in contrast, believe that Muslims schooled in the Qur'an and *hadith* should practice *ijtihad* and not blindly conform to legal judgments a millennium old. They argue that Revolutionary Islamists are loathe to accept unquestioningly any practice, tradition, or judgment coming after the classical era of Islam.

Fatalists

The Traditionalist Islamists, like all Muslims, believe that God is omnipotent, omnipresent, just, and merciful; a person is merely an *abd* (obedient servant) of God, and only God retains absolute sovereignty over His creation; God's commands are always just and right; and all determinations of right and wrong are

---

[14]Metcalf, *Islamic Revival in British India*, pp. 14–15.

[15]Binder, *Religion and Politics in Pakistan*, p. 20 (further elaboration on pp. 24, 26, 42–43, 74); Freeland Abbott, *Islam and Pakistan* (Ithaca, N.Y.: Cornell University Press, 1968), pp. 89, 225.

[16]Ahmad, *Islamic Modernism in India and Pakistan*, p. 107.

embodied in the Qur'an. However, carrying these beliefs to the logical extreme, many Traditionalist Islamists believe that to allow a person freedom to decide questions of right and wrong trespasses against God's omnipotence.[17] A quotation from Abul Hasin Ali bin Ismael al-Ashari (873–935 CE), the Iraqi-born *alim* (Islamic scholar) who spearheaded a Traditionalist Islamist movement, vividly illustrates this point:

> We believe that God created everything by bidding it 'Be' [*kun*] . . . that nothing on earth, whether a fortune or misfortune, comes to be save through God's will; that things exist through God's fiat; . . . and that the deeds of the creatures are created by Him and predestined by Him; . . . that the creatures can create nothing but are rather created themselves; . . . We . . . profess faith in God's decree and fore-ordination.[18]

Thus to al-Ashari, expressing even the concept of chance, of randomness, or of bad luck was unpardonable blasphemy, since "this was to imply that an event might occur otherwise than the will of God, or that the will of God was unjust. The correct response was an immovable claim and a reference to **kismet** [fate] or **taqdir** [destiny]."[19]

The Traditionalist *ulama*'s rigid viewpoint emphasizing *taqlid* and predestination was caused in part by the Asharite movement, which gained ascendency during the reign of the Abbasid caliph al-Mutawakkil (847–861 CE). The movement impeded the revision and reform of Islamic theological law and tradition, often branding revisionists and reformists as heretics, *kafirs* (infidels), or enemies of Islam. Furthermore, it stifled creative and critical thought and action among the public while sanctioning corruption, nepotism, and tyranny as demonstrated by its leaders. The Traditionalist Islamists, believing in predestination, reasoned, "It is God's eternal decree that these men must rule; all their actions are inevitable and destined by God. . . . A believer could not very well rebel against that."[20] They expressed similar dogmatic attitudes after the destruction of Baghdad, the center of Islamic knowledge and learning, in 1258 CE by the Mongols under Hulaku. By considering humankind insignificant and powerless, the Traditionalist Islamists undermined the self-esteem of the Muslim people and dampened their spirit of dynamism and creativity. Belief that humans could not conquer and control their environment led the Traditionalist Islamists, often considered as the spiritual guides of the Muslim community, to adopt a passive and scholarly orientation. In moments of crisis or during distressing times, they encouraged the *ummah* to seek refuge and spiritual strength in the omnipotence and generosity of God. This stance was challenged by the gross corruption and hypocrisy of politics and the

---

[17]Peter Hardy, "Traditional Muslim Views of the Nature of Politics," in C. H. Phillips, ed., *Politics and Society in India* (London: George Allen and Unwin, 1963), pp. 32–33, 36.

[18]Ibid.

[19]Richard H. Pfaff, "Technicism vs. Traditionalism: The Developmental Dialectic in the Middle East," in Carl Leiden, ed., *The Conflict of Traditionalism and Modernism in the Muslim Middle East* (Austin: University of Texas Press, 1966), p. 104.

[20]Ignaz Goldzihar, *Introduction to Islamic Theology and Law*, trans. Andras and Ruth Hamori (Princeton, N.J.: Princeton University Press, 1981), p. 76; D. S. Roberts, *Islam: A Concise Introduction* (San Francisco: Harper and Row, 1981), pp. 48–49.

decline of central authority. The Traditionalist Islamists rationalized that the well-developed and appealing religion of Islam could easily survive the loss of power manifested in Muslim rulers and the depoliticization of Islam.[21] In disengaging themselves from active politics and the worldly temptations of power and wealth, the Traditionalist Islamists sincerely believed that they were protecting the integrity and cherished ideals of Islam. Thus they tolerated the de facto separation of "church and state," though no such idea existed in Islamic theory or history. Sometimes they were co-opted and reduced to impotent passivity by shrewd rulers.

Traditionalist Islamists' apolitical and fatalistic orientation was manifested in the Farangi Mahallis, with the notable exception of Abdul Bari. Most of the time the Barelvis had a similar orientation, though they became political with their involvement in the Pakistan Movement from 1940 to 1947, in the 1968–1969 anti–Ayub Khan movement in Pakistan, and in the *Nizam-i-Mustafa* (Islamic Order of Prophet Muhammad) movement against Prime Minister Zulfikar Ali Bhutto's Pakistani regime in summer 1977. Finally, the Deobandis had a similar apolitical and fatalistic orientation, with the exception of their involvement in the Khilafat Movement and their opposition to the Pakistan Movement, to Ayub Khan in the spring of 1969, and to Zulfikar Ali Bhutto in the summer of 1977.

Fatalism by Traditionalist Islamist standards cannot be reconciled with activism. To accept God's will is to take no action opposing it but rather to submit fully. The Revolutionary Islamists, however, reject this interpretation of predestination. They argue instead that God specifically enjoined Muslims to fight injustice, thus laying the foundation for *jihad, ijtihad*, and political and social activism. While Revolutionary Islamists also believe in the ultimate authority of God over all things and in all matters, they insist that God invested humanity with free will—to choose between right and wrong, belief and disbelief. The Traditionalist Islamists, in contrast, generally reject "worldly" political activity as unseemly and un-Islamic. Nevertheless, when Islam is attacked or when Revolutionary Islamists spark Islamic revivalist movements and revolutions, Traditionalist Islamists will not stand idly by but will protect and defend the *ummah* from aggression.

Opponents of Modernization

Traditionalists are often learned scholars of Islamic theology, law, and civilization who lead austere and pious lives. They can be spellbinding in their extemporaneous renditions of the Qur'an or the sayings of Prophet Muhammad, his **Sahabah** (companions), and many Islamic theologians and jurists throughout Islamic history. Traditionalists impress Muslims with their detailed knowledge of the lives and accomplishments of Prophet Muhammad and the major figures in Islamic history. They also have an authoritative grasp of *fiqh*.

Nevertheless, these respectable scholars have serious limitations when viewed in a contemporary light. They are often naive, if not ignorant, of modern natural and

---

[21]S. Alam Khundmiri, "A Critical Examination of Islamic Traditionalism," *Islam and the Modern Age*, Vol. 2, No. 2 (May 1971), p. 7.

social sciences. If they read modern scientific theories at all, they either accept or reject these themes according to the Qur'an and the *sunnah*. Traditionalist Islamists are generally oblivious to the complexities, institutions, and processes of modern governments and international relations in an interdependent world—and they do not perceive this ignorance as a shortcoming. They are convinced that the perfect religion of Islam, in which they are well versed, reveals all truths and can help to resolve all internal crises and external threats facing Muslim societies around the world.[22]

Despite huge differences, both Revolutionary Islamists and Traditionalist Islamists are strong opponents of modernization, secularization, and Westernization, all of which they attribute to the *dar al-harb* and the enemies of Islam. Given their narrow, almost parochial attitudes, the Traditionalist Islamists, like the Revolutionary Islamists and even many Modernist Islamists, express serious concern about the increasing secularization of the critically important educational, legal, economic, and social realms of their Muslim societies. Secularization to them is tantamount to the elimination of the divine *shariah*; they believe secularization will eventually erode the Muslim community's very foundations. In the educational sphere, Traditionalist Islamists, like Revolutionary Islamists, demand the generous funding of *madrassahs*; advocate syllabi that contain mainly Islamic disciplines and few, if any, modern Western sciences; and promote the segregation of the sexes and extreme modesty in dress in educational institutions. In the legal sphere, Traditionalist Islamists demand rigid adherence to their respective schools of *fiqh*. They want an Islamic constitution drawing heavily upon the Qur'an, the *sunnah*, and the *shariah* and the establishment of Islamic law courts presided over by *qadhis* and based on the *shariah*. In the economic sphere, they advocate the institution of the *zakat* and *ushr* taxes, as well as the prohibition of *riba* (usury). Unlike the Revolutionary Islamists, however, the Traditionalist Islamists do not engage in a sustained political crusade for these beliefs.

In the social realm, Traditionalist Islamists, like Revolutionary Islamists, encourage monogamy while at the same time allow Muslims who meet certain criteria to have up to four wives. In keeping with their belief in the timelessness of morality, Traditionalist Islamists categorically reject the right of any Muslim to tamper with the practice of polygamy.[23] Like most Revolutionary Islamists, the

---

[22]Ibid., p. 11.

[23]Most Modernist Islamists urge severely restricting polygamy, while Muslim Secularists advocate abolishing polygamy on the grounds that there no longer exists (for all practical purposes) the two major reasons for early Islamic condoning of polygamy. First, when Islam began, there was a widely prevalent practice among Arab men to marry a number of women at the same time. Prophet Muhammad realized that he could not ban the practice completely and still make Islam attractive to the majority, so he restricted polygamy by limiting husbands to four wives, with the important qualification that all wives should be treated with complete equality, justice, and compassion. Second, during the early years of Islam there were numerous tribal and religious wars in which many men lost their lives, leaving numerous widows and orphans without husbands and fathers to support them. All Muslim Secularists, and even many Modernist Islamists, conclude that because these two reasons are gone and because they believe it is humanly impossible for any man to treat four wives equally, the practice of polygamy should be abolished.

Traditionalist Islamists promote the segregation of the sexes. Both Islamists groups enjoin women to adopt **purdah** (veiling, segregation, and seclusion). Furthermore, the Traditionalist Islamists and the Revolutionary Islamists believe that the court testimony given by one man is equal to that of two women.

The Traditionalist Islamists manifest a detached attitude in their reluctance to adapt Islamic viewpoints to contemporary eras. A significant number of Muslims frown upon this detachment and reluctance to change and believe that this fatal flaw in Traditionalist Islamists' worldview has contributed to the stagnation of the Muslim world, as well as to the impotence of the *ummah* on the world stage. The Traditionalist Islamists forcefully reply that Islam has not, cannot, and should never change, for it is founded on God's comprehensive and immutable words and laws. Consequently, they argue that immutability is not the cause of the Muslim world's decline, but that the problem arises from the Muslim world's inherent imperfections and from Muslims' failure to steadfastly follow the letter and spirit of the religion.

Summary

The emphasis given by Traditionalist Islamists to Islamic scholarship, teaching, and preaching, as well as their firm belief in *taqlid* and predestination, often gives them a passive and apolitical orientation. Thus, few Traditionalist Islamists are in the vanguard of Islamic revivals. However, Islamic revivals often spark them to abandon temporarily their passivity and to try to leverage the revival toward their theocratic and theocentric orientation.

Internet Sites

http://www.sunnah.org/articles/Imam_raza_ahmed_khan.htm

http://www.rediff.com/news/1998/jan/21maha.htm

http://www.milligazette.com/Archives/01072001/28.htm

http://www.milligazette.com/Archives/01072001/28.htm

http://www.al-islam.org/beliefs/practices/taqlid.html

http://www.al-shia.com/html/eng/books/taqlid_meaning_and_reality/taqlid meaning-and-reality.htm

http://www.people.virginia.edu/~aas/article/article5.htm

http://65.193.50.117/index.php?ln=eng&ds=qa&lv=browse&QR=7216&misc=& offset=0&sort=d

http://www.al-islam.org/begin/intro/rahim.html

http://www.hf.uib.no/smi/paj/vikor.html

http://www.ummah.org.uk/khoei/shia/author.htm

CHAPTER FIVE

Modernist Islamists

The third category of Islamists or Islamic Revivalists are the Modernist Islamists, who are referred to variously as "adaptationists," "apologists," "syncretists," and "revisionists." Modernist Islamists are devout and knowledgeable Muslims whose mission is threefold: first, "to define Islam by bringing out the fundamentals in a rational and liberal manner"; second, "to emphasize, among others, the basic ideals of Islamic brotherhood, tolerance and social justice"; and third, to interpret the teaching of Islam in such a way as to bring out its dynamic character in the context of the intellectual and scientific progress of the modern world.[1]

In contrast to Traditionalist Islamists, concerned with maintaining the status quo, and to the puritanical Revolutionary Islamists, Modernist Islamists sincerely endeavor to reconcile differences between traditional religious doctrine and secular scientific rationalism, between unquestioning faith and reasoned logic, and between the continuity of Islamic tradition and modernity.

Ardent Opponents of *Taqlid*, Vigorous Proponents of *Ijtihad*

Modernist Islamists, like Revolutionary Islamists, vehemently disagree with Sunni Traditionalist Islamists, who believe in the dogma of *taqlid*, which implies the unquestioning and rigid adherence to one of the four schools of Sunni *fiqh* developed in the postclassical period. The Modernist Islamists attribute the decline of

---

[1]Cited in *Muslim World*, Vol. 50, No. 2 (April 1960), p. 155; also cited in Donald Eugene Smith, "Emerging Patterns of Religion and Politics," in Donald Eugene Smith, ed., *South Asian Politics and Religion* (Princeton, N.J.: Princeton University Press, 1966), pp. 32–33.

Islamic culture and power mainly to the inhibition of independent, creative, and critical thought and to the lack of vigorous discussion about Islamic laws and issues that resulted from what Traditionalists consider the closure of "the gates of *ijtihad*" a millenium ago. Convinced that Islam is a progressive, dynamic, and rational religion, Modernist Islamists denounce the inhibiting dogma of *taqlid*. Consequently, they advocate an unconditional reopening of "the gates of *ijtihad*," thus facilitating the reinterpretation and reformulation of Islamic laws in the light of modern thought. Modernist Islamists reinforce their appeal for the restoration and exercise of *ijtihad* with Qur'anic quotations: "And to those who exert we show the Path" (29:69). Additional evidence comes from Qur'anic verses stating that "God would never change His favor that He conferred on a people until they changed what was within themselves" (8:53) and "Verily, God changes not what is in a people until they change what is in themselves" (22:10). Modernists insist these verses indicate that Islam is not a confining and inhibiting force but an inspiration and spur to progress. Indeed, dynamic change in Islam is not only possible but desirable. Therefore, according to most Modernist Islamists, Islamic laws must be carefully revised and be flexible and adaptable enough to incorporate modern political, economic, social, cultural, and legal conditions.

Jamal ad-Din al-Afghani (1838–1897), considered by many the father of Islamic Modernism or Modernist Islamism, was extremely critical of the Traditionalist Islamist *ulama* who believed in *taqlid* and who discouraged any new and creative thought. Convinced that the medieval mentality of Traditionalist Islamists was primarily responsible for the decline of Muslim power and influence in the world,[2] al-Afghani wrote:

> The strangest thing of all is that our ulema in these days have divided knowledge into two categories: one they call Muslim knowledge and the other European. . . . Because of this, they forbid others to learn some useful knowledge. They just do not understand that knowledge which is a noble thing, has no connection with any particular group. . . . How strange it is that Muslims study with great delight those sciences that are ascribed to Aristotle, as if Aristotle were a Muslim author. However, if an idea is related to Galileo, Newton, or Kepler, they consider it unbelief. . . . In fact . . . when they forbid [modern] knowledge with a view of safeguarding the Islamic religion . . . they themselves are the enemies of religion. Islam is the closest religion to knowledge and learning and there is no contradiction between [modern] knowledge and the basic principles of Islam.[3]

Thus, according to al-Afghani, "intellectual decline first penetrated" through the ranks of the influential *ulama*, who were narrowly educated in the outdated, limited, and archaic Islamic studies imparted in *madrassahs* and who were unexposed to the outside world. Consequently, "through them destruction has fallen upon the entire nation."[4]

---

[2]Rashid Ahmad (Jullundhri), "Pan-Islamism and Pakistan: Afghani and Nasser," *Scrutiny*, Vol. 1, No. 2 (July–December 1975), pp. 31–32.

[3]Ibid., p. 32; Mortimer, *Faith and Power: The Politics of Islam* (New York: Vintage, 1982), p. 121.

[4]Rashid Ahmad, "Pan-Islamism and Pakistan," p. 32.

BOX 5.1   Sayyid Jamal ad-Din al-Afghani

The Father of Islamic Modernism

Sayyid Jamal ad-Din al-Afghani (1838–1897) was born into a Shi'ah family in the village of Asadabad in northwest Persia. Throughout his life, however, al-Afghani concealed his Persian Shi'ah origins and intimated that he was born in predominantly Sunni Afghanistan.

In his studies he became familiar with a variety of Islamic disciplines and supported the **Usuli** school of thought in Persia, which favored the use of *ijtihad* to develop the Islamic theory of jurisprudence. The Traditionalist *ulama* of the **Akhbari** school, however, opposed the Usuli school, holding that traditional judgments were adequate.

Al-Afghani traveled from Iraq to Afghanistan, India, Egypt, Turkey, France, Britain, and Russia. His travels gave him a cosmopolitan perspective. He spent eight years in Egypt as an instructor at Al-Azhar in Cairo (1871–1879), where he met Muhammad Abduh, who became his most prominent pupil. In his teaching, Al-Afghani emphasized the threat of Western imperialism, the need to unify the *ummah*, and the necessity of constitutional limits on political power. Al-Afghani also introduced his students to Western intellectual thought and scientific achievement.

Although a critic of the *ulama* and the archaic and obsolete Islamic education it provided in *madrassahs*, al-Afghani was also critical of Muslim apologists and pro-Western Modernist Islamists who promoted Western education (like Sir Sayyid Ahmad Khan). Formal and secular Western education, al-Afghani believed, made Muslims insensitive to the injustices of pro-Western rulers. He also felt it fostered elitism and excessive individuality while promoting a materialistic lifestyle.

However, al-Afghani did not denounce nationalism as un-Islamic. He felt that pan-Arabism, pan-Islamism, and local nationalism were all appropriate ideologies, provided they promoted Muslim self-determination and solidarity. Al-Afghani returned to Persia in the late 1880s, but he was soon expelled for opposing the tobacco concessions granted by the Persian monarchy to British businessmen. While in Iraq, Al-Afghani continued his opposition to the concessions. His efforts were vindicated in 1892, when the Iranian monarchy canceled the concessions. Al-Afghani's opposition inspired a revolutionary fervor in Persia that eventually led to the constitution of 1907.

Al-Afghani's primary goal was to establish pan-Islamic regimes free from imperialism and colonialism. He looked forward to the reconciliation between sects within Islam, the rebirth of Islamic nationalism, and the development of an Islamic confederation ruled by a devout, progressive, just, and tolerant caliph. This, al-Afghani reasoned, would more effectively counter imperialism than a plethora of divided nation-states.

http://www.cis-ca.org/voices/a/afghni.htm
http://www.nmhschool.org/tthornton/jamal_ad.htm
http://www.muslimphilosophy.com/rep/H048.htm

Al-Afghani, in common with most subsequent Modernists, attributed the dynamic vitality, strength, progress, and prosperity of the West to its freer use of reason and its encouragement of scientific and technological processes that the impoverished and weak Muslim world refused to adopt.[5] Therefore, al-Afghani, like most Modernist Islamists, strongly recommended acquiring Western learning, technology, and services, as long as borrowing from the West was selective and served the basic needs and aspirations of the Muslim people. In this undertaking, which he believed would raise all Muslims' standard of living, al-Afghani struggled to initiate an Islamic reformation similar to the successful Christian Reformation sparked by Martin Luther.[6]

The seeds of *ijtihad* planted by al-Afghani in his most prominent Egyptian student and ardent follower, Muhammad Abduh (1849–1905), bore fruit when the latter assumed positions of great official religious responsibility and influence in Egypt. Like his mentor, Abduh made a dedicated and sustained effort to liberate Islam from the dogma of *taqlid*. He insisted that Muslims could improve their lives and their society only by returning to its source, the Qur'an, and by carefully studying this source in the light of reason and rationality. He indicated that the Qur'an gives all Muslims the right to differ with even the *ulama*, if the latter were unreasonable or irrational. He justified this stance by maintaining that "Islam had liberated man from the authority of the clergy; it has put him face to face with God and has taught him not to rely on any intercession."[7] He further said:

> The supposed superiority of the ancients was a mere pretext to keep intact the absurdities of the past, and such a pretext of infallibility must necessarily mean the thwarting of human intellect.[8]

Reacting to the uninspiring and stultifying Islamic education based on rote learning that he had received in *madrassahs*, Abduh constantly exhorted Muslims to approach problems in the true spirit of Islam through analysis, reason, and logic. In one instance, he declared that "when reason and [Islamic] tradition are in conflict, the right of decision rests with reason."[9] On another occasion, he said:

> Of all religions, Islam is almost the only one that blames those who believe without proofs, and rebukes those who follow opinions without having any certainty. . . .

---

[5] Albert Hourani, *Arabic Thought in the Liberal Age, 1798–1939*, 2nd ed. (Oxford: Oxford University Press, 1979), p. 109.

[6] Nikki R. Keddie, *Sayyid Jamal ad-Din al-Afghani: A Political Biography* (Berkeley and Los Angeles: University of California Press, 1972), p. 141.

[7] Quoted in Osman Amin, "Some Aspects of Religious Reform in the Muslim Middle East," in Carl Leiden, ed., *The Conflict of Traditionalism and Modernism in the Muslim Middle East* (Austin: University of Texas Press, 1966), p. 91.

[8] Mahmudul Haq, *Muhammad Abduh: A Study of a Modern Thinker of Egypt* (Aligarh, India: Institute of Islamic Studies, Aligarh Muslim University, 1978), p. 181.

[9] Muhammad Abduh, *al-Islam wa'l-nasraniya ma'af-'ilm wa'l-madaniya*, Cairo, n.d. [posthumously printed], p. 56; also quoted in Ignaz Goldziher, *Introduction to Islamic Theology and Law*, trans. Andras and Ruth Hamori (Princeton, N.J.: Princeton University Press, 1981), p. 110.

Whenever Islam speaks, it speaks to reason . . . and the holy texts proclaim that happiness consists in the right use of reason.[10]

Because of Abduh's emphasis on reason and rationality, he considered Islam and constructive science the twin offspring of reason, which "God gave us to guide us in the right path."[11]

Muhammad Rashid Rida (1865–1935), an Egyptian disciple of Abduh, vigorously pursued his mentor's mission for Islamic reform. He urged the *ulama* to come together, to intelligently utilize *ijtihad*, and to produce a comprehensive revision of Islamic laws based on the Qur'an and *hadith*. He wanted the *ummah* and Muslim countries to progress and acquire the positive aspects of European civilization, and he exhorted Muslims to reclaim their glorious heritage. Islamic civilization had sown the seeds that subsequently flowered in the European Renaissance.[12]

The famous Indian Modernist Sir Sayyid Ahmad Khan (1817–1898) maintained that a revitalized Islam was indispensible to the intellectual, economic, social, and political progress of Muslims. Sir Sayyid, like other Modernists, dismissed the contention of Sunni Traditionalists that the "gates of *ijtihad*" had been eternally sealed a millennium earlier, and he vehemently denounced the inhibiting force of *taqlid*. Sir Sayyid declared:

If people do not shun blind adherence, if they do not seek that light which can be found in the Qur'an and the indisputable *Hadith* and do not adjust religion to the science of today, Islam will become extinct in India.[13]

Although Sir Sayyid was a devout Sunni, his idealization of *ijtihad* led him to accept the Shi'ah belief that every generation must have its *mujtahids* (Islamic scholars with authority to exercise *ijtihad*), with one significant reservation: *ijtihad* was not the exclusive right of a privileged few *ulama* but the right of all devout and enlightened believers to interpret the Qur'an in the context of prevailing circumstances. The overwhelming benefit derived from diverse opinions outweighed possible errors of judgment and enhanced Muslim self-esteem.[14]

Another well-known Modernist Islamist of South Asia, Muhammad Iqbal (1873–1938), admired al-Afghani's ideas and tireless efforts for betterment of the *ummah* and criticized the Traditionalist Islamists for debating issues of abstract Islamic theory that had little relevance to the realities of life. He also scathingly criticized them for their belief that scientific, technical, and technological knowledge corrupt and weaken Muslim society and undermine the faith. Iqbal pointed out that this misrepresented Islam, since there had been numerous Muslim scientists in the heyday of Islamic power who did not leave Islam but were inspired

---

[10]Osman Amin, "Some Aspects of Religious Reform in the Muslim Middle East," p. 91.

[11]Ibid.

[12]Albert Hourani, *Arabic Thought in the Liberal Age*, p. 236; D. E. Smith, *Religion and Political Development*, pp. 216–217.

[13]Bashir Ahmad Dar, *Religious Thought of Sayyid Ahmad Khan* (Lahore, Pakistan: Sheikh Muhammad Ashraf, 1957), pp. 113, 247–248, 264.

[14]Ibid.

BOX 5.2   Muhammad Abduh

Preeminent Muslim Modernist of Egypt

Muhammad Abduh (1849–1905) was born in Lower Egypt into a lower-middle-class farming family. In 1862 he started school at the Ahmadi Mosque in Tanta. He was disappointed in his courses of instruction and briefly left school. During this period, Abduh's great-uncle, Shaykh Darwish, instilled in Abduh an appetite for Sufism. Abduh returned to school in Tanta, now motivated to acquire a religious education. Within a year, Abduh left for Al-Azhar in Cairo, where he studied for the next four years.

In 1871 Abduh became associated with al-Afghani and abandoned his absorption in the passive and mystical realm of Sufism. With al-Afghani as his mentor, Abduh championed religious reform. In 1874 he began to write newspaper and journal articles and books. In his writings, he criticized the traditionalist *ulama* for their dogmatic and doctrinaire stand on Islamic theology and jurisprudence. Abduh also emphasized the need for Muslims to study modern science and Western progress.

After obtaining his degree, Abduh taught at Al-Azhar, where he continued to promote reform. In 1882, however, Abduh was suspected of involvement in a nationalist revolt against British and French influence in Egyptian politics and was exiled. Within a few years, Abduh joined al-Afghani in Paris. The two published a strongly pan-Islamic, modernist, and anti-imperialist newspaper called *Al-Urwat Al-Wuthqa (The Indissoluble Link).* The paper was soon banned, and al-Afghani and Abduh were exiled from France.

In 1889 Abduh promised the Egyptian authorities to work within the system to bring about reform and to eschew revolution, and he was allowed to return home. Abduh's ideas grew in popularity and he was made grand **mufti** (supreme religious guide) of Egypt. In this and other positions, Abduh introduced a number of significant reforms, including a reinterpretation of the Qur'an and the *hadith* in light of modern developments, a reformation of higher education, and protection of Islam against Western influences.

Throughout his life, Abduh also sought to liberate Muslims from the inhibiting doctrine of *taqlid,* urging them to interpret the Qur'an and *hadith* on the basis of reason and rationality. Abduh also encouraged Muslims to read not only the classical Arabic works of theology and jurisprudence but also the works of Western scientists and intellectuals, which, Abduh insisted, were compatible with Islam.

Muhammad Abduh promoted many of al-Afghani's ideas, although Abduh's manner was more moderate, sustained, and effective. In due course, the Islamic reforms that he supported helped adapt Islam to a rapidly changing world. Thus, Abduh shares with al-Afghani the status as one of the two parents of Islamic modernism.

http://www.cqpress.com/context/articles/epr_muhammadabduh.html
http://www.nmhschool.org/tthornton/muhammad_abduh.htm
http://www.muslimphilosophy.com/rep/H049.htm

■
BOX 5.3   Al-Azhar

The *masjid*-university of Al-Azhar in Cairo, Egypt, is one of the oldest and most prestigious Islamic centers of learning in the world. It was first built as a *masjid* on the orders of the Fatimid caliph al-Muizz between 970 and 972 CE and was formally organized as an Islamic university by 988 CE. After the Mongol destruction of a number of Islamic educational institutions in Iraq, Al-Azhar became the focus of attention for its scholarship and received generous grants and endowments from Muslims all over the world. It also became the bastion of Traditionalist Islamism, with its conservative and Traditionalist *ulama*, and sanctioned a syllabus of medieval Islamic studies. Starting in the late nineteenth century, some Modernist Islamist *ulama*, the most prominent of whom was Muhammad Abduh, tried to reform the curriculum despite formidable opposition. That reform was greatly accelerated by Gamal Abdel Nasser's secular socialist regime in 1961, when the syllabus was modernized, faculties of modern social and natural science were added, and a new campus was built. Under Egyptian government patronage, Al-Azhar began to send scores of Traditionalist *ulama* and teachers of the Arabic language to other Muslim countries and to receive thousands of foreign students from all over the world. The student body has been coeducational since 1962.

http://lexicorient.com/m.s/egypt/azhar.htm

---

by it, helped the *ummah*, and spread Islamic influence.[15] According to Iqbal, it was Islam's dynamism that had made it a potent force in the world. However, he attributed both the decline of Islam as a dynamic faith and the decline of the Muslim world in recent centuries largely to the Traditionalist Islamists' insistence on stultifying conformity and orthodoxy. At times he denounced the conservative *mullah*: "For the shortsighted [and] narrow-minded *mullah* the concept of religion is to brand others as *kafirs*."[16] The *mullah's* obscurantist worldview served no other function than "sowing corruption, perverseness and disruption in the name of God."[17]

Iqbal, like the Modernist Islamists that preceded him, did not consider the *shariah* sacrosanct, since it had been formulated by fallible *ulama* three centuries after the death of Prophet Muhammad.

He appealed to devout and educated Muslims schooled in Islam and modern Western ideas to apply *ijtihad* judiciously to revise the *shariah* in the light of the Qur'an and *sunnah* and to meet the requirements of contemporary Muslim societies.[18] According to Iqbal, *ijtihad* should reflect the opinion of society and meet

---

[15]Allama Muhammad Iqbal, *The Reconstruction of Religious Thought in Islam* (Lahore, Pakistan: Sheikh Muhammad Ashraf, 1977), pp. 9–14.

[16]Quoted in Masud-ul-Hassan, *Life of Iqbal*, Vol. 2 (Lahore, Pakistan: Ferozsons, 1978, p. 386.

[17]Ibid.

[18]Freeland K. Abbott, *Islam and Pakistan* (Ithaca, N.Y.: Cornell University Press, 1968), pp. 166–167.

■

BOX 5.4   Muhammad Rashid Rida (1865–1935)

Muhammad Rashid Rida was born near Tripoli in present-day Lebanon in 1865. He received a traditional religious education and then attended an Islamic school founded by scholars who felt it important to combine religious learning with a thorough knowledge of modern science. Rida excelled as a student of Islam, the natural sciences, and languages. During his education he was increasingly inspired to reform what he perceived to be the declining state of Islam.

While still a young man, Rida joined the **Salafiyyah** movement, led by Jamal al-Din al-Afghani and Muhammad Abduh. Rida agreed with the movement's desire to reinvigorate Islam by resisting tyranny and foreign domination and by promoting Muslim solidarity and the adoption of modern sciences to improve the lives of all Muslims. In 1897 Rida joined Muhammad Abduh in Egypt and proved to be his most prolific disciple. Rida began publishing the magazine *Al-Manar (The Lighthouse),* in which he explained and elaborated upon the essential compatibility of modern science and Islam as well as the need to exercise *ijtihad* (independent judgment) in interpreting Islam to enable Muslims to adopt their faith to modern circumstances.

Unlike his mentor Abduh, however, Rida believed that Muslim Secularists posed a greater threat to Islam than the Traditionalist Islamists. He urged the *ulama*—Traditionalist, Revolutionary, and Modernist—to come together, undertake *jihad,* and produce a comprehensive revision of Islamic laws based on the Qur'an and *hadith* that would meet contemporary requirements. Rida dreamed of a Muslim world that could acquire the positive aspects of European civilization without westernization or secularization.

Rashid Rida supported the concept of a progressive, liberal, tolerant, and pluralist Islamic state in which non-Muslims would be treated equitably and justly. He even suggested the establishment of a "caliphate of necessity" to coordinate Muslim countries' efforts against foreign threats, and ultimately the restoration of a genuine caliphate with a wise, pious, honest, and just ruler who would consult a broad spectrum of *ulama* and use *ijtihad* before making decisions. Rida spent his life urging Muslims to acquire what he considered the most useful aspects of Western education—the sciences and technical skills. His emphasis on education as the key to real reform in the Muslim world was underscored by his establishment of a school to combine religious teachings with modern education. Later in his life, Rida emphasized the place of Arabs in his reform movement, feeling that they would represent the vanguard of a new and revitalized Muslim world. Rida's influence is still felt today. Rida was ultimately an important bridge between al-Afghani and Abduh and today's Modernist Islamists.

its interests.[19] Iqbal believed that if the Qur'an were interpreted in an enlightened, rational, and liberal way, it could awaken a person's higher consciousness in his or

---

[19]Riaz Hussain, *The Politics of Iqbal: A Study of His Political Thoughts and Actions* (Lahore, Pakistan: Islamic Book Services, 1977), p. 42.

BOX 5.5   Sir Sayyid Ahmad Khan

Torchbearer of Islamic Modernism in the Indian Subcontinent

Sayyid Ahmad Khan (1817–1898) was educated in a conservative, religious environment. When Sayyid Ahmad turned twenty-one, he went to work as a record writer in the East India Company's court of justice at Delhi. In 1841 he rose to the position of a subordinate judge. In 1846, at age twenty-nine, he began to seriously study the Qur'an, the *sunnah*, Islamic jurisprudence, and Arabic literature. He wrote several works, including a biography of Prophet Muhammad, a defense of the *sunnah*, and a denunciation of *bid'ah* (innovation).

After the suppression of the Indian Mutiny (1857–1858), Sayyid Ahmad Khan was saddened by British retaliation against disaffected Muslims in rebellious regions. Consequently, Sayyid Ahmad became an outspoken reformer of Indian Muslim conditions. Sir Sayyid dedicated his efforts to reducing the distrust between Indian Muslims and the British. Because he believed that the British had prevented communal strife and Hindu oppression of Muslims, he viewed British-Muslim rapprochement as possible. Sir Sayyid encouraged Muslims to abandon self-pity and futile denunciations of the British and to emulate the forward-thinking Hindus by learning English, acquiring Western education, seeking government jobs, and entering the professions of journalism, law, medicine, and engineering. In essence, he urged Muslims to adapt to the realities of modern times. In his six-volume commentary on the Qur'an, Sir Sayyid argued that Islam was a dynamic and flexible faith, fully compatible with science, technology, justice, freedom, and other enlightened and humane Western concepts.

Sir Sayyid's political and sociocultural accomplishments include encouraging Indian Muslims to learn English and study Western education, reducing British-Muslim tensions, discouraging Muslim cooperation with the Hindu-controlled All-India Congress Party, advocating and supporting separate Hindu and Muslim electorates, and promoting the "two-nation" separatist concept. Today he is credited as the initiator of India's Islamic Renaissance. Consequently, he is widely recognized as a Modernist Islamist and one of the founding fathers of Pakistan.

http://www.cis-ca.org/voices/k/syydkhn-mn.htm
http://www.slider.com/enc/1000/Ahmad_Khan_Sir_Sayyid.htm

---

her relationship with God and other human beings and assist humanity in the changing environment. Therefore, for a Modernist Islamist like Iqbal,

> Islam properly understood and rationally interpreted is not only capable of moving along with the progressive and evolutionary forces of life, but also of directing them into new and healthy channels in every epoch.[20]

---

[20]Donald E. Smith, ed., *Religion, Politics and Social Change in the Third World: A Sourcebook* (New York: Free Press, 1971), p. 73.

BOX 5.6   Allama Muhammad Iqbal

Islamic Modernist Poet and Philosopher

Allama Muhammad Iqbal (1873–1938) was born in Sialkot, India. In his youth, Iqbal was an Indian nationalist who advocated Hindu-Muslim cooperation and collaboration in a united India. However, by 1909, the thirty-six-year-old Iqbal began to consider the desirability of separating the Muslim community from the Hindu one. He feared that Indian Muslims were in danger of losing their distinct faith, culture, and identity in a predominantly Hindu nation and became convinced that the Muslims of the Indian subcontinent should have their own nation-state. He defined the possible boundaries of this proposed Muslim state as incorporating Punjab, the Northwest Frontier Province, Sindh, and Baluchistan.

Iqbal developed this concept further by describing a distinct Muslim nation based on a common language, history, race, and religion. Muhammad Ali Jinnah, the future leader of the Muslim League and of Pakistan, adopted the separatist ideas of Iqbal and of Sir Sayyid Ahmad Khan as his own and promoted the "two-nation theory," which became the justification for the new "Islamic State" of Pakistan. While Iqbal had traveled and studied in the West, he remained critical of Western secular education and preferred the traditional Islamic education taught in *madrassahs*. Although impressed by the achievements of Western technology and of Western intellect, he disliked the excessive competition, selfishness, materialism, hedonism, and deterioration of spiritual values found in the West. Moreover, he denounced Western secular education for its lack of humanism, which is inherent in Islam. In Iqbal's view, Western education tended to make Muslims feel Islamic culture was reactionary, backward, and inferior to Western culture and civilization. Iqbal believed that Western technological, economic, social, and political advancements were admirable but that secularization of Muslim societies was responsible for creating a spiritual void among Muslims and for promoting the decay and decline in the Muslim world.

Iqbal was a famous poet, a philosopher, and a founding father of Pakistan. He conceived of the Muslim state in 1930 and encouraged the Muslim League leadership to pursue the establishment of such a homeland, inspiring millions of Indian Muslims through his poetry. In this manner, Iqbal played a pivotal role in fostering an Islamic revival on the Indian subcontinent and creating Pakistan.

http://members.tripod.com/islamica/index.html
http://www.pak.org/person/iqbal.html
http://www.geocities.com/junaid_hassan25/iqbal.htm
http://www.merawatan.com/iqbal/
http://www.storyofpakistan.com/person.asp?perid=P007

Ali Shariati (1933–1977), the Shi'ah Modernist Islamist, Iranian sociologist and revolutionary Islamic ideologue, followed in the footsteps of al-Afghani and Iqbal by criticizing the Traditionalist Islamists in the ranks of the *ulama* for promoting the "old-fashioned way" of "believing without thinking" and discouraging new ideas.[21] When attacked by the conservative *ulama* as an agent of "Wahhabism," "communism," or "Christianity," he noted that moribund and stagnant organizations generally defended themselves by engaging in character assassination of the agents of change.[22] When the denunciation of Shariati by the conservative *ulama* continued, he retorted that

> Islam had abolished all forms of official mediation between God and man. . . . We have scholars of religion; they do not constitute official authorities. . . . Islam has no clergy; the word clergy [*ruhaniyun*] is recent, a borrowing from Christianity.[23]

In his lecture "Independent Reasoning and the Principle of Perpetual Revolution," Shariati implored *mujtahids* to recognize the contemporary world's changed realities and to meet the pressing demands with enlightened Islamic solutions. He understandably angered the *ulama* when he promoted the idea that devout Muslim laymen should not unquestioningly follow *mujtahids* but carefully assess the rationality of their opinions. In fact, by blindly following *mujtahids*, Shariati contended, they were committing the sin of *shirk* (polytheism), which greatly undermines Islam's most cardinal principle of *tawhid* (oneness of God).[24]

Reformers of Islamic Thought and Practice

In addition to being devout Muslims and knowledgeable about Islam, Modernist Islamists have been exposed to modern non-Islamic (especially Western) ideas in their formal and/or informal education, either in their homeland or abroad. Most Modernist Islamists, including al Afghani, Abduh, Sir Sayyid, and Shariati, were filled with new ideas and insights after exposure to the West and were eager to introduce them into their own societies. In this respect, they lived up to Iqbal's belief that "the West's typhoon turned a Muslim into a true Muslim [in the] way waves of the ocean nourish a pearl in the oyster."[25]

Consequently, unlike the Revolutionary Islamists and Traditionalist Islamists, Modernists do not fear or dislike Western ideas and practices. On the contrary, they welcome all non-Islamic ideas and practices that they consider beneficial to the progress and prosperity of Muslim societies. The resultant amalgamation of Islamic and Western ideas is then imaginatively synthesized to produce a reasonable and relevant reinterpretation of Islamic thought noted for its enlightened cosmopolitan, liberal, and realistic perspectives. This approach represents a tolerance

---

[21]Mangol Bayat-Philipp, "Shi'ism in Contemporary Iranian Politics: The Case of Ali Shariati," in Elie Kedourie and Sylvia G. Haim, ed., *Towards a Modern Iran: Studies in Thought, Politics and Society* (London: Frank Cass, 1980), p. 156.

[22]See Ali Shariate, *We and Iqbal* (Tehran: Husainiyeh Irshad, 1979), p. 207.

[23]Ali Shariati, *On the Sociology of Islam* (Berkeley: Mizan Press, 1979), p. 115.

[24]Abdulaziz Sachedina, "Ali Shariati: Ideologue of the Iranian Revolution," in John Esposito, ed., *Voices of Resurgent Islam* (Oxford: Oxford University Press, 1983), p. 203.

[25]Quoted in Hafeez Malik, *Sir Sayed Ahmad Khan and Muslim Modernism in India and Pakistan* (New York: Columbia University Press, 1980), p. 99.

BOX 5.7   Ali Shariati

The Intellectual Father of Modern Revolutionary Shi'ahs

Ali Shariati (1933–1977) was born in Persia. On graduating from school, he joined the Research Center for the Propagation of Islamic Teachings. There he wrote, lectured, and translated works from Arabic and French into Persian while earning a degree in Persian literature. During this period, he actively supported Prime Minister Muhammad Mossadegh (1951–1953). After the shah forced Mossadegh to resign, Shariati continued his political activities and in 1957 was incarcerated for a short time. In 1959 he traveled to Paris to pursue a doctorate in the sociology of religion at the Sorbonne. He remained politically active during this period, supporting the Algerian and Iranian student movements. After completing his doctorate in 1964, Shariati returned to Iran and was jailed for six months for his antimonarchical activities abroad. After his release, Shariati lectured, wrote, and taught at the University of Meshad. In 1965 he established the Husainiyeh Irshad Research Center, where he continued to lecture and write.

In 1973, the *shah*'s regime reacted to Shariati's antigovernment rhetoric by closing his research center and once again jailing him. Pressured strongly by domestic and international forces, the *shah*'s government released Shariati two years later but prohibited him from lecturing or publishing. Shariati fled Iran for London, where he died in 1977 under mysterious circumstances.

Shariati believed that Islam's central message was to fight for justice and freedom. For Shariati, Shi'ism represented not only a metaphysical religion or a dogmatic theology but a progressive and revolutionary political ideology that emphasized protest, revolution, holy war, and martyrdom—all for the sake of justice and brotherhood. Shariati also criticized the traditionalist *ulama* for promoting *taqlid*, which he argued was a form of *shirk*, undermining Islam's fundamental principle of *tawhid*. While Shariati proposed to integrate Islamic concepts with Western social sciences in an effort to make Islam relevant in the modern age, he nevertheless criticized Westernized Muslim Secularists in Iran and the Muslim world. Shariati argued that foreigners had politically and economically exploited Iran and the entire Muslim world.

Ali Shariati, considered by many Iranians as the intellectual father of the revolutionary Islam of 1979, was a lay Modernist Islamist inspired by the progressive Islamic theology and political activism of such men as Abu Dhar al-Ghaffari, Jamal ad-Din al-Afghani, and Muhammad Iqbal. Shariati integrated their ideas in so creative and dynamic a manner that he profoundly influenced Iranian youth, and his thoughts permeated the 1979 Islamic Revolution in Iran.

---

for diversity and a willingness to adjust rapidly to a changing environment, and thereby contributes to the emancipation of the individual Muslim and to the progress of Muslim societies.

While al-Afghani was teaching part-time at the Al-Azhar in Cairo for eight years (1871–1879), he introduced his pupils to Arabic translations of Western intellectual and scientific thought and achievement; encouraged them to examine, analyze, and critique whatever they read; motivated and trained them to write and publish articles on a wide variety of subjects in order to influence public opinion; and coached them in the art of public speaking.[26]

In 1892, when Muhammad Abduh joined Al-Azhar's Administrative Committee, he successfully reformed the curriculum by introducing several courses in the modern natural and social sciences.[27] In 1899, when Abduh became Egypt's Grand Mufti, he used his authority as Egypt's supreme official interpreter of the *shariah* to initiate the process of progressively revising Islamic law and reforming the entire court system. Three of his *fatwas* (authoritative legal rulings) were particularly famous. In one *fatwa*, he granted Muslims permission to eat the flesh of animals slain by Jews and Christians, because they were also "People of the Book." In another *fatwa*, he noted that, although the Qur'an permits a man to have as many as four wives, it does not endorse this practice. Further, as the Qur'an specifically enjoins husbands to treat all wives equally, Abduh felt this was a clear, albeit indirect, prohibition of polygamy, as it is impossible for any man to treat his wives equally. Similarly, Abduh strongly disapproved of the way *talak* (repudiation of marriage) was arbitrarily and unilaterally misused by Muslim men. He forcefully argued that the Qur'an orders the appointment of arbitrators in the event of "discord" between husband and wife. Since *talak* implies discord between the spouses, repudiation of marriage should not be permitted unless the court authorizes it.[28]

Indeed, Modernist Islamists today are generally saddened by the discrepancy between the revolutionary reforms improving the status of women during Islam's classical period and their second-class status in the Muslim world of the nineteenth and twentieth centuries. In this respect, they would definitely concur with Abduh when he said: "To be sure, the Muslims have been at fault in the education and training of women, and of acquainting them with their rights in our religion."[29] Shariati, for instance, denounced the excessive independence, materialism, and sexual permissiveness of Western women but was equally critical of Muslim societies for not giving women adequate opportunities to grow, develop, and participate in all spheres of life. He offered the Prophet Muhammad's daughter Fatimah as the role model because she was the ideal daughter, wife, mother, and social worker.[30]

---

[26]Charles C. Adams, *Islam and Modernism in Egypt: A Study of the Modern Reform Movement Inaugurated by Muhammad Abduh* (New York: Russel and Russel, 1933), pp. 34–35.

[27]Ibid, pp. 70–78.

[28]M. K. Nawaz, "Some Aspects of Modernization of Islamic Law," in Carl Leiden, ed., *The Conflict of Traditionalism and Modernism in the Muslim Middle East* (Austin: University of Texas Press, 1966), p. 74.

[29]Quoted in John L. Esposito, *Islam and Politics* (New York: Syracuse University Press, 1984), p. 49.

[30]Sachedina, "Ali Shariati: Ideologue of the Iranian Revolution," pp. 220–221; Ali Shariati, *Fatima is Fatima*, trans. Laleh Bakhtiar (Tehran: Shariati Foundation and Hamadami Publishers, 1980); Adele Ferdows, "Shariati and Khomeini on Women," in Nikki R. Keddie and Eric Hoogland, eds., *The Iranian Revolution and the Islamic Republic: Proceedings of a Conference* (Washington, D.C.: Middle East Institute, in cooperation with Woodrow Wilson International Center for Scholars, 1982), pp. 75–77, 81; Shanin Tabatabai, "Women in Islam," *Islamic Revolution*, No. 1 (1979), pp. 14–17.

Sir Sayyid, like Abduh, argued that Islam encouraged monogamy and allowed polygamy only in specific and exceptional cases. He concurred with Abduh that certain types of interest were not "usurious" and consequently were permissible in trade and commerce. Sir Sayyid even claimed that in the classical period of Islamic history, punishment by amputation of hand or foot was seldom, if ever, imposed and therefore should be discontinued in the modern age.[31]

To popularize modern ideas among Indian Muslims, Sir Sayyid established in 1864 the Literary and Scientific Translation Society in Ghazipur for the translation of Western books (primarily in the natural and social sciences) into simple Urdu.[32] He also created the Muhammadan Anglo-Oriental College at Aligarh in 1875 after the pattern of institutions of higher learning in England. This college provided a modern education tempered with training in Persian, Arabic, and Islamic studies. The products were well-rounded graduates who, as part of the Aligarh movement of enlightened and dynamic Muslims, played a stellar role in the birth of Pakistan and subsequently assumed elite roles in governmental, financial, and educational institutions.[33]

Sir Sayyid advocated the separation of the religious and secular realms in clear violation of the "organic" and holistic nature of conventional Islamic theory and practice. He justified his argument by referring to a *hadith* in which Prophet Muhammad himself is believed to have recommended that Muslims separate the secular and religious domains. In the *hadith* the Prophet came across farmers pollinating some palm trees. The Prophet recommended that they not do so. Following the Prophet's advice, the farmers discontinued this method of pollination and harvested far fewer ripe fruit than before. On hearing this bad news the Prophet is said to have remarked: "I am only a human being; if I order you to do something regarding your religion, you must accept it. . . . You know better in matters concerning your worldly affairs."[34] In the same vein, one of many examples of a Western idea presented in an Islamic framework is Iqbal's recommendation to expand the scope and authority of *ijma* (consensus) to encompass not only the *ulama* but also the nation-state's legislative assembly—comprised of elective representatives of the people. Iqbal stated:

---

[31]Michael Nazir Ali, *Islam: A Christian Perspective* (Exeter, England: Paternoster Press, 1983), p. 108; James A. Bill and Carl Leiden, *Politics in the Middle East*, 2nd ed. (Boston: Little, Brown, 1984), pp. 50–51.

[32]Safdar Mahmood, *A Political Study of Pakistan* (Lahore, Pakistan: Shaikh Muhammad Ashraf, 1972), p. 124; Safdar Mahmood and Javaid Zafar, *Founders of Pakistan* (Lahore, Pakistan: Publishers United, 1968), p. 31.

[33]Aziz Ahmad, *Islamic Modernism in India and Pakistan*, p. 37.

[34]Quoted from Sahih Muslim and said to have been reported by Prophet Muhammad's wife, Aysha, Rafi bin Khadij, and Moosa bin Talhah. The quotation has been taken from Ali Abdel Wahid Wafi, "Human Rights in Islam," *Islamic Quarterly*, Vol. 11, Nos. 1 & 2 (January–June 1967), p. 66; also see Dar, *Religious Thought of Sayyid Ahmad Khan*, pp. 245–247.

The transfer of the power of *ijtihad* from the individual representatives of the [medieval] school of Islamic law to a Muslim legislative assembly . . . in view of the growth of opposing sects, is the one possible form *ijma* can take in modern times.[35]

Unlike the Revolutionary Islamists and Traditionalist Islamists, who often insist on devout and learned Muslims helping in formulating and ratifying legislation, Iqbal did not object to assigning an advisory role to the *ulama* but insisted on vesting the elected representatives of the people with the final authority of the modern-day nation-state's governance. They, in turn, are required to legislate in a manner that does not contravene the basic "spirit of Islam." Interestingly, Iqbal's novel idea has now come to be accepted by a majority of Muslims.

Modernist Islamist Muhammad Rashid Rida (1865–1935) supported the concept of a progressive, liberal, and tolerant Islamic state in which non-Muslims would be treated in an exemplary way. Rashid Rida suggested the establishment of a "caliphate of necessity" to coordinate efforts of Muslim countries against foreign threats. He even envisioned the ultimate restoration of a genuine caliphate ruled by a wise, pious, and just caliph who would consult a broad spectrum of *ulama* and who would practice *ijtihad* before making decisions.[36]

Advocates of Reconciliation among Islamic Sects

As Modernists have been concerned about the divisions and frictions between the various *madhabs* (sects), they have spent considerable effort advocating Muslim reconciliation and unity. Al-Afghani spent his entire adult life preaching pan-Islamism, minimizing Shi'ah-Sunni differences, and stressing the commonalities between the two major Islamic sects. In fact, al-Afghani, who was born into a Shi'ah family in the Iranian village of Asadabad, in his ceaseless effort to unite the worldwide *ummah*, concealed his Shi'ah heritage and alluded to having been born into a Sunni family in Afghanistan.[37] Like al-Afghani, Shariati believed that the worldview of many Traditionalist and Revolutionary Islamists accentuated the divisions in the "House of Islam." Therefore, he did his utmost to promote the *ummah*, advocating the reconciliation and acceptance of various schools of Islamic *fiqh* to promote unity.[38] At times he angered the Shi'ah *ulama* by saying that the succession of Ali after Prophet Muhammad's death was merely a difference of opinion between the Shi'ah belief in **wisaya** (designation of Ali as Prophet Muhammad's religiopolitical successor) and the Sunni belief in *shura* (election or

---

[35]Muhammad Iqbal, *The Reconstruction of Religious Thought in Islam*, pp. 174–176.

[36]Hourani, *Arabic Thought in the Liberal Age*, pp. 243–244.

[37]Nikki R. Keddie, *An Islamic Response to Imperialism: Political and Religious Writings of Sayyid Jamal ad-Din "al-Afghani"* (Berkeley: University of California Press, 1983), pp. ix, 5–8; Keddie, *Sayyid Jamal ad-Din "al-Afghani": A Political Biography*, pp. 10–12, 427–433; M. A. Zaki Badawi, *The Reformers of Egypt* (London: Croom Helm, 1978), p. 7.

[38]Nikki R. Keddie, *Roots of Revolution: An Interpretive History of Modern Iran* (New Haven: Yale University Press, 1981), p. 220.

BOX 5.8   Hasan al-Turabi

Hasan al-Turabi was born in 1932 in central Sudan, south of Khartoum. He received an Islamic education from his devout family but also pursued a modern education. At universities in Khartoum, London, and the Sorbonne, Turabi studied law. As a student in the 1950s, Turabi joined Sudan's Muslim Brotherhood and became prominent during subsequent uprisings and in political activities in which Turabi demanded that Sudan adopt an Islamic constitution.

In 1977 Sudan's President Numeiri made peace with the Revolutionary Islamists in Sudan and appointed Turabi as his attorney general. Turabi encouraged members of the Muslim Brotherhood to take more active roles in the military and in commerce. Turabi also was behind Numeiri's attempt to adopt Islamic law in 1983. However, Numeiri turned against the Islamists shortly after this and imprisoned Turabi. In 1985 Numeiri was overthrown, and Turabi was released from prison. Turabi's political party did well in Sudan's 1986 elections and took part in subsequent coalition governments. Nevertheless, Turabi remained committed to the idea of establishing an Islamic state, in spite of the possibility of renewed civil war with the predominantly non-Muslim population in the south of Sudan. In 1989 General Omar Hasan Ahmed al-Bashir, also an Islamist, over-threw Sudan's elected government. With Turabi's backing, al-Bashir reestablished Islamic law and appointed Turabi as speaker of Sudan's parliament. For ten years, from 1989 to 1999, Turabi ruled Sudan hand-in-glove with President Bashir.

In various writings, speeches, and interviews, Turabi has presented himself as a fairly liberal and moderate Islamist who embraces such notions as democracy, tolerance, and women's rights. However, there is another side to Turabi. After his call for an Islamic legal code pushed southern Sudan into civil war, Turabi set up Islamic militias to fight a *jihad* there. Turabi has actively participated in several governments that were among the most repressive, belying his commitment to democracy and liberalization. His views of an Islamic state, as he helped outline it in the 1998 constitution, were far more Revolutionary than Modernist. Likewise, he has shown support for Revolutionary Islamist groups from outside Sudan. It was while Turabi was at the height of his power that Osama bin Laden was a welcome guest in Sudan, establishing training camps for Revolutionary Islamists. Turabi's Sudan has also harbored members of Hamas and Hezbollah. And although Turabi condemned the 1993 bombing of the World Trade Center, its prime suspect had spent time in Sudan as Turabi's guest.

By 1999, Bashir began to view the charismatic Turabi as a threat to his power. In late 1999, Bashir declared a state of emergency, removed Turabi from his posts, took over Turabi's political party, and by early 2001, placed Turabi under house arrest. Many of Turabi's followers either kept quiet or betrayed him and sided with President Bashir.

http://www.witness-pioneer.org/vil/Articles/
shariah/interview_on_apostasy_hasan_turabi.htm

http://www.wam.umd.edu/~gsanders/text/alturabi.html

nomination of a leader through consultation and consensus). In fact, Shariati concluded that Shi'ahs and Sunnis were both correct, since both had valid and persuasive arguments to support their contentions.[39]

Summary

The differences between Modernist Islamists and their Traditionalist and Revolutionary counterparts are distinct. Nevertheless, each recognizes the other as truly Muslim. The Modernist Islamists, unlike the Muslim Secularists, are devout and practicing Muslims whose proclivity for Westernization and modernization is tempered by their hostility for secularization. The Modernist Islamists have struggled to reappraise and reform a comprehensive religion revealed to mankind nearly fourteen hundred years ago, so that constructive and feasible solutions to the new problems of a dramatically changed socioeconomic and political environment can be found. This extensive and difficult task, intensified during the Islamic revivals, has often been pursued at the cost of many cherished beliefs and traditions and in the face of unrelenting opposition from the Traditionalist Islamists and Revolutionary Islamists. Finding innovative insights into the Islamic scriptures or emphasizing ideas that may have long been dormant in the substantive body of Islamic scripture is bound to continue indefinitely while yielding dividends for the entire *ummah*.[40]

Internet Sites

http://www.icna.org/tm/greatmuslim3.htm

http://www.muslimedia.com/archives/book99/synthesbk.htm

http://www.geocities.com/Athens/Cyprus/8613/index.html

http://www.encyclopedia.com/articlesnew/32332.html

http://www.cqpress.com/context/articles/epr_muhammadabduh.html

http://www.nmhschool.org/tthornton/muhammad_abduh.htm

http://www.cis-ca.org/voices/k/syydkhn-mn.htm

http://www.slider.com/enc/1000/Ahmad_Khan_Sir_Sayyid.htm

http://www.pak.org/person/iqbal.html

http://www.geocities.com/junaid_hassan25/iqbal.htm

http://www.merawatan.com/iqbal/

http://www.dawoodi-bohras.com/perspective/islam-plu.htm

http://lexicorient.com/cgi-bin/eo-direct.pl?erbakan.htm

---

[39]Sachedina, pp. 192–196.

[40]Abbott, *Islam and Pakistan*, p. 23.

TABLE 5.1 A Typology of Islamists

Major Characteristics	Revolutionary Islamists	Traditionalist Islamists	Modernist Islamists
I. Belief in the Fundamentals of Islam	All three believe in (a) *tawhid* (oneness of God); (b) the omnipotence, omnipresence, justice, and infinite mercy of God; (c) Prophet Muhammad as the last in a long line of God's Prophets starting with Adam and including Abraham, Moses, and Jesus; (d) the Holy Qur'an as revealed to Prophet Muhammad as the last of God's Holy Books along with the Torah as given to Moses and the Bible to Jesus; and (e) the Last Day of Judgment.		
II. Degree of Devoutness	1. Practicing Muslims--		
	2. Extremely devout, austere, and often puritanical.	2. Extremely devout, relatively dogmatic and orthodox but tolerant of some local customs in varying degrees.	2. Devout to very devout, eclectic, and not rigid or puritanical.
III. Education and Learning	1. Formal education acquired in Islamic educational institutions. Informal learning also primarily, but not exclusively, religious.		1. Formal and informal education not confined to religious learning.
	2. Minor influence of some non-Islamic (e.g., Western) ideas, ideals, and practices among Revolutionary Islamists in the modern period.	2. Often reject non-Islamic (e.g., Western) ideas, ideals, and practices.	2. Significantly influenced by non-Islamic (especially Western) ideas, ideals, and practices.
IV. Clerical Affiliation	Not exclusively from the ranks of the *ulama* (Islamic scholars); many non-clerics among them.	Virtually all come from the ranks of the *ulama*.	Though they may come from the ranks of the *ulama*, the majority have been non-clerics.
V. Normative Periods	1. Look primarily to classical period of Islam for inspiration and emulation; secondary emphasis on medieval Islamic era.	1. Look nostalgically to both classical and medieval periods of Islam for their ideas, ideals, and practices.	1. Look to classical period of Islam as well as to Western capitalist and socialist worlds for their ideas, ideals, and practices.
	2. Consider true Islam's immutability and perfection to transcend time and space. Determined to prove that many popular and beneficial ideas, ideals, and practices across cultures, ideological systems, and time are Islamic in essence or have Islamic roots or influences.		2. Place all adopted popular and beneficial non-Islamic/foreign concepts, practices, and institutions within Islamic framework.

(Continued)

TABLE 5.1 *(Continued)*

Major Characteristics	Revolutionary Islamists	Traditionalist Islamists	Modernist Islamists
VI. Respect for Tradition and Openness toward Change	1. Opposed to doctrine of *taqlid* (whereby legal rulings of one or more schools of Islamic jurisprudence are blindly and unquestion-ingly followed) and all accretions and innova-tions in Islam from postclassical period.	1. Adhere to doctrine of *taqlid* and often support or condone conservation and pre-servation of "Islamic" customs and traditions popular among Muslims in their particular locality or region.	1. Against *taqlid* and all those traditions that they consider to inhibit the progress of Muslim societies. Believe in the continuity of essential, useful, and popular tra-ditions, along with com-prehensive progress (including structural change) that they deem compatible with the spirit of Islam.
	2. Advocate *ijtihad* (independent reasoning, especially in matters of Islamic law).	2. Opposed to *ijtihad* except for some minority Shi'ah sects, which restrict that practice to *mujtahids* (highly qualified *ulama* exercising *ijtihad*).	2. Advocate *ijtihad*. Often believe that *ijti-had* should be exer-cised by all devout, enlightened, and pro-gressive Muslims who are knowledgeable about Islamic thought and practice.
	3. Opposed to modern secular (especially Western or socialist) ideas, practices, and institutions that are contrary to Islam.		3. Opposed to Modern secular (especially Western or socialist) ideas, practices, and institutions that are contrary to Islam. However, in practice, often tolerate them in varying degrees.
	4. Seek compatibility of policies and programs with the letter and "spirit of Islam."		4. Seek compatibility of policies and programs with the "spirit of Islam."
VII. Tolerance of Secularization	Opposed to secular-ization. Often launch a *jihad* (crusade) to stop and reverse secularization pro-cesses. Their active political involvement is often taken into account by regimes in power.	Opposed to secular-ization of Muslim societies. The majority, however, do little to retard or reverse secularization pro-cesses. The few that do get politically involved do so because they perceive that Islam and the Muslim community of which they are a part are in danger.	Opposed to seculariza-tion in principle, theory, and rhetoric, but con-veniently tolerate secu-larization with either benign neglect or as a necessary evil that must be accomodated in con-temporary times.

Major Characteristics	Revolutionary Islamists	Traditionalist Islamists	Modernist Islamists
VIII. Principal Reasons for the Muslim World's Decline	1. Ascribe decline of Muslim world (including its poverty and impotence) to two commonly shared reasons: (a) colonialism and neo-colonialism (especially by Western powers) and (b) disunity within the "House of Islam."		
	2. Believe that decline is also due to (a) failure on the part of Muslims to adhere to letter and spirit of Islam; and (b) "corrupt," "incompetent," and often "dictatorial" leadership of Secularists (and thus wayward Muslims).		2. Believe that decline is due to rigid, doctrinaire, and dogmatic orthodoxies promulgated by Revolutionary Islamists and Traditionalist Islamists.
	3. Also believe that it is due to the lackluster leadership and inhibiting influences of the detached Traditionalist Islamists.		3. Emphasize inhibiting of *ijtihad* and banning of *bid'ah* (innovation in Islamic beliefs, practices, and laws) as counterproductive practices.
IX. Manifestations of an Islamic State	**A. Type of Islamic State:** 1. Advocate an Islamic state, though its character differs significantly in each case.		
	2. Prefer one with puritanical manifestations.	2. Prefer one with traditional theocratic manifestations.	2. Prefer one with liberal democratic manifestations.
	B. Who Should Govern?: Convinced that enlightened, sincere, and dedicated Revolutionary Islamists would do the best job of governing the truly Islamic state. Often very critical of non-Revolutionary Islamists.	Believe that Traditionalist *ulama* ought to govern the Islamic state as they are the guardians and principal interpreters of the divine *shariah*. In practice have become somewhat tolerant of Revolutionary Islamists, Modernist Islamists, and Secularists governing Muslim societies.	Believe that enlightened and competent Modernist Islamists would do the best job of governing the modern-day Islamic state. In practice are very tolerant of and even support competent Secularists in leadership positions.
	C. Nature of Constitution and Laws: 1. Would like to formulate and implement a constitution that is Islamic in both letter and spirit.		1. Would like to formulate and implement a constitution consonant with the letter and especially the spirit of Islam.
	2. Would like the Islamic state to be governed by the *shariah*, which for them is sacrosanct, immutable, and capable of successful application to all given situations regardless of time and place.		2. Believe in revision of Islamic legal system in order to cope with contemporary problems. Would not remove many secular laws already implemented.

(Continued)

TABLE 5.1   *(Continued)*

Major Characteristics	Revolutionary Islamists	Traditionalist Islamists	Modernist Islamists
IX. Manifestations of an Islamic State	**D. Basis of Sovereignty**: 1. Believe that sovereignty primarily rests with God. Believe all devout Muslims should reject sovereignty of humanity. With few exceptions, have come to accept (Western) parliamentary democracy in the modern period, implying that they do give importance to "popular sovereignty" (especially in the post–World War II period) after sovereignty of God.		1. Believe above all in God's ultimate sovereignty but next in "popular sovereignty." The latter is manifested in a form of (Western) parliamentary democracy legitimized as essentially Islamic.
	E. Integration of Society: 1. Believe in integrating a predominantly Muslim country's citizenry on the basis of Islam, although the character of that Islam differs markedly in each case.		
	2. Based on revolutionary Islamism.	2. Based primarily on Islamic orthodoxy with a minimum of custom and occasionally on custom-laden "popular Islam" or "folk Islam."	2. Based on progressive Islamism and/or Islamic nationalism.
X. Degree of Fatalism and Activism	1. Vary in their fatalism, believing in such notions as *kismet, taqdir* (fate), predestination, and preordination.		
	2. Very fatalistic but extremely active religiopolitical crusaders for revolutionary Islamism, piety, and puritanism.	2. Very fatalistic; often passive, apolitical, contemplative, and mystical scholars, teachers, and preachers of traditional Islamic doctrine and practice. However, do get involved in politics if and when they perceive that Islam is threatened by non-Muslims or by "wayward" Muslims.	2. Moderately to very fatalistic, though extremely dynamic reformers of Islam and Muslim societies. Imbued with and desirous of promoting the spirit of Islam.
XI. Major Foreign Policy Orientation	1. Often extremely insular and parochial.--------------		1. Often relatively cosmopolitan, broad-minded and highly principled pragmatists.
	2. Exponents of a united Muslim world/Islamic bloc---------------------------------		
	3. Believe in *dar al-Islam* (abode of Islam) versus *dar al-harb* (abode of the war) dichotomy of the World. Thus end up with a We-They, Us-Them, Good-Evil dichotomous orientation toward outside world.		3. Hardly preoccupied with *dar-al-Islam* and *dar al-harb* dichotomy.

Major Characteristics	Revolutionary Islamists	Traditionalist Islamists	Modernist Islamists
Common Stereotypes	**A. Critics**: fundamentalists; fanatics; militants; religious zealots; puritans; and iconoclasts.	obscurantists; reactionaries.	apologists; revisionists; syncretists.
	B. Defenders: purists; literalists; scripturalists; religious ideologues/revolutionaries; restorationists; restitutionists.	Islamic scholars; learned theologians; conservatives.	progressives; reformers; modernizers; adaptationists; realists; liberals; pragmatically oriented Islamists
Prominent Islamists	Shaykh Ahmed Sirhindi (1564–1624)	*The Farangi Mahallis*	Jamal ad-Din al-Afghani (1838–1897)
	Shah Waliullah (1702–1762)	The most prominent of whom was:	Sir Sayyid Ahmad Khan (1817–1898)
	Muhammad ibn Abd al-Wahhab (1703–1792)	Qayam-ud-Din Muhammad Abul Bari (1878–1926)	Muhammad Abduh (1849–1905)
	Sayyid Ahmed Shahid (1786–1831)	*The Barelvis*	Muhammad Rashid Rida (1865–1935)
	Mir Nisar Ali (1782–1831)	The most prominent of whom was:	Muhammad Iqbal (1873–1938)
	Haji Shariatullah (1781–1840)	Ahmad Raza Khan Barelvi (1856–1921)	Ali Shariati (1933–1977)
	Mohsenuddin Ahmed (1819–1860)		
	Muhammad ibn Ali al-Sanusi (1787–1859)	*The Deobandis*	Mehdi Badar Bazargan (1905–)
	Hasan al-Banna (1906–1949)	The most prominent of whom were:	Abul Hasan Bani-Sadr (1933–)
	Muhammad Ahmad Abdullah al-Mahdi (1844–1885)	Haji Imdadullah (1815–1899)	Ali Akbar Hashemi Rafsanjani (1934–)
	Sayyid Abul A'la Maududi (1903–1979)	Muhammad Qasim Nanautwi (1833–1877)	Abdul Karim Saroush (1945–)
	Sayyid Qutb (1906–1966)	Rashid Ahmad Gangohi (1829–1950)	Mohammed Khatami (1942–)
	Ayatollah Ruhollah Khomeini (1902–1989)	Mahmud al-Hasan (1850–1921)	Burhanuddin Rabbani (1940–)
	Ayatollah Sayyid Ali Khamenei (1939–)		Ahmad Shah Massoud (1956–2001)

(Continued)

TABLE 5.1   (Continued)

Major Characteristics	Revolutionary Islamists	Traditionalist Islamists	Modernist Islamists
Prominent Islamists	Muhammad Zia-ul-Haq (1924–1988)	Sayyid Kazem Shariatmadari (1905–1986)	
	Hasan al-Turabi (1932–)		
	Muammar al-Qaddafi (1942–)		
	Omar Hasan al-Bashir (1935–)		
	Gulbuddin Hekmatyar (1947–)		
	Shayleh Ahmad Yassin (1938–)		
	Mullah Muhammad Omar (1962–)		
	Sheikh Omar Abdel Rahman (1938–)		
	Aiyman Zawahiri (1951–)		
	Osama bin Laden (1957–)		

CHAPTER SIX

Failure of Muslim Secularists in the Postcolonial Muslim States

By the ninth century, the Islamic empire stretched from the Indus River in the east to the Atlas Mountains in northwest Africa. Europe, the stronghold of Christendom, saw the Crescent rising over its stone walls. Islamdom included Spain, southern France, part of Italy, and the Mediterranean islands of Crete, Corsica, Sicily, and Sardinia. Muslims led the world in science and art, in mathematics and might. The Islamic empire was first intellectually, economically, and politically—its supremacy was unequaled.

One thousand years later, Islamdom's conspicuous glory was faded, and the Crescent eclipsed by an inexorably modernizing Europe that had surpassed the Islamic empire in military and industrial technology. One Muslim land after another fell into Western hands as Europeans gradually dismembered the debilitated empire of the Ottoman Turks and imposed colonial rule throughout the Muslim world. The Europeans not only exploited these colonies, rich in cheap raw materials and labor, but used them as export markets for their surplus capital goods (like machines) and consumer goods. Moreover, the Europeans introduced modernization[1] and Western secular education. In the process, they

---

[1]The terms *modernization* and *development* are often used interchangeably in scholarly literature and popular media to refer to the movement of a society or country from the traditional, through the transitional, and into the modern stage of economic, social, and political development. Some scholars (like Samuel Huntington), however, see a major difference between the two terms. In Huntington's words, development is "an evolutionary process in which indigenous institutions adapt and control change and are not simply caught up in imitating and reacting to outside forces. Modernization is often contemporary, imported, and creates a dependency on the technologically advanced urban-industrial centers without helping local political and social institutions to grow and adapt. Development means that a system has some ability to be selective in the type and pace of changes, often imported, that occur in a country" (Herbert Winter and Thomas Bellows, *People and Politics*, New York: Wiley, 1977, pp. 352–353; Samuel P. Huntington, "Political Development and Political Decay," *World Politics*, Vol. 17 (1965), p. 389).

penetrated all levels of society and regulated the political, economic, social, and cultural lives of their Muslim subjects. The indigenous elite, simultaneously impressed and antagonized by European power, both emulated and cooperated with their colonial masters. They embraced Westernization and secularization: they served the Western powers that governed their people while they sent their own children to European universities. The elite, armed with thoroughly Western attitudes, lifestyles, and ideologies, were poised to take power following independence.

World War I marked the decline of colonial rule. The Europeans promised the Muslims independence in exchange for their cooperation against the Axis nations in general, and the Ottoman Turks in particular, igniting nationalist passions throughout the Muslim world. Following the Allied victory, however, the promised independence was not forthcoming. Instead, the West enlarged its colonial possessions at the expense of the defeated countries. For example, in the 1916 Sykes-Picot Agreement, Britain and France divided the former Ottoman territories between themselves and justified the action under the League of Nation's mandate system.

Following the final dismemberment of the Ottoman Empire and the termination of the Khilafat, disappointed Muslims traded Ottoman Turkish Muslim rule for European Christian colonialism. Even the Western-allied elite grew restless with colonial rulers and despaired of rousing themselves from stagnation. Thus, anticolonial sentiment gathered momentum throughout the Muslim world. Finally, following World War II, the West, exhausted spiritually, economically, and even militarily by the war, initiated the process of decolonization hoping to extricate itself from its increasingly troublesome and strife-filled colonial possessions.

Despite formal independence, the newly emerging Muslim nation-states of Asia and Africa were not yet independent of Western ideologies and Western notions of secular, territorial nationalism. These independent Muslim nation-states emphasized the "national interest" and abandoned the traditional Islamic *ummah*. Instead, ultimate authority rested in the state—and the state demanded total political obedience. This concept was understood by the governing Westernized elite but lost on the governed, who identified themselves not according to Western-delineated national boundaries but on the basis of the *ummah*.

Moreover, these newly independent and predominantly Muslim states were economically poor and politically fragile. To survive and to consolidate power, they turned to the competing superpowers. The West needed allies and military bases throughout the world to contain and combat communism. In turn, most Muslim states in need of aid and hostile to the characteristic atheism of communism joined the Western-sponsored antisocialist and anticommunist alliance scheme. A much smaller number tilted, instead, toward the socialist camp, while the rest chose nonalignment. Thus, although the colonial era was over, the impoverished states of the Muslim world grew dependent on foreign aid, were drawn into geopolitical conflicts, and were divided among themselves both on a national and an ideological basis.

Box 6.1   Who Are the Muslim Secularists?

Muslim Secularists are generally Muslims by name and birth who often cherish Islamic ideals and values, identify with the Muslim community and culture, and are perceived as Muslims by non-Muslims. In most cases, it is the Muslim Secularists who have governed Muslim countries since these developing countries gained their independence from Western colonial rule. This box will summarize some of the hallmarks of Muslim Secularists.

Nonreligious Muslims

While faithful to Islam, albeit sometimes without much theological grasp of its details, and fully aware of the basic tenets of their faith, Muslim Secularists often do not observe the ritual obligations incumbent on all Muslims, such as offering daily prayers, fasting during Ramadan, paying the annual *zakat*, and performing the *hajj* at least once in a lifetime. Despite their nonchalant attitude toward the faithful adherence to and dutiful observance of their religion, they fall back on it in moments of personal crisis or when they find it necessary to conform to social or political pressure exerted by devout Muslims. The Secularists are nonpracticing nominal Muslims with a veneer of a liberal and eclectic version of Islam. Frequently their faith is reduced to various basic ethical, moral, and spiritual principles emphasized by Islam and other religions, such as equality, justice, liberty, freedom, honesty, integrity, brotherhood, tolerance, and peace. The Secularists' liberal and lax approach to Islam is decried by devout Muslims, who consider them "wayward souls" at best and "unbelievers" at worst.

Secular Politicians

Most Secularists have been educated in the secular Western tradition at home or abroad and consequently are more knowledgeable of and sympathetic with Western intellectual thought than with Islamic concepts. Their formal and informal Western educational experiences encourage them to view classical and medieval Islamic doctrines and practices as anachronistic, reactionary, and impractical for contemporary purposes. If chastised for acquiring non-Islamic Western knowledge and training, Secularists, like many Modernist Islamists, might easily quote the popular saying of Prophet Muhammad: "Seek knowledge even if you have to go to China" (China not only was a distant foreign land in those days of very slow transportation and communications but was inhabited by non-Muslim foreigners who had a polytheistic religion and their own distinct culture). Instead of taking the nostalgic Islamist stance that the "Islamic state" of Prophet Muhammad and the Khulafa-i-Rashidin was the golden age of Islam, Secularists wish to modernize their societies and believe that secularization is not only inevitable but desirable.

Influential Members of the Elite

Though a minority in all Muslim societies, the Muslim Secularists wield a disproportionate degree of wealth and power and hold leadership positions in their countries' influential institutions. They are in the upper echelons of their governments' civil service and

(Continued)

Who Are the Muslim Secularists? *(Continued)*

armed forces. They are heavily represented in the mass media, in educational institutions, in the business community, among landlords, and throughout a broad spectrum of professions. They keep abreast of events in their country and in the world at large, and they constitute the most assertive and vocal segment of their societies.

Believers in the Separation of Religion and Politics

Secularists are pleased that Islam does not give a privileged status to the *ulama* in the governance of Muslim societies. Secularists iterate the view that there is no institutionalized clergy in Islam but that all Muslims are responsible to God for their thoughts and deeds. While Secularists constitute the privileged class, they point to Islam's emphasis on equality and have an aversion to the formation of any privileged class (including a priestly one) that fosters elitism and encourages differentiation between individuals. According to Secularists, the *ulama* are experts in the Islamic religion only and are therefore fully entitled to their invaluable religious guidance in the affairs of the state. However, the Secularists contend that, in economic, political, technical, international, and non-Islamic legal matters, the *ulama* have no right to impose their viewpoint on the nation.

Some Effectively Manipulate Islam

Some Muslim Secularists use Islamic rhetoric and symbolism to promote their economic, social, and political policies and programs of modernization and Westernization to an often hostile population; to draw support away from the Revolutionary Islamists, Traditionalist Islamists, and Modernist Islamists; to enhance their own legitimacy; to integrate and unite their fragmented citizenry; and to inspire and galvanize the Muslim masses.

Failure of Secular Ideologies

In the immediate aftermath of independence, the Muslim Secularists, who were influenced by Western ideologies, often Western educated, and impressed by the Western nations' order and progress, comfortably filled the political void left by the departing colonial administrators. The euphoria of independence from the West initially endeared these Muslim Secularists to the masses, and they were enthusiastically swept into power. However, these Secularists no longer saw through the eyes of the masses; they saw their nations as backward and sought to emulate the Western model of progress. Muslim Secularists worked to transform the predominantly rural and traditional Muslim world into modern urban nation-states by pursuing programs of modernization, Westernization, and secularization.

Despite the Muslim Secularists' early popular support, within a few decades the credibility and legitimacy of their government had dangerously eroded. Their poorly implemented modernization programs have proved incompatible with traditional Islam and Islamism. The Secularists carelessly and thoughtlessly imposed secular socialism, secular capitalism, or a mixture of both, but have failed to

■

BOX 6.2   Mustafa Kemal Atatürk

Mustafa Kemal Atatürk was born in 1881 in Salonika (now in Greece, but then part of Ottoman Turkish Macedonia). He began his studies in a traditional religious school but soon switched to a school with a more modern and Western-oriented curriculum. In 1893 young Mustafa enrolled in a military high school where he excelled in mathematics and earned his nickname "Kemal," which means perfection.

Mustafa Kemal attended the War Academy in Istanbul. He graduated in 1905 with the rank of staff captain. The young officer founded an underground political movement, called "Homeland and Freedom," in opposition to the tyranny of the Ottoman sultan. Kemal was a colonel during World War I, when Turkey was allied with Germany. He repelled allied invasion forces in the Dardanelles in 1915 and liberated two eastern provinces. He rose quickly in rank to general and became commander of several Ottoman armies.

After the Ottoman Empire's capitulation and dismemberment at the war's end, Kemal defied the sultan's government and began a war for Turkish national independence in 1919. By 1922 Kemal was made commander-in-chief with the rank of marshal and led Turkish armies to liberate the Turkish mainland. Kemal's impressive military successes against invaders led ultimately to the independence of the new state of Turkey. He abolished the Ottoman dynasty, which had ruled for more than six hundred years, and established the Republic of Turkey, with its capital in Ankara, in 1923. In 1924, he abolished the Ottoman caliphate, thus breaking Turkey's last ties to its imperial Ottoman past. Considered a national hero, Kemal was Turkey's first elected president. In foreign policy he made efforts to secure peace for his nation. Although Kemal died in 1938, his pro-Western legacy also assured that Turkey would be aligned with the West during the Cold War and even become a member of NATO.

Kemal began his fifteen-year presidency with programs of dramatic modernization and Westernization that came later to be associated with the ideology of Kemalism. Kemal was agnostic and considered Islamic traditions an impediment to Turkey's progress. He did away with Turkey's Islamic legal system and instituted a new legal and political system based on Western principles. He secularized education and adopted the Western calendar. He prohibited such symbols of Ottoman culture as the fez cap in favor of more fashionable Western hats. Kemal gave women the right to vote, discouraged the wearing of veils, and abolished polygamy. He also abolished the Arabic script and replaced it with a specially developed Latin alphabet. Turkey under Kemal also made impressive strides in agricultural and economic development. The changes he successfully instituted were dramatic and unparalleled in the Muslim world. In 1934 Kemal took the surname Atatürk, which means "father of Turkey." Today, he is still regarded by many as having single-handedly founded the modern state of Turkey.

http://www.demokrasivakfi.org.tr/ataturk/index_eng.html
http://www.ataturk.com/index2.html
http://www.sporum.gov.tr/English/Ataturk/ata2.asp
http://www.cs.umd.edu/~kandogan/FTA/Ataturk/ataturk.html
http://www.secularislam.org/books/ataturk.htm
http://www.columbia.edu/cu/tsa/ata/ata.html
http://www.mrdowling.com/608-ataturk.html
http://www.turizm.net/turkey/history/ataturk.html

deliver on their promises of economic, social, and political development.[2] Even the rapid economic growth registered in some Muslim countries has not significantly benefited the impoverished majority. Instead, any economic gains have been enjoyed almost exclusively by the wealthy elite. The Secularists have interpreted modernization as the adoption, not the adaptation, of Western ideology and industry. This modernization has not occasioned development, which involves finding the best use of a nation's potential in order to mitigate poverty and raise the majority's standard of living.[3] In fact, in the Muslim world, rapid modernization has precluded appropriate development.

Muslim Secularists, hoping to become partners with the Western industrial world, have espoused the Western idea of nationalism to integrate and to unify their fragmented societies and to consolidate political power. However, nationalism instead has further divided the Muslim world as a whole, and the leadership has pursued national interests at the expense of the *ummah*. In the interests of realpolitik, Muslim nations have ignored fellow Muslims in distress, whether starving in Ethiopia and Somalia or bearing Israeli assaults in southern Lebanon.

The ideology of pan-Arabism, pursued by Muslim Secularists to rectify the failure of nationalism, enjoyed popularity in the 1950s and 1960s. However, the ideology lost favor when Arab Muslims realized that pan-Arabism was a thinly disguised extension of secular nationalism promoted primarily by those leaders who sought to dominate the Arab world. Pan-Arabism neither unified Arabs against Israel nor settled the Palestinian problem. Pan-Arabism was discredited first with the Arab defeat in the 1967 Arab-Israeli War, second by its failure to increase trade and commerce between Arab nations, and third by the failure of Arab governments to break the bonds of dependency with the West or, in a few cases, with the communist bloc.

Muslim Secularists have also failed to fulfill their post-independence promise of implementing liberal parliamentary democracy. Of all Western values and ideologies, democracy was the first discarded by Muslim Secularists from their modernization policies. Most regimes in the Muslim world are authoritarian and dictatorial; some are as callous, oppressive, and tyrannical as prior colonial

---

[2]The example of secular socialism implemented in the communist world has disappointed the Muslim masses as they have learned more about the lack of political, economic, and social freedoms prevalent in the communist bloc. Moreover, the Muslim elite has also stopped looking at socialism and communism as model ideologies because the former Soviet-dominated communist bloc itself has repudiated communism. The Muslim masses, however, have been equally disappointed by the example of secular capitalism practiced in the West. Many Muslims feel that capitalism breeds excessive greed, individuality, materialism, and hedonism, as well as a lack of compassion for the poor and needy.

[3]E. Bradford Burns, *Latin America: A Concise Interpretive History*, 5th ed. (Englewood Cliffs, N.J.: Prentice-Hall), 1990, p. 357. Although a Latin Americanist, Burns's views on and definitions of key concepts like "modernization" and "development" are applicable throughout the Third World; too many other studies are based heavily on the experience of the developed West. See also E. Bradford Burns, *The Poverty of Progress: Latin America in the Nineteenth Century* (Berkeley and Los Angeles: University of California Press, 1983), which details the Positivist-inspired, elite-mandated modernization process in Latin America and its disastrous consequences; and E. Bradford Burns, "The Modernization of Underdevelopment: El Salvador, 1858–1931," *Journal of Developing Areas*, Vol. 18 (April 1984), which chronicles a similar struggle in El Salvador.

BOX 6.3   Ba'athism and Nasserism

The Arab **Ba'ath** (Rebirth) movement was founded in Damascus in the early 1940s with dreams of unifying the Arab world into a single Arab nation that would glorify Arab culture, guard Arab identity, and grant Arabs a significant place in the world. The party advocated the extirpation of colonialist influence in the Arab world, redistribution of government-controlled lands, nationalization of industries and banks, and the improvement in social services. The Ba'athist ideology appealed across class lines to the peasantry, urban labor, the intelligentsia, the middle class, and young army officers.

By the late 1950s, Ba'athism—which emphasized Arab nationalism, Arab socialism, and pan-Arabism—had spread from Syria to Iraq, Jordan, and Lebanon, reaching its zenith by the 1960s. Yet Ba'athism was used to justify and perpetrate tyranny and demagoguery. Today, Ba'athism is no longer associated with the utopian ideals of its founders. Instead, the Ba'athist regimes in Syria and Iraq are at odds with one another and, under these regimes, the people have suffered economic, spiritual, and cultural impoverishment. The Arab people no longer turn to Ba'athism as an alternative to their destitution.

Nasserism, like Ba'athism, enjoyed its greatest prestige during the 1960s. Although ideologically almost identical, Nasserism and Ba'athism diverge with regard to the person of Egypt's President Gamal Abdel Nasser, without whom Nasserism would be but the Egyptian chapter of the Ba'ath party. The preeminent tenets of Nasserism were Arab nationalism, Arab socialism, pan-Arabism, and opposition to colonialism. Using his considerable charisma, Nasser portrayed himself as a hero leading the Arab quest for unity, dignity, and sovereignty. As an ideology attached to Nasser's personality, Nasserism lived and died with Nasser, its popularity among the masses intertwined with Nasser's own. Thus, when Nasser's prestige and popularity were at their height after the 1956 Suez War, Nasserism was a powerful and attractive ideology to Arabs everywhere. Iraq's Saddam Hussein, Syria's Hafiz al-Assad, and Libya's Colonel Muammar al-Qaddafi were influenced profoundly by Nasser and, in turn, embraced elements of Nasserism shared by Ba'athism. Indeed, Hafiz al-Assad and Saddam Hussein became staunch Ba'athists as a result of early Nasserist influences. Nasser, whose Free Officers Movement never had much ideology to support it, adapted elements of Ba'athism as his own. But the star of Nasserism, so bright for a decade, fell in 1967 when Nasser was crushed by the Israelis in the Six Day War. Coupled with Nasser's authoritarian tendencies, a troubled economy, and foreign policy failures, the disastrous war with Israel discredited Nasserism throughout the Arab world.

http://www.digbib.uio.no/publ/vikan/51/57/58.html
http://www.ahram.org.eg/weekly/archives/parties/nasser/nass90.htm

---

regimes. Muslim Secularist Saddam Hussein is the leader of one such regime in Iraq (see Box 6.4)

Nor have Muslim Secularists delivered on their promised postindependence goal of ending poverty and bridging the gap between the rich and poor. Their

■

BOX 6.4   Saddam Hussein

Saddam Hussein was born on April 28, 1937. Saddam, whose education was sporadic, joined the Ba'ath party, which was based on an ideology of revolutionary nationalism. In 1958 the Iraqi military, with Ba'ath support, overthrew the Iraqi goverment. The military government, however, turned against the Ba'athists and drove them underground. After an assassination attempt on the new president, Saddam fled Iraq and moved to Egypt, where he was influenced by Nasser's anti-Western, pan-Arab revolutionary rhetoric and ideology.

In 1963, after Ba'athist military officers overthrew the Iraqi government, Saddam returned to Iraq and began to study law. However, the Ba'athists were driven from government, and Saddam was imprisoned. In 1966, after escaping from prison, Saddam went underground and dedicated himself to reorganizing the Ba'ath party. When the Ba'ath party returned to power, Saddam became vice president and oversaw Iraq's day-to-day affairs. Acting as virtual master of Iraq during the 1970s, Saddam nationalized the Iraq Petroleum Company—which had been owned by British, American, French, and Dutch firms—and thereby gained direct control of approximately 10 percent of Middle Eastern oil. He repaired relations with the West during the mid-1970s, but his diplomacy was always based on the exigencies of self-interest.

In mid-1979 Saddam Hussein became president and initiated his dictatorship by executing five hundred Ba'athist leaders in Iraq. Saddam also used his absolute power to create a cult of personality. He promoted himself as the future leader of a united Arab world. When Iraq invaded Iran, his country was seen as a bulwark against the spread of Revolutionary Islamism. The West and the Arab states, including Saudi Arabia and Kuwait, sided with Iraq against the Iranians.

The war went badly for Iraq and ended in a bloody and expensive stalemate. Neither the Iraqis nor the Iranians achieved much in the way of their expressed objectives. Learning well the lessons of the war with Iran, Saddam chose next to victimize a smaller, weaker, and much more vulnerable nation: Iraq's oil-rich neighbor to the south, Kuwait. Iraq invaded Kuwait in 1990 and proceeded to loot that wealthy country. However, the United States led a multinational coalition to expel Iraq from Kuwait in Operation Desert Storm. The war cost Iraq dearly: over 400,000 Iraqi dead, thousands wounded, and the country in ruins. It was a crushing and humiliating military defeat for Saddam, but he remains in power.

http://www.uruklink.net/iraq/bio.htm
http://www.top-biography.com/9004-Saddam%20Hussein/index1.asp
http://www.pbs.org/wgbh/pages/frontline/shows/saddam/
http://www.danielpipes.org/reviews/19910809.shtml

desire to modernize has retarded the process of breaking dependency relationships with the West and instead reinforced dependency.

The Muslim Secularists, who assumed the levers of power in postcolonial Muslim countries, have not delivered on the economic, political, and social development that they promised their citizens during the independence struggle. The secular pan-Turkism, pan-Arabism, Kemalism (Ataturkism), Ba'athism, Nasserism, capitalism, socialism, nationalism, modernization, and Westernization have utterly failed to achieve the high level of development that the Muslim masses in the Muslim world looked forward to at the time of independence from colonial rule. Instead, the rapid modernization and secularization process that has been undertaken in most Muslim countries has diminished the role of traditional belief in public schools; eroded the traditional, comprehensive, and holistic belief system of Islam; transplanted alien and secular Western institutions, laws, and procedures; and created an acute identity crisis in the minds of millions of Muslims. It's not surprizing, then, that there is an Islamic revival and that Islamism has become the primary idiom of protest to Muslim Secularist regimes and their modernization policies.

Seeing the resurgence of Islam, some astute Muslim Secularists have exploited Islamic rhetoric and symbolism in domestic and foreign policy to shore up wavering support. Yet instead of appeasing the sincere and committed Islamists, the Muslim Secularists' political use of Islam has legitimized Islamism and, thus, undermined government secularization programs—the linchpin of the secularists' modernization policies. Moreover, rather than being perceived as devout "born-again Muslims," the Secularists are seen as hypocrites and opportunists not to be trusted.[4] Egypt's President Muhammad Anwar al-Sadat was a good example of a Muslim Secularist, who used Islamic rhetoric and symbolism, and thereby contributed to an Islamic revival in his country during the 1970s. He was assassinated by Revolutionary Islamists in October 1981 (see Box 6.5). Another Muslim secularist, who lost power in a military coup d'etat in 1985 but not his life, was Sudanese President Ja'afar Muhammad al-Numeiri (see Box 6.6).

Manifestations of Six Developmental Crises in Muslim States

While Muslim states are undergoing rapid modernization, their development is neither holistic nor healthy. What may seem at first a paradox is the effort that has been made to transplant a developed Western system in a totally alien, non-Western environment. In the West, where modernization and development have proceeded gradually and simultaneously, many equate the two and bundle them together under the value-laden term "progress." In contrast, modernization has occurred rapidly in the Muslim world, while appropriate and holistic development has not taken place.

In essence, modernization is a complex, multidimensional, prolonged, and unsettling process of technological, economic, political, social, and cultural innovation. Since modernization in a temporal sense has succeeded in the West, it has become identified in the minds of the Muslim elite with Westernization, secularization, and the sweeping adoption of Western industry, ideology, and institutions.

---

[4]Fouad Ajami, *The Arab Predicament: Arab Political Thought and Practice since 1967* (Cambridge: Cambridge University Press, 1981), p. 171.

■

BOX 6.5   Muhammad Anwar al-Sadat

Muhammad Anwar al-Sadat (1918–1981) was born in Lower Egypt. The young Sadat entered Cairo's Royal Military Academy in 1936, where he met and became a friend of Gamal Abdel Nasser. Sadat became a lieutenant in the Egyptian army but was dismissed and imprisoned when the government discovered Sadat's anti-government political activities. Sadat escaped from prison but was arrested again in 1946 and charged in several assassination attempts. After Sadat's acquittal, he was reinstated as an officer in the army.

While in the army, Sadat joined Nasser's Free Officers Movement, dedicated to liberating Egypt from British influence. In 1952 the Free Officers Movement overthrew the Egyptian monarchy. Nasser ruled Egypt for the next eighteen years (1952–1970) and appointed Sadat to several government posts. In 1954 Nasser banned the Ikhwan, which had actively supported the Free Officers Movement in the 1952 coup, and turned increasingly to the left while aggressively espousing Egyptian nationalism and Arab socialism.

In 1969 Nasser appointed Sadat vice president. Sadat became interim president of Egypt when Nasser died in 1970 and was elected president by the ruling clique to avoid a polarizing power struggle among rightist and leftist candidates for the presidency. In order to neutralize the more powerful Secularist left, Sadat encouraged and assisted Islamic organizations, particularly the Ikhwan, which harbored deep grudges against the Nasserites and pro-Soviet leftists. While Sadat relaxed political restrictions on Islamic organizations, he purged Nasserites and leftists from the Egyptian government in 1971.

Sadat was behind the surprise invasion of Israel in 1973 to recover Arab lands. At the height of the war, Sadat persuaded Saudi Arabia and the Organization of Arab Petroleum Exporting Countries (OAPEC) to embargo oil to the United States, resulting in OPEC's quadrupling of oil prices. The Saudis also agreed to accept thousands of Egyptian workers into the Saudi workforce. Following the moderately successful 1973 Arab-Israeli War, Sadat became popular at home and abroad. Having outmaneuvered his rivals, Sadat transformed Egyptian foreign and domestic policy by distancing himself from the Soviet Union and improving relations with the West.

In 1979 Sadat signed the Camp David Accords and committed his country to peace with Israel, while Israel promised to return the Sinai Peninsula to Egypt. Muslims around the world condemned the Egyptian-Israeli peace agreement as a "separate peace" that undermined the Palestinian cause, Arab solidarity, and the *ummah*. Egypt was expelled from the Arab League and the Organization of the Islamic Conference (OIC). In 1981, while reviewing a military parade in Cairo commemorating the 1973 war against Israel, the sixty-two-year-old Sadat was assassinated by Revolutionary Islamists belonging to Al-Jihad (the Holy Struggle).

http://www.ibiblio.org/sullivan/bios/Sadat-bio.html
http://www.us-israel.org/jsource/biography/sadat.html
http://www.geocities.com/CapitolHill/9361/sadat.htm

BOX 6.6   Ja'afar Muhammad al-Numeiri

Ja'afar Muhammad al-Numeiri was born on January 1, 1930, in Sudan. Numeiri's family was humble, but his tribe, the Dongolawi, had traditionally supplied prominent Sudanese political leaders. In May 1949, Numeiri was accepted to the Military College of Khartoum. After graduating, Second Lieutenant Numeiri became increasingly involved in political activity and took Nasser as his role model. He imbibed Nasser's ideologies of Arab socialism, pan-Arabism, and anti–Western imperialism.

After some training missions and other assignments in Cyprus, Libya, West Germany, the United States, and Egypt in the 1960s, Numeiri returned to the Sudan, where he continued his political activities. In 1969 Numeiri and his supporters in the army overthrew Sudan's ineffective and unpopular parliamentary regime. The military regime nationalized key industries and introduced land reform. Like his Arab hero, Numeiri pursued secular nationalism and Arab socialism at home and pan-Arabism and pro-Soviet policy abroad.

Numeiri's greatest achievement was an early one—the 1972 Addis Ababa Accord, which ended the country's fifteen-year civil war by giving the southern Sudanese rebels (made up of Christians and animists) a wide local-regional autonomy. But his regime did not attain real stability.

The first serious challenge to Numeiri's Secularist regime came from the Revolutionary Islamists in the Ummah party (the political wing of the Ansar religious sect). Numeiri turned to the Sudanese Communist Party to strengthen his position. After dealing harshly with the Islamists, he turned against his Communist supporters. The leftists overthrew Numeiri, but most of the army still supported him, and he was quickly restored to power. Numeiri reversed his socialist policies and privatized the industries his government had originally nationalized.

In the late 1970s, Numeiri grew increasingly insecure because of several factors: (1) he was one of the few Muslim leaders who had openly supported Muhammad Anwar al-Sadat's controversial trip to Jerusalem and the Camp David Accords; (2) Libyan leader Muammar al-Qaddafi was attempting to undermine his rule by aiding the powerful Islamic movement in Sudan; (3) the *shah* had been overthrown by the Islamic Revolution in Iran; and (4) Numeiri's original socialist and later capitalist experiments had failed to resolve Sudan's chronic socioeconomic problems (poverty, unemployment, underemployment, inflation, mounting debt, corruption, lack of national integration, and the increasing emigration of educated and skilled workers).

Sadat's assassination by Revolutionary Islamists, in October 1981, convinced Numeiri that the only way to survive politically was to launch a government-sponsored Islamization campaign of his own. Numeiri replaced Sudan's secular legal system with the *shariah*. This policy reignited the anti-government rebellion in the south. Numeiri was overthrown in April 1985 in a coup mounted by the army in collaboration with his political foes, including the Islamists he had attempted to court. Numeiri escaped to Egypt and received political asylum there.

Western technology, introduced into the Muslim world by European colonialists and the Muslim Secularists who assumed power when the colonialists left, instantaneously supplanted the simple, nonmechanized, and nonautomated indigenous technology. Within two generations, industrialization and urbanization rapidly progressed; transportation and communications were revolutionized; public and private education spread; formal, differentiated, and specialized roles and institutions emerged to replace informal, personalistic administration; and Muslims were asked to adopt more rational, secular, and modern attitudes. Old centers of power disintegrated, giving way to new and emerging power centers. Modernization involves a comprehensive transformation in all sectors and at all levels of society. Nevertheless, in the Muslim World old ideas, ideals, traditions, institutions, and processes, often sanctified by Islam, have resisted the encroachment of modernization. Continuity persists with change.[5]

Development, in contrast to modernization, encompasses the relative welfare of a nation's population. In the West, modernization accompanied the growth of a large middle class. In this respect, development occurred because a large number of Westerners enjoyed the fruits of modernization. However, in the Muslim world, modernization has not coincided with the growth of a substantial middle class. Although small "middle sectors" have emerged, they lack class consciousness and tend to ally themselves with the elite, whom they emulate, against the "rabble," whom they disdain. Modernization throughout the Muslim world has led to politicoeconomic polarization and social fragmentation. Resources have not been freely or fairly distributed. Instead, the elite has been the primary beneficiary, while the impoverished masses have borne the burden of subsequent underdevelopment. In effect, the Muslim Secularists, convinced or deluded about the benefits of modernization, have unwisely neglected appropriate holistic development. As a result, they have sacrificed the welfare of the many for the prosperity of a few.

Political development, a more specific distillation of general development, involves the formation of political institutions to improve popular participation in government and to incorporate new power contenders. Political development signifies a government's capacity not only to sustain and adapt to the stresses of modernization but also to direct the course and rate of economic, social, and political change.[6] The problem of achieving political development is particularly relevant in the Muslim world as the modernization process has undermined and overwhelmed existing political institutions. Political development is usually associated with the secularization of government, which in turn often involves the differentiation of governmental institutions and processes from religious organization, influ-

---

[5]James A. Bill and Robert Springborg, *Politics in the Middle East*, 5th ed. (New York: Longman, 2002), pp. 2–4.

[6]Since political development is defined here as relative to the process of modernization, it becomes impossible to discuss political development prior to the Industrial Revolution. Although the empires of the Romans, the Byzantines, and the Incas, for example, may have had, at their height, ample capacity to meet the demands made upon them, they did not suffer the numerous stresses and crises of accelerated modernization, and therefore, the concept of political development, circumscribed in time, is inapplicable (Huntington, "Political Development and Political Decay," p. 389).

ence, and control.[7] The same process of secularization in the Muslim world is often perceived as the chief perpetrator of underdevelopment. Moreover, since such political development in conjunction with modernization has been achieved only in the West, it is generally associated with the formation of Western democratic institutions. The capacity of a government to absorb change and solve problems, however, may have nothing to do with Western-style democracy. For example, political participation can be realized through referendums or plebiscites, which bypass representative institutions.

Theoretically, the problem of achieving political development is linked to the imperatives of differentiation, equality, and capacity.[8] Differentiation is linked to political development to the extent that, the more highly developed a political system becomes, the greater the specialization of roles and functions within its administrative and political structures.[9] Equality, the second imperative of political development, involves national citizenship (equality as a participating member of society), a universalistic legal order (equality under the law), and achievement norms (equal opportunity).[10] The third imperative, capacity, signifies a polity's ability to adapt to the pressures inherent in pursuing equality and differentiation. More than mere adaptation, capacity indicates proficiency in planning, organizing, implementing, and manipulating new changes while striving to achieve new goals. The main attributes of "creative capacity" are scope and effectiveness, which are aspects of a developing polity's performance and rationality.[11] In this manner, capacity is not only an adaptive but a creative force.

Unless the imperatives of differentiation, equality, and capacity are satisfied as a polity modernizes, specific developmental crises will arise. The crises of identity, legitimacy, penetration, distribution, and participation are interrelated; one can give rise to another and any number can occur simultaneously.

The Identity Crisis

The ancient admonition "Know thyself" is an enduring feature of human history and a recurring theme of philosophy. The search for personal identity begins with an assessment of one's past (What are my roots?), one's present (Who am I?), and one's future (What is the purpose of my life?). Only when these questions are answered does the quest for self-knowledge end.

During periods of rapid modernization (especially industrialization and urbanization), when the familiarity of traditional society is broken, a widespread identity crisis can ensue. People are uprooted from their tightly knit rural communities and migrate to the cities, where many become victims of unemployment

---

[7]James S. Coleman, "The Developmental Syndrome: Differentiation-Equality-Capacity," in Leonard Binder et al., eds., *Crises and Sequences in Political Development* (Princeton, N.J.: Princeton University Press, 1971), p. 77.

[8]Ibid., pp. 74–75.

[9]Ibid., p. 75.

[10]Ibid., p. 76–78.

[11]Ibid., p. 78–79.

or underemployment, inflation, and unhygienic living conditions. Often these individuals arrive in the cities with high expectations; instead they find a world of excessive materialism, selfishness, and crime. The depersonalization, alienation, and frustration of the "urban jungle" disillusion them and threaten their security and identity. For Muslims, this identity crisis often draws them closer to the religion into which they were socialized as children. Their religion acts as an anchor, alleviates their fears, and gives them a sense of stability, direction, and faith in the future. Therefore, Islam, as both a "historical" and an "organic" religion, is especially significant in the modernizing Muslim world.

Just as the identity crisis must be resolved by individual Muslims if they are to develop into mature and stable adults, so the first and most crucial hurdle facing a new nation-state is to achieve a common or "national" identity. This means that citizens of a new nation-state must come to recognize their national territory as their homeland and must feel that their personal identities are in part defined by their identification with their country.[12] In essence, only when a nation's citizens identify themselves with the nation can a stable yet adaptable and mature political system be realized.[13] This entails a government's effort to integrate its citizenry into a single patriotic political community owing its primary loyalty to the national entity rather than to its primordial groups, which include the extended family and tribal, racial, linguistic, religious, sectarian, class, or regional communities. Most individuals in a traditional developing society are closely tied to their primordial groups and find it difficult to shift allegiance to the nation-state. In the process of political development, individuals and groups within a multiethnic nation-state must transcend traditional kincentric loyalties and become patriotic citizens. Thus it is imperative that the government translate the loose and uncoordinated sentiments of nationalism into a cohesive spirit of patriotism, citizenship, and solidarity. In this respect, political development entails nation building.[14]

Traditional community loyalties are not so easy to overcome, however. In fact, they often become intensified under the pressures of modernization. Identity crisis in the traditional community involves profoundly ambivalent feelings about the modern world and one's own historical, religious, and cultural traditions.[15] An appropriate resolution of the identity crisis must then involve reconciliation of one's own sociocultural traditions and modern practices. Until and unless there is a satisfactory reconciliation of tradition and modernity, people remain ambivalent, conflicted, and rootless. This rootlessness, in turn, hinders the development of the identity that is necessary for building a stable and modern nation-state.[16]

---

[12]Lucien W. Pye, *Aspects of Political Development* (Boston: Little, Brown, 1966), p. 53.

[13]Lucien W. Pye and Sidney Verba, *Political Cultural and Political Development* (Princeton, N.J.: Princeton University Press, 1965), p. 529; and Lucien W. Pye, *Politics, Personality and Nation Building: Burma's Search for Identity* (New Haven, Conn.: Yale University Press, 1962), pp. 52–53.

[14]Pye, *Aspects of Political Development*, p. 38

[15]Meenakshi Gopinath, *Pakistan in Transition: Political Development and Rise to Power of the Pakistan's People's Party* (New Delhi: Manohar Book Service, 1975) p. 7.

[16]Pye, *Aspects of Political Development*, p. 63.

Most Third World countries, including those in the Muslim world, have yet to resolve their identity crisis. Thus, they are plagued by periodic sociopolitical explosions.

A major factor that has contributed to an identity crisis among Muslims all over the world is the preeminence of the *ummah* in Islamic theory. Derived from the Arabic word *umm*, meaning "mother," the term *ummah* in Islam refers to "the community of believers." In the *ummah*, Muslims all over the world are brothers and sisters despite their particular histories, regions, cultures, colors, languages, or socioeconomic and political status. Both *ummah* and nationalism involve a peoples' sense of group identity and loyalty due to shared heritage. Both demand the prime loyalty of their followers. However, the Western secular ideology of nationalism attempts to engender solidarity among the diverse people living within the territorial boundaries of a particular nation-state, rather than grouping persons by their religious beliefs.[17] People in countries all over the world are indoctrinated to love their country, often referred to as the motherland, from an early age. They are thus influenced, manipulated, and even coerced into being or becoming patriotic, owing their allegiance to their government, and fighting for their country's national interests.[18] The Islamic *ummah*, in contrast, is concerned with improving the welfare of and forging a sense of solidarity among all Muslims. While this pan-Islamic vision seems utopian and difficult to achieve today, it is nevertheless the dream that figures prominently in the Islamist's worldview.

The Legitimacy Crisis

Closely related to the identity crisis is the legitimacy crisis, the problem of reaching a consensus on the legitimacy of a nation's political institutions.[19] Legitimacy can be defined as "the basis on which and the degree to which the decisions of government are accepted by the populace of a society because of normative beliefs as to the rightness of the ways in which decisions were made."[20] The population must acknowledge, without coercion, their regime's authority to govern. People may disagree with specific governmental decisions or actions without necessarily

---

[17]Many developing countries cannot be considered "nations," as the term was initially used by Western scholars and media. Instead, developing countries are more or less artificial aggregates of various ascriptively defined communities (tribal, ethnic, racial, linguistic, and religious). However, the national integration of these multiethnic and multinational societies still remains the principal goal of all Third World governments.

[18]National interests involve the critically important and enduring considerations that lie at the very core of a nation's value system. These include such matters as national security against external and internal threats; protection of the country's political, economic, and sociocultural system; enhancement of the country's economic well-being or the development of a higher standard of living; and protection and promotion of a country's honor and ideology.

[19]Pye, *Aspects of Political Development*, p. 63.

[20]Monte Palmer and William R. Thompson, *The Comparative Analysis of Politics* (Itasca, Ill.: F. E. Peacock, 1978), p. 74.

denying the right of the regime to remain in power. Yet the population will support existing political institutions only as their values correspond. Thus, the greater the public's conviction that a regime is honest, fair, and interested in the general welfare, the more popular that regime will be, the more power it can exercise, and the more effective it can be. The moment a regime loses the people's confidence, its political institutions will be perceived as illegitimate and the regime will either fall or become increasingly repressive.

Legitimacy is a moral bond between the government and the governed. The greater that bond, the more likely that the people will see the government's existing political institutions as appropriate for their society and will obey those institutions, even when obeying may be unpleasant or harmful to the individual. A political system that enjoys no legitimacy is forced to resort to increasing degrees of coercion to maintain itself.

Establishing legitimacy is the first best step toward political development. A government that is legitimate will be more able to adapt to and overcome developmental crises. Conversely, developmental crises can erode legitimacy.[21]

A legitimacy crisis exists in the Muslim world because of immense differences in values between the rulers and the ruled. The governing Muslim Secularists are in varying degrees Westernized and secularized. They speak Western languages and have acquired Western education either at home or abroad. In contrast, the culture of the people is permeated with the religious tradition of Islam, which is in direct conflict with secularism and a secular society. Most Muslims are uneducated and therefore do not understand the language (figuratively and, at times, even literally) of their elitist leaders. Hence Muslim Secularists are unable to legitimize their rule, mobilize their populations behind their policies and programs, or integrate their multiethnic citizenry. Lacking mass support, the Secularists are ever vulnerable to overthrow. Thus, to stay in power they have resorted to a mixture of secular indoctrination, cooptation, and coercion. However, these strategies have further divided the power elite from the governed and, in turn, further destabilized existing political institutions.

The Penetration Crisis

The penetration crisis is the problem faced by central governments of all modernizing nations to reach down to the level of their citizenry.[22] Governments that are unable to enforce their decisions at the local level are inherently unstable. Effective penetration by a national government involves controlling previously insulated institutions and segments of society. This is often accomplished with the help of political institutions, such as governmental agencies, political parties, and local village councils, that link the governing elite with the governed in order to

---

[21]Raymond Grew, "The Crises and Their Sequences," in Raymond Grew, ed., *Crises of Political Development in Europe and the United States* (Princeton, N.J.: Princeton University Press, 1978), p. 25.

[22]Pye, *Aspects of Political Development*, p. 64.

implement the country's laws and the regime's policies and programs. This process of state building results in a centralized bureaucracy with increased coercive capacity to effectively enforce national authority, secure public compliance, and govern the society.

All political systems are created and controlled by the governing elite. Yet the long-term survival of these systems depends on popular support. The penetration crisis can be resolved only by bridging the conspicuously wide gulf between the governing and the governed so that the developmental needs of the country can be met. This task in the developing Muslim world is particularly formidable as the ambitious modernization programs of the governing elite far exceed the comprehension of people accustomed to old parochial ways. The wide "cultural gap" or "cultural cleavage," which blocks any resolution of the legitimacy crisis, is also impeding leaders from developing a rapport with the people they govern and from reaching down to the grassroots to change old values and behaviors. Hence, the Muslim Secularists are unable to mobilize support for their modernization programs.

Paradoxically, when governments successfully resolve the closely related crises of penetration, legitimacy, and identity, widespread pressures for greater popular participation in government decision making are unleashed.

The Distribution Crisis

The most visible and extended crisis in political development involves the division of the nation's economic wealth. In essence, the distribution crisis involves the vitally important question of how government powers are to be used to allocate, distribute, and redistribute values, material goods, services, and other benefits in society.[23] The processes and policies of distribution are what government is all about. The distribution crisis is the most difficult of the developmental crises to resolve because the wealthy and powerful elite are seldom willing to surrender their privileges. Their resistance to redistribution can manifest itself by lowering their economic investment and productivity. Sometimes they even provide monetary support to demonstrators who oppose reform-minded regimes and play a role in toppling them. Thus, the ultimate gauge of a government's political performance is its management of the distribution crisis in terms of national security, general welfare, and individual liberties.

The distribution crisis is compounded in the Muslim world by the population explosion characteristic of developing countries. The population explosion has meant that the working population carries a larger "dependency load." In Muslim countries, nearly half the population is under fifteen years of age. As a result, a high percentage of the countries' capital is expended on feeding, housing, clothing, educating, and training these young individuals. Moreover, the demographic

---

[23]Pye, *Aspects of Political Development*, p. 66.

preeminence of youth in Muslim countries indicates that fertility rates will not soon decline.[24]

Since the population of the major cities in the Muslim world is doubling every fifteen years, rapid urban growth is putting heavy pressure on food and water supplies, housing, sanitation, health care, education, and employment. Given the current inadequate distribution of goods and services and its relation to sociopolitical instability and violence, it is likely that cities throughout the Muslim world will be the focal points of future revolutions.

The population explosion contributes to a chronic shortage of resources (such as food, drinking water, clothing, housing, education, health care, consumer goods, and electricity); leads to the chronic overcrowding of cities and towns; contributes to inflation and a sharp rise in the cost of living; greatly reduces the opportunities that job seekers will have obtaining relevant job training programs and work; and accelerates ecological degradation. Shortages of food, consumer goods, and services drive up the prices of these goods and services, making them less accessible to the needy majority, more of whom are slipping into the category of the "absolute poor" who are eking out an existence at bare subsistence levels. This, in turn, results in a chronic distribution crisis that most Muslim governments are finding difficult to resolve. Robert McNamara, former president of the World Bank, summarized the consequences of the population explosion best:

> All are rightly viewed by governments as threats to social stability and orderly change. Even under vigorous economic growth, managing the demographic expansion is difficult; with a faltering economy it is all but impossible.[25]

Muslim governments for various reasons have been unwilling to crusade against the explosive population growth. Some Muslim Secularists have placed their faith in the "demographic transition" theory positing that economic and social modernization will inevitably lower population growth rates, as it has done in the West. Also, Muslim leaders are seriously concerned about the enormous influence that the conservative clerical establishment has over the illiterate masses in opposing population control. Muslim leaders are also wary of the costs involved in instituting a successful family-planning program. Other leaders, usually nationalist and socialistic, are suspicious of the West's emphasis and propaganda on the population issue and are opposed to the encroachment of secular Western governments or groups in their internal affairs.

The distribution crisis is accentuated by the problem of "relative deprivation," or heightened expectations, which causes sociopolitical instability. Prominent

---

[24]Dorothy Nortman, *U.N. Reports on Population/Family Planning*, No. 2, September 1976, p. 4; Lester Brown, *World without Borders* (New York: Vintage Books, 1972), p. 134; J. Faaland and J. R. Parkinson, *The Political Economy of Development* (New York: St. Martin's Press, 1986), p. 168; Gerald O. Barney, *Global 2000* (Arlington, Va.: Seven Locks Press, 1991), pp. 1, 8–9; Michael P. Todaro, *Economic Development in the Third World* (New York: Longman, 1989), p. 187; Helen Low and Howe Low, "Focus on the Fourth World," *The U.S. and World Development: Agenda for Action 1975* (New York: Praeger Publishers, 1975), pp. 38–39.

[25]Robert S. McNamara, "The Population Problem," *Foreign Affairs*, Summer 1984, pp. 119.

intellectuals of the last twenty-three centuries have said that people act aggressively, and even violently, not only because they are poor and deprived in an absolute sense but also because they feel deprived relative to others or relative to their own expectations. Thus, feelings of relative deprivation result when people realize that others have done better than they in the past, are doing better now, and/or are expected to do better in the future.[26] Aristotle, for instance, contends that the principal cause of revolution is the desire of the entrenched oligarchy for more power and wealth conflicting with the desire of the poor for greater equity and justice.[27] *Relative deprivation* is today defined as

> the discrepancy between those conditions of life to which people in society think they are justifiably entitled (value expectations) and those desirable social circumstances which they feel they are capable of achieving and maintaining (value capabilities). This discrepancy induces social discontent, which may lead to widespread anger, which, in turn, may be triggered into collective political violence.[28]

Rebellions and revolutions may also occur when a society, having enjoyed a prolonged period of rising expectations and gratification, suddenly experiences a sharp reversal. A period of rapid growth often heightens people's expectations of continuing improvement in their lives. When a sudden reversal occurs, the gap between the accelerating expectations and the realities of plummeting gratifications is far more distressing and intolerable than if the reversal had followed a period of relative stagnation. These accumulated and intolerable frustrations eventually seek violent outlets. If frustration and bitterness have been festering for a long time and are sufficiently widespread, intense, and focused on the established regime in power, violence may explode into revolution that may displace the ruling regime, undermine the old and discredited power structure, and radically transform the entire society through coercion and attendant bloodshed. If, however, the outbreak of violence is not focused, intense, or widespread enough, the the unpopular regime may stay in power by intimidating, crushing, or coopting its opposition. In the latter case, potential rebels may prefer to live with their frustrations than endure job loss, long prison terms, torture, or execution. Just as often, the government partially or completely addresses the grievances of the discontented masses.[29]

In Muslim societies today, the distribution crisis is particularly acute because the gap separating the rich and powerful few from the poor and powerless majority has grown wider. In the case of the Middle East, which is a microcosm of the

[26]Bruce Russet and Harvey Starr, *World Politics: The Menu for Choice*, 4th ed. (New York: W. H. Freeman, 1992), p. 89.

[27]J. E. C. Weldon, trans., *The Politics of Aristotle* (New York: MacMillan, 1905), p. 338.

[28]Ted R. Gurr, *Why Men Rebel* (Princeton, N.J.: Princeton University Press, 1970), p. 37.

[29]James C. Davies, "Satisfaction and Revolution," in David H. Everson and Joann Popard Paine, eds., *An Introduction to Systematic Political Science* (Homewood, Ill.: The Dorsey Press, 1973), pp. 158–160. For a much more detailed discussion of the hypothesis forwarded by James Davies and others on the subject of relative deprivation, see James Chowning Davies, ed., *When Men Revolt and Why: A Reader in Political Violence and Revolution* (New York: Free Press, 1971).

Muslim world, the gap between modernization on one hand and socioeconomic and political dimensions of development on the other has been consistently much larger than in other regions of the world. For instance, although the Middle East has a higher GNP per capita than Latin America, Latin American countries are placed higher on the United Nations' Human Development Index.[30]

Since Islam emphasizes socioeconomic equity and justice and enjoins devout Muslims to play an active role in politics, religion has become a powerful revolutionary ideology used by the poor, disenfranchised, exploited, frustrated, and alienated masses (socialized in Islam) to challenge the governing elite. Some of the poor adopt violent measures to pressure the government to improve the distribution of goods and services in the society. This was vividly evident during the fifteen-year Lebanese civil war (1975–1990), when the Muslim majority gave up on the peaceful and legal parliamentary means of pressuring the Christian-dominated government to improve their economic, social, and political welfare. The same distribution crisis manifests itself in most other Muslim countries. However, major sociopolitical upheavals are prevented and contained by the authoritarian civil, monarchical, and military regimes ruling the Muslim world.

The Participation Crisis

Although relative deprivation is primarily an economic concept, people can also suffer from relative political deprivation. The population in a modernizing, secularizing, and Westernizing society inevitably asks for greater political participation, particularly when such participation is routine in Western nations. Relative political deprivation, or a participation crisis, occurs when the governing elite refuses to accommodate the aspirations and expectations of citizens to participate in the political system's decision-making process. In reaction to pressures for increased participation, a government may become more authoritarian as it struggles to stay in power or may organize a rigged election or referendum. Sometimes the participation crisis will cause a military coup d'etat or, more rarely, a broad-based revolution.[31]

Rapid modernization intensifies relative political deprivation "when there is uncertainty over the appropriate rate of expansion and when the influx of new participants creates serious strains on the existing institutions." The pressures accompanying increased participation upset the status quo and the "continuity of the old

---

[30]The United Nations Development Programme's Human Development Index (HDI combines the scores of three indices: life expectancy, adult literacy, and educational enrollment) reveals that although the per-capita GNP of a Middle Eastern country is generally twice that of countries of Latin America, the HDI of Latin American societies is over 20 percent higher than in the Middle East. The GNP per capita is one measure of the overall wealth of a nation, while the HDI indicates the true distribution of that wealth (data cited in Bill and Springborg, *Politics in the Middle East*, p. 5). Also see United Nations Development Programme, *Human Development Report, 1997* (New York: Oxford University Press, 1998), pp. 146–148.

[31]Myron Weiner, "Political Participation: Crisis of the Political Process," in Leonard Binder et al., eds. *Crises and Sequences in Political Development*, p. 187.

polity is broken and there is the need to reestablish the entire structure of political relations."[32] The consequent political chaos and dislocation could easily overwhelm the fragile nation-states of the Muslim world.

The participation crisis is often related to the legitimacy and penetration crises. Legitimacy can become untenable either under conditions of severely limited participation, which are common in the Muslim world, or under conditions of widespread participation outside existing political institutions. Although Indonesia, Malaysia, Turkey, Lebanon, Jordan, and Bangladesh have controlled forms of pluralism and democracy, there are no functioning democracies among the other forty-four predominantly Muslim countries. Most authoritarian leaders, whether civilian or military, are Muslim Secularists who sometimes manipulate Islamic rhetoric and symbols to stay in power. To encourage mass participation, these opportunistic Secularists often mask modernization with indigenous concepts (like Islamic democracy or Islamic socialism), rather than hold general elections based on Western-oriented liberal parliamentary democracy. Moreover, the Secularist's efforts usually are intended to mobilize support for government programs, seldom to give the masses any real say in the governance of society.[33]

In Muslim societies, few democratic institutions exist through which the masses can vent their grievances or from which they can expect justice. This institutional void has been filled by the *masjid*, which has served throughout the Muslim world as an oasis of freedom in a desert of despotism. Most Muslims— whether rulers or ruled—respect the sanctity of the *masjid* and are loathe to shed blood therein. The most cruel and dictatorial tyrant will hesitate in his repression under the shadow of the minaret. To do otherwise, to murder in a house of worship, invites political suicide.

Masjids in the Muslim world often require no government license to operate, and authoritarian Muslim governments generally refrain from closing even politically objectionable *masjids*. Since Prophet Muhammad strongly urged congregational prayer, especially on Friday afternoons, disallowing such prayer or barring the doors of the mosque would cause a furor among worshipers. Because *masjids* are to this degree immune from blatant government repression, the *masjid* has become the focal point of anti-government, anti-Secularist, and anti-Western opinion in the Muslim world. Many Muslim clerics, following the example of Muhammad, utilize the sacred premises of the *masjid* not only to worship God, but as a political platform from which to enlighten the faithful and to mobilize political action. Some Muslim clerics deliver sermons sharply critical of government policies, programs, and leadership. Thus, the clerics in the Muslim world have risen to positions of leadership in opposition to unpopular and tyrannical Secularist regimes and their corrupt and unrepresentative political institutions. This clerical class often has little or no knowledge of Western intellectual thought,

---

[32]Pye, *Aspects of Political Development*, p. 65.

[33]Norman D. Palmer, "Changing Patterns of Politics in Pakistan: An Overview," in Manzooruddin Ahmad, ed., *Contemporary Pakistan: Politics, Economy, and Society* (Durham, N.C.: Carolina Academic Press, 1980), pp. 48–49.

has not traveled abroad, and can speak no Western languages. Therefore, when the clerics communicate with the people through Islamic symbols, they are seen as sincere, unlike the Muslim Secularists. These Islamists have risen repeatedly throughout Islamic history, leading mass movements against foreign and domestic despots. The last decade represents a cyclical renewal of this Islamism or Islamic revivalism. The Revolutionary Islamists and the Traditionalist Islamists, often insulated from direct government control in the *masjids*, have effectively used the potent Islamic concepts of *khurooj* (the right to revolt against an unjust and tyrannical ruler), *jihad* (the right to engage in a holy struggle against nonbelievers and the unrighteous), and of *shahadat* (martyrdom attained in a *jihad*) to agitate and mobilize Muslims against repressive regimes throughout Islamic history.

Aware of this history, the Muslim Secularists have not stood idly by in the face of *masjid*-instigated anti-government activity. Government troops have been placed within sight of *masjid* entrances to deter possible spontaneous demonstrations following congregational prayer. The Egyptian government has taken this strategy a step further and exercises direct control over urban *masjids*. The Egyptian government pays the salaries and screens the Friday sermons of as many as one-third of Egypt's mosque *imams* (preachers). Thousands of other *imams* serving in mosques throughout Egypt, especially in rural areas, regularly denounce the government for being "un-Islamic."[34] Egypt's control of the *masjid*, perhaps the most extensive of any Secularist regime, is truly inadequate. The dynamism of Islamism in Egypt is undampened, the clerics are undeterred, and the mosque remains the focal point of opposition to Muslim Secularists and their Modernist Islamist supporters. Thus, in Egypt and throughout the Muslim world, the *masjid* represents a safe haven for anti-government opposition.

The nations of the developed Western world are fortunate to have become modernized gradually over the centuries, giving the West sufficient time to resolve each developmental crisis in turn. In the Muslim world, modernization is occurring at such an accelerated pace that centuries of transformation are condensed into a single generation. Hence, the crises that occurred serially in the West are coming simultaneously in the Muslim world and are imposing intolerable demands on political systems that have neither the time nor the opportunity to adapt. Sociopolitical explosions are frequent, usually leading to authoritarian civil or military regimes and sometimes even to civil wars and revolutions.

Iran experienced all five crises simultaneously and with such elevated intensity that the compound mixture reached "critical mass" and exploded in an Islamic Revolution in 1978. Iran's Muhammad Reza Shah Pahlavi had initiated a process of rapid modernization but had been unwilling to resolve the consequent developmental crises. The youth of Iran questioned the legitimacy of the *shah*'s authoritarian regime, the lack of popular participation, and even their own identity. Meanwhile, the distribution crisis worsened as the material needs and wants of an expectant population went consistently unfulfilled. The crises of development

---

[34]Caryle Murphy, "Islam's Crescent of Change," *Washington Post National Weekly Edition,* May 25–31, 1992, p. 7.

became cumulatively acute in the final years of the *shah*'s regime, despite U.S. president Jimmy Carter's encouraging the Iranian monarch to liberalize his political system. Overwhelmed by the developmental crises, the *shah* fled and his regime collapsed. Ayatollah Khomeini, representing the "Islamic" alternative, assumed power and promised to reverse the pro-Western policies of the *shah* and to establish a "true" Islamic state.

Sudan, like Iran, is experiencing all five developmental crises simultaneously; however, the identity crisis is particularly acute. Southern Sudan, which is primarily Christian and animist, does not identify with the predominantly Muslim north, which governs Sudan. The overwhelming majority of southern Sudanese resent the authoritarian control exercised by the army in the north and have waged guerrilla warfare for autonomy for nearly two decades. The situation worsened in the late 1970s, when Sudan's Secularist president Ja'afar al-Numeiri imposed the *shariah* and started an aggressive Islamization program. Though Numeiri was overthrown in a military coup in 1985, subsequent Sudanese regimes have continued his Islamization program. The current military regime of Omar Hasan al-Bashir has appointed several prominent Islamists in the National Islamic Front (dominated by the *Ikhwan al-Muslimun*) to high-level government positions and is seriously committed to instituting Islamic policies and programs and making Sudan an Islamic state. However, Sudan's economy has been in the doldrums since the early 1990s, when the oil-rich Arab kingdoms of the Persian Gulf discontinued all their aid in retaliation for the Sudanese regime's refusal to send soldiers to fight in the U.S.-led military coalition against Iraq in 1991. Moreover, the U.S. government accused the Sudanese regime of using its diplomats in the United States to aid and abet some Sudanese terrorists in New York, who were arrested on charges of planning to blow up the Lincoln and Holland Tunnels, and the United Nations and take prominent Americans hostage. The economic sanctions have further aggravated and compounded all five developmental crises in Sudan (see Box 6.7).

The fifteen-year civil war in Lebanon (1975–1990) also can be attributed to the convergence of the five developmental crises. First, this predominantly Muslim country has been controlled by its Christian minority since it gained independence on November 22, 1943. Over time, the Muslim population grew faster than that of the Christians, while individual Muslims became more conscious of their Islamic identity and their state of relative deprivation vis-à-vis the governing Christian elite. Next, the Palestine Liberation Organization (PLO), which had been targeted by King Hussein's army in Jordan, escaped into Lebanon in September 1970. The PLO and their families were first treated as refugees by the Lebanese Shi'ahs of South Lebanon; however, by the late 1970s the PLO had assumed control of the Shi'ah heartland of South Lebanon and were perceived by the Lebanese to be a state within the state of Lebanon.

The Lebanese identity crisis worsened after the Israeli invasion of Lebanon in 1982. Initially, the Shi'ah majority welcomed the Israeli invaders as liberators from the PLO infrastructure in southern Lebanon. Yet when the Israelis, like the PLO, overstayed their welcome and victimized the Lebanese Shi'ahs, the Shi'ah majority of Lebanon, emboldened by the successful Islamic revolution in Iran, rose and

■

BOX 6.7   Hasan al-Turabi

Hasan al-Turabi was born in 1932 in central Sudan, south of Khartoum. He received an Islamic education from his devout family but also pursued a modern education. At universities in Khartoum, London, and the Sorbonne, Turabi studied law. As a student in the 1950s, Turabi joined Sudan's Muslim Brotherhood and became prominent during subsequent uprisings and in political activities in which Turabi demanded that Sudan adopt an Islamic constitution.

In 1977 Sudan's President Numeiri made peace with the Revolutionary Islamists in Sudan and appointed Turabi as his attorney general. Turabi encouraged members of the Muslim Brotherhood to take more active roles in the military and in commerce. Turabi also was behind Numeiri's attempt to adopt Islamic law in 1983. However, Numeiri turned against the Islamists shortly after this and imprisoned Turabi. In 1985 Numeiri was overthrown, and Turabi was released from prison. Turabi's political party did well in Sudan's 1986 elections and took part in subsequent coalition governments. Nevertheless, Turabi remained committed to the idea of establishing an Islamic state, in spite of the possibility of renewed civil war with the predominantly non-Muslim population in the south of Sudan. In 1989 General Omar Hassan Ahmed al-Bashir, also an Islamist, overthrew Sudan's elected government. With Turabi's backing, al-Bashir reestablished Islamic law and appointed Turabi as speaker of Sudan's parliament. For ten years, from 1989 to 1999, Turabi ruled Sudan hand-in-glove with President Bashir.

In various writings, speeches, and interviews, Turabi has presented himself as a fairly liberal and moderate Islamist who embraces such notions as democracy, tolerance, and women's rights. However, there is another side to Turabi. After his call for an Islamic legal code pushed southern Sudan into civil war, Turabi set up Islamic militias to fight a *jihad* there. Turabi has actively participated in several autocratic governments, belying his commitment to democracy and liberalization. His views of an Islamic state, as he helped outline it in the 1998 constitution, were far more Revolutionary than Modernist. Likewise he has shown support for Revolutionary Islamist groups from outside Sudan. It was while Turabi was at the height of his power that Osama bin Laden was a welcome guest in Sudan, establishing training camps for Revolutionary Islamists. Turabi's Sudan has also harbored members of Hamas and Hezbollah. And although Turabi condemned the 1993 bombing of the World Trade Center, its prime suspect had spent time in Sudan as Turabi's guest.

By 1999, Bashir began to view the enlightened, charismatic, and popular Turabi as a threat to his power. In late 1999, Bashir declared a state of emergency, removed Turabi from his posts, took over Turabi's political party, and by early 2001 placed Turabi under house arrest. Many of Turabi's followers either kept quiet or betrayed him and sided with President Bashir.

http://www.witness-pioneer.org/vil/Articles/shariah/
interview_on_apostasy_hasan_turabi.htm

http://www.wam.umd.edu/~gsanders/text/alturabi.html

challenged an unjust status quo. The fact that Lebanon is a poor country and its society a complex mosaic of different ethnic groups has complicated its tragic fate. The divided Christian elite, the fragmented Palestinians, the polarized Shi'ah (with moderates and pro-Iranian Revolutionary Islamists), the Sunnis, and the Druze are all proud of their identity, highly politicized, and heavily armed. As though these divisions and rivalries were not bad enough, the Lebanese system is also deeply penetrated by Syria, Israel, Iran, France, the United States, and the PLO. Each external power manipulates its surrogates in the Lebanese system, often to Lebanon's detriment. The penetration of the Lebanese system by outside powers has greatly destabilized the fragile ethnic balance of a once peaceful and prosperous country and has contributed to the prolongation and exacerbation of its fifteen-year civil war. Today, Lebanon is plagued by all five developmental crises; they will be difficult to alleviate.

The civil war that has consumed Ethiopia since 1962 involves the simultaneous combustion of all five crises. As in some other Muslim nations, the identity crisis manifested itself first. Over half the population of forty-four million is in rebellion (four million Eritreans, five million Tigreans, and fifteen million Oromoans). Eritrea, increasingly populated by Arabic-speaking Muslims, became a province of Ethiopia with Western help following World War II. When the Ethiopian government formally and permanently annexed Eritrea in 1962, the Eritreans rose in rebellion against the Marxist-Leninist regime in Addis Ababa. At first the Muslims were in the vanguard of the rebellion; however, in the 1970s, a Christian Eritrean rebel movement usurped the leadership role. Besides the Eritreans, the Ethiopian government has had to suppress the movement for self-determination among the Tigrean people (one-third of whom are Muslim). Government mismanagement and callousness cost over a hundred thousand Tigrean lives to hunger and disease in the Ethiopian famine of 1972–1973. The Tigreans vowed never to die quietly again and have since engaged in guerrilla warfare against the government. Ethiopia's military government has spent over seventeen years trying to crush the Eritrean and Tigrean movements. In this effort it received enormous help from the Russians and Cubans. When these two benefactors stopped supporting Mengistu Haile Miriam's regime in Addis Ababa, the Ethiopian regime fell. The Eritreans took over control of all of Eritrea, the Tigreans took over the Tigre province, and the country slid into anarchy.[35]

Algeria has been rocked since spring 1992 by legitimacy and participation crises. Beginning with the massive uprisings in October 1988, in which more than six hundred people were killed and over ten thousand were injured, the military regime of Chadli Benjedid relented and in February 1989 announced its decision to adopt a multiparty system. This was the first time since Algeria's independence from France in 1962 that Islamists had been allowed to organize themselves into political parties. The Islamic Salvation Front (FIS), which advocated an Islamic state with the Qur'an as the constitution, won 55 percent of the vote in the June

---

[35]James F. Dunnigan and Austin Bay, *A Quick and Dirty Guide to War: Briefings on Present and Potential Wars*, rev. ed. (New York: William Morrow/Quill, 1991), pp. 308–310.

1989 regional elections and 49 percent of the vote in the first round of the general election on December 26, 1991. In fact, the FIS won 188 out of 430 seats in the national legislature and needed only an additional 28 out of 199 seats in the second round of runoff voting, to be held on January 16, 1992. The Secularist-socialist National Liberation Front, in contrast, won only 15 seats in the parliament. Although the party has governed Algeria since independence, the National Liberation Front was perceived by the Algerian masses as guilty of authoritarianism, corruption, nepotism, close ties with France (Algeria's unpopular former colonial master), and above all, gross mismanagement of an economy suffering from 100 percent inflation and 25 percent unemployment.[36]

Western leaders and Secularists in the Muslim world were shocked that the Islamists walked away with almost half the national vote in Algeria despite competition from forty other political parties. The Secularists in the top brass of the Algerian army, fearing, at the very minimum, the victory of the Islamists and the loss of their positions, privileges, and comfortable lives, pressured Benjedid to resign and cracked down on the FIS. On the day Algerians were to celebrate the occasion of the Arab world's first genuine multiparty democracy, the army called on Muhammad Boudiaf—a hero from Algeria's war of independence against France who had just returned to Algiers after three decades of exile in Morocco—to head an army-backed, five-member "collegial presidency" and run the country in place of the elected leaders until new elections were held. Boudiaf was assassinated by Revolutionary Islamists in early July 1992, and since then tens of thousands of Algerians have been killed in a bloody civil war between a despotic, corrupt, and incompetent secular regime, on one hand, and a grassroots movement of radicalized Islamists, on the other. As Iran was, Algeria seems headed for an Islamic revolution because of legitimacy, participation, and distribution crises.[37]

Summary

The unhappy predicament of the nation-building, state building, modernizing, and secularizing Muslim world invites certain conclusions. The five developmental crises, in no discernible or definitive sequence, have afflicted the fragile nation-states of the developing world. However, the identity crisis is often the precipitating crisis in the Muslim world; it triggers political chaos and national catastrophe. Nevertheless, the identity crisis is not a priori; it is both a symptom of and a contributor to the other crises. In essence, it serves as a catalyst.

---

[36]Alfred Hermida, "Algeria: Fundamentalists Sweep to Near Victory," *Middle East International*, January 10, 1992, pp. 7–9; "Algeria: An Alarming No Vote," *Time*, January 13, 1992, p. 28; "Fundamentalist Leaders Reported Arrested in Algeria," *New York Times*, January 20, 1992, p. A-3; Stephen Budiansky, "Democracy's Detours: Holding Elections Does Not Guarantee That Freedom Will Follow," *U.S. News & World Report*, January 27, 1992, p. 49; Howard La Franchi, "Algeria's Leadership Chooses Head of Ruling Council," *Christian Science Monitor*, January 16, 1992, p. 3; "Algerian Islamic Parties," *The Minaret*, Vol. 10, No. 3, Summer 1989, p. 36.

[37]Ibid.

The apparent primacy of the identity crisis suggests the government's failure to achieve political development, establish valid political institutions, or instill a national consciousness; it is a failure of nation building. Regimes throughout the Muslim world have been incapable of understanding or undertaking successful political development. Unlike Europe and the United States, the Muslim world was initially conceived as a single political and religious unit. The creation of nation-states from the dismemberment of this unit was an artificial and arbitrary contrivance of the colonial powers; it was not wholly consensual. Consequently, the resulting false borders were rejected as truly legitimate among Muslims. This rejection has been exacerbated by the oppressive, but otherwise ineffectual, leadership of Muslim Secularists who are loyal to the secular nation-state and want their citizens to be as well.

In reaction, Muslims have sought more legitimate, more comforting, and more effective definitions of identity and community—definitions excluding "nation-state" and including everything from tribe and race to language and religion. The question becomes, On what basis and at what level should "community" be delineated? Sincere Islamists wish to unify Muslims under the banner of the universal *ummah*, under the universal law of the *shariah*; they advocate pan-Islamism. At the other extreme, community units smaller than the nation-state are arising—units based on family, a religious sect, a tribe, or a village. But whether the pull is toward utopian universalism or narrow parochialism, the pull is decidedly away from the nation-state. As an appropriate and acknowledged unit of community, the nation-state, like the Muslim Secularist leadership advocating it, is discredited.

The developmental crises are cumulatively hastening the dissolution of the Muslim nation-state. The Muslim secularists have been unable to establish national institutions to forestall or resolve the developmental crises or to satisfy the imperatives of differentiation, equality, and capacity. Hence, these nations are politically underdeveloped and are today held together by raw force alone. The Muslim Secularists have failed to build working political institutions or cohesive nations. Their regimes are illegitimate and their ideologies inappropriate, and they have chosen to oppress the masses rather than to submit to the inevitable—the dissolution of the nation-state.

Internet Sites

http://www.demokrasivakfi.org.tr/ataturk/index_eng.html

http://www.ataturk.com/index2.html

http://www.sporum.gov.tr/English/Ataturk/ata2.asp

http://www.cs.umd.edu/~kandogan/FTA/Ataturk/ataturk.html

http://www.secularislam.org/books/ataturk.htm

http://www.columbia.edu/cu/tsa/ata/ata.html

http://www.mrdowling.com/608-ataturk.html

http://www.turizm.net/turkey/history/ataturk.html

http://www.business-with-turkey.com/tourist-guide/ataturk.htm

http://www.digbib.uio.no/publ/vikan/51/57/58.html

http://www.ahram.org.eg/weekly/archives/parties/nasser/nass90.htm

http://www.ibiblio.org/sullivan/bios/Sadat-bio.html

http://www.us-israel.org/jsource/biography/sadat.html

http://www.geocities.com/CapitolHill/9361/sadat.htm

http://www.uruklink.net/iraq/bio.htm

http://www.top-biography.com/9004-Saddam%20Hussein/index1.asp

http://www.pbs.org/wgbh/pages/frontline/shows/saddam/

http://www.danielpipes.org/reviews/19910809.html

http://lexicorient.com/e.o/sad_huss.htm

http://www.witness-pioneer.org/vil/Articles/shariah/interview_on_apostasy_hasan_turabi.htm

http://www.wam.umd.edu/~gsanders/text/alturabi.html

CHAPTER SEVEN

Islamic Politics in the Arab-Israeli Conflict

The Arab-Israeli conflict has contributed to Islamism around the Muslim world in two principal ways. First, the Secularist Palestinian leadership, since the Palestinian Liberation Organization (PLO) was established in 1964, has failed to wrest any substantive concessions from the Israeli government through peaceful negotiations or guerrilla warfare. The failure of Yasser Arafat's Secularist Palestinian Authority (PA) to end Israeli occupation, pauperization, and isolation of Palestinians has profoundly disillusioned Palestinian Muslims in particular and disappointed Muslims all over the world. Second, the ineffectiveness of secular Arab regimes in four wars with Israel (1948, 1956, 1967, and 1973) has frustrated and alienated many Muslims. Consequently, the people of the Muslim world are turning increasingly to Islam as the answer to this complex, long-festering, and seemingly intractable conflict.

The Palestinian Catastrophe (al-Nakba)

The Palestinians refer to the creation of Israel, which is celebrated by Israelis and Jews all over the world, as **al-Nakba** (the Catastrophe). This is because the biggest victims of the unresolved Arab-Israeli conflict are the Palestinians—a people who have lost much of their homeland. They are stateless, friendless, and without hope. Although they had nothing to do with the anti-Semitism, pogroms, and holocaust against the Jewish people, the world nevertheless expects Palestinians to pay the price for it. They are not only the unfortunate victims of both geography and history—living in the wrong place at the wrong time—but have also been ill-served by incompetent and unscrupulous leaders in the Muslim world and by the Great Powers. Moreover, their most basic human needs for food, clean water, clothing, shelter, health care, education, and jobs have gone largely unmet.

In 1948, as the state of Israel took its first breath, thousands of Palestinians were driven from their homes by overzealous Zionists. Jews maintain that these Palestinians fled on the urging of neighboring Arab governments, who initially rejected Israel's right to exist and considered the Jewish state a foreign neocolonial cancer in the heart of the Arab world.

Despite these conflicting accounts of the initial Palestinian diaspora (dispersion), it is indisputable that many thousands of Jews from all over the world migrated to Palestine, and then after 1948 Israel, while nearly a million Palestinians became refugees, living in squalor in Egypt's Gaza Strip, Jordan's West Bank, Syria, and Lebanon. As the Jews returned to Zion (a symbol for Jerusalem during King David's reign of biblical Israel), the Palestinians lost their state and home. The Arab-Israeli wars of 1948, 1956, 1967, and 1973 contributed to the Palestinian exodus from Israel, and to swelling refugee camps in neighboring countries. Likewise, many Palestinians were killed, wounded, and terrorized in the Jordanian Civil War of 1970 and in two Israeli invasions of Lebanon in 1978 and 1982. Although these conflicts targeted the Palestine Liberation Organization, many innocent Palestinians suffered. For example, following the PLO evacuation of Beirut in 1982, over two thousand Palestinians, mostly old men, women, and children, were killed in the Sabra and Shatila refugee camps in Lebanon. The attackers were members of the paramilitary wing of the Christian Phalangists—a tightly organized rightist political party committed to preserving the Maronite Catholic control of Lebanon—acting with Israeli army complicity.

The 1.2 million Palestinians who remained in what had been Palestine and was now under Israeli jurisdiction were hardly any better off. Through a systematic policy of discrimination and persecution, the powerless Palestinians in Israel were relegated to second-class Israeli citizenship or became little more than refugees in the occupied West Bank and Gaza Strip. A stepped-up effort in the Israeli government's heavily subsidized settlement policy in those territories uprooted thousands of Palestinians to make way for newly arriving Zionists from around the world.

The predicament of the Palestinians in the last fifty years has been politically and psychologically devastating. They have been stripped not only of the land of their ancestors but also of their very identity and self-respect. While they have focused primarily on the Israelis in their struggle to establish a secular and democratic state in place of the Jewish/Zionist state of Israel, or adjacent to it, their enemies are not always Zionists.

Serious and sometimes explosive tension underlies the relationship between Palestinians and other Arabs. While Egypt, Syria, and Jordan have warred with Israel ostensibly in the name of the Palestinian plight, Palestinians recognize that Egyptian, Syrian, and Jordanian motives are not altruistic. National interests motivate the actions of the Arab states neighboring Israel. Their promotion of the Palestinian cause is often symbolic. It rarely takes the form of substantive eco-

TABLE 7.1   Characteristics of Middle Eastern and North African Countries

Country	Population (thousands)	Population Growth Rate (%)	Infant Mortality Rate (per 1,000 live births)	Population under 15 Years of Age (%)	Life Expectancy (years) (males)	Urban Population (%)	Literacy Rate (%)	Arable Land (%)	Per-Capita GNP ($U.S.)
Middle East									
Bahrain	603	2.6	16.4	31	72	91	85	2	6,200
Iran	67,540	2.4	51	44	67	60	72	8	2,068
Iraq	22,219	3.0	58	47	66	75	58	12	1,036
Israel	5,535	1.4	8	28	76	91	95	17	15,920
Jordan	4,325	2.4	31	44	71	72	87	4	1,510
Kuwait	2,077	2.6	77	37	59	39	97	7	17,390
Lebanon	3,859	1.3	35	35	68	88	92	21	2,660
Oman	2,265	3.8	26	46	71	78	59	2	4,820
Qatar	665	2.3	19	29	70	92	79	3	15,040
Saudi Arabia	20,008	3.3	44	43	68	84	63	1	7,040
Syria	16,138	2.7	39	46	66	53	71	28	1,120
Turkey	63,528	1.4	41	31	70	71	82	30	2,780
United Arab Emirates	2,262	2.2	16	33	73	84	79	0	17,400
Yemen	13,972	3.3	68	48	59	34	43	6	260
North Africa									
Algeria	29,830	1.7	47	39	67.5	56	61.6	3	1,600
Egypt	64,792	1.6	71	36	59.8	45	51	3	790
Libya	5,648	3.2	58	48	63	86	76	2	4,755
Morocco	30,391	1.6	41	37	68	53	44	18	1,110
Tunisia	9,183	1.5	34	33	72	63	67	20	1,820
Comparison States									
Canada	29,123	0.6	6	20	76	77	97	9	19,380
Poland	38.7	0.3	12	22	68	64	99	48	2,790
Italy	57,534	-0.1	7	15	75	67	97	32	19,020

Source: Adapted from the World Bank and *The World Almanac and Book of Facts, 1998.*

nomic or military assistance. Meanwhile, the Palestinians are "reviled by self-pro-claimed sympathizers."[1] One Palestinian explained that

> the real enemy of the Palestinians is the other Arabs. That is because we know the Zionists are against us, but the Arabs say they are friends and brothers, but the truth is that they just use us for what they need.[2]

Thus, the alienation of the Palestinians is complete; their identity, uncertain. They cannot identify themselves by reference to a homeland. They have none. Yet most Palestinians consider themselves people of a once and future Palestine. Their current situation is best characterized as being in limbo, with their security and survival at stake. In fact, many Palestinians refer to their struggle as not merely an independence movement but an unfolding revolution.[3] Given this chronic and unresolved crisis of identity, the stateless and victimized Palestinians are susceptible to Islamism—Islam as a source of identity and strength, a security blanket in a climate of terrible insecurity, and an anchor in a rootless and hopeless existence.

In their struggle, the Palestinians have traditionally embraced secular nation-alism and have fought ceaselessly since 1948 to establish a homeland in any part of the former Palestine. They have trusted politically adept leaders like Yasser Arafat and have avoided Islamism as an idiom of their struggle. Nevertheless, the Palestinians are predominantly Muslim, and their fifty-four-year failed struggle against Israel has led to the empowerment of Revolutionary Islamists within the Unified Leadership of the Uprising (UNLU), which the traditionally secular PLO has long controlled. In response PLO chairman Yasser Arafat has tried hard to appease the influential Islamist leadership of Hamas and Islamic Jihad. These organizations enjoy significant support among the Palestinians both in the occu-pied territories and abroad. The conflict, therefore, between Islamism on one hand and Palestinian secular nationalism on the other remains unresolved. Arafat seeks to establish a sovereign, secular, democratic Palestinian nation-state. This is conceptually irreconcilable with Revolutionary Islamism.

Although secular in orientation, Arafat realizes that secular nationalism has become increasingly discredited among Palestinians as a motivating force in the struggle against Israel. A chief advisor to Arafat, Hani Hassan, told journalist Alan Hart in 1988 that "we discovered that not less than sixty percent of our young peo-ple in the occupied territories were thinking that Islamic fundamentalism had more to offer than the PLO."[4] Although Arafat is respected by most Palestinians, the failure of the PLO to achieve appreciable success in its struggle against Israel, even as it has moderated its policy toward the Jewish state, has deeply disheart-

---

[1]Nels Johnson, *Islam and the Politics of Meaning in Palestinian Nationalism* (London: Kegan Paul International, 1982), p. 61.

[2]Ibid.

[3]Ibid.

[4]Quoted in Alan Hart, *Arafat: A Political Biography* (Bloomington and Indianapolis, Ind.: Indiana University Press, 1989), p. 519.

BOX 7.1   Yasser Arafat

Yasser Arafat was born in Egypt in 1929. His father was an enterprising merchant, and his mother was related to the Grand Mufti of Jerusalem. In the early 1950s, while a civil engineering student at Cairo University, Arafat founded and became president of the Palestinian Students' Federation. After graduating with a civil engineering degree, he served in the Egyptian army during the 1956 Suez War. Subsequently, he went to Quwait, where he worked as an engineer for the Ministry of Public Works and ran a successful private construction company.

In 1957 Arafat cofounded the Al-Fatah (the Victory) resistance group with Khalil Wazir (Abu Jihad). Al-Fatah's mission was to engage in guerrilla struggle against Israel and achieve a homeland for the Palestinian people. From 1957 to 1965, Al-Fatah was a network of secret underground cells, which found its support among Palestinians living in Arab countries. Al-Fatah became a functioning guerrilla organization with a Central Committee in 1963. Arafat was displeased when, one year later, the Arab League established the Palestine Liberation Organization (PLO) and made Ahmad Shuqairi, the Palestinian-born Saudi Arabian representative to the United Nations in the early 1960s, its leader. After the humiliating Israeli defeat of Arab armed forces in the Six Day War, of 1967, the Palestinians decided to intensify their own struggle to achieve a Palestinian homeland and not put all their faith in Arab states to do it for them. In 1968 Arafat's effective leadership of Al-Fatah—the oldest, largest, and most influential guerrilla group within the PLO—helped him emerge as the leader of the multimember Palestine Liberation Organization. The following year, he was elected by the PLO as its chairman and commander-in-chief.

Israel effectively eliminated the organized existence of the PLO in Palestinian territory by the late 1960s. Arafat and the PLO were forced to attack Israel from other states, including Jordan. Friction between Arafat's PLO and the Jordanian government culminated in armed conflict in Jordan and the expulsion of the PLO from there. Arafat relocated to Lebanon, but during the Israeli invasion of Lebanon in 1982, the PLO was again expelled from its base of operations. The PLO guerrillas relocated to several Arab countries, but maintained their headquarters in Tunis, the capital of Tunisia.

Divisions within the PLO caused Arafat to lose control over the organization in the early 1980s. Arafat regained control of the PLO within a few years, but he seemed no closer to securing independent Palestinian statehood. Over time, Arafat became more moderate in his views and slowly began to acknowledge Israeli statehood. These views only further alienated the PLO's more radical factions, whose activities Arafat found difficult to control. During the Persian Gulf War, of 1990–1991, Arafat sided with Iraq. As a result, his oil-rich benefactors, particularly Saudi Arabia, cut all aid to the PLO. In these circumstances, Arafat was more open than ever to a negotiated settlement to the Israeli-Palestinian dispute. In the 1990s, Arafat participated in the Madrid Peace Conference and signed the Oslo Document of Principles, which resulted in mutual recognition between Israel and the PLO. In 1994 Arafat signed the Cairo Agreement with Israel, which outlined the process by which Israel would withdraw from Palestinian territory and the Palestinian Authority would be established. For his peacemaking efforts, Arafat—along

(Continued)

Yasser Arafat   *(Continued)*

with Israeli prime minister Yitzhak Rabin and foreign minister Shimon Peres—was awarded the Nobel Peace Prize.

When the Palestinian National Authority (PNA) was established in 1996, Arafat was elected president of the embryonic Palestinian state. Since that time, however, Arafat has been unable to expand on these successes. The Palestinian Authority (the term often used term for the PNA) remains weak and relatively powerless to control the Palestinian militants engaging in urban guerrilla warfare against Israelis in the Gaza Strip and the West Bank. Israel's Prime Minister Ariel Sharon blames Arafat personally for the continuing Palestinian attacks on Israeli targets, including civilians; Sharon seems committed to severely punishing the Palestinian Authority generally and Yasser Arafat in particular for the suicide bombings engaged in by Palestinian militants. Whether Arafat will survive this latest challenge to his political survival remains to be seen.

http://www.us-israel.org/jsource/biography/arafat.html
http://lexicorient.com/e.o/arafat.htm
http://www.nobel.se/peace/laureates/1994/arafat-bio.html
http://www.la.utexas.edu/chenry/aip/fall01/bibs01/msg00030.html
http://history1900s.about.com/cs/yasserarafat/
http://www.toptown.com/hp/jaber/Arafat.htm

ened Palestinians. Defeat after defeat, in combat and in negotiation, have gradually eroded Palestinian support for the secular, pragmatic, and accommodationist direction of Arafat and his influential wing of the PLO. Secularists like Arafat have been ineffectual. They have failed to improve the conditions of the Palestinians under PA control despite negotiating with the Israeli government for over eight years. Therefore, desperate and alienated Palestinians has been turning to political Islam as their new idiom of protest.

Muslims all over the world are understandably exasperated with their leaders for having failed to defeat the Israelis, either militarily or diplomatically, in over five decades. Politically active Revolutionary Islamists are today attacking this status quo and mobilizing the masses with promises to defeat and destroy Israel. The Muslim people, tired of their dictatorial regimes—mainly governed by Secularists and Modernist Islamists—are heeding the call of the Revolutionary Islamists. Thus, the Arab-Palestinian-Israeli conflict, unresolved after over fifty years, is not only contributing to the strength of political Islam but is radicalizing and revolutionizing it.

The First Arab-Israeli War (1948–1949)

In November of 1947 the United Nations General Assembly adopted Resolution 181, which called for the partition of Palestine into two sovereign states, one Jewish and one Arab. The Palestinian Arabs and the Arab League rejected the UN resolution, and conflict between Palestinians and Jewish settlers in the region intensified. The British, who for decades had administered Palestine, evacuated their forces on May 15, 1948, unable to referee the conflict any longer. Jewish settlers proclaimed the establishment of the state of Israel. At the same time, five Arab armies, in the name of the Arab League, invaded Palestine to destroy the new Jewish state. However, the Arab advantages in numbers, strategic positioning, and surprise were squandered by inadequate planning for the military campaign, insufficient military training, the poor quality of their equipment, incompetent leadership, and their failure to mount a joint offensive. The Israelis won the war in December of 1948.

The results of the first Arab-Israeli war were significant. First, the land allocated to the Palestinians by UN Resolution 181 had been either conquered by the Israelis or divided between Egypt and Transjordan. Obviously, no Palestinian state, with three foreign powers occupying it, could come into being. Arab-Palestinian tension was rooted in this development. Arab defense of Palestinian rights had degenerated into a land grab—Transjordan took the West Bank and Egypt took the Gaza Strip. The Palestinians grew increasingly aware that they could count on no one but themselves. Second, the Palestinian refugee problem became acute. Banished from their homes in Israel, the Palestinians were now truly homeless and nationless. And third, the victory of tiny Israel against numerically superior Arab forces was both surprising and embarrassing to the Muslim world.[5] The people accused their governments of incompetence and corruption. Proving themselves incapable of defending either the Palestinians or themselves, these corrupt governments were toppled by military coups and populist leaders.

The failure of Arab regimes to defeat Israel and the consequent internal upheaval were especially significant in Egypt. Different groups coalesced in common opposition to King Farouk's discredited government. In this atmosphere of despair, Egypt's Gamal Abdel Nasser, leader of the Free Officers Movement, overthrew Farouk's regime in 1952. Nasser rose to power with an ideology of Arab socialism, pan-Arabism, and anti-Zionism, becoming president in 1954.

Ironically, the Revolutionary Islamist Ikhwan al-Muslimun originally supported Nasser and the Free Officers movement in 1952. The Ikhwan had been consistently outspoken in its displeasure with the Farouk government, which it blamed for the Israeli victory in the 1948 Arab-Israeli war. Moreover, the Revolutionary Islamist Ikhwan at that time compromised and accepted the secular vision of pan-Arabism, in contrast to "ideal" Islamism, but only as a first step toward pan-Islamism. Nevertheless, relations soon became strained when the Ikhwan demanded to select representatives to the new, Secularist revolutionary government. The Secularist Revolutionary Command Council (RCC), governing Egypt at the time, rejected these demands. In 1953 the government outlawed all political parties except its own. Then, in early 1954, the Ikhwan and the RCC

---

[5]Itamar Rabinovich, "Seven Wars and One Peace Treaty," in Alvin Z. Rubinstein, ed., *The Arab-Israeli Conflict: Perspectives* (New York: Praeger, 1988), p. 46.

came to blows again. As Nasser struggled to assume control of Egypt, the Ikhwan rose in protest.

Politically threatened by the revolutionary Ikhwan, Nasser began to systematically suppress the organization in the first year of his presidency. Using as his pretext an assassination attempt by an Ikhwan member, Nasser condemned the entire organization and arrested its activists. With most of its leaders behind bars and Nasser rising in popularity throughout the Muslim world, the Ikhwan, and like-minded Islamists, saw a decade-long decline in their fortunes. Within two years, Nasser emerged as a charismatic Arab statesman—an emergence effected by his defiance of the West and of Israel in the 1956 Suez War.

The Suez War (1956)

On July 26, 1956, Nasser nationalized the strategically vital Suez Canal, that was British-owned and controlled, in order to pay for the planned Aswan Dam on the Nile River, a decision that prompted British, French, and Israeli forces to stage a military strike against Egypt. Although the Israelis performed well, the Anglo-French operation floundered. The United States, fearing anti-Western (including anti-American) sentiments spreading through the Middle East and the Soviets gaining influence in the region, forced the British and the French to abandon their attempt to retake the Suez Canal. The United States also persuaded the Israelis to evacuate the Sinai Peninsula and the Gaza Strip.

The results of the brief Suez War were threefold. First, Israel proved, again, that it was militarily powerful. Second, the Egyptians agreed to the demilitarization of the Sinai and the stationing of UN forces in the Gaza Strip. Third, the war was a major political victory for Nasser.[6] By standing up to two Western powers and Israel, Nasser now enjoyed unequaled stature throughout the Muslim world. He became the idol of the masses. The popularity of his ideologies of pan-Arabism and Arab socialism became widely known as "Nasserism."

Nevertheless, the voices of Islamist discontent could still be heard within Egypt. As Nasser undertook the socialist transformation of his country and improved relations with the Soviet Union, the Egyptian religious establishment feared their country was drifting toward atheistic communism. To defend his policies from the attacks of the Traditionalist Islamist *ulama*, Nasser co-opted clerics (with such offers as money or jobs for relatives). When this failed, he intimidated them. Thus, Nasser persuaded a number of the *ulama* either to endorse his foreign and domestic policies or to abstain from criticizing them.

The Ikhwan, meanwhile, was unsatisfied. In August 1965, fearing a resurgence of the Revolutionary Islamist organization, Nasser spread a story of a second Ikhwan-sponsored plot to assassinate him. Again, Nasser's security forces arrested and imprisoned Ikhwan leaders and activists. This, however, was hardly

---

[6]Leon Carl Brown, "The June 1967 War: A Turning Point?" in Yehuda Lukas and Abdalla M. Battah, eds., *The Arab-Israeli Conflict: Two Decades of Change* (Boulder, Colo.: Westview Press, 1988), p. 133.

■

BOX 7.2   Gamal Abdel Nasser

Gamal Abdel Nasser was born in 1918 in Alexandria, Egypt. As early as elementary school, tradition has it, Nasser was involved in political activity, protesting the British occupation of Egypt. In 1938 Nasser graduated from the military academy in Cairo as an officer. Five years later, he became an instructor at the academy and would later take part in the Arab attack from 1948 to 1949 on the newly established state of Israel.

The failure of the Arab military effort against Israel inspired Nasser to continue his political activity in opposition to the corrupt, Western-influenced government of King Farouk. Nasser was a leader of the Free Officers Movement that ultimately ousted Farouk in 1952. By 1954 Nasser had consolidated his position in the regime and became the first president of the new Republic of Egypt. Nasser's dreams of pan-Arabism, his socialist leanings, and his stringent opposition to Western interference in Egyptian affairs became the core of a political ideology ultimately termed "Nasserism." Nasser, however, was sensitive to political opposition and banned all political groups except his own party. Nasser also turned against the Revolutionary Islamist Ikhwan al-Muslimun, despite its support for Nasser's overthrow of Farouk. Nasser ruthlessly suppressed the Ikhwan.

In 1956, Nasser nationalized the Suez Canal, thereby bringing down on him the combined wrath of Britain, France, and Israel. However, both the Soviet Union and the United States opposed the Suez War, and the British, French, and Israeli forces were compelled to withdraw. This humiliation of the Israelis and the former imperial rulers of the Arab world made Nasser popular in the Middle East. Nasser hoped to parlay this popularity into the realization of his vision of pan-Arabism. In 1958, Egypt and Syria were merged into the United Arab Republic, with Nasser as president. This pan-Arabic political union ended quickly; Syria seceded in 1961, dashing Nasser's hopes of uniting and ruling the Arab world.

In 1966 Nasser signed a defense pact with Syria, providing for joint command of Egyptian and Syrian forces in case of war. In 1967 Jordan also signed a mutual defense agreement with Egypt. These pacts brought Nasser to the apogee of his prestige and power. In 1967, however, Israel launched a surprise attack on all three countries, defeating them in six days. Nasser was humiliated and his profile in the Arab world fell. By 1968, Nasser launched a war of attrition against Israel in occupied Egyptian territory, but he could claim no spectacular Egyptian successes.

After the 1967 war with Israel, Nasser reached out to former enemies, including King Faisal of Saudi Arabia. Additionally, Nasser served as a mediator between the PLO and Lebanon in 1969 and between the PLO and Jordan in 1970. Perhaps in time, he would have restored his standing in the Arab world. However, it was not to be; Nasser died of a heart attack in September 1970.

http://www.geocities.com/CapitolHill/Lobby/5270/index2.htm
http://i-cias.com/e.o/nasser.htm
http://www.cnn.com/SPECIALS/cold.war/kbank/profiles/nasser/
http://www.ahram.org.eg/weekly/gallery/nasser/
http://www.geschichte.2me.net/bio/cethegus/n/nasser.html
http://www.arab.net/egypt/history/et_nasser.html
http://www.palestinehistory.com/intbio03.htm
http://www.mrdowling.com/608-nasser.html

the end of the Ikhwan or Revolutionary Islamism in Egypt. Events in 1967 would favor the reemergence of Islamism and would discredit Nasser's ideologies of Arab socialism and pan-Arabism.

The 1967 Arab-Israeli War

For ten years following his good fortune in the aftermath of the 1956 Suez War, Nasser decided to avoid direct military confrontation with Israel while he strengthened the Egyptian military and gloried in his position of preeminence among Arab leaders. Nevertheless, by 1967 events overtook the charismatic Egyptian president, resulting in a war that humiliated his military and tarnished his glory.

Unable to resist either challenges to his reputation or Soviet reports of a fictitious Israeli attack planned against Egypt and Syria, Nasser took steps that would test the legitimacy of his regime and of his ideology and that would provoke the Israeli leadership.[7] Nasser sent UN forces packing, remilitarized the Sinai Peninsula, and proclaimed a blockade, which he never enforced, of the strategically important Strait of Tiran. Initially, these steps restored Nasser's standing as the leader of Arab nationalism.[8] However, Nasser's decisions would soon embarrass and humble him.

Considering Nasser's actions as equivalent to a declaration of war, Israel launched a preemptive air attack against Egypt and Syria that destroyed the Arab air forces on the ground. Israel then took the Sinai Peninsula from Egypt, the West Bank and East Jerusalem from Jordan, and the Golan Heights from Syria. The Arab military response was inconsequential. Within six days, Israel crippled the military capability of Egypt, Syria, and Jordan; conquered much Arab land to use in future peace negotiations; and seized the holy city of East Jerusalem. Having achieved its objectives, Israel accepted a United Nations–brokered ceasefire.

In Egypt and throughout the Muslim world, the psychological injury inflicted by the Israelis was enormous. A period of intense self-examination descended upon Muslims. Nasser, his secular socialist ideologies discredited by the overwhelming defeat, turned to Islamic themes and ritual observances to heal the wounds and relieve the trauma plaguing the Egyptian people. He stopped using socialist rhetoric and resorted to an Islamic idiom to rationalize the astounding Arab defeat on the battlefield.[9]

---

[7]Rabinovich, "Seven Wars and One Peace Treaty," p. 49.

[8]Ibid., p. 50.

[9]John Waterbury, "Egypt: Islam and Social Change," in Philip H. Stoddard, David C. Cuthell, and Margaret W. Sullivan, eds., *Change and the Muslim World* (Syracuse, N.Y.: Syracuse University Press, 1981), p. 54; Ali E. Hillal Dessouki, "The Resurgence of Islamic Organization in Egypt," in Alexander S. Cudsi and Ali E. Hillal Dessouki, eds., *Islam and Power in the Contemporary Muslim World* (Baltimore: Johns Hopkins University Press, 1981), p. 114.

Nasser maintained that defeat had been God's will and, therefore, not preventable by any precaution or preparation. He stressed Islamic virtues, like patience and perseverance in the face of adversity.[10] The government even encouraged Islamic activities to help the nation cope with its failure and shame.[11] On June 19, 1967, Nasser personally participated in the festivities marking the Prophet Muhammad's birthday. This event was heavily covered by the Egyptian media, which prior to the 1967 war had been discouraged from covering such religious events. Moreover, as Nasser continued to emphasize Islam, he fired his secular socialist advisors or encouraged them to resign; he introduced economic liberalization; and he made fraternal overtures to the wealthy, traditional, pro-Western, monarchical regimes of the Persian Gulf, whom he had denounced and even subverted in the previous decade (1957–1967).[12] Meanwhile, numerous Islamic institutions, *masjids*, and the *ulama*, which had been tightly controlled by the government, were now allowed to function with relative freedom in the prevailing environment of shock, humiliation, and sadness. Even restrictions on the Islamist Ikhwan were relaxed, and many of its members were released from jails.[13]

Islamists quickly took advantage of their newfound freedom and the emotional religious atmosphere to offer a simple explanation for the Arab world's shattering defeat: Egypt and other countries had strayed from the "straight path" of Islam that had brought progress and glory in the past. By importing and embracing alien Western ideologies like nationalism and socialism, the Muslim world suffered chronic divisiveness, greater poverty, lack of freedom, and a weaker belief in Islam.[14]

The Ikhwan al-Muslimun went further and declared that Arab defeat in the 1967 war was an effective condemnation of the secularist policies characteristic of present regimes that ignored or violated the principles of the *shariah*; a sign of God's revenge for the oppression Muslims had endured under Nasser's dictatorial regime; and God's punishment for Nasser's alliance with the atheistic Soviet state.[15] The Ikhwan, in essence, attributed defeat to a lack of faith and stated, "Israel is a religious state, based upon the tenets of Judaism. The Egyptians, who had depended upon a secular ideology, could not hope to withstand the power of

---

[10]Hassan Hanafi, "The Relevance of the Islamic Alternative in Egypt," *Arab Studies Quarterly*, Vol. 4, Nos. 1–2 (Spring 1982), p. 61.

[11]Waterbury, "Egypt," p. 54.

[12]Dessouki, "Resurgence of Islamic Organization," p. 114; Nazih N. M. Ayubi, "The Political Revival of Islam: The Case of Egypt," *International Journal of Middle East Studies*, Vol. 12 (1980), p. 490.

[13]Raphael Israeli, "Islam in Egypt under Nasir and Sadat: Some Comparative Notes," in Metin Heper and Raphael Israel, eds., *Islam and Politics in the Modern Middle East* (New York: St. Martin's Press, 1984), p. 70.

[14]Ali E. Hillal Dessouki, "Arab Intellectuals and *Al-Nakba*: The Search for Fundamentalism," *Middle Eastern Studies*, Vol. 9, No. 2 (May 1973), p. 189.

[15]Abd al-Monein Said Aly and Manfred W. Wenner, "Modern Islamic Reform Movements: The Muslim Brotherhood in Contemporary Egypt," *Middle East Journal*, Vol. 36, No. 3 (Summer 1982), p. 345; Dessouki, "Resurgence of Islamic Organization," p. 114.

religious faith."[16] The Ikhwan believed firmly that the imported Western ideologies of socialism, nationalism, and secularism—enshrined in Nasserism—had been defeated, and the only cure for the Muslim world's ills lay in Revolutionary Islamism. Only the staunch practice of Islam would renew Egyptian dignity and courage or would inspire Egyptians to give their lives as martyrs in a martial *jihad* against Israel.[17] Thus, Islamism gained favor as had Nasserism before it, on the promise to vanquish Israel.

Arson at Al-Aqsa Mosque and Nasser's Death

After the 1967 Israeli occupation of Jerusalem's eastern section, frustration and anger steadily built throughout the Muslim world. This frustration was aggravated by the Israeli government's attempts to Judaize the city after 1967 by expropriating Arab lands, demolishing Arab homes, expelling eminent political and intellectual leaders of the Arab community, and requiring Arab schools to teach a history that distorted Arab claims to Palestine. On August 21, 1969, a deranged Australian Christian Zionist set fire to the al-Aqsa Mosque in East Jerusalem, and the Muslim world rose up in protest. The arsonist's sacrilege seemed to many Muslims symptomatic of Israeli abuses on East Jerusalem.

Two days following the fire, Nasser penned a letter rife with Islamic imagery and symbolism to his defense minister.

> We shall return to Jerusalem and Jerusalem will be returned to us . . . we shall not lay down our arms until God grants His soldiers the victory and until His right is dominant, His house respected and true peace is restored to the city of peace.[18]

Meanwhile, there was a vigorous discussion in the Egyptian mass media and a proliferation of literature examining the centrality of Jerusalem for Islam. Later, in 1970, the fifth conference of Al-Azhar's Academy of Islamic Research devoted a substantial part of its proceedings to a discussion of the Islamic nature of Jerusalem and Palestine.[19] In essence, in Egypt and throughout much of the Muslim world, the arson and desecration of the Al-Aqsa Mosque reinforced the Islamist trend already pronounced since the 1967 war. Likewise, it reminded Islamists that Israel stood between the *ummah* and sacred Jerusalem. Israel, therefore, remained a significant enemy.

The death of Nasser in 1970 increased the Egyptian regime's reliance on the politics of Islam and thus directly contributed to Islamism. Nasser's successor, Muhammad Anwar al-Sadat, heightened Islamism by fully lifting the ban of the political activities of the Ikhwan al-Muslimun. Sadat's motives were simple:

---

[16]Aly and Wenner, "Modern Islamic Reform Movements," p. 345.

[17]Dessouki, "Resurgence of Islamic Organization," p. 114.

[18]Quoted in Yvonne Yazbeck Haddad, *Contemporary Islam and the Challenge of History* (Albany: State University of New York Press, 1982), pp. 35–36.

[19]Ibid., p. 36.

unleashing the Ikhwan effectively neutralized the influence of the socialists who sought to topple the Sadat government. Sadat, like Nasser following the 1967 war, was an adept Secularist who astutely manipulated the politics of Islam in domestic and foreign policies. Many of Sadat's speeches, statements, and actions were intentionally given Islamic overtones. Sadat's emphasis on the Islamic idiom reached its peak in the 1973 war with Israel.

The 1973 Arab-Israeli War

While the defeat inflicted on the Arabs by Israel in 1967 led to a period of intense self-evaluation and laid the groundwork for political Islam in several Arab nations, the Arab-Israeli War of October 1973 added great impetus to the popularity of Islamism. Although the 1973 war was fought to a military stalemate and the Arabs regained none of the lands lost to them in 1967, the conflict began with a successful Arab invasion of Israel's fortified military positions. Throughout the Muslim world the Arab effort was perceived as a victory, though it was a limited one. The widely held myths of Arab disunity and military inferiority were dashed. The myth of Israeli invincibility was similarly discredited.

An important feature of the 1973 war was the Arab emphasis on religious symbolism, an emphasis indicative of religion's influential role in Egyptian society following the 1967 war. For example, Sadat launched the 1973 war during Islam's holy month of Ramadan. The operational code name for the crossing of the Suez Canal by Egyptian forces was "Badr," a reminder of the first Islamic victory under Prophet Muhammad against the pagan Makkans in 623 CE. The battle cry in the 1973 Ramadan War was *"Allahu Akbar"* (God is Great). The battle cry of the Arabs in the Six Day War of June 1967 had been the less-than-inspiring "Land, Sea and Sky," which implied protecting the territory of the Arab world—a secular nationalist idea rather than a religious one. The 1967 battle cry also implied faith in military equipment and the tactics of military engagement, rather than in God. Many Muslims throughout the world attribute the 1973 Arab victory to God and His modern-day holy warriors.[20] Thus, Islamists could later point out that trust in Islam is the surest way to defeat any of Islam's foes.

Israel's 1982 Invasion of Lebanon

Following the 1979 Camp David Accords, in which Egypt made peace with Israel, the Arabs no longer posed a viable military threat to Israel. Having secured its border with Egypt, Israel could prosecute a limited war on its northern border without risking a substantial regional escalation of hostilities. In this context, Israel invaded Lebanon in 1982 with the following objectives: first, to prevent the PLO

---

[20]Yvonne Haddad, "The Arab-Israeli Wars, Nasserism, and the Affirmation of Islamic Identity," in John L. Esposito, ed., *Islam and Development: Religion and Sociopolitical Change* (Syracuse, N.Y.: Syracuse University Press, 1980), p. 120.

from further shelling northern Israel by expelling it from its last "autonomous territorial base"; and second, to establish a Lebanese government favorably disposed to Israel.[21]

The war in Lebanon lasted three months, beginning in June of 1982 under the code name "Operation Peace for Galilee." By early September, Israeli forces laying siege to West Beirut forced the PLO to evacuate from Lebanon. The PLO's departure, however, did not signal an end to the Israeli-Lebanese war. Instead, the war entered a new phase, marked by Israeli conflict with the majority Lebanese Shi'ah population.

When the Israelis first invaded Lebanon in 1982, Lebanese Christians and Shi'ahs alike welcomed the Israeli soldiers for ridding Lebanon of the overbearing PLO. However, while the Lebanese Shi'ahs had begun to dislike and resent the PLO for destabilizing their lives, they distrusted and feared the Israelis.[22]

Although a "tacit understanding" did exist between the Israelis and Lebonese, this understanding ended abruptly when, after the Israelis had expelled the PLO, the conquerors overstayed their welcome and began to oppress the local population. Although welcoming the elimination of the PLO as a political and military presence in Lebanon, the Shi'ahs soon realized they had merely witnessed the substitution of one occupation force for another.[23]

Various Shi'ah guerrilla organizations began a long and sustained *jihad* against the Israelis. The Shi'ah group Amal represented, at least initially, the most popular and moderate Shi'ah guerrilla group. Other, more radical organizations, however, had significant support among Lebanon's Shi'ahs and soon eclipsed the Amal. These radical groups included the Islamic Amal and **Hezbollah** (Party of God).[24] These two Islamist organizations represented Revolutionary Islamism in the struggle against the Israeli invaders and enjoyed friendly relations with Iran's newly founded Islamic Republic. Whereas the goal of the Amal was to stabilize Lebanon and transform it into a secular sovereign state ruled by the Shi'ah majority and resistant to undue outside influence, the goal of the Revolutionary Islamist Islamic Amal and Hezbollah was an Islamic revolution in Lebanon and the establishment of an Islamic republic.[25]

The Shi'ahs' campaign inflicted heavy Israeli casualties, which made the Israeli-Lebanese war increasingly unpopular in Israel. By 1985 Israel evacuated

---

[21]Rabinovich, "Seven Wars and One Peace Treaty," p. 52; Daniel C. Diller, ed., *The Middle East*, 7th ed. (Washington, D.C.: Congressional Quarterly, 1990), p. 33.

[22]Augustus Richard Norton, *Amal and the Shi'a: Struggle for the Soul of Lebanon* (Austin: University of Texas Press, 1987), p. 85.

[23]Ibid., p. 86.

[24]Clinton Bailey, "Lebanon's Shi'is after the 1982 War," in Martin Kramer, ed., *Shi'ism, Resistance, and Revolution* (Boulder, Colo.: Westview Press, 1987), p. 220.

[25]Ibid.

most of Lebanon, having achieved only the expulsion of the PLO. Even this success, however, was tarnished. The PLO fighters in southern Lebanon were replaced by Amal, Islamic Amal, and Hezbollah fighters, whose skill in harassing the Israelis has impressed even the exiled PLO. The Islamists' success on the battlefield in Lebanon proved to many Muslims that Israel could be checked not by secular leaders and secular forces but only by true, Revolutionary Islamist *mujahids* (those engaged in a *jihad*). The Shi'ahs had achieved the success against the Israelis that had eluded the PLO. The lesson was not lost on the PLO or on Palestinians living in the occupied territories. Taught by example and distraught by the consistent failures of the past, the Palestinians turned more fully to Islam and to Revolutionary Islamism.

The First Palestinian Intifadah

According to the 1947 UN Partition Plan, the territories of the West Bank and the Gaza Strip were to be integral components of the Arab Palestinian state. However, following the 1948 invasion of Palestine by Arab armies ostensibly in support of the Palestinian cause, the Egyptians assumed control of the Gaza Strip and King Abdullah of Transjordan officially annexed the West Bank.

The 1967 war replaced the Arab occupiers of Palestinian land with Israeli occupiers, and Israel has controlled both the West Bank and the Gaza Strip ever since. Originally, Israel considered the occupied territories as bargaining chips to exchange with the Arabs for peace. The stunning victory of 1967, however, emboldened the Israeli government to reject the Arab peace overtures. Israeli intransigence hardened, while the Palestinians living in the West Bank and the Gaza Strip continued to endure occupation.

Although West Bank Palestinians enjoyed material economic gains in the late 1960s and early 1970s, benefiting from a boom in the Israeli economy, they still recognized their occupiers as foreigners. In fact, the Palestinians in the occupied territories paid in taxes the cost of the Israeli occupation. Add to that a litany of human rights abuses perpetrated on the Palestinians, and a portrait of resentment, frustration, and alienation emerges, a portrait that no material gain can erase or obscure.[26]

The first anti-Israeli uprising occurred immediately following the Israeli victory and occupation in June 1967. As civil-disobedience campaigns in the occupied territories devolved into rebellion in Gaza, the Israeli army stepped in, forcefully suppressed the demonstrators, and restored order. The West Bank experienced popular upheaval after the 1973 Arab-Israeli War. The Israelis responded with arrests and deportations. In the early 1980s, protests and demonstrations again erupted in the occupied territories. The Israeli expulsion of the

---

[26]Charles D. Smith, *Palestine and the Arab-Israeli Conflict*, 2nd ed. (New York: St. Martin's Press, 1992), pp. 241–243.

PLO from Lebanon, however, quieted the desperate and demoralized populace. In addition, Israeli treatment of demonstrators toughened under Defense Minister Yitzhak Rabin's "Iron Fist" policy, inaugurated in 1985.[27]

Fearing eradication as a political and social unit, the Palestinians, provoked by a relatively minor incident, rose against their Israeli occupiers. The *intifadah* (translated as "shaking off" or "uprising") of Palestinians, which began in December 1987, for the first time in the Arab-Israeli conflict drew world attention to the plight of the long-forgotten Palestinians living in the Israeli-occupied territories. Israel's tempestuous relations with its Arab neighbors were suddenly eclipsed. Now the focus shifted to "Israel's relations with the Arabs who lived under its occupation."[28]

On December 8, 1987, four Palestinian workers driving into the Gaza Strip were rammed by an Israeli military tank transport and killed. This traffic accident ignited the *intifadah*—the widespread and sustained Palestinian uprising against Israeli occupation. Soon after the *intifadah* began, Palestinian activists from various groups and factions formed the Unified National Leadership of the Uprising (UNLU) to coordinate their strategy and tactics. While local grassroots committees were the backbone of the UNLU, the PLO was its dominant member. Acting as an umbrella organization, the PLO-UNLU invited the participation of Islamist groups, who represented the most serious opponent to the PLO's secular nationalism and to its overtures of peace and compromise with Israel, embodied in the Palestinian National Council's Palestinian Declaration of Independence of November 1988. PLO-UNLU realized that the major organizational and political challenge to the UNLU came from Revolutionary Islamist groups.[29]

While most Palestinians remained loyal to the PLO, Islamists increasingly gained adherents in the occupied territories, particularly in the Gaza Strip. At first, Islamist activities centered around local *masjids*, schools, colleges, and universities, where Muslim clerics and teachers inculcated Palestinian youth with a politically activist Islamic message. Ironically, Islamists established effective institutions in Gaza with Israeli complicity. Revolutionary Islamist and Traditionalist Islamist leaders were seldom harassed by the Israelis to the extent that PLO members were. Apparently, the Israelis hoped to undercut PLO support and divide and weaken the Palestinian movement by pitting the Islamists against the secular-leaning PLO. However, this strategy backfired when the Revolutionary Islamists entered the forefront of the opposition to the occupation.[30] Even the

---

[27]Ann Mosely Lesch, "Anatomy of an Uprising: The Palestinian Intifada," in Peter F. Krogh and Mary C. McDavid, eds., *Palestinians under Occupation: Prospects for the Future* (Washington, D.C.: Georgetown University Press, 1989), pp. 90–91.

[28]Diller, *The Middle East*, p. 37.

[29]Helena Cobban, "The PLO and the Intifada," in Robert O. Freedman, ed., *The Intifada: Its Impact on Israel, the Arab World, and the Superpowers* (Miami: Florida International University Press, 1991), p. 76.

[30]Don Peretz, *Intifada: The Palestinian Uprising* (Boulder, Colo.: Westview Press, 1990), p. 43.

PLO itself supported the more revolutionary Islamic Jihad in 1989 to undermine the relatively moderate Islamist Ikhwan's growing popularity in Gaza.[31]

The growth of Islamism in the West Bank and Gaza increased after the Iranian Islamists succeeded in defeating and overthrowing the *shah*, establishing an Islamic republic, and remaining in power against formidable odds. The success of the Lebanese Shi'ah Islamists, inspired by the example of the Iranian Revolution, in expelling the Western multinational forces and Israelis from southern Lebanon in the fall of 1983 further accelerated the growth of the Islamic movement in the occupied territories. Thousands of young, energetic, and zealous Palestinian students joined Islamic student organizations and youth groups in the Gaza Strip and West Bank during the 1980s.[32]

Despite Islamist groups' growing appeal and power in the Israeli-occupied territories, the Islamists played no role in the first days of the *intifadah*. Initially, the Ikhwan termed the uprising inappropriate "Muslim social behavior" and took a nonactivist approach to the *intifadah*. The formerly Revolutionary Islamist Ikhwan had mellowed with age. Although accepting compromise with the Israeli state and openly hostile to the secular nationalist PLO, the Ikhwan backed up its rhetoric not with militarism but by espousing "an essentially educational and social role for its adherents."[33] The Ikhwan controlled three universities in the occupied territories with a moderate and modernist Islamist curriculum.[34] Consequently, the Ikhwan, having become moderate in its orientation, was left behind in the *intifadah*.

Shaykh Ahmed Yassin, the Ikhwan's influential spiritual leader and the head of the Islamic Center in Gaza, was unhappy with the Ikhwan's emphasis on apolitical activity. He was inspired by the example of Ayatollah Khomeini defying the Western powers and came to believe that Palestinian Muslims should actively struggle to achieve an Islamic state in Palestine and should fight in the front lines of the *intifadah*. Therefore, in August 1988 he founded the Revolutionary Islamist Harakat al-Muqawama al-Islamiyya (Islamic Resistance Movement), known better by its Arabic acronym, Hamas.[35] Shaykh Yassin's Hamas dubbed itself the newest in a historical chain of militant Islamist organizations.[36]

Hamas portrayed itself as the Muslim answer to Jewish Zionism. Hamas considers Palestine as a **waqf**, an "Islamic trust" to be governed by Muslims until the Day of Judgment. According to Yassin, Palestinian Muslims were obliged to undertake a *jihad* against the Israeli occupiers, who had usurped Muslim land. Yassin's view is remarkably similar to the Zionist ideology, which views the same

---

[31]Cobban, "The PLO and the Intifada," p. 78.

[32]Lisa Taraki, "The Islamic Resistance Movement in the Palestinian Uprising," *Middle East Report*, Vol. 19, No. 1, (January–February 1989), p. 30.

[33]Cobban, "The PLO and the Intifada," p. 77.

[34]Charles D. Smith, *Palestine and the Arab-Israeli Conflict*, p. 295.

[35]Ibid., p. 299.

[36]Taraki, "The Islamic Resistance Movement in the Palestinian Uprising," p. 30.

land as a divine trust granted to the Jewish people for all time.[37] In contrast to the Ikhwan, Hamas assumed a more aggressive political role in opposing the Israeli occupation of the West Bank and Gaza Strip. Hamas became a powerful organization mobilizing and agitating Palestinians in the *intifadah*.[38]

The PLO-UNLU attempted to coopt the Palestinian Islamists.[39] However, while the Islamic Jihad accepted UNLU membership and by extension PLO leadership, Hamas rejected active membership in UNLU. Both Hamas and Islamic Jihad differ with the PLO, first by virtue of their Revolutionary Islamism and second in their ultimate goals. The Islamists favor the liberation of all Israel and replacement of the Jewish state with a Revolutionary Islamist one. In the short run, however, the PLO and the Islamists shared the cause of liberating the occupied territories from the common Israeli foe.

Sensitive to the belligerence of Revolutionary Islamists, the Israelis ceased to give preferential treatment to Hamas and Islamic Jihad. The Israelis have labeled Hamas a "terrorist organization," arrested Yassin, and sought to destroy the Revolutionary Islamist movement they themselves once cultivated.[40] Such efforts, however, have been largely ineffectual against the growing political appeal of Islamism in the territories and have failed to quell the Palestinian uprising; instead, they have "unified it, solidifying ties that had been tenuous."[41] Israeli repression brought the Islamists and the secular nationalists together, spread the *intifadah* from the Gaza Strip to the West Bank, and attracted all classes of Palestinians to the ranks of the uprising. In contrast to Israel's violent and brutal methods, the Palestinians in this first *intifadah* reacted rarely with lethal force but with stones, strikes, economic boycotts, and resistance to taxes.[42]

The Gulf War and the Palestinians

By mid-1990 the Palestinian *intifadah*, in its third year, had begun to founder, and the Palestinians had grown increasingly desperate. Although the *intifadah* had attracted international attention, the world community took no concrete steps. This explains the ebullient Palestinian response to Iraqi president Saddam Hussein's invasion and occupation of neighboring Kuwait, beginning August 2, 1990. After all, "any shakeup in the Arab world could only help the Palestinian cause; things couldn't get worse."[43]

Enthusiasm for Saddam Hussein's actions cut across ideological lines within the Palestinian community and united, if briefly, secular nationalists and Islamists. The Traditionalist Islamists and Revolutionary Islamists in occupied Palestine raised

---

[37]Ibid., p. 31.

[38]Cobban, "The PLO and the Intifada," p. 79.

[39]Ibid., p. 81.

[40]Ibid.

[41]Charles D. Smith, *Palestine and the Arab-Israeli Conflict*, p. 298.

[42]Ibid., pp. 298–299.

[43]Daoud Kuttab, "Emotions Take Over," *Middle East International*, No. 382, (August 31, 1990), p. 13.

BOX 7.3   Shaykh Ahmed Yassin

Born in 1938 in what is now Israel, Shaykh Ahmed Yassin fled Palestine with his family after the 1948 Arab-Israeli War. He relocated in the Gaza Strip, which was then under Egyptian control. In 1952 Yassin injured his back and he has been in a wheelchair ever since.

Unable to afford college, Yassin became a teacher. He joined the Ikhwan al-Muslimun (Muslim Brotherhood) in his early twenties, yet even after Israel occupied the Gaza Strip, he avoided the growing military and political struggle against Israel, focusing instead on social and economic issues. He established the Islamic Center in 1973 to coordinate programs sponsored by the Ikhwan. The center received funding from oil-rich Persian Gulf states and was not harassed by the Israelis since they saw Yassin's peaceful organization as a counterweight to the PLO's growing popularity.

The PLO painted the Ikhwan as a tool of the Israeli government and as collaborators. By the early 1980s, however, Yassin and his followers decided to participate in political and military action to remain credible in the eyes of Palestinians. Israel arrested Yassin for his activities but released him within a year. In 1987 Yassin established a separate faction called Hamas, which means "zeal."

Yassin was arrested again in 1989 and sentenced to life in prison. His imprisonment, however, backfired on Israel. The power vacuum left in Hamas by Yassin's arrest brought more militant leaders to the fore. During the early 1990s, Hamas's power and influence grew. In opposition to the Oslo Peace Accords between the PLO and Israel, Hamas carried out a series of suicide attacks against Israeli civilians. This created considerable tension between the Israelis and Palestinians and ultimately derailed the peace process.

Because Yassin was more moderate than the new leadership in Hamas and because his health was failing, Israel released him from prison in 1997. Initially, Yassin made conciliatory statements about Israel on behalf of Hamas. However, other Hamas leaders remained committed to the armed struggle to free Palestine, and Yassin's own views became gradually more revolutionary. Acknowledged as Hamas's spiritual leader, Yassin began to defend suicide attacks on Israeli citizens by arguing that, although Islam prohibited such attacks, the Israelis had started it and that Palestinians were the real victims. Israel used further Hamas suicide attacks on civilians in December 2001 to justify attacks on Yasser Arafat's Palestinian National Authority (referred to by Israel and the West simply as the Palestinian Authority [PA]). Arafat attempted to place Yassin under house arrest in response to Israeli demands, but this attempt met fierce resistance by Palestinians in the Gaza Strip. Hamas's attacks and Israel's response to those attacks served hardliners in both camps insofar as they undermined Arafat's credibility and authority in Gaza and the West Bank.

http://members.tripod.co.uk/alquds/yasin_interview.htm
http://www.skynews.co.uk/skynews/article/0,,30000-1037422,00.html

their voices during Friday congregational prayers in support of the secularist Saddam Hussein. Islamist support for Hussein, however, represented no love for the Iraqi dictator's pan-Arabism or Arab nationalism; it represented a more intrinsic rejection of Western intervention in the *ummah* and an attack on "the presence of foreign troops in Saudi Arabia," which defiled "the holiest land for Islam."[44]

Yasser Arafat joined the Islamists in their condemnation of Western interventionism. The ubiquitous PLO chairman, taking an enormous political risk in relations with most Arab countries, threw his support behind Saddam Hussein. Yet Arafat's stance was widely misinterpreted in the West and in Arab capitals. In response, Arafat hastily announced

> the Palestinians' principled position against taking land by force, but at the same time opposing a foreign military presence in Arab countries and the demand that the Gulf crisis should be solved within an Arab context.[45]

Palestinian support for Saddam Hussein, bolstered by the Iraqi president's attempt to link Iraqi withdrawal from Kuwait to simultaneous Israeli withdrawal from the West Bank and Gaza, was rooted not in dislike of Kuwait but in Palestinians' "deep desire for national liberation, their feeling of having been victimized, betrayed, or ignored by the West, and their deep sense of despair at the failure of their leadership, its moderation, and rational political processes to produce tangible change in their living conditions under a brutal occupation."[46]

The PLO, Hamas, and other Palestinian organizations paid dearly for the so-called "principled position" that the Palestinians took during the Gulf crisis (1990–1991). Significant aid from Kuwaiti and Saudi benefactors ended abruptly after the Palestinians gave their support to Saddam Hussein. In addition, thousands of Palestinian workers and students who were expelled from the Persian Gulf kingdoms returned to the occupied territories, requiring places to live and jobs and, above all, placing further burdens on an already struggling economy.[47] Since earlier survey information in the occupied territories indicated that the Islamist trend was most evident among the youth and the college-educated generation,[48] the Islamists received a political boost with the Palestinian "in-gathering" of young workers and students.

The *intifadah*, meanwhile, increasingly stagnated. One journalist observed, "the Gulf crisis has so absorbed everyone's attention that the *intifadah* has been almost completely forgotten."[49] Before the crisis, the uprising had been receding.

---

[44]Ibid.

[45]Daoud Kuttab, "Forgotten Intifada," *Middle East International*, No. 383 (September 14, 1990), p. 16.

[46]James J. Zogby, "The Strategic Peace Initiative Package: A New Approach to Israeli-Palestinian Peace," *American Arab Affairs*, No. 35 (Winter 1990–1991), pp. 181–182.

[47]Kuttab, "Emotions Take Over," p. 14; Kuttab, "Forgotten Intifada," p. 15; Daoud Kuttab, "The Palestinian Economy and the Gulf Crisis," *Middle East International*, No. 383 (September 14, 1990), p. 16.

[48]Cobban, "The PLO and the Intifada," p. 77.

[49]Kuttab, "Forgotten Intifada," p. 15.

During the crisis it was eclipsed. After the crisis, it became "a kind of permanent state" that began "to harden and to lose the bright colors of its early days."[50]

Conflict within the Palestinian community after the end of the Persian Gulf War increased. The *intifadah* faltered, and unity between Islamists and secular nationalists disintegrated. On June 2, 1991, for example, Hamas and PLO supporters battled in the streets and suburbs of Nablus. Although the conflict was patched up with promises to work together against the common Israeli foe, the days of "national unity" were past.[51]

The keen attraction of Islamist politics in the West Bank and Gaza can be dulled only if Israel satisfies a few Palestinian demands. Otherwise, political Islam will continue to grow and will replace a discredited PLO. Islamism offers Palestinians "ethnic identity, attachment to the land, and cultural purity as Palestinians."[52] If the isolation of the West Bank and the Gaza Strip continues indefinitely, the Revolutionary Islamists will sweep the chairman and his organization away in an ecstasy of fanaticism.

The Madrid Peace Process

In October 1991 President George H. W. Bush's administration—riding the crest of popularity in the United States due to the U.S.-led coalition's smashing triumph during the hundred-day Persian Gulf War and keen to do something that would please the Arabs and Muslims for a change—dropped the incremental (step-by-step) approach that marked U.S. diplomacy in the 1970s and adopted a far more ambitious two-track strategy: bilateral negotiations between Israel, on one hand, and Jordan, Lebanon, Syria, and the Palestinians, on the other; and multilateral negotiations to deal with broad regional issues, such as security, economic development, refugees, water, and the environment.[53]

The bilateral negotiations between Israel and its Arab neighbors got underway at the royal palace in Madrid on November 3, 1991, and had as their foundation UN Security Council Resolutions 242 and 338, passed on November 22, 1967, and October 22, 1973, respectively. Resolution 242 focused mainly on the principle of land for peace, while Resolution 338 called for direct negotiations between Arabs and Israelis. Among the most important and challenging issues that the bilateral negotiations were meant to tackle and resolve were the conditions for signing peace treaties, deciding Israel's national boundaries, disposing of the occupied territories, and deciding the future of the Palestinians. The bilateral meetings

---

[50]Azmy Bishara, "Palestine in the New Order," *Middle East Report*, Vol. 22, No. 2 (March/April 1992), p. 6.

[51]Daoud Kuttab, "Worries about the Intifada," *Middle East International*, No. 402, June 14, 1991, pp. 12–13.

[52]Emile Sahliyeh, *In Search of Leadership: West Bank Politics Since 1967* (Washington, D.C.: The Brookings Institution, 1988), p. 137.

[53]Augustus Richard Norton, "U.S. and the Middle East: Elusive Quest for Peace," *Great Decisions 2002* (New York: Foreign Policy Association, 2002), p. 34.

between Israeli and Arab diplomats continued for the most part in Washington, D.C., under U.S. government auspices. However, other than the Israeli-Jordanian peace agreement, these talks stumbled because of Israel's reluctance to relinquish the Syrian Golan Heights, its inability to reach any agreement with Syrian-controlled Lebanon, and its reluctance to engage in face-to-face talks with Arafat or his PLO representatives. Israeli prime minister Rabin's assassination in 1995 by a Jewish zealot derailed the negotiations.[54]

The multilateral negotiations between Israeli and Arab professionals as well as mid-level bureaucrats and diplomats got underway in Moscow (the capital of post-USSR Russia) in January 1992. These discussions were never intended to address the central and most difficult land-for-peace issues, which could only be settled bilaterally between the adversaries. However, they were the first time that states in the Middle East had begun to dialogue with their former enemies. It was noteworthy to see Israelis talking with Saudis, Kuwaitis, and Omanis.[55]

Israel Attacks Islamists in Southern Lebanon

After the Madrid Peace Conference opened, the pro-Iranian Revolutionary Islamist Hezbollah and Islamic Amal intensified their attacks against Israel's self-declared security zone in southern Lebanon. This fifteen-mile-long security zone was patrolled by the Christian Southern Lebanese Army (SLA) and their Israeli patrons.

Choosing to answer violence with violence, on February 16, 1992, Israeli helicopter gunships attacked a convoy carrying a Hezbollah leader and his family. The Lebanese Shi'ahs, avenging the death of their leader, elected another Revolutionary Islamist to succeed him and launched rocket attacks against Jewish settlements in northern Israel. Unable to break the cycle of violence it had initiated, Israel and its surrogate Lebanese Christian forces invaded Hezbollah villages in South Lebanon, brushing aside poorly armed UN peacekeeping forces stationed on the border. Within twenty-four hours, the Israelis withdrew and "jubilant Muslim militiamen swarmed back into the region."[56] Syria's Hafiz al-Assad, just beginning to enjoy legitimacy over Lebanon, feared another, deeper invasion of Lebanon by the Israelis. He therefore asked Iran to reign in the zealous Hezbollah fighters. Consequently, Hezbollah evacuated the border region with Israel, but a significant political victory had been won within the Muslim community.

In the summer of 1993, trouble flared again in southern Lebanon. Hezbollah expressed its opposition to the ongoing Middle East peace talks by engaging in attacks against Israeli and SLA soldiers in the "security zone" Israel had declared

---

[54]Ibid., p. 34.

[55]Ibid.

[56]Gerald Butt, "Iran and Syria Curb Hizbullah Attacks, but Group Gains," *Christian Science Monitor*, February 25, 1992, p. 5.

in Lebanon. Over a period of months, Hezbollah launched a number of rocket attacks against northern Israel and, in July, killed seven Israeli soldiers in Israeli-occupied southern Lebanon.[57] Using these deaths as a pretext, the Rabin government launched "Operation Accountability" in July 1993.[58] Israeli ships bombarded the Lebanese coastal cities of Sidon and Tyre, and Israeli fighter-bombers and helicopter gunships razed villages and leveled houses throughout southern and eastern Lebanon. Hezbollah answered by firing Soviet-made Katyusha rockets at northern Israel. Two Israelis were killed.[59]

When, after a week of constant bombardment, the Israeli offensive in southern Lebanon ended, 130 Lebanese civilians were dead, 450 to 500 were wounded, and 250,000 were homeless refugees. Ten thousand houses were leveled and thirty thousand damaged in seventy villages. Less than ten Hezbollah guerrillas were reported killed.[60]

Israel's objective, however, was not simply to kill Hezbollah fighters but to intimidate the civilian populace in the south and to create a refugee problem for the government in Beirut. The Rabin government hoped that Syria and its puppet government in Lebanon would rein in Hezbollah to prevent further Israeli incursions into the country. Although Hezbollah received its ideological prompting from Iran, Syria controlled the organization's supply lines and could thus be greatly influential. However, Syria publicly refused. Hezbollah, Syria maintained, had legitimate cause to oppose the Israeli occupation of southern Lebanon.[61]

Nevertheless, Syria did not wish to jeopardize the Middle East peace talks. Assad wanted to regain the Golan Heights, and continued negotiations with Israel were vital. Thus, Syria stayed aloof from the confrontation and was praised by President Bill Clinton for its "considerable restraint," even after Syrian soldiers were killed in the Bekaa Valley, victims of Operation Accountability.[62] Assad then defused the situation by wresting a promise from Hezbollah to refrain from further rocket attacks on northern Israel. Nevertheless, Hezbollah "maintained their right to take action against Israel's 'security zone.' "[63]

The Israelis accepted Hezbollah's promise and ended Operation Accountability. However, Israel also exacted a promise from the Lebanese

---

[57]"Operation Exodus," *The Economist*, July 31, 1993, p. 35; Tom Masland, "Fire on the Border," *Newsweek*, August 9, 1993, p. 17; Bruce W. Nelan, "What's Peace Got to Do with It?" *Time*, August 9, 1993, p. 32.

[58]"Operation Exodus," p. 30.

[59]Ibid., p. 35; Brian Duffy, "Israel Takes on the Party of God," *U.S. News and World Report*, August 9, 1993, p. 16.

[60]Masland, "Fire on the Border," p. 30; Nelan, "What's Peace Got to Do with It?" p. 33; "Assault Course," *The Economist*, p. 42; Jim Muir, "Rabin's Revenge Exacts an Appalling Toll," *Middle East International*, No. 456 (August 6, 1993), p. 3.

[61]Masland, "Fire on the Border," p. 30; Nelan, "What's Peace Got to Do with It?" p. 33; "Operation Exodus," p. 35.

[62]"Operation Exodus," p. 35.

[63]"Assault Course," p. 42.

government to deploy the Lebanese army in the south to offset the power of Hezbollah. To further strengthen the Lebanese military, Arab ministers meeting in Damascus promised $500 million to the government in Beirut.[64]

Israel's periodic bombing of South Lebanon's villages and periodic sweeps of Lebanese villages to arbitrarily arrest young men and incarcerate them indefinitely in Israel greatly embittered the Lebanese Shi'ah population and guaranteed future recruits to Hezbollah. In essence, Israeli attempts to crush the Hezbollah instead strengthened the group's popularity and authority in the Lebanese Shi'ah community. By amplifying the cycle of violence, the Israelis boosted Hezbollah's fortunes and provided Islamists the world over with a role model, particularly among the Palestinians in the Gaza and West Bank.

The Oslo Peace Process

It is ironic that, while the Israelis were struggling to contain the six-year *intifadah* on their home front and punish the Lebanese Hezbollah for firing rockets into Israel, Israeli and PLO negotiators were secretly meeting in the cold Scandinavian city of Oslo, Norway. In this peace initiative, Israeli foreign minister Shimon Peres convinced Prime Minister Yitzhak Rabin to start a back channel with Yasser Arafat's PLO representatives in Oslo. The secret talks between Israeli and PLO representatives began in January 1993 and went on for over seven months.

On August 20, 1993, Israeli foreign minister Peres and the Norwegian foreign minister witnessed the signing of the Declaration of Principles (DOP) by high-level PLO and Israeli representatives. This agreement was undoubtedly the most significant development in the Arab-Israeli peacemaking process since Sadat's momentous visit to Jerusalem on November 19, 1977.[65]

In September 1993 Arafat and Rabin signed the Declaration of Principles at the White House in the glare of global publicity. Israel formally recognized the PLO and gave the Palestinians limited autonomy in Gaza and heavily populated Palestinian areas in return for peace and an end to Palestinian claims to Israeli territory. The agreement also provided for Israel's withdrawal from the Gaza Strip and the West Bank town of Jericho; the establishment of an interim Palestinian Authority (PA) and a five-year period for the negotiation of the so-called "final status" issues (Jerusalem, Palestinian refugees, Jewish settlements, security agreements, and borders). But as often happens in the Middle East, extremists in the region seem to resent the peace process unless the peace is achieved on their unilateral and uncompromising terms.[66]

---

[64]Ibid., p. 42.

[65]Avraham Sela, *Political Encyclopedia of the Middle East* (New York: Continuum, 1999), p. 114.

[66]Norton, *Great Decisions 2002*, p. 36.

The Ibrahimi Mosque Massacre
of Palestinian Worshipers

At dawn on February 25, 1994, a fundamentalist Jewish settler entered the crowded Ibrahimi (Abraham's) Mosque,[67] located in the ancient biblical town of Hebron on the Israeli-occupied West Bank. Dressed in an Israeli Army uniform, he opened fire with his automatic assault rifle on as many as eight hundred worshipers who had just started their Ramadan fast and were kneeling in prayer with their foreheads touching the ground. The anti-Arab ideology that inspired the attack permeates the worldview of a significantly large segment of the gun-toting Jewish settlers in the Gaza Strip and West Bank. The attack was a clear indication that there was madness and zealotry on both sides of the Palestinian-Israeli conflict.

The attacker was a forty-two-year old American-born orthodox Jewish physician named Dr. Baruch Goldstein, who in 1983 immigrated to Israel from the New York City borough of Brooklyn. He had long been a committed follower of the radical Jewish fundamentalist Rabbi Meir Kahane.[68] In Israel, Goldstein became part of Kahane's inner circle and even ran Kahane's political campaign for the Israeli Knesset (legislature). Because the two Zionist soulmates had grown so close, Kahane's assassination in New York City in 1990 left Goldstein seriously disturbed. He must have been further angered by the trial of Kahane's accused assassin. At trial's end, the Arab-born American Al-Sayyid al-Nosair walked away a free man due to insufficient evidence. Goldstein is said to have repeatedly told his friends thereafter that Kahane's murder must be avenged.[69]

As the leader of the local emergency medical team for his Jewish settlement, Goldstein had seen several of his close friends and neighbors die under his care. He therefore considered "Arabs to be Nazis" and refused to treat them when they came in for emergency treatment.[70] Furthermore, the Israeli government's peace accord with the PLO and the Arafat-Rabin handshake on September 13, 1973,

---

[67]The Ibrahimi Mosque, or al-Haram al-Ibrahimi (The Tomb of Ibrahim), is named after Prophet Abraham, who is venerated in Judaism, Christianity, and Islam. Muslims reverentially refer to him as Khalil Allah (God's friend). Adherents of all three faiths believe that Abraham is buried at the site of this mosque. The Bible states that Abraham purchased the site as a burial ground for his wife, Sarah. The Jews called the hallowed site the Tomb of the Patriarchs or the Cave of Machpela because they believe that the sacred tombs of the patriarchs Isaac and Jacob and matriarchs Rebecca and Leah are also to be found there. Both Jews and Muslims worship in separate sections of the same Tomb of the Patriarchs, and therefore the hallowed site has been a flashpoint since 1929, when Arabs massacred sixty-nine Jews there (Joel Greenberg, "Biblical Tomb Long a Site of Arab-Jewish Conflict," *New York Times*, February 26, 1994, p. 6).

[68]Rabbi Meir Kahane, a Brooklyn-born native, had founded the Jewish Defense League (JDL) in 1968. In 1971, the radical and demagogic rabbi immigrated to Israel and founded the right-wing Kach party. The goal of this Jewish fundamentalist party was to expel all Arabs from Israel and from Israeli-occupied lands and to make Israel a truly Jewish state based on the Torah.

[69]Russel Watson et al., *Newsweek*, pp. 34–37; Tom Masland, Carrol Bogert, Robin Sparkman, and Caroline Hawley, "Benjie Was Always an Extremist," *Newsweek*, p. 36.

[70]Richard Lacayo, "The Making of a Murderous Fanatic," *Time*, March 7, 1994, p. 52.

must have enraged and incensed him. He believed that Arafat was a "terrorist" and that the PLO was a "terrorist organization." The Israeli government's negotiations with Arafat was a betrayal of the Jewish people and the Jewish state. Goldstein was determined to sabotage the Israeli-PLO peace talks with a dramatic and explosive event.

He chose a Friday for his attack because Muslims engage in congregational noontime prayers on Fridays. His attack also occured during Islam's holy month of Ramadan, a time when fasting Muslims make every effort to get involved in the congregational prayer sessions. It was also the Jewish festival of Purim, when Jews celebrate the deliverance of Persian Jews from a plot to destroy them in the fifth century BCE.

The cry that went up in the Ibrahimi Mosque just after the Jewish terrorist had emptied three 35-shot magazines into the congregation of worshipers was: "Where are you Arafat? Where is the peace?" This cry, mingled with the Islamic rallying cry of *Allahu Akbar*, was immediately taken up by furious Palestinians venting their disillusionment and anger at the deaths of their brethren and at the disappointing results of the peace talks that Arafat had said would soon give his people a Palestinian state. It was a cry heard by U.S. President Bill Clinton, who invited both Israeli and Palestinian negotiators to Washington, D.C., so that they could tie up all the loose ends of their piece accord on limited Palestinian autonomy. It was a cry likewise heard by Yasser Arafat at his PLO headquarters in Tunis, Tunisia. Immediately suspending the Israeli-PLO peace negotiations, the PLO chairman now made the Israeli settler issue the principal problem requiring urgent attention; no longer, he insisted, could it be a secondary matter to be addressed in 1995, as agreed to in the Israeli-PLO Declaration of Principles.[71]

The PLO and Israel Continue the Peace Process

Despite the efforts of extremists to make it difficult for Palestinians and Israelis to achieve peace, the peace process was boosted in May 1994, when Egyptian President Hosni Mubarak hosted Israeli and PLO representatives in Cairo. The result was the Cairo Accord. This accord allowed Arafat to return to Gaza; established the terms for the transfer of power to the PLO as Israeli forces withdrew from most of Gaza and Jericho on the West Bank; and stated that final-status issues were to be concluded by May 1999.[72]

In October 1994, the courageous and enlightened efforts of Arafat, Rabin, and Peres at achieving peace between their two peoples was recognized with the Nobel Peace Prize. In the same month, Jordan's King Hussein signed a peace treaty between his kingdom and Israel.

On September 28, 1995, Arafat and Rabin signed the Oslo II Agreement in Washington, D.C., in the presence of President Clinton, President Mubarak, and

---

[71]Peter Ford, "The Peace Process after Hebron: Attack Prompts Calls for End to Talks, but Some See New Impetus," *Christian Science Monitor*, February 28, 1994, p. 3.

[72]Norton, *Great Decisions 2002*, p. 36.

King Hussein. The agreement allowed the election of a Palestinian legislative council and divided the West Bank into three zones: the Palestinian Authority (PA) is to exercise complete civil and security control in Zone A; in Zone B, the PA administers towns and villages populated exclusively by Palestinians, under overall Israeli "security control"; and Zone C is under complete Israeli jurisdiction because it covers all Jewish settlements, with 7,000 Jewish settlers living in the Gaza Strip (where there are 1.2 million Palestinians) and over 190,000 Jewish settlers living in the West Bank. Jerusalem was assigned without comment to Israeli control, including former Arab East Jerusalem. Seventy-two percent of the West Bank was now under full Israeli control, although most Palestinians were found in the first two, PA-administered zones. Oslo II also set May 1996 for the beginning of final-status talks, but this was subsequently postponed by Prime Minister Benjamin Netanyahu.

In an effort to derail the Israeli-Palestinian peace process, Yigal Amir, a militant Jewish rabbinical student, assassinated Israeli Prime Minister Rabin on November 4, 1995. Foreign Minister Shimon Peres became prime minister and completed Israel's promised withdrawal from Palestinian towns in the West Bank, except for Hebron.

In January 1996, radical Islamist parties boycotted scheduled Palestinian elections: this effectively threw the PA entirely into Arafat's hands. Arafat was elected president of the Palestinian Authority, and his supporters won two-thirds of the eighty seats in the Palestine Legislative Council. At its first session, held in the PA-controlled West Bank city of Ramallah (about ten miles north of Jerusalem) on April 24, the Palestine National Council formally removed from its charter all the articles incompatible with Israel's right to exist.

However, the peace process suffered a setback when Prime Minister Shimon Peres lost the May 1996 national election to hawkish Benjamin Netanyahu, his right-wing Likud Party, and the religious right. But due to President Clinton's constant efforts to bridge the differences between the Israelis and Palestinians, the peace process was sustained. In January 1997, the representatives of Israel and the PA signed the Hebron Protocol, which returned most of Hebron to the PA. However, Hebron's central district, where several hundred Jewish fundamentalist settlers of the **Gush Emunim** (Hebrew for Bloc of the Faithful) reside, was to be protected by the Israeli military authority. Then, on October 23, 1998, Arafat and Netanyahu signed the Wye River Memorandum, which commited Israel to hand over 13 percent of the West Bank territory to the Palestinian Authority within three months in exchange for Palestinian enforcement of peace.

Prime Minister Netanyahu became enmeshed in a corruption scandal, and elections in May 1999 removed him from power. Labor Party leader Ehud Barak, one of Israel's most decorated soldiers, espoused a peace platform and defeated Netanyahu by a substantial number of votes. In September 1999, Barak and Arafat signed the Sharm el-Shaykh Memorandum in Egypt. This agreement created a timetable for the delayed Israeli withdrawals to begin immediately and conclude January 2000; allowed for the opening of two safe passages between Gaza and the West Bank; released Palestinian prisoners from Israeli jails; and established September 2000 as the deadline for final-status talks.

Prime Minister Barak also worked with Syrian president Hafiz al-Assad's trusted foreign minister, Farouk Sharah, in mid-December 1999 and in March 2000 in an effort to conclude a lasting peace between Israel and Syria. However, on both occasions, the negotiations broke down.

On May 24, 2000, Barak decided to abruptly end Israel's eighteen-year occupation of the fifteen-mile-deep "security zone" in South Lebanon (north of the Israeli border). Israel had obstinately held this enclave with the help of the Christian South Lebanon Army (SLA). Israel's abrupt decision to completely pull out of Lebanon two weeks before its evacuation was planned was due to the sudden collapse of the SLA, whose Christian fighters began crossing into Israel in search of refuge from Hezbollah and Amal para-military groups.

The Second Palestinian Intifadah

The Israeli-Palestinian peace talks between Barak and Arafat lasted for nearly a year, but ended on July 25, 2000, after President Clinton failed to bridge the irreconcilable differences during a two-week marathon session at the Camp David presidential retreat in Maryland. Israelis were furious with their prime minister's willingness to concede too much to the Palestinians to get a peace deal and some of Barak's coalition partners withdrew from his government. Barak insisted that Palestinians had to agree formally to Jerusalem as Israel's capital in return for receiving most of the West Bank (minus most of the areas with Jewish settlements) and local oversight over Islamdom's holy sites and the Palestinian quarters in the Old City. Negotiations, however, collapsed over the issue of Palestinian refugees' "right of return" to their homes in Israel. The Palestinian negotiators insisted on it, but the Israelis were adamantly against it.[73]

On September 28, 2000, Ariel Sharon, the right-wing Likud Party leader, accompanied by many Israeli security guards, strode provocatively onto the hallowed grounds of the *Haram al-Sharif* (the Noble Sanctuary) or the Temple Mount in Jerusalem. Palestinians loathed Sharon for having spent much of his adult life militarily attacking them or expropriating their best land for Jewish settlements in the West Bank. In the summer of 1982, Sharon and his troops invaded South Lebanon, liquidated the PLO infrastructure (including schools and medical clinics), and killed nearly 20,000 people (most of them Palestinian and Lebanese civilians). (Sharon was later found indirectly responsible for the Christian Phalangist massacre of Palestinian refugees in the Sabra and Shatila camps.) Thus, Sharon's visit to the Haram al-Sharif precinct—where the *Al-Aqsa Mosque* (the furthest mosque) and the Dome of the Rock are located—conjured up unpleasant memories about Sharon's past and pointed to the future Israeli control of these bitterly disputed sacred sites (see Box 7.4). This is what triggered the second *intifadah*, the al-Aqsa *intifadah*, and ended the seven-year-long Oslo peace process.

---

[73]Norton, *Great Decisions 2002*, pp. 37–38.

BOX 7.4   Jerusalem: A Flashpoint in the Middle East

Muslims reverentially call **Jerusalem** *Al-Quds* ("The Holy") because it has sacred sites associated with such biblical prophets as Abraham, David, Solomon, Moses, and Jesus. Prophet Muhammad is also associated with Jerusalem because of his *isra* or night journey from Makkah to Jerusalem and *mi'raj* or ascension to heaven for a meeting with God (17:1–4). Muhammad enjoined Muslims to turn in the direction of Jerusalem to say their prayers for the first thirteen years of his prophethood (610–623 CE). Jerusalem is the third holiest city in Islamdom after Makkah and Madinah.

Known as "the Noble Sanctuary" to Muslims and "the Temple Mount" to Jews and Christians, **Haram al-Sharif** is a thirty-five acre hallowed precinct on biblical Mount Moriah located in the southeast corner of historic Jerusalem's Old City. Haram al-Sharif is sacred to Muslims, Jews, and Christians. The Qur'an mentions Prophet Muhammad's night journey from Makkah to *Masjid al-Aqsa* ("the furthest mosque") in Jerusalem and ascension to heaven for a meeting with God from the Foundation Rock where the *Qubbat al-Sakhra* ("Dome of the Rock") is located. Jews and Christians believe Adam was buried in the enclosure, and Abraham brought his son, Isaac, for sacrifice to this compound (Genesis 22). Muslims believe Adam's burial site and Ishmael's (not Isaac's) proposed sacrifice was close to Makkah in the Arabian peninsula. Christians consider the southeast corner of the Temple Mount overlooking the deep Kidron Valley as the site of the second temptation of Christ, the site where the Devil "took Jesus to Jerusalem, and set him upon the pinnacle of the Temple, and said to him, 'If you are the Son of God, throw yourself down from here' " (Luke 4:9).

The **Dome of the Rock** is an imposing blue-tiled octagonal building with a glittering golden dome that dominates old Jerusalem's skyline. It is known as *Qubbat al-Sakhra* in Arabic and was built by Umayyad caliph Abd al-Malik ibn Marwan (685–691 CE). This venerable shrine—one of the oldest and most important artistic monuments of Islamic civilization—stands in the sacred sanctuary that Muslims reverentially refer to as Haram al-Sharif and what Jews and Christians call the Temple Mount. Muslims believe that Prophet Muhammad ascended to heaven for a meeting with God from this site. The Qur'anic inscriptions inside the shrine declare the Islamic doctrine about Jesus as prophet, not the son of God, and glorify the triumph of the Islamic empire over the Byzantine and Persian empires. There are three fictional stories that Muslims associate with the Dome of the Rock: the story of the Foundation Rock that bears the imprint of Muhammad's winged horse that leapt heavenward; that the reliquary inside the building holds hair from Muhammad's beard; and that God will send one of His angels to the shrine to sound the trumpet call to signal the end of the world and the Day of Judgment. Jews believe that Solomon's temple once stood at this site and that the Foundation Rock, which the shrine houses, was the center of Solomon's temple. Jews also believe that the Ark of the Covenant (which contains the tablets with the Ten Commandments that God gave to Moses on Mount Sinai) was brought to Solomon's temple.

(Continued)

Jerusalem: A Flashpoint in the Middle East   *(Continued)*

The **Al-Aqsa Mosque**, "the furthest mosque" in Arabic, stands at the south end of the Temple Mount and has prayer niches dedicated to Moses and Jesus. The Qur'an mentions Prophet Muhammad coming from Makkah to this site before ascending to heaven for a meeting with God. Michael Rohan, an Australian Christian fundamentalist, torched and attempted to burn down the Al-Aqsa Mosque in August 1969, an event that shocked the Muslim world enough that Muslim leaders assembled and established the Organization of the Islamic Conference (OIC) to represent the Islamic bloc.

Barak decided to use military force to suppress quickly the Palestinian demonstrations because he wanted to show his citizens that he was a strong leader despite the fact that he had abruptly withdrawn Israeli troops from Lebanon, tried but failed to resolve the Israeli-Syrian dispute over the Golan Heights, and failed to get a peace agreement in the final status talks with the Palestinians at Camp David. The Revolutionary Islamist organizations and the Al-Aqsa Martyr's Brigades (which was made up of revolutionary and armed activists from Arafat's secular Fatah organization) responded to Barak's crackdown by cooperating with and competing against each other in a series of suicide bombings that began to take a terrible toll on Israeli society. Considering Barak's catalogue of failures, his government quickly lost support in the Israeli Knesset, the 120-member unicameral legislature, and was forced to call early elections. During the brief election campaign, Sharon successfully claimed that Barak had not only failed to achieve peace with Israel's enemies but had jeopardized Israel's security instead. In February 2001, Israelis gave Sharon a mandate to do what it would take to punish Israel's enemies and bring back stability and security. Sharon formed a national unity government with several prominent Labor Party members (including the liberal and moderate Shimon Peres, who became foreign minister), greatly escalated the Israeli government's policy of assassinating radical Palestinian activists, and meted out severe retribution and collective punishment against entire Palestinian cities, towns, and refugee camps after every act of Palestinian violence.

The Mitchell and Tenet Plans

In April 2001, President George Bush sent former U.S. Senator George Mitchell (who had played a leading role in the successful negotiations between the Protestants and Catholics in Northern Ireland) to lead an inquiry into the Al-Aqsa *intifadah*. On May 5, 2001, highlights of the Mitchell Report were released. The report called on Arafat to do much more to stop suicide bombings and to imprison those engaging in terrorism. It also called on Israel to cease all Jewish settlement activity. Sharon, who had dedicated his entire political career to advocating, planning, and building Jewish settlements to maintain control of Judea and Samaria—

the biblical terms right-wing Israelis use for the West Bank—was unlikely to agree to these terms.[74]

To resume security cooperation between Israel and the Palestinian Authority, Bush sent CIA director George Tenet to meet Sharon and Arafat and to lead a negotiation of a cease-fire. Tenet produced a plan in June 2001 that the Israelis and Palestinians accepted but had not implemented as of June 2002 because of Sharon's precondition that the committee's recommendations be preceded by seven days of no Palestinian violence against Israelis.[75]

After the September 11, 2001, terrorist attacks, the United States launched a "war on terror" worldwide. On October 7, 2001, the United States started its military campaign in Afghanistan to end Taliban rule and root out al-Qaeda training camps. America's war on terror gave Sharon the pretext and license to refer to all Palestinian violence as "terrorism" and to declare a war on Palestinian terrorism.

In November 2001, U.S. Secretary of State Colin Powell called on Arafat to reign in the suicide bombers and appealed to the Palestinians to stop their suicide bombings. At the same time, Powell requested Sharon to halt the building of Jewish settlements in the West Bank and to withdraw immediately from Palestinian villages and towns that it had reoccupied. Powell also dispatched retired Marine general Anthony Zinni as his special representative to the Holy Land to try to bring the Palestinians and Israelis to the negotiating table. Zinni made several trips to the region but failed to bridge the gulf of distrust and hostility that had grown between the Israelis and Palestinians since Sharon's coming to power.

Despite the agreements reached by previous Israeli governments, Sharon, under the pretext of fighting a war on terror, has undermined the limited Palestinian autonomy in the West Bank and Gaza. By continuing his heavy-handed military operations and pick-ups of hundreds of Palestinian men for questioning, Sharon may believe he will reduce the problem of Palestinian terrorism. He may also believe that with the passage of time conditions in the West Bank and Gaza will become so unbearable for the Palestinians that they will prefer to leave the area rather than stay, and Israel will once again end up controlling the Judea and Samaria (West Bank). However, the overwhelming majority of Palestinians in the young and highly politicized under twenty-five years of age group does not bode well for good relations between the Palestinians and Israelis for years to come.

The Israeli Security Fence on the West Bank

Another issue that is bound to worsen relations between Palestinians and Israelis is the Israeli government's erection of a security fence to seal off Israel from the West Bank along the old Green Line marking Israel's border before the 1967 war.

---

[74]Norton, *Great Decisions, 2002* pp. 40–41.

[75]Ibid, p. 40

When completed, this elaborate 225 mile border of trenches, barricades, walls, watchtowers, patrol roads, high-technology surveillance equipment (including electronic motion detectors and other sensors), and beefed-up border patrol on both sideroadss at an estimated cost of $350 million may constitute a unilateral declaration of a border.[76]

The few Jewish settlers on the West Bank who are on the outside of the fence being constructed believe their own Jewish state is keeping them out of the land of Judea and Samaria that God gave the Israelis. Palestinians also object to the establishment of the fence, and they are furious that terror against the Jewish people resulted in the catonization of the land of Israel. Palestinians believe that the fence will restrict their freedom of movement, including preventing them from commuting to jobs and further crippling the Palestinian economy: it is estimated that 25,000 Palestinians cross into Israel each day to find work.[77] Palestinians believe the fence will physically divide some towns and split families. Furthermore, much of the fence will be built on large tracts of Palestinian land and many Palestinians believe that the fence could potentially finalize a border that should be decided through negotiations. Saeb Erekat, a Palestinian cabinet minister and peace negotiator, believes that the fence would divide Palestinian territories into small cantons and start a new apartheid system like the one that existed in South Africa. Indeed, the fence could very well leave 30,000 Palestinians in an expansive buffer zone straddling both sides of the line, isolating them from Israel and the West Bank.[78]

Hamas, Islamic Jihad, and the Al-Aqsa Martyr's Brigade believe that if they can maintain their war of attrition through guerrilla warfare and suicide bombings, like Hezbollah did in South Lebanon, Israel's harsh colonization or cantonization of Palestinian areas (especially in the West Bank) will radicalize future generations of Palestinians into the armed struggle. Eventually, the cost in terms of blood and treasure could prove unbearably high for the Jewish state, and the majority of Israelis themselves may reject either the colonialization or cantonization of the West Bank in favor of a two-state solution.

The Abdullah and Bush Peace Plans

In late February 2002, Crown Prince Abdullah ibn Abdul Aziz al-Saud (Saudi Arabia's de facto ruler due to King Fahd bin Abdul Aziz al Saud's illness) put forward a Middle East peace proposal that had the Arab states normalizing relations with Israel if the latter relinquished the Arab lands it conquered in the 1967 Arab-Israel War. This included the return by Israel of the Golan Heights to Syria, and the Gaza Strip and West Bank to the Palestinians. The twenty-two member Arab

---

[76]John Ward Anderson, "Israel Begins Work on Controversial Fence," *Mobile Press Register*, June 17, 2002, p. 1A, 4A;.

[77]John Kifner, "Palestinian Bomber Blows Himself Up Near Fence Site," *New York Times*, June 18, 2002, p. 6A.

[78]Anderson, "Israel Begins Work on Controversial Fence," *Mobile Press Register*, p. 4A.

League endorsed the Saudi Middle East peace proposal at its Beirut Summit at the end of March 2002, and the United States, the European Union, and even the Israelis diplomatically praised the "land for peace" formula (which, incidently, is as old as UN Resolution 242, passed in 1967, and approved by participants attending the 1991 Middle East peace conference in Madrid, Spain). Sharon, though, apparently had no intention of accepting the Saudi proposal, and the peace plan was shelved. Many believe that Prince Abdullah wasn't interested in helping the Palestinians or resolving the Middle East dispute but rather wanted to appear like a statesman and thus help to improve Saudi Arabia's image, which was tarnished because 15 of the 19 hijackers in the September 11 terrorist attacks were Saudis; the Saudis backed the Taliban financially and diplomatically; Saudis provided Islamic literature and funding for many *madrassah* schools in developing Muslim countries that may well have graduated Revolutionary Islamists; and the Saudis in and out of government may have directly or indirectly funded al-Qaeda.[79]

After much delay, President Bush delivered his speech on the Israeli-Palestinian conflict on June 24, 2002. Bush reiterated his vision of a Jewish state and a "provisional" or "interim" Palestinian state living side-by-side within the next three years, but Bush made this conditional on the Palestinians electing a new set of leaders that are committed to political and economic liberalization as well as an end to terrorism, corruption, cronyism, nepotism, and incompetence. All this may be highly unrealistic, but Bush's speech did indicate that his administration has come to the conclusion that Arafat is part of the problem rather than part of the solution, and therefore they will have to deal with one of the secular technocrats around him, who have been helpful in the past, whether in the negotiating process or in maintaining security on the West Bank and Gaza.

In Bush's Middle East plan, Sharon does not have to negotiate a political settlement with the Palestinians until they elect new leaders, stop attacking Israel, initiate political and economic reforms, and implement free enterprise. In fact American leaders are telling the Palestinian people not to elect Arafat and his friends; if they do, the United States will give them no economic and humanitarian aid and no "provisional" state within three years. There was no reference in Bush's speech to a previously promised international peace conference (which would involve the United States, the European Union, and/or the U.N.) that explores the paths to a comprehensive peace settlement, a regional conference (involving only Middle Eastern countries), or the placement of international monitors and peacekeepers to separate the antagonists. What is significant is that Bush did not tell the Israelis to stop building settlements in the West Bank, to stop using heavy American weapons against the Palestinians, to stop reoccupying heavily populated Palestinian towns, villages, and refugee camps, or to stop engaging in a policy of collective punishment against the Palestinians living in the West Bank and Gaza. The Bush plan also may do little to stop the cycle of violence that has adversely affected both the Israelis and the Palestinians. As of July 2002, it seems all hopes of future peace talks are pinned on the Palestinian elections scheduled

---

[79]Scott Macleod, "The Man Behind the Plan," *Time*, March 11, 2002, p. 47.

for January 2003. What will happen if Arafat is reelected or if Revolutionary Islamists from Hamas or Islamic Jihad win the popular vote and come to power? Will Israel respect the will of the Palestinian people, or will the democratic process be aborted and a crack down ensue? If that happens, more Revolutionary Islamism could probably be expected.

Summary

Explosive conflicts and dramatic peace agreements between the Arabs and Israelis have both contributed to the growth and spread of Islamism. The Six Day War (June 1967) inspired and was boosted by the limited victory of the Arabs in the 1973 war with Israel. The Israeli invasion of Lebanon in the summer of 1982 accelerated the development of Islamism, particularly in Lebanon but more generally in the entire Muslim world, as television pictures of that invasion were broadcast all over the world. Israel's periodic bombing of Lebanese villages and towns by air, sea, and land for much of the 1980s and early 1990s has helped keep Islamism alive in Lebanon.

In Israel, the attack and counterattack by Muslim and Jewish extremists has weakened the legitimacy of moderate secular alternatives to Revolutionary Islamism. At the same time, Arab-Israeli peace agreements have failed to quell the appeal of political Islam. Sadat's trip to Jerusalem and the Camp David Accord between Sadat and Begin were perceived by a significant portion of the *ummah* as a betrayal of the Arab and Muslim cause. Sadat's efforts at peace with Israel reinforced Islamism's appeal, not only in Egypt but in the Middle East at large. Just as Sadat lost his leadership of the Arab world and then his life to Revolutionary Islamists, Arafat was in danger of losing his leadership of the Palestinian movement and his life to Revolutionary Islamists as a result of signing the Declaration of Principles for limited Palestinian self-rule in the Gaza Strip and West Bank. Many Palestinians in the Israeli-occupied territories and in the diaspora saw the Oslo Peace Process and the Arafat-Rabin handshake as a "raw deal" because Palestinians are worse off today than they were in 1993. The Arafat-Rabin peace agreements brought new recruits into the ranks of Revolutionary Islamist Palestinian organizations such as Hamas and Islamic Jihad. With the Hebron massacre of Palestinian worshipers in the Ibrahimi Mosque, Hezbollah's success in driving Israel and its SLA allies out of South Lebanon, and the continuation of the Al-Aqsa *intifadah*, Islamism in the West Bank and the Gaza Strip looks more and more like an Islamic resurgence—or will it convert the struggle for an independent Palestinian state into an Islamic resurgence and the continuation of a Jewish-Islamic crusade for years to come? This nightmare scenario is one that intolerant extremists and soldiers of God from both the Palestinian and Israeli side embrace, but most rational, moderate, and peace-loving Palestinians and Israelis fear.

Ramallah on several occasions may have temporarily lifted the sagging popularity of the Palestine Authority's president. But the Bush administration's decision to freeze out Arafat as the principal spokesman and interlocator for the Palestinian people, while dealing with a few secular Palestinian technocrats around him, may be the end of a long and eventful career for the father of Palestinian nationalism. The Bush administration's intelligence suggests that the Palestinian people are deeply disillusioned with Arafat's leadership of the Palestinian Authority. The majority of Palestinians (including the Palestinian Islamists) accuse Arafat's administration for having been autocratic, corrupt, and incompetent. He is also accused of cronyism and collaboration with Israel, the United States, and the West in general. Therefore, it is quite possible that Arafat may not be reelected president of the Palestinian Authority in January 2003.

The ultimate consequence of Israeli success in killing and capturing many militants; undermining the moderates and pragmatists, like Arafat; and making life more miserable for the Palestinians, will be the creation of an entire generation of Palestinian extremists and suicide bombers intent on depriving Israelis of peace, stability, security, and prosperity. The injustices the Palestinians suffer are covered by the mass media not only in the Arab world but in the Muslim world in general. As it is, the Muslim world is angry with Israel for taking over much of Palestine and depriving Palestinians of their human rights. The Bush administration's decision to align itself with Sharon in his strategy of meting out collective punishment against the Palestinian people may have hurt America's image of an "honest broker" in the Arab-Israeli conflict.

Finally, if the Bush administration indiscriminately targets Arab and Muslim countries and organizations in the name of a war on terrorism, the U.S. government will only be broadening and deepening Revolutionary Islamism among the Palestinians, Arabs, and Muslims all over the world. In the medium- to long-term, such a strategy will result in not only a much more turbulent and dangerous Middle East, but a much more dangerous Muslim world, for U.S. diplomats, members of America's armed forces, business people, bankers, tourists, and other innocent American citizens to venture into and deal with.

Internet Sites

http://www.ict.org.il/arab_isr/frame.htm

    The Interdisciplinary Center (ICT), in Herzliya, Israel, provides information on terrorist organizations, terror attacks, and the Palestinian-Israeli peace process.

http://www.time.com/time/europe/timetrails/israel/

    Time Europe magazine's summary of the Arab-Israeli conflict.

http://www.middleeastbooks.com/html/books/b-arabisraeli.html

    AET Book Club provides searches for books on the Arab-Israeli conflict through author's name or book title.

http://www.mepc.org/journal/0103_gazitandabington.htm

    Middle East Policy Council Web site that provides journal articles and archives of Arab-Iraeli conflict.

http://www.washingtoninstitute.org/pubs/battlsum.htm

The Washington Institute for Near East Policy provides articles, book excerpts, and policy information.

http://www.assr.org/vlibrary/peace

This Arab Social Science Research Web site includes links to international, Arab, and Israeli resources.

http://www.birzeit.edu/links/

Birzeit University provides Palestinian Web links to business, advocacy, travel, education, research, and other topics.

http://www.arts.mcgill.ca/MEPP/meppnet.html

Web site that provides various links to Palestinian-Israeli resources and issues.

http://www.historyguy.com/arab-israeli_war_links.html

Collection of many Web links that discuss the Arab-Israeli conflict.

http://www.wbz-net.org/islinks.htm

Collection of many Web links that discuss Israeli resources and issues.

Palestine and Israel

http://www.masada2000.org/historical.html

http://www.dean.usma.edu/history/dhistorymaps/Arab-Israel%20Pages/aitoc.htm

http://www.regiments.org/milhist/mideast/israel.htm

http://www.cactus48.com/truth.html

http://www.mideastweb.org/biblio.htm

http://www.globalissues.org/Geopolitics/MiddleEast/Palestine.asp

http://www.incore.ulst.ac.uk/cds/countries/israel.html

http://www.ariga.com/peacewatch/iscyber.htm

http://www.wafa.pna.net/EngText/IndexE.htm

http://www.oneworld.net/specialreports/palestine/

http://members.tripod.co.uk/alquds/kataib.htm

http://www.adl.org/Israel/advocacy/gl_jihad.asp

http://www.military.com/Resources/ResourceFileView?file=HAMAS-Organization.htm

Arab and Israeli Wars

http://www.mfa.gov.il/mfa/go.asp?MFAH00us0

http://www.historyguy.com/arab_israeli_wars.html

http://www.historyguy.com/suez_war_1956.html

http://www.factmonster.com/ce6/history/A0804479.html

http://www.palestinehistory.com/war.htm

http://www.science.co.il/Arab-Israeli-conflict.asp

http://ebooks.whsmithonline.co.uk/htmldata/ency.asp?mainpage=HTTP:// EBOOKS.WHSMITHONLINE.CO.UK/ENCYCLOPEDIA/12/M0002912.HTM

Gaza

http://www.palestinehistory.com/gaza.htm

http://www.gazanews.com/

http://www.gaza.net/pages/History/

http://www.wikipedia.com/wiki/Gaza_Strip/History

Hamas

http://www.needham.mec.edu/NPS_Web_docs/High_School/cur/kane97/P1/alcg/ ALCGp1.html

http://www.pallinks.com/history/

http://home.talkcity.com/YosemiteDr/mole333/history.html

http://www.cdn-friends-icej.ca/isreport/hamas.html

Hezbollah

http://www.mg.co.za/mg/books/nov97/10nov-hezbollah.html

http://www.military.com/Resources/ResourceFileView?file=Hezbollah-History.htm

http://www.historyguy.com/new_and_recent_conflicts.html

http://www.adl.org/Israel/advocacy/gl_hezbollah.asp

Oslo Accords

http://almashriq.hiof.no/general/300/320/327/oslo.html

http://www.wisdom.weizmann.ac.il/~hand/Oslo.html

http://www.palestinecenter.org/palestine/osloaccords.html

http://www.earlham.edu/~pols/17Fall96/walkejo/homepage.html

http://www.washingtoninstitute.org/media/latimes.htm

http://www.claremont.org/precepts/277.cfm

http://www.us-israel.org/jsource/Peace/treatytoc.html

Wye River Accords

http://www.mideastweb.org/mewye.htm

http://www.jonathanpollard.org/wye.htm

http://www.loga.org/WyeLttr.htm

http://www.twf.org/News/Y1998/19981117-WyeNotPeace.html

http://www.likud.nl/viol.html

http://www.nad-plo.org/eye/moments.html

Arab-Israel Peace Summits

http://english.peopledaily.com.cn/200010/16/eng20001016_52759.html
http://www.csmonitor.com/durable/1997/11/14/intl/intl.3.html
http://www.la.utexas.edu/chenry/aip/archive/debriefing96/0028.html
http://www.washingtoninstitute.org/watch/Peacewatch/peacewatch1997/134.htm

Camp David Peace Treaty

http://www.usembassy-israel.org.il/publish/peace/peace1.htm
http://www.mideastweb.org/history.htm
http://www.usembassy-israel.org.il/publish/peace/peaindex.htm
http://www.us-israel.org/jsource/Peace/egtoc.html
http://www.arabicnews.com/ansub/Daily/Day/990309/1999030908.html
http://www.jewishgates.org/history/modhis/cdavid.stm

Palestinians

http://davenet.userland.com/2001/09/14/palestinians
http://www.ifc.org/camena/wbgaza.htm
http://www.usip.org/pubs/PW/1296/profile.html
http://www.palestine-net.com/
http://www.ptimes.com/
http://www.birzeit.edu/links/
http://www.palestinechronicle.com/
http://www.palestine-info.com/
http://www.arab.net/palestine/palestine_contents.html
http://www.visit-palestine.com/

Other

http://www.ju.edu.jo/campusnews/4jun2001/jerusalem
http://www.palestinehistory.com/intbio03.htm
http://www.cfr.org/public/pubs/MitchellComm_Report.pdf
http://www.fmep.org
http://www.state.gov/p/nea/rt/index.cfm?id=2829
http://www.mideasti.org
http://www.ahram.org.eg/weekly
http://www.alternativenews.org
http://www.birzeit.edu/links
http://www.electronicintifada.net
http://indymedia.org.il/imc/israel/webcast/index.php3

http://www.merip.org

http://www.palestinemonitor.org

http://mail.jmcc.org/media/reportonline

http://www.zmag.org/meastwatch/meastwat.htm

http://www.badil.org

http://www.fmep.org

http://www.ipsjps.org

http://miftah.org

http://www.arts.mcgill.ca/mepp/prrn/prfront.html

http://www.upmrc.org

http://www.adalah.org

http://www.adameer.org

http://www.alhaq.org

http://www.mezan.org

http://www.amnesty.org

http://btselem.org

http://www.cesr.org/index.html

http://hrw.org

http://www.lawsociety.org

http://www.pchrgaza.org

http://www.phrmg.org

http://www.derechos.net/ngo/phr

http://www.unhchr.ch

http://www.al-awda.org

http://www.adc.org

http://www.batshalom.org

http://www.prairienet.org/cpt

http://www.gush-shalom.org

http://www.ittijah.org

http://www.junity.org

http://www.cactus-48.com

http://www.rapprochement.org

http://www.nimn.org

http://www.skynews.co.uk/skynews/article/0,,30000-1037422,00.html

CHAPTER EIGHT

OPEC, OAPEC, and the OIC: Institutionalizing Pan-Islamism

The Organization of Petroleum Exporting Countries (OPEC) was established in 1960 by Saudi Arabia, Iran, Iraq, Kuwait, and Venezuela. Many Westerners erroneously believe that OPEC (1) completely monopolizes and manipulates the world's oil market; (2) consists solely of wealthy harem-keeping kings, *amirs,* and shaykhs; (3) is united in purpose, identity, and ideology; and (4) is bent on undermining Western economic and political stability. Despite these popular misconceptions, OPEC has had a significant impact on the West as an organization comprising important oil producers and consumers of Western products.

Within the Muslim world, OPEC has enriched a few Arab Muslim nations, like Saudi Arabia and Libya, while the vast majority of Muslims throughout the Muslim world remain destitute and impoverished. This, in turn, has fueled Islamism in particular and the politics of Islam in general on several levels. First, devout Muslims have perceived OPEC's relative success during the 1970s, despite Western interference, as God's blessing for pursuing the "straight path" following the disastrous 1967 Arab-Israeli War. OPEC's success, in their eyes, has vindicated them and testified to the will of God. Second, the money that OPEC has brought to the oil producers of the Muslim world has in limited amounts found its way through the agency of OPEC member nations to various and often competing Islamist organizations—whether to build *masjids* or to buy mortars. And third, the failure of OPEC member nations to redistribute their oil wealth throughout the Muslim world, regardless of national delineation, has engendered envy and frustration among impoverished Muslims. Accordingly, Islamists have sometimes turned against the oil-rich OPEC nations, labeling them corrupt and un-Islamic.

The creation of OPEC has contributed to global Islamic politics in often contradictory and ironic ways, yet OPEC's connection to the global Islamic revival is seldom made in either the popular or the scholarly literature. To understand the true and substantive effects of OPEC on the development and growth of global Islamism requires a thorough examination of OPEC, its origins, and its actions.

Prelude to OPEC's Ascendency

The oil-producing nations of the Muslim world after years of struggle following World War II achieved full political independence. They immediately sought economic independence from the West as well. At the time, the Seven Sisters[1] dominated and monopolized the oil industry, acting sometimes arrogantly and disrespectfully to their host nations and denying them fair and appropriate compensation. This situation aggravated tensions between the foreign oil companies and the governments of the nations in which they operated and in which "oil as a commodity represented the primary, and often only, resource . . . and an important, and often prime, energy input for the countries in which it was consumed."[2] Savoring their newfound political independence, these governments began to give precedence to their own economic interests at Western oil companies' expense. By the 1950s, host governments fought the foreign oil companies for "basic modifications in the concessions terms, which originally granted the companies, in addition to the right of exploiting the oil, extraordinary privileges."[3] The era of the virtual sovereignty of the Western oil companies in the region was coming to a close.

The establishment of OPEC was the result of increasing anger among oil-producing nations over the reduction of the posted price for oil by Western petroleum companies, which in turn threatened to cut into producer nations' desperately needed oil revenue. OPEC's stated resolutions were (1) that the governments of oil-producing nations needed to assume a more direct and active role in the determination of oil prices and not leave the decisions to the private companies; (2) that sudden price fluctuations were intolerable and oil prices must be stabilized; and (3) that oil policies among OPEC member nations needed to be reconciled and unified in order to benefit the organization generally and each member individually. In brief, OPEC was founded with the express purpose of coordinating the petroleum policies of member states and thereby safeguarding their individual and collective interests.[4]

Since stabilizing oil prices and maintaining steady oil revenues were OPEC's immediate short-term goals, the organization was successful in the 1960s despite

---

[1]A nickname for seven of the biggest oil corporations in the world: Exxon, Royal Dutch-Shell, Texaco, Standard Oil of California (Socol, marketed as Chevron), Mobil, Gulf, and British Petroleum.

[2]Ian Skeet, *OPEC: Twenty-Five Years of Prices and Politics* (New York: Cambridge University Press, 1991), p. 2.

[3]Yaacov Shimoni, *Political Dictionary of the Arab World* (New York: Macmillan, 1987), p. 358.

[4]See Resolutions I 1.2 and I 3.4 adopted at the first OPEC conference in Baghdad, Iraq, on September 1966, quoted in Abdul Kubbah, *OPEC: Past and Present* (Vienna, Austria: Retro Economic Research Center, 1974), p. 21.

a continuing worldwide recession and a declining demand for oil. In fact, as oil prices fell, OPEC's market share increased, and OPEC members' revenues rose. Lower oil prices meant that oil companies found it less profitable to search for more oil, small oil, companies went bankrupt, and potential oil men decided to wait for better days before venturing into the oil business. However, since demand for oil remained weak for the first decade of OPEC's existence, the organization was yet incapable of showing economic or political muscle.

Egypt's demoralizing defeat in the Six Day War with Israel in 1967 cost Nasser and his ideologies of pan-Arabism and Arab socialism much of their attraction among the masses. In turn, Islam strengthened as a source of identity and solace. Egypt's defeat, coupled with long-standing economic problems, compelled the once proud Nasser to turn to his erstwhile ideological foes, the oil-rich members of OPEC, which were conservative antirevolutionary proponents of Islamic, not Arab, solidarity. In exchange for desperately needed financial assistance, Nasser embraced the oil producers and compromised his own ideological zeal.[5] To further appease the Saudis and their allies and also to enhance his own legitimacy at home, Nasser began to utilize Islamic symbols and rhetoric. Thus, conservative oil-producing OPEC-member nations like Kuwait and Saudi Arabia emerged as new centers of regional power, handing out money and aid to gain friends and partisans throughout the Muslim world.

Accompanying these successes was a notable failure. During the 1967 War OPEC attempted to turn the "oil weapon" against those nations supporting Israel. This first short-lived oil embargo collapsed as the economic consequences for the oil producers became too burdensome. Therefore, in 1968, Saudi Arabia, Kuwait, and Libya established the Organization of Arab Petroleum Exporting Countries (OAPEC)—an organization similar to OPEC except that it excluded non-Arab oil producers—to achieve Arab political unity within the cartel and to employ that unity and Arab control of substantial oil resources as a weapon.[6] Thus, the stage was set for the vastly more successful oil embargo of 1973.

OPEC Ascendant

A confluence of factors, many rooted in the events of the 1960s, brought OPEC to the apogee of power and influence during the 1970s. First, the 1970s were years of remarkable and unprecedented economic expansion both in the industrialized West and in the Third World. As industry grew, after a long decade of worldwide recession, demand for oil grew, as well, and OPEC members prospered. Second, this prosperity underscored OPEC's predominant position in the oil industry. Prior to the establishment of OPEC, not even one oil-exporting nation accounted for more than one-third of total world exports, and no single oil-producing nation

---

[5]Shireen T. Hunter, *OPEC and the Third World* (Bloomington, Ind.: Indiana University Press, 1984), pp. 58–60.

[6]Shimoni, *Political Dictionary of the Arab World*, p. 361.

BOX 8.1   Organization of Arab Petroleum Exporting Countries (OAPEC)

Established in 1968 by Kuwait, Libya, and Saudi Arabia, the Organization of Arab Petroleum Exporting Countries (OAPEC) is a regional intergovernmental organization dedicated to the petroleum industry. OAPEC sponsors joint ventures among members and supports the integration of the petroleum industry among its membership. OAPEC sees this integration as the key to the future integration of the economies of the Arab world. OAPEC is also intended to act to resolve conflicts between its members and to present a unified Arab perspective on energy and development policies to the outside world. OAPEC also promotes scientific and technological advances in the oil industry.

OAPEC's charter describes its primary mission as one of creating and maintaining close cooperation among its members. This is achieved by promoting the exchange of information and holding seminars to review technological developments and address technical problems. OAPEC also sponsors five ventures that together are intended to act as a solid foundation for joint Arab action and economic integration. These ventures include the Arab Maritime Petroleum Transport Company (AMPTC), which covers all operations related to marine transport of oil; the Arab Shipbuilding and Repair Company (ASRC), which builds, repairs, and maintains seagoing vessels used in the transportation of oil; the Arab Petroleum Investments Corporation (APIC), which provides needed capital for petroleum projects; the Arab Petroleum Services Company (APSC), which specializes in drilling, logging, and oil exploration; and the Arab Petroleum Training Institute (APTI), which conducts research related to techniques of industrial organization, training, and education.

OAPEC's current members are Algeria, Bahrain, Egypt, Iraq, Kuwait, Libya, Qatar, Saudi Arabia, Syria, and the United Arab Emirates. The 1990–1991 Persian Gulf War, which directly involved member states Iraq, Kuwait, and Saudi Arabia, disrupted the operations of OAPEC. Ongoing sanctions against Iraq, as well as tensions between member states, continue to undermine the economic unity that OAPEC was created to promote.

http://www.oapecorg.org/
http://www.iet.com/Projects/HPKB/Web-mirror/OAPEC_EST_FCT/est_fct.html

---

accounted for more than one-fifth of world petroleum production. Yet by 1974, more than half the world's oil production and more than three-quarters of the world's exports were concentrated in the hands of the OPEC cartel.[7] Third, the world had begun a transformation from bipolarity—in which the two superpowers, the United States and the USSR, completely dominated their spheres of influence—to global multipolarization, in which numerous powerful countries act with

---

[7]Jeffey Hart, "Three Approaches to the Measurement of Power in International Relations," *International Organization*, Vol. 30, No. 2 (Spring 1976), p. 303.

relative independence from the superpowers. Hence, oil producers like Saudi Arabia and Kuwait, feeling no particular affinity for Moscow or for Washington, felt comfortable rejecting the blandishments and threats of both superpowers. Fourth, smaller independent oil companies had started to deal with the OPEC cartel. These companies offered larger royalties and higher taxes to the governments of the oil producing countries, giving the cartel greater clout in negotiations with the Seven Sisters. Fifth, in May 1970, the Trans-Arabian Pipeline (TAPline), bringing Saudi Arabian crude oil to the Eastern Mediterranean overland, was temporarily closed, and long-haul Gulf crude oil was shipped in to satisfy excessive demand. A tanker shortage ensued and freight rates skyrocketed. This situation, coupled with the closure of the Suez Canal after numerous ships were sunk there in the 1967 Arab-Israeli War, also pushed up the value of the low-sulphur Libyan crude oil that independent oil companies were taking to European markets.[8] While these new conditions resulted in the tightening of the oil supply, which increased the profits of the oil corporations, the revenues of the oil-producing countries' governments did not much increase. OPEC members discovered that they prospered only when they exercised control.[9]

In 1969, Libya's Colonel Muammar al-Qaddafi rose to power through a military coup and began his long tenure as leader of Libya, replacing the conservative regime of King Idris with his own peculiar brand of political Islam. The increasingly favorable winds of OPEC prosperity were at Qaddafi's back; he had ascended to leadership at an especially propitious time for the oil producers. Qaddafi was in a unique position to improve OPEC leverage vis-à-vis the oil companies. As leader of OPEC's Mediterranean Group, Libya cut petroleum production in order to raise prices and increase the revenue taken in by OPEC-member nations. Libya's position of prominence and leadership in OPEC was bolstered by the fortuitous bulldozer accident in May 1970 that temporarily closed Saudi Arabia's TAPline and increased the value of Libyan oil. Qaddafi took this opportunity to demand larger revenues and higher taxes from foreign oil corporations operating in Libya.

Libya's unprecedented success exacting concessions from the oil companies changed the pattern of compliance that had prevailed for the previous six decades, injected new life and vigor into OPEC, and spurred other OPEC members into action. The twenty-first meeting of OPEC in Caracas, Venezuela, in December 1970 resulted in an across-the-board increase in posted prices of 33 cents per barrel and a tax rate increase in each member nation to a minimum of 55 percent.[10]

Although the balance of power between the oligopolistic multinational oil corporations and the oil-producing nations had shifted decidedly in favor of the latter in the early 1970s, this shift did not attract international attention until OPEC

---

[8]Philip Connelly and Robert Perlman, *The Politics of Scarcity: Resource Conflicts in International Relations* (London: Oxford University Press, 1975), p. 72.

[9]Abbas Alnasrawi, "Arab Oil and the Industrial Economies: The Paradox of Oil Dependency," *Arab Studies Quarterly*, Vol. 1, No. 1 (Winter 1979), p. 5.

[10]Kubbah, *OPEC: Past and Present*, p. 54; Connelly and Perlman, *Politics of Scarcity*, p. 72.

BOX 8.2   Muammar al-Qaddafi

Muammar al-Qaddafi was born in 1942 in an arid region of Libya near the Mediterranean. His family was engaged in goat and camel herding and were members of the Bedouin tribe of Qaddafah. Qaddafi received a traditional Islamic education but was also inspired by Nasserism and the idea of a pan-Arab state. While completing his high school education, Qaddafi organized an underground political movement aimed at overthrowing the Libyan monarchy. Qaddafi and other members of his movement enrolled in the Royal Libyan Military Academy, where they actively recruited members for Qaddafi's Free Unionist Officers.

In 1969, while King Idris was out of the country, the Free Unionist Officers on Qaddafi's order overthrew the monarchy. Qaddafi proclaimed the Libyan Arab Republic and became commander-in-chief of Libya's armed forces. Political opposition to his regime was ruthlessly crushed.

Like his idol Nasser, Qaddafi began to nationalize industries in Libya. His nationalization of Libya's oil industry proved particularly lucrative. His opposition to Western political influence and interference in Libya culminated in the closing of U.S. and British bases in Libya and the expulsion of large numbers of Italians in 1970. Although committed to principles of pan-Arabism and socialism, Qaddafi is a devout, if somewhat eccentric, Muslim. He embraced political Islam early in his rule. In 1973, he proclaimed the *shariah* to be the supreme law of Libya. Between 1976 and 1979, Qaddafi published his "Green Book," in which he enumerated and elaborated upon his political and social theories. Qaddafi claimed that these theories derive from the Qur'an. He denounced Western representative democracy and proposed a socialist economic system in opposition to both Western capitalism and Marxism-Leninism. This system, Qaddafi declared, would be in complete harmony with Islam.

Qaddafi's foreign policy was erratic and confrontational. He made many enemies in the Arab world, particularly with his high-handed attempts to promote political union at various times with Egypt, Sudan, Syria, Tunisia, and Morocco. But Qaddafi's dreams of a pan-Arab state with himself at its head came to nothing. Qaddafi's relations with the West were also troubled by accusations that he supported terrorists operating in Western Europe. Qaddafi denied these accusations yet failed to convince the United States of his sincerity. In 1986 the United States bombed Libyan installations in retaliation for a terrorist attack in West Berlin. Although the U.S. attack was unpopular in both Europe and the Muslim world, Qaddafi's government has been implicated in a number of assassination and coup attempts in the Arab world as well as terrorist attacks on Europeans and Americans. However, in the late 1980s, Qaddafi's views began to moderate, and he made efforts to repair relations with his Arab neighbors.

http://www.geocities.com/LibyaPage/gadhafi.htm
http://www.nfsl-libya.com/English/Studies/LisaAnderson.htm
http://www.emergency.com/qaddafi.html
http://www.mathaba.net/info/mqadhafi.htm
http://www.cairotimes.com/news/qaddafi.html
http://www.abcnews.go.com/reference/bios/gadhafi.html

flexed its economic muscle during and after the Arab-Israeli War of October 1973. Within two weeks of Egypt's surprise attack on Israeli positions in the Sinai Peninsula, OAPEC instituted an oil embargo against the United States and the Netherlands. OAPEC members, indignant at the United States for its previous substantial economic, political, military, and moral support for Israel, imposed the embargo after President Nixon requested from the U.S. Congress $2.5 billion in immediate arms deliveries to the besieged Israeli state. Meanwhile, a Dutch offer to provide a relay center for emigrating Soviet Jews and charter flights to Israel on the official Dutch airline, KLM, triggered Arab antipathy toward the Netherlands.[11]

The oil embargo, coupled with a simultaneous OAPEC cut in oil production, occurred at a time when demand for oil in the industrialized world was already stretching OPEC production, refining, and transportation beyond capacity. Taking advantage of this development, OPEC exercised its formidable market power by raising the posted price of oil to $5.11 a barrel in October 1973. Sensing no reaction among the powerful industrialized oil-consuming nations that might threaten OPEC members' collective or individual interests, OPEC again raised the price of crude to an unprecedented $11.65 in January 1974, thus quadrupling the price since the outbreak of the Ramadan War in October 1973. All of this occurred without the oil companies' consent.[12]

The immediate U.S. reaction was to "bite the bullet." Even after the imposition of the embargo, the Nixon administration increased its arms shipments to Israel. Nonetheless, the sudden and devastating oil-price increases undermined economies around the world. The disruption resulting from OPEC and OAPEC actions induced a worldwide recession between 1974 and 1975. Meanwhile, OPEC member nations were enjoying oil revenues that before they could never have imagined.[13]

Although the Arab combatants' relative success (or at least avoidance of outright failure) in the 1973 war boosted morale throughout the Muslim world, OPEC's unmistakable success positively electrified Muslims. OPEC's ability to quadruple oil prices and OAPEC's embargo of oil to a superpower gave Muslims the world over a sense of pride, a taste of power, and a vision of a more promising future. For devout Muslims, OPEC's economic and apparent political empowerment was a token of divine providence—vindication for their belief that God was at last granting His believers a reward after years of fruitless struggle and hardship. OPEC thus directly contributed to Islamic politics.

---

[11]George Lenczowski, "The Oil-Producing Countries," in Raymond Vernon, ed., *The Oil Crisis* (New York: Norton, 1976), p. 68. The embargo against the United States was lifted in March 1974 (Bill and Leiden, *Politics in the Middle East*, p. 426).

[12]James A. Bill and Carl Leiden, *Politics in the Middle East* (Boston: Little Brown, 1984), p. 426; Ramon Knauerhase, "The Oil Producing Middle East States," *Current History*, Vol. 76, No. 443 (January 1979), p. 9.

[13]Lawrence Ziring, *The Middle East Political Dictionary*, 2nd ed. (Santa Barbara, Calif.: ABC-CLIO Information Services, 1992), pp. 292–293.

While OPEC's economic success in the 1970s was extraordinary, its political success was dubious at best. OPEC achieved few of its political objectives. Although member Muslim regimes were able to influence subtly the domestic and foreign policies of needy Muslim and non-Muslim Third World countries and even to persuade Europe and Japan to tilt, at least symbolically and rhetorically, toward Arab anti-Israeli and pro-Palestinian causes, little headway was made in wringing substantive concessions from the West on any big issue. Moreover, the major political objectives of the oil embargo—the withdrawal of Israel from all territories captured in the 1967 war, the "affirmation of the Arabism of Jerusalem," and the restoration of the "legitimate rights" of Palestinians—were not achieved. [14] The United States, meanwhile, encouraged OPEC members to invest their wealth in petrodollars in U.S. producer goods, consumer goods, military hardware, and agricultural produce. Consequently, OPEC's economic health became tied to the well-being of the U.S. economy. From this point on, OPEC discouraged and dismissed any attempts to destabilize the U.S. economy with excessive price hikes or an oil embargo. Saudi Arabia, the most influential OPEC member, for example, had become the largest importer of American military hardware, with purchases totaling $5.1 billion in 1980.[15]

Since the end of the oil embargo in 1974, OPEC has failed repeatedly to take action in the face of bold Israeli aggression and unqualified U.S. support for Israel. While OPEC has done nothing, Israel has built more settlements on the West Bank, made Jerusalem the unified capital of Israel, attacked OPEC-member Iraq's nuclear reactor at Osirik, annexed the Golan Heights, repeatedly invaded Lebanon, dismantled the PLO infrastructure, driven the PLO fighters out of Lebanon, and attacked Palestinians in Gaza and the West Bank without any concerted united action from the regimes in the Muslim world. This in turn has disillusioned many Islamists, even those receiving financial assistance from OPEC-member nations.

Of the prominent Muslim nations of OPEC, only Iraq is secular in its ideological orientation. The rest are religious conservatives promoting distinct brands of Islamic Revivalism through the disbursement of petrodollar aid.[16] Despite an apparent unity of interest in Islamic politics, no uniform policy of aid disbursement has ever emerged from an OPEC meeting. OPEC-member nations have preferred overwhelmingly to channel their petrodollar aid to recipients on a bilateral rather than a multilateral basis. Joint development projects are, by comparison, rare and underfunded. Furthermore, the promotion of Islam by individual OPEC nations is sometimes no more than the promotion of selfish national interest through the agency of a particular brand of Islam. However, in the process,

---

[14]Joseph A. Szliowicz, "The Embargo and U.S. Foreign Policy," in Bard E. O'Neil, ed., *The Energy Crisis and U.S. Foreign Policy* (New York: Praeger, 1975), pp. 185, 204.

[15]George Thomas Kurian, *Encyclopedia of the Third World*, 3rd ed. (Facts on File, 1987), p. 1698.

[16]Roy R. Anderson, Robert F. Seibert, and Jon G. Wagner, *Politics and Change in the Middle East: Sources of Conflict and Accomodation*, 3rd ed. (Englewood Cliffs, N.J.: Prentice-Hall, 1990), p. 239.

OPEC has strengthened the Islamic revival to such an extent that it too can no longer overlook Islam's demands.[17]

Libya's Qaddafi has taken keen interest in exporting his version of radical political Islam, and consequently his personal influence, to non-Arab African nations with substantial Muslim populations. In addition, a Libyan payroll tax has long supported the Jihad fund, which distributes money to militant, anti-Israeli Muslim groups and to Muslim guerrillas in the Philippines and in Ethiopia.[18] Ideologically, Qaddafi believes that "Islam is the best answer to the Third World's problems, and for the Islamic countries a return to Islamic principles is the best solution to their difficulties."[19]

Iran, like Libya, has supported militant and clandestine Islamist organizations that are anti-Western and anti-Zionist in ideology. As a nation calling itself an Islamic republic and governed by Shi'ah religious clerics, Iran considers itself the greatest benefactor to Islamism and has expended substantial oil revenues to prove it.[20] Radical Lebanese Shi'ah organizations, for example, look to Iran not only for petrodollar aid but for leadership as well. Iran has also involved itself in the Central Asian Muslim republics newly independent from Moscow. Iran has vied with Turkey and Saudi Arabia for influence in Central Asia by promoting commercial ties. More important, Iran has sent clerics and religious teachers to the former Soviet Muslim republics to heighten and politicize the Islamic revival taking place there.

Of all OPEC members, Saudi Arabia provides the best-documented case for the use of petrodollar aid to promote Saudi national interests and to disseminate Islamic Revivalism, two essentially compatible goals. Saudi Arabia's King Faisal (1906–1975) promoted a moderate brand of pan-Islamism in the 1960s to counter Nasser's attempts to destabilize pro-Western regimes by exporting radical Arab socialism. Faisal greatly increased and expanded monetary loans and grants to needy Muslim countries and to Muslim minorities in non-Muslim countries during the 1970s. Through aid, the Saudi government subsidized (a) the building of *masjids* and *madrassahs;* (b) the publication of Islamic books, journals, magazines, and newspapers; and (c) the activities of clandestine revolutionary Islamist groups like the Ikhwan, which was outlawed in Egypt, Sudan, and Syria. Saudi loans and grants were partly responsible for influencing Egypt's Sadat, Sudan's Numeiri, and Somalia's Said Bari to remove their countries from the Soviet sphere of influence and embark on a more pro-Western foreign policy. Partly to counter and neutralize entrenched socialist elements in Egypt and partly to please Saudi patrons, Sadat allowed Islamic groups to operate freely in Egypt again. He also introduced a policy entitled *infitah*, or "open door policy," in which Western multinational corporations were encouraged to invest in Egypt. Similarly,

---

[17]Hunter, *OPEC and the Third World,* p. 68.

[18]Kurian, *Encyclopedia of the Third World,* p. 1206.

[19]Hunter, *OPEC and the Third World,* p. 68.

[20]Anderson, Seibert, and Wagner, *Politics and Change in the Middle East,* p. 239.

Pakistan's Prime Minister Zulfikar Ali Bhutto was no doubt courting Saudi aid when he adopted an uncharacteristically strong Islamic emphasis in Pakistan's foreign and domestic policy.

Saudi aid often influenced political decisions. With the promise of millions of dollars in aid, the Saudis convinced the leadership of the newborn and needy nation of Bangladesh to abandon its desire for revenge against Pakistani army officers—some already marked for execution—languishing in Bangladeshi jails, to forego demanding war reparations from Pakistan, and to try to improve relations with Pakistan. The Saudis also offered the regime of Ferdinand Marcos' aid in return for his promise to soften the Philippine government's militaristic policy against the Muslim rebels in Mindanao.

In essence, OPEC members have used their vast petrodollar wealth and petroleum resources to support and encourage their particular views of Islam and their national interests. Unified OPEC disbursement of petrodollar aid has failed to occur since views of Islam and national interests vary from country to country. Consequently, OPEC has evoked envy and resentment by giving petrodollar aid selectively to the governments of a few Muslim countries, while most Muslim countries suffer privation from high oil prices, global inflation, rising unemployment, and a heavier debt burden. Some members of OPEC have further incurred the anger of many Muslims by squandering petrodollar wealth on the purchase of huge quantities of Western arms; on industrialization and urbanization on the materialistic Western model; on investment in Western banks, real estate, and corporations; on the purchase of gold; and on imported luxuries. Moreover, throughout the Muslim world, Muslims have come to regard OPEC as a paper tiger, unwilling or unable to force substantive concessions from Israel or the West. Instead, OPEC has aggravated and perpetuated poverty and inequality by failing to share its enormous wealth with less fortunate Muslims, as enjoined by Islam. Thus, while the oil embargo of 1973 to 1974 and the oil-price increases of 1973 to 1981 contributed positively to Islamism, the disillusionment inspired by OPEC's failure to improve the lives of most Muslims, in turn, further fueled the global Islamism.

The Future of OPEC

The spike in oil prices from 2000 to 2001 was the result not of OPEC's calculated planning but rather of years of depressed oil prices. The oil price collapse of 1998 to 1999 kept Western capital investment in exploration and production to a bare minimum. OPEC members themselves made no efforts to increase their own production capacity. OPEC therefore maintained its leverage over oil markets. The cartel made some efforts to manage its oil supply and bring prices up; by 2000, prices did begin to climb. However, the danger to OPEC of increasing oil prices was twofold. First, high oil prices might induce or prolong recessions in the Western markets that represent OPEC's biggest customers. In a recession, demand for oil and other energy sources necessarily drops—and with it, the price of oil. Second and alternatively, Western markets facing higher oil prices become more likely to invest large sums of money necessary to find alternative forms of energy or cheaper sources of oil—new sources of oil located outside OPEC nations. In fact, the longer OPEC maintains higher prices for oil, "the more response there will be towards promoting competing supplies, alternative fuels, conservation, greater energy efficiency, and falling demand."[21] Therefore, discovery and extraction of new oil sources will not only depress the price of oil but also decrease the percent of the market over which OPEC exerts direct control. Prior to September 11, 2001, Caspian Sea oil was considered well worth exploiting; but U.S. friction with Russia and Iran, who are the region's major power brokers, and the continuing unrest in Afghanistan, which would serve as a transit route for Caspian Sea oil to Western markets, mitigated against development.

The U.S. recession that began in March 2001, sparked in part by higher energy prices, represented the fulfillment of the first danger to OPEC. For example, Saudi Arabia failed to make investments in increasing its own oil production capacity "to try to fill government coffers [and] to stave off political problems at home and social unrest."[22] Meanwhile, Western economies felt the pressure of higher oil prices, and recession loomed on the economic horizon. The higher prices ultimately hurt demand. The further economic jolt that followed the attacks on the United States on September 11 made it clear that the West was in recession; demand for oil fell, and as a result the price of oil collapsed.

Add to the lower oil prices the U.S. war in Afghanistan, and it becomes clear that a confluence of factors, including closer and friendlier U.S. relations with Russia as well as stabilization of Afghanistan politically, could have a long-term impact on OPEC's market share, which was 50 to 55 percent of worldwide crude oil production in the 1970s but is currently less than 40 percent. More significantly, Russia initially refused to play along with OPEC plans to reduce production. Russia's Vladimir Putin characterized his country's unrestricted oil production as "an act of solidarity with the antiterrorist coalition," in which Russia serves "as an alternate source of energy to the unstable Middle East."[23] One effect of Russia's refusal to cooperate with OPEC in reducing production was to drive oil prices down. If prices go much lower, the effect on OPEC members' revenues could be devastating. In the late 1990s, when oil prices dropped to $10 a barrel, "Saudi Arabia had to borrow money for the first time in its history to cover its welfare-state budget."[24] Should OPEC fail to bolster petroleum prices, the Saudi government may face significant internal dissension—headed by the same militant and Revolutionary Islamists its petrodollars once supported to fight in Afghanistan.

By December 2001, OPEC nations agreed to cut daily output of oil in an effort to stabilize the price of petroleum and to prevent it from dropping further. This agreement was made only after nonmembers Russia, Norway, Mexico,

---

[21]Steven Poruban, "Special Report: OPEC's Evolving Role: Analysts Discuss OPEC's Role." *Oil and Gas Journal*, Vol. 99, No. 28, July 9, 2001, p. 64.

[22]Ibid.

[23]Daniel Schorr, "Cheap Fill-Ups? Thank Russia," *Christian Science Monitor*, November 30, 2001.

[24]Ibid.

Oman, and Angola agreed to cut their production. By December the political situation had already changed. The U.S.-led bombing campaign in Afghanistan met with surprising success and was winding down. Moreover, the U.S. economy had shaken off the effects of the September 11 attacks. The recession, which predated the attacks by six months, was expected to continue no more than six months. Russia was more amenable to persuasion, and OPEC forced the issue by threatening non-OPEC countries with a price war that OPEC members, with their greater capacity for oil production, would surely win. Whether Gulf State governments could survive a prolonged price war in which revenues would, at least in the short term, dramatically fall remains to be seen. Furthermore, OPEC members were not optimistic about Russia's compliance with the agreement to cut production. Russia remains "engaged in a major push to find new markets for its oil exports."[25] In any event, OPEC member compliance itself is questionable. OPEC secretary general Ali Rodriguez noted: "Compliance by OPEC members is voluntary. . . . It's a question of honor for countries. Sometimes, for different reasons, compliance is not satisfactory."[26] Whether these attempted production cuts will achieve the goal of stabilizing oil prices or not, the involvement of non-OPEC members in the agreement demonstrates how the cartel has lost its ability to unilaterally control the value of petroleum. Nevertheless, the United States considers protecting OPEC countries, particularly the states in the Persian Gulf, from political instability as part of its own national interest. It is this U.S. national interest in the availability of oil from the region that inspires U.S. policy to support governments it would otherwise consider reprehensible; thus, militant and Revolutionary Islamists consider the United States just as much an enemy of their cause as the governments that repress them.

The OIC and Pan-Islamism

Religion in society has always inspired two contradictory tendencies: the first toward union, the second toward distinctness. In Islam, for example, believers are united in the *dar al-Islam* (abode of Islam) as distinguished from the *dar al-harb* (abode of conflict). Pan-Islamism represents the most modern ideological expression of these tendencies and is enshrined in the idea of the *ummah*—an idea as ancient and as compelling as the Qur'an. An integral component to Islamic revolution, pan-Islamism reflects the ultimate aspirations of today's devout Muslims. It is an ideology that calls upon believers to cast aside the veils of secular nationalism and racial, linguistic, and tribal loyalties to reunite the long-divided *ummah*. In this sense, Islam asks for more than personal devotion and submission to the will of God; Islam demands the devotion and submission of the community of believers to the precepts revealed in the Qur'an and set forth in the *shariah*.[27] It

[25]Alan Riding, "OPEC Cuts Oil Output in Pact with Rivals," *New York Times*, December 28, 2001.

[26]Ibid.

[27]Shimoni, *Political Dictionary of the Arab World*, p. 397.

is upon this fourteen-hundred-year-old concept of community, of the universal *ummah* so alien to the West, that the modern Organization of the Islamic Conference (OIC) is based.

The *ummah* is more than some distant or utopian goal rooted deeper in faith than in immediate fact. It represents more than a divine promise, like the Kingdom of God foretold in Judaism, Christianity, and Islam alike. After Prophet Muhammad's death, in 632 CE, the Muslim world, which spanned the Arabian peninsula, retained its unity as the *ummah*. The basis of this unity was brotherhood and equality among believers, as well as the primacy of Islamic law and ummaic loyalty over the tribal claims to individual fealty that for millennia had prevailed among the pagan Arabs. Muhammad's death did briefly inspire a challenge to ummaic authority, vested in the institution of the Khilafat, mounted by rebellious Arab tribes. Abu Bakr, Islam's first caliph and Muhammad's immediate successor, quickly suppressed this defiance. Thus, Abu Bakr established the superiority of ummaic over tribal identity and reminded Muslims that their first loyalty lay in submission to God and to his earthly *ummah*.[28]

Over the centuries, as Islam spread, the *ummah* remained intact. Nevertheless rivalries for power within the Khilafat eroded its effectiveness, and the *ummah* as a designation of the political unity of the Muslim world gradually dissolved. As the Khilafat crumbled, its political authority disintegrating in the hands of those who had paid every price to wield it, the vacuum was filled increasingly by Westerners. Finally, in 1924, the Turks terminated the Khilafat as a political entity. This dissolution of ummaic authority and the continued role of non-Muslim Western colonial powers in the Muslim world engendered the "romance" of the *ummah*, the popularization of the Muslim world's political unity. A number of prominent Muslim rulers took advantage of this renewed popularity to attain the position of caliph of the Muslim world.[29] Among the most notable were Makkah's Sharif Husayn at a conference in 1924, Egypt's King Fu'ad in 1926, Saudi Arabia's King Abd al-Aziz Ibn Saud also in 1926, and the *mufti* Amin al-Husayni in 1931.[30] Yet these efforts came to naught. Instead, the secular ideal of the nation-state was adopted without modification from the West, dashing hopes for a reborn Khilafat. Yet Muslims could not so blithely cast their history and their culture aside nor so easily reconcile their new political identity with their identity as members of the community of Islam—the *ummah*.

If pan-Islamism had no longer a political reality, it retained a psychological one. As the boundaries of nation-states in the Muslim world divided the *ummah*, learned Islamists advanced the notion that the secular nation-state, as a Western imposition, had rendered impotent the formidable power that the *ummah*, in the vesture of the Khilafat, had once wielded. Only pan-Islamism, they argued, could

---

[28]Abdullah al-Ahsan, *OIC: The Organization of the Islamic Conference*, Islamization of Knowledge Series (Herndon, Va.: International Institute of Islamic Thought, 1988, pp. 8–9.

[29]Shimoni, *Political Dictionary of the Arab World*, p. 398.

[30]Trevor Mostyn, ed., *The Cambridge Encyclopedia of the Middle East and North Africa* (Cambridge: Cambridge University Press, 1988), p. 477.

BOX 8.3   Organization of the Islamic Conference (OIC)

Following the arson attack against the al-Aqsa Mosque in Jerusalem, the OIC was established in 1969 to promote Islamic solidarity and foster political, economic, social, and cultural cooperation among member Muslim states. According to the OIC charter, the objectives of the organization are as follows:

1. To promote Islamic solidarity among member states
2. To consolidate cooperation among member states in economic, social, cultural, scientific, and other vital fields of activities, and to carry out consultations among member states in international organizations
3. To eliminate racial segregation and discrimination and to eradicate colonialism in all its forms
4. To take necessary measures to support international peace and security founded on justice
5. To strengthen the struggle of all Muslims with a view to safeguarding their dignity, independence, and national rights
6. To create a suitable atmosphere for the promotion of cooperation and understanding among member states and other countries

The OIC charter advocates additional principles, including total equality between member states; respect of the right of self-determination; noninterference in the domestic affairs of member states; respect for the sovereignty, independence, and territorial integrity of member states; settlement of conflicts by peaceful means, such as negotiation, mediation, reconciliation, or arbitration; and abstention from the threat or use of force against the territorial integrity, national unity, or political independence of any member state.

Besides OIC's International Development Bank (IDB) other subsidiary and affiliated OIC institutions include the Al-Quds Fund, founded to resist Israeli-sponsored Judaization policies in Arab Jerusalem and to support the Palestinians generally; the Islamic Commission of the International Crescent, which is the OIC's answer to the Red Cross; the Islamic Solidarity Fund, founded to build *masjids, madrassahs,* and hospitals; the International Islamic Law Commission, charged with the promotion of the *shariah;* the Islamic Center for the Development of Trade founded to encourage mutually beneficial commercial ties among member nations; the Islamic Center for Technical and Vocational Training and Research, which trains individuals, conducts research in relevant technologies, and encourages exchanges of technologies between member nations; the Islamic Civil Aviation Council, which promotes member-nation cooperation in air transport; the Islamic Jurisprudence Academy, established to study the problems besetting the modern Muslim world, to devise solutions in accordance with the *shariah,* and more generally, to promote the unity of the Muslim world; the Islamic Foundation for Science, Technology and Development, which promotes research in science and technology within an Islamic framework; the Research Center for Islamic History, Art and Culture, founded to research the common past of the Muslim world; and the Statistical, Economic and Social Research and Training Center for the Islamic Countries, which collects and evaluates

(Continued)

Organization of the Islamic Conference (OIC)   (Continued)

socioeconomic data on member nations.* Among additional OIC-related institutions are the International Islamic News Agency; Islamic States Broadcasting Organization; Islamic Capitals Organization; Islamic Chamber of Commerce, Industry and Commodity Exchange; Islamic Educational, Scientific and Cultural Organization; and the Islamic Shipbuilders Association.**

The OIC comprises fifty-seven countries (see Table 8.1).

http://www.oic-oci.org/
http://www.irna.com/oic/oicabout.htm
http://www.forisb.org/oic.html

*al-Ahsan, OIC, pp. 30–37; The Middle East and North Africa, p. 204.
**The Middle East and North Africa, p. 204

TABLE 8.1   OIC Member States

Currently the OIC has fifty-seven members.

State	Year of Admission
Member States	
Afghanistan	1969
Albania, Republic of	1992
Algeria, People's Democratic Republic of	1969
Azerbaijan, Republic of	1991
Bahrain, State of	1970
Bangladesh, People's Republic of	1974
Benin, Republic of	1982
Brunei Dar-us-Salaam, Sultanate of	1984
Burkina Faso	1975
Cameroon, Republic of	1975
Chad, Republic of	1969
Comoros, Federal Islamic Republic of the	1976
Cote d'Ivoire, Republic of	2001
Djibouti, Republic of	1978
Egypt, Arab Republic of	1969
Gabon, Republic of	1974
Gambia, Republic of the	1974
Guinea, Republic of	1969
Guinea-Bissau, Republic of	1974
Guyana, Republic of	1998
Indonesia, Republic of	1969
Iran, Islamic Republic of	1969
Iraq, Republic of	1976
Jordan, Hashemite Kingdom of	1969
Kazakhstan, Republic of	1995
Kuwait, State of	1969
Kyrghyzstan, Republic of	1992

State	Year of Admission
Member States	
Lebanon, Republic of	1969
Libya (Socialist People's Libyan Arab Jamahiriya)	1969
Malaysia	1969
Maldives, Republic of	1976
Mali, Republic of	1969
Mauritania, Islamic Republic of	1969
Morocco, Kingdom of	1969
Mozambique, Republic of	1994
Niger, Republic of	1969
Nigeria, Federal Republic of	1986
Oman, Sultanate of	1970
Pakistan, Islamic Republic of	1969
Palestine, State of	1969
Qatar, State of	1970
Saudi Arabia, Kingdom of	1969
Senegal, Republic of	1969
Sierra Leone, Republic of	1972
Somalia, Democratic Republic of	1969
Sudan, Republic of the	1969
Surinam, Republic of the	1996
Syrian Arab Republic	1970
Tajikistan, Republic of	1992
Togo, Republic of	1997
Tunisia, Republic of	1969
Turkey, Republic of	1969
Turkmenistan, Republic of	1992
Uganda, Republic of	1974
United Arab Emirates, State of	1970
Uzbekistan, Republic of	1995
Yemen, Republic of	1969

reverse the damage inflicted by secular nationalism and loosen the bonds of Western domination. In effect, Islamists recognized the great inherent potential of an Islamic bloc and, indeed, derided secular nationalism, the foundation on which the Muslim world was now being rebuilt, as un-Islamic. After all, they pointed out, the glory of Islam was historically the glory of the *ummah*, the fragmentation of which had undermined the strength of Islam and opened the doors to Western colonialists.

Moreover, Muslims throughout the world continued to feel a special bond with their coreligionists, without regard to race, tribe, language, or even nation. Islam, after all, turned all Muslims to the **qiblah** (the direction of Makkah, toward which Muslims must pray), called all Muslims from the minaret, and brought all Muslims to the Ka'abah, irrespective of homeland. Spiritually, Islam was their home. The psychological and spiritual unity of Muslims continued despite the dissolution of their political unity.

The psychological *ummah*, however, could not give life to its political manifestation. After the Muslim nations achieved independence from the West, secular nationalism enjoyed greater popularity than did the ideology of pan-Islam. Abu
Bakr was not alive to lead armies against Nasser, and Nasserism for a time waxed
triumphant. Arabism, not Islam, Nasser insisted, was an appropriate framework on
which to construct unity.

Nasser's political rivals, particularly the Saudis, who resented Nasser's interference in Yemen and his threats to their legitimacy, also became his ideological
rivals. The obvious alternative to Nasser's pan-Arabism, Arab socialism, and personal cult of secular leadership was pan-Islamism. The attempts of King Faisal to
promote and popularize pan-Islamism were welcomed by many Muslim nations,
at least in principle, but were condemned vigorously by the regimes of Egypt,
Syria, and Iraq. Nasser, meanwhile, had reached the height of his popularity
among the masses. The Saudis, using their credentials as the guardians of Islam's
two holiest cities, Makkah and Madinah, countered Nasser's vast appeal and kept
the Egyptian president at bay.

The Saudi royal family's sponsorship of pan-Islamism before 1967 resulted in
the creation in 1962 of the Rabitat al-Alam al-Islami (Muslim World League), a
pan-Islamic organization. However, this organization served as little more than "a
propaganda forum for the Saudis" against Nasser.[31] Despite Saudi Arabia's continued efforts, pan-Islamism made little progress during the height of pan-Arab
nationalism and did nothing to diminish Nasser's soaring popularity.

Ironically, what the Saudis could not in a decade accomplish with pan-Islam
and the creation of pan-Islamic organizations, the Israelis accomplished in six
days. The 1967 war with Israel humiliated Egypt, humbled Nasser, and undermined the credibility of nationalism, Arab socialism, and pan-Arabism. Nasser's
popularity plummeted; no more could he impede the development of an institutionalized international organization devoted to promoting Islamic unity.[32] The
political ascendancy of Saudi Arabia at Nasser's expense, coupled with the devastating psychological trauma inflicted upon the Muslim world by the swift defeat in
1967, granted pan-Islamism and the concept of the *ummah* a renewed ideological
life; secularists and secularism had utterly failed to defeat Israel. A profound sense
of despair pervaded the Muslim world, a despair assuaged by renewed faith in
Islam, by Islamism, and by the promise and potential of pan-Islamism.

Several years passed between the 1967 war and the establishment of the OIC.
Although pan-Islamism was growing in popularity—even in Nasser's Egypt—the
creation of the OIC occurred only after a second shock to the Muslim world: the
August 21, 1969, arson at the al-Aqsa Mosque in Jerusalem. Although the fire and
its consequent damage were the work of Denis Michael Rohan, a lone and fanatical Australian Zionist, Muslims all over the world were outraged and, in one way
or another, held the Israeli government responsible for the crime.[33] A conference

---

[31]Mostyn, *Cambridge Encyclopedia of the Middle East and North Africa*, p. 479.

[32]Ibid., p. 480.

[33]Ibid.

of twenty-five Muslim nations was convened in Rabat, Morocco, on September 22, 1969. Then a March 1970 meeting of the foreign ministers of Muslim countries directed the creation of the OIC, a pan-Islamic organization based upon the philosophy of the *ummah* and charged (1) to protect Islamic holy sites (like the al-Aqsa Mosque), (2) to encourage Islamic solidarity among Muslim states, (3) to end all manifestations of colonialism and imperialism, and (4) to assist Palestinians in the liberation of their land.[34] These, in abbreviated form, represent both the immediate reasons and the ultimate objectives for which the OIC was formed.

The OIC's Role in Institutionalizing the Islamic Revival

Today the OIC consists of fifty-seven member states and at least twenty subsidiary bodies and affiliated specialized associations. By organizing conferences that periodically bring Muslim leaders, government officials, and nongovernmental groups of the fifty-seven member nations together, the OIC plays a vitally important organizational role not only by fostering a greater sense of solidarity in the fragmented Islamic bloc but also by institutionalizing the Islamic revival. Muslims the world over no doubt feel pleased and hopeful when they learn through the media that leaders of the Muslim countries—with sometimes diametrically opposite ideological orientations and national interests—are sitting down to discuss their common problems, coming up with unanimous resolutions, and formulating solutions for the Muslim world in the true spirit of Islamic unity. The OIC has also published a considerable amount of literature on Islam in its twenty-three-year existence. This Islamic literature has been disseminated not only in predominantly Muslim countries but also in non-Muslim countries with significant Muslim minorities.

Because the OIC was established as a consequence of the Israeli occupation of Jerusalem, the Arab-Israel conflict is central to OIC members. Indeed, the fifth stated objective in Article 2 of the OIC charter is "to coordinate efforts for the safeguard of the Holy Places and support of the people of Palestine, and help them regain their rights and liberate their land."[35] The OIC has remained true to this founding principle; for example, in 1981 it announced a *jihad* and an economic boycott against Israel.[36] Nevertheless, despite the great emphasis placed on the Arab-Israeli conflict, the organization since its establishment has cultivated the more ancient and agreeable traditions of the *ummah*. Consequently, the first and second objectives of the OIC, defined in Article 2, are "to promote Islamic solidarity among member states" and "to consolidate co-operation among member states in economic, social, cultural, scientific and other fields of activities, and facilitate consultation among member states in international organizations."[37] Thus, the OIC was founded primarily on principles of Islamic unity and is rooted,

---

[34]al-Ahsan, *OIC*, pp. 23–24.

[35]Ibid., p. 128.

[36]*The Middle East and North Africa, 1984–85* (London: Europa, 1984), p. 205.

[37]al-Ahsan, *OIC*, p. 128.

at least theoretically, in the tradition of the *ummah*. In practice, however, the OIC's roots in the ideal, politically united *ummah* are weak. The organization, fragmented and poorly anchored, is often powerless and ineffective in the face of political storms.

While the OIC is hardly a vision of pan-Islamism or of a sturdy Islamic solidarity, the organization has made serious and concerted strides toward greater unity culturally, intellectually, economically, and politically over the last two decades, often through various subsidiary or affiliated institutions. The Islamic Development Bank (IDB), for example, was established in 1975 by the finance ministers of OIC member nations in an effort "to encourage economic and social progress of member countries and Muslim communities in accordance with the principles of the Islamic *shariah*."[38] The IDB, abiding by Islamic law, forbids usury and provides interest-free loans, charging only a service fee. These loans are granted to the poorest member states so that they can attend to their most urgent socioeconomic problems. The IDB also encourages investments within and joint ventures among member states.[39] Moreover, the IDB's special assistance account renders emergency financial aid and promotes Islamic education for Muslims outside OIC member countries.[40]

Although many OIC organizations specifically encourage the cooperation of OIC member nations in cultural, economic, and political realms, their success has been hindered by questions of national interest in even less ambitious projects. The IDB, for example, is not funded or equipped to bridge the gulf separating the rich Muslim states from the poor. But because rich OAPEC nations prefer to promise and disburse aid money to poorer states on terms conducive to their national interests, the IDB, which does not promote any one Arab country's national interest, is not their major benificiary. Meanwhile, the success of organizations promoting sociocultural unity in the Muslim world is, when possible to gauge, undermined by dictatorial regimes that can endure only by drawing distinctions between "us" and "them" within their own nations and between their nations and others within the Muslim world. Iraq, for example, won support from the oil-rich Gulf states in its war with Iran only by portraying itself as an impediment to Persian-dominated Iran's revolutionary Shi'ah brand of political Islam. Underlining the essential sociocultural similarities between Iran and Iraq would, in contrast, have been an unproductive strategy.

In essence, the national interests of OIC member states far outweigh any commitment to Islamic solidarity. The OIC's attempt to study and coordinate Muslim affairs, particularly in political matters, may prove unproductive since the OIC itself is handicapped by significant internal contradictions. The OIC purports to represent its members, but its members prefer to represent themselves; the OIC wishes to unify the *ummah*, but the *ummah* and the modern nation-state sys-

---

[38]*The Middle East and North Africa*, p. 196.

[39]al-Ahsan, *OIC*, pp.95–96.

[40]*The Middle East and North Africa*, p. 196.

tem have a difficult time coexisting. Consequently, constant internal squabbling, turmoil, and dissension have rendered the OIC a pale shadow of its own ideals.

The OIC's chronic inability to enforce the collective will over the objections of specific member nations represents the subordination of international Islamic law to Western international law in the Muslim world. In the days of the Khilafat, the *ummah* was ruled entirely on the basis of the *shariah*. Member states of the OIC, in contrast, today "are stronger authorities than the OIC itself."[41] The law of individual states—whether secular or religious—takes precedence over *shariah* law at the global level. Submission of member nations to OIC rulings based on the *shariah*, no matter if there is overwhelming support from most members, is wholly voluntary. Therefore, the OIC, unlike the *ummah* during the Khilafat, is not a sovereign entity but, like other equally impotent international organizations, is obeyed, manipulated, or ignored by member nations according to their perceived best interests. Thus, while the OIC brilliantly and lucidly transcribes the ideal of the universal *ummah* into its finely worded charter, it is unable to translate that ideal into action.

The OIC succeeds and fails according to the dictates of sovereign nation-states, which are able on the surface to make common cause, but which all too often pursue national interests that are essentially irreconcilable with the interests of their neighbors and with the OIC. Even on the issue of Israel, the issue that directly inspired the creation of the OIC, member states have fallen into argument and disunity. When Egypt signed the Camp David agreement with Israel in 1978, the OIC suspended Egyptian membership for its "flagrant violation of the U.N. and OIC Charters."[42] Egypt, to regain the Sinai Peninsula, to secure its border with Israel, and to end the devastating cycle of war in the region, jettisoned, in the view of many Muslims, the very principles on which the OIC was founded. Thus, Egypt was deprived of its OIC membership for having sacrificed collective objectives for national benefit. Yet no other penalties were exacted, and within five years Egypt was reinstated. In fact, the reinstatement required no compromise by Egypt of the Camp David peace and was based on no conditions. The OIC had no power to enforce its most basic decisions.[43]

The Soviet invasion of Afghanistan in 1979 further complicated the Israeli issue within the OIC and damaged the organization's credibility as a consistently just and principled organization. Many OIC members likened the Soviet invasion and occupation of Afghanistan to Israeli occupation of Palestine and therefore condemned the Soviet action on terms no less explicit. Other OIC members, however, refused to offend their Soviet patron and remained silent, despite the cries of their Afghan coreligionists. The OIC, in turn, demanded Soviet troop withdrawal "without condemning the Soviet Union for the invasion."[44] Consensus

---

[41]al-Ahsan, *OIC*, p. 48.

[42]"Islam Spreads Political Mantle," *Middle East,* No. 57 (July 1979), p. 5.

[43]"Egypt to Rejoin Islam Group," *Philadelphia Inquirer,* January 31, 1984, p. A-3.

[44]al-Ahsan, *OIC*, pp. 71–72.

building in the highly diverse and fragmented OIC has compromised the organization's ideological integrity. Deep divisions within the Muslim world have greatly undercut the OIC's power on the world stage. Furthermore, the authoritarian leaders of several Muslim nations have merely paid lip service to the OIC's noble principles and goals.

Since Operation Desert Storm, the OIC has been predominantly in the hands of Saudi Arabia, Egypt, and Kuwait. OIC conferences have been little more than formal get-togethers in which the delegates dutifully repeat old rhetoric of fraternity and solidarity but do little to help the poor and needy or redress the inequality and tyranny widely prevalent in the Muslim world. The OIC has both harshly denounced and issued sanctions against Iraq. During the OIC's sixth meeting, in 1991, Pakistan inserted a resolution condemning the Indian government for its harsh treatment of the Kashmiri Muslims. OIC members promised to resist the repeal of the UN resolution equating Zionism with racism—a promise few of them kept. The OIC demanded Israeli withdrawal from the occupied territories but, despite a five-hour speech by Yasser Arafat, omitted the word *jihad* from that demand. Terrorism was denounced at the meeting and U.S.-backed peace talks were encouraged. Divisions in the OIC appear greater than ever, and the Islamist dream of pan-Islam remains unfulfilled. In the aftermath of September 11, 2001, this dream is further than ever from realization.

Summary

The predominantly Muslim OPEC, established in 1960, did not flex its muscles until the early 1970s. It was Libyan leader Qaddafi's success in demanding larger revenues and higher taxes from foreign oil companies operating in Libya that inspired other OPEC members to follow suit. Then came the 1973 Yom Kippur/Ramadan War, which was soon coupled with the OAPEC oil embargo against Israel's allies in the West. The resulting oil shortage put upward pressure on oil prices. The oil-price explosion that the world witnessed from 1974 to 1982 helped in the rapid modernization of oil-rich countries. The Muslim members of OPEC (especially, Saudi Arabia, Libya, Kuwait, U.A.E., and Iran) donated much aid to poverty-stricken Muslim countries, gave a number of financially strapped Muslim countries a discount on oil, purchased food and had it distributed among starving Muslims, financed a number of Islamic organizations, built mosques, and purchased and distributed copies of the Qur'an to *madrassahs*. The *ummah* interpreted OPEC's success during the "oil boom" years as Allah coming to the assistance of His "chosen people."

But the euphoria was short-lived. The governments of many Muslim countries complained that they were promised far more by their oil-rich brethren than they received. Moreover, OPEC's dramatic oil price increase contributed to global inflation, followed by higher interest rates and recession. All three of the aforementioned economic problems plagued the oil-poor Muslim countries many times more than the developed Western world and made the Third World far worse off than before the oil price explosion. Furthermore, a number of additional factors have tended to virtually emasculate the once powerful oil cartel: division in OPEC ranks between pro- and anti-Western member states; Western oil companies finding new sources of petroleum in different parts of the world almost every year (for instance, the huge oil discovery in the Caspian Sea was particularly good news for the Central Asian republics and the world); and more oil being exported to the Western world from such non-OPEC countries as Russia, China, Mexico, and Angola.

There is a widespread perception in the Muslim world that both OPEC and the OIC have failed to protect and defend the rights of the global *ummah*. Among other things, these organizations have failed to achieve their principal objective of persuading Israel to withdraw from all territories captured in the 1967 war and restoring the legitimate rights of the Palestinian people; failed to stop the periodic Israeli aggression in Lebanon, until Israel itself decided to leave its self-declared "security zone," in May 2000, after eighteen years; have failed to halt the rapid growth of Israeli settlements in the West Bank and Gaza Strip; have failed to prevent two disastrous Persian Gulf wars; have been unable to end the Western world's decade-long sanctions against Iraq, which have resulted in the death of as many as one million Iraqi babies and infants; did little, if anything, to prevent the starvation of Muslims in Somalia or the killings of hundreds of Muslims in Palestine, Bosnia-Herzegovina, Kosovo, Chechnya, Kashmir, Burma, and other parts of the world; were unable to end the fratricide of Muslims in Algeria, Tajikistan, and Afghanistan; were unable to convince Afghanistan's Taliban regime not to destroy the Buddha statues or hand over Osama bin Laden and his associates in al-Qaeda; and have failed to unite the Muslim world and improve the lot of the *ummah*.

Internet Sites

http://www.opec.org

http://www.opec.com

http://www.eia.doe.gov/emeu/cabs/opec.html

http://www.opecnews.com/

http://www.opecfund.org/

http://www.infoplease.com/ce6/history/A0836844.html

http://www.oic-oci.org/

http://www.irna.com/oic/oicabout.htm

http://www.forisb.org/oic.html

http://www.oapecorg.org/

http://www.arab.de/arabinfo/opec.htm

CHAPTER NINE

The Islamic Revolution in Iran

In 1978 the people of Iran, led by Iran's Shi'ah clerical establishment and its theological students, rose in demonstrations throughout the country to challenge the forty-year tyranny of the *shah*. A little more than a year later the *shah*, overwhelmed by the revolutionary tide, fled Iran on an "extended vacation," and his secular, pro-Western monarchical regime, long considered by Western analysts an anchor of stability in the stormy Middle East, collapsed unconditionally, catching the West by surprise. Suddenly, a political void opened in Iran, and the Shi'ah *ulama* stepped in, assuming total power, setting up an Islamic model of development, breaking Iran's ties of dependency with the West, and forging a sovereign and nonaligned Islamic republic on the anvil of past Iranian grievances against despot and imperialist alike. The Islamic Revolution signified a watershed in world history, its repercussions shaking both East and West. Seizing the attention of all Muslims, the Iranian Revolution became the "source of emulation" for Islamists throughout the world. Inspired by its success and stirred by its utopian appeal to pan-Islamism, Revolutionary Islamists were emboldened by the revolution to remake their countries after the "Iranian model." Muslim Secularists trembled at the Islamic Revolution's triumph. Western analysts, in turn, perceived a new threat to Western hegemony: the specter not of communism but of Revolutionary Islamism.

Although the West, particularly the United States, was surprised by the Iranian Revolution, its roots were deep in Iranian soil. Political, social, and cultural inequities and their synergistic impact undid the Iranian monarchy, overturned the status quo, and enabled the Shi'ah religious hierarchy to supplant the government of the *shah*. An exploration of this synergism reveals the genesis of the Iranian Revolution and exposes the anatomy of Islamism.

The Genesis of a Revolution

In 1953, the U.S. Central Intelligence Agency (CIA) engineered the ouster of Iran's popular prime minister Muhammad Mossadegh. Although Mossadegh was respected by Iranians for his uncompromising nationalism, the United States worried that Mossadegh's regime was opening Iran to communist influence. Thus, the staunchly pro-Western *shah*, who had escaped to Paris, returned triumphant to the Peacock Throne. The unmistakable U.S. role in deposing Mossadegh would later poison relations between the United States and the Islamic Republic of Iran after the fall of the *shah* and would contribute to decades of anti-U.S. sentiment among the Iranian people. Iranians believed, following the overthrow of the popular Mossadegh, that the meddlesome Americans were but "leasing" the Peacock Throne to the *shah*, who, with the support of a powerful and oppressive U.S.-trained State Organization for Intelligence and Security—called Sazeman-i-Ettelat wa-Amniyat-i-Kashvar in Farsi/Persian and known by the acronym SAVAK—apparatus maintained his tyrannical and absolute dominion over Iran. Indeed, the Pahlavi *shah* permitted no form of political dissent.

U.S. motives in supporting the *shah* were simple. The *shah* had been the West's steadfast ally and owed the West his political survival. Iran's strategic value amplified the *shah*'s importance to Washington. During the Cold War, the United States was determined to contain the USSR and to deny it influence in the oil-rich Persian Gulf region. Possessing large oil and gas reserves, sharing a sixteen-hundred-mile border with the Soviet Union, and hugging the critical Persian Gulf and the narrow mouth of the Strait of Hormuz, Iran represented an irreplaceable strategic asset. The *shah* became the United States' ally in Tehran, his autocratic style notwithstanding.

By 1976 the *shah* began to realize the necessity of modest and gradual political liberalization after decades of harsh autocratic rule. Increasingly frequent attacks against government targets by urban guerrillas disturbed the *shah*. His closest security advisors, among them General Hussein Fardust, counseled him to moderate his repressive policies. Furthermore, the *shah* was ailing and wished to ensure the succession to the Peacock Throne of his eldest son, sixteen-year-old Crown Prince Muhammad Reza. By gradually building legitimate democratic institutions, the *shah* hoped that his son could govern Iran in a less authoritarian manner than he had and that the longevity of the Iranian monarchy would be ensured. The persistence of despotism was simply counterproductive. The *shah* was moved to adopt a more moderate government also by events in the West. The Western media, long friendly to the *shah*, began to decry his shameful human-rights record. The emphasis of President Jimmy Carter also forced the *shah* to rethink his policies of repression. Thus, from 1976 onward, the *shah* replaced a number of his old advisors with younger, more progressive, and more able technocrats. Concomitantly, he liberalized Iran's long-restrained political system enough to allow his oppressed and resentful subjects an opportunity to vent their frustration. The *shah*, however, had waited too long to liberalize. Forty years of rage and alienation could not so easily be assuaged by the *shah*'s momentary indulgence.

BOX 9.1   Reza Shah Pahlavi (1877–1944)
and Muhammad Reza Shah Pahlavi (1919–1980)

Born in 1877, Reza Shah Pahlavi became a soldier in a regiment of cossacks in the Persian Army. During his service as an officer, he acquired a reputation for bravery and leadership and was quickly promoted. Reza opposed Shah Ahmad's lack of resistance to the influence of European powers during World War I. In 1921 he led a coup against the *shah* and became prime minister in 1923. Between 1921 and 1924, he negotiated the evacuation of British and Russian troops from Persia. In 1925 Reza officially deposed Shah Ahmad and was made the new *shah*. He changed his name to Reza Shah Pahlavi. In 1935 Reza Shah changed the name of Persia to Iran.

Early in his reign, Reza Shah promoted Westernization and centralization of his government. He broke the political power of the clerical establishment and adopted a Western legal system. Reza Shah also imposed European dress on Iranians, opened schools and the workplace to women, and abolished the wearing of the veil. To accomplish these reforms, Reza Shah took power from the Majlis (Iranian Parliament), censored the press, and ruthlessly suppressed opposition. Meanwhile, his taxation policies made him extremely unpopular in Iran. During World War II, Reza Shah made his biggest mistake, establishing close ties to Germany. Both British and Soviet forces invaded Iran in 1941 and forced him to abdicate in favor of his son, Muhammad Reza Shah Pahlavi.

Muhammad Reza Shah Pahlavi became crown prince of Iran in 1926, when his father was crowned *shah*. He was sent overseas for his education and attended the LeRosey school for boys in Switzerland. In 1936 he returned to Iran and entered military school. After his father was deposed by occupying Soviet and British forces in 1941, Muhammad Reza became *shah* of Iran. During and immediately after the war, the new *shah* had to provide political balance and moderation in the polarized struggle between Iran's pro-Soviet Tudeh Party and the pro-British National Will Party. By 1946 Muhammad Reza Shah was able to negotiate the evacuation of British and Soviet soldiers from Iran.

During the early 1950s, relations between the relatively young and weak pro-Western *shah* and his relatively old, paternalistic, and nationalist Prime Minister Mosaddegh reached a breaking point. The *shah* briefly left Iran but was able to return when Mosaddegh was overthrown, with considerable help from the United States. After his return, the *shah* became more reactionary. He undertook a Westernization program later called the "White Revolution," which called for nationalization of some industry, land redistribution, and greater political rights for women. The clerical establishment opposed the *shah*'s program, but Iran remained relatively stable during this period and prospered owing to its oil wealth.

By the 1970s, however, the *shah*'s popularity had failed, and opposition to his autocratic rule was actively promoted by the clerical establishment. The 1979 revolution in Iran forced the *shah* into exile; he died a year later in Cairo.

http://persepolis.free.fr/iran/personalities/shah.html
http://novaonline.nv.cc.va.us/eli/evans/his135/MODULES/events/shah80.htm
http://www.rezapahlavi.org/index.htm
http://www.80s.com/Icons/Bios/mohammed_reza_shah_pahlavi.html
http://www.sedona.net/pahlavi/rezashah.html
http://www.sedona.net/pahlavi/
http://www.farahpahlavi.org/content2.html
http://www.farsinet.com/tambr/pahlavi1.html
http://www.angelfire.com/home/iran/
http://www.stanford.edu/class/history187b/mrshah.htm

The Iranian people began openly to criticize their government's domestic and foreign policies. Iranians protested their nation's trade with Israel and South Africa and criticized Iran's dependence on the United States. They denounced the presence of U.S. military advisors and technicians and the expenditure of billions of dollars on the purchase of U.S. weapons. The feeling was widespread that the *shah* was nothing more than a puppet of a meddlesome imperial power. Enraged by such criticism and fearing a loss of control, the *shah* changed his mind and ordered SAVAK to crush dissent. It was too late. Two ill-conceived public statements, both made within one week, inspired Iranians to rise against the Pahlavi monarchy. On December 31, 1977, President Carter misread the depth of the anti-*shah* sentiment in Iran and praised the *shah*'s "great leadership" for bringing stability to Iran. "This is a great tribute to you, Your Majesty," Carter said, "and to your leadership, and to the respect, admiration and love that your people give to you."[1] Distrusting the United States, the Iranian people saw Carter's statement as American government support and encouragement for the Pahlavi regime's repressive methods. Despite his talk of human rights, Carter's praise for the *shah* earned the United States only Iranians' hatred.

Within a week of Carter's shortsighted statement, the *shah*'s ministry of information planted a rash personal attack against Ayatollah Khomeini, the prominent Shi'ah cleric and uncompromising opponent of the *shah*. The Iranian newspaper Ittila'at ran an article on January 7, 1978, entitled "Iran and Red and Black Colonialism," which read in part:

> In order to acquire name and fame, Ruhollah Khomeini became a tool for the red and black colonialists who have sought to discredit the revolution of the Shah and the people. . . . Actually, Khomeini is known as the Indian Sayyid (Sayyid Hindi). . . . He lived in India for a time where he was in touch with British colonial circles and it is said that when young he composed love poems under the pen name of Hindi.[2]

The article reflected the *shah*'s suspicions that Khomeini was the agent of both "red" leftist intellectuals and "black" religious reactionaries. Although the article was planted in a transparent effort to slander Khomeini and thereby to deprive him of popular support, its publication had precisely the opposite effect. Indeed, after the article's publication, crowds of Iranians demonstrated in defense of the *ayatollah*'s reputation.

From January 1978 to February 1979 anti-*shah* demonstrations rocked Iran, shaking the foundations of the Pahlavi monarchy. During this fourteen-month period, the *shah*'s security forces confronted and killed as many as twelve thousand unarmed men, women, and children and wounded another fifty thousand. The "extended family phenomenon" increased casualty figures and broadened the

---

[1]Quoted in James Bill, "The Shah, The Ayatollah, and The U.S.," *Headline Series,* No. 285 (New York: Foreign Policy Association, June 1988), p. 21.

[2]Ibid.

BOX 9.2   Ayatollah Khomeini and Gamal Abdel Nasser Compared

Although Iran's Ayatollah Khomeini and Egypt's Gamal Abdel Nasser differed in many respects, particularly in their ideological proclivities, the fascinating commonalities in their lives become that much more worthy of examination. Nasser and Khomeini were of humble birth; neither was a prince, neither had the world handed to them. Both men lived simple and austere lives. The material trappings of power had no hold over them. Both were unpretentious in speech. Nasser spoke the language of the people, inspiring millions of Arabs in colloquial, not classical, Arabic. Likewise, Khomeini eschewed the classical Persian in which he was proficient in favor of colloquial Persian. Identifying themselves with the poor and underprivileged masses, both overthrew unpopular, pro-Western monarchies. Neither explicitly assumed political power in the initial phase of their revolutions, but both were kingmakers and wasted no time assuming power themselves. Khomeini and Nasser alike exercised supreme power within and beyond the borders of their nations.

As a revolutionary, Nasser utilized a growing Arab nationalist sentiment to take power in Egypt. Similarly, Khomeini, as the senior Muslim divine in Iran, stood in the vanguard of revolutionary upheaval in his country. Khomeini and Nasser were transformational revolutionaries who overturned the status quo and inaugurated massive social changes. But they shook not only their countries but the world around them as well. Both were supremely self-confident. Self-assurance was Nasser's undoing in the 1967 war with Israel, and it brought Khomeini's despair in the fruitless war with Iraq. Nevertheless, Khomeini and Nasser both stood up to the Great Powers. Nasser faced down Britain, France, and Israel in the Suez crisis (with a little help from Eisenhower), while Khomeini defied the United States. Their repudiation of Western assistance endeared both men to the masses, and their attempts to export revolution throughout the Muslim world frightened their pro-Western neighbors. Moreover, Khomeini and Nasser piqued Western anger with blatantly anti-Western policies and inflammatory rhetoric, promising and delivering on promises to break dependency with the West and to take positions of leadership in the Muslim world. Both repudiated imported Western political, economic, and social systems and values. They opted instead to pursue their own models and ideologies.

Khomeini and Nasser will both be remembered as uncompromising autocrats, as ideologues, and as revolutionaries. Although both were poor administrators who mismanaged their economies, they remain charismatic figures who appealed to the masses with their populist style and with their fearlessness in the face of incredible odds. Destiny, they believed, was theirs and history will remember their names and deeds.

---

opposition to the Pahlavi regime. When an Iranian died during the demonstrations, his relatives engaged in public mourning processions every forty days, as is the Shi'ah custom. These traditional processions for the dead became overtly political and occasioned the violent and frequently lethal response of government security forces. The revolution was thus cumulative in character and spread rapidly in major Iranian cities.[3]

Ayatollah Khomeini, safe from the *shah* while in exile in the Iraqi city of Najaf, encouraged the revolutionary fervor without ever personally leading the revolution. He gave angry sermons denouncing the Pahlavi regime and calling for revolution. Tapes of these sermons were then disseminated throughout Iran, where they inflamed the Iranian people.[4]

The *shah* turned to the United States for advice. When the Iranian people learned this, their anger further escalated, and they turned to the streets in rage. U.S. National Security Advisor Zbigniew Brzezinski counseled the *shah* to crack down harder. Following the torching of a public theater in the city of Abadan, which the shah's opposition alleged had been done by SAVAK agents, hundreds of thousands of Iranians protested in the streets. The *shah,* taking Brzezinski's advice, declared martial law. However, the *shah* had lost effective control over the country and demonstrators continued to take to the streets.[5]

With his government and the Iranian economy paralyzed by mass strikes and student demonstrations, the *shah* became increasingly conciliatory. Desperate to save the monarchy, the *shah* made an unprecedent public plea:

> I commit myself to make up for past mistakes, to fight corruption and injustices and to form a national government to carry out free elections. . . . Your revolutionary message has been heard. I am aware of everything you have given your lives for.[6]

After a year of terrible bloodshed, the Iranian people were not prepared to forgive the *shah.* The aging monarch realized by mid-January 1979 that his position in Iran was untenable. His subjects universally despised him; his continued suppression of them had only strengthened their resolve. There was nothing left for the *shah* to do. On January 16, 1979, the last Pahlavi monarch left Iran on an "extended vacation."[7] The Iranians were left with bitter memories of the *shah's* terrible reign and of the United States' part in perpetuating it.

Western analysts failed to predict the revolution. That failure has been often justified by the Westerners' conviction that the Islamic Revolution was nothing more than barbaric madness against a leader too ahead of his time. In reality, however, Western analysts were surprised by the revolution because they had

---

[3]George Lenczowski, *American Presidents and the Middle East* (Durham, N.C.: Duke University Press, 1990), pp. 188–189.

[4]Ibid., p. 189.

[5]Robert D. Schulzinger, *American Diplomacy in the Twentieth Century* (Oxford: Oxford University Press, 1984), p. 333.

[6]An extract of Muhammad Reza Shah Pahlavi's speech quoted in *Newsweek,* November 20, 1978, p. 38.

[7]Philip Lee Ralph, Robert E. Lerner, Standish Meacham, and Edward McNall Burns, *World Civilizations: Their History and Their Culture,* Vol. 2, 8th ed. (New York: Norton, 1991), p. 691.

■

BOX 9.3   The Role of Shariati and Khomeini in the Iranian Revolution

The catalytic role of Ali Shariati and Ayatollah Khomeini is principal to understanding the timing, direction, and temperament of the Islamic revival and revolution that swept Iran in the late 1970s.

An Iranian sociologist with a degree from the Sorbonne in Paris, Shariati was never the leader of an Islamic movement or party, though a party was built around his Modernist Revolutionary Islamist ideology. Shariati formulated a popular and attractive synthesis of the ideals of Islamic theology and Marxist ideology, adapted to the contemporary Iranian environment. Shariati's revolutionary and populist Islamic ideology appealed to restless and confused university students, offering an exciting alternative to the sometimes tiring and abstruse sermons of the *ulama*. Shariati's ideas were influential during and immediately after the Iranian Revolution. His mysterious death in London in 1977, perhaps at the hands of the *shah*'s agents, was eulogized by the Shi'ah *ulama* in their sermons—no doubt increasing his popularity among the Iranian people.

Ayatollah Khomeini was revered by the Iranian people as a most senior Shi'ah religious leader and an early opponent of the Pahlavi dynasty. The *shah* exiled Khomeini from Iran following the cleric's vociferous opposition to the Pahlavi regime's surrender to demands that all U.S. military and civilian personnel in Iran be governed by U.S., not Iranian, law. But exile, for Khomeini, was a hidden blessing. While in Iraq and later in France, Khomeini was out of the *shah*'s reach and could speak against the Pahlavi regime with impunity.

Khomeini's influence was likewise strengthened by his connections with friends inside Iran. While a religious leader in Qom, Khomeini earned the respect of innumerable theological students over the years. These students, many of whom became Islamic clerics themselves, became eager disciples of the Ayatollah and transmitted Khomeini's ideas and teachings to Iranians while he languished in exile. When the revolutionary fuse was lit in the first week of 1978, Khomeini's many clerical supporters (Revolutionary, Traditionalist, and Modernist alike) agitated and mobilized the people in *masjids* throughout Iran. Demonstrators against the *shah* carried huge posters of the *ayatollah* through the streets. His portraits bedecked the walls of city slums, and many booksellers and street vendors sold Khomeini's writings, speeches, and statements. In the public eye, the *ayatollah* became the living embodiment of the Islamic Revolution against the *shah* in a way that Shariati never did.

neglected to study the crisis adequately. Indeed, the media emphasized immediate political history while slighting the economic, sociocultural, and religious factors contributing to the revolution. If only the political features of Iran are examined, the revolution is mysterious and unpredictable. However, introducing Iran's economic woes and sociocultural disharmony helps make sense of the Iranian Revolution and dispels many of the misconceptions and much of the mystery.

As a major oil-producing country, Iran benefited greatly from the 1973 oil price explosion, which triggered a fivefold jump in the nation's oil revenues.

Flushed with a $20 billion inflow of petrodollars in 1974, the *shah* inaugurated a development plan that over a period of five years would cost $70 billion. The plan dangerously inflated the expectations of most Iranians. The government promised expensive new weapons for the armed forces, the latest technology and foreign expertise for industrialists, and employment and expanded social services for the Iranian people. The *shah* bragged that he would fashion Iran into the world's fifth greatest industrial power by the turn of the century.[8] The *shah* and his subjects, however, were in for a terrible disappointment.

To transform Iran into a modern nation-state by the turn of the century, the *shah* accelerated the pace of modernization and dismissed the wise advice of technocrats who counseled a more gradual and holistic approach to socioeconomic development. Consequently, the *shah*'s unrealistic, hasty, and haphazard modernization policies and goals induced shortages in manpower and material. A lack of skilled and professional manpower prompted the Pahlavi monarchy to recruit thousands of foreigners by offering handsome salaries to work in Iran. Simultaneously, soaring petroleum prices increased prices of all imports from the petroleum-importing West, while excessive government spending coupled with ballooning manpower costs fueled an inflationary spiral that devastated the majority of Iranians' incomes.[9]

Preoccupied with the *shah*'s modernization policies, the Iranian government gave inadequate attention to agrarian development in the countryside, where the majority of Iranians resided. Economic stagnation resulted in villages throughout rural Iran. Meanwhile, members of the royal family, royal courtiers, and highly placed bureaucrats accepted payments from Western agribusiness corporations to open large tracts of valuable food-growing tillage for the cultivation of cash crops. Consequently, large numbers of unemployed farmers and peasants fled rural poverty and flooded into towns and cities in search of work. By the mid-1970s, rural to urban migration numbered 250,000 people annually. As a result, the bad situation in housing, health, and education in the cities worsened; unemployment and inflation soared; and the gap between rich and poor widened and was alarmingly evident in the growth of slums.[10]

The *shah*, meanwhile, set an example of garish extravagance that contrasted obscenely with the poverty of migrants to the cities, who lived on the edge of existence in the slums. The *shah* reasoned that his personal dearth of charisma could be remedied by building a cult of worship around the institution of the monarchy itself. Such a cult could be built, the *shah* imagined, by continually and flamboyantly displaying the royal family's riches. The *shah*'s ostentation, however, did nothing to increase his popularity. For instance, the bacchanal celebration at Persepolis to mark the 2,500th anniversary of the Persian monarchy was a memorable insult to Muslim sensibilities throughout Iran. The history of Zoroastrian

---

[8]Akbar Husain, *The Revolution in Iran* (East Sussex, England: Wayland, 1986), p. 41.

[9]Ibid.

[10]Ibid., pp. 42, 45, 47; Ralph et al., *World Civilizations,* p. 690.

Persia was honored in the feasts and festivities while Islamic precepts were flouted. Western-dressed men and women drank alcoholic beverages; dancing was encouraged; and pork was served during the banquets.[11] Expenditures on the festival ran into the millions of dollars. Meanwhile, the *shah* maintained five palaces for his family, bought shares in powerful Western corporations, and stashed away millions of dollars abroad in Western banks.[12] The *shah*'s ostentation inspired not love of the monarchy among Iranians; it inspired resentment. Acting on this resentment, the Shi'ah *ulama* easily turned the *shah*'s penchant for big spending against him. But as long as the petrodollars continued to pour into the Iranian economy, the *shah* could afford to throw Iran's money away and pursue shortsighted modernization policies.

The United States nurtured the *shah*'s ambition to modernize Iran. U.S. leaders saw the conservative, anticommunist, pro-Western government of the *shah* as a reliable ally against the spread of Soviet communism. In fact, Iran served the United States as a well-situated listening post from which Soviet missile activity could be scrutinized. Moreover, during a time when the United States was haunted by the "Vietnam syndrome," fearing direct military intervention in the developing world, the *shah* cultivated an image as America's policeman in the oil-rich Persian Gulf region. Accordingly, Iran's armed forces grew to half a million men, and the regime eagerly purchased $20 billion worth of U.S. armaments between 1973 and 1978.[13] The *shah* also spent considerable amounts of money to beef up his internal security forces, including both local and national police agencies. Likewise, Iran's intelligence service, SAVAK, benefited from a generous and paranoid monarchy.[14]

Accompanying the unprecedented exploitation and export of petroleum, the heavy inflow of petrodollars, the excessive military spending, the rapid industrialization and urbanization, and the *shah*'s ambitious but unrealistic modernization programs was massive and widespread corruption. When hard times returned to Iran in 1976, the disillusioned Iranian people were convinced that the nation's oil wealth had been squandered by the unscrupulous royal family, the Iranian elite, and Westerners. Indeed, increasingly indignant Iranians viewed the hundred thousand Westerners living and working in their country as neocolonialist interlopers exploiting Iran in the grand imperialist tradition.[15] Educated and ambitious Iranians resented that a growing population of foreigners enjoyed responsible, influential, and high-paying positions in the Iranian government and in the private business sector. Iranians' resentment was heightened when they learned that foreigners were earning far more than Iranian citizens in comparable positions. The

---

[11]Karl W. Deutsch, Jorge I. Dominguez, and Hugh Heclo, *Comparative Government: Politics of Industrialized and Developing Nations* (Boston: Houghton Mifflin, 1982), pp. 419–422.

[12]Ibid.

[13]Glenn E. Perry, *The Middle East: Fourteen Islamic Centuries* (Englewood Cliffs, N.J.: Prentice-Hall, 1983), p. 297.

[14]Deutsch et al., *Comparative Government*, pp. 419–422.

[15]Husain, *The Revolution in Iran*, pp. 42–43.

effect of this realization was profound for the future of Iran and of Iranian-Western relations. Ayatollah Khomeini capitalized on antiforeign sentiment; he consistently condemned foreign domination of Iran and became, in Iranian eyes, an authentic Iranian patriot.[16]

The belief was widespread that the *shah* had mismanaged Iran's economy, and every class that bore the burdens of the 1976 recession blamed the Pahlavi monarchy and the West for its economic ills. In fact, the *shah* had made enemies even of the well-to-do *bazaaris,* the largely conservative and religious entrepreneurs. They never forgave the *shah* for undercutting them by establishing state-purchasing corporations selling wheat, meat, and sugar; for establishing government-subsidized supermarkets that decreased the **bazaars'** clientele; for engaging in town planning and road construction programs that destroyed sections of the *bazaars*; and above all, for dispatching aggressive young government inspectors to the *bazaars* in 1977 who arbitrarily fined and jailed those *bazaaris* suspected of price gouging.[17]

Despite the incredible petrodollar windfall beginning in 1974, the *shah* earned the anger of nearly every economic class except the Iranian elite. Impoverished peasants who had hopefully migrated to the cities remained jobless. *Bazaaris* felt their economic status slipping. The Iranian people in general saw none of the expected social services promised by the *shah.* Indeed, the *shah*'s modernization policies had turned the petrodollar blessing into Iran's curse.

While the *shah*'s modernization policies during the 1970s damaged the economic standing of the middle and lower classes, they also had a social and cultural impact on Iran. Indeed, the *shah*'s transformational approach to Iranian life precipitated an identity crisis among Iranians (see Chapter 6), the vast majority of whom did not enjoy a standard of living comparable to the West's and who therefore could not emulate Western lifestyles. Consequently, many Iranians sought redefinition: just what was it to be Iranian when Iran was turning upside down?

The poor who thronged to the slums of Iran's cities and who grew daily more cognizant of the widening gap between their standard of living and that of the foreigners and wealthy Iranian elite, were lost and alienated in their new environment. Their traditional ways of life were disrupted by the move from village to city, and they hungered for a renewed sense of belonging and of self. Consequently, they represented an enormous pool of anti-*shah* sentiment from which the opposition could and did draw support.[18]

As petrodollars inundated Iran during the 1970s, Western goods and cultural influences transformed Iranian cities. Materialistic and hedonistic elements of Western culture infiltrated Iran and undermined the country's traditional Islamic sociocultural values. The royal family led the way. Queen Farah Deeba herself became a patron of the Annual Arts Festival, which showed Western avant-garde

---

[16]Ibid., pp. 37–41.

[17]Ibid., p. 38.

[18]Deutsch et al., *Comparative Government,* pp. 419–422; Lenczowski, *American Presidents and the Middle East,* p. 185.

and X-rated films. Nightclubs, dance halls, cinemas, bars, and brothels proliferated in major Iranian cities to serve foreigners and wealthy Iranians looking for a good time, and pornographic literature was widely available in city streets. Bikini-clad Iranian women displayed themselves on beaches around the nation, Iranian cities teemed with prostitutes, and upper-middle-class Iranian women infuriated many conservative Iranians by aping prurient and unseemly Western ideas, dress, and behavior.[19] In reaction to widespread immorality and permissiveness, many Iranian women, even in universities, were veiling themselves by 1978. Asked why she had donned the traditional veil, one young Iranian woman at Isfahan University in 1977 responded, "I am making a statement."[20]

The backlash against the Westernization, secularization, materialism, hedonism, and widespread permissiveness prevalent in Iranian cities was especially strong within the Shi'ah clerical establishment. After all, the Shi'ah *ulama* nursed a grudge against the *shah* for usurping a significant portion of their rural landholdings during the "White Revolution" in the early 1960s. Furthermore, the fire of their anger was stoked again during the oil bust of the late 1970s, when the *shah* terminated all subsidies to the clerics as part of a severe austerity program.[21]

Although the *shah*'s policies had effectively reduced the Shi'ah clerics' central role as educators, judges, and advisors, the clerical establishment still maintained a vast network of *masjids,* through which they now politicized and mobilized their discontented congregations against a corrupt and increasingly illegitimate monarchy.[22] The clerics' appeal to Islamic socioeconomic equity and justice swayed many unhappy Iranians—and in no part of Iran did this appeal go unheard. Wherever stood a *masjid* stood a bastion of opposition against the policies of the *shah.* Furthermore, the Shi'ah clerical establishment had contributed to the political, spiritual, and intellectual development of the Iranian people. Politically conscious and armed with their faith, the Iranian masses made an Islamic Revolution in their country.[23] Indeed, the Shi'ah *ulama* in Iran were particularly suited to assuming the reins of government after the fall of the *shah.* Many years prior to the revolution, the *ulama* had "emerged as a class providing not only religious leadership in the narrow and technical sense but also leadership of a national and political nature, given increasingly to contesting the monarchical institution."[24] In fact, the Shi'ah *ulama* had a long history of political involvement in protests between 1891 and 1892 and during the constitutional revolution of 1905–1911. The Pahlavi monarchy, which began in 1925, harassed and persecuted the *ulama,* but to little avail. The Shi'ah clerical establishment rose again to challenge the gov-

---

[19]Akbar Husain, *The Revolution in Iran,* p. 45.

[20]Bill, "The Shah, The Ayatollah, and The U.S," p. 12.

[21]Ibid., p. 11.

[22]Ibid., p. 41.

[23]Kalim Siddiqui, Iqbal Asaria, Abd Al-Rahim Ali, and Ali Afrouz, *The Islamic Revolution: Achievements, Obstacles and Goals* (Toronto: Crescent International, 1980), p. 40.

[24]Ibid.

■

BOX 9.4   A Comparison of *Ayatollahs* Khomeini and Shariatmadari

Sayyid Ruhollah al-Musavi al-Khomeini and Sayyid Kazem Shariatmadari were born into conservative Shi'ah households in Iran. Both had the title *Sayyid* because they could trace their lineage back to Prophet Muhammad. Their fathers and grandfathers were respected members of the Shi'ah clerical establishment in their hometowns. However, while Ruhollah was born in Khomein into a Persian-speaking family, Kazem was born into a Turkish-speaking family in the northern city of Tabriz.

Both were given a solid grounding in Islam at home and were serious about their formal *madrassah* education. Both spent some of their most memorable years studying Islam in the Shi'ah holy cities of Qom in Iran and Najaf in Iraq. Shariatmadari completed his advanced Islamic education in Najaf under the tutelage of two of the most learned Shi'ah *alims*, while Khomeini spent over fourteen years of his life in Najaf after the *shah* exiled him in 1964.

After concluding their advanced Islamic studies, both taught in the *madrassahs* of Qom. Shariatmadari mainly taught *fiqh* (Islamic jurisprudence) and Islamic *akhlaq* (etiquette), while Khomeini taught Islamic philosophy, mysticism, ethics, and even the *shariah*.

Both clerics climbed the Shi'ah clerical establishment in Iran to became part of a highly select association of Grand Ayatollahs. On one hand, Khomeini built a reputation for himself as a revolutionary and an uncompromising political critic of the Pahlavi monarchy's despotism, Westernization, secularization, corruption, and dependency on the United States. On the other hand, the mild-mannered, moderate, and apolitical Shariatmadari's criticism of the Pahlavi monarchy was far less strident and often couched in essentially religious terms, such as advising the *shah*'s regime to abide by Islamic principles.

Shariatmadari accepted the *shah*'s nomination of Shahpour Bakhtiar as prime minister and was willing to trust the *shah*'s promise to establish a constitutional monarchy based on the 1906–1907 constitution. In this regard, the *shah* agreed to become a reigning monarch or ceremonial head of state, to give the prime minister the power to govern the country, and to grant the leading Shi'ah clerics virtual veto power over government policies. Ayatollah Khomeini, in contrast, was totally against that compromise and considered it too little too late. While Khomeini advocated the establishment of an Islamic government fusing religion and politics, Shariatmadari believed that the place of the clergy was not in government but in disseminating the peaceful and enlightened message of Islam among the people.

When the Islamic Revolution began in spring 1978, Khomeini was willing to accept the loss of lives of his supporters as they engaged in an intense nonviolent struggle to overthrow the Pahlavi monarchy and establish an Islamic state. In sharp contrast, Shariatmadari, while agreeing with the goal of establishing an Islamic state, was totally opposed to a revolutionary upheaval in which many lives would be lost, people wounded, and much property destroyed. He also opposed the implementation of traditional Islamic punishments for crimes, including amputations and stoning. Furthermore, Shariatmadari preferred women in his presence to be veiled but had no desire to impose

(Continued)

A Comparison of *Ayatollahs* Khomeini and Shariatmadari   *(Continued)*

this style of dress on every woman in Iran, as Khomeini's regime had done. And while he refrained from attending cinemas, neither did he demand they be closed, as Khomeini did.

Although Shariatmadari approved of the senior clerics advising a democratically elected political leader, he was against clerics governing Iran. He had strong reservations about Khomeini's doctrine of Vilayat-e-Faqih (Supreme Law Giver), which would make Khomeini the ultimate arbiter of Iran's destiny, and strongly disapproved of the revolutionary political role of the Islamic Republican Party (IRP). In essence, Shariatmadari, the quintessential Traditionalist Islamist, had a very different vision of an Islamic Republic than the Islamic theocracy that he saw emerging under Khomeini's Revolutionary Islamists.

There is no doubt that both these learned and revered Grand Ayatollahs made a significant contribution to Iranian society, Islam, and Islamic history during their long and productive lives. While both died in their eighties (Shariatmadari at 81 and Khomeini at 87) Iranians gave Khomeini a hero's funeral, while they gave Shariatmadari a much more subdued, solemn, and uneventful burial. Also the huge and impressive mausoleum in which the architect and "strong man" of Iran's Islamic state lies buried contrasts starkly with the small, simple, and unimpressive tomb of the low-keyed, gentle, and scholarly *alim* from Tabriz.

---

ernment in 1963, when it was suppressed, and in 1978, when it emerged victorious.[25]

The *shah*, aware of the *ulama*'s political interests and its opposition to his policies of land redistribution, women's rights, secular education, and modernization, attempted to check clerical influence among the Iranian people.[26] Stripping the clerics of their special perquisites, closing down Islamic presses, breaking up religious assemblages, and imprisoning, exiling, and even executing clerics, the *shah* hoped to undermine clerical power. Instead, his suppressive policies strengthened it.[27] The *shah* could not easily enforce his edicts within the sacred *masjid*. Thus, while the *masjids* became safe forums for political dissent, the Shi'ah clerical establishment became an alternative government.

The role of the *masjid* in the genesis of the Iranian Revolution is central to an understanding of the *ulama*'s political functions in Iran. Despite the *shah*'s cultural campaign to modernize and secularize his country, most Iranians remained resolute in their religious faith and traditions. Shi'ah Islam was heavily reinforced by the central role played by the *masjid* in Iranian communities. In the *masjid*,

---

[25]Nikki Keddie, "The Revolt of Islam and Its Roots," in Dankwart A. Rustow and Kenneth Paul Erickson, eds., *Comparative Political Dynamics* (New York: HarperCollins, 1991), pp. 292–293.

[26]Robert W. Strayer, Edwin Hirschmann, Robert B. Marks, and Robert J. Smith, *The Making of the Modern World: Connected Histories, Divergent Paths (1500 to the Present)* (New York: St. Martin's Press, 1989), pp. 321, 323.

[27]Deutsch et al., *Comparative Government*, pp. 421–422.

daily prayers were recited, sermons delivered, weekly religious assemblies held, and community activities planned. These organized religious gatherings often had political overtones, especially during the 1970s.[28]

The Shi'ah clerical establishment had the only truly nationwide organization in Iran, penetrating deeper than even the *shah*'s regime. *Masjids* stood in every community in Iran and remained independent of the government and relatively free to operate in the *shah*'s repressive police state. By 1978, 180,000 clerics (one Iranian cleric for every two hundred Iranians) communicated their displeasure with the *shah*'s policies directly to the Iranian people in every community in Iran.[29]

The *ulama*'s function as an alternative government was girded during the revolutionary period of 1978–1979 with the generous financial assistance of the *bazaaris*. The clerics, in turn, distributed the money honestly and efficiently to the unemployed, poor, and needy and to the families of murdered antiregime demonstrators. Increasingly, district and neighborhood *masjids* gained control over the daily affairs of their communities. Prior to the overthrow of the *shah*, *masjids* operated as local power centers that brought together all opposition to the *shah* under their banner, including the dispossessed, the *bazaaris*, the intelligentsia, the nationalists, and even the leftists. During this twilight of the Pahlavi monarchy, Islam permeated the Iranian consciousness. No secular ideology emerged as a rival to the *ulama* against the *shah*. Leftists and nationalists, for example, could not match the widespread influence of the *masjid* on Iran. Thus, following the collapse of the *shah*'s regime, Revolutionary Islamist clerics who had stood in the vanguard of the revolution were well positioned to step into the political vacuum. Indeed, it was only natural.[30]

The collective grievances of the Iranian people, compounded by decades of oppression under the *shah*, erupted in 1978 like a match dropped in a sea of gasoline. During his reign the *shah* had angered and alienated nearly all sectors and classes of Iranian society. The educated, politically conscious, and ambitious middle class felt economically excluded and politically stifled in the police state of the Pahlavi monarchy. The middle class also resented the presence of a hundred thousand Westerners who enjoyed positions of power and influence in the Iranian government and who earned higher wages than native Iranians. The *bazaaris* were angry with the *shah* for his policies to undercut them economically. The clerics were aroused by the *shah*'s secularization policies and his sometimes blatantly anticlerical programs. Workers in the cities were infuriated by the *shah*'s crackdown on organized-labor movements. Even the upper middle class was dissatisfied with the *shah*'s inept, unprofessional, and often corrupt government.[31] The poorest 40 percent of the population was incensed by the *shah*'s government not

---

[28]Ramy Nima, *The Wrath of Allah: Islamic Revolution and Reaction in Iran* (London: Pluto Press, 1983), p. 77.

[29]Ibid.

[30]Ibid., p. 142.

[31]Deutsch et al., *Comparative Politics*, pp. 419–422.

only for ignoring their plight, but for contributing to it. The *shah*'s failure to earn the support of any class or to root his regime in anything more substantial than promising handouts cost him the Peacock Throne. Unified against his tyranny, the Iranian people cast the *shah* aside. The *bazaaris* rendered financial assistance, the clerics provided the leadership, and the frustrated and disaffected urban poor became the foot soldiers of the Islamic Revolution in Iran.[32]

Ironically, the *shah* precipitated the final revolutionary crisis himself. Relative deprivation, fueled by the *shah*'s extravagant promises to remake Iran into a modern, Western-style nation-state, exploded into popular discontent following the oil bust. The *shah* had lifted Iranian expectations and reality had dashed them. Therefore, the *shah* became the target of popular anger. When the recession hit Iran in 1976, the *shah*'s policies of Westernization were considered failures. Indeed, millions of devout Iranian Muslims considered the *shah*'s secular ideologies unsuitable for Iran and felt vindicated by the widespread dissatisfaction they precipitated. The perceived failure of "imported" development plans strengthened the appeal of Islam as the only alternative to the *shah* and his U.S. masters.

Moreover, the *shah*'s modernization policies aggravated and amplified the five common crises of development (see Chapter 6). The *shah* never had the legitimacy the clergy held. The *shah*'s government did not penetrate far into Iran; *masjids* were everywhere. The government failed to secure a fair and equitable distribution of goods and services during the 1970s; the Shi'ah clerics gave the impression that they were doing more than the government to help the poor. The government of the *shah* permitted no popular participation; all Muslims were welcomed in the *masjid*. And the *shah*'s policies precipitated a crisis of identity that the monarchy could not resolve; the clergy could. Therefore, the fall of the *shah* was inescapable, and the rise of the Shi'ah clerical establishment in his place, inevitable.

Exporting Revolutionary Islam

With the *shah* permanently exiled, Khomeini returned triumphantly from exile in Paris on February 1, 1979—where he had resided from late October 1978 after being expelled from Iraq—to preside over a new phase of the Iranian Revolution: the establishment of an Islamic government. To this end, Khomeini appointed the respected and devout Mehdi Bazargan (See Box 9.5) as Iran's prime minister. Bazargan's government was short-lived, however. Meant only to be an interim prime minister, Bazargan was directed to lay the foundations for the Islamic form of government that Khomeini envisioned. The new Islamic Republic would be ruled not by the people but by the precepts of Islam as interpreted by the Revolutionary Islamist Shi'ah *ulama*. Khomeini, assuming the title *Velayat-i-Faqih*, appointed himself and was accepted by most Iranians as the last word in scriptural interpretation. In essence, the new government of Iran would be a

---

[32]Ibid.; Rod Hague, Martin Harrop, and Shaun Breslin, *Political Science: A Comparative Introduction* (New York: St. Martin's Press, 1992), pp. 80–81.

BOX 9.5   Mehdi Badar Bazargan

Bom in 1905, Mehdi Badar Bazargan studied engineering in France and received his degree in thermodynamics. Bazargan returned home and taught at Tehran University. Following World War II, Bazargan became involved in the National Front's opposition to the *shah* and was allied with Muhammad Mossadegh. During Mossadegh's nationalist government (1951–1953), the Iranian government nationalized the Anglo-Iranian Oil Company. Mossadegh appointed Bazargan to oversee its operations. After Mossadegh was ousted and the *shah* restored to power, Bazargan cofounded the Islamist-oriented Iran Freedom Movement and continued his opposition. Bazargan organized Islamic discussion groups and lecture series and wrote articles and books in which he advocated Islam's compatibility with modern science and technology. Bazargan felt that the West's scientific and technological advances were worth emulating, though he opposed Western secularism. He believed that religion should function as the guiding star of politics. Still, Bazargan was no advocate of theocracy and preferred a liberal and tolerant brand of Modernist Islamism in which the best elements of Western civilization would be adapted to function within an Islamic context.

In 1979, after the fall of the *shah,* the Ayatollah Khomeini capitalized on Bazargan's reputation by appointing him prime minister of Iran's provisional government. Bazargan's administration spanned the turbulent period between the old monarchical regime of the *shah* and the new Islamic state about to be born. Bazargan selected as ministers men who were devout Muslims but qualified and competent technocrats and who had actively opposed the *shah's* regime.

Bazargan's authority was increasingly undermined, however, by radical Islamist and secular political parties, by ethnic uprisings throughout Iran, and by the Revolutionary Council, which frequently organized large-scale street demonstrations, local revolutionary committees, Islamic courts, and the *pasdaran* (Revolutionary Guards)—which together served as an alternative government challenging Bazargan. These organizations, coupled with the newly created Islamic Republican Party (IRP), finally brought down the Bazargan government. The prime minister had been photographed and filmed during an official visit to Algeria shaking hands and speaking amiably to U.S. National Security Advisor Zbigniew Brzezinski—notorious in Iran as a staunch supporter of the *shah* and an opponent of the revolution. The outcry against Bazargan for his friendliness with the Americans forced him to resign the premiership and to return to his position of leadership in the Iran Freedom Movement. His criticism turned from the deposed *shah* to zealous Revolutionary Islamists, whom he accused of misgoverning Iran. Bazargan would survive to be one of the few voices of dissent permitted in Iran.

theocracy. The Revolutionary Islamist *ulama,* Khomeini especially, advocated direct clerical rule of Iran. Given Khomeini's incomparable popularity in the flush of victory against the *shah,* few Iranians were willing to question the eighty-year-old *ayatollah's* judgment. The Traditionalist *ulama's* view that the Shi'ah clerical establishment should not rule but should only advise temporal rulers was abandoned. Traditionalists like the Ayatollah Shariatmadari and Modernists like interim prime minister Bazargan, who felt the *ulama* should maintain only an advisory role in Iranian government, lacked the stature and popularity among the Iranian people enjoyed by the Revolutionary Islamist *Ayatollah* Khomeini and were left by the wayside.

In Khomeini's mind and in the minds of most Iranians, the Iranian Revolution was more than a popular revolt against the tyranny of the *shah*. The Iranian Revolution was synonymous with an Islamic revolution. The monarchy was discarded, certainly, but to be replaced by an Islamic theocracy. The Islamist *ulama* sought to transform Iranian society from the top down. Iran would be "Islamized." The clerics would reorganize and reform Iran's legal system, its cultural institutions, its system of education, and even its economic system according to the letter and spirit of Islam.[33]

Consolidating the gains of the Iranian Revolution meant securing Ayatollah Khomeini's personal power over the nation while simultaneously pursuing policies of Islamization in all sectors of society. Almost immediately following Khomeini's assumption of power in February 1979, Revolutionary Islamists began systematically and thoroughly to purge any individuals suspected of loyalty to the *shah* from the military and government. Paranoid of a military coup against the nascent Islamic Republic and determined never to trust the *shah*'s U.S.-trained armed forces, the ruling clerics purged the officer corps repeatedly. Furthermore, tens of thousands of young and unemployed supporters of the revolutionary government were recruited to serve in a paramilitary group known variously as the **Pasdaran**, the Revolutionary Guards, or Guardians of the Islamic Revolution. These young soldiers comprised the Praetorian Guard of clerical government, loyal only to the *ulama*.

During the Islamic Revolution, committees were established in workplaces to organize strikes protesting the Pahlavi monarchy. With the victory of the Revolution, these committees undertook to run those workplaces whose owners and management had fled the country or to share control with owners and managers who remained in Iran.[34] Meanwhile, the clerical establishment also inaugurated committees, known as *komitehs*, in numerous *masjids*. In larger Iranian cities, two forms of *komitehs* were established: the first based in the *masjid* to control and organize the neighborhood and the second, called a central *komiteh*, with far greater powers to coordinate and direct the policies of Islamic Revolution throughout the city. Central *komitehs* rapidly became the primary governing bodies in large urban centers. They controlled the prices and distribution of goods; policed city streets; enforced law and order; and meted out justice based on the *shariah*. The central *komitehs* combined the administrative and judicial functions of government, while higher authorities, like the Islamic Revolutionary Council and Khomeini himself, exercised legislative powers.[35]

---

[33]Strayer et al., *The Making of the Modern World*, pp. 326–327.

[34]Nima, *The Wrath of Allah*, p. 79.

[35]Ibid., pp. 77–79.

BOX 9.6   Abul Hasan Banisadr

Abul Hasan Banisadr was born in northwestern Iran in 1933. He attended Tehran University and completed his undergraduate education in theology, economics, and sociology. He aligned himself with Islamic groups in the underground opposition to the *shah*. His political activity resulted in several years of imprisonment. In 1963 he left Iran and joined a doctoral program in economics in France.

While in France, Banisadr continued to oppose the *shah* and postulated that Iran was a "tributary," dependent on foreign patrons since Iran exported oil to buy consumer goods while neglecting agriculture. Banisadr proposed to build an independent and egalitarian Iran by founding Iranian national development on principles of Islamic socialism that, he argued, corresponded to the Qur'an.

In 1972 Banisadr met Ayatollah Khomeini and joined his inner circle. Banisadr helped bring together the secular nationalists, socialists, and communists, on one hand, and the Revolutionary Islamists, Traditionalist Islamists, and Modernist Islamists, on the other. Recognized for his contribution to the Iranian Revolution, Banisadr joined Khomeini on his triumphant return to Iran in 1979.

Labeled an Islamic socialist, Banisadr favored nationalization and proposed to expand the public sector at the expense of the private sector. As finance minister, Banisadr brought about the nationalization of banks and insurance companies in the summer of 1979. As foreign minister, Banisadr worked to free the American hostages held in Tehran. His Revolutionary Islamist opponents, however, criticized Banisadr as soft on the United States and too critical of the Iranian militants who had stormed the U.S. Embassy and detained the American diplomats.

In 1980 Banisadr became Iran's first popularly elected president and, thereby, assumed the responsibility of commander-in-chief of the Iranian armed forces as well. However, Banisadr had neglected to develop a base of support in the Majlis (Parliament) and had repeatedly angered the Revolutionary Islamist clerics who dominated the government.

Banisadr benefited politically from the 1980 Iraqi invasion of Iran because he enjoyed greater popularity with the armed forces than did the Revolutionary Islamist clerics. Nevertheless, his Revolutionary Islamist foes in Tehran defeated his domestic programs. When even Khomeini turned against him, Banisadr declared that the Revolutionary Islamists were establishing a dictatorship and the people should show their support for their beleaguered president. The Revolutionary Islamists perceived this statement as a call for a counterrevolution and influenced Khomeini to dismiss Banisadr from the powerful position of commander-in-chief.

Afraid for his personal safety, Banisadr fled for Paris in late June 1981. The Majlis officially removed him from office, while Banisadr continued to oppose the direction of the Islamic Revolution in Iran.

In institutionalizing the Islamic Revolution, Iran's Shi'ah clerical establishment hurriedly formulated an Islamic constitution and an Islamic legal system in which clerics would officiate as judges over criminal cases and would punish offenders according to *shariah* law. The ruling clerics also established a new political organization, called the Islamic Republican Party (IRP), under the astute leadership of the Ayatollah Beheshti. Revolutionary Islamists elected under the IRP banner became a new breed of politician in Iran.

True to his Revolutionary Islamist credentials, Khomeini undertook a "cultural revolution" in 1980 to "Islamize" Iran domestically. Khomeini's Revolutionary Islamist partisans attacked leftists in Iranian colleges and universities. In June 1980 Khomeini closed all Iranian institutions of higher education to expedite a purge of Westernized and secular elements. Public education from kindergarten up was also revamped. Secular teachers and administrators were fired to make room for devout Muslim teachers who were more amenable to the new Islamic curriculum. Khomeini also purged the Iranian bureaucracy and staffed ministries with "good" Muslims.[36]

Both domestically and internationally, Khomeini pursued a policy of unwavering opposition to Western influences of any sort. Indeed, for Khomeini, everything beyond Islam was truly *dar al-harb;* the Muslim world was beset by various un-Islamic evils that included Secularist Muslim regimes and meddlesome imperialist powers like the United States and the USSR. In fact, Khomeini perceived the U.S. government as the "Great Satan," the leader of the immensely powerful West that was a controlling force in Iran and the Muslim world. He called on Muslims all over the world to engage in a ceaseless *jihad* against their pro-Western and pro-Russian rulers and against dependency on the powerful but morally "degenerate" powers of the West and the communist world.[37]

Despite Khomeini's death in 1989, his anti-Western and anticommunist rhetoric continues to attract and inspire Islamists throughout the world. His call to eradicate Western and communist influence from the Muslim world remains powerful and popular even though many Revolutionary Islamists, particularly of the Sunni sect of Islam, resist emulating the "Iranian model" because of its Shi'ah overtones and adverse publicity in the world. For Islamists throughout the Muslim world, the victory of the Islamic Revolution in Iran signified a new type of revolution in which secularization, modernization, and Westernization did not prevail but were, in fact, overthrown in the name of non-Western Islamic values and cultures. The appeal of such a victory even in the most general sense generated widespread outbursts of Islamist militancy throughout the Muslim world, including Egypt, Saudi Arabia, Kuwait, Sudan, and Algeria, even though Khomeini's leadership itself was rejected. Consequently, Iran's Islamic Revolution has had an unprecedented international impact. Its reverberations are still being felt throughout the Muslim world. Furthermore, Muslims worldwide were affected by Khomeini's Islamic message of justice, equality, and Islamic purification. His frequent admonitions to Muslims to overthrow the Secularist Muslim regimes that oppress them greatly emboldened both legitimate and revolutionary Islamic political movements in nearly all Muslim countries.

---

[36]John L. Esposito and James P. Piscatori, "Introduction," in John L. Esposito, ed., *The Iranian Revolution: Its Global Impact* (Miami: Florida International University Press, 1990), p. 3.

[37]Ralph et al., op. cit., pp. 691–692.

Khomeini's proclamations that he would export the Islamic Revolution to all Muslim countries alarmed the regimes of those countries and angered the status quo governments of the West and of the communist world. Fear that Khomeini or his successors might make good on threats to undermine and overthrow secular or conservative neighboring governments by spreading Islamism has motivated and directed U.S. policy toward the Muslim world for over two decades now.

The U.S. Embassy Hostage Crisis

Although he despised the West and the Communist bloc with equal vigor, Khomeini focused his xenophobic rage against the United States, the longtime ally of the hated *shah*. Generally, Khomeini decided that Iran must rely neither on West nor East; all foreign non-Islamic influence was to be eschewed. However, Iran emerged from its partly self-imposed isolation from the international community in 1988, when Iranian president Ali Akbar Hashemi Rafsanjani repaired Iran's ties with several European nations. Rafsanjani's efforts to improve U.S.-Iranian relations since then have failed because the two nations' relations have been contaminated by mutual mistakes and misconceptions. Years of Khomeini's rhetoric deriding the "Great Satan" were answered by equally irrational anti-Iranian outbursts in the United States. For Iran the trouble with the United States had begun in 1953. In U.S. eyes, however, Iran had started trouble in 1979 by taking U.S. diplomats hostage.

The fall of the *shah* and the "loss" of Iran was traumatizing for the West. The U.S. government was thoroughly unprepared to deal with the new government in Tehran, especially one consisting of Muslim clerics.[38] Worse than that, however, the United States totally undermined the chances of a U.S.-Iranian reconciliation after the Iranian Revolution by permitting the *shah* to enter the United States for medical treatment on October 22, 1979. The United States justified the action on "humanitarian grounds." Furthermore, the *shah* still commanded the friendship of men like Henry Kissinger and David Rockefeller. Nevertheless, the *shah* had no friends in Iran. By admitting the *shah* into the United States, President Carter stoked the paranoia of the Iranian people, who remembered the U.S. role in the 1953 ouster of Mossadegh. Playing on this paranoia, Khomeini called for mass demonstrations, which he got. Three million Iranians marched on the U.S. Embassy in Tehran on November 1, 1979. Three days later, hundreds of young Revolutionary Islamists stormed the embassy, and took U.S. diplomats hostage. So powerful was the image of Iranians attacking the U.S. Embassy that similar attacks were made against U.S. diplomatic offices in Libya and Pakistan.[39]

The radical Iranian youths in control of the U.S. Embassy in Tehran accused the United States of spying in Iran and of supporting the *shah* while he massacred

---

[38]Ralph et al., *World Civilization*, p. 691.

[39]Schulzinger, *American Diplomacy*, pp. 333–334.

BOX 9.7   Ali Akbar Hashemi Rafsanjani

Iran's Ali Akbar Hashemi Rafsanjani was born in 1934 in the southwestern desert village of Rafsanjan, near the city of Kerman. He received an Islamic education and studied under Ruhollah Khomeini and other clerics. He was influenced by and ultimately reflected Khomeini's revolutionary anti-Western Islamic worldview. When the *shah* exiled Khomeini, Rafsanjani was among those clerics who kept his former mentor informed about developments within Iran.

After Khomeini's return to Tehran from exile in 1979, Rafsanjani became speaker of the Majlis (Parliament), a position of considerable influence. In 1988 Ayatollah Khomeini appointed Rafsanjani commander-in-chief of the armed forces. After Khomeini's death in 1989, Rafsanjani was elected president of Iran. As president, he endeavored to preserve Iranian unity and maintain the balance between rival factions. However, Rafsanjani dismissed most of the Revolutionary Islamist ministers and surrounded himself with progressive technocrats. Instead of exporting Iran's brand of Revolutionary Islamism, Rafsanjani expanded oil exports, improved economic relations with the West and with the former Communist bloc, signed economic cooperation agreements with the former Soviet Union, and even expressed a willingness to improve relations with the United States—a willingness he illustrated when he persuaded the Lebanese Shi'ah leaders of Hezbollah and Islamic Amal to release their Western hostages. During Operation Desert Shield and Desert Storm, Rafsanjani maintained a position of strict neutrality that ultimately benefited Iran, despite calls from many Iranians to join with Iraq to fight the United States and the coalition.

Rafsanjani faced harsh opposition within Iran from Revolutionary Islamists. Although the late Ayatollah Khomeini was Rafsanjani's patron, mentor and student could not have differed more in temperament and outlook. Khomeini was a charismatic leader given to controversial decisions and momentous gambles. Rafsanjani, in contrast, was more moderate and pragmatic, with a keen political sense. Khomeini's worldview was idealistic, radical, dogmatic, doctrinaire, and even xenophobic. Rafsanjani was a realist with a remarkably progressive, open-minded, and cosmopolitan Islamic worldview. Both men are Islamists. Rafsanjani, however, avoided Khomeini's brand of messianic Revolutionary Islamism and addressed the existential needs of his people.

http://inic.utexas.edu/menic/oil/game/simulation/profiles/sp1993/0013.html
http://school.discovery.com/homeworkhelp/worldbook/atozhistory/r/457970.html

---

protestors, tortured political prisoners, squandered and plundered the nation's wealth, and introduced Western values at the expense of Islamic values. Although they originally detained ninety persons in the embassy, the hostage takers released all non-U.S. hostages, all African Americans, and all women except one. The remaining fifty-two were branded as spies and held prisoner for 444 days. The "hostage crisis" enraged and humiliated the United States and became a lesson in the limits of U.S. power. The inability of the United States, the world's foremost military and industrial power, to resolve the crisis expeditiously or to pressure a Third World Muslim country to submit to U.S. demands sobered Americans. The world watched, captivated and bewildered, as the drama of the hostage crisis dragged on and on. Never before had the United States appeared so absolutely helpless, particularly when, in April of 1980, the Carter administration bungled a military rescue attempt to free the hostages. The United States itself was held hostage by Revolutionary Islamists in Tehran. The sight of U.S. powerlessness, in turn, encouraged Revolutionary Islamists around the world and terrified Muslim Secularist leaders, who, seeing that Islamism could paralyze the United States, feared what it could do to "un-Islamic" regimes in the Muslim world itself.

The hostage crisis poisoned Iranian relations with the outside world. The United States and its Western allies successfully used the United Nations and the Western media to portray Iran as a "pariah state" and isolated it in the world community for its breach of international law. Nevertheless, the spectacle of the hostage crisis amazed Muslims throughout the world, who saw the Khomeini regime courageously (some said "imprudently") defying a preeminent superpower equipped with the most advanced military technology in the world and with a truly frightening nuclear arsenal. Khomeini's gamble of supporting the hostage taking was thus a big one. However, when the U.S. attempt to free the hostages failed in an Iranian desert sandstorm, Revolutionary Islamists were convinced that the tide was turning against the West at last and that God was fighting in Iran's corner.[40]

The hostage crisis represented the inauguration of a new phase of the Iranian Revolution: its export. Although Iran was in no condition to spread its Islamic Revolution militarily, it commanded significant influence in the world among Revolutionary Islamists.

The hostage crisis ended peacefully and all American hostages were released on January 20, 1981, after 444 days of incarceration. While America's superpower status was called into question, the major losers were President Carter, Khomeini, and Iran. The hostage crisis coupled with the serious economic problems facing the United States, made Carter look weak and incompetent and cost him the 1980 presidential election. However, Ayatollah Khomeini, Iran, Islam, and the Shi'ah sect were hurt far more.

Iran's violation of international law was universally condemned. Many Iranians—including Modernist Islamist Mehdi Bazargan, who was Khomeini's choice for first interim president of Iran (February 1 to November 6, 1979), and Modernist Islamist Abul Hasan Banisadr, who was the first popularly elected president of the Islamic Republic (January 25, 1980 to June 22, 1981)—disagreed with their supreme spiritual leader on the hostage crisis. While the hostage crisis may have contributed to shortening Bazargan's and Banisadr's presidencies, it damaged Ayatollah Khomeini's reputation and greatly undermined Iran's Islamic Revolution. Khomeini was demonized in the non-Muslim world, and even many Muslims felt that his confrontation with the West was hurting Islam and, more

---

[40]Richard H. Foster and Robert V. Edington, *Viewing International Relations and World Politics* (Englewood Cliffs, N.J.: Prentice-Hall, 1985), p. 18.

particularly, Khomeini's Shi'ah sect—to which the majority of Iranians belong. Iran was isolated in the world community and was blacklisted as a "terrorist state." This, in turn, emboldened Iraq's Saddam Hussein to invade Iran on September 22, 1980. The Iran-Iraq War dragged on for eight long years, resulting in over 500,000 Iranian casualties, bankrupting the Islamic Republic's treasury, and distracting the Khomeini regime from the vitally important task of economic and social development.

A number of prominent leaders in Iran—including Ali Akbar Hashemi Rafsanjani, speaker of Iran's Majlis (Parliament)—convinced Khomeini to end the Iran-Iraq War and save the Islamic Republic. On July 18, 1988, Khomeini reluctantly agreed to accept United Nations Security Council Resolution 598, calling for an immediate cease-fire. A formal cease-fire went into effect on August 20, 1998.

With the end of the Iran-Iraq War, Iran's foreign ministry went into high gear and started a major diplomatic "peace offensive" in order to end their country's isolation in the world. Iran's relations with the rest of the world were improving when Ayatollah Khomeini infuriated the West again by issuing a *fatwa* (edict) on February 14, 1989, calling on Muslims to execute Salman Rushdie for insulting Islam in his novel *The Satanic Verses.*

The Post-Khomeini Era in Iran

Ayatollah Khomeini died on June 3, 1989, and with his burial Iranians put to rest a turbulent decade in their country's history. Because he had successfully used his enormous charisma not only to institutionalize the Islamic Revolution but to anoint his successor as well, Khomeini's death was not followed by an intense power struggle or sociopolitical turmoil. There was a remarkably peaceful, smooth, and efficient transition of power.

Two clerics, both of whom had been familiar and influential actors on the Iranian political stage throughout the Khomeini era, assumed key positions in the post-Khomeini era: Ayatollah Sayyid Ali Khamenei (see Box 9.8), who had been Iran's president for eight years, became the supreme spiritual leader; and Ali Akbar Hashemi Rafsanjani, the Speaker of Iran's *Majlis* for over nine years, assumed the presidency. Khamenei and Rafsanjani both had been former theological students and protégés of Khomeini; had both played an active role in the Iranian Revolution by carrying out Khomeini's instructions and successfully organizing the influential clerical establishment; both remained part of Khomeini's close-knit inner circle from the time of the Grand Ayatollah's return from exile until his death; both officiated as provisional leaders of the Friday congregational prayers in Tehran; both held several important government positions in Khomeini's Islamic Republic; both were savvy and experienced politicians who believed in free enterprise at home and good relations with the world in order to break out of the U.S.-inspired isolation of Iran due to the "hostage crisis"; both were criticized by radical Islamists for their pragmatism and "open-door policy" that even included covert dealings with the United States during the Iran-Contra Affair; and both Khamenei and Rafsanjani were responsible for persuading

■

BOX 9.8   Ayatollah Sayyid Ali Khamenei

Sayyid Ali Khamenei was born in 1939 into a family of Islamic scholars in northeastern Iran. As a young man, he pursued a religious education in the Shi'ah holy city of Najaf, Iraq. In 1958 he became a student of Ayatollah Ruhollah Khomeini. In 1963 Khamenei came out in opposition to the *shah*'s Westernizing reforms. The student protests that followed were crushed by the *shah*'s regime, and Khomeini was sent into exile. Khamenei, however, continued his Islamic studies and became a *hojatolislam* (authority of Islam), the Shi'ah clerical rank just below *ayatollah*.

Khamenei's opposition to the *shah* resulted in his arrest and imprisonment. But by 1979 Khamenei was free and helped organize nationwide protests that ended with the fall of the *shah* and Khomeini's return from exile.

In Khomeini's new government, Khamenei cofounded the Islamic Republican Party and became a member of the Majlis (Iranian Parliament). Khamenei also established the Revolutionary Guards and defended the hostage takers who stormed the U.S. Embassy. In 1981 Khamenei was elected president of Iran. His authority seemed mostly symbolic, though he did contribute to ending Iran's diplomatic isolation with his "open door" policy. Khamenei was even denounced by hardliners in the Iranian government for his attempts to improve relations with the United States. Khamenei and Majlis speaker Rafsanjani both contributed to Iran's acceptance of a cease-fire in its long and fruitless war with Iraq. Khamenei also suggested that condemned author Salman Rushdie could be forgiven if he repented; Khomeini, however, reversed him.

After the death of Ayatollah Khomeini, Khamenei, an *ayatollah* himself now, was named the new supreme leader. Khamenei's views, however, seemed to harden after Khomeini's death. He accused the United States of interference in Iranian affairs, banned several Western consumer products in Iran, and increased censorship of the Iranian media. Khamenei warned President Rafsanjani not to lose sight of the revolution's principles and maintained a level of revolutionary fervor that Iranian society had already tired of. During the 1997 presidential elections, Khamenei backed Ali Akbar Nateq-Nuri. However, Khamenei's pick was defeated by Mohammad Khatami in a clear signal from the electorate that Iranians wanted greater freedoms, not new restrictions on political expression.

Khomeini to end the war with Iraq in August 1988. There was, however, one major difference between Khamenei and Rafsanjani. As supreme spiritual leader since June 1981, Khamenei (see Box 9.8) has been far more conservative in his domestic and foreign policies than he had been as president (1981–1989). It was Rafsanjani, as president for two four-year terms, who remained the moderate and pragmatic politician that he was as Speaker of the *Majlis*.

During the 1990s Abdul Karim Soroush (see Box 9.9), a passionate Revolutionary Islamist and Khomeini's protégé in the 1980s, became disillusioned with the Revolutionary and Traditionalist Islamists in the clerical establishment. Like Ali Shariati before him, Soroush became an eloquent spokesman for Modernist Islamism, pluralism, human rights, and a multiparty democracy.

BOX 9.9   Abdul Karim Soroush

A bdol Karim Soroush was born in 1945 in Tehran to a lower-middle-class family. Soroush pursued an education that combined instruction in the modern sciences with coursework on matters of religion, particularly Islamic law and exegesis. In high school, Soroush concentrated on mathematics but occupied his free time with religious studies. Soroush went on to receive a degree in pharmacy and spent two years in the Iranian army. Later he returned to Tehran to work in the Laboratory for Medicine Control and then moved to London to pursue higher studies and familiarize himself with the West.

While in London, he completed a degree in analytical chemistry and then pursued another advanced degree in history and philosophy of science. During his years in the U.K., opposition to the *shah* in Iran became more open, and Soroush attended gatherings with other Iranian students. Important opposition leaders from Iran often spoke at these meetings, including Ayatollahs Muhammad Husseini Beheshti and Murtaza Mottahari. When Shariati died under suspicious circumstances, Soroush attended his funeral service in London.

Soroush was no mere bystander to the events of the Iranian Revolution, however. He delivered speeches on religious and philosophical subjects, hoping to mitigate against leftist influences on Iranian intellectuals. He wrote several books based on his lectures, which were well received by Mutahhari and Ayatollah Khomeini. Soroush returned to Iran and, after the fall of the *shah,* was appointed by Khomeini to serve on the Cultural Revolution Institute. The institute's purpose was to revise university curricula in Iran and to reopen universities closed by the clerical establishment during the Revolution. Soroush later held research and teaching positions at Tehran University; he also began to publish again but no longer concentrated on the anti-Marxist writings that had endeared him to Iranian leaders. Now Soroush concentrated on work, critiquing the clerical establishment and its inflexible interpretation of Islam. Soroush has denied that there is a direct role for religion in politics. He has argued, furthermore, that Iran should selectively borrow from Western culture, rather than rejecting it altogether.

Although expressing these opinions has been made possible by more liberal and tolerant trends in Iranian society, Soroush faces substantial opposition from the entrenched Iranian clerical establishment. Because the clerics still hold the levers of power in Iran, Soroush has several times been prohibited from writing, teaching, and traveling. However, the election of President Khatami, who himself is a Modernist Islamist, has emboldened Soroush to respond to his critics forcefully. Nevertheless, Soroush recognizes that religion informs the political culture of Iran; reforming that political culture is as much a question of religion as it is of politics. Should the more liberal trend continue in Iranian politics, Soroush will remain a tremendous influence and a powerful voice of Modernist Islamism.

http://www.seraj.org/biog.htm
http://www.seraj.org/papers.htm
http://www.iranian.com/Opinion/Oct98/Soroush/
http://www.ait-cec.com/jebhe10mesg/4856.html
http://www.isim.nl/newsletter/8/jahanbaksh.htm
http://www.mideasti.org/html/b-sourush.html
http://www.theestimate.com/public/082500.html

One of Soroush's most important intellectual contributions is that Khomeini's version of a theocracy governed autocratically by clerics could not be an ideal Islamic state. Only Islamic democracy—with its emphasis on freedom of thought, tolerance, and pluralism—could create a popular, legitimate, and healthy government for Muslim societies.[41]

Furthermore, Soroush advanced the idea that Islamic democracy is based on two essential principles. The first was to be a true believer, one must be free. To be coerced into becoming a believer is not true belief. Therefore, freedom precedes religion. This freedom is also the basis of democracy. Thus, the beliefs, opinions, and will of the majority of people shape the ideal Islamic state. An ideal Islamic state should not and must not be imposed from above because it is legitimate only if the majority of people, both believers and nonbelievers, have elected it. The second principle Soroush posited was that the human interpretation of sacred texts is always in a state of flux because it is influenced by the changing times and conditions in which believers live. No interpretation from the seventh century, or any earlier era, was absolute and fixed for all time. Believers, then, did not have to follow one single truth. Furthermore, since human beings should be free, this freedom entitles them to their own understanding of the truth. No group or class of people, however learned (including the clergy), has the exclusive monopoly to interpret or reinterpret the faith. While some interpretations may be more enlightened than others, no version is more authoritative than another. Using this reasoning, Soroush criticized the clergy's claim to be the supreme power in any Muslim society.[42]

When national elections for the president were held in May 1997, Muhammad Khatami (see Box 9.10) won a landslide victory of gaining nearly 70 percent of the vote. His reformist platform, calling for greater freedom of expression and liberalization of the mass media as well as pluralism and civil rights (especially women's rights), endeared him to the younger generation; while Ali Akbar Nateq-Noori, the Revolutionary Islamist Speaker of the Iranian *Majlis* and Khatami's main opponent in the election, was the choice of the upper echelons of the clerical establishment.

In his 1977 inaugural address as president, Khatami said that Iran should have "clearly defined rights and duties for citizens and the government"; that its government should "officially recognize the rights of the people and the nation within the framework of law"; and that such a government needs "organized political parties, social associations, and independent free press." He went on to say that this is a society "where the government belongs to the people and is the servant of the people, not their master, and is consequently responsible to the people."[43]

---

[41]See Robin Wright, *Sacred Rage: The Wrath of Militant Islam* (New York: Simon and Schuster, 2001), pp. 283–285; see also Valla Vakili, "Abdol Karim Soroush and Critical Discourse in Iran," in John L. Esposito and John O. Voll, eds., *Makers of Contemporary Islam* (Oxford: Oxford University Press, 2001), pp. 150–176.

[42]Ibid.

[43]Muhammad Khatami, *Hope and Challenge: The Iranian President Speaks* (Binghamton, N.Y.: Institute of Global Cultural Studies, Binghamton University, 1977), pp. 77–78.

BOX 9.10   Muhammad Khatami

Muhammad Khatami was born in the town of Ardakan in the province of Yazd, Iran, in 1943, the son of Ayatollah Ruhollah Khatami. He spent his early school years in the town of his birth but attended Qom Theology School in 1961. He received a degree in philosophy from Isfahan University and pursued higher degrees at Qom. His religious studies ultimately earned him the rank of *hojatolislam*.

In the 1970s, Khatami went abroad to complete a doctorate. He served as head of the Islamic Center of Iran in Hamburg, where he learned German. He was already fluent in English and Arabic. Following the 1979 Islamic Revolution, Khatami was elected a representative of his native region in the Majlis (Iranian Parliament). In 1982 he was minister of education and Islamic instruction. During the war with Iraq, he served as head of the Joint Command of the Armed Forces and chair of the War Propaganda Headquarters. Under President Rafsanjani, he served as presidential advisor and chair of the national library.

Before the 1997 presidential elections, Khatami was not well-known. He ran for president on a platform of change that appealed strongly to younger voters and women. This alone was enough to secure him 70 percent of the vote, humiliating Natek-Nouri, the conservative candidate supported by the senior clerics. However, President Khatami found it easier to talk of change than actually to implement it. He faced the opposition of Revolutionary and Traditionalist Islamists, especially in the Shi'ah clerical establishment, who continued to control Iran's important institutions, including the military and the judiciary. Even the Majlis, which is now also in the hands of the Modernist and progressive Islamists, has been unable to implement any reform, and its liberal members are cowed by the threat of arbitrary arrest and imprisonment. Khatami, however, was patient and considered gradual change to be the best approach, despite his own supporters' demands for more immediate action. However, by the end of his first term, he had little to show for his efforts. The Revolutionary and Tradtionalist clerics had blocked every reform; dozens of his supporters were jailed; newspapers friendly to Khatami and to reform were banned. Still, Iranians were optimistic.

In June 2001 Khatami was reelected with 77 percent of the vote. Clearly, the Iranian people supported his reforms, which conservatives nevertheless made every effort to block. Khatami's landslide election has not made reform easier to achieve. The Revolutionary and Traditionalist Islamists will continue to block him; his most eager supporters will continue to demand faster action on behalf of reform. The question now is, Which side is Khatami most likely to disappoint?

http://inic.utexas.edu/meclass/aipol/mail/profiles97/0084.html
http://www.ain-al-yaqeen.com/issues/19980121/feat2en.htm
http://lexicorient.com/cgi-bin/

During the 1997 meeting of the Organization of the Islamic Conference in Tehran, Khatami impressed the dignitaries of Muslim countries with an eloquent speech about a "new Iran" that wanted to "live in peace and tranquility with other peoples and nations."

In February 2000, the sociopolitical climate in Iran had changed so much that President Khatami's supporters won 170 of the 290 seats in *Majlis* elections, thus taking control of the legislative body from the Revolutionary Islamists and Traditionalist Islamists who had dominated it since the 1979 Islamic revolution. In the June 2001 presidential election, President Khatami was re-elected for a second four-year term, winning 77 percent of the vote. Under his enlightened leadership, Iran is a far freer society today and enjoys good relations with much of the world (except the United States).

In a speech he delivered to American religious leaders in New York City in November 2001, President Khatami condemned those exploiting religion to engage in terrorist acts:

> Vicious terrorists who concoct weapons out of religion are superficial literalists clinging to simplistic ideas. They are utterly incapable of understanding that, perhaps inadvertently, they are turning religion into the handmaiden of the most decadent ideologies. While terrorists purport to be serving the cause of religion and accuse all those who disagree with them of heresy and sacrilege, they are serving the very ideologies they condemn. . . .[44]

Khatami concluded his speech by appealing to religious scholars and leaders of all faiths to initiate an interfaith dialogue and become the vehicle of social solidarity.

The Islamic state of Iran has a more lively debate about the role of Islam in a modern society than most Middle Eastern countries. It surprised many people around the world, then, when President George W. Bush's January 2002 State of the Union address lumped Iran, along with Iraq and North Korea, as being part of the "axis of evil." Ironically, in the short run at least, Bush's statement tended to strengthen the position of the Revolutionary and Traditionalist Islamists—who felt vindicated that the U.S. remained the "Great Satan"—while it undermined the position of the Modernist Islamists and Secularists who are trying to improve relations with the West (including the United States).

Summary

The significance of Iran's Islamic Revolution in Iran for Islamism throughout the Muslim world is simple: the Iranian Revolution was an Islamic movement to topple a secular, Western-looking government "in the name of Islamic purification." For Muslims around the world, and especially those enduring suppression, repression, and oppression at the hands of the secular Muslim regimes that predominate in Muslim nations, the Islamic Revolution in Iran was truly "an inspiring feat for devout men who have seen their aspirations for political and religious reforms crushed repeatedly in the 20th century."[45] Indeed, Islamism, particularly that having radical fringe elements, is especially active in countries that have suffered the

---

[44]"Khatami's View: The refreshing voice of moderate Islam," *The Economist,* November 24, 2001.

[45]William Beeman, "Khomeini's Call to the Faithful Strikes Fear in the Arab World," *Philadelphia Inquirer,* May 29, 1992, p. 12-A.

ills of "rapid economic growth and subsequent dislocation; . . . massive inequalities in urban areas; and a . . . period of pro-Western and relatively secular rule."[46] The conditions that contributed to the Islamic Revolution in Iran exist in much of the Muslim world, although the *shah's* ouster gave a much needed boost to the Islamic revival. In fact, the Islamic Revolution in Iran directly and indirectly inspired and motivated many Muslims and Muslim groups around the world. It accelerated and fortified the forces of Islamism and even initiated a revitalization of Islam among Muslims in both Muslim and non-Muslim countries. In essence, the Islamic Revolution in Iran provided a banner around which the oppressed and impoverished people of the Muslim world have rallied to protest the continued influence of the West in their societies and the continued rule of usually Western-supported governments that have persecuted the people they were created to serve.[47]

Key Events in the History of Iran

1502: Safavid dynasty (1501–1736) introduced Shi'ah Islam as the official religion of Iran.

1907: Persia became a constitutional monarchy due to the "constitutional revolution," which limited royal absolutism

1908: The first large oil fields were discovered in Iran. One year later, the Anglo-Persian Oil Company (renamed the Anglo-Iranian Oil Company in 1935) was established.

1921: Reza Khan, a military commander, overthrew the Qajar monarchy and became prime minister.

1925: Reza Khan convinced the Parliament to make him king.

1926: The coronation of Reza Khan took place, and he assumed the title of Reza Shah Pahlavi (the latter dynastic name was derived from an ancient province and language of the Persian Empire). The Shah's eldest son, Muhammad Reza, was proclaimed crown prince.

1935: The *shah* officially changed the name of his country from Persia to Iran.

1941: Anglo-Russian pressure forced Reza Shah to abdicate the throne (due to his pro-German sympathies during World War II) in favor of his eighteen-year-old son, Muhammad Reza.

1951: Muhammad Mossadegh—a Muslim Secularist, nationalist, and populist—became prime minister. The Anglo-Iranian Oil Company (and Britain) boycotted the purchase of Iranian oil after Mossadegh nationalized Iran's petroleum industry.

---

[46]Keddie, "The Revolt of Islam and Its Roots," p. 304.

[47]Hague et al., *Political Science*, pp. 80–81.

1953: The U.S. Central Intelligence Agency (CIA) overthrew Mossadegh and put Muhammad Reza Shah Pahlavi back on the throne.

1962: Reza Shah started the "White Revolution," which was an ambitious program of land reform and socioeconomic modernization.

1963: Ayatollah Ruhollah Khomeini (along with other prominent Shi'ah clerics) instigated anti-government demonstrations in response to the seizure of lands belonging to the clerical establishment, Westernization, and growing American influence in Iran.

1964: The *shah* exiled Khomeini to Iraq.

1971: The *shah* celebrated 2,500 years of the Persian monarchy at the ancient Persian capital of Persepolis. The vast amount of money spent on the spectacular affair and the glorification of a pre-Islamic era angered devout Iranian Muslims.

1974: Taking advantage of the influx of petrodollars due to increasing oil prices, the *shah* started a rapid modernization and Westernization program.

1978: An article published in early January in the popular national daily newspaper *Ittila'at* slandered Khomeini. This, in turn, sparked demonstrations in the religious city of Qom and, a month later, in Tabriz. These protests were then emulated by pro-democracy protestors in other cities.

1978 (March 30): Day of Mourning demonstrations in fifty-five Iranian cities.

1978 (August 19): Four hundred Iranians were burned alive in the Rex Cinema in Abadan. People blamed the *shah*'s SAVAK.

1978 (September 7): Despite the *shah*'s September 6 ban on demonstrations, half a million people marched, carrying placards calling for Ayatollah Khomeini's return and an end to the Pahlavi monarchy. The *shah* imposed martial law.

1978 (September 8): Millions defied martial law and marched in peaceful demonstrations all over Iran. The *shah*'s troops opened fire, killing hundreds in Zhaleh Square. Since the massacre was on Friday, that day is commonly referred to as "Black Friday."

1978 (October 6): On the *shah*'s request, Iraqi president Saddam Hussein expelled Khomeini from Iraq, where the *ayatollah* had lived since 1965. On October 23, the seventy-seven-year-old Shi'ah cleric in exile flew to Paris, where he had much easier access to the media.

1978 (October 18): After Khomeini's appeals to the Iranian working class to stop working and topple the *shah,* forty thousand petroleum workers went on strike. This was the largest single anti-government movement in the oil fields.

1978 (November 5): Students attacked Western banks, airline offices, hotels, and the British Embassy.

1978 (December 1): People defied the curfew, and hundreds of protestors were killed by the *shah*'s troops.

1978 (December 11): Two million people demonstrated in Tehran against the *shah*'s monarchy.

1978 (December 29): The *shah* appointed Shahpour Bakhtiar as prime minister.

1979 (January 16): The *shah* and his family went into exile.

1979 (January 19): Khomeini called for demonstrations against the Bakhtiar government. One million Khomeini supporters marched in Tehran.

1979 (February 1): Khomeini made a triumphant return to Iran after fourteen years of exile for opposing the *shah*'s regime.

1979 (February 9): Militant Islamists attacked military bases.

1979 (February 11): Following two days of clashes between Khomeini supporters and government troops, the army's high command declared neutrality in the political crisis to prevent further bloodshed and ordered troops to return to their barracks. The Bakhtiar government resigned after the withdrawal of army support, and Khomeini became the supreme religiopolitical leader of Iran.

1979 (March 30–31): A national referendum was held on the establishment of an Islamic Republic, which reportedly received 90 percent support.

1979 (April 1): The Islamic Republic of Iran was proclaimed, and Khomeini declared it "the first day of the government of God."

1979 (May 5): The *Pasdaran* (Revolutionary Guards) was established to protect the Islamic Revolution.

1979 (June and July): The Islamic Republic took over private banks (June 5), then nationalized private insurance companies (June 25), and then took over more private industry (July 5).

1979 (July 9): Khomeini declared a general amnesty for anyone who had committed offenses during the *shah*'s rule, except those charged with murder or torture.

1979 (August 3): Elections were held for the seventy-three seats on the new Assembly of Experts, responsible for finalizing a new Islamic constitution. Shi'ah clerics won fifty-five seats on that powerful decision-making body.

1979 (October 14): The Assembly of Experts approved a constitutional clause that provided for Khomeini to assume the Velayat-e-Faqih (Guardianship of the Islamic Jurist) and become commander-in-chief of the armed forces. There was also a clause that he would have ultimate veto power over selection of candidates, including those for the presidency.

1979 (October 23): David Rockefeller and Henry Kissinger convinced President Carter to allow the *shah* to come to the United States for cancer treatment.

1979 (November 4): Islamic militants feared that the United States was planning to put the *shah* back on the Peacock Throne (as in 1953). As a result, they seized the U.S. Embassy in Tehran and demanded the extradition of the *shah* to face trial in Iran for his theft of billions of dollars and his systematic murder of many thousands of Iranians during his thirty-eight-year rule.

1979 (December 2–3): In a national referendum, more than 99 percent of Iranian voters accepted a new constitution based on the *shariah* (Islamic Law).

1980 (January 25): The first national presidential elections were held on the basis of adult franchise; Abul Hasan Banisadr, a French-educated economist, received more than 75 percent of the vote. However, he did not get the prime minister of his choice. After a six-month power struggle with the influential Islamic Republican Party (IRP), Banisadr yielded to a lackluster candidate of the IRP, Muhammad Ali Rajai.

1980 (February 19): Khomeini appointed President Banisadr commander-in-chief of the armed forces.

1980 (April 24): The U.S. hostage rescue attempt began. But mechanical malfunctions and the crash of a helicopter into a transport plane at an Iranian desert staging area led President Carter to cancel the mission. To prevent any future rescue attempt, the Iranian captors dispersed the American hostages to several locations in the country.

1980 (March 14): The first parliamentary elections were held since the election. The Islamic Republic's first Majlis (parliament), comprising many clerics, convened on May 28, with Ali Akbar Hashemi Rafsanjani as the first speaker of the Majlis.

1980 (July 27): The exiled *shah* died of cancer in Egypt.

1980 (September 22): Iraq invaded Iran, starting a war that would last eight years.

1981 (January 20): Militant Iranian students released the fifty-two American hostages after 444 days.

1981 (June 22): Khomeini dismissed President Banisadr, and the latter fled to France.

1981 (July 24): Elections were held for the presidency, and Prime Minister Rajai overwhelmingly won with the backing of the Islamic Republican Party.

1981 (October 2): New presidential elections—the third time in twenty-one months and the second time in ten weeks—were held because of the assassination of President Rajai. Sayyid Ali Khameini, former Supreme Defense Council member and leader of the Islamic Republican Party, won, becoming Iran's fourth President (after Bazargan, Banisadr, and Rajai).

1986 (January 17): President Reagan gave the go-ahead to secretly win the release of American and European hostages held by the Iranian-backed Hezbollah (Party of God) in Lebanon by offering spare parts and ammunition for Iran's American weapons. This later came to be known as the Iran-Contra affair.

1986 (March 2): To commemorate Women's Day, Khomeini opened the way for greater participation of women in public life, including military service.

1986 (May 25): Former U.S. national security advisor Robert McFarlane, Lieutenant Colonel Oliver North, and others made a secret trip to Iran to deliver a secret arms shipment to the Iranian government.

1986 (November 3): The Lebanese magazine *Al-Shara'a* revealed McFarlane's secret trip to Tehran.

1986 (November 13): President Reagan said in a televised address that reports about the United States selling arms to Iran in exchange for hostages were "utterly false." He said that a small shipment of arms was sent to start "a new relationship" with Iranian "moderates." The next day, President Khamenei said Iran could not help the United States with hostages "under the present circumstances."

1986 (November 25–26): The Reagan administration disclosed that profits from arms sales to Iran had been diverted to the Contras and confirmed that the third country involved in the Iran arms sales was Israel.

1987 (July 31): Iranian *hajj* pilgrims in Makkah carried placards of Khomeini and criticized the Saudi regime's alliance with the United States and Saddam Hussein during the Iran-Iraq War. Saudi security forces were ordered to fire at the demonstrators, which resulted in the death of four hundred Iranians.

1988 (July 3): The United States damaged three Iranian gunboats, and less than an hour later, the USS *Vincennes* fired at an Iran Air plane, downing it and killing all 290 passengers on board.

1988 (July 20): Khomeini formally accepted a cease-fire agreement with Iraq following negotiations in Geneva under the aegis of the UN secretary general Javier Perez De Cuellar. Khomeini referred to his endorsement to end the war against Iraq worse than "drinking poision."

1989 (February 14): Ayatollah Khomeini issued a *fatwa* (religious edict) ordering Muslims to kill British author Salman Rushdie for his novel *The Satanic Verses,* considered blasphemous to Islam.

1989 (June 3): Ayatollah Khomeini died; two million people turned out for his funeral.

1989 (June 4): President Ayatollah Sayyid Ali Khamenei was appointed as the new supreme spiritual leader.

1989 (August 17): Ali Akbar Hashemi Rafsanjani, the speaker of the *Majlis* (Parliament), was sworn in as the new president.

1990 (August 2): The Iraqi army invaded and occupied Kuwait. Less than a week later, U.S. president George H. W. Bush announced Operation Desert Shield to force the Iraqi withdrawal from Kuwait. The Iranian government denounced Iraq's conquest of Kuwait and also stated its opposition to any long-term presence of U.S. forces in the region.

1997 (May 23): Muhammad Khatami won 70 percent of the popular vote in national elections for president. What is more, he defeated his conservative opponent, who was backed by much of the clerical establishment.

1998 (September): Iran deployed thousands of troops on its border with Afghanistan after the Taliban admitted killing eight Iranian diplomats and a journalist in Mazar-i-Sharif.

1999 (July): Pro-democracy students at Tehran University demonstrated following the closure of the reformist newspaper *Salaam*. Clashes with the security forces lead to six days of rioting and the arrest of over a thousand students.

2000 (February 18): Modernist Islamists and President Khatami's supporters won 170 of the 290 seats in *Majlis* elections and thus took control of the legislative body from the Revolutionary Islamists and Traditionalist Islamists who had dominated it since the 1979 Islamic Revolution.

2000 (August 1): Senior Shi'ah clerics issued a *fatwa,* allowing women to lead religious congregations of women worshippers.

2001 (June 8) President Khatami was reelected for a second term after winning 77 percent of the vote. He was sworn into office on August 8.

2002 (January): President George W. Bush described Iran (along with Iraq and North Korea) as being part of the "axis of evil" in his first State of the Union address. He warned Americans and the world that the development of long-range missiles in these three countries posed a threat to their neighbors and the United States. The speech outraged Iranians in and out of government, undermined the Modernist Islamists and Secularists, and strengthened the position of the Revolutionary Islamists who felt vindicated that the United States remained the "Great Satan."

2002 (February): The Iranian government rejected the appointment of David Reddaway, the British diplomat chosen by the United Kingdom to be its new ambassador to Tehran. This move threatened to worsen relations (which had been improving steadily since 1998) between the two countries.

Internet Sites

http://inic.utexas.edu/menic/countries/iran.html

http://www.farsinet.com/news/

http://www.madison.k12.wi.us/elib/Themes/Western_Asia/Individual_Countries/

http://c-library.um.ac.ir/Iransite.htm

http://memory.loc.gov/frd/cs/irtoc.html

http://www.time.com/time/daily/special/iran/

http://www.islamic-studies.org/Historical%20grounds.htm

http://www.newschool.edu/centers/socres/vol67/issue672.htm

http://www.macalester.edu/courses/russ64/pdf/daneshvarev.pdf

http://www.irvl.net/

http://globetrotter.berkeley.edu/Islam/iranB.html

http://www.bbc.co.uk/persian/revolution/biogs.shtml

http://news.bbc.co.uk/hi/english/world/middle_east/country_profiles/
newsid_790000/790877.stm

http://www.merip.org/mer/mer212/mer212.html

http://www.ifes.org/eguide/country/iran.htm

http://www.washingtoninstitute.org/pubs/menaexec.htm

http://persepolis.free.fr/iran/personalities/shah.html

http://novaonline.nv.cc.va.us/eli/evans/his135/MODULES/events/shah80.htm

http://www.rezapahlavi.org/index.htm

http://www.80s.com/Icons/Bios/mohammed_reza_shah_pahlavi.html

http://www.sedona.net/pahlavi/rezashah.html

http://www.sedona.net/pahlavi/

http://www.farahpahlavi.org/content2.html

http://www.farsinet.com/tambr/pahlavi1.html

http://www.angelfire.com/home/iran/

http://www.stanford.edu/class/history187b/mrshah.htm

http://www.seraj.org/biog.htm

http://www.seraj.org/papers.htm

http://www.iranian.com/Opinion/Oct98/Soroush/

http://www.ait-cec.com/jebhe10mesg/4856.html

http://www.isim.nl/newsletter/8/jahanbaksh.htm

http://www.mideasti.org/html/b-sourush.html

http://www.theestimate.com/public/082500.html

http://inic.utexas.edu/meclass/aipol/mail/profiles97/0084.html

http://www.ain-al-yaqeen.com/issues/19980121/feat2en.htm

http://lexicorient.com/cgi-bin/

http://inic.utexas.edu/menic/oil/game/simulation/profiles/sp1993/0013.html

http://school.discovery.com/homeworkhelp/worldbook/atozhistory/r/457970.html

CHAPTER TEN

Afghanistan:
One Nation, Divisible

Before September 11, 2001, most Americans would have been hard-pressed to find Afghanistan on a map or describe it in terms more telling than a vague recollection of Soviet defeat there. Afghanistan's location, however, is of strategic interest. Although landlocked, Afghanistan borders six other states: China, Pakistan, and Iran as well as the former Soviet republics of Turkmenistan, Tajikistan, and Uzbekistan. Afghanistan's history reflects its importance as a commercial route. Its people are a mixture of some twenty-two ethnicities further subdivided into tribal groups speaking about thirty different languages.

The Pashtuns are the largest ethnic group. Afghanistan also includes populations of Tajik, Uzbek, Hazari, and several other much smaller ethnic groups. These nationalities, with the exception of the Hazari, have sizeable populations that inhabit territory beyond Afghanistan's borders. Therefore, a unique "Afghan" identity has been difficult to establish on the basis of nationality. However, the Pashtuns of Afghanistan "are the historical founders of the Afghan state, its rulers, and its backbone."[1] The Pashtuns are the dominant ethnic group, and their culture has profoundly influenced Afghanistan's other nationalities and the modern form of Afghan nationhood. Tribal groups further divide Afghanistan's many ethnic communities.[2] The ethnic groups and tribes of Afghanistan have long managed their independence from each other, from the great powers, and from the central governments that claim their allegiance from the capital of Kabul. Divisions among the peoples of Afghanistan, and the frequent internecine warfare that

---

[1]Frederick Barth, "Cultural Wellsprings of Resistance in Afghanistan," in Rosanne Klass, ed., *Afghanistan: The Great Game Revisited*, rev. ed. (New York: Freedom House, 1990), p. 190.

[2]While the majority of Afghans are tribally organized, several nationalities are not, including the Tajiks, Uzbeks, Turkomans, and Farsiwans. See Ibid., pp. 195–196.

accompanies those divisions, are based as often on clan and tribal rivalries within ethnic groupings as they are on rivalries between the ethnic groups themselves.

Afghans are also divided on the basis of religion. For example, the majority Pashtuns are Sunni Muslims; the Hazaris are Shi'ah. Yet in spite of differences of religious orthodoxy and ethnic and tribal affiliation, Islam is the common bond that unites Afghans, particularly against foreign invaders. Because Muslim religious figures in Afghanistan stand outside the tribal system, they have been crucial unifying elements bringing clans together. These religious leaders operate also as military leaders against foreign interlopers, partly because they can "command a combined army without threatening the parity of the temporarily united clans and ethnic groups."[3] However, Afghanistan has a long history of temporary military alliances among ethnic groups and tribes; this history explains the weakness of unity within the Afghan resistance during the Soviet invasion and the collapse of that unity after the Soviets withdrew. This has been the cause of considerable misery for Afghans.

Afghanistan has been portrayed as "a country impossible to conquer: a small army would be beaten there and a large one starved."[4] This has proven true for hundreds of years and for countless armies defeated by Afghanistan's intractable tribes and inhospitable terrain. However, Afghanistan has been conquered before, most notably by Alexander the Great and by Genghis Khan and numerous regional empires. "Afghanistan has been the focus of the powers of the day."[5] This rugged country connects India with the Mediterranean and Middle Eastern worlds. It could not be ignored then. We ignore it at our peril today. A primarily rural society even in the twentieth century, Afghanistan's tribal populations were converted to Islam only after Arab armies conquered the region; the primarily Turkic peoples of Central Asia (which includes Afghanistan) resisted both the encroachment of the Arabs and the adoption of their faith. However, Islam in time became as precious a source of identity to the Afghans as their own tribal traditions—until faith in Islam became indistinguishable from their ancient social and cultural practices, even where that faith and those practices contradicted one another.

In the nineteenth century, Afghanistan became the focus of a seventy-year struggle between the Russian and British Empires—a struggle remembered as the "Great Game." The British Empire at the time included India, and the British wanted to secure their frontiers and protect trade routes. They hoped to expand those frontiers into Afghanistan. The Russians, meanwhile, sought a warm water port, and Afghanistan was the surest route for them to reach the Persian Gulf and Arabian Sea. The British opposed Russian moves in the region, fearing a Russian challenge to Britain's position in India and to its naval superiority in the Indian Ocean. Despite several regional wars in which the British and Russians clashed,

---

[3]Ibid., 198.

[4]Mohammed Ahsen Chaudhri, "Afghanistan and Its Neighbors," in Mohammed Ayoob, ed., *The Middle East in World Politics* (New York: St. Martin's Press, 1981), p. 140.

[5]Ibid.

Afghanistan stubbornly maintained its independence, routing a British army during the First Afghan War (1839–1842) and serving as a buffer state against Russian expansion following the Second Afghan War (1878–1880). The Afghans quickly learned that the key to independence from both these powers was to play them against each other, thus "obtaining support from one neighbor to check pressures from the other."[6] This policy served the Afghans well.

Afghanistan maintained its neutrality during World War I. It developed strong relations with the Bolshevik regime in Russia to counteract growing British influence.[7] During the Third Afghan War in 1919 the Afghans made significant overtures to Soviet Russia for aid in fighting the British. Hoping to avoid any expansion of the conflict, the British, exhausted by the world war, conceded Afghanistan's independence in the Treaty of Rawalpindi in 1919. In 1921 Afghanistan signed the Treaty of Friendship with the Soviet Union. Independence, however, did not put an end to internal conflict. The ruler of Afghanistan, Amanullah, was concerned about his country's backwardness; he began a program of modernization that included attempts to introduce Western dress codes and coeducation. Armed rebellion, which took on Islamist overtones, broke out in the countryside, and Amanullah was overthrown. A Tajik warlord briefly ruled Afghanistan but was soon replaced by a former commander of Amanullah's army, Muhammad Nadir Shah, who was Pashtun. In 1930 Nadir Khan called together a *loya jirga*, which is a council of Afghan tribal and religious leaders, and was made king. *Shariah* law was imposed, but the constitution of 1931 established a parallel secular system of law. Nadir Khan had been persuaded, by Amanullah's example, that "reform had to be tackled with extreme caution in the face of the ultra-conservatism of rural society."[8] Zahir Shah succeeded his father, Nadir Khan, as king of Afghanistan in 1933. Zahir Shah's forty-year reign was to be the longest period of peace his country would enjoy during the twentieth century.

Nevertheless, these years were not entirely free of conflict. In 1947 the two independent states of Pakistan and India emerged from the partition of a newly independent Indian subcontinent. The British were no longer on the border; now the Afghans faced the Islamic Republic of Pakistan. However, relations between Afghanistan and the newly formed Pakistan were unfriendly. Pakistan includes a sizeable Pashtun minority in the northweat frontier province (NWFP) bordering Afghanistan. For this reason, the Pashtun dominated Afghanistan repeatedly and made irredentist claims on Pakistan's NWFP.[9] This issue hampered good relations

---

[6]Ibid.

[7]The government of Afghanistan was quick to recognize the new Bolshevik government and to establish friendly relations with Moscow. "The Russians supplied Afghanistan with money, arms, ammunition and technical assistance," and not for the last time. See Ibid., pp. 142–143.

[8]Peter Marsden, *The Taliban: War, Religion and the New Order in Afghanistan* (New York: Zed Books Ltd., 1998), p. 21.

[9]Pakistan's minority population of Pashtuns is in fact greater than the number of Pashtuns in Afghanistan, where they are the largest ethnic group. See Chaudri, "Afghanistan and Its Neighbors," p. 144.

between Afghanistan and Pakistan for many years, leading nearly to war in 1955 and a three-year closure of the border beginning in 1961. Afghan trade carried on through Karachi suffered as a result of mounting tensions; Afghanistan was thus pushed into Soviet arms. The USSR eagerly accommodated Afghanistan with free and unobstructed transit through Soviet territory as well as "financial and technical assistance in building a network of roads in the country."[10] Interestingly, these were the very roads on which Soviet armies marched into Afghanistan several decades later. In fact, the Soviets built a highway toward the Khyber Pass, which would provide access from Afghanistan through Pakistan to the warm water ports of the Arabian Sea.

Most histories of Afghanistan focus on the rivalries among pro-Soviet political associations within Afghanistan prior to the Soviet invasion of Afghanistan in 1979. Such histories, while factually accurate, by their nature tend to overlook the power of Islam as a source of political identity in the countryside. The political competition between the Marxists in the 1960s and 1970s lacked a powerful ethnic or tribal component. These struggles took place primarily in the capital city of Kabul and were the reflection of urban political ideologies within a tiny minority of Afghanistan's population. Consequently, pro-Soviet political leaders in Kabul paid lip service to notions of social justice and political participation that derived from Islam rather than from Marxism. Yet in spite of their use of Islam to explain and justify new economic and social policies, the Marxists found few friends in the countryside. The rural tribes were hostile to the central government, particularly when its policies violated tribal traditions or tribal practices of Islam. But during Zahir Shah's reign, pro-Soviet policies and Marxist political leanings were not allowed to interfere with life in the countryside. As a monarch and an autocrat, Zahir Shah himself had no warm feelings for communism. Nevertheless, he recognized the need to placate, and to extract economic aid from, his communist neighbor to the north.

In the 1960s and early 1970s, Zahir Shah hoped to decrease his country's dependence on Soviet aid for its programs of economic development. While Zahir Shah wanted to maintain a close association with the USSR, "he and his closest advisors were convinced of the necessity to balance this relationship with arrangements involving the western countries."[11] By the early 1970s, Zahir Shah made visits to the West, where he expressed a desire for better relations with the British and the Americans. The Soviets, however, frowned on Zahir Shah's flirtations with the West. In 1973, while Zahir Shah was receiving medical treatment in Italy, former Prime Minister Muhammad Daud overthrew the monarchy with the support of two Marxist parties—the Khalq (Masses), led by Nur Muhammad Taraki, and Parcham (Flag), led by Babrak Karmal. However, the monarchy had been the only institutionalized source of Afghanistan's unity and sovereignty. New sources of

---

[10]Ibid., 145.

[11]Lawrence Ziring, *Iran, Turkey and Afghanistan: A Political Chronology* (New York: Praeger, 1981), p. 92.

national unity had to be found.[12] Daud consequently emphasized the importance of Afghanistan's Islamic identity. He declared that his new government would be truly democratic and would operate in accordance with the tenets of Islam. In fact, Daud sought to maintain and strengthen his alliance with the Leftist parties. Business and religious leaders in Afghanistan viewed this alliance as a threat and did not hesitate to oppose Daud politically.[13] This, in turn, pushed Daud more firmly to the left, while the Soviets provided significant economic aid as well as military advisors.

The *shah* of Iran tried to weaken Daud's ties to the left and to the Soviet Union. The *shah*, no friend of the Soviets, promised significant developmental aid to Afghanistan as well as construction of a railway linking Afghanistan with the Iranian port of Bandar Abbas. Had these plans gone forward, Afghanistan would no longer have had to choose between friendship with Pakistan and friendship with the Soviets. Of course, the pro-Soviet Khalq and Parcham parties opposed Daud's Iranian connection and, in 1978, had enough support from pro-Soviet elements in the Afghan armed forces to overthrow Daud and establish a new government under the leadership of Taraki. Once in power, however, Taraki de-emphasized his Marxist sympathies and promised he would "promote genuine Islamic tradition."[14] He, like Daud before him, hoped to use Islam as glue to hold his fractious country together. Although Taraki had the support of elements of Afghanistan's army (and, of course, its Soviet advisors), he nevertheless determined that Islamic political sympathies were strong both in the army's rank and file as well as in the countryside. Taraki made sure to appeal to those sympathies. The West, however, interpreted the coup against Daud as evidence of Soviet intervention on behalf of Taraki and his Marxist supporters.[15] Meanwhile, the Muslim world was "divided between traditional regimes that sensed the immensity of the communist threat and radical administrations that saw new opportunities for themselves."[16]

---

[12]Some credit the Soviets for making a conscious move by supporting Daud against a monarchy that represented "the one institution of national unity in a multilingual, multi-ethnic country." In fact, Muhammad Daud was Zahir Shah's cousin and brother-in-law. Although Daud did not make himself king, it might be argued that his rule represented a muted continuation of the Afghan monarchy. Whether Zahir Shah's overthrow was in fact a "Communist trap" ascribes to Moscow a level of Moriarty-like ingenuity that probably did not exist in any case. See Leon B. Poullada, "The Road to Crisis 1919–1980: American Failures, Afghan Errors and Soviet Successes," in Klass, *Afghanistan: The Great Game Revisited*, p. 54.

[13]Political opposition in Afghanistan took the form primarily of coup attempts (Ziring, *Iran, Turkey and Afghanistan*, p. 94).

[14]Ibid., p. 99.

[15]It is likely that Soviet Mig aircraft and heavy armor were used in the coup against Daud. "Judging from what is known about links between [the Khalq and Parcham factions of] the People's Democratic Party of Afghanistan (PDPA) and the Soviet KGB, there can be little doubt that the operation was meticulously planned by Soviet experts." See Poullada, "The Road to Crisis," p. 55.

[16]Ibid., p. 100.

■

BOX 10.1   Muhammad Zahir Shah

Muhammad Zahir Shah, a Pashtun by birth, was born in Kabul in 1914, the son and heir of Muhammad Nadir Shah, the king of Afghanistan. Zahir Shah was not yet twenty when his father was assassinated and he ascended the throne, although he had served briefly as a cabinet minister in his father's government. For a number of years, Zahir Shah's uncles, Muhammad Hashim and Shah Mahmud, were the real powers behind the throne. Zahir Shah acquired a reputation for being indecisive and vacillating. With the dismissal of his cousin, Muhammad Daud, as Afghanistan's prime minister in 1963, Zahir Shah came into his own and asserted his power through the constitution of 1964, which prohibited relatives of the king from holding public office.

For the next ten years, Zahir Shah, with foreign aid from the Soviet Union and the United States, undertook numerous projects of economic development, with a special emphasis on agricultural and transportation infrastructure. Zahir Shah struggled to maintain Afghanistan's independence in the face of considerable pressure, particularly from the Soviets. His reforms had little impact on most Afghans, however. In 1973, Muhammad Daud, whom Zahir Shah had dismissed as prime minister ten years prior, deposed the king and proclaimed Afghanistan a republic and himself its president.

After his removal from power, Zahir Shah spent his exile in Italy. After the failure of the Soviet invasion but even before the collapse of Muhammad Najibullah's Communist government, both the Communists and some of the monarchists among the *mujahideen* considered asking Zahir Shah to return to establish a government of national reconciliation. Even after Najibullah's fall and the capture of Kabul by the *mujahideen*, many Afghans, looking for a truly national leader to rally behind, saw their best hope in Zahir Shah. The rise of the Taliban and their decidedly anti-monarchist sentiments, due particularly to Zahir Shah's familiarity and comfort with the West, prevented Zahir Shah from considering a return to his native land. However, when the Taliban fell, talk returned of restoring Zahir Shah, now in his late eighties, to power. The interim government established in Bonn in December 2001 chose Hamid Karzai as Afghanistan's new leader. Karzai's family was close to Zahir Shah and the royal family, and Karzai was not known to oppose the idea of bringing Zahir Shah back, if necessary. Zahir Shah has returned to Afghanistan. However, after taking to the new Afghan leadership and the tribal leaders, the elderly Zahir Shah decided not to attempt to resurrect his monarchy or assume any official position in the democratically elected Karzai goverment.

http://www.afghan-info.com/Politics/King_ZahirShah/ZahirShah_Profile.htm
http://www.afghan-web.com/bios/today/zahirshah.html
http://www.islamonline.net/English/Crisis/2001/11/article3.SHTML
http://www.gl.iit.edu/govdocs/afghanistan/KingMuhammadZahirShah.html

The Taraki government embarked on significant economic and social reform. Taraki's deputy prime minister, Hafizullah Amin, pursued programs intended to bring about wholesale social change—including the eradication of class distinctions. These programs, however, had the immediate effect of alienating Muslims in the countryside, who saw attacks, even limited to traditions unrelated to Islam, as a sign that "Islam in Afghanistan was in mortal danger."[17] Amin's policies represented an attack on traditions; in the insurrection that followed, "the defense of a traditional society was expressed in the garb of a defense of Islam, because Islam was inextricably bound to tradition in the worldview of the Afghan peasantry."[18] The Soviets warned Amin against moving too quickly and discouraged offending Muslim sensibilities. The Soviets had learned in Muslim Central Asia to move slowly or risk insurrection. Amin, who was now the real power in the government of Afghanistan, did not heed these warnings. As a result, armed Muslim resistance in the countryside rose against the government. This resistance was not unlike that raised against Amanullah and his programs of social and cultural reform in the 1920s.

Because the members and leadership of the Taraki government were primarily Pashtun, the initial insurrections were launched by the nontribal ethnic groups in the north. The Pashtuns, in fact, did not join the resistance in any real numbers until the Soviet invasion. In the meantime, however, the Afghan army was suffering massive losses in casualties and desertions to guerrilla fighters who now styled themselves *mujahideen*, or "holy warriors." The rebels also targeted foreigners generally and Russians specifically. In response to this insurgency, Amin became increasingly oppressive and dictatorial. As the rebellion grew, large numbers of refugees, often families of the insurgents, fled to the borders of Iran and Pakistan. This was the beginning of a humanitarian crisis that was to last decades and reach unbelievable proportions. The refugee camps that sprang up on the borders of Pakistan and Iran also served as breeding grounds for fresh recruits of young and angry *mujahideen*.

In 1978, U.S. Ambassador Adolph Dubs was kidnapped in Kabul by "dissidents" and killed in a botched rescue attempt headed by Soviet advisors. Dubs had been making overtures to the Amin government to improve U.S. relations with Afghanistan and to wean it from Soviet influence. His death, however, effectively ended diplomatic relations between Washington and Kabul. The United States reduced its aid to Afghanistan and canceled a program of military assistance. Suspicion remains that the ambassador's death was not entirely accidental but that the Soviet "rescue" team might have deliberately endangered Dubs in an effort to short-circuit potentially cordial future relations between the United States and the government of Afghanistan.[19]

Taraki, whose role by now was almost ceremonial, was summoned to Moscow. The Soviets were increasingly uncomfortable with Amin's methods, which they

---

[17]Ibid.

[18]Olivier Roy, "Afghanistan: An Islamic War of Resistance," Martin E. Mary and R. Scott Appleby, *The Fundamentalism Project*, Volume 3: *Fundamentalisms and the State: Remaking Politics, Economies, and Militance* (Chicago: University of Chicago Press, 1993), p. 496.

[19]In fact, the Soviets considered the possibility that Amin was working for the CIA—though this was improbable at best.

blamed for the intensifying insurgency of the spring and summer of 1979. They urged Taraki to eliminate Amin; the Soviets themselves would take direct control of the Afghan armed forces. Taraki was then to offer amnesty to all insurgents, release all political prisoners, and make reassuring statements about the importance of "Islamic traditions." Amin caught wind of Moscow's plan, and before Taraki could act, Amin had him killed. Realizing that Moscow opposed him, Amin sought to make a quick peace with the Muslim rebels to restore order in Afghanistan. The Soviets interpreted Amin's move as a dangerous flirtation with Revolutionary Islamism. But the war with the insurgents had been too brutal; the *mujahideen* refused to work with Amin. In December 1979 the Soviets invaded, murdered Amin and his supporters, and installed Babrak Karmal as the new leader of Afghanistan.

The Soviet Invasion 1979–1989

The Soviet gamble in Afghanistan ended ultimately in disaster for the USSR and Afghanistan. At the time, however, the Soviet invasion seemed strategically sound. After all, the United States was, considering its difficulties in Iran, unlikely to intervene. The few steps the Carter administration did take had little impact on the Soviets. Moreover, the Soviet presence in Afghanistan would give Moscow leverage over developments in Iran and Pakistan. And perhaps most significant, the Soviets would be closer to direct access to the Persian Gulf and could establish air bases in Afghanistan that would put the Soviet air force within easy striking distance of shipments of Western oil. The Soviets also argued that this invasion was intended to preserve Soviet influence in Afghanistan—influence that the Soviets had jeopardized by siding with Taraki over Amin and thus ultimately alienating the otherwise pro-Soviet government in Kabul. The Kremlin feared that Amin was cultivating contacts with the United States within the framework of the 'more balanced foreign policy course' balancing the Soviets against the Americans."[20] This was unacceptable.

The Soviet invasion was also a response to the Islamic insurgency against the central government in the countryside. Moscow sought to prevent the possibility that a Revolutionary Islamist government would be established with so near access to the Soviet Central Asian republics. The Central Committee of the Communist Party of the Soviet Union (CPSU), in a top-secret report on the invasion of Afghanistan, noted, "Amin tried to strengthen his position by reaching a compromise with the leaders of the internal counterrevolution." If that wasn't clear enough, the report continued: "Through his entrusted persons he got in contact with the leaders of the right-wing Muslim opposition."[21] The "scourge" of

---

[20]John K. Cooley, *Unholy Wars: Afghanistan, America and International Terrorism* (London: Sterling Press, 2001), p. 278.

[21]Ibid.

Revolutionary Islamism would not be allowed to spread. Ultimately, what the Soviets counted on was a short and quick victory and the installation of a friendly government. They expected something on the scale of their interventions in Hungary and Czechoslovakia. What the Soviets did not anticipate was that they were to inherit the desperate insurgency that Amin had started. Amin's war with tribal rebels became for Moscow more than just a "Soviet Vietnam." The decision to invade Afghanistan was taken in the Politburo, the highest decision-making group in the USSR, without a clear understanding of the situation on the ground in Afghanistan and in spite of serious differences among the top Communist Party members. This was to be a fatal mistake for the Soviet Union.

The United States did see an opportunity in the Soviet invasion of Afghanistan. Carter's national security advisor Zbigniew Brzezinski believed that the war in Afghanistan could become a proxy war for the United States "against the Soviets, using Muslim mercenaries."[22] He endorsed a plan, which Carter approved, of supplying arms to the insurgents. The operation, however, was to be covert. The United States decided to arm the *mujahideen*, but only with weapons that appeared Soviet in origin, appeared to have simply been captured on the battlefield by the *mujahideen*. The United States could then deny it had armed the Afghan resistance. By 1980 the United States turned to Egypt for its stockpile of old Soviet weapons there and was manufacturing new weapons that would be indistinguishable from those produced in the Communist bloc. Even Israel pitched in by supplying the *mujahideen* with weapons it had captured during previous wars with Egypt and its Arab allies. Notably, Israel was to pay a price for this assistance. Palestinians who fought with the Afghan resistance were to return after the defeat of the Soviets and join the Revolutionary Islamist groups like Hamas and Islamic Jihad.[23]

To reach the Afghan fighters, military supplies from the United States and its allies had to pass through Pakistan. Pakistan's porous border with Afghanistan and the location of refugee camps along that border, where the *mujahideen* actively recruited young men, made it relatively easy to reach the various factions of the *mujahideen*. During the 1980s, Zia-ul-Haq, a Revolutionary Islamist, became leader of Pakistan. Rising to power after a military coup against Pakistani president Zulfikar Ali Bhutto, Zia enjoyed the support of Revolutionary Islamist parties in his own country. Although relations with those parties were strained by his consistent refusal to hold new elections, Zia became the single most significant supporter of the Afghan resistance and was primarily responsible for the strength of its more Revolutionary Islamist factions. Zia's intentions were more than simply to expel the Soviet invaders from Afghanistan. He was equally interested in backing the factions of the *mujahideen* that he considered most appealing in terms of both Pakistan's national interest and the Revolutionary Islamization of Pakistan, which Zia supported. During a 1980 meeting with Brzezinski in Islamabad, Zia agreed to

[22]Ibid., p. 29.

[23]Ibid., p. 34.

serve as a conduit for U.S. supplies to the Afghan *mujahideen*, on the single condition that "arm supplies, finance and training of the fighters *must be provided through Pakistan and not directly from the CIA.*"[24] The Carter administration, and the Reagan administration after it, agreed to these terms. Subsequently, Pakistan's military intelligence institution, the Inter-Services Intelligence (ISI), maintained rigid control of disbursement of supplies to the *mujahideen*. This provided Pakistan with an influence over the Afghan resistance far greater than any influence enjoyed by the West and guaranteed that support for the *mujahideen* would serve two interests—the fight against the Soviet invaders and support for Revolutionary Islamists among the Afghan resistance. Zia, his successors learned more than a decade later, was playing with fire; both Pakistan and the United States were ultimately burned. Permitting Pakistan absolute control over the U.S. operation to support the *mujahideen* proved to be the first mistake made by the United States in Afghanistan. It was not to be the last.

One of the greatest obstacles to Afghan victory against the Soviet invasion was lack of unity among the *mujahideen*. Even prior to the invasion, no fewer than six different organizations claimed to represent the *mujahideen* opposition to the Communist government in Kabul. The subsequent Soviet invasion made it crucial for them to combine their operations to more effectively resist the modern, mechanized Soviet armed forces. Impressively, these political factions, based in Peshawar, Pakistan, announced their unification only six weeks after the Soviet invasion. The six parties (later seven) officially created the Islamic Alliance for the Liberation of Afghanistan and declared "their ability to mount an effective, well-organized resistance to the Soviet-backed regime in Kabul."[25] In reality, however, this show of unity was a sham intended to impress the Muslim world and its Western friends. While proclaiming the alliance, "the leaders unashamedly resumed the bickering that . . . kept them apart."[26] The factions and their leaders acknowledged the need for common leadership, without which they could not hope to replace the Kabul government with an Islamic republic. However, each faction's leader saw himself as the appropriate "chairman" of the alliance. Moreover, ethnic and tribal differences compounded ideological ones. Hatred of the Soviets and political Islam remained the only bonds that effectively tied these groups together. But the factions could not even agree on the form that their eventual Islamic republic might take—moderate and pro-Western Modernist Islamist, or Revolutionary Islamist. The only thing these groups could, in fact, agree upon without discussion was "hatred for the atheistic communists in Kabul and their Soviet cohorts."[27] As one prescient Western observer remarked, "hatred may eventually provide the required unity to fight the Soviets, but it seems doubtful

---

[24]Ibid., p. 55 (emphasis added).

[25]Edward Girardet, "Afghans Struggle to Present United Front," *Christian Science Monitor*, February 15, 1980.

[26]Ibid.

[27]Ibid.

that it will provide a healthy atmosphere for the creation of a peacetime government once the communists are thrown out."[28]

Despite the infighting and disunity of the Afghan resistance, the war went badly for the Soviets. Soviet armies often won pitched battles against organized forces of the *mujahideen*. However, the Soviets had no effective defense against the *mujahideen*'s frequent and unpredictable hit-and-run attacks. These attacks sapped the strength and morale of Soviet soldiers in the field. Nevertheless, the Soviets and the government of Babrak Karmal maintained the offensive from 1979 to 1986.

The Soviets Withdraw

By 1986 the tide was turning against the Soviets. U.S. President Reagan increased overt aid to the *mujahideen*, providing them with arms and supplies—including Stinger anti-aircraft missiles. The Stingers were to have a devastating impact on Soviet airpower in Afghanistan. *Mujahideen* possession of the Stingers, an effective countermeasure against helicopters and low-flying aircraft, cost the Soviets one aircraft every day.[29] This, in turn, undermined Soviet public support for the war effort. After years of war, Soviet forces appeared no closer to victory than on the first day of the invasion. Pacification of the countryside had failed; so too had ruthless prosecution of the war against Afghan civilians. A million Afghans were dead, another million wounded, and nearly six million were in refugee camps. Thirty thousand to forty thousand Soviet soldiers had died. Yet the war showed no sign of ending.

When Mikhail Gorbachev came to power, he viewed the war as "an open sore." Military action was not working; public support was gone, and continuing the war in Afghanistan would be disastrous to Gorbachev's policies of openness and economic reform. Gorbachev began to look for a way out. He began by replacing Karmal with Muhammad Najibullah as president. The pro-Soviet Kabul government, like the rebels in the field, had been sapped by infighting. Gorbachev chose Najibullah, who was the former head of the feared Afghan secret police, known as the Khad, to bring unity and efficiency to the Kabul government. Najibullah quickly pushed for a cease-fire with the *mujahideen*. In January 1987 he called on the *mujahideen* to join him in forming a coalition government of "national reconciliation." Although Najibullah had little expectation that the coalition of the seven *mujahideen* parties would join him, he hoped at least to lure tribal groups and monarchists into his government, thus broadening his base of

---

[28]Ibid. For a concise treatment of the Peshawar-based political factions, as well as specifics on the regions where they drew support, see ibid. See also Marsden, *The Taliban*, pp. 31–34, and Curtis Cate, ed., *Afghanistan: The Terrible Decade, 1978–1988* (New York: American Foundation for Resistance International, 1988), p. 79. See also Gail Russell, "Afghanistan on the Eve of Soviet Withdrawal," *Christian Science Monitor*, May 12, 1988.

[29]Gail Russell, "Afghanistan on the Eve of Soviet Withdrawal," *Christian Science Monitor*, May 12, 1988.

■

BOX 10.2   The Afghan Resistance

The Jami'at-i-Islami-Afghanistan was the first of the Islamist parties. Burhanuddin Rabbani, formerly a lecturer in Islamic theology at Kabul University, led the party. The Jami'at-i-Islami's brand of political Islam was moderate and pragmatic and emphasized consensus building. Rabbani, however, was an ethnic Tajik and therefore had little base of support among Afghanistan's majority Pashtun population. Another prominent member of the Jami'at-i-Islami was Ahmed Shah Massoud, also an ethnic Tajik. He was widely regarded as the most successful commander in the war against the Soviets.

Hizb-e-Islami was originally a single party but split into two separate factions, each bearing the original name, in 1979. Golbuddin Hekmatyar, formerly an engineering student, led one faction. An ethnic Pashtun, Hekmatyar's organizational skills were superb. His ideology was more radical than that of the Jami'at-i-Islami. He supported the immediate creation of an Islamic state and rejected the gradualist approach of his rivals Rabbani and Massoud. Unlike the Jami'at-i-Islami, Hekmatyar's organization lacked a base of support within Afghanistan. He drew his strength from the disaffected millions of refugees in camps along the Pakistani border with Afghanistan. Despite his virulent anti-U.S. views, Hekmatyar received the greatest portion of U.S. assistance through the agency of Pakistan's Inter-Services Intelligence (ISI). Interestingly, Massoud was a far more effective commander in the field than Hekmatyar; but Hekmatyar's more radical brand of political Islam and his Pashtun ethnic background made him more palatable to Pakistani president Muhammad Zia-ul-Haq.

Younos Khalis, another Pashtun with a fondness for radical Islamic politics, led the other faction of Hizb-i-Islami. Unlike Hekmatyar, Khalis leadership style was based on tribal models. He enjoyed greater regional support within Afghanistan, particularly in the southeast.

Abdul Rabb Sayyaf led a fourth Islamic faction, the Itihad-i-Islami-Baraye-Azad-i-Afghanistan. Originally serving under Rabbani, Sayyaf escaped to Pakistan when the Soviets invaded and founded his own party dedicated to *jihad* against the USSR. Like Hekmatyar, Sayyaf lacked a real territorial base within Afghanistan but received significant backing from Saudi Arabia.

The three other main factions in the *mujahideen* were the Jabha-i-Nejat-i-Melli-Afghanistan, led by Sibghatullah Mujadidi; the Mahaz-i-Milli-i-Islami, led by Pir Gailani; and the Harakat-i-Inqilab-i-Islami, led by Muhammad Nabi Muhammadi. The first two factions were less Islamist in their ideological orientation and were influenced by monarchist tendencies. Of all seven parties, the Harakat-i-Inqilab-i-Islami was the closest in ideology to the Taliban, which did not yet exist during the war with the Soviets.

Although other parties, some with Shi'ah rather than Sunni leanings, were active during the war with the Soviet Union, these seven factions were the most prominent, had the greatest number of adherents, and were loosely united together in an Alliance of Afghan *Mujahideen*. It was well-known that leaders like Hekmatyar and Massoud were on less than friendly terms. While the Soviets had troops in Afghanistan, however, they were united with a single purpose—to drive the communist (agnostic or atheistic) and colonialist "infidels" out.

http://www.gl.iit.edu/govdocs/afghanistan/
http://www.afghanmagazine.com/afghanhistory/royalfamilies.pdf
http://www.cia.gov/cia/publications/factbook/geos/af.html
http://www.infoplease.com/spot/taliban-time.html
http://www.afghan-web.com/
http://news.nationalgeographic.com/news/2001/10/1009_afghanfacts.html

support. He offered a unilateral cease-fire to last six months, beginning on January 15.[30] Najibullah also implied that a timetable for withdrawal of Soviet forces had been established, although he gave no specifics.

The seven parties rejected both the offer to join the Najibullah government and the cease-fire. Before the end of January, in a renewed show of vigor and unity against the Soviets, the leaders of the seven parties appeared together, a rare event, before a mass rally in Pakistan of a hundred thousand refugees and fighters. Renewed fighting also broke out within Afghanistan. There was to be no cease-fire; there was to be no government of "national reconciliation." The Afghan *mujahideen* intended to fight Najibullah, not share power with him. Najibullah's offer, in fact, pushed the factions of the Islamic Alliance for the Liberation of Afghanistan closer together. The leadership of the alliance held a mass rally in which they appeared together, for the first time, before one hundred thousand fighters and refugees. "Their united public stand was meant to be a vivid affirmation of their resolve to continue fighting until the Soviets withdraw."[31] By the end of the year, improved field cooperation among the *mujahideen* was responsible for the fall of strategic Soviet–Afghan government garrisons to the resistance. The Soviets continued to fish for "peace with honor." They made contact with Zahir Shah, the exiled former Afghan king, to help form a coalition government to bring the *mujahideen* together with the Najibullah government. Both Moscow and the West saw Zahir Shah as the single Afghan leader "with the necessary nationwide support to head a transitional government that could oversee Soviet withdrawal and free elections."[32] Zahir Shah, sensitive to the opposition of *mujahideen* factions to his return, refused.

As it became clearer to the *mujahideen* that the Soviets intended to withdraw, disunity among the seven factions increased. One of them, the *Hizb-e-Islami*, headed by Golbuddin Hekmatyar, began attacking other resistance factions in the field and robbing and murdering Western journalists and aid workers. Hekmatyar also avoided conflict with Soviet forces, allegedly saving his faction's strength for future battles with his *mujahideen* rivals. The United States and Pakistan had been strong supporters of Hekmatyar's group and had supplied his *Hizb-e-Islami* with more than one-third of total aid earmarked for the resistance. Meanwhile, Hekmatyar stepped up criticism of the United States, decrying its "imperialism."[33] Hekmatyar was already jockeying for position in a post-Soviet Afghanistan.

With the *mujahideen* in control of over 70 percent of the countryside and with the Afghan Communists dug into Kabul and other garrison cities, Soviet troops

---

[30]Paul Quinn-Judge, "Soviet, Afghan Leaders Push for Resolution of Conflict," *Christian Science Monitor*, January 6, 1987.

[31]Edward Girardet, "Guerillas and Refugees Wage War on Their Own Disunity: Resistance Mounts Rare Show of Unity, Vows to Fight On," *Christian Science Monitor*, January 26, 1987.

[32]Edward Girardet, "Afghanistan War Defies Political Solution," *Christian Science Monitor*, December 21, 1987.

[33]Edward Girardet, "Radical Afghan Group Undercuts Resistance Efforts," *Christian Science Monitor*, December 30, 1987.

began their "orderly and disciplined" withdrawal from Afghanistan in May 1988. Moscow speculated that the Communist regime in Kabul would not survive without the Soviet army in the field. The Soviets were aware of infighting within the Najibullah government and expected that, if internal divisions in Kabul did not lead to the collapse of the Afghan Communists, *mujahideen* entry into Kabul would.

However, neither of these occurred. Government forces in urban strongholds were effectively resisting the *mujahideen*, even as the Afghan resistance negotiated defections of commanders and soldiers from the Afghan government's armed forces.[34] By February 1989 the Soviet pullout was nearly complete. The Najibullah government, however, held on to a few major cities, including Kabul. Fears in Moscow that Hekmatyar would come to power and establish a Revolutionary Islamist state on the Soviet's predominantly Muslim southern borders were premature. Defections from the Afghan government army continued, however. And the regime in Kabul relied upon the army to stay in power, as Najibullah lacked broad-based support in any part of the country. Yet the growing disunity within the ranks of the *mujahideen* contributed significantly to Najibullah's ability to hang on. Now that the Soviets were gone, the war was, in the eyes of many *mujahideen*, no longer a "true" *jihad*. Unity seemed less important than ever. Najibullah felt strong enough to purge his government of ministers who did not belong to the ruling Communist party.[35] He had no interest in dealing with disagreements in his own government and sought to deprive the *mujahideen* every advantage they might derive from such disunity.

The Warlords

As the last Soviet forces left Afghanistan, the Afghan resistance factions, under pressure from Pakistan, at last agreed on the formation of an Afghan government in exile. The new interim government was intended to operate until elections might be held. Sibghatullah Mujadidi, leader of the Jabha-i-Nejat-i-Melli-i-Afghanistan party in Peshawar, was named president of the interim government. His moderate and pro-monarchist tendencies, however, were offset by the new prime minister, Abdul Rabb Sayyaf, of the Revolutionary Islamist Itihad-i-Islami-Baraye-Azad-i-Afghanistan faction. The other five parties divided up the remaining government ministries. But in spite of this renewed show of unity, Najibullah's government continued to hold Afghanistan's cities. Disunity in his own government, however, at last resulted in a coup attempt against Najibullah in March

---

[34]See Edward Girardet, "Mujahideen Find Kabul Can Put Up a Tough Fight," *Christian Science Monitor*, June 28, 1988. See also Paul Quinn-Judge, "Afghan Ruling Party Digs In," *Christian Science Monitor*, November 25, 1988.

[35]"Afghans on Both Sides Maneuver for Power: Resistance vs. Ruling Regime," *Christian Science Monitor*, February 22, 1989.

1990, led by his defense minister, Shahnawaz Tanai, who had been in contact with Hekmatyar.[36] Tanai's defection underscored years of rivalry between the urban Parcham faction of the Afghan Communist party and the more rural Khalq faction led by Najibullah. Western observers considered this to be another example of "clan" warfare, this time on the Communist side of the war, rather than among the *mujahideen*.[37] Najibullah arrested hundreds and purged his regime, but the damage done by Tanai's defection to the resistance was significant and would foreshadow the ultimate downfall of Najibullah's government.

By 1991 Western interest in the war in Afghanistan reached a low point. President Bush's proposed budget for 1992 included no aid to the Afghan resistance. More than two years had passed since the Soviets had withdrawn; the *mujahideen* continued to bicker among themselves in the countryside, and the Najibullah government continued to control the cities. The Bush administration lacked the will or the interest to pressure the *mujahideen* to seek a peaceful political settlement with the Najibullah government, and the *mujahideen* showed no interest in such a settlement in any case. Moreover, the West no longer saw the *mujahideen* as "freedom fighters" against the Soviet Union; they were now characterized as extremist Muslim fundamentalists or bandits or both. The Bush administration therefore opted to unilaterally disengage from Afghanistan—a policy that one analyst warned was "bound to reduce the strength of the pro-Western Afghan groups and enhance the power of those groups that are supported by Pakistan and Iran."[38]

In April of 1992 Kabul finally fell to the *mujahideen*; the transfer of power from the Communist government to the *mujahideen* forces on the city's outskirts was relatively peaceful. Unfortunately, the *mujahideen* factions, Hekmatyar's ethnic Pashtun forces to the south and Ahmed Shah Massoud's coalition of ethnic Tajik and Uzbek fighters to the north, immediately began battling in the streets. Najibullah's ability to stay in power for the three years since the Soviet withdrawal was a surprise. More surprising still was the sudden collapse of Najibullah's government in 1992. The cause was, as might be guessed, internal divisions within Najibullah's government and army. During the year prior to the fall of Kabul, high-ranking commanders in Najibullah's army were negotiating their defections to Massoud.

The negotiations began to bear fruit in February 1991. Najibullah decided to dismiss General Abdul Rashid Dostum, who commanded the government's militia forces in the north. Dostum formed an alliance with other officers dissatisfied with the Najibullah regime and defected with them to Massoud's forces. Massoud

---

[36]Sheila Tefft, "Afghan Leader Najib Rebounds Solidly after Coup Attempt," *Christian Science Monitor*, March 15, 1990.

[37]Sheila Tefft, "Afghanistan: Return of Warlords," *Christian Science Monitor*, April 5, 1990.

[38]Anwar-ul-Haq Ahady, "US Shouldn't Just Abandon Afghanistan," *Christian Science Monitor*, June 11, 1991. See also Sheila Tefft, "US, Other Afghan Patrons Back Out of Proxy War," *Christian Science Monitor*, August 6, 1991.

and his new allies, calling themselves the Islamic Jihad Council, cut Kabul's supply routes. Najibullah could not be resupplied, and his regime slowly starved. By April all of Afghanistan's major cities had fallen to the *mujahideen*, except Kabul. Massoud's coalition was camped north of Kabul; Massoud negotiated with Najibullah's vice president for its peaceful surrender.

Hekmatyar's forces, meanwhile, gathered to the south of Kabul. Najibullah attempted to flee the city, but was able to find refuge only in Kabul's UN offices. When Hekmatyar arrived on the scene, he rejected forming a coalition with Massoud's Islamic Jihad Council and demanded that the city surrender directly to him. The Communist government slipped into oblivion as the two rival factions of the *mujahideen* stormed Kabul in an effort to seize strategic locations. What had been a peaceful surrender of Kabul erupted into violence between Hekmatyar's men and Massoud's. The interim government in exile, headed by Mujadidi, prepared to fly into Kabul to take over from the previous government. Hekmatyar, however, warned that the interim government need not bother since "power had already been transferred to the *mujahideen*."[39] Mujadidi paid no attention to this comment and appointed Massoud as his defense minister and head of security for Kabul.

Burhanuddin Rabbani and Massoud were members of the Jami'at-i-Islami, the most powerful faction, but their hold on power was slender. Both Rabbani and Massoud were ethnic Tajik, the second largest minority in Afghanistan. Eighty years before, the last ethnic Tajik leader to rule Afghanistan lasted only nine months before being pushed out of power by a Pashtun. Hoping to avoid a repeat of history, Rabbani made concessions to the Pashtun majority, who were typically more conservative Muslims. Although himself a moderate, Rabbani did not resist efforts to apply Islamic law in Kabul. Afghanistan's Islamic republic banned alcohol and narcotics, ordered women to cover up, and closed movie theatres on Fridays, the Muslim holy day.[40] Hekmatyar and his party, the Hizb-e-Islami, remained unreconciled to the interim government, and their personal animosity toward Rabbani and Massoud did not diminish. As the interim presidency of Afghanistan was intended to rotate among the individual leaders of the *mujahideen* factions, Rabbani assumed the position in June. Hekmatyar did not recognize the interim government and remained camped with his forces in Charasyab, twelve miles south of Kabul. Conflict between Hekmatyar and Massoud intensified. By August Hekmatyar's forces were firing artillery and rocket-propelled cluster bombs into Kabul.[41] Hundreds of civilian casualties were the result, but Rabbani and Massoud remained in control.

---

[39]Farhan Bokhari, "Afghan Rebels Engage in Battle for Capital City," *Christian Science Monitor*, April 27, 1992. See also "Afghan Rebels Form Coalition to Oust Government," *Christian Science Monitor*, April 20, 1992; "Acting President Calls for Peaceful Transfer," *Christian Science Monitor*, April 22, 1992; and Justin Burke, "Afghan Envoy Says Ethnic Rivalry Threatens a Peaceful Transition," *Christian Science Monitor*, April 22, 1992.

[40]Justin Burke, "Afghan Capital Adjusts to Life under Islam," *Christian Science Monitor*, May 13, 1992.

[41]"Afghan Faction Offers Ceasefire," *Christian Science Monitor*, August 14, 1992.

■

BOX 10.3   Ahmed Shah Massoud

Ahmed Shah Massoud (1956–2001) was born in Panjshir, a primarily ethnic Tajik region north of Kabul. Massoud attended a French-language high school in Kabul and studied engineering at Kabul University. After the Soviet invasion of Afghanistan in 1979, Massoud became involved in the war against the Soviets in the early 1980s. During the Afghan *jihad* against the Soviets and the Communist regime in Kabul, Massoud joined the Jami'at-i-Islami party, headed by Burhanuddin Rabbani.

Unlike Gulbuddin Hekmatyar and Rabbani, Massoud spent the entire war in Afghanistan and in the field fighting Soviet forces. His personal charisma, his fluent French, and his moderate and modernist views of political Islam made him popular in the West. His success in battle and his defeat of Soviet forces earned him popularity among his troops, and the nickname the "Lion of Panjshir." Massoud was the most successful of the *mujahideen* commanders, earning him the hatred of Hekmatyar, whose Hizb-i-Islami (Islamic Party) was more revolutionary and whose hunger for power was more obvious.

After the withdrawal of the Soviets in 1989 and the final collapse of Muhammad Najibullah's government in 1992, Rabbani established an interim government over which he presided as President. Massoud was Rabbani's "sword arm," serving as defense minister in that government. Hekmatyar rejected the interim government, and his forces clashed repeatedly with Massoud's. Afghans blamed both Hekmatyar and Massoud for the continuing civil war. Massoud's position was also weakened by his unfamiliarity with the territory in and around Kabul, and his Tajik ethnic background won him no friends among Pashtuns like Hekmatyar and, later, the Taliban.

When the Taliban first appeared on the scene, Massoud is rumored to have assisted them, hoping that they might finally rid him of Hekmatyar and join him and Rabbani in governing Afghanistan. The Taliban obliged initially but then turned against Massoud and drove him out of Kabul in 1996. Massoud retreated with his forces to his redoubt in the Panjshir Valley. There he organized his forces against the Taliban and was able to keep them at bay, even as they swallowed nearly 90 percent of Afghanistan. Massoud joined forces with Dostum, the Uzbek general in northern Afghanistan, and formed what was ultimately called the "Northern Alliance." Massoud traveled overseas, particularly to Europe, to appeal for funding to fight the Taliban. Massoud's stubborn resistance to the Taliban earned him the enmity of Osama bin Laden, who is rumored to have sent two Algerians posing as reporters to kill him. Bin Laden's assassins succeeded on September 9, 2001. The Northern Alliance's chances to survive never looked worse. However, two days later, al-Qaeda's attacks against the United States gave the Northern Alliance the most powerful ally they could have had against the Taliban. Little did Massoud realize before September 9 that, within four months, his cause would be victorious.

By December 1992 Rabbani was scheduled to step down as president of the interim government, and the position would rotate to the next faction leader. Rabbani, however, did not step down. Instead, he moved forward with plans to convene 1,335 delegates in Kabul to dissolve the interim government and elect

Afghanistan's first president since the Soviet invasion. In spite of accusations of bribery and fraud, the assembled delegates voted for Rabbani as the new president. Other factions of *mujahideen* accused Rabbani of manipulating the election to maintain himself in power. Both Dostum and Hekmatyar rebelled against the Rabbani government, and civil war continued.[42]

Hekmatyar and Dostum vigorously disputed the legitimacy of Rabbani's December election. Hekmatyar's forces wasted no time in making their displeasure known—the fighting began the day after Rabbani was sworn in. Rockets and artillery shells again rained on Kabul, killing hundreds of civilians and driving half a million residents out of the city. Hekmatyar continued to frame the conflict as a *jihad* and declared that Rabbani was "frustrating the wishes of the Afghan people for an Islamic state."[43] This, of course, flew in the face of Rabbani's background as an Islamic scholar and his application of Islamic law in Kabul. Nevertheless, from Hekmatyar's more Revolutionary Islamist point of view, Rabbani wasn't doing enough. Heavy fighting in February 1993 in western Kabul finally convinced Rabbani and Massoud to come to terms with Hekmatyar. President Rabbani invited Hekmatyar to be prime minister. This solution, however, did not fully satisfy Hekmatyar and further alienated Dostum, who by January 1994 was allied with Hekmatyar. The two joined forces in an attempt to unseat Rabbani, and again rockets rained down on Kabul, this time for an entire year—though Hekmatyar came no closer to replacing Rabbani. Thousands of Afghan civilians died; tens of thousands were wounded; and one-third of Kabul's population fled the fighting. President Rabbani himself was forced to admit, two years after the end of the Communist regime in Afghanistan, "There are people who waited for the coming of the *mujahideen*. Now they are suffering."[44]

Meanwhile, the international community had given up. The United Nations closed its offices in Kabul. The U.S. Embassy had long since been boarded shut. Other foreign embassies were likewise closed. Kabul faced more devastation and destruction in two years under the government of the *mujahideen* than it had for over a decade under the Communists. It seemed as though the fighting might never end.

The Rise and Reign of the Taliban

By early 1996 Hekmatyar agreed to join the Rabbani government as prime minister. For three months, the Rabbani administration ruled Afghanistan before the Revolutionary Islamists Taliban drove the *mujahideen* out of Kabul. Prior to 1994,

---

[42]Scott Baldauf, "Afghan Fighting Erupts over Delayed Power Transfer," *Christian Science Monitor*, December 10, 1992. See also, "New Afghan President Sworn In," *Christian Science Monitor*, January 4, 1993.

[43]Jim Muir, "Afghanistan Faces Disintegration as Rebel Factions Fight Each Other," *Christian Science Monitor*, February 23, 1993.

[44]Greg Gransden, "War Grinds on in Kabul, Crumbling Buildings and Lives," *Christian Science Monitor*, July 6, 1994.

BOX 10.4   Gulbuddin Hekmatyar

Gulbuddin Hekmatyar was born a Pashtun in the Kharoti tribe in the northern province of Kunduz in 1947. He attended Kabul University in the late 1960s, where he studied engineering. Hekmatyar was inspired by the writings of Sayyid Qutb, among others, and was actively involved in campus politics. He cofounded the Organization of Muslim Youth in opposition to the Marxist parties that dominated Afghan politics.

Hekmatyar's political activities resulted in his arrest in 1972. Released in 1973, Hekmatyar went into exile to Peshawar, Pakistan, where he was involved in plots against the governmet of Muhammad Daud. These plots ultimately failed, and the plot leaders were imprisoned or executed by the Daud government and by the Marxist government that replaced it in 1978. Hekmatyar eluded capture and became the leading figure in what finally became known as the *Hizb-i-Islami* (Islamic Party). From 1978 to 1992 Hekmatyar and the *Hisb-e-Islami* actively opposed the Communist government in Kabul. Hekmatyar was recognized for his outstanding organizational skills, and Pakistan's Inter-Service Intelligence (ISI) provided him with much of the aid supplied by the United States to fight the Soviets. However, Hekmatyar was a controversial leader, extremely anti-Western in his orientation and more interested in acquiring power than fighting the Soviets. Moreover, during the war against the Soviets, Hekmatyar was recognized as the most extreme of the Revolutionary Islamists among the *mujahideen.*

After the overthrow of the Communist government in Kabul, Hekmatyar turned against fellow *mujahideen* leaders Rabbani, Massoud, and Dostum. As alliances came and went, Hekmatyar occasionally joined Rabbani's coalition government and occasionally shelled Kabul in opposition to it. By 1996, when the Taliban entered the political and military scene, Hekmatyar, though he shared with them a fondness for revolutionary Islamic politics, was pushed out of power. The Taliban considered him "un-Islamic" for failing to establish a truly Islamic government with the other leaders of the *mujahideen.* Hekmatyar fled Afghanistan and was given asylum in Iran. During the brief U.S. bombing campaign against the Taliban in 2001, Hekmatyar pledged to return to Afghanistan to fight the Americans. However, Iran prevented him from traveling, and many in Afghanistan breathed a sigh of relief.

http://rawa.fancymarketing.net/gul-kgb.htm
http://www.afghanradio.com/news/2001/november/nov7k2001.html
http://www.janes.com/defence/interviews/dw011024_i.shtml
http://www.afghanhero.com/afghanan/biographies/hekmatyar.htm
http://www.afghan-web.com/bios/today/ghekmatyar.html

---

no one had ever heard of the Taliban. Their meteoric rise stunned the world; but they brought a measure of stability to Afghanistan that the people needed and wanted, even if the admission price was the most stringent and punishing interpretation and enforcement of Islamic law ever known.

Different stories have circulated about the Taliban's origins. The word *Taliban* literally means "seeker" and, more specifically, "seeker of religious truth"

■

BOX 10.5   Burhanuddin Rabbani

Burhanuddin Rabbani, an ethnic Tajik, was born in 1940 in the Afghan province of Badakhshan. His schooling began in his native province. Later he pursued a religious education in Kabul. He attended Kabul University, where he studied Islamic law and theology. In 1963 he became a professor at Kabul University. In 1966 he attended the Al-Azhar University in Cairo, where he earned a masters degree in Islamic philosophy.

Rabbani returned to Afghanistan in 1968 and became a member of the Jami'at-i-Islami (Islamic Party). While teaching at Kabul University, he recruited university students to join the party's ranks. By 1972 Rabbani was made leader of the Jami'at-i-Islami. Rabbani's outspoken opposition to the Marxist political parties that had begun to dominate politics in Kabul made him a target for arrest. In 1974 he eluded police and escaped to the countryside.

Ultimately, Rabbani's opposition to the Communists, and to the subsequent Soviet invasion, forced him into exile. He spent much of the war against the Soviets in Peshawar, Pakistan, where he raised funds and organized his party one day to return to Kabul. Rabbani's prominence was due in part to the battlefield success of Jami'at-i-Islami member Ahmed Shah Massoud. When Massoud's *mujahideen* captured Kabul in 1992, Rabbani returned to Afghanistan and, with Massoud's backing, became president of the new *mujahideen* government. Rabbani made Massoud defense minister.

Unfortunately, Gulbuddin Hekmatyar, an ethnic Pashtun, had substantial forces south of Kabul and demanded a prominent place in the Rabbani government. Unsatisfied with Rabbani's offers, Hekmatyar began shelling Kabul and his forces clashed frequently with Massoud's. The conflict between Hekmatyar and Rabbani, with its strong ethnic component, was also based on their different views of Islam. Although Rabbani was an Islamic scholar, his vision of political Islam was moderate; Hekmatyar, in contrast, was a Revolutionary Islamist who regularly denounced the West and insisted on strict implementation of Islamic law in Kabul. Rabbani and Massoud both conceded to a more stringent application of the *shariah* in Kabul but only in response to Hekmatyar's demands.

Rabbani's government remained in turmoil until 1996, when the Taliban drove Hekmatyar and Massoud out of Kabul. Rabbani escaped, but was still acknowledged by most foreign countries as the legitimate president of Afghanistan. Following the terrorist attacks on the United States in September 2001, the U.S.-led campaign successfully ousted the Taliban. Rabbani's position as president was in jeopardy. His government's inability to unite quarreling *mujahideen* factions and prevent the consequent leveling of much of Kabul made him an unpopular figure among most Afghans. His ethnic Tajik background was also an impediment to his acceptance among the primarily ethnic-Pashtun population of Afghanistan. After meetings in Bonn, Germany, among the various factions opposing the Taliban, Hamid Karzai was chosen as chair and leader of a new interim government intended to replace Rabbani. Initially, Rabbani rejected the legitimacy of Karzai's appointment but ultimately accepted the inevitable. Rabbani attended Karzai's inauguration in Kabul and publicly embraced Afghanistan's new leader.

http://www.afghan-web.com/bios/today/brabbani.html

or "religious student." This concurs with suggestions that the original members and leaders of the Taliban were Afghan students of Islam attending *madrassahs* in Pakistan. Adherents to the Taliban cause were drawn from the refugee camps along the Pakistani border. In Pakistan, the Taliban were taught a particularly conservative, radical, and militant form of Revolutionary Islamism. However, the Taliban did not yet exist as a national political movement. They were a latent force with primarily local interests. But as frustration with the warlordism of the *mujahideen* increased, the Taliban mutated into a Revolutionary Islamist military organization. The *mujahideen* lost considerable public support as their factions continued to battle one another even six years after the defeat of the Soviets. The Taliban, like all Afghans, were frustrated with civil war, insecurity, and corruption, for all of which they held the *mujahideen* factions collectively responsible.

The Taliban's political and military goals were therefore simple: to throw out the *mujahideen* government (which in its final form was a shaky coalition dominated by Tajiks and headed by Rabbani with Massoud, Hekmatyar, and Dostum) and to unite Afghanistan under a strict version of *shariah* law. Initially, their unyielding opposition to the *mujahideen* factions and their apparent drive for peace and unification under a new order of strict Revolutionary Islamism appealed to the exhausted people of war-ravaged Afghanistan. Taliban support also had an ethnic component. Although claiming to be open to Sunni Muslims of any ethnicity, the Taliban were overwhelmingly Pashtun, and their interpretation of Islam was partly informed by their own ethnic and tribal traditions. As a result, they were quickly accepted in November 1994 when they came to power in Kandahar, a Pashtun city in southern Afghanistan.

The Taliban's sudden rise to prominence in Kandahar tends to obscure Pakistan's role in supporting the group. Pakistan had for years favored Hekmatyar's *mujahideen* faction but was losing patience with Afghanistan's instability. The Pakistani government, therefore, gambled on the Taliban's popularity and their promise to bring peace and stability to Afghanistan once in power. Pakistan in the mid-1990s hoped to reestablish lucrative trade routes through Afghanistan to Central Asia. Benazir Bhutto, prime minister of Pakistan during that period, explained that her support of the Taliban was based on Pakistan's desire to gain access to Turkmenistan through Kandahar: "We were trying to bypass Kabul and establish an enclave in the south. The Taliban were supposed to give us safe passage."[45]

In October 1994 the first Pakistani convoy began its trek to Central Asia along this route. Local bandits attacked but were quickly repelled by Taliban soldiers. The convoy was able to proceed, and the Taliban moved into Kandahar, quickly eliminated the *mujahideen* factions fighting among themselves there, and took control of the city. The population respected Taliban orders to turn in their weapons, based in part on the Taliban's announcement of its mission "to free Afghanistan of its existing corrupt leadership and to create a society that accorded

---

[45]Benazir Bhutto, "One View of the Taliban," *Newsweek Web Exclusive*, September 22, 2001.

with Islam."[46] Law and order came to Kandahar under Taliban leadership, and the Taliban gained a regional reputation for incorruptibility and religious piety. This reputation made it relatively easy for the Taliban, in about a year's time, to conquer half of Afghanistan. The *mujahideen* were unable to repel the Taliban for several reasons, not the least of which was the *mujahideen*'s inability to stand united even against a threat to them all.

The Taliban's movement toward Kabul began when Taliban soldiers pushed Hekmatyar's forces out of their base in Charasyab in the southern outskirts of Kabul. In this action the Taliban were backed by Massoud, who supplied them with political and military support in their advance against his rival.[47] Massoud came to realize, however, that the Taliban did not play favorites. They advanced against the Tajik warlord and took western Kabul but were forced out by Massoud's stronger army. The Taliban lost Charasyab and fell back. In the meantime, Kabul experienced a lull in fighting while the Taliban concentrated on consolidating their conquests throughout Afghanistan.

By the end of 1996, the Taliban were strong enough to try again. By then, Hekmatyar, realizing the disaster that was to encompass all the *mujahideen*, joined forces with Massoud in Rabbani's government as the Taliban continued their sweep of other cities throughout Afghanistan. Within two weeks of taking Jalalabad, the Taliban turned their attention again to Kabul. The real battle for Afghanistan's capital took place between the *mujahideen* and the Taliban seventy-five miles south of Kabul, in the town of Sarobi. Hekmatyar's Pashtun soldiers quickly retreated into the hills or defected and joined the Taliban. Massoud was unfamiliar with the terrain, and the Taliban pushed back his Tajik soldiers. Small units of Taliban troops in pickup trucks swept from their victory in Sarobi into Kabul. Massoud, realizing the battle was lost, led his troops in retreat to the Panjshir Valley, far north of Kabul. Here Massoud hoped to regroup and fight on; but Massoud never saw Kabul again.

The Taliban's victorious entry into Kabul was met with no resistance among the civilians. There was no shelling; there was no looting; only well-disciplined Taliban soldiers. The first act of the new Taliban regime, however, was to kidnap Najibullah, who had never bothered to leave Kabul, beat him to death, and hang his body from a traffic control tower. The Taliban also immediately introduced the city to their stringent interpretation of Islamic law. Female government employees were ordered not to report to work, and all women were required to cover themselves from head to toe; failure to do so merited a beating at the hands of the Taliban. Ultimately, the Taliban decreed that men must grow their beards out and women were not permitted to work. The Taliban also prohibited "un-Islamic" practices, such as watching television, playing music (whether recorded or live), and kite flying. To underscore their adherence to extreme and Revolutionary Islamism, the Taliban established what they called the Ministry for the Promotion

---

[46]Marsden, *The Taliban*, p. 46.

[47]Peter DeNeufville, "Afghanistan's Long Civil War Shaken Up by Islamist Purists," *Christian Science Monitor*, December 2, 1994.

of Virtue and the Prevention of Vice, an organization feared in Afghanistan and reviled around the world. The Taliban's harshness, however, was based as much on their interpretation of Islamic law as on ethnic differences. The residents of Kabul were ethnically mixed, with large concentrations of Tajiks and Shi'ah Hazaris. The primarily Pashtun fighters with the Taliban felt considerable animosity toward these ethnic groups and suspected them of collaboration with Massoud, a fellow Tajik. Yet even Pashtuns in Kabul were different from the Taliban. The residents of the city were generally less conservative and more cosmopolitan than their country cousins and were also less inclined toward militant and Revolutionary Islamism. In the history of Afghanistan, Islamism had always been the voice of the countryside, never of the capital. The Taliban sensed this difference and were hostile to it. This hostility led to incidents of violence in Kabul, forcing the Taliban's supreme leader, Mullah Omar, to appeal to his followers in Kabul not to mistreat the residents of Kabul.[48]

Massoud's retreat from Kabul effectively ended Rabbani's government. The fiction of the old *mujahideen* government remained alive, although it governed virtually nothing. However, the West, Russia, and China were sufficiently hostile to the Taliban to continue to recognize Rabbani as the legitimate president of Afghanistan. The forces of Uzbek warlord Rashid Dostum and Tajik commander Massoud now became what was called the Northern Alliance. There was no effective southern alliance, insofar as the south was dominated by the Pashtun tribes and the Taliban were Pashtun. There was, of course, resistance to the Taliban among some Pashtuns, Pashtun tribal leader Hamid Karzai, for example. It wasn't until U.S. intervention in 2001 that Pashtun tribal resistance took a military form. Moreover, the Taliban did deliver much of what they promised—particularly an end to the fractious and incompetent *mujahideen* government and the unification of (most of) Afghanistan under their rule.

The Northern Alliance, meanwhile, held on to smaller and smaller portions of Afghan territory. By early 2001, despite support from Iran, Russia, Central Asia, and China, the Northern Alliance was holding on to less than 10 percent of Afghan territory, all of it in the north along the border with Central Asia. Massoud made trips to Europe attempting to shore up international aid and support for the Northern Alliance. He recognized how little time the alliance had before it would be snuffed out by the Taliban.[49] The Northern Alliance received some aid and comfort, but its greatest advantage was the ethnic makeup of the northern reaches of Afghanistan and the local populations' hostility toward the Pashtun Taliban. The city of Mazar-i-Sharif, in the north, was a city of strategic importance to the Northern Alliance. Although the Taliban had taken it in early 1997, the local population had driven them out. However, disunity, the hallmark of the Rabbani gov-

---

[48]Marsden, *The Taliban*, p. 52.

[49]As Massoud lobbied for international aid for the Northern Alliance, he contended that the Taliban itself was the puppet of a foreign power—specifically Pakistan, without whom, Massoud noted, "the Taliban cannot last for six months." In this Massoud was prescient. See "The Lion Clawed," *The Economist*, September 13, 2001.

ernment when it occupied Kabul, were not absent in the Northern Alliance. Defections and squabbles among rival warlords continued to arise and hamper effective campaigns against the Taliban.

In February 1998 an earthquake struck the Afghan province of Takhar, a region beyond the Taliban's control and in the hands of the Northern Alliance. The earthquake killed thousands and left tens of thousands homeless. Russia offered its "unlimited" support to the region, partly because it recognized the Rabbani regime as the legitimate government of Afghanistan but mostly because Russia feared the spread of the Taliban's form of Revolutionary Islamism into Central Asia and the Muslim regions of Russia itself. Uzbekistan also offered support for the same reasons that Russia did. Uzbekistan also had a friend in Rashid Dostum, the Uzbek warlord who, allied with Rabbani and Massoud, opposed the Taliban and held onto territory in northern Afghanistan.

Iran also provided significant aid to the Northern Alliance. Its support was based primarily on tensions between the puritanical Sunni Taliban and the Shi'ah theocracy of Iran. Although both Iran and the Taliban espoused Revolutionary Islamism, their understanding of its form differed significantly, and friendly relations were further undermined by Taliban oppression of the Hazari minority, who were Shi'ites like the Iranians. Iran also opposed the consolidation of the Taliban regime for economic reasons: a stable Afghanistan could serve as a conduit for Caspian Sea oil from Russia and Central Asia. Pipelines bringing oil to the West through Afghanistan would necessarily undermine Iranian influence in the region, particularly if the Taliban were the beneficiaries.[50]

Pakistan's offers of support to the region were seen by the international community as disingenuous at worst, puzzling at best. That Pakistan would provide aid and supplies to a region controlled by forces at war with the Taliban did not necessarily indicate a lack of Pakistani support for the Taliban, a political movement to a large extent supported and cultivated by Pakistan's Inter-Services Intelligence (ISI). However, it did indicate that Pakistan's support of the Taliban was not the sole factor in the country's political calculations in the region. The Taliban themselves, nearly at the height of their power in Afghanistan, had "begun to shrug off Pakistan's influence."[51] Although originally a creature of the ISI, by 2001 the Taliban were acting independently of Islamabad.

The Taliban regime seemed at times of two minds concerning its public image in the international community. Despite hostile relations with all its neighbors except Pakistan, the Taliban sought international recognition and hoped for international aid. Mullah Omar, the supreme spiritual leader of the Taliban, and his lieutenants repeatedly declared that they had neither intention nor desire to spread their form of Revolutionary Islamism beyond the borders of Afghanistan. In any case, their first and most pressing priority was to unite all of Afghanistan under Taliban rule. Foreign affairs would be worked out later. Thus the Taliban hoped to assuage Western fears of "fanatical Islam" and to encourage a normal-

---

[50]"Bearers of Gifts," *The Economist*, March 12, 1998.

[51]Ibid.

ization of relations with the West. Yet even in its fifth year of power and with control of more than 90 percent of Afghanistan, the Taliban were recognized as the legitimate government by only three countries: Saudi Arabia, the United Arab Emirates, and Pakistan. Despite their protestations to the contrary, the Taliban had alienated virtually the entire world, including other Muslim states, with their extremist version of Revolutionary Islamism.

The Taliban's initial attempts to project a friendlier face to the outside world were fruitless. In July 2000 the Taliban's leadership issued a *fatwa* (religious ruling) that prohibited the growth of the poppy flower, which is the essential ingredient of opium. Afghanistan's farmers were easily addicted to the poppy, not for its narcotic qualities but because of its tremendous value as a cash crop; in the poorest country in the world, that was sufficient incentive.[52] In 2000 Afghanistan cultivated three-quarters of the world's supply of opium. The United Nations lobbied the Taliban regime to crack down; by July 2000 the Taliban complied quite effectively, in fact. Although the Taliban had itself profited from taxes on the opium trade, systematic cultivation of the poppy crop nevertheless came to a halt in 2001, according to UN sources.[53] The result, however, was a nearly tenfold increase in the value of opium. So long as the demand for opium and heroin remained, the Taliban were able to profit from the opium trade, even as they curtailed production. Moreover, the Taliban's *fatwa* was welcomed in the West but proved insufficient to achieve international recognition for their government.

Other attempts to improve relations with the outside world included talks with Western investors to build pipelines through Afghanistan bringing Caspian Sea oil to the Indian Ocean. By October 2000, however, these attempts to normalize relations collapsed.

Even before 9/11, Osama bin Laden's al-Qaeda terrorist cells had been tied to previous attacks on U.S. targets around the world. Bin Laden, his lieutenants, and his training camps were in Afghanistan. The Taliban refused to turn their "guest" over. In 1998 the United States fired cruise missiles into Afghanistan, hoping to disable bin Laden's network and kill bin Laden himself. The attack produced few tangible results except to increase tensions between the Taliban and the United States. Meanwhile, Taliban support for the rebels in Chechnya alienated the Russians. Similar Taliban support for Revolutionary Islamists in China's Xinjiang province alienated the Chinese. The result was an unusual confluence of U.S., Russian, and Chinese interest in punishing the Taliban. The UN Security Council, dominated by this rare triumvirate, approved new sanctions against Afghanistan— sanctions that included the severing of international air links with Afghanistan and the closing down of Taliban embassies overseas, including the UN office the Taliban maintained in New York.[54] Moreover, this triple alliance against the Taliban began to provide more active support to the Northern Alliance. However,

---

[52]Afghan farmers earn approximately $5,000 per hectare for poppy production. They earn roughly a quarter of that per hectare of wheat (Robert Marquand, "The Reclusive Ruler Who Runs the Taliban," *Christian Science Monitor*, October 10, 2001).

[53]"Afghanistan's Opium Fields," *The Economist*, February 22, 2001.

[54]"The Afghan Iconoclasts," *The Economist*, March 8, 2001.

BOX 10.6 Mullah Muhammad Omar

According to some members of the Taliban, Mullah Muhammad Omar was born in 1959 in Urzugan, a province of Afghanistan. Others claim he was born in the village of Singesar, near Kandahar. His supporters believe he studied Islam in schools outside Afghanistan, most probably in Pakistan. He joined the *jihad* against the Soviet invasion of Afghanistan in the early 1980s as a deputy commander in the Harakat-i-Inqilab-i-Islami party led by Muhammad Nabi Muhammadi. Of all the *mujahideen* factions fighting the Soviets, the Harakat-i-Inqilab was closest in ideology to the future Taliban. During the war, Mullah Omar was wounded four times and lost an eye to shrapnel.

Mullah Omar became leader of the Taliban no later than 1994, when the group first took over Kandahar. His friendship with Osama bin Laden began earlier, during the war against the Soviets. The two maintained close relations while the Taliban governed most of Afghanistan. However, in the late 1990s, Mullah Omar criticized bin Laden and condemned the export of *jihad* to neighboring countries. To some extent, this criticism was for overseas consumption. Even before September 11, 2001, Mullah Omar refused to turn over bin Laden, suspected in the embassy bombings in Africa and the attack on the USS *Cole* in Yemen, to U.S. officials and described the Saudi exile as an "honored guest."

Mullah Omar had never been interviewed by a Western journalist, and few photographs of him are known to exist. He rarely appeared in public and, when the Taliban were in power, lived in Kandahar, rather than Kabul, the capital of Afghanistan. Although some doubted he even existed or considered him a pliant tool of Pakistan's intelligence agency, the Taliban followed the man they called Mullah Omar without question. They called him "Mullah," though he was not a Muslim cleric, and they called him "Commander of the Faithful."

The Taliban followed Mullah Omar's strict interpretation of Islamic law, which they implemented throughout Afghanistan. His edicts included the death penalty for adultery, prostitution, homosexuality, and apostasy. He also supported the repression of women. Women were not allowed to work; they were as much as possible to remain in the home; and if they were to go out, they were to be completely covered in a **burqa.** Women who violated these strictures were summarily flogged in the street.

Mullah Omar first gained widespread attention in the West when he ordered that Afghanistan's ancient Buddha statues be destroyed as idols. Although initially welcomed by many in Afghanistan as the last chance for peace and order, Mullah Omar initiated policies of repression that sapped the Taliban's popularity. Moreover, the Taliban's substantial and influential core of Arab and Pakistani fighters inspired resentment among Afghans. When the U.S.-led bombing campaign began in early October 2001, after Mullah Omar's refusal to turn Osama bin Laden over to the United States for his part in the attacks on the World Trade Center and the Pentagon, his regime quickly crumbled, losing support even among fellow Pashtuns. Despite Mullah Omar's exhortations to the Taliban to "fight to the death" in Kandahar, by December 6, 2001, he was actively negotiating with Pashtun leader Hamid Karzai for the surrender of the city and his own safe passage. When Kandahar, the Taliban's last stronghold, fell a few days later, Mullah Omar quietly escaped but was suspected of being somewhere in the region.

http://www.afghan-web.com/bios/today/momar.html
http://www.deccanherald.com/deccanherald/nov11/f1.htm

that support was late in coming; by the middle of 2001, the Northern Alliance had lost Mazar-e-Sharif and was in desperate straits.

The Taliban's reaction to continued international ostracism was to announce in early 2001, in the name of Islam, that two ancient stone statues of the Buddha were idols and would be destroyed. The international community reacted with horror and outrage. Even Pakistan opposed the Taliban's plans, fearing that destruction of these statues, one of them the largest standing Buddha in the world, would give Islam a reputation for intolerance it did not deserve.[55] Despite international pleas that the statues be spared, the Taliban proceeded with their destruction. On a smaller scale, the Taliban damaged and destroyed precious arti- facts and works of art long stored in a museum in Kabul, again with the excuse that icons, representations of human and animal forms, were incompatible with Islam.[56]

Relations with the outside world grew even more strained by August 2001. The Taliban arrested twenty-four aid workers with Shelter Now International, a German-based Christian aid organization, with attempting to convert Afghan Muslims to Christianity. If convicted of the charge, the aid workers, including two Americans, would be put to death. This too seemed a reaction to mounting inter- national pressure on the Taliban. New UN sanctions were soon to take effect that would prevent arms shipments to the Taliban, although not to the Northern Alliance. For the Taliban, however, this was not to be the worst of it. While there was considerable Western revulsion to the Taliban's treatment of women and destruction of Afghanistan's cultural treasures, Western—particularly American and Russian—animosity was primarily engendered by the Taliban's "aid and com- fort" to "Afghan Arabs" like Osama bin Laden and Ayman Zawahiri. The Taliban's collapse and the failure of their particular brand of political Islam in Afghanistan were inextricably tied to their closeness with al-Qaeda and its leaders. That close- ness was partly the result of the Taliban's isolation from the rest of the world and partly the result of the Taliban's Revolutionary Islamism, which was shared by bin Laden and Zawahiri.

The Afghan Arabs: With Friends like These

During the 1980s and early 1990s, Arab volunteers arrived in Afghanistan to assist the Afghan *mujahideen* in their *jihad* against the Soviets and the Communist gov- ernment of Kabul. Saudi Arabia,[57] other Muslim countries, and the United States

---

[55]Ibid. See also Marquand, "The Reclusive Ruler Who Runs the Taliban."

[56]"Afghanistan's Art: Missing," *The Economist,* December 22, 2001.

[57]Saudi support for the *mujahideen* was well documented during the war against the Soviets in Afghanistan. Saudi Arabia also provided modest support to the Taliban regime, whose strict interpre- tation of *shariah* law counts as its forebear the strict Wahhabi form of Islam that is the official religion and sect of Saudi Arabia. In the 1990s, the Saudis turned a blind eye toward those thousands of young Saudi recruits that became *jihadis* in conflicts around the world or joined Osama bin Laden's al-Qaeda network. See Douglas Jehl, "Holy War Lured Saudis as Rulers Looked Away," *New York Times International*, December 27, 2001.

supported these Arab volunteers. Osama bin Laden's activities were encouraged, even those that had less to do with fighting the Soviets in Afghanistan. With complicit support from the United States, bin Laden established recruitment centers in over fifty countries to find volunteers to fight a *jihad*—a *jihad* that bin Laden did not define as strictly against the Soviet Union.[58] Of course, U.S. support for these activities made perfect sense during the Cold War, but these volunteers were inclined politically to more extreme versions of Revolutionary Islamism than even the Afghans were. When the Najibullah government fell in 1992 and the *mujahideen* commanders began fighting among themselves, the Arab volunteers moved on. Nevertheless, the withdrawal of the Soviets made the Afghan Arabs feel nearly invincible. They had, after all, defeated the Soviet Union; shortly after, the USSR ceased to exist. Drawing conclusions out of context, bin Laden himself believed that "the myth of the superpower was destroyed."[59] Without any perception that other events had been no less responsible for the demise of the Soviet Union, bin Laden noted, "Allah defeated them. They became non-existent. There is a lesson to learn from this. . . . We now predict . . . the end of the United States."[60] Bin Laden and his followers in al-Qaeda perpetuated two myths—first, that the Afghan Arab volunteers had contributed significantly to the defeat of the Soviets, a contention that many Afghans considered ludicrous; and second, that the United States, like the Soviet Union before it, could be destroyed by men like bin Laden and organizations like al-Qaeda. Many of the Afghan Arab *"jihadis,"* meanwhile, continued their fight elsewhere in the world, in Chechnya, Azerbaijan, Kashmir, China, and Central Asia.[61] Bin Laden himself was also active, heading to Sudan. He was involved in Somalia in the early 1990s, where attacks on U.S. soldiers abruptly ended the American humanitarian mission in that country. Again, he drew dangerous conclusions about the U.S. withdrawal from Somalia, declaring, "American soldiers are paper tigers. After a few blows, they ran in defeat."[62]

When the Taliban came to power, however, foreign volunteers, both Arab and Pakistani, returned. Bin Laden himself, expelled from the Sudan, took up residence in Afghanistan again in 1996 and set up new training camps for thousands of *jihadis* and al-Qaeda operatives. The intimacy between bin Laden and the Taliban was greater than ever. Arab and Pakistani soldiers added a new dimension to the conflict in Afghanistan. They were recognized as foreigners, and *mujahideen* commanders like Massoud resented their interference in what was now Afghanistan's civil war. But, unlike the *mujahideen* in the war with the

---

[58]Robin Wright, *Sacred Rage: The Wrath of Militant Islam* (New York: Simon and Schuster, 2001), p. 249.

[59]Ibid., p. 250.

[60]Ibid., p. 257.

[61]These *jihadis* were not necessarily under the control of bin Laden or even part of al-Qaeda. In Chechnya, for example, bin Laden supplied tactical support and military aid to the most militant of the Chechen rebels; he did not, however, supervise their operations or act as their leader. See "The Spider in the Web," *The Economist*, September 22, 2001.

[62]Wright, p. 254.

■

BOX 10.7   Osama bin Laden

Osama bin Laden was born in Saudi Arabia in 1957 to a Yemenite father and a Syrian mother. His father was an extremely successful businessman, a personal friend of Saudi king Faisal and a cabinet minister for the Saudi royal family. His father's business was construction; during his youth, bin Laden worked for his father as a laborer and attended King Abdul Aziz University in Jedda. In 1979 bin Laden graduated with a degree in civil engineering.

In the 1980s, bin Laden traveled to Afghanistan to fight with the *mujahideen*. His contribution to the *jihad* in Afghanistan was less as a warrior than as a wealthy benefactor and builder. However, as the war progressed, bin Laden commanded thousands of battle-hardened soldiers, mostly Arabs who had come to Afghanistan, as he had, to wage *jihad* against the Soviets.

In 1988 bin Laden founded al-Qaeda but returned to Saudi Arabia the next year. When Iraq invaded Kuwait in 1990, bin Laden encouraged the Saudis to repulse the Iraqis by activating the Arab veterans of the war in Afghanistan and to embark on a new *jihad* against Saddam Hussein. The Saudis preferred to enlist U.S. support. During the Gulf War in 1991, bin Laden was incensed that U.S. soldiers were stationed in Saudi Arabia; he considered this an occupation force of infidels who were defiling Muslim holy sites and protecting the corrupt Saudi royal family from overthrow. Bin Laden's opposition, and his ties to subversive political groups, angered the Saudi government. Bin Laden escaped to the Sudan. In 1994 the Saudi government stripped bin Laden of his citizenship. By 1996 Sudanese authorities buckled to U.S. pressure and asked bin Laden to leave the country. He returned to Afghanistan and settled in Jalalabad. In 1997 bin Laden survived several assassination attempts; he moved to the mountains and built several underground caves. In the meantime, he had built a strong relationship with the Taliban, particularly with their supreme leader, Mullah Muhammad Omar. Their friendship sealed, bin Laden relocated to a camp outside Kandahar, the de facto capital of Afghanistan. Bin Laden actively supported the Taliban's fight against the Northern Alliance, supplying loyal Arab-Afghan troops, supplies, and training.

In 1998 Ayman al-Zawahiri joined bin Laden and merged his organization, Islamic Jihad, with al-Qaeda. The umbrella organization, led by bin Laden, was called the "World Islamic Front for the Struggle against the Jews and the Crusaders." He and Zawahiri issued a *fatwa* (religious decree) demanding that Muslims everywhere are obligated to kill Americans on sight. Al-Qaeda then embarked on the terrorist attacks on U.S. embassies in Africa. The success of these attacks, and al-Qaeda's links to them, resulted in U.S. cruise missile attacks on suspected al-Qaeda training camps. The Taliban continued to protect bin Laden, even while the United Nations imposed strict sanctions on the impoverished country.

Following the September 11, 2001, attacks on the World Trade Center and the Pentagon, the United States put a $25 million price on bin Laden's head. When the bombing campaign began in Afghanistan, bin Laden released a videotape denouncing the United States. However, as the Taliban were thrown out of power, bin Laden fled with his troops to Tora Bora. U.S. warplanes relentlessly bombed the site, and Northern

(Continued)

> ## Osama bin Laden   *(Continued)*
>
> Alliance troops forced al-Qaeda soldiers to surrender. However, there was no sign of bin Laden. Rumors circulated that he was in Pakistan or was with Mullah Omar hiding in the Kandahar region. As of this writing, whether he is dead or alive no one is sure.
>
> http://www.top-biography.com/9007-Osama%20Bin%20Laden/
> http://www.pbs.org/wgbh/pages/frontline/shows/binladen/who/bio.html
> http://www.infoplease.com/spot/osamabinladen.html
> http://users.skynet.be/terrorism/html/laden.htm
> http://www.adl.org/terrorism_america/bin_l.asp
> http://abcnews.go.com/sections/world/DailyNews/binladen_profile.html

Soviets, the Taliban relied heavily on these fighters and their leaders, like bin Laden and his lieutenant, Ayman Zawahiri. Nevertheless, many Afghans sympathetic to the Taliban deeply resented the Afghan Arabs, who, on occasion, mistreated the local Taliban, ordering them around and generally being abusive.[63] Moreover, their presence in 1999 and 2000 became increasingly obvious. One Pakistani journalist noted that the Afghan Arabs "are seen on the streets, in the restaurants, everywhere."[64] And although Mullah Omar initially condemned bin Laden's attempts to "export *jihad*," Zawahiri, who took up residence near Omar, strongly influenced the Taliban's supreme leader and helped maintain Omar's support for and dependence upon bin Laden personally and al-Qaeda operations in general.

The Taliban's continual conflict with the Northern Alliance and their inability to conquer the remaining 5 to 10 percent of Afghanistan's territory sapped support among Afghans tired of turning their sons over to the Taliban to fight endless *jihads*. The paucity of willing recruits forced the Taliban to rely even more heavily on Arab Afghan fighters.[65] By 2001 Western intelligence sources estimated that 25 to 50 percent of the Taliban's force was not Afghan but Arab and Pakistani.[66] Bin Laden had established numerous redoubts in the mountains in eastern Afghanistan and had thousands of Arab soldiers at his disposal. By the summer of 2001, bin Laden's forces increasingly dominated the war against the Northern Alliance. Bin Laden's financial resources were also useful in bribing commanders to defect to the Taliban. Furthermore, bin Laden sent assassins on their success-

---

[63]Marquand, "The Reclusive Ruler Who Runs the Taliban." See also "Honoured Guest," *The Economist*, September 22, 2001.

[64]Ibid.

[65]Ibid.

[66]Edward Girardet, "A More Dangerous Afghanistan," *Christian Science Monitor*, September 20, 2001.

■

BOX 10.8 Ayman Al-Zawahiri

Born in Egypt to a well-educated upper-class family in 1951, Ayman al-Zawahiri was a precocious and deeply religious child. Zawahiri's education was modern, though he was involved early on in Revolutionary Islamist politics. After graduating from medical school, Zawahiri spent time in Afghanistan as a surgeon.

In 1981, Zawahiri was back in Egypt, actively opposing Egyptian President Muhammad Anwar al-Sadat, who had made peace with Israel. Zawahiri founded Islamic Jihad and played a role, however small, in the assassination of Sadat on October 6, 1981. After the assassination, Revolutionary Islamists were arrested and tried. Zawahiri was caught up in a second wave of arrests but was acquitted of conspiracy to murder Sadat. However, he was found guilty on an unrelated weapons charge and spent three years in prison.

While in prison, Zawahiri's charisma, plus his fluency in English, made him a natural spokesman for other imprisoned Revolutionary Islamists. By the time Zawahiri was released from prison, he had already become a prominent leader of the Revolutionary Islamist opposition to the Egyptian government. He left Egypt in 1985 and lived in Afghanistan and Pakistan, where he continued his efforts in the *jihad* against the Soviets. It was at this time that Zawahiri first met Osama bin Laden, who, like Zawahiri, had abandoned a life of privilege for war in the mountains. While in Afghanistan, Zawahiri also reestablished Islamic Jihad, an originally Egyptian Revolutionay Islamic organization. Zawahiri traveled abroad to raise funds and recruit members, venturing even to California in 1995.

In 1998 Zawahiri merged his organization with bin Laden's al-Qaeda network. The combined organization was given the name *World Islamic Front for the Struggle against the Jews and the Crusaders*. Zawahiri and bin Laden signed a *fatwa* (religious declaration) stating: "The judgement to kill and fight Americans and their allies, whether civilian or military, is an obligation for every Muslim." These words were given greater meaning when the U.S. embassies in Kenya and Tanzania were bombed. The United States indicted both Zawahiri and bin Laden for those attacks. Despite cruise missile attacks on suspected al-Qaeda training camps in Afghanistan, the United States made no concerted effort to capture or kill either Zawahiri or bin Laden. Experts agreed that Zawahiri was probably the mastermind of those attacks and of several to follow.

The attacks on the World Trade Center and Pentagon in September 2001 inspired renewed interest in the United States to find and capture or kill Zawahiri. After the U.S.-led bombing campaign began, Zawahiri appeared in two videos with Osama bin Laden angrily denouncing the United States. Since the Taliban's fall in December 2001, Zawahiri has not been heard from.

ful mission to murder Massoud, whose elimination was a huge boost to Taliban morale and a devastating blow to the leadership of the Northern Alliance. Bin Laden always found ways to make himself indispensable to the Taliban, and after the attacks on September 11, his indispensability cost the Taliban dearly.

The Fall of the Taliban

On September 11, 2001, al-Qaeda operatives hijacked four U.S. commercial jets. Two of those jets destroyed the twin towers of the World Trade Center in New York City, killing thousands. A third jet was flown into the Pentagon in Washington, D.C., killing several hundred. The fourth airliner crashed in Pennsylvania; the passengers had discovered what the hijackers were up to and prevented them from carrying out their mission. There was never much doubt in the West that Osama bin Laden was responsible. The immediate economic repercussions looked severe but proved short-lived; the U.S. recession had in fact begun in March 2001, and by January 2002, the stock market recovered ground it had lost since September. The primary goal of the attacks, as bin Laden later described it, was to undermine the U.S. economy and bring down the last superpower by striking at its "economic" heart. The attempt was insufficient, and the goal itself unrealistic, based as it was on bin Laden's surprisingly naïve view of the sources of American power, a power which was not contained in a single wing of the Pentagon or found in two 110-story buildings in Manhattan. These were but symbols of American power, and the attacks on these symbols profoundly impacted the American pscyhe. The Bush administration, resisting the urge many Americans felt to lash out immediately, began careful preparations to destroy bin Laden and al-Qaeda, goals that were, comparatively speaking, far more feasible than any of bin Laden's own. The difficulty for the Bush administration was, of course, that the attacks did not have a "return address." There was no specific nation against which to turn U.S. wrath. However, the Taliban's inexplicable desire to play host to bin Laden, even after the attacks, provided sufficient evidence for the United States to go to war with the Taliban. In October the United States began bombing; by December, the Taliban ceased to function as a government.

Although he initially denied direct involvement in the attacks, bin Laden and his al-Qaeda network were already wanted by the international community for staging previous attacks. September 11 fit their methods perfectly, and bin Laden himself had crowed just before the attacks of "an unprecedented 'action' against the United States."[67] The Bush administration, meanwhile, needed little convincing of bin Laden's role. If his goal was to attack U.S. targets, al-Qaeda was sufficiently organized to fulfill that goal. The Bush administration immediately referred to the events of September 11 as "acts of war" and, in statements directed primarily at the Taliban leadership, declared that the United States would "make no distinction between the terrorists who commited these acts and those who harbor them." This statement was also a warning to other countries, among them Iraq, Iran, Syria, Pakistan, Yemen, Saudi Arabia, Somalia, and Sudan, just to name a few, that terrorist activities tied to organizations operating out of their countries would invite U.S. military attack.

---

[67]"Who Did It?" *The Economist,* September 13, 2001.

The United States demanded that the Taliban turn Bin Laden and the other leaders of al-Qaeda over. Mullah Omar, in what was the beginning of amazingly bad judgment on the part of the Taliban leadership, called for "negotiations" while declaring that the United States was just looking for an excuse to eliminate his regime. Nevertheless, the Taliban made conciliatory gestures, convening an assembly of senior clerics to determine whether bin Laden should be turned over. Although the assembly finally decided that the Taliban government should persuade bin Laden to leave Afghanistan of his own accord, there would be no extradition. The United States rejected this solution out of hand. In the meantime, Afghans began to pour out of their country into Pakistan, fearing U.S. attacks on Afghanistan and expecting casualties on the scale inflicted by the Soviet Union twenty years prior. The Taliban's behavior during this crucial period is bewildering. Their refusal guaranteed U.S. military action against their country. Of course some believed the myth of a weakling America, whose soldiers were "paper tigers." Others realized the extent to which bin Laden had become a power in his own right in Afghanistan, perhaps even the real power behind the Taliban.

Nearly two weeks after the attacks on the United States, international diplomatic isolation of the Taliban was nearly complete. On September 22, the United Arab Emirates cut its diplomatic ties to the Taliban regime. Three days later, the Saudis followed suit. By the end of December, the only country in the world to maintain diplomatic relations with the Taliban was Pakistan. And even Pakistan took the side of the United States. Pakistani president Pervez Musharraf, who had come to power two years before in a military coup against the civilian government, had committed his country to supporting the United States and its allies, permitting even the use of its territory and airspace for possible attacks on the Taliban. In the last days of September, the United States received the support of the European Union in what was becoming known as the "war against terror." Japan followed suit. NATO had already invoked Article 5 of its charter, in which the attack on the United States was considered an attack on all NATO countries. There was no direct NATO involvement in the war; the United States and Britain were to handle the war themselves, with only logistical support from European and Asian allies. Iran, meanwhile, offered no real support and made public statements critical of the coalition but essentially acquiesced to the inevitable.[68]

In the meantime, the U.S.-led coalition had built an impressive military presence in the region.[69] U.S. and British special forces were already rumored to be

---

[68]When the bombing began on October 7, Iran declared the U.S. campaign "unacceptable" but did not reject the possibility of global cooperation against terrorism. The possibility of the Taliban's destruction did not displease Iran; its negative comments regarding U.S. air strikes seemed more like an instinctive reaction to all things American rather than true opposition. The U.S. success against the Taliban would solve several problems for Iran, especially the refugee crisis on its borders with Afghanistan. See "Saying One Thing, Meaning Another," *The Economist,* October 11, 2001.

[69]By the first days of October, more than fifty thousand U.S. and British soldiers were in the region, along with nearly five hundred aircraft, three aircraft carrier battle groups, and two U.S. carriers on the way. See "Paving the Way," *The Economist,* October 3, 2001.

inside Afghanistan, presumably working with the Northern Alliance. With Russian permission, several former Soviet republics, including Uzbekistan, Tajikistan, and Turkmenistan, all bordering Afghanistan, permitted U.S. and British use of their bases.[70] Although Russia declined to join the coalition as a military partner, it promised to increase aid to the Northern Alliance, which was to do the real fighting on the ground with coalition air cover. Russia's cooperation was not absolutely vital to the operation; but Russia embraced the opportunity to be rid of the troublesome Taliban, to secure the borders of its Central Asian "clients," and to persuade the United States that its brutal war against Revolutionary Islamists in Chechnya was both appropriate and necessary. Russian claims that the Chechen rebels were supported by bin Laden and al-Qaeda were now readily accepted by the United States and its allies.[71] Russian President Vladimir Putin required little evidence of bin Laden's direct involvement in the September 11 attacks, declaring that he recognized bin Laden's "signature."

The Taliban maintained its refusal to turn over bin Laden and was defiant in the face of imminent attack by the United States. Mullah Omar continued to send mix signals. He backed the decree issued by an assembly of clerics asking bin Laden to leave Afghanistan of his own free will. However, the Taliban said they could not find bin Laden in order to deliver this important message. At the same time, the Taliban claimed to have raised more than a quarter million troops to fight a *jihad* against the United States. Although it was impossible to gauge support for the Taliban regime within Afghanistan itself, anti-American protests around the Muslim world demonstrated a feeling of solidarity with the Taliban in the face of U.S. "aggression." Pakistan's Musharraf had his hands full containing the anger of his own citizens at the prospect of U.S. attacks on Afghanistan launched from their own country. Bin Laden himself released a statement in which he urged Pakistanis to help Afghanistan resist any attack undertaken by the United States. In using Uzbekistan as a forward base, the United States recognized that the political situation in Pakistan was potentially unstable. U.S. operations carried out from Pakistan might inspire nationwide demonstrations that could destabilize the Musharraf regime and ultimately replace it with a government much less pliable.

The Taliban's last chance to avert U.S. military action came on September 28. A delegation of clerics and government officials from Pakistan visited Kandahar to persuade the Taliban to turn over bin Laden to the United States. Although they had claimed previously to have lost contact with bin Laden, the Taliban now admitted that they had delivered to the al-Qaeda leader a message asking him to

---

[70]The Russian media reported that U.S. transports were landing in Uzbekistan within days of September 11. Uzbekistan's autocratic president, Islam Karimov, was eager to offer the United States whatever it asked for in exchange for the possibility that the Taliban would be eliminated. See "Paving the Way." Karimov's government was facing internal insurgency framed in Revolutionary Islamism, presumably supported by bin Laden and the Taliban. The opportunity to eliminate that threat was too good for Karimov to pass up, even in the face of initial Russian opposition to the hosting of U.S. forces in Central Asia.

[71]"Paving the Way."

leave. Beyond that, the Taliban were unwilling to go. Pakistan's final attempt to prevent its erstwhile clients, the Taliban, from a suicidal confrontation with the United States came to the nothing. British prime minister Tony Blair made a final plea a few days later, explaining that the Taliban had a stark choice, to "surrender the terrorists, or surrender power."[72] The Taliban chose the latter.

On October 7, the U.S. air campaign began against the Taliban. The Bush administration attempted to cast the conflict as a war against terrorists, not against the Afghan people, nor against Islam, nor against the Muslim world. Bush himself characterized the Taliban and al-Qaeda as "barbaric criminals who profane a great religion by committing murder in its name."[73] Bin Laden likewise had choice words for the Americans. In a videotape broadcast on October 7, bin Laden ran through his usual denunciations of the West and of the United States, boasted of American "fear" after the terrorist attacks of September 11, and asked all Muslims to undertake a *jihad* against the United States. The overwhelming response in the Muslim world was tepid support at best and a growing realization that bin Laden was most likely behind the previous month's attacks. The Taliban's insistence that the United States supply them with evidence of bin Laden's guilt was tempered by Pakistan's insistence that the evidence it had seen was sufficient to justify an indictment.

The Northern Alliance greeted U.S. intervention in Afghanistan with delight. With U.S. bombers pounding Taliban positions in the field, Northern Alliance commanders felt certain they could roll back the Taliban's advances. Rashid Dostum's Uzbek militia was determined to retake Mazar-e-Sharif, a strategic city that would open the road to Uzbekistan and ease the entry of U.S. and British troops. The successful capture of Mazar-e-Sharif would also demonstrate the Taliban's vulnerability and might inspire regional leaders to defect to the Northern Alliance.

The initial weeks of the bombing campaign showed little evidence of progress. While the United States and Britain bombed Taliban targets in Afghanistan, including Kandahar, where the Taliban leadership operated, Russia busily supplied convoys of material to the Northern Alliance, including ammunition, rifles, and surface-to-air missiles. A little more than a week after the bombing campaign began, the U.S. military insisted that the "combat power of the Taliban has been eviscerated." Such statements were contradicted by the Taliban's continued defiance. Mullah Omar promised that the Taliban would ultimately defeat the "infidel," meaning presumably the United States. Meanwhile, a former *mujahideen* commander, Abdul Haq, who had gone into Afghanistan to persuade Pashtun tribal leaders to turn against the Taliban, was captured and executed. Nor was the Northern Alliance making any progress. Its attempt to take Mazar-e-Sharif had foundered, and Northern Alliance commanders on the ground complained that U.S. bombing was inaccurate or insufficiently intense and had the effect of raising the morale of Taliban troops. The only good news the United States had was in

---

[72] Ibid.

[73] "America Strikes Back," *The Economist,* October 7, 2001.

Pakistan. Demonstrations in Pakistan had been large but were not a threat to the government of President Musharraf. Nevertheless, Musharraf and the Pakistani military urged the United States to keep the campaign as brief as possible, perhaps stopping during the month of Ramadan, which would begin on November 17.

After a full month of bombing and little to show for it, the United States decided not to stop bombing during Ramadan, or over the Afghan winter. However, the United States did not want the war to last any longer than its allies in the Muslim world did. As U.S. Defense Secretary Donald Rumsfeld said, "We will take the least possible time." How long the "least possible time" might be was anybody's guess. The Taliban were bracing for intense fighting against what they presumed would be the introduction of U.S. ground troops into the war, much as the Soviets had invaded in 1979. But this was not the U.S. strategy. U.S. Special Forces were on the ground in Afghanistan with Northern Alliance troops, but only to direct more accurate bombing on Taliban positions. But the U.S. decision not to introduce massive numbers of ground troops initially heartened the Taliban; one Taliban official declared, "If they have the strength and if their soldiers are not men used to a soft life, why are they not fighting face-to-face?"[74] Afghan refugees recently arrived from Kabul, and other cities in Afghanistan described the arrival of large numbers of Arab and Pakistani fighters.[75] Moreover, the Taliban claimed that, while civilian casualties were high, U.S. bombing had killed few of their soldiers.

Throughout the months of November and December, the United States, despite an expressed distaste for "nation building" began the process of finding a new government to ultimately replace the Taliban. Two options faced the United States, either to support the reinstallation of Burhanuddin Rabbani's government or to establish a new government under Afghanistan's former king, Zahir Shah. Neither option was particularly palatable. Although Rabbani had behind him the Northern Alliance, the mismanagement and fractiousness of Rabanni's government in the mid-1990s had made the rise of the Taliban possible in the first place. Moreover, Rabbani was an ethnic Tajik and thus unacceptable to Afghanistan's Pashtun majority. Zahir Shah, who was Pashtun, had been living in exile in Italy for nearly thirty years and lacked troops or territory. Nevertheless, Zahir Shah represented the best hope for a stable future government after the Taliban were defeated. Both Russia and Iran seemed to prefer a continuation of the Rabbani regime, but Pakistan opposed this, hoping that a broad-based government, which should include repentant and moderate Taliban leaders, would be established.

The United States also preferred the establishment of a new, broad-based government with Pashtun representation, but without a place for the Taliban, whom they expected to defeat in the battlefield. However, relying strictly on Zahir Shah was untenable. The United States began to fish around for possible anti-Taliban Pashtun leaders. They found one quickly in Hamid Karzai, a tribal leader

---

[74]"Escalation," *The Economist,* November 7, 2001.

[75]Ibid.

who had close ties to Zahir Shah but who enjoyed support within Afghanistan. By mid-November the search for a new interim government took on greater urgency. On November 9, with the help of more aggressive and more accurate U.S. bombing of Taliban front-line positions, Mazar-e-Sharif fell to the Northern Alliance. Northern Alliance advances thereafter occurred with great speed, far faster than anyone, including the United States, expected. On November 11, the Alliance captured the city of Taloqan. The next day, they took the city of Heart and expanded their control of Afghan territory to approximately 40 percent. The capture of Kabul, which was imminent, would give the alliance control of over half the country and an important psychological victory as well. The fall of Mazar-e-Sharif had done precisely what the United States and the Northern Alliance had hoped; after their decisive defeat in Mazar-e-Sharif, the Taliban's resistance throughout Afghanistan simply collapsed, revealing both their military weakness and widespread unpopularity. By November 13 the Northern Alliance was in Kabul, after the Taliban quit the city without a fight. Crowds of jubilant city residents came out to greet the alliance fighters. Music, banned by the Taliban, was heard throughout the city, and men began to shave their beards. Although some in Kabul were wary of the return of the *mujahideen,* Kabul's Pashtun, Tajik, and Hazari populations nevertheless greeted the removal of the Taliban as a positive development.

In a period of four days, with U.S. bombers at their disposal, the alliance "recaptured territory that it took the Taliban four years, from 1994 to 1998, to conquer from them."[76] Essentially, the Northern Alliance had routed the Taliban from the northern half of Afghanistan, although small pockets of Taliban fighters remained in the region. In the south, meanwhile, hostile Pashtun tribes, with leaders like Hamid Karzai, rose against the Taliban and fought them for control of parts of Kandahar, the Taliban's stronghold. Mass defections of Taliban fighters also undermined their control. Local warlords in the east and south were also wresting control of territory from the Taliban; some estimated that the Taliban's writ extended to no more than a fifth of the country. With the end of the Taliban in sight, the United States redoubled its efforts to establish an effective interim government that might enjoy widespread support in Afghanistan. Without that government in place, the United States could not meet its objectives of dismantling al-Qaeda, eliminating bin Laden, and bringing an end to the lawlessness and bloodshed that made Afghanistan a source of terrorist activity.

Despite their sudden losses of territory, the Taliban remained defiant. In an interview, Mullah Omar expressed his hope that the Taliban would regain the territory they had lost but said that these events were inconsequential in comparison to the ultimate outcome of the conflict, which he described as the "destruction of America." With few exceptions, however, organized Taliban resistance had ceased.

On November 27, the United Nations convened a conference on Afghanistan in Bonn, Germany. Four groups were represented: the Northern

---

[76]"The Fall of Kabul," *The Economist,* November 13, 2001.

■

BOX 10.9 Hamid Karzai and Afghanistan's Interim Government

In December 2001, representatives of the various forces fighting the Taliban met in Bonn, Germany, to work out power sharing in a post-Taliban government. Under United Nations auspices and with substantial prodding from the United States and its allies, the Bonn agreement established a new interim government.

Hamid Karzai, an ethnic Pashtun, was selected as the new government's leader. Karzai, a traditional tribal chief from Kandahar, first rose to prominence while a member of the *mujahideen* during the war against the Soviet Union. Karzai was the son of the tribal leader of one of the largest Pashtun tribes, the Popolzai. Karzai's family had ties to the family of Zahir Shah, and Kharzai is known for monarchist tendencies.

After the fall of the Najibullah government, Karzai joined the interim government of Burhanuddin Rabbani in 1992 as deputy foreign minister. However, Karzai was disillusioned by the internal divisions of the *mujahideen*. When the Taliban emerged in 1994, he initially supported them, though he was a moderate and Modernist Islamist with little fondness for Revolutionary Islamism. Karzai, like many Afghans, hoped the Taliban might bring order and peace to Afghanistan. As the Taliban became more powerful, Karzai began to suspect that they were tools of Pakistan. The Taliban tried to court Karzai, offering him the post of UN ambassador. Karzai refused and went into exile in 1996.

In 1999, Karzai's father was assassinated, allegedly by agents of the Taliban. In spite of great danger to himself, Karzai returned to Afghanistan to bury his father. Now the leader of the Popolzai tribe, Karzai slipped back across the border to Pakistan. When the U.S.-led bombing campaign began in October 2001, Karzai supported it fully and reentered Afghanistan. By December 2001, he was commanding troops attempting to expel the Taliban from Kandahar. Just as the Taliban were negotiating the terms of their surrender with him, Karzai was named chair of the interim government.

Hamid Karzai's cabinet includes:

Muhammad Fahim, defense minister, Tajik. Fahim was deputy to Ahmed Shah Massoud. When Massoud was assassinated, Fahim became the leader of Massoud's forces.

Abdullah Abdullah, foreign minister, Tajik. During the U.S.-led bombing campaign, Abdullah became a familiar face to Westerners thanks to his fluency in English. Abdullah served the Rabbani government and took part in the Bonn negotiations.

Yunus Qanooni, interior minister, Tajik. Qanooni was a close aide to Massoud and was head of the Northern Alliance delegation in Bonn.

Sima Samar, minister of women's affairs, Hazara. Samar, a doctor by training, has lived in exile in Pakistan since 1984. There she managed schools and clinics for women in both Afghanistan and Pakistan.

Hedyat Amin Arsala, Finance Minister, Pashtun. Arsala served as foreign minister in the *mujahideen* government in 1992.

Almost immediately after his inauguration, Karzai made an addition to his cabinet by appointing Rashid Dostum, the powerful Uzbek warlord who had been criticizing the new government, as deputy defense minister.

http://www.afghan-info.com/Politics/Hamid_Karzai_Profile.htm
http://www.pbs.org/newshour/bb/asia/afghanistan/karzai.html
http://ap.tbo.com/ap/breaking/MGAZJKH2VUC.html
http://www.washingtonpost.com/wp-srv/nation/graphics/attack/zone_30.html
http://cgi.citizen-times.com/cgi-bin/story/united/2520

Alliance, the "Rome process" (which represented Zahir Shah), the "Cyprus process" (representing Afghan intellectuals and politicians living in exile), and the "Peshawar convention" (representing primarily moderate members of the seven-party *mujahideen* government that took power in 1992). Each faction had its supporters in the international community. Russia, India, Uzbekistan, and Tajikistan backed the Northern Alliance. Iran supported elements within both the Cyprus process and the Peshawar convention. Pakistan, meanwhile, was willing to support any faction in opposition to the Northern Alliance. The talks in Bonn moved, like the collapse of the Taliban, with surprising speed. Agreement was quickly reached that an interim executive council of thirty people would be established to govern Afghanistan. After six months, this executive council would convene a grand council, or *loya jirga,* to create a transitional regime that would hold power another eighteen to thirty-six months until regular elections could be held. Significant pressures from Western states facilitated concessions and compromises among the four groups in the Bonn talks. Without Western support the talks could not hope to succeed, and the West threatened to withhold the aid vitally needed in Afghanistan if a broad-based government were not established.

The four groups also agreed to the presence of foreign peacekeepers in Kabul, despite initial resistance from the Northern Alliance. The final issues to be covered included the allocation of seats and portfolios in the cabinet of the new interim government. On December 5, the conference selected Pashtun tribal leader Hamid Karzai, who was busy negotiating the surrender of the Taliban in Kandahar at the time, as chair of the executive council. His ministers were divided among the ethnic groups. The representatives of the Northern Alliance in Bonn acted independently of their leader, Burhanuddin Rabbani, and secured key cabinet seats for themselves in the executive council. For once, the divisions and factionalism within the Northern Alliance proved useful to the establishment of a relatively broad-based government. Rabbani's initial objections were ignored; his own ministers transferred their loyalty from Rabbani to the council under Karzai, and Rabbani could do nothing about it. In any case, Rabbani at last acceded to the inevitable and relinquished power with surprising graciousness.

Following the fall of Kandahar and the reduction of Taliban resistance to mere scattered pockets, Karzai was inaugurated as chairman on December 22 and was publicly embraced by outgoing President Rabbani. Karzai also invited Uzbek warlord Rashid Dostum into the executive council, as a sign of Karzai's commitment to power sharing and national reconciliation. Within weeks of his inauguration, Karzai released tens of thousands of Taliban fighters, allowing them to return home. Karzai explained, "They were not responsible for anything. They are just common soldiers." He had no such words of reconciliation for Mullah Omar or Osama bin Laden, promising to hunt them down, capture them, and turn them over to the United States.

By early January, scattered pockets of Taliban and al-Qaeda resistance remained in Afghanistan. Moreover, in portions of Afghanistan, lawlessness and banditry replaced the law and order that the Taliban had imposed. Such conditions had made the Taliban seem like a positive alternative in 1996. The job before Hamid Karzai and the executive council was to avoid the mistakes of the past, to restore order to Afghanistan, to legitimize the authority of the interim government, to eliminate remaining Taliban resistance, and to provide food, shelter, and security to a people long deprived of basic necessities. International aid for national reconstruction is a crucial component of Karzai's task, without which he cannot hope to succeed.

Conclusion

Before the Soviet invasion in 1979, Afghanistan was among the world's poorest countries in terms of such indicators as income, health care, and education. After twenty years of warfare, the situation had worsened; Afghanistan's agricultural base had been devastated by three years of drought. The country's infrastructure was in ruins. The most highly educated Afghans had left the country years before. And warlordism and lawlessness were rampant. Today, starvation in Afghanistan is as great a threat as it has ever been; law and order needs to be restored to the countryside, civil institutions (including a working government) need to be reestablished, and massive amounts of food aid are required to stave off a humanitarian catastrophe. Nation building does not begin to describe the financial cost and level of commitment required of the world community to redeem Afghanistan from more than twenty years of warfare.

In this environment of destruction, poverty, and human tragedy, it seems foolish to talk of Islamism or the various manifestations of Islamism as a topic of serious concern to Afghans. Whether or not the *shariah* is implemented as the law of the land is of precious little relevance to families that have nothing to eat and nowhere to live. Even in relatively more prosperous times, the average Afghan never demanded Revolutionary Islam. Islamism, in any of its forms, was seldom more than an idiom of dissent or a defense of traditional and conservative mores in the countryside, mores that sometimes even *contradicted* Islamic law. A careful observation of Afghanistan's history in the last two hundred years has potent predictive value, but Western policy makers focused their attentions on the Cold War

---

BOX 10.10   Blowback!

Chalmers Johnson, a former U.S. naval officer stationed in Japan, the president of the Japan Policy Research Institute, and author of several books—has written *Blowback: The Costs and Consequences of American Empire*. *Blowback* is a term that the CIA invented to refer to the unintended consequences of U.S. policies overseas that were in many cases kept secret from the American public. In this thought-provoking book, Johnson lays out the dangers facing the American "global empire" and "economic colonialism" if it insists on projecting its military, political, economic, and cultural power all over the world based on its hegemonic self-interests (including our so-called mission to protect the "free world"). Brazenly expanding our defense budget, encouraging our multinational corporations, and imposing harsh IMF conditions on developing countries (like Indonesia), we are fueling an "anti-globalization time bomb," Johnson argues, that could explode in the future with severe consequences for the United States, Americans, and U.S. interests. Examples of blowback abound. The United States' support of Chiang Kai-shek and then our strong opposition to Mao Zedong and the People's Republic of China (PRC) from 1949 to 1971 contributed to the Korean War (1950–1953) and later to our quagmire in Southeast Asia. The overthrow of Iran's prime minister Mossadegh and return of Muhammad Reza Shah Pahlavi to the Peacock Throne in 1953 made the Iranian Revolution and the rise of Ayatollah Ruhollah Khomeini's theocratic and anti-American regime possible. Plots to overthrow and assassinate Fidel Castro contributed to John F. Kennedy's assassination. Expanding the Vietnam War into Cambodia resulted in the rise of Pol Pot and the holocaust in Kampuchea from 1975 to 1979; support for the Afghan *mujahideen* and Afghan Arabs, whom the United States trained to expel the Soviet invaders, contributed to the rise of the Revolutionary Islamist Taliban in Afghanistan and al-Qaeda's terrorist campaign against U.S. interests, including the September 11, 2001, attacks against the United States itself. Johnson's chilling conclusion, backed by much supporting evidence, is that a nation reaps what it sows.

---

and then on fears of Revolutionary Islamism and, for a period, paid no attention to the region at all. The human cost for this shortsightedness and inattention was a terrible one.

One of the difficulties in understanding the role of Revolutionary Islamism in modern Afghanistan is the ambiguity of the Afghan war against Soviet occupation. Was it a war of national liberation? Was it a *jihad* against the infidel? Was it a war between ethnic groups? Was it a revolutionary reaction to internal despotism? Was it comparable to the Iranian Revolution or the civil war in Lebanon? It was, in fact, all of these things, not any one of them exclusively. While the Soviets occupied Afghanistan, the conflict helped tie together such disparate factions as tribes, ethnicities, and Secularists, as well as the Revolutionary Traditionalists and Modern Islamists. All these factions unfurled Islam as a banner of unity, though none of them could agree on the other's definition of Islam. When the Soviets withdrew, however, this careful construct of group identity and solidarity crumbled. The Communist regime therefore remained in power even years after the Soviets withdrew. When the *mujahideen* finally took Kabul, they could not agree to the establishment of a government.

Previous *jihads* had been declared in Afghanistan, several times in the nineteenth century in response to invasions of non-Muslim forces and again in 1924 in response to King Amanullah's modernization policies, which threatened tribal and communal traditions. These *jihads,* however, had nothing to do with Islam as a political ideology; it was traditional and folk Islam but not Islamism. These *jihads* were waged strictly to preserve the social and political framework of Afghanistan, not to upset that framework. The call to *jihad* in 1978 was no different. As an internal domestic force, the call to *jihad* was "not directly linked with religion, but Islam provided the intellectual framework that allowed the peasants to articulate and legitimize their grievances against the new regime."[77] The Soviet invasion altered the appeal of Islam as an idiom of dissent and considerably broadened it to include defense of Islam as a war against non-Muslim "infidels." In neither case did Afghans intend *jihad* to represent a revolutionary upheaval of society, to overturn the social and political framework and replace it with something new. However, certain leaders of the Afghan *mujahideen* did intend *jihad* against the Soviets to mean exactly that: true Revolutionary Islamism. The withdrawal of the Soviets undermined "the only common objective of all these groups."[78] When the *mujahideen* actually came to power, however, the old tribal and ethnic affiliations and animosities resurfaced, "transforming even the supposedly modern political parties, as the fundamentalist parties were supposed to be, into networks of patron/client relationships based on common traditional identities."[79] In spite of their efforts and the unifying force of Islam and the articulation of Islamism, the *mujahideen* were unable to construct a government of national unity on the basis of political Islam. The factions were held together only by temporary alliances; ideology meant nothing.

The Taliban's rise to power seemed to confirm the possibility that national unity could be achieved on the basis of political Islam generally and Revolutionary Islamism specifically. The truth was far more complicated. The Taliban's ties to the Pashtun tribes was as much a part of their success and support as was political Islam. After all, few Tajiks, Uzbeks, or Hazaris joined their ranks. The civil war in Afghanistan remained predominantly a war between ethnicities and tribes, not a *jihad* at all. There were no fewer devout Muslims fighting with Massoud, Rabbani, and Dostum than were supporting the Taliban. The real issues were about representation of Afghanistan's many nationalities in a national government and the incompetence and inability of Rabbani's interim government to provide what Afghans most wanted—peace and stability. By 1996, many Afghans were willing to accept Revolutionary Islamism provided it came with law and order and an end to constant internecine fighting. In the end, the Taliban were able to offer only

---

[77]Olivier Roy, "Afghanistan: An Islamic War of Resistance," p. 496.

[78]Ibid., p. 499.

[79]Ibid.

intolerance, brutality, and continued fighting. Revolutionary Islamism was there-fore too high a price, and when under attack by the United States and Britain, the Taliban's autocratic and puritanical Islamic state collapsed.

So what does all this mean for the future of Islamism in Afghanistan? What new forms will it take? Until basic services are restored to Afghans, until jobs and food and shelter are provided, Modern Islamism has a much better future in Afghanistan than Revolutionary Islamism.

Afghanistan Timeline

1919: After the third Afghan War, Afghanistan gained its independence from British interference and military intervention.

1926: Pashtun leader Amanullah became king of Afghanistan and attempted to modernize and Westernize his country with a program of social reforms. These reforms sparked an insurrection in the conservative countryside that eventually overthrew Amanullah.

1933: Muhammad Zahir Shah became king and ruled Afghanistan for forty years.

1953: Zahir Shah's cousin and brother-in-law, Prince Muhammad Daud, became prime minister. He made overtures to the Soviet Union for aid and military assistance. Daud was forced to resign in 1963.

1964: Zahir Shah became a constitutional monarch. Politics in Afghanistan became unstable, and pro-Soviet Marxist political parties, with little sup-port in the countryside, vied for political power in urban areas.

1973: Muhammad Daud, with Soviet assistance and in alliance with Afghanistan's Communist party factions, overthrew Zahir Shah, who went into exile in Italy.

1978: Daud was overthrown and murdered by the factions of the Communist party in Kabul, with Soviet backing. The new Communist government began to initiate reforms, to which conservative Islamic and ethnic leaders objected. Armed insurrection against the government began. Primarily northern nontribal populations declared a *jihad.*

1979: Continuing insurrection in the countryside and a power struggle within the Afghan government led to a Soviet invasion. The Soviets restored order in the Afghan Communist party and appointed Babrak Karmal as the head of Afghanistan's government.

1980: Resistance to the Communist regime in Kabul and the Soviet troops in Afghanistan spread to Pashtun territory. Refugees fled the countryside while various factions of *mujahideen* fought Soviet forces. The *mujahideen* received covert aid and support from the United States and its allies through Pakistan.

1985: Mikhail Gorbachev, the new leader of the Soviet Union, decided to withdraw Soviet troops from Afghanistan.

1986: The United States supplied Stinger missiles to the *mujahideen*. The war turned in favor of the Afghan resistance. Gorbachev removed Babrak Karmal and made Muhammad Najibullah the head of the Afghan government.

1989: The last Soviet troops withdrew from Afghanistan. Najibullah's regime held on to power as the *mujahideen* forces intermittently fought among themselves.

1992: Najibullah was overthrown. Rival factions of the *mujahideen* continued to fight among themselves. Burhanuddin Rabbani established a coalition government in Kabul. Civil war continued.

1994: Factional fighting continued to devastate Kabul and terrorize civilians. The Taliban emerged and took control of Kandahar in the south.

1995: The Taliban conquered more territory and expressed their aim of ousting the Rabbani government.

1996: The Taliban took Kabul; the Rabbani government went into exile. Anti-Taliban forces headed north and formed the Northern Alliance.

1997: The Taliban controlled 70 percent of the country. War between the Taliban and the Northern Alliance, headed by Ahmed Shah Massoud, continued.

1998: Osama bin Laden was targeted by the U.S. government for his role in the embassy bombings in Africa. U.S. cruise missiles were launched against bin Laden's bases inside Afghanistan.

1999: The United States imposed sanctions against Afghanistan to force the Taliban to surrender bin Laden to the United States for trial.

2001 (September): Ahmed Shah Massoud, leader of the Northern Alliance, was killed by assassins sent by Osama bin Laden. Bin Laden was accused of masterminding the attacks on New York and Washington, D.C. The United States sent the Taliban an ultimatum to turn bin Laden and leaders of al-Qaeda over or face a U.S.-led attack.

2001 (October): The U.S.-led coalition began bombing Taliban positions throughout Afghanistan.

2001 (November): The Northern Alliance, with air support from the U.S.-led coalition, took the Afghan cities of Mazar-i-Sharif and Kabul.

2001 (December): The Taliban surrendered their last stronghold in Kandahar. The post-Taliban interim government of Pashtun Modernist Islamist Hamid Karzai took power and agreed to let U.S. forces remain in Afghanistan "for as long as it takes" to capture bin Laden and Taliban leader Mullah Omar.

2002 (April): Former Afghan king Zahir Shah returned from exile in Rome, Italy, but made no effort to reclaim his throne.

2002 (June): The *loya jirga* elected Hamid Karzai as interim head of state until elections are held in 2004. President Karzai picked his cabinet to help him govern and reconstruct war-torn Afghanistan.

Internet Sites

http://www.a-l-o.org/historical.htm

http://www.aijac.org.au/updates/Nov-01/081101.html

http://shell.spqr.net/islam/kabbani2.html

http://www.afghancriminals.com/members.htm

http://www.alternet.org/story.html?StoryID=12012

http://www.comebackalive.com/df/dplaces/afghanis/index.htm

http://www.afghan-web.com/

http://web.nps.navy.mil/~library/tgp/qaida.htm

U.S. State Department summary of the terrorist group al-Qaeda.

http://web.nps.navy.mil/~library/tgp/hua.htm

U.S. State Department summary of the terrorist group Harakat al-Mujahideen.

http://web.nps.navy.mil/~library/tgp/algama.htm

U.S. State Department summary of the terrorist group Gamaʻa al-Islamiyyah.

http://cns.miis.edu/research/wtc01/algamaa.htm

Center for Nonproliferation Studies profile of the terrorist group Gamaʻa al-Islamiyyah.

http://web.nps.navy.mil/~library/tgp/asc.htm

U.S. State Department summary of the terrorist group Abu Sayyaf.

http://web.nps.navy.mil/~library/tgp/jihad.htm

U.S. State Department summary of the terrorist group Al-Jihad.

http://lexicorient.com/cgi-bin/eo-direct.pl?osama_b_laden.htm

Encyclopedia of the Orient's summary of al-Qaeda leader Osama bin Laden.

http://lexicorient.com/cgi-bin/eo-direct.pl?qaida.htm

Encyclopedia of the Orient's summary of the terrorist organization al-Qaeda.

http://www.cia.gov/cia/publications/factbook/geos/af.html

CIA summary information on Afghanistan.

http://www.pcpafg.org/Organizations/undp/

United Nations Development Program's: PEACE—rebuilding Afghanistan's urban centers, promoting food security and sustainable agriculture, and helping disabled Afghans.

http://devdata.worldbank.org/external/dgprofile.asp?RMDK=82662&SMDK=1&W=0

World Bank's population, environment, economic, technology, and development statistics for Afghanistan.

http://www.lib.berkeley.edu/SSEAL/SouthAsia/afghan_US.html

University of California at Berkeley's collection of Web links dealing with Afghanistan, the Taliban, Osama bin Laden, Afghan government statements, Afghan opposition groups, and more.

Miscellaneous

http://www.afghan-info.com/Politics/King_ZahirShah/ZahirShah_Profile.htm

http://www.afghan-web.com/bios/today/zahirshah.html

http://www.islamonline.net/English/Crisis/2001/11/article3.SHTML

http://www.gl.iit.edu/govdocs/afghanistan/KingMuhammadZahirShah.html

http://www.gl.iit.edu/govdocs/afghanistan/

http://www.afghanmagazine.com/afghanhistory/royalfamilies.pdf

http://www.cia.gov/cia/publications/factbook/geos/af.html

http://www.infoplease.com/spot/taliban-time.html

http://www.afghan-web.com/

http://news.nationalgeographic.com/news/2001/10/1009_afghanfacts.html

http://rawa.fancymarketing.net/gul-kgb.htm

http://www.afghanradio.com/news/2001/november/nov7k2001.html

http://www.janes.com/defence/interviews/dw011024_i.html

http://www.afghanhero.com/afghanan/biographies/hekmatyar.htm

http://www.afghan-web.com/bios/today/ghekmatyar.html

http://www.afghan-web.com/bios/today/brabbani.html

http://www.afghan-web.com/bios/today/momar.html

http://www.deccanherald.com/deccanherald/nov11/f1.htm

http://www.top-biography.com/9007-Osama/%20Bin/%20Laden/

http://www.pbs.org/wgbh/pages/frontline/shows/binladen/who/bio.html

http://www.infoplease.com/spot/osamabinladen.html

http://users.skynet.be/terrorism/html/laden.htm

http://www.adl.org/terrorism_america/bin_l.asp

http://abcnews.go.com/sections/world/DailyNews/binladen_profile.html

http://www.afghan-info.com/Politics/Hamid_Karzai_Profile.htm

http://www.pbs.org/newshour/bb/asia/afghanistan/karzai.html

http://ap.tbo.com/ap/breaking/MGAZJKH2VUC.html

http://www.washingtonpost.com/wp-srv/nation/graphics/attack/zone_30.html

http://cgi.citizen-times.com/cgi-bin/story/united/2520

CHAPTER ELEVEN

Perceiving Islam

The Causes and Consequences of Islamophobia in the Western Media

In the hours and days following the attacks on the Pentagon and World Trade Center, symbols of American military and economic preeminence, Americans were asking themselves, "Why do they hate us?" Trying to make sense of the biggest terrorist attack on American soil, they asked themselves: why did the terrorists strike at us? What conceivable grievances could they have? Do all Muslims hate us? Or were these criminal acts merely the work of a few misguided Muslim zealots? Was the problem poverty or oppression? Or was Islam itself to blame for the national catastrophe of September 11, 2001?

Many Westerners today, if they possess any perception of Islam at all, often imagine it as a monstrous force stretching its arms over the face of the world. Revolutionary political Islam, or Revolutionary Islamism or Islamic fundamentalism, is as thoroughly feared in the West today as Soviet and Chinese Communism were before it. Islam is seen as a monolithic force threatening not only the West's way of life but also its survival. Yet Western fear of the Islamic "threat" or the "green peril"[1] is rooted not in reality but in misperception and misunderstanding. Western politicians, scholars, and of course, the mass media habitually focus on the most sensational aspects of Islamism, and this by itself has contributed to a tragic distortion of Islam and of devout Muslims around the world. Islam is erroneously characterized as both inconceivable to the Western mind and inherently opposed to the Western way of life.[2]

---

[1] The color green is a symbol of Islam.

[2] We talk about "the West" and "Islam" as though history, politics, and culture can be reduced to these terms and yet remain comprehensible. However, these are the words that are used to frame most discussions, whether scholarly or journalistic, of Western and Muslim encounters with one another. Of course these terms are inadequate and misleading, and this chapter specifically addresses the gross oversimplification that necessarily results when using the word "Islam" to convey the complexities and contradictions of the Muslim world. I leave it to the reader to understand the equivalent argument: that talking about "the West" is equally inadequate.

Clash of Western and Islamic Civilizations: Historical Roots

The notion that Islam, as a religious and cultural force in the world, stands some-how intrinsically opposed to all things Western is nothing new. Western scholars have for centuries weighed the "Islamic threat," wondering when again the Saracens would be at the gates of Vienna or threatening Paris. Western scholarly perception of Islam has historically been hostile. Islam is "other," alien; it is incom-prehensible; it is hostile politically, militarily, and culturally to things Western. The clash between the Christian West and the Muslim world is more than a thou-sand years old. Islam's Prophet Muhammad himself faced vehement opposition to his mission not only from idol worshippers but also from Jews and Christians. This conflict between the Christian West and the Muslim world intensified when Muslims conquered portions of Europe and the Holy Land and when the Muslim Ottoman Empire dismembered the Christian Byzantine Empire—the same fate, ironically, that later befell the Ottomans. Although the Crusaders themselves rarely were a picture of Christian unity in opposition to various Muslim empires,[3] the Crusades profoundly affected Western thinking about Islam. Even during the European Renaissance (1350–1650)—sparked in part by Muslims engaging not in war but in peaceful trade and commerce with Europe—and during the European Enlightenment of the eighteenth century, Islam continued to be maligned as a threat to Christendom or even as a threat to reason and rationality. The men of letters and guiding lights of the Enlightenment, while courageously debunking Christian Church propaganda, which had stigmatized Islam as a perverse hedo-nistic faith, were themselves particularly unenlightened about Islam, Muslims, and the Muslim world. Voltaire, one of the Enlightenment's prominent figures, for instance, wrote a play entitled *Fanaticism, or the Prophet Muhammad* and referred to Prophet Muhammad in his *Philosophical Dictionary* as "a brazen impostor who deceived imbeciles."[4] Meanwhile, the paintings of Jean-Auguste-Dominique Ingres portrayed Ottoman Turks lolling around in their harems with their female concubines and thereby conjured up and reinforced the distorted image of Muslims as permissive and promiscuous misogynists.

Christian Europeans had for centuries viewed Islam as a dangerous and threatening adversary both on the field of battle and in the realm of ideas. Indeed, "until Karl Marx and the rise of communism, the Prophet [Muhammad] organized and launched the only serious challenge to Western civilization. . . ."[5] As Roman might ebbed in the fifth century, the Muslim world rose in the seventh century as a formidable political, ideological, and military force threatening the very heart of

---

[3]The Fourth Crusade, led by Doge Dandolo of Venice, involved no skirmishes with Muslims in the Holy Land. Instead, it ended when the Crusaders sacked the Christian city of Constantinople in the thirteenth century.

[4]Voltaire, *The Portable Voltaire*, edited by Ben Ray Redman (New York: Viking Press, 1961), p. 187.

[5]Fathi Osman, "Ayatullah Khomeini: A Genuine 'Alim-Leader' in the Contemporary World," *The Minaret*, Vol. 10, No. 3 (Summer 1989), pp. 19–20.

Europe, at different times conquering Spain and southern Italy, central Europe and southern France. Muslim powers represented an alarming thousand-year threat that not only enjoyed considerable military success against Europeans but posed an ideological challenge as well, winning converts away from Christianity by the tens of millions.[6] Nothing before or since—with the exception of communism—has so alarmed the West as this steady westward push of a massive, relentless and frequently victorious challenge.[7] Unable fully to subdue Muslim armies on the field of battle, Christian Europeans vilified Muslims and denigrated Islam, describing it as a dangerous monolithic force, a faith founded on deception and clumsy plagiarism of Judaism and Christianity, and depicting its believers as frightful caricatures.

By the nineteenth century, advances in military and industrial technology favored the West. The Muslim world suffered gradual conquest by European military forces. Muslim economic and political power declined.[8] This eventual technological superiority of secular Western nation-states over the expansive but fragmented Muslim world ushered in an era of imperialism and colonialism. Western nations conquered, administered, and exploited the developing Muslim societies in spite of considerable opposition from the Muslims themselves. Western fear of Islam abated; the alleged "threat" of Islam had been tamed by superior Western technology. During the period of Western imperialism and colonialism, Muslims who dared challenge Western dominance were branded subversive agitators; they were hunted down and imprisoned or killed in their own lands. Even after gaining nominal independence from Western colonial rule in the twentieth century, the secular pro-Western nationalists, who assumed power in these Muslim countries, felt greater affinity with their former Western masters than with the people they governed.

In the closing decades of the twentieth century, the Western relationship with the Muslim world changed. States in the Muslim world were revealed as friends or foes through the prism of the Cold War. The intense ideological struggle between the West and the Communist bloc inspired greater American aid to strategically located and resource-rich Muslim countries to maintain pro-Western, anticommunist regimes. Whenever Islamists challenged the governing pro-Western Muslim Secularists, they were suppressed with Western help. The Western mass media justified this suppression by branding them "Marxists," "Fundamentalists," or "terrorists."[9] No attempt was made to explore the meaning of these terms; the universal understanding of Westerners was that these revolu-

---

[6]Ibid., pp. 19–20.

[7]Ibid.

[8]Yvonne Yazbeck Haddad, *Contemporary Islam and the Challenge of History* (Albany: State University of New York Press, 1982), p. xiii.

[9]Of course, the Soviets did likewise. As an ideology firmly and openly committed to atheism, communism necessarily was incompatible with Islamism, and the suppression of Muslim religious expression in Central Asia was but the mildest form of Soviet oppression of Islam. The more severe form was displayed in Afghanistan. See Chapter 10.

tionaries were a threat to their interests, indeed to the Western way of life.[10] Thus, when authoritarian Muslim regimes' security forces, trained and equipped by the West, crushed opposition movements that threatened the status quo, the West either ignored the repression or applauded it as though the troublemakers had no right to revolt but were merely communist dupes. Law and order were to be preserved as a hedge against Soviet expansion, no matter the people's grievances.

Western interest in the Muslim world is sensible and appropriate today given the geostrategic interests of the West in the region, the region's possession of natural resources vitally important to the West, the sizeable market that more than 1.2 billion Muslims present, and the history of Arab and Turkish Muslim armies conquering the Holy Land and parts of Europe. All this is coupled with modern Western ignorance, insensitivity, and misunderstanding of justifiable Muslim frustration. Moreover, Westerners are constantly reminded that Muslims, holding fast to the anchor of Islam as best they understand it, have often rejected modernization and secularization.

However, with the end of the Cold War and the conclusion of the Gulf War, Western interest in the Muslim world briefly declined. Incidents of terrorism, a common news item in the 1980s, seemed to abate. Oil prices were low. The troubled history of the Middle East seemed of little importance, and Westerners, particularly in the United States, turned their attention to domestic priorities. During the 1990s, however, Revolutionary Islamists were very active. Defeat of the Soviets in Afghanistan, war with the Russians in Chechnya, and a hasty U.S. withdrawal from Somalia emboldened some Revolutionary Islamists who were preparing for another battle with the West.

Events such as the OAPEC oil embargo, the OPEC oil price explosion, the destruction of the U.S. Marine barracks in Lebanon, the Islamic Revolution in Iran, the Iranian hostage crisis, the kidnapping of American hostages in Lebanon, the assassination of Egypt's President Muhammad Anwar al-Sadat, and the Persian Gulf War, to name only a prominent few, briefly resurrected that sense of an "Islamic threat" antithetical to U.S. interests. Yet nothing less than the attack on the Pentagon and the World Trade Center was required to rekindle Western interest in the Muslim world. The attack on the USS *Liberty* by Israeli aircraft in 1967 and the Jonathan Pollard affair, in which case, an American Jew in U.S. navy intelligence handed over a significant amount of sensitive information about the Middle East to Israel: should these events have been described as evidence of a "Jewish threat"? Of course not, nor should acts of terrorism, even when carried by Muslim militants, be considered signs of a "Muslim threat" or an "Islamic threat." After the events of September 11, discussions of a "Muslim threat" or "Islamic terrorism" became commonplace. But Western concern about "Islamic rage," is by no means a new phenomenon. Immediately after the Cold War and the emascu-

---

[10]Of course, when Revolutionary Islamists were in active opposition to the Communist regime of Afghanistan during the 1980s, Western media and policy makers were quick to use the term *freedom fighters*, rather than *fundamentalist fanatics* or *Islamic terrorists*.

lation of communist ideology, Western scholars and policy makers went fishing for a new adversary worthy of Western attention.

Although the ideological context within the Western world has shifted from a parochial and conservative Christian worldview to a secular and liberal worldview over the last three hundred years, deep-seated negative perceptions of Islam fed by a millennium of anti-Muslim propaganda have tenaciously endured, and the Western image of Muslims and the Muslim world remains a distorted caricature of reality. But how has this image been conveyed and who is responsible for it? Insofar as most Westerners, including journalists, are poorly informed of the thousand-year history of clashes between the West and the Muslim world, the true descendants of the Crusader mentality are modern Western scholars and policy makers, sometimes mistaken as "experts."

Samuel Huntington identified Islam as the West's new adversary in his 1993 article "The Clash of Civilizations" (see Box 11.1). Relying heavily on works by Bernard Lewis, Professor Emeritus of Near Eastern Studies at Princeton University, Huntington described "Islam" in a fashion that assumed that such an entity could be comprehensible without reference to the myriad opinions and doctrinal viewpoints held by the world's 1.2 billion Muslims. Huntington's daring and compelling proposition turned out to be nothing more than a rehash of the Cold War paradigm, with Muslims filling in for the villain. Judith Miller's contention in a 1993 opinion piece for *Foreign Affairs* that Islam does indeed represent a threat to the West offers a similarly unimpressive view of the worldwide conspiracy of Islam against the West. But scholars like Lewis, Miller, and Huntington tread dangerous ground by promoting overly simplistic explanations of Islam. Their absurd reductionism of Islam as enemy convey nothing of the richness or nuance or complexity of Islam as a religious faith, whether today or during its long and eventful history. Their understanding of Islam as an entity that is at once quickly recognized as opposed to all things Western is in fact no understanding at all. It is a clumsy, prefabricated conspiracy theory that "ties together isolated events and trends." As Leon Hadar—an adjunct scholar at the Cato Institute at Washington, D.C.—notes, "all changes and instability in the post–Cold War Middle East and its peripheries are described as part of a grand scheme perpetrated by 'Islam International.' "[11]

Such a conception of Islam rests on a foundation of wilful ignorance and lazy scholarship. It is not, for example, Bernard Lewis's contention that Revolutionary Islamists have perverted and mutilated Islam but rather that these fanatics who twist Islam into a means of attaining political power are in fact the true exemplars of what Islam is. Of course, it is no myth that individuals and organizations supporting particular forms of Islamic militancy against the West have, in fact, attacked Westerners and the West. The myth is that this violent activism is representative of Islam as a religion of 1.2 billion people, or for that matter, that the

---

[11]Leon T. Hadar, "What Green Peril?" in John T. Rourke, ed., *Taking Sides: Clashing Views on Controversial Issues in World Politics*, 5th edition (Guilford: Dushkin, 1994), p. 101.

■

BOX 11.1   "The Clash of Civilizations"

Professor Samuel P. Huntington, director of the John M. Olin Institute for Strategic Studies and chair of the Harvard Academy for International and Area Studies, wrote a seminal and provocative article for the journal *Foreign Affairs* in summer 1993 entitled "The Clash of Civilizations?" In his book *Clash of Civilizations and the Remaking of the World Order* (1996), Huntington elaborates his controversial thesis that cultural identity or civilization is becoming the central force shaping the patterns of integration, conflict, and disintegration in post–Cold War international relations. To be more precise, civilization (defined primarily in terms of religion), rather than ethnicity, borders, or nationality, represents an individual's or a group's deepest source of loyalty and identity. He posits that the potential for major and minor clashes between at least eight competing cultural systems or "civilizations"—Western, Confucian, Japanese, Islamic, Hindu, Slavic-Orthodox Christian, Latin American, and African (sub-Saharan black Africa)—has replaced the bipolar East-West ideological conflict (between the communist totalitarian world and capitalist democratic world) as well as the realist paradigm of competing states and national interests that dominated international relations since the end of World War II. He gives examples of the balkanization of Yugoslavia, when all-out war broke out between the Orthodox Christian Serbs, Roman Catholic Croats, and Bosnian Muslims; the war in Russian Chechnya between the Chechen Islamists and the Orthodox Christian Russians; the war in Kashmir between the Muslims and the Hindus; and the Arab Muslims and Jewish Israelis that goes on generation after generation, among others.

Huntington sees the West's attempt to push "modernization" (Westernization), "globalization," and its own continued global dominance (economic, military, political, and sociocultural) on the world as dangerous because it could lead to a backlash against the West, especially in light of the reassertion of religion. He is particularly concerned about an "intercivilizational war" between the Muslim world and the other civilizations. Not only are Muslim countries involved in far more intergroup violence due to the modernization revolution, but the world of Islam is "a different civilization whose people are convinced of the superiority of their culture and are obsessed with the inferiority of their power."

Huntington calls for reducing Western intervention in other civilizations, which is a big departure from the aggressive foreign policy that he advocated during the Cold War. He also considers the emphasis on "multiculturalism" in the West to be a dangerous delusion that could contribute to conflict and fragmentation. In the West, Huntington recommends reemphasizing the core European values on which its culture is based.

In Asia and Africa, Huntington's thesis has been referred to as "the West against the rest." Some have criticized Huntington for underestimating the conflict between the "haves" and "have-nots" in the world as well as the "fault lines" within civilizations or the ongoing and more dangerous intracivilizational conflicts. For instance, take the chronic conflict within the Islamic civilization itself between Muslim countries (Iran versus Iraq; Iraq versus Quwait) as well as within Muslim countries (Islamists versus Secularists; Revolutionary Islamists versus Modernist Islamists; elite versus proletariat; rich versus poor).

world's Muslims are somehow more dangerous than the world's Protestants or Hindus or Roman Catholics. Hardly unified, Islamic politics is better described as "a kaleidoscope producing shifting balances of power and overlapping ideological configurations" that defy central control.[12]

Tragically, it is the scholarship of oversimplification that informs the West about Islam. People predisposed to distrust what they do not understand readily embrace inaccurate shorthand explanations of a religion they know nothing about.[13] This is the understanding of Islam that gave us, in the days immediately following the 1995 Oklahoma City bombing, "experts" who claimed that it was the work of Islamic terrorists—a claim that proved wholly untrue.[14] This is the scholarship that inspired Newt Gingrich to denounce the "worldwide phenomenon of Islamic totalitarianism funded and largely directed by the state of Iran."[15] It is to such "experts" and political personalities that the Western mass media turn to understand the complexities of the Muslim world. The little that Americans know about Islam has been fed to them by the Western mass media. The Western mass media served as the conduit through which medieval anti-Muslim propaganda and nineteenth-century Orientalist Western prejudice against the Orient/East (including Islam, Muslims and the Muslim world) have been translated into modern Western anti-Muslim press. The preponderance of Western-born and educated reporters, editors, writers, and producers in the Western media establishes the apparatus by which the Western viewpoint prevails in news reporting. Although most reporters genuinely attempt to be objective in their interpretation of events, few can can erase their political socialization or deny their culture and the voice that a subconscious bias lends it. Given the inordinate influence the media wield in the West, negative images of Islam, however unrepresentative or dishonest, only reinforce ancient stereotypes.

Thus, a long and traumatic history of conflict between the Western world and the Muslim world has clouded Western and Muslim sensibilities with regard to one another. And just as many Muslims hastily decry the West and all things Western, so do many Westerners with comparable haste decry all things Islamic. Furthermore, the recent memory of the Cold War has only reinforced a Western us-versus-them worldview, lent credence by scholars like Huntington and Lewis. In the Muslim world, distrust, frustration, and resentment of the West run deep and is periodically manifested in acts of anti-Western protest and violence. Westerners, for whom the era of colonialism was largely beneficial, are insensitive to the feelings of downtrodden and persecuted Muslims. Westerners are inclined

---

[12]Ibid.

[13]Edward W. Said's excellent critique of the Huntington article appears in "The Clash of Ignorance," *The Nation*, October 22, 2001, pp. 11–13. Another critique of both Lewis's and Huntington's views can be found in John L. Esposito, *The Islamic Threat: Myth or Reality?* 3rd edition (New York: Oxford University Press, 1999), pp. 219–222.

[14]Greg Noakes, "Muslims and the American Press," in Yvonne Yazbeck Haddad and John L. Esposito, eds., *Muslims on the Americanization Path?* (Oxford: Oxford University Press, 2000), pp. 289–290.

[15]Newt Gingrich quoted in Esposito, *The Islamic Threat*, p. 213.

to think that Muslim demonstrations against Western hegemony in ostensibly sovereign Muslim states are a reflection of ingratitude, parochialism, and ignorance and, worse still, are irrational and barbaric outbursts of an "Islamic threat."

Anti-Islamic Bias in the Western Mass Media

Unwilling to divine the wellspring of Muslim anger or ever to fathom its abyssal depths, the West has devised an alternate terminology that vilifies Muslims for actions or attitudes that Westerners praise in themselves. Zionists in the Hagannah, the Irgun, and the Stern Gang, fighting often ferociously for the independent Jewish state of Israel, were referred to not as "Jewish terrorists" but as patriots, nationalists, guerrillas, the Jewish underground, and freedom fighters. Their struggle was treated with considerable sympathy in the context of a history of virulent Western anti-Semitism. Following the Holocaust, few Westerners in good conscience could deny the Jewish people their long-awaited homeland, where they might freely practice their religion, enjoy their own culture, and govern themselves. Consequently, their military activities were portrayed as an "independence struggle."

In contrast the military activities of members of the Palestine Liberation Organization (PLO) were never called by the Western mass media a "liberation struggle" or seen in light of a similar history of injustice and victimization suffered by Palestinian Arabs. Until only recently, the Western mass media has referred to Palestinians only as "terrorists," so often that *terrorism* and *Palestinian* are nearly synonymous in the Western vocabulary. Unable to accept that Jews and Palestinians have both been persecuted, many Westerners have reduced a complex political situation into simple black and white. How easy the world is to understand when the "good guys" (the Israelis) engage in "counter-terrorism," "retaliation," "preemptive strikes," "commando raids," or an "iron-fist policy" against the "bad guys" (the Palestinians) who are always "terrorists"; the Palestinian Authority, Hamas, and Hezbollah are forever branded as the instigators of violence who murder Israelis. Israeli bombing of Lebanese villages, always with civilian casualties was, in contrast, depicted by the mass media clinically and unfeelingly. When a Palestinian suicide bomber in Haifa murdered innocent Israelis on a bus, there was understandable international outcry and indignation. But when the Israelis responded with much heavier military attacks on Palestinian police headquarters and killed innocent civilians, the Western commentary is much different—at best, an urging of restraint and call to both sides in the dispute to "end the cycle of violence."

This double standard in terminology occurs not only in the Arab-Israeli conflict but also throughout the world. In the former Yugoslavia, the Western press rightly decried Serbian attacks on Bosnian and Kosovar Muslims but never made reference to them as "Christian terrorists," though the Serbs called themselves Christian soldiers defending Europe from the scourge of "Islamic fundamentalism." Religion is as central a feature in the conflict between the Serbs and the Bosnians as it is between the Arabs and the Israelis. Yet the Serbs were always called "nationalists," while the Palestinian Islamists are defamed as "Islamic terrorists." When the Serbs committed genocide against Bosnian Muslims and Kosovars (Muslims of Kosovo), the Western mass media constantly referred to it as "ethnic cleansing," not genocide or mass murder of innocent Muslims. However, if Muslims had done the same thing, it would probably have been called "Islamic terrorism" or genocide.

The mass media ought to know that words have power. We must therefore empathize with the victims and try to end their victimization rather than accept the language of the aggressor and victimizer. Still, the press has convinced both itself and the public that only Muslims (Islamists) are "terrorists." Strangely, there are no "Christian" or "Jewish" terrorists! The Catholic Irish Republican Army, which has carried out attacks against Irish and English Protestants, was never called an organization of "Christian terrorists," nor is the Protestant Ulster Defense Association so termed, though it too carried out acts of terror against Catholics. In the United States, Christian antiabortion zealots firebombing health clinics are never portrayed as "Christian terrorists," and for good reason. They are not acting as Christians or in the loving spirit of Christianity when engaging in acts of fanatical violence. Logically, then, the mass media should refrain from decrying "Islamic terrorism." Moreover, the mass media should remember that kidnapping, incarcerating, and torturing innocent civilians of any religion, race, color, or nationality is totally reprehensible, whoever does it. Killing innocent civilians, of course, is heinous and barbaric no matter the perpetrator, whether it is the Israeli Defence Forces, the Mossad, the CIA, the Serbs, militant Hindu fundamentalists, the Palestinian Authority, Hamas, or Hezbollah. The selective perceptions of the Western mass media, however, cause many Westerners to condemn strongly the alleged crimes of their enemies, while overlooking or rephrasing euphemistically the "human rights abuses" of their allies and friends.

Some Muslim observers of the Western mass media have declared its biases and prejudices indicative of a neocolonialist conspiracy against Islam. In general, however, there may occasionally be an absence of malice in Western mass media coverage of Islam, though never a shortage of the prejudice, bias, and ignorance in the cultural baggage we all carry. Certain universal psychological factors, acting often subconsciously, work behind mass media misperception of Islam. Ingrained since birth with negative images of Islam and Muslims, the ordinary Westerner is predisposed to maintaining and justifying certain convenient stereotypes. Stereotyping Muslims as harem-keeping oil-rich shaykhs, as angry mobs, or as fanatics and terrorists occurs for several reasons. First, such stereotypes are easy; they make actual thinking unnecessary. Instead of a thorough examination of Islam, instead of worrying about the many sects and schools of Islam that render it a faith as fragmented, varied, and rich as Christianity, Islam is reduced to a few negative images. This, in turn, transforms the innocent Muslim into a convenient scapegoat for the ills of modern Western civilization.

The "greedy" and "ruthless" Muslims, for example, are blamed for rising oil prices and for the West's poor economic performance in the 1970s. Meanwhile, the West's inordinate demand for and self-imposed dependence on oil are not addressed. Someone else is always to blame, and our stereotypes of Muslims as avaricious oil rich shaykhs make them an easy target. The social and economic troubles of the United States in the 1970s become the fault of the Muslim world— a world predominantly of destitute urban workers, small farmers, and peasants who must pay the same prices for oil as do Westerners. Western stereotypes that portray Islam as a religion of fanatics reinforces the Muslim conviction that the West is determined to frustrate the Islamic quest for identity. Muslims point to the outpouring of Western sympathy for the aspirations and suffering of the Eastern Europeans and the Caucasians of the Baltic states (Lithuania, Latvia, and Estonia) and Russians and to Westerners' apparent indifference to what happens to Muslims in many parts of the world. Implicit is the attitude that Muslims are very different from "us," and probably even against "us" and our national interests. Western military intervention to stop Serbia from carrying out genocide in Kosovo represented a step in the right direction but was by no means an expression of Western support for Kosovar independence from Serbia. Western policy remains that Kosovo is unquestionably a part of Serbia. In the case of predominantly Muslim Chechnya, which the United States recognizes as part of the Russian Federation, sympathy for Chechen Muslims and opposition to Russian brutality in the region have enjoyed some play in the Western media. But even this lukewarm support ended entirely with the attacks on the Pentagon and World Trade Center. In any event, Western media support for the Chechens was likely more representative of residual Cold War fear of and opposition to Russia.

A process called *cognitive consistency*, which is based on the notion that human beings, by and large, resist change and prefer stability, perpetuates established stereotypes. When a person is used to a particular stereotype, when it is comfortable, he or she enjoys cognitive stability with regard to the subject of the stereotype. This saves him or her the mental effort and anguish of rethinking not only that stereotype but also his or her entire worldview. Cognitive consistency is thus the frequently subconscious effort human beings naturally make to avoid potentially contradictory perceptions. Whenever an image is inconsistent with one's established stereotype, one simply disregards the new information, and the stereotype goes unaltered. Although the stereotypes are wrong, they become firmly entrenched at all levels of society—particularly in academia, where young scholars simply force new information to fit old perceptions and paradigms.[16] The *evoked set*, much like *cognitive consistency*, is another psychological process by which the West's perception of Islam, Muslims, and the Muslim world has been colored. Having grown accustomed to the Cold War and the difficulty of retrenching millions of people employed in the enormously influential military-industrial complex, Westerners have tended to recycle the obsolete Cold War, us-versus-them mentality and applied it to other trouble spots. Once upon a time, the "Reds" were our greatest adversary, and now by drawing an imperfect historical analogy, called an "evoked set," we believe that Revolutionary Islamism is an enemy comparable in every way to revolutionary Communism and thus must be at all costs

---

[16]William Montgomery Watt, *Muslim-Christian Encounters: Perceptions and Misperceptions* (New York: Routledge, 1991), p. 111.

contained and neutralized. Certainly Huntington's description of Islam as an entity that exists for apparently no reason other than to defy the West falls into this category.

The "blindness of the instant" concept also explains Western mass media misperceptions of the angry outbursts of some Muslims. Individuals tend to perceive and interpret unanticipated events out of historical context. In fact, they sometimes wholly disregard causality. Thus, the West, while rightly condemning Iranian hostage-taking in 1979, conveniently overlooked the prominent U.S. role in propping up the *shah* for thirty-eight years. In fact, a long history of callous and shortsighted U.S. support for the tyrannical and unpopular *shah* contributed directly to the callous and shortsighted Iranian retaliation during the Islamic Revolution. The attack on September 11, 2001, which differs in that it is strongly pathological, does not excuse the United States from trying to determine the motivations of the attackers and potentially changing Western policy to prevent future attacks.

All the above tendencies are buttressed by the *black-white diabolical enemy image* that transforms "us versus them" into a sweeping "good versus evil" paradigm. The adversary is demonized and dehumanized. It becomes impossible to understand or empathize with "them." One disregards the possibility that this adversary may be just like "us," that "they" may be hoping for peace or spoiling for war for reasons that are readily explicable, provided we put ourselves in their place. Moreover, the black-white diabolical enemy image is compounded by its reciprocity. It is, like all the above-mentioned psychological processes of misperception, double-edged. All human beings are subject to their own parochial caprices. Just as some Westerners sense the "Islamic threat" as an evil best contained, so do some Muslims perceive Westernization and secularization as an evil best dismantled—whether personified by the Israeli state or by Western-supported puppet governments like that of the *shah* of Iran, President Hosni Mubarak of Egypt, or the late King Hussein of Jordan and the late King Hassan of Morocco. Moreover, this reciprocity of hostility lends itself to a *conflict spiral*, in which the perceived hostility of a foe is matched by hostility in return. The consequent cycle, the action-reaction syndrome, thereby reinforces untrue, unsavory, and unsympathetic stereotypes, generates reactionary policies, and undermines efforts to bring disputants together.[17] Like Sisyphus perpetually rolling the stone up the hill, the combatants expend everything in their struggle with one another, but it avails them nothing.

The persistence of stereotypes, related directly to the human need for cognitive consistency, haunts us today despite, or perhaps because of, the communications revolution and the shrinking of our global village. Two hundred years ago Revolutionary Islamism was irrelevant to the newly created American republic.

---

[17]For a concise discussion of these psychological processes, see Bruce Russet and Harvey Starr, *World Politics: The Menu for Choice*, 4th edition (New York: W. H. Freeman), pp. 274–279; also see Ralph K. White, *Nobody Wanted War: Misperception in Vietnam and Other Wars*, rev. edition (New York: Doubleday, 1968); John G. Stoessinger, *Why Nations Go to War?* 7th edition (New York: St. Martin's, 1998).

Islam was a distant, mysterious, but intriguing force that never intruded into an American's world. Now *everything* concerns us. During the 1980s and 1990s Cable News Network (CNN) frequently carried stories dwelling on the "Islamic threat." Today this fear of some universal and monolithic "Islamic threat" is not only perpetuated but is amplified far out of proportion to its reality by the Western media. Western reporters and journalists who cover and portray the Muslim world are either predisposed to condemn Islamism outright or totally unprepared to comprehend it. And with scholars like Huntington and Lewis informing Western journalists, no wonder that many consumers of Western media confidently proclaim the backwardness and barbarism of Islam and the cultural superiority of the West.

Imagine a world in which prominent scholars were better informed and more balanced in their discussions of Islam. The Western media, in an effort to say as much as possible in the least amount of time, would still lack the capacity to distinguish between Islam and criminally insane fanatics who purport to be God's warriors on Earth. Not all Muslims are militant and violent religious fanatics, nor for that matter are all militant and violent religious fanatics Muslims. Edward Said—the Palestinian-American Professor of Literature at Columbia University—asks, when analyzing the September 11 attacks, why not "see parallels, admittedly less spectacular in their destructiveness, for Osama bin Laden and his followers in cults like the Branch Davidians or the disciples of the Rev. Jim Jones at Guyana or the Japanese Aum Shinrikyo?"[18]

Westerners have been convinced that Osama bin Laden, Ayatollah Khomeini, and Saddam Hussein epitomize Islam—that these men are true representatives of the faith. Yet in truth, Islam is in spirit as kind and gentle a faith as its two predecessors—Judaism and Christianity. One strain of the Revolutionary Islamist interpretation of Islam should be seen as the violent reaction to perceived Western (including American) imperialism and neocolonialism. Nor should anyone confuse the totality or essence of Christianity with the examples of David Koresh and Jim Jones. Nor are many radical fundamentalist Jews like Baruch Goldstein or Rabbi Meir Kahane (who founded the Jewish Defense League) representative of the totality of Judaism. Why then does much of the Western mass media take Osama bin Laden's extremist Revolutionary Islamism out of context or, worse still, label Islam and all devout Muslims as irrational zealots and fanatics? Islam is as diverse, rich, and meaningful a monotheistic and peaceful belief system as the monotheistic religions of Judaism and Christianity. There is just as much diversity in the worldview of Muslims as there is in the worldview of Jews, Christians, and members of other religious faiths.

Western mass media have also engendered a confusion of *Arab* with *Muslim*. Although as many as 10 percent of all Arabs worldwide are Christians and Jews and although as many as 75 percent of Muslims are non-Arabs, the West invariably equates all Arabs with Muslims—even such prominent non-Arab Persian Muslims like Ayatollah Khomeini are subject to this misconception. In the bombing campaign in Afghanistan, most Westerners were not aware that the Afghans

---

[18]Edward W. Said, "The Clash of Ignorance," p. 12.

are themselves not Arabs. Arabs in Afghanistan are foreigners. Perhaps the greatest misconception perpetrated by the Western mass media is that the Muslim world consists of wild and murderous people seething with inexplicable anti-Western rage. Camera crews went looking for a few Palestinians celebrating the September 11 attacks or a crowd of Pakistanis chanting their allegiance to Osama bin Laden and denouncing the West. Little mention was made of the overwhelming majority of Muslims who express no support for bin Laden and who sympathize with the victims of the attacks. Instead, 1.2 billion Muslims scattered the world over with different and unique historical backgrounds, cultures, traditions, and worldviews are conveniently reduced to a series of simple stereotypes immediately recognizable by the dimmest wits.

Western media rarely engage in a substantive examination or appraisal of the Muslim world. Instead, they often portray Muslims—whether in movies, news programs, or television sitcoms—as negative, one-dimensional caricatures and tend to represent them "in unqualified categorical and generic terms: one Muslim is therefore seen to be typical of all Muslims and of Islam in general."[19] Through the media looking glass, all Muslims are mysteriously transformed into oil shaykhs, terrorists, or uncivilized, bloodthirsty, book-burning, stone-throwing, placard-waving anti-Western mobs. Thus, Western media disregard Islam as a holistic religion in the objective sense and use it instead to describe all aspects of the diverse Muslim world, "reducing all aspects of Islam to a special malevolent and unthinking essence."[20] In the Western worldview, therefore, Islam becomes "them" in an easily understood us-versus-them equation.

All forms of the Western mass media are responsible for perpetuating certain ridiculous stereotypes of the Muslim. Television programs and Hollywood motion pictures have been instrumental in giving Westerners a distorted picture of Islam and its adherents. Given these media's alleged reputation for liberal and politically correct inclinations, one might expect that they would know better. After all, the American mass media has taken great pains to eliminate most negative, unpleasant, and untrue stereotypes of Jews, African Americans, and Native Americans. Yet the Muslim "stock character" persists in movies and television. Far from eliminating such negative stereotypical characters, "Hollywood films preserve traditional stereotypes and television shows follow Hollywood's lead."[21] Indeed, "assiduous research has shown that there is hardly a prime-time television show without several episodes of patently racist and insulting caricatures of Muslims."[22] Western mass media depictions of Islam and of Muslims have been generally shallow, callous, and often racist. The Arab-Israeli conflict, for example, helped to popularize films, such as "Exodus," depicting the founding of Israel. These films,

---

[19]Edward W. Said, *Covering Islam: How the Media and the Experts Determine How We See the Rest of the World* (New York: Pantheon Books, 1981), p. 69.

[20]Ibid., p. 8.

[21]Jack G. Shaheen, *The TV Arab* (Bowling Green, Wis.: Bowling Green State University Popular Press, 1984), p. 5.

[22]Said, *Covering Islam*, p. 69.

instead of using drama to explain the conflict's complexities, relied instead on creating an ambience reminiscent of World War II. In fact, "these movies present the Israeli-Arab conflict in much the same way as cowboys and Indians: the Arabs are always the bad guys, the Israelis, the good guys."[23]

Cinema stereotypes persisted during the 1970s. Several years after the murder of Israeli Olympic athletes by secular Palestinian extremists in Munich, the movie *Black Sunday* postulated an Arab attack on an American Superbowl crowd by means of a blimp.[24] OPEC price hikes in the late 1970s also engendered the film *Rollover,* in which "the Arabs destroy the world financial system." As a star of *Rollover,* Jane Fonda, the then-future wife of CNN founder Ted Turner, declared in an interview: Arabs "are unstable, they are fundamentalists, tyrants, anti–women, anti–free press."[25]

During the 1980s and 1990s, popular Hollywood movies depicted Muslims solely as terrorists bent on humiliating or conquering the United States. The lesson that movies like *Navy SEALs, Iron Eagle, Delta Force, Invasion USA, Death before Dishonor, True Lies, Rules of Engagement,* and *Executive Decision*[26] teach is that diplomacy is worthless, seeing an adversary's point of view has no value. Instead, "violence serves as the main vehicle for plot development and plot resolution."[27] And in Hollywood, "it doesn't take long to figure out which side is going to win the shootout."[28] Not surprisingly, the spirit of these movies lived on not just in future films but in future U.S. relations with Iraq. By the early 1990s, Iraqi conscripts became the victims of ten years of Hollywood dehumanization.[29] Notwithstanding the impact of television and film depictions of Muslims on the Western image of Islam, the news media—both print and electronic—are the primary source of information in Western society and thus the greatest perpetrator of "Islamophobia." Television shows and motion pictures have portrayed Muslims negatively and simplistically not only because these media trade in comfortable and convenient stereotypes but because they too rely on the Western news media. Fictional television and movie depictions of Muslims are merely the popular cultural expression of Western antipathy toward "Islam." Humiliating stereotypes of Muslims constructed for entertainment provide a catharsis through which Western paranoia and "Islamophobia" is expressed and partly relieved. The news media is the instigator of that paranoia and "Islamophobia."

---

[23]Laurence Michalak, "Cruel and Unusual: Negative Images of Arabs in American Popular Culture," *ADC Issues,* January 1984, pp. 14–16.

[24]Michael Parenti, *Make-Believe Media: The Politics of Entertainment* (New York: St. Martin's Press, 1992), p. 30.

[25]Ibid.

[26]For a complete listing of Hollywood movies that slander Arabs and Muslims, see Jack G. Shaheen, *Reel Bad Arabs: How Hollywood Vilifies a People* (New York: Olive Branch Press, 2001).

[27]Parenti, *Make-Believe Media,* pp. 31–32.

[28]William Claiborne, "Hollywood's Mideast Policy," *Washington Post,* July 14, 1986, p. 29.

[29]Parenti, *Make-Believe Media,* pp. 31–32.

For the most part, the mass media have unintentionally fabricated the "threat of Islam" in the guise of extremist Revolutionary Islamism. The psychological motivations previously discussed have facilitated this demonization of Islam and dehumanization of Muslims. But cognitive consistency and other such processes are alone not sufficient to explain the news media's bias in their coverage of Islam. Western media typically provide a simplistic, monochromatic picture of the Muslim world because of commercial constraints inherent in their operation. Journalists and reporters in the Western press, for example, tend to prefer sensational and exciting news events that will capture and hold the viewer's interest rather than slower-paced, more deliberate, more substantive stories—the kind that require time-consuming research and draw smaller audiences. The Muslim "types," which include terrorists, angry mobs, and oil-rich emirs, no matter how unrepresentative they are of Muslims at large, are common fixtures in news coverage of Islam and represent Islam to Westerners. The inherent newsworthiness of isolated incidents in the Muslim world will, on television screens, be perceived by Westerners as typical fare. Hostage taking, bomb throwing, and rioting mobs chanting "Down with America" come to epitomize the Western view of "Islam." Western news media rely on inherently sensational events to attract viewers. Endless stories of planes taking off and landing every hour without incident will likely drive viewers and advertising dollars away, if it does not kill viewers with boredom first. Unfortunately, lacking an informed and intelligent picture of the Muslim world, Westerners are likely to mistake the act of terrorism or the crowd run amuck for the everyday reality of Islam. Imagine Westerners' surprise if Muslims were to perceive the Los Angeles riots of 1992 as everyday reality all over the United States.

Certainly the great fault of the electronic news media is a lack of time and a consequent lack of depth. CNN's *Headline News*, for example, has only half an hour to explain important international events; and that brief thirty minutes must be shared with domestic news, business news, and sports and entertainment segments; add to that a hearty portion of commercials, and it is not surprising that the coverage of Islam and the Muslim world gets short shrift. Of course, viewers could eschew the sound bites and turn to more in-depth news coverage from, for example, National Public Radio's *All Things Considered*. But only a tiny fraction of the American population has time for news and analysis that is totally devoid of entertainment. We have patience only for the easily digestible, beautifully packaged, half-hour helping of network news. And while such news is not inherently bad, it is demonstrably insufficient, and worse, most Western viewers are unaware of its limitations as a source of valuable or reliable information. ABC, CBS, NBC, CNN, MSNBC, and Fox promise to give us the world if we give them half an hour. But the world they give us lacks depth and substance. Headline news has time enough only for the finely crafted headline—the story itself is sacrificed in Western haste.

The Western news media's inability and/or unwillingness to present an unbiased view of Islam, Muslims, and Muslim societies is a tragedy not only for Westerners who come away with a poor understanding of the Muslim world but for Muslims as well. The impact of the Western news media is felt around the world. During the Gulf War, that impact was magnified and compounded. Since the war, Muslims and Muslim nations, no longer strictly "the source of news . . . have become consumers of [Western] news."[30] Thus the Muslim world is today "learning about itself by means of images, histories, and information manufactured in the West."[31] Muslims now are being emotionally and psychologically affected by watching Westerners vilify and belittle Islam, Muslims, and the Muslim world on television. This has, understandably, shaped Muslim perceptions of the West.[32]

The communications revolution that brought CNN into Muslim households during the 1990s has been accompanied by "an over-all Muslim delay in understanding the reasons for Muslim dependence" on the Western mass media; this delay "prevents their doing something about it."[33] Well-organized, well-funded, and assertive Israeli interest groups have had a positive impact on media coverage of Jews and Israel, while no effective organization of pro-Muslim sympathies has improved coverage of Islam, Muslims, and Muslim states. Muslims themselves share some of the blame for this misfortune. First, Muslims living in democratic Western nations who decry unfair and unfavorable media coverage have done little to redress the problem. They have remained relatively disorganized, parsimonious with their money, nonpolitical, and therefore, powerless. Second, authoritarian leaders of most Muslim countries, fearful of their own unsavory human rights, economic, and social records, are unwilling to provide access to the Western mass media within their own countries. Third, some of the blame falls on those oil-rich Muslim nations that possess the money but lack the interest or will to improve the Western media's depiction of Islam, Muslims, and the Muslim world.

The establishment of Al-Jazeera, the twenty-four-hour Arabic language news channel based in the tiny emirate of Qatar, was one response to Western media bias in its coverage of the Muslim world. Founded in 1996 with $140 million from the Qatari government, this Arab equivalent to CNN and Fox reaches 35 million viewers in the Muslim world. During the U.S. war in Afghanistan (October to December 2001), Al-Jazeera was the sole foreign broadcaster allowed in Taliban-controlled territory. Osama bin Laden made use of the media outlet to supply videotapes of his denunciations of the West in the aftermath of the September 11 attacks. Al-Jazeera's anti-Western coverage of the conflict concerned Western policy makers, but attempts by the Bush administration to stifle Al-Jazeera were viewed in the Muslim world as hypocritical, considering that many Muslims consider Western news media "fundamentally partisan and biased in their own right."[34] Al-Jazeera's anti-Western slant is best answered not by attempts to quash

---

[30]Said, *Covering Islam*, p. 52.

[31]Ibid.

[32]Ibid.

[33]Ibid., p. 62.

[34]Joel Campagna, "Between Two Worlds: Qatar's Al-Jazeera Satellite Channel Faces Conflicting Expectations," http://www.cpi.org/Briefings/2001/aljazeera_oct01.html.

the network's independence (curbed somewhat by the channel's reliance on funding from the Qatari government) or to censor its message but by genuine Western attempts to convey the Western message to the Muslim world. That message can be persuasive to Muslims only insofar as it rejects blanket statements about Islam and terrorism that have no basis in reality.

Presently, Western fear of the "threat of Islam" is the overwhelming theme of Western media treatment of the Muslim world. Sensational and misleading information selectively perceived and transmitted by the news media could make Huntington's prophecy of a clash of civilizations self-fulfilling. While the West continues to portray Islam in a bad light and to give it a bad name, "the irony is that Western views of Islam on the whole prefer to associate Islam with what many Muslims themselves are opposed to in the current scene: punishment, autocracy, medieval modes of logic, theocracy."[35] Therefore, deliberate Western vilification of Islam, many Muslims reason, is nothing more than cultural imperialism, a Western-instigated and -funded conspiracy against them and their faith. Such views find a voice on Al-Jazeera.

Misperception is reciprocated by the Muslim world toward the West. Muslims are not immune to cognitive consistency and the black-white diabolical enemy image, by which the West is made into "the Great Satan." Just as the Westerner condemns "Islam" and its medievalism and barbarity, so does the Muslim condemn the "West" and its arrogance and consumerism. The conflict spiral of misperception soon becomes one of real hostility, increasingly difficult to defuse. And global Islamism feeds upon and fuels that conflict spiral. Real and perceived provocation by the West against "Islam" is answered with real and perceived hostility by frustrated and angry Muslims. Thus, the West and the Muslim world demonize each other, transforming the other into what each fears most. A political and cultural polarization occurs and the chasm separating "us" from "them" becomes ever more unbridgeable. The most radical demagogues rise to power spouting inflammatory religious rhetoric to win over the masses—and Islamic politics, militant or otherwise, takes on a more anti-Western temperament. Thus in response, the Western mass media, instead of denouncing the acts of a few radical and relatively parochial Muslims, begin ridiculing Islam, Muslims, the Muslim world, and a rich and varied civilization.

The Western Mass Media and the Iranian Revolution

Of all the upheavals gripping the Muslim world none has been more misread and misinterpreted by the Western mass media than the Iranian Revolution and the consequent hostage crisis in the twilight of the Carter presidency. The Western media totally misunderstood the motivations and dynamics animating the Iranian Revolution and therefore contributed to a conflict spiral and to policies implemented by both the United States and Iran that were shortsighted and often irrational. As the ultimate source of public information, the Western media blundered

---

[35]Said, *Covering Islam,* p. 64.

famously in its coverage of the Iranian Revolution specifically and Islam in general. The failure of the media rested not so much in its ignorance as in the failure to concede its ignorance to the viewer. With the Iranian Revolution and the hostage crisis, suddenly every journalist and pseudointellectual was an expert on Islam and on the causes of the Iranian Revolution. In short, the media and its "experts" erred in "pretending that a great deal was known and in presenting a view of Iran's revolution that was dictated more by official Washington than by reality."[36]

In truth, the Iranian Revolution was a monster of the United States' own making. It was the likeliest reaction to decades of senseless, short-term U.S. policy toward Iran. The ultimate success and ascendancy of the Revolutionary Islamist Ayatollah Khomeini over such Modernist Islamists as Mehdi Bazargan and Abul Hasan Banisadr and Muslim Secularists as Shahpour Bakhtiar was partly made possible by a long history of Western interference and intervention in Iranian internal affairs. Holding the line against communist expansion at all costs—even the life, liberty, and happiness of the Iranian people—insured not only the Revolution against the repressive *shah* but its decidedly anti-American temperament.

Yet both the Western media and Western policy makers were surprised by the Iranian Revolution and by the overthrow of the "iron-fisted" *shah.* Only months before, the Western news media were assuring readers and viewers that the *shah* maintained full control of Iran and enjoyed widespread popular support. Even President Carter praised the *shah* as a beloved and enlightened leader. Most Westerners accepted this public relations spectacle, but the Iranian people were not only unconvinced but incensed by favorable Western press coverage of the hated *shah.* When, for example, the *shah* in a last-ditch compromise move appointed Bakhtiar as prime minister and the new leader was lauded in the Western media, Bakhtiar found his position of authority in Iran abruptly untenable. The Iranian people did not trust the Western media. The government-controlled Iranian media was itself directly responsible for triggering the Iranian Revolution when, in a "spectacular case of bad judgment," the shah's men planted a story which called into question the ancestry of opposition leader Ayatollah Khomeini. This false report sent Iranians into the streets to protest angrily but peacefully in defense of the *ayatollah*'s honor.[37]

The consequent Iranian Revolution interested a Western mass media that sought to determine the motivations and ultimate intentions of the Iranian people. Conveniently overlooking a long history of U.S. support for a regime with a deplorable human rights record, the news media decided that the culprit behind "senseless" revolutionary upheaval was Islam, currently typified by "a disturbingly neurotic Iran," which was "writhing in self-provoked frenzy."[38] Unsatisfied even with the explanation that Muslims were insane and that their behavior was inexplicable, some journalists and scholars entertained the ridiculous idea that "the

---

[36]William A. Dorman and Mansour Farhang, *The U.S. Press and Iran: Foreign Policy and the Journalism of Deference* (Berkeley and Los Angeles: University of California Press, 1987), p. 179.

[37]Ibid.

[38]Edward Said, "Inside Islam," *Harper's,* January 1981, p. 27.

diabolism of communism" was acting "in natural alliance with the devilish PLO and the satanic Muslims."[39] Haunted by the Cold War paranoia that had cost the United States Iranian friendship in the first place, scholars, journalists, and policy makers evoked the 1950s-era notion of a worldwide conspiracy of "them against us." Consequently, the media swallowed "the regime's and Washington's contention that the *shah*'s problems were wholly the work of Islamic reactionaries and Marxists," their alleged cooperation and their fictional friendship producing what the *Washington Post* described as "a poisonous brew."[40] In reality, however, the Shi'ah leadership in the vanguard of the Iranian Revolution succeeded and prevailed only "as a result of widespread disillusionment with Western reforms and Soviet Marxism—two of the main sources of opposition ideology in Iran for fifty years."[41] Moreover, the *mullahs* were equally happy to characterize the USSR as the Great Satan as they were to demonize the United States—particularly after the Soviet invasion of Afghanistan in December 1979. The belief that Soviet Marxism motivated the fervor and the rage of the Iranian Revolution was unsupported by the evidence. Indeed, by 1979 it had grown obvious that "alleged Marxist influence among oil workers [was] more a product of Western press panic than a reality in the oil fields."[42] Nevertheless, the Western mass media—in thrall to a Cold War worldview and to an historical ignorance of and antipathy to Islam—sustained the incredible fiction of a communist-PLO-Shi'ah conspiracy against the West.

The Western media perpetuated another popular myth, that the Ayatollah Khomeini "had made the revolution instead of the other way around."[43] The Western media as usual simplified information to the extent that the simplification bore little resemblance to reality. The Western news media, immediately and unthinkingly reducing any event of consequence to the work of one man, determined that the aging *ayatollah* from Khomein had cleverly "masterminded" the revolution entirely by himself from exile and was, therefore, "the man who brought down the *shah*" and who would send Iran hurtling into medieval barbarity.[44] The role of the Iranian people individually and en masse was, according to the Western mass media, inconsequential and irrelevant to the story of the Iranian Revolution. In fact, U.S. dislike of the Revolution was first founded in that "single-minded media caricature of the Ayatollah Khomeini, a caricature that sends ethnocentric chills through Americans."[45] The news media by far preferred the simplicity of a story in which "our man in Tehran," the *shah*, was subverted and

---

[39]Edward W. Said, "Islam Rising," *Columbia Journalism Review,* March–April 1980, p. 26.

[40]Dorman and Farhang, *The U.S. Press and Iran,* p. 153.

[41]Ibid., p. 171.

[42]William A. Dorman and Mansour Farhang, "Nobody Lost Iran," *Politics Today,* May–June 1979, p. 37.

[43]Dorman and Farhang, *The U.S. Press and Iran,* p. 160.

[44]Ibid., pp. 160–161.

[45]Dorman and Farhang, "Nobody Lost Iran," p. 37.

overthrown by a fanatical *ayatollah*. And if Khomeini was bad, then conversely, the *shah* must have been good, if the world as portrayed by the Western media is truly black and white.

Consequently, mass media depictions of the *shah* were shallow and misleading. The *shah* cleverly portrayed himself the sturdy dam containing the Red deluge, as well as the enlightened, benevolent, and paternalistic dictator, like a latter-day Peter the Great, introducing his ignorant, backward, and stubborn subjects to the bounties of modernization and secularization. Thus, the king on his Peacock Throne enjoyed decades of relatively favorable press at the expense of the truth. The impression he left with the Western mass media was strong and endearing. At his downfall, the Western media, long feted and pampered by an indulgent *shah,* depicted the ruler as a "saddened, tearful, and ill-treated sovereign whose ungrateful people, in mindless fashion, had driven him from his country."[46] Looking back, the media described, but never discredited, the *shah*'s rule as "stern" and "iron-fisted"—terms that are euphemisms for what was really going on in Iran and, indeed, even appealing to law-and-order-minded Americans. Conversely, the press very rarely used unpalatable terms like "bloody" and "tyrannical," although they were equally appropriate descriptions of the *shah*'s rule.[47] Moreover, Iranians in opposition to the *shah* viewed Western media coverage with disappointment. They believed that the Western press had "misinterpreted and oversimplified their motives" while denying them "the legitimacy they believed their cause deserved."[48]

The American Hostage Crisis

The Western news media, however, did not turn definitively against the revolution until the seizure of U.S. diplomats in Iran by zealous Iranian students. The embassy takeover occurred in response to years of perceived interference, intervention, and abuse perpetrated by the United States against Iran. The mass media thought otherwise. American anchors and journalists—who were, after all, patriotic Americans—abandoned the pretense of objectivity in news coverage of Iran. They took personal offense at the taking of American hostages by Iranian militants. Their loyalties and their empathy rested fully with the hostages. In response to this Iranian attack on U.S. sovereignty, American reporters stigmatized the Iranian Revolution specifically, and Islam generally. Iran, in effect, "came to symbolize . . . American relations with the Muslim world."[49] In turn, Islam came to symbolize Iranian behavior. Blinded by the instant, unwilling to submit their attitudes to analysis, unable to escape the prison walls of their prejudices, Americans made the Iranian Revolution and the hostage crisis the basis on which Islam was

---

[46]Ibid., p. 163.

[47]Ibid., p. 164.

[48]William A. Dorman and Ehsan Omeed, "Reporting Iran the Shah's Way," *Columbia Press Review,* January–February 1979, p. 27.

[49]Said, *Covering Islam,* p. 77.

reduced to a militant, monolithic, and anti-American menace of explosive passions. As far as the Western press was concerned, "resentment, suspicion, and contempt were characteristic of 'Islam.' "[50]

The vilification of Islam was pronounced, not only because the Iranian students had taken hostages in the name of their own national pride but also because vilification was so easy. The news media, trading in simple and convenient stereotypes and stock characters could translate the revolution and all its complexities into a cartoon in which unreasonable mobs of self-flagellating Muslims confronted all things decent and American. The Iranian Revolution was portrayed as Islam out of control—a threat, like communism, best contained. Consequently, "the media had a field day in attacking Iran, even using abusive language against its leader. . . . Any dissent from the view that Iran was solely to blame for the crisis was considered bordering on unpatriotism."[51]

Wondering aloud how Iranians could hold America itself hostage, the press delved into the perceived cause of the frustration of efforts to free the hostages—Islam. A plethora of five-minute reports purporting to explain Islam crossed American T.V. screens. The impression these reports left with most Americans, who knew little or nothing of the Islamic faith, was shallow at best, grossly inaccurate at worst. Islam itself became the enemy because the Western media could not and/or would not explain the depth of or even the reasons behind Iranian anger with the United States. Instead of explaining Iranian anger, news organizations invented "the ugly Muslim" and his or her "hatred of this country," thereby slandering Islam to make the us-versus-them equation add up simply and without reference to tiresome complexities. Islam was fictionalized into a force within which "murder, war, [and] protracted conflict involving special horrors" were praiseworthy and commonplace.[52] And this force, Americans were informed, had set itself against Americans and their way of life and, hence, warranted only our enmity and disdain. And as Muslims likewise viewed the gross fallacies attributed to Islam by Western journalists, the realization increased throughout the Muslim world that the West had set itself against all Muslims and, hence, warranted only their enmity and disdain. It was cultural imperialism, many Muslim charged, and the Western model was further discredited as something inherently anti-Islamic.

Western Coverage of the Iran-Iraq War

Although "media antipathy towards the Iranian Revolution [was] a continuation of past hostility," Western media misperceptions of Iran ended neither with the consolidation of the Islamic regime nor with the peaceful resolution of the hostage crisis during the inauguration of Ronald Reagan. Instead, encouraged by an American public strongly against Iran, the Reagan administration embarked on policies meant to punish the Iranians. The mass media rarely questioned these

---

[50]Said, "Inside Islam," p. 20.

[51]Mushahid Hussain, "How Western Media Didn't Report Islam," August 15, 1980, p. 26.

[52]Said, *Covering Islam*, 79.

policies even when they involved lending support to Saddam Hussein following the 1980 Iraqi invasion of Iran. Only when George Bush faced a stubborn and dangerous Saddam Hussein a decade later were those policies critically examined by the media. During the 1980s, however, anger with Iran was rooted so deeply in the American psyche that the press further demonized the Iranians even at the cost of coddling the ambitious tyrant of Baghdad.

When the Iraqi advance into Iran began to flounder and Iraqi armies suffered dramatic setbacks at Iranian hands less than five months after the initial invasion, the Western mass media began to consider the prospect of total Iranian victory over Iraq. News stories from Western correspondents in Tehran described Iranian military forces repelling Iraqi invaders as "a barbaric and fanatical army on the rampage." Analysts in Washington, D.C., used such images "to conjure up an image of imminent danger to the globe that must be contained at any cost."[53] Consequently, in the eyes of many Muslims, "rather than appreciating the Islamic qualities which triumphed over Ba'athism, the readers of the western media once again prepared to accept and more likely welcome a concerted western attempt to destroy the Islamic Revolution."[54]

Perhaps the crowning error of the Western news media during the long Iran-Iraq War rested in coverage of the 1980 destruction of a commercial Iranian airliner by the USS *Vincennes*. To engage high-speed but easily outclassed Iranian gunboats operating within Iranian territorial waters, the *Vincennes* willfully and intentionally crossed "into Iranian waters, . . . in violation of international law"; however, the captain of the U.S. ship "was not paying attention to juridical niceties."[55] While pursuing the Iranian gunboats, the *Vincennes* picked up a radar blip that was initially and correctly identified as a commerical airliner. The 290 passengers and crew of Flight 655 had taken off from Iran's Bandar Abbas Airport heading for Dubai along a routine and prescheduled flight path from which it never deviated. Unfamiliar with Iranian flight schedules over Iranian territorial waters, the *Vincennes* now mistakenly identified the Iranian airbus as a possible F-14 Iranian airforce jet fighter. The *Vincennes* fired on the plane; there were no survivors.

The destruction of Flight 655, empathy for the captain of the *Vincennes*, and discussion by some in the American mass media (especially on radio talk shows) that the Khomeini regime had intentionally sent the civilian airplane with dead Iranians on board to embarrass the United States, infuriated Iranians and "surely caused Iran to delay the release of the American hostages in Lebanon."[56] More important, it brought grief to the families of the innocent dead and reinforced the conviction among many Muslims around the world that the United States was "out to get them." Indeed, when the mass funeral for the victims was conducted in

---

[53]Iqbal Asaria, "Media Proves Mightier Than the Sword and Penetrates Islamic Defenses," *Crescent International*, Vol. 11, No. 4 (May 1–15, 1982), p. 4.

[54]Ibid.

[55]John Barry and Roger Charles, "Sea of Lies," *Newsweek*, July 13, 1992, p. 33.

[56]Ibid., p. 29.

Tehran, "it was an article of faith in Iran that the Americans deliberately attacked the plane."[57]

The Pentagon and White House, while expressing remorse, explained the tragedy solely in terms of a technical error and praised the captain of the *Vincennes* for his commendable service to his country. And the press in its initial coverage of the event engaged in no investigative journalism or critical analysis. It should be emphasized, however, that the American news media is not necessarily subservient to the U.S. government; it is often a prisoner, rather, of it own ethno-centric worldview. Consequently, "the news stories about the U.S. downing of an Iranian plane called it a technical problem while the Soviet downing of a Korean Jet (Flight 007 in 1983) was portrayed as a moral outrage."[58]

The 1983 Soviet attack on Korean Airlines Flight 007 was branded "Murder in the Air" by *Newsweek* magazine. In contrast, for a situation with eerily similar circumstances, but with roles reversed, *Newsweek* on its July 18, 1988, cover laid no blame but merely "promised to disclose, about Iran Air, 'Why It Happened.' "[59] The press blamed the government of the USSR at every level for the KAL disaster while shifting the blame for the U.S. attack on the Iranian plane either to technical error or, worse yet, on (nonexistent) Iranian provocation. The underlying tone in the Western media was that the Iranians had somehow been asking for it. The Western media described victims of the KAL tragedy as "innocent human beings" who could tell "269 tales of personal poignancy." Discussion of the Iranian victims was bloodless and sterile, as though the *Vincennes* had inadvertently swatted a fly.[60] While the attack on the KAL was described as "brutal" and "barbaric" by the U.S. media, the U.S. attack on Iran Air was "fatal" but "understandable."[61] In fact, one retired navy captain insisted that "the Iranian airliner was placed in a dangerous situation that was created by its own government."[62]

Newsweek's investigation took four years to determine that the attack on the Iranian airbus was only superficially the result of technical error. Despite Pentagon assertions to the contrary, *Newsweek* determined that the *Vincennes* was in Iranian coastal waters in clear violation of international law—just as Iran had been by taking American diplomats hostage. Muslims around the world, distressed by the United States' nonchalant attitude to Muslim deaths, were further inclined to see the Western mass media as yet another tentacle of the imperialist leviathan. The mass media's reporting was hypocritical but not devious or conspiratorial. In short, "news organizations shape their reports to elicit favorable reactions from readers and viewers, and the anticipated reactions of the public also affect the rhetoric and actions of political elites, who are the primary 'sponsors' of news

---

[57]Ibid., p. 39.

[58]Robert M. Entman, "Framing U.S. Coverage of International News: Contrasts in Narratives of the KAL and Iran Air Incidents," *Journal of Communication*, Vol. 41, No. 4 (Autumn 1991), p. 6.

[59]Ibid., p. 11.

[60]Ibid., p. 17.

[61]Ibid., p. 19.

[62]Quoted in "The Navy Returns Fire," letters to *Newsweek*, August 3, 1993, p. 8.

frames."[63] The opinions of the public, the media, and the policy makers were thus founded on the basis of conformity.

The mutual derision and distrust sowed by the mass media coverage of Iran's Islamic Revolution, Khomeini's Islamic regime, the Iran-Iraq War, and the 444 days that Americans were held hostage in Tehran surfaced again with the Rushdie controversy in the late 1980s. The war of words and between the two worlds—the Western and the Muslim—was rejoined.

The Rushdie Controversy

"The author of *The Satanic Verses* book, which is against Islam, the Prophet and the Koran, and all those involved in its publication who were aware of its content, are sentenced to death."[64] With this declaration, Iran's Ayatollah Khomeini baited the West, gave the Revolutionary Islamists and Traditionalist Islamists a new issue with which to attack Western animosity toward Islam, polarized the Muslim world, and made Salman Rushdie's novel an international best-seller, in nations where it was not banned.

Born a Muslim, Rushdie was no longer practicing his faith when he wrote *The Satanic Verses*. He was educated in Britain, where he resided until driven into hiding by Khomeini's death sentence. His 1988 novel, *The Satanic Verses*, was roundly condemned throughout the Muslim world as an affront to Islam. But it was the eighty-eight-year-old Ayatollah Khomeini who, more than anyone, thrust the Rushdie controversy onto the world stage, polarizing world opinion, and contributing to a confrontation of rhetoric between Islam and the West.

The Muslim world was justifiably galled by Rushdie's inflammatory book. The very title, *The Satanic Verses*, questions the validity of the Qur'an as holy scripture. Rushdie consciously impugns the Qur'an and imputes upon it satanic overtones—that it is the work of the Devil. Likewise, the second part of the book is entitled "Mahound," a derogatory name for Muhammad given by medieval Christians to discredit Islam. "Mahound" is an intentional caricature of Muhammad insofar as Rushdie parallels the life of the fictional "Mahound" with the life of Muhammad. Moreover, Rushdie insinuates that Muhammad manufactured the Qur'an for his own benefit under "Satanic" influence and thus that the holiest book of Islam is not the revealed Word of God. Hence, the "businessman-turned-prophet" is portrayed as a fake, and Islam a work of clever forgery. Along the way, Rushdie gratuitously names twelve prostitutes after Muhammad's wives and thereby even further infuriates Muslims. In essence, "to devout Muslims, this book challenged and even violated the centrality of their beliefs, the very words of God, the integrity of their religious doctrine, and the image and dignity of the person of prophet Muhammad."[65] Harvard professor William Graham explains that "it's as

---

[63]Entman, "Framing U.S. Coverage of International News," p. 7.

[64]Quoted in Russel Watson, et al., "A Satanic Fury," *Newsweek*, February 27, 1989, p. 34.

[65]Mahmood Monshipouri, "The Islamic World's Reaction to *The Satanic Verses*: Cultural Relativism Revisited," *Journal of Third World Studies*, Vol. 3, No. 1 (Spring 1991), p. 205.

if you took the Bible, and in the middle of the Sermon on the Mount, you showed Jesus fantasizing copulation with whores."[66]

It is a testament to the Western media's culturally myopic worldview that, upon publication of *The Satanic Verses*, the Muslim world's vehemently negative reaction was unanticipated and totally misperceived. Immediately, calls came from Muslim communities to ban Rushdie's novel, and many developing nations obliged—among them Egypt, Saudi Arabia, Pakistan, India, and South Africa.

To Westerners and Muslims alike, the Rushdie controversy warranted outrage, but for different reasons. Westerners, particularly those in the liberal media, viewed Muslim attempts at censorship as at least unseemly, at most an affront to principles of freedom of speech and expression. Islamists viewed Western defense of Rushdie as the continuation of a fourteen-hundred-year-old cultural crusade against Islam. Above all, the Rushdie controversy became a rallying cry of Revolutionary Islamists to reject all things Western. The West, meanwhile, watched in horror as Muslims in Britain staged book burnings and protestors marched on the American Cultural Center in Islamabad, Pakistan, throwing stones, roughing up a few Americans, and demanding Rushdie's death. For the West, the coup de grâce came February 14, 1989, with Khomeini's "Valentine's Day" death sentence.

Sadly, the West responded to these unreasonable emotional outbursts with a few of its own. Western commentators and politicians heralded Rushdie's "inalienable" right to offend even one billion Muslims, while the Western news media, with an eye to the sensational, portrayed all Muslims as primitive religious fanatics burning books, donning shrouds, and proposing to hunt Rushdie down and "send him to Hell."

Death threats aside, Muslim calls for censorship of *The Satanic Verses* are easily explicable. Since Muslims identify themselves not according to the nation-state, as Westerners do, but according to the *ummah*, according to Islam and its community of believers, the charge against Rushdie of cultural treason is reasonable, while suppression of his book, which represents an obscene attack on that community, is understandable.[67] If, after all, the United States can plot to kill Fidel Castro of Cuba, Ngo Dinh Diem of South Vietnam, Rafael Leonidas Trujillo of the Dominican Republic, and Muammar al-Qadaffi of Libya; if it can overthrow Jacobo Arbenz Guzman of Guatemala, Salvador Allende of Chile, and Muhammad Mossadeq of Iran; and if it can invade Panama, Granada, and Iraq in the name of "democracy" and "human rights," why cannot the Muslim world in the name of the Qur'an, which "is the ultimate constitution of the community of believers,"[68] prohibit publication of Rushdie's libelous book, given that permitting publication is analogous to inciting a riot? Indeed, for the sake of the public order

---

[66]Quoted in Donna Foote, "At Stake: The Freedom to Imagine," *Newsweek*, February 27, 1989, p. 37.

[67]Ali Mazrui, *The Satanic Verses or a Satanic Novel? The Moral Dilemmas of the Rushdie Affair* (Greenpoint, N.Y.: Committee of Muslim Scholars and Leaders of North America, 1989), p. 6.

[68]Ibid., p. 10.

in predominantly Muslim countries, banning Rushdie's book is not a repressive act; it is a responsible act. If "American political morality expects its citizens to be ready to 'uphold, protect and defend the Constitution of the United States' "[69] against enemies foreign and domestic, how can the West deny the right of Muslims to uphold, protect, and defend the integrity of the Qur'an? Western media, bent on insulting the villain of the day, never addressed these questions. Instead, the news media turned to simple stereotypes in which once again "Islam is reduced to terrorism and fundamentalism and now, alas, [was] seen to be acting accordingly, in the ghastly violence prescribed by the Ayatollah Khomeini."[70]

Both Britain and the United States, whose staunch defense of individual freedoms is admirable, consistently censor information whether for reasons of national security (i.e., Britain's ban of the book *Spycatcher*) or to avoid unduly offending minority groups. Although the latter form of censorship is practiced less by government than by private corporations and interest groups, it is still censorship. Moreover, thoughtful censorship in a free society is not necessarily harmful so long as reasonable limits are observed. Likewise, the "political correctness" fad currently sweeping U.S. campuses is based on gagging individuals who might otherwise give offense to women and minorities. In sum, this is all characteristic of the struggle between individual and corporate rights.

Muslims naturally wonder why censorship of culturally treasonous material is commonplace in the West (see if you can find a legally displayed swastika in Germany), while the reasonable concerns and requests of Muslims are either ignored or deemed unreasonable. Meanwhile, Rushdie wins literary awards, more for pity than for merit. Thus, the Muslim world rightly perceives Western hostility toward Islam. The West bestows upon Rushdie the right to blaspheme Islam and slander its 1.2 billion believers, in fact congratulates him for it, while the right of those 1.2 billion believers to apply their community standards against Rushdie's heretical, hate-inspiring book is denied.

In contrast, when Irish singer Sinead O'Connor tore up a photograph of Pope John Paul II on an airing of *Saturday Night Live* in 1992, press sympathy was clearly for millions of rightly offended American Catholics. No mention was ever made of O'Connor's right to free speech while a mob cheered on a steamroller as it crushed hundreds of O'Connor CDs—a picture analogous to the burning of Rushdie's book by a handful of Muslims in different parts of the world.

There was no question in the Muslim world, or even in the West, that Rushdie maligned Islam. However, there was a question among Muslims regarding what constituted an appropriate response to Rushdie's blasphemy. While the Western mass media characterized riots, book burning, and death sentences as the universal reaction of Muslims to *The Satanic Verses*, this was simply not the case. And while all Muslims justly condemned Rushdie's book, not all demanded Rushdie's death.

---

[69]Ibid., p. 6.

[70]Edward W. Said, quoted in Lis Appignanesi and Sara Maitland, eds., *The Rushdie File* (Syracuse, N.Y.: Syracuse University Press, 1990), p. 165.

Many Muslims openly supported Khomeini's death edict and made comments that truly shocked Western sensibilities and that therefore enjoyed great exposure in the mass media. According to one zealot: "I think we should kill Salman Rushdie's whole family. . . . His body should be chopped into little pieces and sent to all Islamic countries as a warning to those who would insult our religion."[71] But many more Muslims, offered no such publicity in the Western mass media, regretted and repudiated the *Ayatollah*'s actions: "[Rushdie] should never have said those things against the prophet. . . . But it is also not right to call for his death."[72] And in India, where the Rushdie book had been banned, prominent Muslims denounced Khomeini's death sentence and felt that the anti-Rushdie movement had been co-opted by the Iranian *ayatollah*.[73] Furthermore, they conceded that "this ban has made the book more popular. Just ignoring it would have been better for Muslims."[74] Another Muslim expressed similar misgivings about the Rushdie uproar: "It has set back Islam. It conveys to non-Muslims a picture of Islam that is barbaric, rabid, and extreme."[75]

Few Muslims felt any warmth or sympathy for Rushdie's partly self-imposed plight, and many Westerners were similarly inclined to denounce Rushdie's insensitivity. Former president Jimmy Carter, for example, insisted that "while Rushdie's First Amendment freedoms are important, we have tended to promote him and his book with little acknowledgement that it is a direct insult to those millions of Muslims whose sacred beliefs have been violated."[76] Rushdie had insulted the most sacred beliefs of Islam. Nevertheless, the news media refused to acknowledge the contention that blasphemy and apostasy were at the heart of Muslim anger. Instead, a story was widely disseminated that Khomeini's death sentence was no better than a cynical effort to prop up the floundering Iranian Revolution, not a measure to defend the integrity of Islam. Western journalists perceived hidden motives behind Khomeini's death threats, particularly in statements the *ayatollah* made indicating that "the dispute over *The Satanic Verses* proved that it was pointless [for Muslims] to pursue moderate policies."[77]

There is little doubt that Khomeini's behavior can be partly attributed to his falling stature in the Muslim world by 1989. His nation was in economic shambles and social decline; he had been forced by prolonged and bloody stalemate to accept a cease-fire with sworn enemy Iraq; and Khomeini's own probable successors had begun to decry the failures and shortcomings of the Islamic Revolution.

---

[71]Quoted in Watson, "A Satanic Fury," pp. 35–36.

[72]Quoted in Sheila Tefft, "Muslims Debate Rushdie Uproar," *Christian Science Monitor*, February 27, 1989, p. 3.

[73]Ibid.

[74]Ibid.

[75]Quoted in John Hughes, "Authors, Death Threats, and Islam," *Christian Science Monitor*, February 22, 1989, p. 18.

[76]Jimmy Carter quoted in Appignanesi and Maitland, eds., *The Rushdie File*, p. 237.

[77]Youssef M. Ibrahim, "Khomeini Assails Western Response to Rushdie Affair," *New York Times*, February 22, 1989, p. 1.

By seizing the anti-Rushdie banner from those who first unfurled it and making it his own, the aging *ayatollah* sought to stoke the smoldering embers of the Islamic Revolution in Iran and reassert himself and his brand of militant Islamism on the Muslim world.[78]

Unfortunately, many analysts seized upon this interpretation of the *ayatollah's* actions as though Rushdie's blasphemy was irrelevant to the story or as though 1.2 billion offended Muslims were the brainwashed minions of the Shi'ah *imam*. The Rushdie controversy was symptomatic of the ever widening chasm of perception between the West and the Muslim world. When, on February 12, 1989, enraged Muslims marched on the American Cultural Center in Islamabad, Pakistan, they "carried placards attacking Zionism as well as Rushdie's book and its publisher."[79] Evidently, the Rushdie book represented only the latest in a series of perceived Western-instigated affronts to Muslims and their faith. Just as the West had used the Rushdie controversy to vilify Islam and to ridicule its alleged "medievalism," so did Islamists on the same basis justify their rejection of Westernization and secularization as evils inherently incompatible with the "straight path" of Islam. The Rushdie controversy did not occur in a vacuum but must be considered in the context of Islamic politics insofar as, "given the interrelatedness of culture, religion, and politics in the Muslim world, the reactions to [*The Satanic Verses*] have taken on understandably explicit political forms."[80] In fact, the Rushdie controversy represents "the spark which set alight an explosive mixture already present."[81] Thus, Revolutionary Islamists, like Khomeini, utilized the Rushdie book to galvanize mass support against Western influence generally, and against the Muslim Secularists and Modernist Islamists specifically. By extrapolation then, the Rushdie controversy is not merely a manifestation of Revolutionary Islamism but a positive contribution to its strength and popularity.

The Gulf War

The 1990 Iraqi invasion of Kuwait and the subsequent U.S.-led Operation Desert Storm were of profound significance in the short history of Western news media coverage of Islam and Muslims. Of course, Operation Desert Storm was not an explicitly anti-Muslim crusade, nor was it portrayed as such, primarily because Kuwait itself was a Muslim nation and other Muslim countries, including Saudi Arabia and Egypt, fought with the U.S. coalition to expel Iraqi forces from Kuwait. Yet there remained an undercurrent of anti-Muslim sentiment that affected Western public opinion to the war.

---

[78]Alex Efty, "Khomeini Aimed His 'Verses' Attack to Stop Liberal Trends," *Birmingham News*, February 26, 1989, p. 5A.

[79]Barbara Crossette, "Muslims Storm U.S. Mission in Pakistan," *New York Times*, February 13, 1989, p. 12.

[80]Monshipouri, "The Islamic World's Reaction," p. 205.

[81]William Montgomery Watt, *Muslim-Christian Encounters: Perceptions and Misperceptions* (New York: Routledge, 1991), p. 121.

This war, called the first "media war" because of the round-the-clock cover-age it received, was both brief and, at least from the Western perspective, blood-less. Support for the war was based primarily on propaganda generated by the exiled rulers of Kuwait, who made a media spectacle of terrible atrocities com-mitted by the occupying Iraqi forces in Kuwait. Recognizing the willingness of the Western mass media to serve as a conduit for Iraqi atrocity stories, the Kuwaiti government hired the public relations firm Hill and Knowlton. In October 1990, Hill and Knowlton provided the U.S. House of Representatives with a witness to the Iraqi invasion who claimed that Iraqi soldiers had removed babies from incu-bators and had let them die on the hospital floor. As it turned out, the "witness" was, in fact, the daughter of the Kuwaiti ambassador to the United States. She had not been in Kuwait during the invasion and had witnessed no atrocities commit-ted in Kuwait by Iraqi forces. But before the Western news media became aware of the shaky credibility of the story's teller, the story itself had been accepted, like so many other xenophobic rumors, by the Western public and by Western policy makers, including U.S. senators who made reference to the incubator atrocity in support of war against Iraq. In fact, ABC discovered, some years after the war, that Hill and Knowlton had used focus groups to determine which atrocities would most upset Americans: they discovered that baby atrocity stories were effective.[82]

The Hill and Knowlton firm played a significant role in galvanizing U.S. sup-port for war against Iraq. Prior to their campaign of atrocity stories, public opin-ion was opposed to possible war, and Congress was inclined against military intervention.[83] The Hill and Knowlton media blitz, however, tipped the scales of public opinion toward war. The Western mass media sold viewers on the likeli-hood of war and the Bush administration's prosecution of that war. Atrocity sto-ries circulated, although many were exaggerations or simply untrue, with the Western media's connivance. Douglas Kellner, Professor of Philosophy at University of Texas at Austin, argues: "The media which repeated these lies with-out scepticism or inquiry also revealed itself to be a naïve instrument of U.S. (gov-ernment) propaganda."[84] In reality, however, both the Western news media and U.S. policy makers turned out to be the naïve instruments of the Kuwaiti govern-ment through the offices of the public relations firm Hill and Knowlton.

There is no question, however, that Western news media were largely uncrit-ical of the U.S. government's prosecution of the war. When U.S. deployment of troops in the region began, the news media agreed to limitations on access to sol-diers in the field by accepting the press pool system. Coalition military forces restricted media access by organizing journalists into pools "that were taken to sights selected by the military itself, and then reporters were allowed to interview troops with their military 'minders' present."[85] The pool system had been adopted

---

[82]Douglas Kellner, *The Persian Gulf TV War* (Boulder, Col.: Westview Press, 1992), pp. 67–69.

[83]Ibid., p. 70.

[84]Ibid., p. 71.

[85]Ibid., p. 80.

by the U.S. military, partly due to British success with such a pool system in the Falkland Islands war and partly because the media had enjoyed virtually unrestricted access to the field in Vietnam. Unflattering media reports in Vietnam, so the military believed, had undermined Western public support for the war. The U.S. government saw to it that it wouldn't happen again; their control of the media during the Gulf War "was unprecedented in the history of U.S. warfare."[86] Moreover, "press and video coverage were also subject to censorship, so that, in effect, the military tightly controlled press coverage of the U.S. military deployment in the Gulf and then the action in the Gulf war."[87]

The imposition of press pools was not necessary to keep the Western media under control. The very fact that journalists were so accommodating to the military's use of pools was evidence enough that the pools themselves were a formality. Critics of the Western media have claimed "[i]n its framing of the 'national debate,' the media cooperated with the government in limiting public understanding of the conflict."[88] The media acted almost as another branch of the armed services or a government department. The Western news outlets were quick to report sensational stories, sometimes untrue. Months or years later, more in-depth Western reports would reveal the falsity of those initial stories. But it was too late—the damage had been done. Of course, Western media scepticism and criticism is unlikely in times of war—the journalists are almost universally American or European in background and are likely to be patriotic in the face of war or crisis. Thus, there is good reason to expect that "when the United States undertakes an especially dramatic foreign policy action, such as the bombing of another country, the media tend to be compliant mouthpieces of administration policy."[89] Unfortunately, it is at precisely these times that the Muslim world is most likely exposed to Western news accounts. And these accounts necessarily do not reflect the anger and resentment of the Muslim world toward the West. Rather, they tend to demonize the Muslim world and thus alienate non-Western news consumers. This apparent connivance of Western media with Western governments was further reinforced by the tendency of U.S. and UK reporters to identify themselves with government policies and coalition forces by using the words *we* and *our* in Gulf War coverage.[90] This blurring of distinction has been more pronounced during the recent "war on terror."

Other media critics point out that Western public opinion supporting war with Iraq was based on popular Western anti-Arab and anti-Muslim cultural

---

[86]Ibid., p. 81.

[87]Ibid., p. 80.

[88]Lee Wigle Artz and Mark A. Pollock, "Limiting the Options: Anti-Arab Images in the U.S. Media Coverage of the Persian Gulf Crisis" in Yahya R. Kamalipour, ed., *The U.S. Media and the Middle East: Image and Perception* (Westport, Conn.: Praeger, 1997), p. 120.

[89]Douglas Kellner, "The U.S. Media and the 1993 War against Iraq," in Kamalipour, ed., *The U.S. Media and the Middle East*, p. 117.

[90]Kellner, *The Persian Gulf TV War*, p. 87.

stereotypes. Although ostensibly coming to the defense of an Arab country against Iraq, the U.S. public was swayed "by media employment of culturally acceptable anti-Arab images."[91] The Western mass media did not offer balanced perspectives of the buildup to war or the war itself. Instead, it relied on traditional and commonplace references from popular culture. Attacks on the character and humanity of Saddam Hussein, which were largely true, unfortunately were "accompanied by commonplace images of other Arabs—including U.S. allies—as incompetent, weak, self-centered, and incapable of diplomacy in their own region."[92] Interestingly, these fearsome caricatures of Iraqis and other Arabs were accompanied by a second commonplace: "the righteousness of a civilized Western world courageously defended by U.S. soldiers."[93]

The Western media's use of these disparaging stereotypes was made considerably easier by their uncritical reporting of stage-managed press briefings in which footage of the war was presented in a way more evocative of a video game than a conflict in which people were dying. The use of so-called "smart bombs" that, at least in footage supplied by the U.S. military, could strike targets with exacting precision was presented by Western media in a manner that convinced many that this was the reality of the Gulf War. Images of collateral damage (i.e., civilian casualties) appeared on occasion but were downplayed as the regrettable exception rather than the rule. Grainy footage of laser-guided bombs striking Iraqi air force buildings emphasized an impression of the Gulf War as a "clean" war that would upset few Western sensibilities; the technology permitted the coalition "to provide good family entertainment without offending the viewing public."[94]

Apart from being a misleading portrayal of the war's realities, at least for those civilians and soldiers under the bombs, the footage removed any possibility of empathy for victims. The war was "an attack on things—weapons, transporters, bridges, buildings—but not on people."[95] But it was because Westerners were not subjected to the horrors that this war visited on Iraqi civilians and soldiers—who, incidentally, wanted nothing to do with a conflict with the world's remaining superpower—that Western stereotypes of Muslims could go undisturbed. Western minds could remain untroubled by the realization that these were fellow human beings and their suffering, even if not their culture, was real. Such feelings of empathy for the avowed enemy would have been counterproductive to the task at hand, which from the U.S. government's point of view was not only to cripple Saddam's power to make war on U.S. allies but to win U.S. public support.

---

[91]Artz and Pollock, "Limiting the Options," p. 119.

[92]Ibid., p. 120.

[93]Ibid. .

[94]Haim Bresheeth, "The New World Order," in Haim Bresheeth and Nira Yuval-Davis, eds., *The Gulf War and the New World Order* (London: Zed Books, 1991), p. 252.

[95]Martin Shaw and Roy Carr-Hill, "Public Opinion and Media Coverage in Britain," in Hamid Mowlana, George Gerbner, and Herbert I. Schiller, eds., *Triumph of the Image: The Media's War in the Persian Gulf—A Global Perspective* (Boulder, Colo.: Westview Press, 1992), p. 146.

Ultimately, the most significant casualty in the Gulf War was public opinion in the Muslim world.[96] Anti-U.S. demonstrations against the war in Algeria, Egypt (which was a coalition partner), Libya, Mauritania, Morocco, Sudan, Tunisia, and Yemen received scant attention in the Western news media. Although the United States was able to find allies in the governments of many Muslim countries, the populations themselves seemed at best wary of U.S. intervention in the Gulf and objected to the U.S. military presence in Saudi Arabia. In fact, it was this very objection that motivated Osama bin Laden to denounce the United States and carry on a *jihad* against the West that ultimately culminated in the attacks on New York and Washington, D.C.

The War on Terror

On September 11, 2001, Revolutionary Islamists, most probably trained by the al-Qaeda terrorist network led by Osama bin Laden in Afghanistan, destroyed the twin towers of the World Trade Center in New York City and destroyed a portion of the Pentagon building in Washington, D.C. Western media coverage began that morning, and as bin Laden's connection to the attacks became clear, war became inevitable. But the war was to be a very different one. The al-Qaeda network was not a nation-state but an affiliation of militant Revolutionary Islamists, headquartered in Afghanistan but spread among terrorist cells in many other countries both in the West and in the Muslim world. The attacks were devastating to the West, not so much in terms of their actual physical impact as psychologically.

In the days immediately following the attacks on the United States, Western media reporting was thoughtful in a way it had avoided before. The overwhelming response was one of terrible sadness and reflection on the loss of life. Calls for revenge were relatively muted, particularly given that in the first several days little was known about the perpetrators or their motives. Throughout the country—indeed, throughout the West—there were outbursts of anti-Muslim violence. But this ignorant racist violence was often misdirected; victims in the United States included Sikhs, who aren't Muslims but wear turbans. Additionally, the Western media was quick to carry extensive reports on anti-Muslim attacks in the West. The media reported on statements made by President Bush and other national and local leaders who warned Americans not to attack Muslim immigrants or Muslim Americans. Newspaper editorials around the country urged restraint and cautioned Americans "not to repeat the tragic injustice that occurred when we detained Japanese Americans during World War II, just because of their race."[97] Even Western popular culture resisted the urge to renew Arab and Muslim bashing and adhered instead to more conscientious programming, intended not to inflame passions but to calm fears and raise money for victims.

---

[96]Khawla Matter, "Western Media: Guilty until Proved Innocent," in Mowlana, Gerbner, and Schiller, eds., *Triumph of the Image*, p. 104.

[97]Amital Etzioni, "A Proud American Moment," *Christian Science Monitor*, October 11, 2001, p. 1

Amnesty International also warned of the danger of xenophobia and applauded steps taken to avert it. In its annual report, the organization noted, "there is a danger that as the world's political leaders focus on combatting 'terrorism' from abroad, a climate is engendered in which racism and xenophobia can flourish."[98] The report also listed hate crimes in the aftermath of the attack committed in the United States and other Western countries against Muslims and people mistaken for Muslims. Like the victims in the World Trade Center towers and the Pentagon, these Muslims were similarly "victims of an attack carried out in the name of Islam."[99]

In the following weeks, Western news media focused increasingly on Osama bin Laden's connection to the terror attack. Bin Laden's ties with the Taliban regime governing 90 percent of Afghanistan were close enough that the West turned to the Taliban leadership and demanded it turn over bin Laden and his chief lieutenants. Even Pakistan, which had nurtured the Taliban, made it clear to the Taliban leadership that the regime would be attacked by a new U.S. coalition of primarily Western powers if the Taliban failed to comply with the West's demands. This, in fact, is precisely what happened. The bombing campaign against Afghanistan's ruling Taliban began within a month of the attacks on the United States. The Taliban crumbled within another month, and members of al-Qaeda fled or were taken prisoner by various Afghan factions that opposed the Taliban. The Western media's role in all this was primarily one of support for Western action and a patriotism that tended to defer to the U.S. government. This was predictable and not necessarily inappropriate, given the magnitude of the attacks on New York and Washington, D.C., and the willingness, shared by most Americans, Europeans, and Russians, to root out al-Qaeda whatever the cost.

Owing to the Taliban regime's quick collapse, the Western bombing campaign was briefer than anticipated. But in spite of the campaign's short duration, public opinion in the Muslim world, while often sympathetic with the United States, was opposed to what most Muslims viewed as the futility and devastation of a Western bombing campaign against impoverished Afghanistan. Al-Jazeera's anti-Western coverage of the bombing campaign, which began on October 7, finally motivated U.S. policy makers to find a way to convince Muslims around the world that the bombing of Afghanistan was not a crusade against Islam. In an October Gallup poll in Pakistan, 83 percent of Pakistanis supported or sympathized with the Taliban. Only 3 percent sided with the United States.[100] Demonstrations and street violence in Pakistan underscored the anti-Western leanings of many Pakistanis, despite their government's support of the Western campaign against the Taliban.[101]

---

[98]Peter Ford, "Xenophobia Follows U.S. Terror," *Christian Science Monitor*, October 11, 2001, p. 1.

[99]Ibid.

[100]Francine Kiefer and Ann Scott Tyson, "In War of Words, US Lags Behind," *Christian Science Monitor*, October 17, 2001.

[101]The Pakistani population, while sympathizing with the Taliban, was generally unwilling to take to the streets or challenge the authority of the Musharraf government to side with the West.

What the Western media has failed to explain to most Westerners is how deeply resentful the Muslim world is toward the West, and toward the United States in particular. While many moderate Muslims view the attacks on the United States as tragic and un-Islamic, they themselves have been critical of U.S. foreign policy and could not comfortably support the West's bombing of Afghanistan—a fellow Muslim nation.[102]

Although President Bush and other Western leaders insisted that the war on terror was not a war on Islam, many Muslims thought differently. Many in the Muslim world see the war on terror as just another phase in an ongoing Western crusade against Muslims. The Russian war in Chechnya is seen as one phase, the Western bombing of the pharmaceutical plant in Sudan, another. Moreover, Western sanctions against Iraq, which have devastated the Iraqi people but have failed to topple Saddam Hussein, are cited as a form of Western genocide against Arabs and Muslims. Many Muslims view Western military support for the Saudi monarchy and Western military presence in Saudi Arabia as an imperialist occupation of Islam's two holiest cities, Makkah and Madinah. Finally, many Muslims consider the West's longstanding support for Israel as Western hostility to Muslims and support for Israeli occupation of Islam's third holiest city, Jerusalem. Bin Laden's entire appeal to militant Muslims is based on this list of complaints. Whether these complaints are fair or have merit is irrelevant; what is relevant is that many rational and reasonable Muslims who would never harm anyone are incensed by what they see as a Western conspiracy against all Muslims. For these moderates, as much as for the Revolutionary Islamists, it all adds up to a Western crusade.

Still, Western media and policy makers are mystified by the fear and hostility found in public opinion in Muslim countries. While Western leaders explain that the terrorists "hate us" because of our freedoms and our democracy and propose to explain those concepts more vigorously to Muslims around the world, the Western media fails to note that most Muslims already long for such freedoms but have been deprived of them by their own governments—governments often supported by or allied with the West. On this basis alone, our protestations that we stand for democracy and civil liberties strike Muslims as hypocritical. The terrorists may list opposition to democracy and freedom as one among their list of grievances against the West; certainly the Taliban were not great democrats even in the eyes of most Muslims.

But there is one thing that most Muslims can agree with Samuel Huntington about: the West is at war with Islam. The Western mass media have conveyed this impression successfully to a generation of both Western and Muslim viewers, and the damage will be difficult to undo. Western ignorance was the cause of this recklessly simplistic distortion of Islam in the Western mass media; those media conveyed this distortion to Muslims around the world; they have responded to our apparent hostility with a hostility of their own—hostility more dangerous because

---

[102]Peter Ford, "Listening for Islam's Silent Majority," *Christian Science Monitor*, November 5, 2001, p. 1.

it is also a reaction to endemic problems of poverty and oppression. Consequently, TV channels like Al-Jazeera will continue enjoying popularity in the Muslim world, and Western viewpoints, once filtered through our own media, will now be interpreted by journalists who themselves are certain of the Western crusade against Islam.

Summary

Western news media coverage of Islam and the Muslim world is decidedly one-sided and usually echoes the policy and the rhetoric of Western governments. Consequently, Muslims who oppose Western policy find themselves and their worldviews at odds with the Western press and are thereby convinced that "the media is as much an arm of imperialism as the Sixth Fleet, nuclear weapons, [or] gunboat diplomacy."[103] However, any collusion between the Western press and Western policy makers is the result not of a tacit alliance or imperialist conspiracy. Instead, Westerners, whether making policy or writing news stories, share an identical view of the Muslim world. Thus, "it is this worldview, projected in the Press, which finds its tangible expression in Western foreign policies."[104]

Images and consequent opinions about Islam are channeled through our media within the context of the unspoken and unchallenged presumptions of Westerners. Such presumptions, perpetually reinforced by a culturally parochial and myopic media, stand as the framework beyond which nothing exists and within which all things operate—public opinion, media coverage, and policy making. This unassailable framework of presumptions is held aloft by an automatically self-reinforcing cycle in which "news and views are put forward by the media, opinion polls reflect the media's news and views, published polls are then highlighted by the same media to indicate 'public opinion' and naturally, the White House responds to this public opinion."[105] The media, therefore, do not engender consistent foreign policy; indeed, they undermine consistency. Foreign policy becomes merely "responses to the 'drama of the moment,' " a drama highlighted briefly by media that jump from one unrelated issue to another.[106]

The attention span of the consumer of news is typically short and has been rendered shorter still by Western news media. Policy, therefore, consists primarily of quick fixes and knee-jerk reactions to problems and provocations. Washington policy makers learned that patience and persistent diplomacy are the recipe for electoral disaster. When Jimmy Carter refrained from applying military force against the Khomeini regime during the hostage crisis and as the crisis dragged on for more than a year, his political fate was sealed despite the eventual success of his diplomatic efforts. Ronald Reagan and George Bush, in contrast,

---

[103]"Tehran Insists on Playing Host to Hostile Media," *Crescent International*, April 16–30, 1982, p. 2.

[104]Mushahid Hussain, "American Mass Media Coverage of Islam," 1980, p. 14.

[105]Ibid., pp. 14–15.

[106]Ibid., p. 15.

wasted no time employing force to address international problems, and Western media heralded military action against countries like Granada, Libya, Panama, Iran, Iraq, and Afghanistan—so long as it was marked by conspicuous success and lasted only briefly. Easy and instant psychic gratification, demanded by the media and the public, is thus the standard by which foreign policy is made.

Having established a direct connection between media images and foreign policy in the West and examined how the press has projected Islamophobia into Western and Muslim cultural and political consciousness, we should consider the implications of that projection on foreign policy and on the perception of policy makers. This unending cycle, the sound bites of "McNews" fueling the engine of "McPolicy," has empowered Revolutionary Islamists in that critical attacks on Islam and Muslims are only likely to strengthen radical Islamist trends. Whether such attacks are conducted by the media or by the military is irrelevant—the result is identical.[107]

Internet Sites

http://www.orst.edu/groups/msa/everwonder.swf

http://www.csis.org/europe/frm990412.html

http://www.ing.org/about_us.htm

http://www.brook.edu/views/op-ed/telhami/19991119.htm

http://free.freespeech.org/manushi/98/islam.html

http://usembassy.state.gov/islamabad/wwwh0005.html

http://www.coloradocollege.edu/dept/PS/Finley/PS425/reading/Huntington1.html

http://www.jochen-hippler.de/Aufsatze/Islam_the_Media_Perceptions/islam_the_media_perceptions.html

http://www.time.com/time/asia/news/column/0,9754,178470,00.html

http://www.canadianislamiccongress.com/media2001/

http://www.runnymedetrust.org/meb/islamophobia/nature.html

http://www.runnymedetrust.org/meb/islamophobia/Religion_and_belief.html

http://www.runnymedetrust.org/meb/islamophobia/Web_bib.html

http://news.bbc.co.uk/hi/english/uk_politics/newsid_1570000/1570106.stm

http://atheism.about.com/library/weekly/aa101701a.htm?PM=n30102501a

http://www.cbsnews.com/now/story/0,1597,314278-412,00.html

http://www.nytimes.com/books/99/04/18/specials/rushdie-verses.html

http://www.nytimes.com/books/99/04/18/specials/rushdie-bombthreats.html

http://www.nytimes.com/books/99/04/18/specials/rushdie-khomeini.html

http://www.nytimes.com/books/99/04/18/specials/rushdie-qualifies.html

---

[107]Watt, *Muslim-Christian Encounters*, p. 124.

http://www.nytimes.com/books/99/04/18/specials/rushdie-cleric.html
http://www.nytimes.com/books/99/04/18/specials/rushdie-mend.html
http://www.nytimes.com/books/99/04/18/specials/rushdie-rally.html
http://news6.thdo.bbc.co.uk/hi/english/world/newsid_56000/56353.stm
http://www.nytimes.com/books/99/04/18/specials/rushdie-visa.html
http://www.nytimes.com/books/99/04/18/specials/rushdie-drops.html
http://www.nytimes.com/books/99/04/18/specials/rushdie-newmoves.html
http://www.hvk.org/
http://www.cpj.org/Briefings/2001/aljazeera_oct01/aljazeera_oct01.html
http://www.meib.org/articles/0006_me2.htm

CHAPTER TWELVE

Conclusion

Islamism is best defined as the transformation of Islam into an ideology. It can also be seen as the reawakening and the resurrection of the Islamic faith as a political idiom in which Islamic symbols, ideas, and ideals are cultivated by practitioners who are both enlightened and unenlightened, sincere and insincere, pacifist and violent, good and bad. In the Muslim world, Islam is a powerful form of identity and political legitimization. Islamism serves as the source of community unification, whether in opposition to or commensurate with nationalism. Manifestations of Islamism invariably include growing interest in political Islam as a key to governing society, grassroots support for an Islamic state, and organizations dedicated to establishing an Islamic state. Sometimes such organizations are national governments, as in Sudan and Iran. More often, however, these Revolutionary Islamist organizations operate in opposition to the government, as in Egypt and Algeria, and the Gaza and West Bank in Israel, and become increasingly revolutionary. A few cases demonstrate a combination of both an Islamic state and Islamists in opposition to it as in Saudi Arabia.

Prominent features of Islamism include the widespread and grassroots dissemination of political Islam from homes and places of worship, observance of Islamic precepts, efforts to establish Islamic governments based on the *shariah,* and the popular discussion and debate of Islamic issues in the media. Islamists emphasize the centrality in Islam of socioeconomic equity and justice while reasserting Islam's relevance to solve contemporary problems in contrast to Westernization and secularization. Most important, political Islam has proved a powerful response to years of real and perceived Western political influence.

Islamists differ significantly regarding the direction political Islam should take and, indeed, about the very meaning of Islamism itself. Thus, an Islamist is defined as any individual who has contributed to the renewal and revitalization of political Islam. Within this extremely broad framework are three categories of

Islamists: Revolutionary Islamists, Traditionalist Islamists, and Modernist Islamists. Sadly, however, the Revolutionary Islamists are often perceived by the West as the only type of Islamist. Therefore, *Islamism* and *Revolutionary* Islamism are mistakenly taken to be synonymous.

Islamism has had profound implications for nations both Muslim and non-Muslim. The long arm of Revolutionary Islamism, one strain of political Islam, has reached across the seas and struck even at the heart of New York City, at the World Trade Center, and at the Pentagon, in Washington, D.C. Such violent and dramatic manifestations of Islamism, however rare and unrepresentative of Islamism at large, demand the world's attention. This attention must be balanced, however, with the realization that such militant and revolutionary Islamism is but one aspect of Islamism. This manifestation of Islamism is shunned by most Muslims, yet it has received overwhelming media exposure. Most Islamists and devout Muslims disparage and repudiate acts of terrorism as inherently irreconcilable with Islam.

There are fifty-five predominantly Muslim nation-states in the Muslim world pursuing sometimes contradictory agendas. Muslims also differ by nationality, history, and culture, and therefore represent a pluralistic and heterogeneous people. Even the Revolutionary Islamists themselves are distinguished from one another according to divisions within Islam, differing interpretations of Qur'anic teaching, and national differences unrelated to Islam. Thus, Revolutionary Islamism specifically and political Islam generally are far from monolithic.

Nevertheless, in every community of Muslims there exists a tendency, inherent in the faith, for politicization of Islam, for making Islam an idiom of dissent against injustice and inequity. Islam, therefore, is one of the keys to understanding Islamic politics, its roots in Muslim communities around the world, and its implications for Muslims and non-Muslims alike. Political Islam need not be violent or revolutionary. It can operate within a democratic context, and many Islamists have worked within that context. It is the war waged against Islamism that has radicalized political Islam and broadened the appeal of Revolutionary Islamists.

Islam is itself the core of political Islam, and the separation of the two is a misleading one. The first Islamic state was founded by Muhammad himself when, after the Hijrah in 622 CE, he governed the people of Madinah. So successful was this first Islamic state under Muhammad's rule that by the time of his death, Muslims were in control of the whole of the Arabian Peninsula. Thus, Muslims today wish to emulate the example of this "once and future" Islamic state by establishing their own, governed by Islamic law encoded in the *shariah*, the comprehensive legal guide to both individual and community life in Islam.

The faith of Islam emphasizes free will and stresses the significance of making "the right decision" in all aspects of life. Thus, Islamic education occupies a central place in the cultivation and appeal of political Islam. For students in Islamic institutions, Islam is presented as a way of life governing every aspect and nuance of existence and thus having significant political implications. For example, in Egypt the most devout, most radical, and most Revolutionary Islamists are young students attending these institutions.

Political Islam's attraction for Muslim students, teachers, and lay persons alike is nothing new. Yet Islamism during the last two decades differs from the many revivals of political Islam preceding it. Islamism today lacks geographic boundaries, and its expression has been varied to an unprecedented extent.

The universality of Islamism has been a significant development in international relations. The communications, transportation, and computer revolutions have shrunk the world drastically. Significant occurrences in Iran, Saudi Arabia, Afghanistan, or Iraq, for example, are communicated to the world through CNN, for example, almost instantaneously. Furthermore, the establishment of non-governmental and transnational Islamic organizations, like the OIC or the Ikhwan al-Muslimun, has spread the message that "Islam is the answer" in all human endeavors. Moreover, global economic and political interdependence have shattered formerly secure borders. No nation's population is long unaffected by events around the world. Today, Islamism is well-known by people throughout the world; Islam has reentered the consciousness of non-Muslims all over the world.

Ironically, the shrinking of the global village has united the people of the Muslim world in common cause but has also made modern Islamism polycentric and heterogeneous, with almost as many aspects as there are Islamists. In this sense, Islamism is hardly conducive to the creation of an Islamic bloc or a unified Muslim *ummah*. Nevertheless, political Islam gains greater vigor and vitality each day. The many faces of Islamism have prevented political Islam from being discredited as a whole. Islamism has remained a popular idiom of political activity among the majority of Muslims. Any action the world takes to try and suppress or eliminate Islamism will only serve to continually legitimize and radicalize it in the eyes of Muslims.

Islam is a vehicle for political action primarily because it is both a "historical" and an "organic" faith. As a "historical" religion, Islam offers a definite direction to human history; every human action becomes another element in the divine scheme. Human history and its direction are important to Islam, and therefore Muslims work to understand history, to emulate it where it has been divinely guided, and to avoid its repetition where it has angered God. Thus, Revolutionary Islamists, for example, insist that Muslims return to the "fundamentals" of Islam as exemplified by the rule of Muhammad and the first four rightly-guided caliphs over the earliest Muslim community. Less dogmatic Muslims likewise see the importance of history to Islam and interpret success and failure in the recent, even immediate, past as indicative of divine grace or anger, respectively.

Islam is also an organic or holistic religion in which, by definition, no distinctions exist between the world of individual worship and community government. Islam sets forth universal principles of human behavior in all its aspects. These principles are binding on Muslims and provide for them an answer in all areas of human endeavor. When secular ideologies and systems cannot answer the political, economic, social, and cultural grievances of Muslims, there is always recourse to Islamism.

Centrally important to Islam as a political idiom is the Islamic emphasis on socioeconomic equity and justice. This emphasis makes Islamism appealing in light of the increasing misery of the population, the polarization of wealth into fewer and fewer hands, and the widespread injustice prevalent in Muslim societies. Like all major religions, Islam stresses honesty, integrity, justice and moderation in all human endeavors, political and otherwise. In Islam no one is above the law of God; all people are equal in the eyes of God, and none goes unpunished for a crime. Furthermore, Islam provides for specific measures in which socioeconomic equity and justice are to be ensured and safeguarded.

The achievement of Islamic justice is possible in Islam through the application of *jihad,* a term much maligned and misunderstood. Three categories of *jihad* exist in Islamic theology: personal, ummaic, and martial. Personal *jihad* is the struggle waged by Muslims to purge themselves of their base desires and evil impulses. *Ummaic jihad* is the peaceful correction of wrongs within the *dar al-Islam* (the community of believers in which Muslims rule). Martial *jihad*—which is, according to most Muslims, the least favored in the eyes of God and the last resort of Muslims according to the Qur'an—is the prosecution of war against un-Islamic oppressors who have precipitated confrontation. Nonpracticing Muslims and other unbelievers are combated in martial *jihad,* at least ideally. However, the misapplication of martial *jihad* has given it a bad name. What *jihad,* particularly *ummaic jihad,* represents to most Muslims is the peaceful means for realizing socioeconomic justice and equity in the Muslim world. Nevertheless, martial *jihad* gains proponents in proportion to the oppression of political Islam in the Muslim world and to the increasing impossibility of nonviolent *ummaic jihad* in the face of such oppression. The question becomes, in which direction will Islamism go? The nonviolent struggle or martial *jihad?*

Central to a prediction of the future of political Islam is an examination of the three different categories of Islamists—Revolutionary, Traditionalist, the Modernist. Revolutionary Islamists are often the more puritanical and radical advocates of political Islam. However, they are not inherently hostile to the West, only to what they consider undue Western influence in the Muslim world. Traditionalist Islamists, usually drawn from the ranks of Islamic scholars, prefer to avoid political activity unless the integrity of Islam is violated and/or when the ummah has been attacked by aggressors. Modernist Islamists—although politically active, like Revolutionary Islamists, and profoundly concerned about the integrity of Islam, like the Revolutionary and Traditionalist Islamists—possess none of their fear of the West and advocate the incorporation of many Western ideas to the current scene in the Muslim world, provided the ideas are not essentially un-Islamic. Although some radical Islamists consider Muslim Secularists to be unbelievers, a few noteworthy Revolutionary and Traditionalist Secularists (like Egypt's Sadat, Sudan's Numeiri, and Pakistan's Muhammad ali Jinnah, and Zulfikar Ali Bhutto) have utilized Islamic rhetoric and symbols to build mass support in order to portray themselves as "defenders of Islam." These Muslim Secularists have also inadvertently contributed to the strengthening of political Islam in the Muslim world. In brief, Islam represents a political idiom accepted, however grudgingly by some, throughout the Muslim world. All three categories of Islamists, and on some occasions even Muslim Secularists, use Islamic symbols and ideals to attract support and build mass movements.

While much of the recent literature on Islamism emphasizes Revolutionary Islamism, it is the dynamic interaction among the three types of Islamists and the Muslim Secularists that fuels the popularity of political Islam. Thus, Islamism today is open to greatly varying interpretation; the meaning, the methods, and the ultimate aim of Islamists differ according to changes in the Muslim world. In this respect, Islamism represents a constructive dialogue in which varied Islamic systems and practices are debated and applied to realities in the Muslim world. Thus, this interaction represents the beginning of both an "Islamic renaissance" and an "Islamic reformation" at the same time!

Following the independence of the Muslim world from colonial rule, the Muslim Secularists were the first to fill the power vacuum. Their emphasis on imported Western ideologies and their policies of Westernization were related to the evident disparity between the strength of the West and the weakness of the Muslim world. However, the policies and programs of modernization, secularization, and sometimes even Westernization that the Secularists initially pursued with such relish have fallen far short of expectations. While the Muslim world has experienced unprecedentedly rapid modernization, appropriate economic, political, and sociocultural development has been lacking.

The Secularists' applications of Western and pseudo-Western ideologies have utterly failed to achieve equitable and holistic development for the Muslim population. Many impoverished Muslims have viewed these imported and "un-Islamic" ideologies as the cause of the inequity in the Muslim world. Western-style policies have not only failed but have largely worsened the ills they were imported to assuage. The ideologies of capitalism, socialism, communism, nationalism, secularism, ataturkism, Ba'athism, Nasserism, and pan-Arabism have thus been discredited in the Muslim world. Political Islam, however, stands ready to fill the developmental void wholly unscathed by the failures of the past. Thus, Muslim Secularists turn to Islam when they need to shore up wavering internal support. This effort has backfired, however. Far from undermining the Islamists, the Muslim Secularists have legitimized political Islam as an idiom of anti-government dissent. Few Muslims are fooled by the Islamic rhetoric of the Muslim Secularists; for instance, the image of Saddam Hussein, a murderer of devout Muslims, kneeling and praying for media consumption is a blatant fraud.

The failure and discrediting of secular ideologies have been precipitated and accompanied by the developmental crises that have beset the Muslim world. By adopting rather than adapting Western technology and innovation, the Muslim Secularists have ignored the uniqueness of the Muslim world, whose potential and pitfalls differ from those of the West. The crises of identity, legitimacy, penetration, distribution, and participation are severe in the Muslim world and have paralyzed the region's governments. Rapid urbanization, immigration, and a frightening population explosion have each contributed to the dire political, economic, social, and religious conditions of most Muslim nations. In contrast to the Western world, where modernization and secularization occurred gradually, the Muslim world is beset by all these developmental crises simultaneously. Consequent civil unrest has therefore brought civil war and revolution, demagogues, and fanatics to the forefront of politics in the Muslim world.

The identity crisis has impeded the resolution of the other four crises and may serve as the key to political, economic and social stability in the region. Yet the processes of modernization pursued by the Muslim Secularists have worsened the identity crisis and need to be suspended. A more effective and attractive idiom of identity is required for Muslims; Islam is their natural alternative. Islamic unity through the agency of the *ummah*, at one end of the spectrum, and narrow community loyalty, at the other, are working together as a centrifugal force tearing apart the nation-states of the Muslim world. Only by force can the Muslim Secularists hold these states together; and force has accelerated the delegitimization of the nation-state as a source of identity for Muslims.

The Arab-Israeli conflict has also contributed significantly to Islamism's attraction for Muslims. The failure of either Arab regimes or secular Palestinians to defeat Israel has reinforced a Muslim inferiority complex, discredited secular and Secularist regimes devoted to Israel's defeat, and contributed to an Islamic backlash against perceived Western neocolonialism through the Israeli "surrogate." Thus the conflict, still unresolved after fifty years, is radicalizing Islamism by playing upon anti-Western sentiment among Muslims and by underscoring the incompetence of Muslim Secularist regimes in the region.

The defeat of Arab forces at Israeli hands in the 1967 Six Day War was a watershed for the global revival of political Islam. After so much boasting and bravado, Egyptian President Nasser in the space of a week discredited himself and his secular and pseudo-Western ideology of Nasserism. Islamic groups throughout the world were quick to ascribe the defeat of the Arabs to the emphasis on the fashionable secular ideologies of the Muslim world's political and economic elites. Political Islam, it was increasingly claimed, could defeat the Israelis—a conclusion bolstered by the improved showing of the Arabs against the Israelis in the 1973 war when Islamic slogans and symbols were used.

The Arab-Israeli conflict also empowered two pan-Islamic international organizations that have played significant roles in the financial enrichment and institutionalization of Islamism: the Organization of Petroleum Exporting Countries (OPEC) and the Organization of the Islamic Conference (OIC). OPEC, which first flexed its economic muscle in the aftermath of the 1973 Arab-Israeli War, fueled the fire of Islamism on several levels: first, by breaking the Arab world's bonds of dependency on the West; second, by providing finances to Islamist organizations around the world; and third, by failing to contribute significant monies to financially strapped Muslim nations, thus underscoring the disparity between the few oil-rich Muslim countries and the many non–oil producing and exporting countries of the Muslim world. The initial satisfaction, indeed euphoria, in the Muslim world for the apparent successes of OPEC were short-lived, tempered by the realization that OPEC, except Iran and Libya, represented status quo powers uninterested in Revolutionary Islamism. Nevertheless, Saudi distribution of oil money has benefited innumerable Islamist groups and has contributed positively to the resurgence of Islam both at the grassroots level and in the corridors of power in the Muslim world.

The 1969 burning of the Al-Aqsa Mosque in Israeli-occupied Jerusalem infuriated Muslims around the world and led to the establishment of the Organization of the Islamic Conference in the same year. Dedicated to principles of Islamic solidarity, the OIC has contributed to Islamic politics by institutionalizing the lost but never forgotten Islamic dream of the universal *ummah*. As with OPEC, however, the promise of the OIC has not yet been realized; yet the OIC's very existence is both the result of and a contribution to the strength of Islamism. Its affiliated institutions, like the Islamic Development Bank, have shown Muslims around the world the potential power of an Islamic bloc dedicated to Islamic politics. Islamists are encouraged to fulfill the potential inherent in pan-Islamism and institutionalized by the OIC.

Iran's Islamic Revolution has, more than any other single event, accelerated and radicalized Islamism. Its implications are felt throughout the world even today, nearly two decades after the fall of the *shah*. The Iranian Revolution traumatized the West and invigorated Islamism in such diverse countries as Egypt, Algeria, Iraq, Syria, and Saudi Arabia. The events leading to the Islamic Revolution, for all its mystery, are commonplace in the Muslim world. The *shah* of Iran pursued Westernization policies incompatible with his people's traditional ways of life, aggravating the five crises of development. He permitted no political participation in the system and thus delegitimized himself and his government. He failed to ensure the just and equitable distribution of resources and goods to all Iranians; the *shah*'s policies and programs benefited the upper middle class far more than it did the masses.

The rapidity of the *shah*'s modernization programs also caused dislocation in the countryside. The cities were suddenly filled with a growing population of job-seeking ex-farmers. This dislocation and the consequent frustration and alienation felt by most Iranians engendered a crisis of identity that left Iranians unsatisfied with the *shah*'s government and more interested in returning to traditions in the countryside, traditions centered around Islam. Moreover, the *shah*'s reign was further undermined by the singular place in Iranian society of the Shi'ah clerical establishment. The clerics' ability to solve, at least to a greater degree than had the Pahlavi monarchy, the developmental crises besetting the nation and the popular leadership of the charismatic Ayatollah Khomeini made the transition of power from the *shah*'s secular government to the Islamic Republic both possible and, in Iranian eyes, desirable.

The implications of the Iranian Revolution extend far beyond Iran's borders. As a classic case study illuminating the causes of Islamism, the Iranian Revolution also provides a model to other Islamists around the world. The anti-Western and anticommunist temperament of the new Islamic regime under the leadership of the Ayatollah Khomeini inspired and excited Islamists everywhere. The victory of the revolution in the face of palpable Western hostility encouraged radical Islamists to struggle for victory. Widespread outbreaks of Revolutionary Islamist militancy have resulted.

The Iranian Revolution also radicalized Islamism both directly and indirectly. Declarations from Tehran that the new government would work actively to export the Revolutionary Islamist revolution throughout the Muslim world infuriated the West and terrified the Muslim Secularist regimes in the Middle East. Their response? Repression of Islamism, regardless of whether it was radical or moderate, without distinction. The result? A self-perpetuating positive feedback of Islamism. This is perhaps the truest significance of the Islamic Revolution in Iran.

Islamism has been radicalized and co-opted by militant demagogues, not because Islam is "barbarous" or "medieval," but because the West is funding oppressive regimes in the Muslim world that detain, torture, and often execute political opponents, including Islamists. By refusing to allow a voice to the people, the Muslim Secularists ruling the Muslim world have strengthened the appeal of an Islamic system in which the Secularists have no place.

The West has deluded itself about the "Islamic explosion" and the much heralded "Islamic threat" to Western interests. The Western media commonly vilifies Islamism and portrays the devout Muslim as some kind of puritanical fanatic. The West has failed to fully appreciate the differences between Islamists. Most of them are not terrorists; in fact, very few of them are interested in waging war on the United States.

The Western mass media, particularly the news media, have covered events in the Muslim world in a manner unquestionably, though not maliciously, one-sided. Muslim viewers of these media have been angered by Western reporters' interpretations of events and personalities in the Muslim world and therefore claim that the Western press is yet another extension of Western imperialism. Although this is not the case, the media and the formulation of policy in the West are closely intertwined.

Meanwhile, the Western media have perpetuated mostly unsavory stereotypes and presented a myopic view of the Muslim world, and Washington has formulated a similarly shallow policy toward the Muslim world. This connection between perception and policy could be solved through more thorough and accurate reporting. Yet the Western media and policy makers continue along this collision course with the Muslim world's people. The West persists in its policies of support for oppressive and corrupt regimes in the Muslim world because the media offers no alternatives. It is better apparently to trust a known tyrant than an unknown popular movement. Making policy on such shallow presumptions is, however, dangerous to the West's long-term interests in the Muslim world.

The United States has pursued a policy not of constructive change for the desperate and impoverished nations of the Muslim world but of no change at all. U.S. foreign policy actually undermines its anti-revolutionary goals. Fearing revolution in the Muslim world, the United States quells revolutionary disquiet by supporting regimes that are the targets of popular revolution. Such a policy prevents immediate revolution but ensures that any revolution that occurs will be violent and decidedly anti-American. That so many revolutions are anti-American should thus come as no surprise.

U.S. foreign policy, emphasizing the "way things are" over the "way things ought to be," is based on the presumption that tinkering with the "status quo" may result in undesirable changes. Better safe than sorry. Thus, U.S. foreign policy emphasizes order and stability over nearly everything—over human rights, over democracy, over poverty alleviation and economic development, over inequality, over corruption and nepotism, and over freedom of worship. By preferring comfortable predictability to possible chaos, U.S. policy makers, Republicans and

Democrats alike, have supported a system in the Muslim world that has been largely to the United States' immediate benefit. In the long view, however, the "system" is far less beneficial. As the United States hurriedly stamps out brush fires from site to site, it may soon discover that it is standing on a volcano.

A peaceful resolution of conflict between the governing elite and the governed masses in the Muslim world is unlikely. Authoritarian regimes there have been established expressly to prevent power sharing with the people and are today supported by Western policy makers. These regimes will not endure for long. Their brutal methods of internal suppression are only alienating opposition groups and hastening the revolutionary upheaval that may topple the Secularist governments of the Muslim world. Secularisms are delegitimized; Ba'athism, Nasserism, capitalism, and socialism are discussed not as solutions to endemic socioeconomic dysfunction but as the causes of such dysfunction. By default, the people look to political Islam as the answer. For the Muslim masses, Islam is associated with the glories of the past. In all likelihood, political Islam will emerge victorious in country after country in the Muslim world; eventually the authoritarian secular regimes of Egypt, Syria, Iraq, Algeria, and Tunisia will fall. Therefore, the United States needs to ensure that future Islamic governments in the Muslim world will not convulse with anti-American fury as they emphasize their independence from "imperial powers." These new regimes may be difficult to get along with at times. Accepting them, taking none of their rhetoric as an affront to U.S. dignity or a threat to U.S. security is the surest way to weather the storm and to avoid entanglements that the United States neither wants nor can afford.

Western analysts and policy makers often overlook the curious history of friendly United States–Islamist relations. Sadly, when Westerners think of Revolutionary Islamism, they inevitably focus on Iran in the first years of its revolutionary rage, or Lebanon in the thick of its civil war, or al-Qaeda hijackers of September 11, 2001. The West forgets its alliance with Zia-ul-Haq's Islamist regime in Pakistan.

Islamist Pakistan was the beneficiary of the third-largest U.S. aid disbursement in the 1980s. Furthermore, the United States allied itself with several Revolutionary Islamist Afghan *mujahideen* factions fighting Soviet colonialism in Afghanistan. The *mujahideen* received substantial military and economic aid from a generous Washington. Moreover, Sadiq al-Mahdi's moderate Revolutionary Islamist Sudanese regime (1986–1989) enjoyed good relations with the United States and received U.S. economic and humanitarian assistance. The moderate Wahhabi rulers of Saudi Arabia and Qatar, who govern Islamic states, have also gotten along well with the United States. Even several Iranian presidents have expressed an interest in reconciliation with the United States. Iran maintained its neutrality during operations Desert Shield and Desert Storm; condemned the terrorist attacks of September 11; and did not actively oppose the U.S. war in Afghanistan. Iran's president Khatami is opening Iran to Western multinational corporations and is trying to open its political process. Is Islamism, even Revolutionary Islamism, so terrible or frightening an enemy? Is it inherently an enemy at all?

In any event, the revolutionary phase of radical Islamism has proven histori-cally to be short-lived after its empowerment. Sustaining revolutionary fervor when the revolution has succeeded is all but impossible. Cultural revolutions, whether on the Saudi, Iranian, or Taliban models, become tiresome to the aver-age citizen and are a drain on popular support. However, when external or inter-nal forces threaten the regime, as Iraq threatened Iran during the 1980s, the revolutionary spirit is prolonged, as it also was in Afghanistan during twenty years of war. Furthermore, when external forces crush Islamist movements as a matter of policy, such movements are popularized and radicalized. Religious and nation-alist passions are easily inflamed when "imperialist" powers meddle in the Muslim world. The Iranian Revolution burned hotter and brighter directly as the result of U.S. meddling and Iraq's war of aggression, supported by the United States among others, on Iran. There was no better way to guarantee that the revolution would be radicalized, uncompromising, and continually anti-American.

The Cold War mentality's persistence has undermined the U.S. image abroad. Although the United States celebrates democratic traditions and cherishes liberty, its fear of change in the Muslim world, even in the name of liberty and democracy, has put it on the losing side of history. The U.S. Cold War policy enjoined the country to support pro-American tyranny and oppose pro-Soviet tyranny in the Muslim world. The details of such ideological warfare, however, are lost on the average Muslim, who feels equally suppressed whether staring down the barrel of a U.S. M-16 or a Russian AK-47. Yet the Cold War is over; such policy, for better or worse, need no longer be pursued. But the United States continues to pursue it. When the Islamist Islamic Salvation Front (FIS) party of Algeria won free and fair democratic elections in 1992 but was cheated of victory by a military coup, the United States said nothing. When the Algerian military rounded up FIS leaders and activists, who had not threatened the government with violent overthrow but had worked legally and peacefully within the system, the United States was silent. Where was the talk of human rights, democracy, or freedom? Was the friendship of Algeria's military regime really worth the United States ignoring everything it stands for? Algeria is now doomed to violent revolution directly as a result of a reactionary, military coup. Unable to operate legally and within the system, the only recourse of the Algerian people generally and the FIS specifically is to revolt against an oppressive and brutal system interested not in serving the people but in perpetuating its own power at the people's expense.

The United States is embarking on a new cold war against Islamism. Dictatorial regimes that promise to cooperate with the United States and keep Islamists at bay receive U.S. aid. During the 1980s, when Iraq invaded Iran, U.S. policy favored Iraq. However, the moment Saddam Hussein invaded Kuwait, the United States turned against the "butcher of Baghdad." Saddam Hussein had not changed. He was the same old butcher the United States had known and sup-ported. Yet when he fought Iran, at least he was "our" butcher. When he invaded Kuwait, he became the new Hitler. Is it no wonder that the people of the Muslim world decry the U.S. double standard?

U.S. policy toward Saddam Hussein, while hypocritical, is easy to understand. While Iraq fought Iran, Saddam was, in U.S. eyes, keeping the revolution-exporting Islamists busy; he was preserving status quo regimes like Egypt and Saudi Arabia from the perils of the "Iranian model." When Saddam invaded Kuwait, however, he was upsetting the status quo. Kuwait was a quiet and conservative nation not much given to making trouble in other countries. Suddenly, Saddam was the troublemaker in U.S. eyes. When the United States turned Saddam out of Kuwait, however, it showed no desire to turn him out of power in Iraq. The status quo demanded that he or another Ba'athist despot remain Iraq's ruler, lest a power vacuum be created that Iraq's Shi'ah majority might fill. When an insurrection threatened to overthrow Saddam's Ba'athist power structure, the United States did nothing. No support was given the insurrection against Saddam's tyranny within Iraq. Saddam Hussein, therefore, remains in power; the status quo and the vaunted "balance of power" in the Persian Gulf region have been preserved. Yet the Shi'ahs of southern Iraq are still seething. U.S. foreign policy, far from assisting and encouraging them and thereby co-opting and befriending them, has instead left them to suffer at Saddam's hands. When Saddam is gone and when the Shi'ahs come to power, as majorities often do, they will remember the U.S. role in their suppression. By supporting the devil it knows, the United States has created the devil it will know. Antiquated and short-term policies toward the Muslim world will haunt the United States for a generation.

Since United States has long-term interests in the Muslim world, it should forge long-term policies in the region. Supporting Secularist dictatorships that ruthlessly suppress their subjects and mismanage their economies is shortsighted policy, as evidenced in Iran. The United States can win the lasting friendship of the Muslim world's people only by staying true to its own democratic ideals and by emphasizing human rights, not ignoring them. If the United States remains on its present course, propping up corrupt, despotic, and unpopular regimes while only paying lip service to human rights, it will earn the wrath of Muslims and will continue to be the favorite target of terrorists. By committing itself to the promotion of human rights, the United States would be making the surest long-term investment for a better world order. The United States would again become a beacon of hope in an increasingly appreciative world. As the single military and economic superpower, the United States has the obligation to stand as the world's moral superpower. After all, the best way to guarantee continued economic prosperity, freedom, and human rights at home is to develop and strengthen them abroad. If the United States continues to support dictators who stifle the freedom and dignity of their people and make peaceful reform impossible, it ensures inevitable revolutions that will assuredly be militantly anti-American. It is far better to make enemies of a hundred Saddam Husseins despised by their own people than to make enemies of the millions of people these despots oppress.

It is unlikely that the United States will abruptly adopt a policy promoting human rights above all else. However, the U.S. government can take realistic and definitive steps to prevent the indefinite perpetuation of prior policies supporting tyrants. The first best step is to promote greater understanding of the Muslim world among American citizens. U.S. policies toward the Muslim world can never change if Americans' perceptions continue to be plagued by so much prejudice and misunderstanding. The U.S. perception of Islam, Muslims, and the Muslim world, built on ancient and deep-seated stereotypes, is a definite impediment to understanding the feelings, wants, and needs of Muslims throughout the world. U.S. attitudes toward Muslims are predominantly negative and prejudiced. Although there is probably little malice in U.S. misperceptions of the Muslim world, there is much that can be done to remedy those misperceptions.

The Muslim world is more than its rare but more sensational aspects, including terrorism, oil wealth, and harems. Muslims are acutely sensitive to Western portrayals of them in both the entertainment and news media. Many Muslims are enraged by unfair and unsavory depictions of their faith and of their brethren in the mass media; even otherwise pro-U.S. Muslims are disinclined to express friendship with a nation that has been cruel in its depictions of Islam and of Muslims. Worse, however, is that, unless U.S. citizens become better educated about the Muslim world and until the Western media puts a truly human face on the Muslim world's tragedies, there can be no appropriate change in U.S. foreign policy. If the United States sees all Muslims as inhuman fanatics, there is no incentive to emphasize "human rights" in its policies toward them. In short, the United States must "rehumanize" the Muslim world. Only through education is this possible.

High schools and universities throughout the United States often give short shrift to the Muslim world in educating young Americans. Both U.S. public schools and the Western media need to dispel stereotypes of Muslims, not perpetuate them. Americans are barely knowledgeable about Islam, a religion whose adherents account for one in five human beings on the planet. On this basis alone, a closer and more equitable treatment of Islam and Muslims is warranted. It is in school and through the mass media that Americans form negative opinions of Islam. Thus, these opinions can be tempered by the portrayal of Muslims as human beings, not as terrorists and religious fanatics.

To create a better understanding between the United States and the people of the Muslim world, the U.S. Department of State, the National Security Council, and the Central Intelligence Agency should employ experts on Islam and the Muslim world. Hiring American Muslims might also improve relations with the world of Islam. Recognizing the central place of the Islamic faith in the cultures of Muslim countries will avert unnecessary misperception and misinterpretation of a region strategically so important to the United States.

The United States must also pursue a strategy of reduced dependency on the Muslim world, in particular, dependency on Middle East oil. Only then will U.S. policy be truly objective and the United States be able to address the wants and needs of the people of the Muslim world, not merely its own wants and needs. More generally, the United States must recover from the current economic recession itself if it is to compete for markets and for products in a world increasingly linked by trade. If the United States succeeds economically, it can abandon its fear of Revolutionary Islamism; after all, Islam and capitalism are almost wholly compatible.

It has long been the United States' intention to encourage its surrogates throughout the world to pursue a measure of political liberalization. However, with some unpopular pro-U.S. regimes, American leaders have simply not done enough to win over their peoples. The people of Egypt, for example, would be unimpressed with U.S. pressure on the Mubarak regime to make cosmetic reforms. Mubarak, like the *shah*, will turn conciliatory only when the revolutionary surge threatens immediately to overwhelm him. The United States would do best to avoid becoming further implicated as a supporter of oppressive regimes in the Muslim world. The United States must abjure its ties with tyrannies of any sort, without regard to their friendship or the benefits they promise to bestow; indeed, where are the casinos in Havana, Cuba, that wealthy and hedonistic Americans frequented during Fulgencio Batista's neo-fascist, corrupt, unpopular rule (1952–1958)? The United States must cut its losses, and cut off its erstwhile dictatorial allies in the Middle East and Central Asia before we are implicated in the oppression and terror they have wreaked upon their subjects. Only then will U.S. rhetoric in support of human rights have the force of truth, not the ring of hypocrisy.

The United States must stand for human rights not only by turning its back to tyrannical regimes that oppress their own people but by applying its standards evenly and without regard to short-term interests. By condemning all who violate human rights and perpetuate abuse on their neighbors and citizens, the United States will better serve its long-term interests, earning the trust and friendship of humankind all over the world.

The United States' foreign policy agenda must come into line with post–Cold War reality. The world's sole surviving superpower must abandon the search for an enemy with whom to grapple for world dominance and must consider new objectives. It must also refocus national security in an interdependent world. The United States must consider the security of the world, and it can safeguard that security by checking the proliferation of weapons of mass destruction. Yet today the United States applies its standards unevenly, sometimes illogically. For instance, if Iraq fails to comply with UN demands for inspection of sites where nuclear material is allegedly hidden, the United States bombs Iraq. Yet the United States has averted its eyes while Pakistan, India, and Israel built nuclear weapons. While Iraqis dig themselves out from the rubble of U.S. anger, the United States threatens a stubbornly noncompliant, indeed defiant, North Korea with a possible economic embargo, and nothing more. The Muslim world is particularly attentive to this double standard, and the outcry against U.S. belligerence toward Iraq might be quieted if only the United States applied such force consistently in the name of world security, not as a bully but as a protector of the common good. Hostility toward, as well as mistrust and mistreatment of, U.S. citizens in the Muslim world would be alleviated. Kosovo was a good first step; but so much more can be done.

The United States is currently perceived in the Muslim world in particular and the developing world in general as a global hegemon or an imperialistic superpower. In order to be perceived as a benign and paternalist global superpower, the United States ought to lift the economic sanctions that it has placed on many developing countries; significantly increase the economic assistance it gives to the Muslim nations; play a leading role in forgiving the debt owed by developing countries to the developed Western world; advise and fund (along with its Western allies) the establishment of numerous *grameen* banks—"poor people's banks" that give small loans to needy people keenly interested in starting a small private enterprise and improving the lives of their extended families—all over the Muslim world; and greatly increase the number of Peace Corps workers going to Muslim countries.

Setting the stage for a rapprochement with the geographically and demographically large as well as strategically located Islamic Republic of Iran deserves serious consideration. Although a loving embrace of Iran is currently unpopular in the United States, especially after President George W. Bush included Iran, along with Iraq and North Korea, in his controversial "axis of evil" statement in the January 2002 State of the Union address, relations with Iran could and should be gradually eased. Petroleum-rich and gas-rich Iran offers a large and hungry market of over 70 million people for American goods and services. Moreover, improving relations with the Revolutionary Islamist theocratic state of Iran will send a positive signal to Muslims all over the world that the United States harbors no ill will toward Islam, Muslims, or the Muslim world; that the United States does not want a clash but a dialogue and cooperation between civilizations. In fact, going ahead then and building an oil pipeline from Central Asia through a relatively stable Iran to the Persian Gulf will make it quicker, easier, and cheaper to get the vast oil resources from the Caspian Sea to the rest of the world via huge oil tankers. Furthermore, President Khatami and the majority of his ministers and advisors are enlightened and moderate Modernist Islamists who prefer to pursue good relations with the United States, if only to lift Iran from decades of isolation and economic stagnation. If the United States misses the opportunity, if it continues its openly hostile policy toward Iran, Khatami and his pragmatic technocrats may be replaced by militant, anti-American Revolutionary Islamists much like the late Ayatollah Khomeini. The United States should remind itself that Khomeini is dead and the hostage crisis over. If the United States could improve relations with Germany and Japan, with whom it fought the costly and bloody World War II; with the Soviet Union and the Peoples Republic of China, its enemies in a forty-year Cold War; and with Vietnam, with which it fought a decade-long war, why not improve relations with Iran?

U.S. policy makers must continue mediating the Arab-Israeli dispute until a comprehensive peace settlement in the Middle East is realized. The Arab-Israeli conflict has gone on too long and cost the adversaries too much in blood and treasure. It has also contributed to the radicalization of Islamism, which is undermining the pro-American regimes of Egypt, Jordan, and Lebanon. The Israel-PLO mutual recognition in September 1993 and the Israeli pledge to give Palestinians limited self-rule in the Gaza Strip and the West Bank town of Jericho is a political breakthrough but has proved insufficient. The United States has the power to ensure Israel's security, and Israelis should enjoy such security, but the Palestinian people are just as entitled to their homeland, peace, and security.

The high expectations of peace between Jewish Israelis and Palestinians that emerged in 1993 have been dashed by a few extremist Palestinian suicide bombers and Israeli Prime Minister Sharon's brutal policies of collective punishment against all Palestinians in the West Bank and Gaza. The Middle East has again become the hotbed of terrorism that it was during the 1970s and 1980s. While the Palestinians are denied their national rights indefinitely, Revolutionary Islamist organizations like Hamas and Islamic Jihad swell with new members. The perpetuity of the Arab-Israeli conflict is coextensive with the perpetuity of radical and Revolutionary Islamism. It is this radicalization the United States should avoid. Otherwise, the United States will continue to have troubled relations with the Muslim world.

The United Nations has a role to play in the Muslim world, and the United States should make certain that the UN can play that role untroubled by a lack of financial, political, or moral support. While the United States can accomplish a great deal internationally on its own, its efforts are bolstered through multilateral and international cooperation. The United States should encourage the UN to expand its peacekeeping missions and to care for the world's millions of refugees. However, the United States must avoid the appearance of controlling the UN. If the people of the Muslim world see the UN as no more than an extension of the U.S. State Department or the Pentagon, then the United Nations' reputation will be undermined and little will be accomplished. The UN must act fairly and consistently.

Can the United States undertake these measures? Does the political will exist? There are few signs of any substantial change in U.S. foreign policy in the near future. During the Clinton administration, policy shifted away from the activist international role pursued by President Bush. With domestic concerns so great, it was a wonder that the "Islamic threat" ever came up at all. That has all changed under President George W. Bush. The attacks on the United States on September 11, 2001, woke the nation from its long slumber. The question now is, will U.S. policy end the threat of terror? Or will it inadvertently perpetuate it? Temptation has grown in the United States to view Islamism in any form as antithetical to U.S. national interest. Is this the beginning of a new Cold War, a new East-West conflict in which the East represents not Communism and the Communist world but Islam and the Muslim world?

The attacks on September 11, 2001, have brought distant events home to Americans. The United States has no personal experience with the authoritarian, corrupt, and unjust regimes ruling many Muslim countries. These regimes are what Muslims the world over despise. These regimes are what Islamists, and not just Revolutionary Islamists, have sacrificed their livelihoods and even their lives to destroy. Why then are some Muslim zealots attacking the United States? The explanation, although insufficient to justify or even fully explain the murder of thousands, is fairly simple. The Muslim world sees U.S. support of Israel as one-sided. The United States has therefore become complicit in the continued denial of Palestinian rights. Moreover, U.S. policy toward Iraq has not harmed Saddam Hussein. Instead, it has been responsible for the deaths of over a million innocent Iraqis, mainly children. And finally, U.S. troops remain in Saudi Arabia; some Muslims see U.S. troop presence there as an affront to Islam. More generally, the United States has supported Secularist governments that deny basic human rights and has singled out Muslim countries such as Iran, Iraq, Libya, Sudan, Syria, and Somalia for punishment.

The destruction of the World Trade Center should alert the United States not only to the dangers of Revolutionary Islamism but also to the tragedy of poverty and oppression wracking the Muslim world. The United States need not embrace Revolutionary Islamists working to throw out oppressive governments at home, but it should not assist oppressive and corrupt Secularist regimes out of an inordinate fear of Islamism. If the United States continues to label sincere and nonviolent Islamists as fanatics and terrorists while describing the despotic and corrupt Secularist regimes as "moderates," friends, and allies, the numbers of the fringe anti-Western Revolutionary Islamist fanatics will only grow exponentially.

Policy decisions in the United States need to be removed from the Cold War atmosphere of the last fifty years. The vaunted "New World Order" looks little better than the old world order minus the Soviets. As the world's last superpower, the United States must remake its foreign policy according to the exigencies of today, not of ten or twenty years ago. The Cold War is over, but the United States has not walked away undamaged. U.S. foreign policy for decades has been one in which the ends justified the means. To eradicate Communism, the United States was willing to support tyrannical, corrupt, and unpopular regimes as well as anti-Communist guerilla organizations all over the world. To encourage capitalism among the oppressed peoples of the world, the United States chose to look aside while "imperfect friends" stripped them of their dignity and humanity. Our proxy wars against Communism left many developing countries (including many Muslim countries) in ruins. The fall of Communism, however, represented a new era and the potential for freedom from such policy constraints. The United States must avoid a new cold war with Islamism, which for most Americans is indistinguishable from the religion of Islam itself—the faith of over 1.2 billion human beings. This new Cold War offers nothing but a further drain of U.S. wealth and a poor utilization of American technology and talent. The United States does not need to deplete its resources in another simmering conflict that promises more pain, more heartache, more loss than the last. Is it possible to wage a war against terrorism without seeming to wage war on Islam, Muslims, and the Muslim world? Only time will tell.

Glossary

Abbreviations

(A) = Arabic word; (P) = Persian word; (U) = Urdu word; sing. = singular; pl. = plural; d = died; r = reign; CE = Common Era.

Abbasids: The Arab Abbasid dynasty came to power after the collapse of the Umayyad dynasty (661–750 CE) and reigned over the Islamic empire from 750 to 1258 CE. They were the descendants of Prophet Muhammad's uncle, Al-Abbas ibn Abd al-Muttalib.

***Abu* (A):** Literally, "the father of"; commonly used in proper names, such as *Abu Abbas*, which means "the father of Abbas."

Abu Bakr: One of the first converts to Islam, Prophet Muhammad's close companion, and the first caliph of Islam (r. 632–639 CE).

Abu Hanifa: The Iraqi-born imam Abu Hanifa (699–769 CE) was the founder of the Hanafi *madhab* (sect) of Sunni Islam. The Hanafi sect was actively promoted by a number of Abbasid and Ottoman rulers. A majority of Sunni Muslims in Turkey, Afghanistan, Egypt, Central Asia, China, and South Asia belong to the Hanafi sect.

Adab: Muslim etiquette, manners, and proper behavior.

***Adhan* (A):** "The call" to prayer made by a *muezzin* (prayer caller).

***Adl* (A):** Equity, fairness, justice, balance, and equilibrium. In Islam, it is often interpreted as justice, an attempt to give everyone his due, and the hallmark of a God-fearing and devout Muslim.

Aggression: An act of force; belligerent actions by one state against another. Iraq committed an act of aggression when it invaded Iran in 1980 and Kuwait in 1990.

Agitation: In a political sense, the term refers to keeping an issue or a debate constantly before the public (e.g., agitation for reform). Usually refers to opposition to the status quo.

A.H.: After the Hijra (Migration) of Prophet Muhammad from Makkah to Madinah, in 622 CE; the abbreviation for the numbering of years in the Islamic calendar.

Ahad (A): The oneness of God. The denial that God has any partner or companion associated with him.

Ahkam (A): Literally, "principles," "directives," "rules," "regulations," or "judgments." In Islam it often applies to the numerous principles, directives, and rules, embodied in the Qur'an and the *shariah*, that Muslims should observe.

Ahl al-Bayt (A): Prophet Muhammad's extended family. Shi'ahs restrict the term to Prophet Muhammad's daughter, Fatimah, Prophet Muhammad's son-in-law and Fatimah's husband, Ali ibn Abu Talib, and the couple's recognized descendants.

Ahl al-Kitab (A): Literally, "People of the Book." The Qur'anic term for Jews and Christians who adhered to God's earlier revelations.

Ahl-i-Hadith (U): From the Arabic term *ahl al-hadith* (partisans of the *hadith*); those belonging to this group are Sunni Muslims who, besides the Qur'an, prefer the authority of the *hadith* over that of a conflicting legal ruling accepted by one of the four Sunni schools of jurisprudence.

Ahl-i-Sunnah (U): Literally, "followers of the *sunnah*"; often refers to Sunnis, although Shi'ahs believe in Prophet Muhammad's *sunnah* (saying and deeds), too. See *sunnah*, Sunni, and Shi'ah.

Ahmadis: An offshoot of Sunni Islam that was founded by Mirza Ghulam Ahmad (1837–1908 CE), who was born in a village in the Indian Punjab called Qadian. Thus Ahmadis are also called Qadianis.

Ajami (A): Those Arabs who, during Prophet Muhammad's life, exhibited strong linguistic nationalism, chauvinistically considering non-Arabic speaking foreigners (especially Persians) as "dumb."

Akhbari: Those Twelver Shi'ahs in Iran who relied primarily on the traditions of the *imams* as a source of religious knowledge, in contrast to the Usuli school, which advocated greater speculative reasoning in Islamic theology and law. See Usuli.

Al (A): Literally, "the" (in article form) or "the clan."

Al-Akhira (A): The life in the hereafter; the other life/world. See Yaum al-Akhir.

Al-Aqsa Mosque: Also called *Masjid al-Aqsa* (the Furthest Mosque), *Bait al-Muqaddas* (the Holy House), or the Dome of the Rock; the beautiful blue-tiled octagonal building in Jerusalem—with bright tiles and mosaics bearing Qur'anic inscriptions inside the building and a glittering gold-leaf dome on top of the shrine—that stands majestically over the site of Solomon's Temple at the peak of the Temple Mount or *Haram al-Sharif* (the Noble Sanctuary). Jews believe that the large rock inside the Al-Aqsa Mosque was in the center of Solomon's Temple during biblical times. Muslims believe that Abraham was willing to sacrifice his son at the site and Prophet Muhammad ascended to heaven in his brief night journey from the rock. Many Muslims believe that the rock bears the imprint of Muhammad's winged horse, *Al-Burak* (the lightening), that soared heavenward from the site carrying God's last prophet. Muslims also believe that God will send one of His angels to the Dome of the Rock to sound the trumpet call to signal the end of the world and the Day of Judgment. From 610 to 630 CE, Muslims prayed in the direction of Jerusalem instead of Makkah out of reverence for this sacred site. The Al-Aqsa Mosque is one of the holiest shrines in Islamdom, and Jerusalem, which Muslims reverentially refer to as *Al-Quds* (The Holy), is the third holiest city in Islamdom after Makkah and Madinah.

Al-Asthma Al-Husna: Literally, "the most beautiful names," in Islam it refers to the ninety-nine names of God, through which people can understand the major hallmarks of God. Many Muslims repeat these names, with the help of the ninety-nine rosary beads that are threaded together.

Al-Bayt al-Haram: Literally, "the holy house"; refers to the cube-shaped shrine that is situated at the center of the Grand Mosque in Makkah. See Grand Mosque, Haram al-Sharif, and Khana-i-Ka'abah.

Al-Dunya (A): Literally, "this world"; life in this world as opposed to life in *al-akhira* (hereafter or next world).

Alawite: Offshoot of the Twelver Shi'ah sect that glorifies Ali ibn Abu Talib to such an extent that its members consider him an incarnation of divinity. Also called Nusayri because the sect was founded by ibn Nusair (d. 873 CE), who was the follower and emissary of the eleventh apostolic Shi'ah *imam* Hasan al-Askari.

Al-Azhar: First built as a mosque in Cairo, Egypt, on the orders of the Fatimid caliph al-Muizz in 970 CE, it is one of the oldest and most prestigious Islamic centers of learning in the world. It was formally organized as an Islamic university around 988 CE.

Al-Nakba: Literally, "the Catastrophe." All Palestinians, and almost all Muslims, tend to agree with the Palestinian characterization of their fate as a result of the creation of Israel in 1948.

Alhamdu lillah: Literally, "thanks be to God."

Ali ibn Abi Talib: Was the son of Abu Talib, the cousin and son-in-law of Prophet Muhammad; one of the first converts to Islam, the fourth caliph of Islam (r. 656–661 CE), and the first Shi'ah *imam*.

Alids: A term used for the recognized descendants of Ali ibn Abi Talib. Those claiming descent from Ali are numerous and spread all over the world. They are distinguished from other Muslims by the title *Sayyid, Sharif,* or *Mir*.

Alim, pl. ulama (A): Literally, "one possessing *ilm* (knowledge)" hence a learned person. In Islam, it refers to a Muslim who is immensely learned in Islam. The term is also used for *muftis, imams, maulvis, mullahs,* and *maulanas*.

Allah: The Arabic/Islamic term referring to the one and only omnipotent, omnipresent, just, and merciful God, who is the Creator and Lord of the universe. Belief in Allah is the first and most essential tenet of Islam.

Allahu Akbar (A): Literally, "God is Great"; many Muslims interpret it as "God is Most Great" or "God is the Greatest."

A'mal (A): Good deeds or good works.

Amin (A): Literally, "trustworthy"; Arabs referred to Prophet Muhammad as *al-Amin* even before he began to propagate Islam.

Amir/emir (A): It is the title given to military commanders, governors, and princes. The title is used by a number of present-day Muslim rulers and leaders of some Islamic political parties.

Amir al-Mu'minin (A): The honorific title of "Supreme Commander of the Faithful," given to the first four rightly guided caliphs.

Amro bil Mahroof: The Taliban's religious police in Afghanistan. The Taliban's Ministry for the Promotion of Virtue and Prevention of Vice (1996–2001).

Anjuman (P): "Assembly," "association," or "political organization."

Ansar (A): Plural of *naseer*, which means "helper" or "supporter." In Islamic history the *ansar* were residents of Madinah who gave asylum to Prophet Muhammad and actively supported him when he emigrated from Makkah in 622 CE.

Aqaid, sing. aqidah (A): Islamic beliefs and doctrines.

Aqida (A): Profession or declaration of the Islamic faith.

Aql (A): Reason, intellect.

Arab: A Semite who most often speaks Arabic and identifies with Arab culture. A majority of the 200 million Arabs are Muslims and live in twenty-one Arabic-speaking countries in the Middle East. Thousands of Arabs also live in non-Arabic-speaking countries worldwide.

Arabic: A Semitic language originating in the Arabian peninsula. Written from right to left, it is spoken by 300 million Arabs living in the Arab world but also by millions of Arabic-speaking Palestinians, Arab minorities, and non-Arabs located all over the world.

Arkan Ad-Din: The five pillars of Islam, consisting of the declaration of faith, prayer, fasting, charity, and pilgrimage to Makkah. See *faraidh, shahadah, salat, sawm, zakat, hajj, Makkah*.

Aryamehr (P): The title of "Sun of the Aryans," assumed by Muhammad Reza Shah Pahlavi in the mid-1960s.

Ashab (A): Companions of Prophet Muhammad.

Asharite: The followers of the Iraqi-born *alim* Abul Hassan al-Ashari (873–935 CE), who spearheaded a traditionalist Islamic movement. Abbasid rulers (833–942 CE) used al-Ashari's theological arguments to silence the liberal rationalism of the Mutazilites and thereby played a role in retarding Islam's dynamism.

Ashraf (A): People who trace their lineage to Prophet Muhammad or his close companions and thus are highly respected.

Ashura (A): The tenth day in the first Islamic month of Muharram, when Muslims commemorate the anniversary of the martyrdom of Prophet Muhammad's grandson, Hussein ibn Ali.

Aslaf (A): Refers to the pious companions of Prophet Muhammad, who are considered to have had special insight into the requirements of the faith because of their close association with the Prophet.

Auliya, sing. Wali (A): Literally, "favorites of Allah"; often applied to prophets, *imams*, and *mujaddids*.

Auqaf, sing. waqf (A): Charitable organizations operated by the government and/or private organizations that help mosques, *madrassahs*, orphanages, and the poor and needy.

Aya (pl. ayat): "Sign," "symbol," "mark," "token," or "miracle" of God's existence and power. The term is often used to refer to any of the 6,200 verses in the Qur'an. See Qur'an and *sura*.

Ayatollah (P): The root term *ayat*, literally means the "sign," "token," or "miracle," such as a verse in the Qur'an. Since *Allah* is the Islamic term for God, *ayat Allah* or *Ayatollah* literally means the "miraculous sign of Allah" on earth. An *ayatollah* is a revered Shi'ah theologian and jurist who studies and interprets God's directives embodied in the Qur'an.

Ba'ath (A): Literally, "rebirth" or "renaissance." The Ba'ath ideology, or Ba'athism, initially emphasized nationalism, pan-Arabism, Arab socialism, anti-Western imperialism, Secularism, and democracy. Authoritarian Ba'ath parties govern Iraq and Syria.

Babism: In 1844, a thousand years after the disappearance of the twelfth Shi'ah *imam*, Mirza Ali Muhammad (1819–1950), a young Shi'ah merchant in Shiraz, Persia/Iran, proclaimed himself the *Bab* (the Gate) to the Hidden Imam/Mahdi, then the Hidden *Imam* himself, and finally God's messiah. The Bab claimed that the *shariah* couldn't remedy the contemporary problems facing humankind and therefore had to be superseded by his teachings, summarized in the Bayan (Sayings). In venerating the Bab as a prophet and the Bayan as God's message, the Babis violate two fundamental Islamic principles, namely, that Prophet Muhammad was God's last messenger, who came with His last message, embodied in the Qur'an.

Bahaism: Around 1863, a leading disciple of the Bab, Mirza Husain Ali Nuri, known as Ba-haullah (1817–1892), or "splendor of God," proclaimed himself the "messiah" in Per-sia/Iran. Bahaullah recognized the Bab as Muhammad's successor and the Bayan as a sacred book. However, Bahaullah claimed that he was the "promised one" whom the Bab had said "God shall make manifest." His persuasive skills won over the majority of Babis, who came to be known as Bahais, or the adherents of Bahaism.

Baitful mal: Islamic charitable/welfare fund raised from a progressive taxation system in an Islamic state.

Bai'ya **(A):** An "oath of allegiance" pledging one's total loyalty and obedience to a reli-giopolitical leader.

Banias: A Hindi term for Indian Hindu moneylenders.

Banu **Adam (A):** Adam's descendents.

Barakah **(A):** The "gift of God's blessing"; spiritual influence emanating from a holy man, a charismatic leader, a place, or a thing, making the person, place, or thing worthy of reverence or veneration.

Basij **(A):** Literally, "mobilization"; In Iran, *basij* is the auxiliary force of the Islamic Revo-lutionary Guards called the Pasdaran (Guardians). See Pasdaran-i-Inqelab-i-Islami.

Basij-i-Mustazafin **(P):** Literally "mobilization of the oppressed"; an organization that was established in Iran in early 1980 by Ayatollah Khomeini's Islamic government.

Bay'a **(A):** Oath of fealty, pledge, or pact.

Bayt **(A):** House or household.

Bazaar **(P):** Market or marketplace.

Bazaari **(P):** A merchant who sells produce and other goods in the market. The Iranian *bazaaris* played an important role in financing Iran's Islamic Revolution in the late 1970s.

Bedouins: Nomadic Arabs who originally inhabited desert areas of the Middle East. Less than 2 percent of the Arab world today is inhabited by bedouins (most of whom are Muslims).

BCE: Abbreviation for Before the Common Era.

Bid'ah **(A):** Literally, "innovation"; some Sunni Revolutionary Islamists consider any "inno-vation" in the purity of Islamic beliefs and practices of the *aslaf* as *bid'ah*, or an "un-worthy innovation," and thus reprehensible.

Bismillah **(A):** Literally, "In the name of Allah," a statement with which Muslims ought to begin any undertaking.

Bismillah ir-rahman ir-rahim (A): "In the name of Allah, the most Merciful and most Kind."

Blowback: A term that the U.S. Central Intelligence Agency (CIA) invented to refer to the unintended consequences of U.S. policies overseas that were in many cases kept se-cret from the American public. In his book entitled *Blowback: The Costs and Conse-quences of American Empire,* Chalmers Johnson lays out the perils ahead if the United States insists on projecting its military, political, economic, and cultural power all over the world.

Burqa: Veil worn by conservative Muslim women in traditional Muslim societies. The *burqa* is a voluminous head-to-toe covering with a mesh grid over the eyes.

Caliphate: The Anglicized term for Khilafat, or rule by a *khalifah* (caliph). See *khalifah.*

CE: Abbreviation for Common Era.

Chador **(P):** The long garment or cloak worn by conservative Iranian Muslim women. The garment covers a woman's head and entire body but not her face. See *hijab.*

"Clash of civilizations": According to Professor Samuel Huntington, cultural identity or civilization (defined primarily in terms of religion) is becoming the central force shaping the patterns of integration, conflict, and disintegration in post–Cold War international relations. Although Huntington discusses the potential for clashes between at least eight competing civilizations—Western, Confucian, Japanese, Islamic, Hindu, Slavic-Orthodox Christian, Latin American, and African—he is particularly concerned about violent clashes between the Islamic and non-Islamic civilizations.

***Dar* (A):** House, abode, tribal territory.

***Dar al-harb* (A):** Literally, "abode of war"; refers to a land ruled by non-Muslims where non-Islamic laws prevail. Until modern times, there was a widespread feeling among Traditionalist and Revolutionary Islamists that in these lands Muslims were not allowed to freely practice their religion, felt insecure, and suffered discrimination. Thus, a state of conflict prevailed between the non-Muslim rulers and their Muslim subjects and between the *dar al-harb* and *dar al-Islam* (abode of Islam or the Muslim world).

***Dar al-Islam* (A):** Literally, "abode of Islam"; often refers to all those lands where Muslim regimes govern and where, ideally, Islamic laws are practiced and Islamic institutions exist.

***Dar al-Ulum* (A):** An institution where Islamic instruction is imparted. In Egypt it often refers to Al-Azhar, in Cairo.

***Dars-i-Nizamiyya*:** The Islamic curriculum developed by Mullah Nizamuddin (d. 1748 CE) of Oudh, India, and popularized by the Traditionalist *ulama* of Farangi Mahall in Lucknow, India, during the eighteenth and nineteenth centuries. It still exerts influence over *madrassah* education in the South Asian subcontinent.

***Da'wa* (A):** The "call," "invitation," or "summons" to acknowledge religious truth and join a religious community, missionary movement, or religiopolitical organization; missionary activity; propagation of Islam.

***Du'a* (A):** Prayer; supplication; making personal requests of God.

***Dhikr* (A):** Literally, "remembrance"; in Islam, it is used for the repetition of certain words or phrases in praise of God and/or Prophet Muhammad. Sufis often chant God's names as a mantra to induce a heightened state of consciousness.

***Dhimmi* (A):** Derives from the Arabic term *dhimma* (an agreement of protection); often applied to free non-Muslims (especially "people of the Book," i.e., Christians and Jews) who lived in Muslim countries and were guaranteed freedom of worship and government protection. *Dhimmis* paid no *zakat* or *ushr* taxes, but paid a capitation tax called *jizya* for the state protection guaranteed them and for not bearing the responsibility of defending the *dar al-Islam* in times of war. See *zakat; ushr; jizya*; and *dar al-Islam*.

Diaspora: From the Greek word meaning "dispersion." It often refers to the protracted exile of the Jewish people after the Romans conquered Israel over 2,000 years ago. The term is also often used by those sympathetic to the plight of the Palestinians after the creation of Israel in 1948 and the four Arab-Israeli wars.

***Din* (A):** Literally, "religion"; in Islam, it is the sum total of a Muslim's faith.

Din-i-Illahi (U): The eclectic "Religion of the Supreme Being," initiated by India's Moghul emperor Jalal-ud-din Muhammad Akbar (r. 1556–1605 CE), combining the best features of the major religions in India. The new religion, however, was accepted by only a few Moghul courtiers and faded away soon after Akbar's death.

***Dua*:** A prayer, blessing, or plea offered by Muslims at any time, anywhere, and for a broad spectrum of reasons. It should not be confused with the obligatory ritual prayer service. However, Muslims do thank God, praise Him, and request His assistance in the form of a brief *dua* after their ritual prayer is over.

***Eid* (A):** Literally, "festival" or "holiday"; Muslims celebrate two *eids* annually: Eid al-Fitr, literally "the festival breaking the fast," which celebrates the completion of a month of fasting, and Eid al-Adha, which celebrates the completion of the *hajj*. See Eid al-Fitr and Eid al-Adha.

Eid al-Adha (A): The "festival of sacrifice," "feast of sacrifice," "Feast of Abraham," or simply "the Great Feast," is the climactic event (when animals are slaughtered) held at the close of the *hajj* season (on the tenth day of the Islamic calendar month of Dhul Hijjah and after three days of *hajj* rituals). It commemorates Abraham's willingness to sacrifice his son Ishmael when commanded by God in a dream to test his faith.

Eid al-Fitr (A): One of the most joyous holidays in the Islamic lunar calendar. It is celebrated on the first day of the Islamic calendar month of Shawal or one day after the month of Ramadan (during which time Muslims fasted from dawn to dusk). See Ramadan.

Eid-i-Milad-un-Nabi (U): Called Maulid or Maulud in Arabic, it is a festival commemorating Prophet Muhammad's birthday. See Maulid or Maulud.

Emirate: A country ruled by an *emir* (monarch or king).

"End of history": In the early 1990s, Francis Fukuyama—a State Department analyst—generated a controversy in intellectual circles when he posited that the triumph of the democratic and free market countries (the Allied Powers) over the totalitarian and corporatist countries (the Axis Powers) at the end of World War II, as well as the triumph of the liberal democratic and capitalist West over the totalitarian command economies of the Communist bloc, suggested that humankind had arrived at the "end of history." The latter concept was based on German philosopher Friedrich Hegel's idea of the dialectical method—thesis, antithesis, and synthesis—that contributes to progress of history in the world. According to Muslims, Islam is the final and ideal synthesis in terms of the Hegelian dialectic and will be embraced by the majority of humankind at the "end of history," and the end of the world as we know it.

Ethnic cleansing: A euphemism for genocide; a systematic policy of terrorizing, expelling, and attempting to liquidate a particular ethnic group. In Yugoslavia, the Orthodox Christian Serbs engaged in the "ethnic cleansing" of Bosnian Muslims (1992–1995) and Muslim Kosavars (1999).

***Fallah*, pl. *fallahun* (A):** Peasant or small farmer.

***Falsafah* (A):** Literally, "philosophy"; an esoteric philosophical movement which tried to reconcile the revealed religion of the Qur'an with the Greek rationalism of Plato and Aristotle. Ayatollah Khomeini taught *falsafah* and his idea of the Velayat-i-Faqih was influenced by his study of Plato.

***Faqih* (A):** An expert in Islamic jurisprudence.

***Faraidh*, sing. *fardh* (A):** Literally, "compulsory duties" or "obligations." In Islam omission of these duties will be punished and the commission of them will be rewarded. The five obligatory *faraidh* enjoined on all Muslims are (a) the *shahadah* (proclamation of one's faith in Islam); (b) *salat* (prayers); (c) *sawm* (fasting during Ramadan); (d) *zakat* (alms to the poor); and (e) *hajj* (pilgrimage to Makkah).

Farangi Mahall: The name of a mansion in Lucknow, India, that was built by a French indigo merchant. It came to be the home of an extended family of Traditionalist Sunni *ulama*—popularly known as the Farangi Mahallis, after their residence—in the late seventeenth century.

***Farsi* (P):** The Persian language, spoken by Persians/Iranians.

***Fatah* (A):** Literally, "conquest" or "victory."

Fatimah bint Muhammad: Daughter of Prophet Muhammad, wife of Ali, mother of Hassan and Hussein, and the woman regarded by all Muslims as a paragon of virtue, piety, and compassion. Many Muslims add the honorific title *Al-Zahra* (The Shining One) to her name.

Fatwa **(A):** A formal and authoritative Islamic decree on a civil or religious issue that is often formulated and promulgated by a *mufti* or a qualified and respected Islamic theologian-jurist.

Fedayeen **(A):** Those Muslims who are willing to sacrifice themselves in a *jihad*.

Fellaheen **(A):** Arab peasants and laborers.

Fertile Crescent: The geographical and political term for the crescent-shaped region stretching along the Mediterranean coast and along the Tigris-Euphrates from Asia to southern Palestine. It includes parts of what are Iraq, Syria, Lebanon, Israel, and Jordan.

Fiqh **(A):** Islamic jurisprudence, which covers all aspects of religious, political, economic, and social life. While a *fiqh* is not as comprehensive, divine, eternal, and immutable as the *shariah*, each *madhab* within the "House of Islam" has its own *fiqh*.

Fiqh-i-Jafariyyah **(A):** The Shi'ah school of jurisprudence that was codified by the sixth Shi'ah *imam*, Ja'far al-Sadiq (d. 765 CE).

Fitna: Civil disorder within the *ummah*; fighting between Muslims.

Fitrah **(A):** Literally, "primordial nature." Islam posits that the original nature of human beings is good. In this respect, Islam disagrees with the Christian view of "original sin." See original sin.

Fundamentalism: This term was initially used in the late nineteenth century for white American Protestants who emphasized the literal interpretation and absolute inerrancy of the Bible as fundamental to Christian life. In the second half of the twentieth century, the Western mass media and scholarly community popularized the term to signify any orthodox, conservative, radical, revolutionary, or zealous religiopolitical movement. Since fundamentalism has come to imply religious bigotry, extremism, fanaticism, and even violence and terrorism, most Muslims in general and Islamists in particular—who firmly believe in and actively practice the fundamentals of their faith—object to the term being used for Islam and Muslims. See Revolutionary Islamism.

Fundamentalist: The term has been popularized in the West to imply an adherent of any religion who believes in the literal interpretation of his or her holy book. Most fundamentalists tend to be pious, moralistic, messianic, autocratic, exclusivist, closed-minded, fanatical, and/or zealous in varying degrees. They are also opposed to secularization, materialism, hedonism, and human-made ideologies (such as Secularism, capitalism, nationalism, Fascism, Marxism, socialism, and communism, to name a few), which they view as corrupting humankind. See Revolutionary Islamist.

Ghair-Muqallid **(P):** A Muslim who does not want to be restricted to only one school of Islamic jurisprudence (such as Ahl-i-Hadith).

Ghayba **(A):** The condition of anyone who has been physically withdrawn by God from the sight of human beings and whose life during that period of disappearance may have been miraculously prolonged. Shi'ah doctrine says the twelfth *imam* disappeared and will reappear at a foreordained time to lead people back to "true" Islam. In the meantime, supreme *mujtahids* have the authority to interpret the twelfth *imam*'s will in his absence.

Ghazi **(A):** A Muslim who fights in a *jihad* to defend his faith, his community, and/or his Islamic state/Muslim homeland. The Ottoman sultans conferred this title upon those generals and warriors who distinguished themselves in the battlefield.

Globalization: The global interdependence of all states in the world due to the revolution in communications, transportation, trade, and finance. The increasing integration of states is contributing to a holistic and single global system in which the process of change increasingly binds people together in a common fate.

Grand Mosque: See Haram al-Sharif.

Hadd: The punishment prescribed by the *shariah* for crimes.

Hadith (A): Prophet Muhammad's recorded saying(s) or statement(s) that were memorized and written down by members of his extended family and *sahabah* (close companions). Later compiled into various collections. The most authentic and popular of these compilations are the Sahih Bukhari and Sahih Muslim.

Hadith al-sahih: An authoritative statement of Prophet Muhammad.

Hafiz-i-Qur'an: One who has memorized the entire Qur'an in Arabic.

Hajar al-Aswad (A): Literally, "black stone"; on the wall near the door at the northeast corner of the Haram al-Sharif is embedded the holy "Black Stone," which was given to Abraham by God. See Haram al-Sharif.

Hajj (A): Literally, "pilgrimage." Adult Muslims of sound mind, health, and financial means have been enjoined by their faith to undertake the spiritual journey to Makkah during the *hajj* season—which falls between the seventh and tenth day of the last Islamic calendar month of *Dhul Hijjah*—and engage in the formal ritual requirements in Islam's holiest city. *Hajj* is the fifth pillar of Islam. See *faraidh*.

Hajji (A): A pilgrim to Makkah who has performed the *hajj* during the annual *hajj* season. Also a title assumed by someone who has successfully completed the pilgrimage.

Halal: That which is lawful, particularly food items. Often applies to meat from animals that have been slaughtered according to Islamic laws and customs. *Halal* meat is very similar to kosher meat in Judaism. The opposite of *haram*.

Hamas: Arabic term for "zeal"; *Hamas* is also the acronym of *Harakat al-Muqawama al-Islamiyah* (Islamic Resistance Movement). Shaykh Ahmed Yassin, a former member of the *Ikhwan al-Muslimun* (Muslim Brotherhood) and spiritual leader of the Islamic Center in Gaza established Hamas in August 1988. It is a Revolutionary Islamist Palestinian organization in the West Bank and Gaza that, along with Hamas, was in the vanguard of the first and second *intifadahs*. Hamas is strongly opposed the Oslo Accords, and has aggressively fought against the Israeli settlers in the West Bank and Gaza, the Israeli army, and even Yasser Arafat's Palestinian Authority. See *Ikhwan al-Muslimun*, Revolutionary Islamists, and *Intifadah*.

Hanafis: Sunni Muslims who follow the teachings of the Iraqi-born *imam* Abu Hanifa al-Nu'man ibn-Thabit (699–569 CE). The Hanafi sect was actively promoted by a number of Abbasid and Ottoman rulers and is widely prevalent in Turkey, Afghanistan, Egypt, Central Asia, China, and South Asia.

Hanbalis: Those Sunnis who follow the teachings of the Iraqi-born theologian and jurist Ahmad ibn-Hanbal (780–855 CE). The puritanism of the Hanbalis, combined with the promotion of the Hanafi *madhab* by the Ottoman rulers, who crushed the Wahhabis (adherents of the Hanbali *madhab*), resulted in the Hanbalis being the smallest of the four Sunni *madhabs*. Hanbalis are concentrated in Saudi Arabia and Qatar.

Haq (A): That which is true or the truth; for example, the Qur'an and Islam itself. In Islamic law it comprises the legal rights, shares, claims, or obligation of an individual. For *sufis* the term refers to the "Divine Essence," or Allah.

Haram: Literally, "restricted" or "forbidden"; that which is unlawful in Islam (like alcohol or pork). By extension, the term also applies to that which is sacred, such as religious sanctuaries or holy places.

Haram al-Sharif (the Noble Sanctuary): Located in the historic old city of Jerusalem, this sacred sanctuary, known as the Temple Mount by Jews and Christians, houses the Dome of the Rock and the Masjid al-Aqsa (the Furthest Mosque). The Dome of the Rock is a blue-tiled octagonal building with a golden dome over the site where Solomon's Temple once stood. Jews believe the Dome of the Rock houses the Rock of

Foundation (of the world), which was in the center of Solomon's Temple. Muslims, Jews, and Christians believe that Abraham was willing to sacrifice his son at the site. Muslims believe that Prophet Muhammad ascended to heaven in his brief night journey from the rock (Qur'an, Surah 17), and that the rock bears the imprint of Muhammad's winged horse, *Al-Burak* (the lightening), that soared heavenward from the site carrying God's last prophet, and that God will send one of His angels to the Dome of the Rock to sound the trumpet call to signal the end of the world and the Day of Judgement. The Al-Aqsa Mosque at the south end of the Temple Mount has prayer niches dedicated to Moses and Jesus. Prophet Muhammad enjoined Muslims to turn in the direction of Jerusalem or *Al-Quds* (The Holy) to say their prayers for the first twenty years of his prophethood. Jerusalem still remains the third holiest city in Islamdom after Makkah and Madinah. The arson attack against the Al-Aqsa Mosque in August 1969 by Michael Rohan, an Australian Christian fundamentalist, shocked the Muslim world and led to the immediate establishment of the Organization of the Islamic Conference (OIC).

Haramain (A): Refers to two of the holiest cities in the Muslim world, namely, Makkah and Madinah. It also refers to the holy mosques, mausoleums, and shrines in those cities.

Hazrat **(A):** A title of respect that is the equivalent of "your reverence" or "his reverence" when applied to eminent spiritual leaders. It is also indiscriminately used for any intellectual.

Hezbollah, (P) Hizb Allah (A): Literally, "Party of Allah." The name was adopted by radical Shi'ah organizations in Iran and Lebanon.

Hijab: The "veil" or covering worn by conservative Muslim women when they are in public. The basic reason for the *hijab* is Islam's emphasis on modesty in dress for both women and men.

Hijaz: A mountainous region of the Arabian Peninsula adjacent to the Red Sea coast that includes the holy cities of Makkah and Madinah, where Islam originated.

Hijra (A): Literally, "migration," "emigration," or "flight." In Islam, it refers to the migration of Prophet Muhammad and his close companions from Makkah to Madinah in 622 CE. The Islamic calendar begins with this migration and the establishment of the first Islamic state in Madinah.

Hijrat **(A):** Literally, "migration," "emigration," or "flight"; In Islam, some devout Muslims have from time to time emigrated from areas ruled by *kafirs*, or "wayward Muslims," to areas where "true" Islam was practiced or would be practiced. See Hijra.

Hilal: Refers to the "new moon" or "crescent." The new moon is important in Islam because of the Islamic lunar calendar. The crescent, analogous to the Christian cross, the Jewish star of David, and other religious symbols, is found on the flags of a number of Muslim countries.

Hisb-e-Islami (A): The name literally means "party of Islam." Led by Golbuddin Hekmatyar, it was one of the Afghan *mujahideen* organizations that was fighting against the Soviet colonialists in Afghanistan during the 1980s.

Hojatoislam **(P):** A mid-level alim (Islamic scholar) in shi'ah Izan.

Hosayniyyeh (P): Religious center for the commemoration of the martyrdom of Imam Hussein and the performance of related ceremonies.

Hujjati (P): Member of the clerical faction in Iran that opposed clerical rule.

Hukumat **(P):** Centralized government.

Human Development Index (HDI): An index that uses life expectancy, literacy, average number of years of schooling, and income to assess a country's performance in providing for its people security and welfare.

Hussein ibn Ali: The son of Ali ibn Abi Talib and Fatimah bint Muhammad, the grandson of Prophet Muhammad, and the third Shi'ah *imam*, who was martyred at Karbala in 680 CE. See Ali ibn Abu Talib, Fatimah bint Muhammad, Shi'ah, Karbala.

Ibadat **(A):** Performance of ritual religious worship/practices or religious obligations, including prayer, fasting, giving alms to the poor, and making the pilgrimage to Makkah.

Iblis (A): The Qur'anic term for Satan, or the Devil.

Ibn **(A):** Literally, "son of"; corresponds to "ben" in Hebrew.

ibn Taimiyyah, Taqi al-Din (1263–1328 CE): A Syrian-born theologian-jurist who spent his life elaborating upon Hanbali teachings in his puritanical writings and sermons. He rejected *taqlid* and *ijma*, insisted on the literal interpretation of the Qur'an and *sunnah*, condemned *bid'ah*, crusaded against the influences of Greek philosophy, denounced Sufism, and censured the cult of Prophet Muhammad and the practice of saint worship.

Ihram **(A):** The two white seamless cotton garments worn by Muslim pilgrims going to perform the *hajj* during the twelfth Islamic lunar month of Dhul Hijjah.

Ihsan: Mercy, kindness, and compassion.

Ijma **(A):** "Agreement," "unanimity," or "consensus"; considered to be the third *usul*, or source, of Islamic law. The consensus can be that of the first generation of Muslims, the great theologian-jurists of the medieval era of Islam, the *ummah* scattered all over the world, or even an entire nation.

Ijtihad (A): The word *ijtihad* derives from the same Arabic root as *jihad* and literally means "to exert oneself." Technically, *ijtihad* implies a Muslim jurist exercising his personal, independent reasoning, knowledge, and judgment to give his opinion on a legal issue where there is no specific order in the Qur'an. The term now commonly implies the independent interpretation or reinterpretation of Islamic laws.

Ikhwan **(A):** Literally, "brotherhood" or "brethren."

Ikhwan al-Muslimun (A): "Muslim Brotherhood" or "Muslim Brethren." Hassan al-Banna founded an Islamic political party by this name in Egypt in 1928. In due course, it spread to other Arab countries.

Ilm **(A):** Literally, "to know," "knowledge," or "learning." It is often used by Muslims for the knowledge of Islam, which is regarded as all encompassing. One possessing *ilm* is called an *alim*.

Imam **(A):** A prayer leader or officiating cleric in a mosque or a very learned and competent *alim*. In the Shi'ah sect, the title *imam* is also used for the divinely guided and rightful religiopolitical successors of Prophet Muhammad, starting with Imam Ali, the Prophet's cousin and son-in-law.

Imamate (A): The divine right of Ali ibn Abu Talib and his male descendents to lead the *ummah*.

Iman **(A):** Refers to the five articles of the Islamic creed, which are (a) belief in Allah; (b) belief in angels; (c) belief in the prophets of Allah, with Adam as the first prophet and Muhammad as the last; (d) belief in the holy books revealed by Allah, that is, the Torah, the Bible, and the Qur'an; and (e) belief in the Day of Judgment.

Infitah **(A):** Literally, "opening up." In 1972, Egypt's President Muhammad Anwar al-Sadat inaugurated an "open door policy" that opened Egypt up to foreign investment and initiated a policy of economic liberalization or capitalism. Attractive tax breaks and duty-free zones lured foreign multinational corporations to a country that had gone through nearly two decades of socialism.

Injil (A): The Qur'anic term for God's revelations to Jesus Christ embodied in the Bible, which is the holy book of the Christians. Muslims believe in the Old Testament, but not in the New Testament. This is because, in the latter, Jesus Christ is mentioned as the son of God, which in Islam is *shirk* (polytheistic, and therefore sinful). See *shirk*.

Insaf (A): Literally, "impartiality," "objectivity," "integrity," and "equity"; refers to a code of ethics and morality that a devout Muslim follows.

Insan (A): Human being.

Insan-i-Kamil (A): Literally, the perfect human being. Often used for Prophet Muhammad.

Intifadah (A): Literally, "shaking off"; it has come to imply a popular grassroots "uprising" or "revolt." The first Palestinian *intifadah* began in Israeli-controlled Gaza (followed soon thereafter in the West Bank) on December 9, 1987, and ended in 1993. The second *intifadah*, also known as the al-Aqsa *intifadah*, began in Gaza and the West Bank on September 28, 2000.

Inshallah (A): Literally, "God willing." Devout Muslims often use this Arabic term when they say they are going to do something in the future.

Isa: Arabic term for Jesus Christ.

Ishmael: The first son of Abraham, from his wife's handmaid, Hagar. Muslims believe that Ishmael, not Isaac, was the son of God's promise to Abraham.

Islah (A): In Islam, the term for reform, purification, and revitalization of the Muslim community based on Islamic principles. The *islah* movement or the movement of Islamic reformism, represented by such Islamic scholars and thinkers as Muhammad Abduh and Muhammad Rashid Rida of Egypt, who attempted to address contemporary problems with the help of the Qur'an and *sunnah*.

Islam (A): Literally, "submission" or "surrender." The aderents of Islam, or Muslims, believe that only by totally surrendering to God's will and obeying His laws can one achieve true inner peace and happiness in this world and the hereafter.

Islamdom: The Muslim world or the world of Islam.

Islamic Calendar: The Islamic lunar calendar begins with Prophet Muhammad's migration from Makkah to Madinah and the establishment of the first Islamic state. The twelve months of the Islamic calendar in proper sequence are: (1) Muharram, (2) Safar, (3) Rabi 'al-Awwal, (4) Rabi 'al-Thani, (5) Jamadi al-Awwal, (6) Jamadi al-Thani, (7) Rajab, (8) Shaban, (9) Ramadan, (10) Shawwal, (11) Dhul-Qadah, and (12) Dhul-Hijjah.

Islamic Jihad: Literally "Islamic struggle." In 1981, disillusioned and militant members of the *Ikhwan al-Muslimun* in Israel's occupied territories of the West Bank and Gaza decided to leave their relatively moderate Islamist organization and form Islamic Jihad committed to Revolutionary Islamism. The Revolutionary Islamists in Islamic Jihad captured media headlines when they threw hand grenades at a military graduation ceremony at the Western Wall in Jerusalem in October 1986. Along with Hamas, Islamic Jihad has been in the forefront of the two Palestinian *intifadahs*; has openly opposed the Oslo Accords; and has aggressively fought Israeli settlers in the West Bank and Gaza, the Israeli army, and even Yasser Arafat's Palestinian Authority. See also *Ikhwan al-Muslimun*, Hamas, Revolutionary Islamists, and *Intifadah*.

Islamic revival: The renewal of heightened interest in Islamic symbols, ideas, and ideals subsequent to a period of relative dormancy of interest.

Islamic Revivalism: See Islamism.

Islamic Revivalist: See Islamist.

Islamism: It can be viewed as the process by which Islam has become a comprehensive political ideology. The generic term for the phenomenon of Islamic revivals occurring around the world. See Islamist; Revolutionary Islamist; Traditionalist Islamist; Modernist Islamist.

Islamist or Islamic Revivalist: A term used generically in the literature on Islamic revivalism to refer to any participant in an Islamic revival. However, it is more specifically used for prominent Islamists or Islamic revivalists who make a significant contribution to Islamism or an Islamic revival. In propagating their perception of the "true" Islam, all Islamists frequently, but not necessarily, promote the creation of an Islamic state by teaching, preaching, and/or writing, and on rare occasions even by the force of arms. There are three types of Islamists: Revolutionary, Traditionalist, and Modernist.

Isma'ilis: A branch of Shi'ism which follows the religiopolitical leadership of Isma'il, a son of Ja'far al-Sadiq and his descendants.

***Isnad*, sing. *sanad* (A):** Literally, "a chain of authorities." In Islam, it refers to the chain of people responsible for transmitting the *hadith*. The validity of the *hadith* depends on the transmitters being perceived as men of honesty and integrity in Islamic history.

Ithna Ashari (A): The Twelver Shi'ah sect, which believes that Ali ibn Abu Talib should have been Islam's first caliph because Prophet Muhammad had nominated him. They follow twelve infallible imams beginning with Ali and ending with Muhammad Mahdi, who disappeared in 873 CE and is promised to reappear as "true" Islam's savior.

Jahannam (A): "Hell," where sinners will go after death.

Jahiliyyah (A): Derived from the Arabic word *jahila*, "to be ignorant." Muslims claim that the pre-Islamic period in Arabia was an "Age of Ignorance" and a state of primitive savagery.

***Jama'at* (A):** A group, association, assembly, congregation, organization, or political party.

Jannah (A): In Islam, Heaven or Paradise.

***Jihad* (A):** Literally, "to strive" or "to struggle"; in Islam it means "to struggle in the way of God." A *jihad* is a "holy struggle," sanctioned by the *ulama* and fought against aggressors and tyrants. Also refers to the spiritual struggle waged against one's own baser instincts.

***Jihad-i-Akbar* (A):** The greatest "holy struggle," to purge one's baser instincts and impulses.

***Jihad-i-asghar* (A):** The smaller "holy struggle"; the military campaign waged against aggressors and tyrants, and "wayward Muslims."

Jirga: A tribal council of respected elders at which major political, economic, social, and legal issues are discussed and decisions made; it plays an important role in Afghanistan and northern Pakistan.

***Jizya* (A):** The poll tax or capitation tax levied on *dhimmis*, or non-Muslims, for protection, exemption from military duty, and full rights of citizenship given to them in an Islamic state.

Ka'abah: This cube-shaped Islamic shrine in the holy city of Makkah (present-day Saudi Arabia) is the most sacred place in the Muslim world. According to Muslims, Abraham and his son Ishmael first built it to worship God, and then Muhammad cleansed it of idols and rededicated it to the worship of one God. Muslims turn to the Ka'abah when they pray and have been enjoined by their faith to make a pilgrimage to the Ka'abah once in their lifetime. See Al-Bayt al-Haram, Haram al-Sharif, Hajj, and Makkah.

***Kafir* (A):** The term was first applied to "unbelieving" Makkans, who rejected Prophet Muhammad's message and denounced him. The term has also been used for non-Muslim enemies of Islam and Muslims as well as for apostates, polytheists, infidels, hypocrites, and "wayward" or nonpracticing Muslims. See *mushrikeen*.

***Kalam* (A):** Literally, "speech" or "dialectic"; in Islam it is applied to Islamic theology, which is the study of God's words, the subject that attempts to give rational proofs for religious beliefs, deals with the problems of God's oneness, His attributes, and human free will and self-determination, among other philosophical issues.

Kalimah: A defining statement or declaration of faith in one God and His last Prophet.

Karbala: A town in southeastern Iraq where in 680 CE a historic battle took place between the armies of Yazid ibn Mu'awiyah, who had become the ruler of the Islamic empire, and Hussein ibn Ali, the grandson of Prophet Muhammad who refused to endorse Yazid as the new caliph. In the ensuing battle, Hussein and his male relatives and followers were killed on the tenth of Muharram. Annually, Muslims all over the world commemorate Hussein's martyrdom, over thirteen hundred years ago, and vow to struggle against corruption, injustice, and tyranny even if it means giving up their lives. Shi'ahs make every effort to visit the tombs and shrines of the martyrs in Karbala once in their lifetime.

Kemalist: Adherent of the Secularist principles of Kemal Atatürk, the founder of modern Turkey, who was against Islamism and advocated Secularism, Turkish nationalism, and modernization instead.

Khadijah bint Khuwaylid: The daughter of a respected chieftain of the Makkan Quraysh tribe. After her father's death, she managed his thriving business. One of her business agents was Muhammad, who had a reputation for being honest and trustworthy. She subsequently married Muhammad. Khadijah was the first to accept Islam and was her husband's staunchest supporter.

Khulafah-i-Rashidun: Or Khulafah-i-Rashidin; most Muslims revere only the first four "rightly-guided" caliphs—Abu Bakr, Umar, Uthman, and Ali—and consider all caliphs thereafter as political rulers, lacking the mantle of spiritual leadership.

Khalifah (A): Caliph; Prophet Muhammad's religiopolitical successors and leaders of the worldwide *ummah*.

Khan: Mongol and Tartar chieftains and tribal leaders were referred to as khans, as were the Ottoman sultans and provincial governors in Safavid Persia. In India, under the Turkish kings of Delhi, *khan* was the title of the principal nobles, especially those of Persian or Afghan heritage. Today it is a common Muslim surname.

Khana-i-Ka'abah: See Haram al-Sharif, Hajr al-Aswad.

Kharijites, sing. *khariji* (A): Derived from the Arabic term *Khuruj*, which means "to rebel" or "to secede." Another possible derivation is the Arabic word *kharij*, which means "to go out." The Kharijites, or Khawarij, became the first Muslim zealots when they initiated a war against Caliph Ali.

Khatam al-Ambiya (A): Literally, "seal of the Prophets"; the title is reserved by Muslims for Prophet Muhammad, who was the last of God's prophets and brought His final message to humankind. See Prophet Muhammad.

Khatamun Nabiyin (A): Same as Khatam al-Ambiya.

Khilafat (A): Caliphate; refers to the religiopolitical rule by a *khalifah* (caliph), which began after Prophet Muhammad's death.

Khulafah-i-Rashidin: Also known as Khulafah-i-Rashidun; literally, "rightly guided *khalifahs*." The religiopolitical rule of the first four righteous *khalifahs* of Islam, namely Abu Bakr, Umar, Uthman, and Ali. In South Asia, it is known as *Khilafat-i-Rashidah*. Also see Khilafat.

Khilafah-i-Rashidun (A): See Khulafah-i-Rashidin.

Khums (A): Besides the voluntary donation of *zakat*; Shi'ahs have been enjoined by their faith to give *khums*, which is a donation of one-fifth of their savings to provide maintenance for and support of the work of needy Sayyids, who are Prophet Muhammad's descendants.

Khutbah (A): In Islam, it is a sermon delivered by a Muslim cleric or a mosque *imam* to a congregation, usually at the Friday congregational prayers.

Kismet: The idea that evolved in the *ummah* that the fate of human beings has been preordained and predestined. It is more a tradition than a principle of faith.

Kufr **(A):** In Islam it means "blasphemy," "hypocrisy," "lies," or "disbelief." A person guilty of *kufr* is a *kafir*.

Laylat ul-Qadr (A): Literally, "the night of power." Muslims believe that Prophet Muhammad received the first divine revelation on one of the last ten nights of the month of Ramadan. Muslims commemorate it most often on the twenty-seventh night of Ramadan.

Loya Jirga: Literally, the "Great Council" in the Pashtun language. In Afghanistan, it is the traditional meeting of tribal chiefs, respected elders, and the *ulama* to choose a new Afghan king. It is also the principal legislative body in the country.

Madhab (A): Literally, "a direction"; in Islam it applies to the four recognized Sunni schools or rites of jurisprudence: the Hanafi, Hanbali, Maliki, and Shafi'i sects. There is also one major school of Shi'ah jurisprudence called *Fiqh i Jafariyyah*.

Madinah: A city in present-day Saudi Arabia that was known as Yathrib before Prophet Muhammad migrated there in 622 CE. Then it was renamed *Madinat al-Nabi* (City of the Prophet) or simply Madinah. It was here that Muhammad established the first Islamic state, where he died in 632 CE, and where he is buried.

Madrassah **(A):** A school, college, seminary, or academy where the primary emphasis is on a broad spectrum of classical Islamic disciplines, which are taught by the *ulama*. Students also learn such subjects as Arabic, astronomy, logic, mathematics, medicine, literature, philosophy, and metaphysics.

Mahdi (A): Literally, "the divinely guided one," "expected deliverer," "redeemer," or "savior." The doctrine of the Mahdi in Islamic history first originated in the Shi'ah sect with their belief in the hidden twelfth *imam*, who will be sent by God to establish "true Islam." In due course, the appealing Mahdist hope also came to be held by many Sunnis and non-Muslims.

Maktabi (P): In Iran, a clerical grouping, faithful to the principles of Ayatollah Ruhollah Khomeini, who believed that clerics should play a leading role in the governance of societies.

Majlis **(A):** Literally, "session," "meeting," "assembly," or "council." In Shi'ah Islam a *majlis* is a religious session in which a knowledgeable Muslim discusses the life and works of the Ahl al-Bayt. It is also the term used for the national legislature in some Muslim countries.

Majlis-i-shura **(A):** Literally, a "consultative body" or an "elected council" to make recommendations to the ruler of an Islamic state or a Muslim homeland. It is also a term used for the national legislature in some Muslim countries.

Makkah: A major city in Saudi Arabia. The holiest city in the world of Islam because it is the birthplace of Prophet Muhammad (570 CE); the city where Muhammad received the first revelations from God and began to propagate Islam; the site of the Ka'abah, to which Muslims from all over the world come to perform the *hajj*; and the direction in which Muslims say their daily prayers.

Maktab **(A):** An elementary school for teaching children recitation of the Qur'an and the *hadith*, and the Arabic language.

Maktabi **(P):** A student or graduate of a *maktab*, or Qur'anic school. In Iran, it refers to the doctrinaire, dogmatic, and orthodox Muslim Revolutionary or Traditionalist Islamist. See Hujjati.

Malikis: Sunnis who follow the Islamic jurisprudence of jurist Abu Abd Allah Malik ibn-Anas (716–795 CE). The Maliki sect spread in Muslim Spain and Africa.

Marabout: A *sufi* leader in Africa.

Marja-i-Taqlid **(P):** Literally, "source of emulation." In the Ithna Ashari Shi'ah sect, any *mujtahid* who has reached the position of Ayatollah can be *marja-i-taqlid*.

Mashallah (A): A phrase occurring in the Qur'an and widely used by Muslims generally meaning "what God does, is well done."

Masjid (A): Derived from the word *sajdah*, meaning "to prostrate oneself." It is the Muslim house of worship, also called a mosque.

Masjid al-Aqsa (A): It is located in Jerusalem and is the site from where Prophet Muhammad is said to have gone on his miraculous nocturnal journey to the seventh heaven and returned. It was also the direction in which Muslims prayed before Prophet Muhammad directed Muslims to pray in the direction of the Ka'abah. See also Al-Aqsa Mosque.

Ma'sum (A): A sinless and infallible person.

Maulana (A): Derived from the Arabic root *maula*, which means "lord," "patron," "master," and "tutor." The title is applied to scholars of Islamic theology, jurisprudence, and history.

Maulid/Maulud (A): The anniversary celebrating the birth of Prophet Muhammad. It is celebrated on the twelfth day of the third Islamic calendar month of Rabi al-Awwal with speeches, writings, and *qawwalis* (poems and hymns praising God, Prophet Muhammad, or a Muslim saint). Muslims regard the birth date (12 Rabi al-Awwal in 570 CE) as one of the most important events in world history. The term could also denote the birth of a religious or sufi saint.

Maulvi (A): Another term for an Islamic teacher or peacher. See *mullah; maulana*.

Mecca: See Makkah.

Meelad-un-Nabi (U): Birthday of Prophet Muhammad. See Maulid/Maulud.

Mehram: A blood relative who should accompany a woman outside the home if the Islamic *shariah* is to be followed rigorously (as it was under the Taliban in Afghanistan).

Messiah (A): Literally, "the anointed one"; the religiopolitical leader who is sent by God to lead people back to the straight path. Jews, Christians, and Muslims believe that it is he who will establish the Kingdom of God on earth.

Middle East: The term *Middle East* is said to have been coined around 1900 by Captain Alfred T. Mahan, the noted American naval historian/strategist. Most Middle East scholars include all the Arabic-speaking countries and Turkey, Iran, and Israel in the region.

Mihrab: A recess in the wall of a *masjid* to indicate the *qibla*, that is, the direction of Makkah, for the correct orientation of ritual prayer. See *masjid, qibla,* and *salat.*

Millet: A religious community in the Ottoman empire; usually used for the *dhimmi* (non-Muslim) communities, which had some measure of autonomy in the Ottoman empire.

Minaret: Steeple or tower of a *masjid*, from which the Muslim call to prayer is sounded five times a day.

Minbar: The pulpit in a *masjid*, from which the *masjid's imam* delivers the *khutbah* (sermon).

Miraj: Literally, "ladder" or "way of ascent." In Islam, it refers to Prophet Muhammad's Laylat ul-Miraj or "night journey." According to the Qur'an, on this night (probably the 27th of Ramadan), Angel Gabriel took Prophet Muhammad from the mosque in Makkah to Mount Moriah in Jerusalem, whence he ascended to heaven, meeting the prophets and, ultimately, God Himself. The latter told him that Muslims should say their prayers five times a day. Modernist Islamists consider this experience to be a dream that Prophet Muhammad had, instead of having physically made this journey. In several Arab countries, there is a holiday entitled al-Isra Wal Miraj marking this miraculous event.

Modernist Islamists: Knowledgeable and religiously devout Muslims who vehemently criticize *taqlid*, pursuasively advocate *ijtihad*, and make a dedicated effort to reconcile the differences between traditional religious doctrine and secular scientific rationalism. Modernists advocate the incorporation of numerous modern day ideas and emphasize major revisions in Islamic laws.

Mu'amalat: Worldly transactions; mutual relations.

***Mudarabah* (A):** Profit and loss sharing in economic transactions.

***Muezzin* (A):** The person who calls people to prayer at the mosque.

***Mufassirin* (A):** The interpreters of the Qur'an.

Mufti: A learned, competent, and respected expert on Islamic theology and jurisprudence. The mufti has the authority not only to interpret Islamic law but also to issue *fatwas*.

***Muhaddith* (A):** A scholar of the *hadith*.

Muhajir: Literally, "migrant" or "refugee"; in South Asia, many Urdu-speaking Indian Muslims migrated or fled to the newborn Islamic homeland of Pakistan when India was partitioned in mid-August 1947.

***Muhajirun* (A):** Literally, "the emigrants"; the name given to the earliest converts to Islam from the Makkan tribe of Quraysh, who went with Prophet Muhammad to Madinah. Also called *muhajirs* in Urdu.

***Muhammadanism* (A):** A term incorrectly applied by non-Muslims to Islam. Prophet Muhammad did not create or start the religion, nor is he worshiped by Muslims. The creator of Islam as well as of everything else, according to Muslims, is Allah.

***Muharram* (A):** The name of the first month in the Islamic calendar. It was the month in which Hussein, son of fourth caliph and first Shi'ah imam Ali ibn Abu Talib, and his seventy-one male followers were martyred on the battlefield of Karbala in 680 CE.

***Mujaddid* (A):** Literally, "renewer," "restorer," or "regenerater" of Islam; Muslims believe that *mujaddids* are sent by God in times of spiritual crisis to set the world on the right path again.

***Mujaddid Alf-i-Thani* (U):** The renewer of Islam in the second millenium of Islamic history.

***Mujahideen* (sing. *mujahid*):** The Qur'anic term for Muslims who fight in a *jihad*.

***Mujtahid* (A):** An *alim* (especially, an expert in Islamic jurisprudence) who practices *ijtihad*, or interpretive reasoning, to inquire into and clarify the intent of the law; and one who has the right to give *fatwas*, or Islamic decrees. See *alim, ijtihad,* and *fatwa*.

***Mulhid* (A):** In the Islamic context, it is a Muslim who has deviated from Islam, hence becoming a heretic, infidel, or *kafir*.

Mullah: Formerly, another term for *alim*; hence someone to be revered. However, now it is commonly used for a Muslim clergyman of the lower ranks who serves as an Islamic teacher, preacher, or *imam* in the *masjid*. Also see *maulana* and *alim*.

Mu'min: Literally, "a true believer"; a God-fearing, practicing, and righteous Muslim.

***Munafiqun* (A):** Literally, "doubters," "waverers," "dissemblers," and "hypocrites." In Islamic history it was a term first used by Prophet Muhammad for those residents of Madinah who, during his first stay in that city, ostensibly joined Islam but were secretly doubting the Word of Allah and were critical of His messenger.

***Muqallid* (A):** A Muslim who considers himself bound by the principle of *taqlid*. Also called "imitators."

***Murid* (A):** Literally, "one who is desirous of knowledge"; a student. In the Islamic context, it applies to the disciple of a *pir*, or *sufi* teacher.

***Murtadd* (A):** One who renounces Islam; an "apostate."

Musa: The Arabic term used for Prophet Moses in the Qur'an.

***Musawaat-i-Muhammadi* (U):** Literally, "the egalitarianism of Prophet Muhammad." It refers to the ideal Islamic system's socioeconomic equality and justice.

***Musharaka* (A):** Profit and loss sharing in economic transactions.

Mushrikeen **or** ***Mushrikun*** **(A):** Literally, "unbelievers," "infidels," "polytheists," or "heretics" who believe in and worship many gods and are perceived as the enemies of Islam and Muslims. See *kafir*.

Muslihun **(A):** Those who work for *islah* (reform).

Muslim, pl. Muslimun (A): Literally, one who submits or surrenders to the will of God. Muslimun worship the same God as do Jews and Christians and share many of the same prophets and ethical traditions, including respect for innocent life. It was a term that came to apply to those who followed the religion of Islam that Prophet Muhammad preached.

Muslim Secularists: Muslims by name and birth who cherish Islamic ideals, identify with the Muslim community and culture, and are perceived as Muslims by non-Muslims. Most are non-practicing Muslims; view the classical and medieval Islamic doctrines and practices as anachronistic, reactionary, and impractical in the modern age; and look to a broad spectrum of ages and philosophies for their models of political and socioeconomic progress. Despite their secular worldview and commitment to promote secularization and Secularism, some Muslim Secularists opportunistically engage in the politics of Islam to enhance their legitimacy; to integrate and unite their fragmented citizenry; and to inspire, mobilize, and galvanize Muslims.

Mustakbirin **(A):** Literally, "the rich and exploitative elite."

Mut'ah **(A):** A temporary marriage for a stipulated period of time. *Mut'ah* is still practiced by some Shi'ah sects. Imam Ali allowed the practice, which was common in Arabia, and it was even condoned by Prophet Muhammad, according to the Ithna Ashari Shi'ah sect. The practice is denounced by Sunnis because Caliph Umar prohibited it.

Mutazilites: A school of Islamic theologians and jurists advocating rationalism and free will. It was founded by Wasil ibn Ata, who separated from the conservative and literalist school of Hasan al-Basri around 732 CE. The school's reasoned arguments were a criticism of those Muslims who read the Qur'an literally. The Mutazilites influenced the intellectual environment in the eighth and ninth centuries.

Muttaqi **(A):** A devout and "God-fearing" Muslim. See *taqwa*.

Muwahiddun, **sing.** ***muwahid*** **(A):** Literally, "monotheists" or "unitarians," who are staunch believers in "the unity and oneness of God." Wahhabis preferred to be known as Al-Muwahidun.

Muztazafin **(A):** A Qur'anic term for the poor, oppressed, and exploited people. A term popularized during the Iranian Revolution.

Nabi **(A):** Literally, "prophet," whose mission lies within the framework of an existing religion. Muslims believe that Adam was the first prophet, Muhammad the last, and that there were 124,000 prophets in between.

Nabuwat **(A):** The office or work of a *Nabi*, who has been directly inspired by Allah and to whom a special mission has been entrusted.

Nafs: Literally "soul."

Nakba: See al-Nakba.

Nahda: Literally, rebirth or renaissance; Arab revival.

Namaz **(P):** See *salat*.

Nation of Islam: An African-American pseudo-Islamic group that Wallace Fard Muhammad founded in the United States in 1931. Fard made Elijah Poole (renamed Elijah Muhammad) his successor and disappeared three years later. Elijah Muhammad developed and popularized the organization among African Americans until he died, forty-one years later. On Elijah Muhammad's death, his son, Wallace D. Muhammad, became leader of the organization. Assuming the name *Warith Deen Muhammad*, he called his father an enlightened teacher instead of a prophet; rejected the organization's racist philosophy; removed all racial restrictions on membership; did away with the rigid dress code; allowed members to participate in American politics and join the U.S. armed forces; renamed the organization the American Muslim Mission; and in 1985 encouraged his followers to join Sunni Islam. Louis Farrakhan, with a relatively small percentage of the former Nation of Islam's followers, has continued to espouse many of Elijah Muhammad's ideas.

Nazr **(A):** Literally, an "offering," "gift," or "present."

New World Order: U.S. President George Herbert Walker Bush used this phrase just before, during, and after the U.S.-led Operation Desert Storm against Iraq. The Bush administration at the time envisioned a new era of U.S.-Soviet cooperation; a bigger role to be played by international organizations (especially the United Nations Security Council); a strengthening of international law and collective security; and a bigger push to promote political liberalization (democratization) and economic liberalization (capitalism) in the new post–Cold War era.

Nizam **(P):** Literally, "system" or "order."

Nizam-i-Mustafa (U): Literally, the "Islamic Order of Prophet Muhammad." It was the rallying cry of the nine opposition parties in the three-month Islamic mass movement in Pakistan just after the "rigged" election of 1977.

Nur: Literally, "light." In Shi'ah Islam it is the light that resides in Prophet Muhammad and the *imams*. See Shi'ah; *imam*.

OAPEC: Acronym for Organization of Arab Petroleum Exporting Countries. Established in January 1968, OAPEC soon included Algeria, Bahrain, Egypt, Iraq, Kuwait, Libya, Qatar, Saudi Arabia, Syria, and the United Arab Emirates (UAE).

OPEC: Acronym for the Organization of Petroleum Exporting Countries. Formed by Iran, Iraq, Kuwait, Saudi Arabia, and Venezuela at the Baghdad Conference (September 1960) to serve as a united bloc for oil producers to achieve their economic objectives. The five founding members were later joined by Libya, Algeria, Qatar, Indonesia, Nigeria, and the United Arab Emirates (UAE).

OIC: Acronym for the Organization of the Islamic Conference. It was established in 1969 after the arson attack at the Al-Aqsa Mosque in Jerusalem and at the initiative of Saudi King Faisal ibn Abdul Aziz. The first meeting of the OIC, attended by twenty-four predominantly Muslim countries, took place in Rabat, Morocco. Currently, fifty-seven countries with majority Muslim populations make up the OIC.

Orientalists: Non-Muslim Western scholars who have studied, researched, interpreted, and written about the Orient (the East), and non-Western cultures in general in an ethnocentric, patronizing, and/or disparaging manner. Islamists believe that the Orientalists have undermined the Qur'an's integrity, Prophet Muhammad's personal character and personality, and the authenticity of the last Prophet's *Hadith*. Islamists also believe that Orientalists have distorted the concept of *jihad* to mean only an aggressive "holy war"; have over-emphasized Islam's conditional permission of polygamy, the veiling and segregation of women, and the second-class status of women in the Muslim world; exaggerated the medievalism and barbarity of *shariah* (Islamic law) punishments; overstated the schisms, heresies, and fanaticism in Islamdom; overplayed the anti-modern and anti-democratic nature of the Islamic state; and denigrated the backwardness of Islamic culture. Finally, Islamists accuse Orientalists of downplaying or marginalizing the achievements of Islamic civilization to humankind and dwelling instead on its weaknesses and problems.

Original Sin: The Christian belief in the sinful state of human nature deriving from the disobedience of Adam and Eve. In Islam, Adam and Eve did disobey God when they ate from the "Tree of Life" (in order to gain immortality). But they repented. And

God, who is famous for His mercy, forgave them. Therefore, unlike Christians, Muslims do not believe that human beings are born into sin or that Jesus came to wash away their sins.

Ottoman: The name given to a member of the Turkish ruling dynasty, descended from Uthman (d. 1324 CE), that ruled over a multinational empire from the fourteenth century. At its height, in the early sixteenth century, the Ottoman Empire ruled much of the Middle East, the Balkan peninsula, and a large part of the Caucasus region. Defeated at Vienna in 1529, the Ottoman Empire slowly declined in power until, allied with Germany, it was defeated in World War I and carved up by the League of Nations in 1919. Mustafa Kemal Atatürk formally ended the Ottoman Empire and Ottoman Caliphate in 1922, after assuming power and proclaiming a Turkish republic. *Ottoman* also refers to any member of the ruling class in the Ottoman Empire or a subject of the Ottoman Empire.

Pahlavi: The language of ancient Persia. It was also the name that Reza Khan—a commander of the Cossack Brigade who assumed power in Persia in 1921—gave his dynasty. Reza Khan was deposed and exiled by the British in 1941 for his pro-Nazi sympathies and replaced by his nineteen-year old son, Muhammad Reza Pahlavi (r. 1941–1979).

Palestinians: Called Filistini in Arabic because they belong to Filistin (Palestine), which in 1948 became the Zionist state of Israel. While most of the 7.5 million Arabic-speaking Palestinians scattered all over the world (including Israel and the Israeli-occupied West Bank and Gaza) are Muslims, there is a significant Christian minority among them.

Palestinian Authority (PA): The Palestinians call it the Palestinian National Authority (PNA), while Israel and the West often refer to it simply as the Palestinian Authority. The PNA, is the first Palestinian self-governing authority or government to be established inside historic Palestine. It was the result of the secret negotiations between Israeli and PLO representatives in Oslo, Norway, and the Declaration of Principles (DOP), formally signed by PLO chairman Arafat and Israel's Prime Minister Yitzhak Rabin on the White House lawn in Washington, D.C., on September 13, 1993.

Pasdaran (P): Literally, security guard; In Iran, the Pasdaran-i-Inqelab-i-Islami (Guardians of the Islamic Revolution) was a paramilitary force that was created by Khomeini's Islamic regime immediately after assuming power in February 1979.

Persia: The name given to Iran by the ancient Greeks. Iran was called Persia until 1935, when the name was changed by Reza Khan (r. 1921–1941, named Reza Shah Pahlavi I in 1925).

Persian: The name given to the national language of Persia, written in a modified Arabic script from right to left. The Persian language is also called Farsi by native Persians, or Iranians. A Persian is also an inhabitant of Persia (called Iran since 1935) and a member of the majority ethnic group of Iran.

Persian Gulf: The body of water separating Iran from the Arabian peninsula and connecting the Shatt al-Arab waterway to the Arabian Sea. Also called the Arabian Gulf or just the Gulf.

Phalangist: A well-organized, right-wing Lebanese political party formed by Pierre Gemayel in 1936 along Fascist lines. It also has a paramilitary wing dedicated to preserving the Maronite Catholic political and socioeconomic control of Lebanon.

***Pir* (P):** A spiritual leader, guide, or teacher. In South Asia, it refers to a *sufi* or a religiopolitical leader of a tribe.

***Purdah* (A):** The term often applies to the "veiling" of women in traditional Islam. In a broader sense, it could also apply to their "segregation" and "seclusion" in traditional Islamic societies.

Qadhi **(A):** An Islamic judge who administers justice under the *shariah*.

Qawwali: Devotional poems or hymns praising God, Prophet Muhammad, or a Muslim saint.

Qiblah **(A):** In Islam, it is the direction, facing the Ka'abah in Makkah, in which a Muslim must turn to perform his or her daily prayers.

Qir'at **(A):** Literally, reading or recitation; in Islam, it often refers to the reading or recitation of the Qur'an.

Qiyas **(A):** Literally, "analogical reasoning"; technically, the fourth *usul*, or founding principle, of the *shariah* after the Qur'an, the *sunnah*, and *ijma*. An Islamic theologian-jurist may use analogical reasoning with situations that are covered in the Qur'an and the *sunnah* to arrive at an Islamic solution.

Qom (A): A world-renowned center of Shi'ah learning in Iran.

Quaid-i-Azam (U): Literally, "Great Leader"; it is the reverential title used by Pakistanis for Muhammad Ali Jinnah, the founding father of Pakistan.

Qur'an (A): Literally, "recitation." According to Muslims, the Qur'an is the collection of revelations sent by God to Prophet Muhammad through the agency of Archangel Gabriel (who recited them to Prophet Muhammad in Arabic). Prophet Muhammad in turn recited these revelations to his companions, who wrote them down and recited them to others. The name *Qur'an* was later given to the holy book containing these revelations. According to Muslims, the Qur'an is the last of all holy books.

Quraysh: The leading Makkan tribe to which Prophet Muhammad belonged.

Rabb (A): Literally, "Allah," "God," or "Lord," who created the universe and all that exists in it. See Allah.

Rahman (A): Literally, "The Merciful"; In Islam, God is always referred to as The Merciful and The Compassionate.

Ra'i **(A):** Literally, "opinion" or "personal judgment" of the *faqih* in interpreting the Qur'an, *hadith*, and *shariah*.

Ramadan (A): The ninth month of the Islamic calendar. The name *Ramadan* is derived from the Arabic root *ramz* (to burn). Thus fasting from dawn to dusk during the month of Ramadan is said to burn away one's sins. It was in the month of Ramadan that God revealed the Qur'an to Prophet Muhammad through the agency of Archangel Gabriel. See *sawm*.

Rasul or Rasul Allah (A): A term used for God's Prophet or a messenger of God who brings His message or revelation. See Nabi.

Revolutionary Islamists: Muslims who are often revolutionary and puritanical in their religiopolitical orientation. They usually are extremely critical of *taqlid* and Western ideas. They often have a passionate desire to establish an Islamic state based on the comprehensive and rigorous application of the *shariah*.

Riba **(A):** The term used for usury, or charging "excessive" interest on loans; it has been prohibited in Islam.

Rukn, pl. *arkan* (A): Literally, "pillar," "principle," or "tenet" of faith. In Islam there are five pillars or tenets of faith called the *faraidh*. See *faraidh*.

Sabbath: The "day of rest" in Judaism and Christianity is premised on the idea that God rested on the seventh day after completing the creation of the universe in six days. Therefore, humans ought also to have a day's rest from work in which they can revitalize themselves and thank God for their blessings. Non-Muslims often refer to Fridays as the Islamic sabbath because Muslims have been enjoined by their faith to perform their midday *zohar* prayers on Fridays in a congregation (preferably at a mosque or Islamic community center). However, Muslims don't believe that God almighty needs rest. Therefore, Muslims and most Muslim countries don't observe a "day of rest" on

Friday's, but carry on their activities before and after their Jummah (Friday) prayers. See Salat-i-Jummah.

Salat-i-Jummah: Literally, "Friday prayers."

Sadaqah (A): The voluntary charitable contribution of money or food for the sake of acquiring merit with Allah and the saints. It is often criticized by Sunni Fundamentalists.

Sahaba (A): Literally, "companions"; in Islamic history, it specifically refers to the companions of Prophet Muhammad.

Salaam (A): Literally means "peace." As-Salaam is one of the ninety-nine attributes or names of God, as well as the name given to the blissful abode of Heaven/Paradise. Prophet Muhammad encouraged Muslims to greet their coreligionists with *"salaam alaykhum"* (peace be upon/with you). See *wa' alaykum as-salaam.*

Salaf (A): A pious companion of Prophet Muhammad. See *aslaf.*

Salafiyyah (A): Those who closely emulate the pious companions of Prophet Muhammad. Two Egyptian Modernist Islamists of Egypt, Muhammad Abduh (1849–1905) and Muhammad Rashid Rida (1865–1935), called their mission to reform Islam "the Salafiyyah movement."

Salat (A): The term often used for ritual prayers in Islam. Each session of prayers comprises a fixed pattern of verse recitations from the Holy Qur'an and prostrations.

Salat al-Jum'ah: Literally, "Friday prayers"; around noon on Fridays, many Muslims offer their midday *zohar* prayers in a congregation at a mosque or an Islamic community center.

SAVAK: Persian acronym for Sazeman-i-Ettelaat-va-Amniyat-i-Kashvar (State Organization for Intelligence and Security). SAVAK was the feared secret police of the Shah of Iran, established in 1955 to combat anti-government activities and cited by Amnesty International in the mid-1970s for the torture and murder of political prisoners. It was disbanded by the Islamic revolutionary government of Iran in 1979.

Sawm (A): The term for fasting from dawn till dusk during the month of Ramadan, which is required of all adult Muslims. See *faraidh,* Ramadan.

Sayyid/Sayed: A title reserved for the descendants of Prophet Muhammad. In some countries, they wear black (as in Iran) or green turbans to show their honorable heritage.

Secular: The civil, nonreligious, or temporal realm in contrast to the ecclesiastical, religious, sacred, or spiritual realm.

Secularism: A government that promotes Secularism clearly separates the church/mosque from the state, refuses to act as the promoter and defender of a particular faith, and rejects religious ideas as the basis of its political legitimacy.

Secularists: Those who believe that religion should not enter into the conduct of governmental affairs and promote secularization.

Secularization: The separation of religion from politics; the government's promotion of Secularism; the gradual transformation of people's values from the strict adherence of religious beliefs and practices to an increasingly secular, rational, and pragmatic orientation; and the gradual decline in the influence of religious leaders and groups in the society.

Semite: In antiquity, this group included the Ammonites, Amorites, Assyrians, Babylonians, Canaanites, and Phoenicians. Some believe that it was used for those who descended from Noah's son Shem. Today it is used for people who speak a Semitic language (Jews and Arabs).

Shafi'is: Those who follow the teachings of Muhammad ibn Idris ash-Shafi'i (767–820 CE), who tried to reconcile the Maliki and Hanafi schools of Islamic jurisprudence.

Shagird (P): A student, apprentice, or novice.

Shah (P): A title that has often been used for Iranian monarchs.

Shahadah (A): A declaration of faith in God and in the prophethood of Muhammad, which reads: *"La ilaha illa 'Llah, Muhammad ar rasul Allah"* (I bear witness that there is no God but Allah and Muhammad is the Messenger of Allah). It is the first pillar of the Islamic faith.

Shaheed (A): A Muslim who dies fighting in a *jihad* is a martyr, who is destined to go to Heaven because he died in "the path of Allah."

Shariah (A): The comprehensive, eternal, and immutable body of law that governs the individual and community life of Muslims.

Sharif, pl. ashraf (A): Literally, "noble," "high-born," or "exalted." Initially applied to a descendant of Prophet Muhammad's family, it now includes a member of a prominent family or a descendant of illustrious ancestors.

Shaykh (A): Literally, "an elderly" and therefore "wise man." It is often used for tribal chieftains, members of the *ulama, sufi* teachers in religious brotherhoods, and generally for men enjoying positions of authority in a Muslim society. Also spelled *sheikh* and *shaikh.*

Shaykhdom: A country ruled by a *shaykh* (monarch or king).

Shaykh al-Islam (A): The highest religious office in Sunni Islam.

Shaytan (A): Satan, or the Devil, is God's principal enemy and humankind's biggest tempter to commit evil deeds.

Shi'ah (A): Members of this minority sect of Islam are "partisans" or "followers" of Ali ibn Abu Talib and believe that God and Prophet Muhammad wanted Ali to be Islam's first caliph.

Shirk (A): From the Arabic verb *shirika* (to associate). *Shirk* often occurs when more than one God is worshiped (polytheism) and/or when anyone or anything other than Allah is assigned divine attributes and powers (idolatory). Those guilty of *shirk* are called *mushrikin.*

Shura (A): The Qur'an recommends "consultation" with erudite and pious Muslims in matters where there is no specific guidance in the Qur'an or the *sunnah.* The term often refers to a group, assembly, or council of knowledgeable and pious Muslims who are consulted by leaders.

Silsilas: See *tariqahs.*

Sirah: Literally, "biography." In Islam the term is often used to refer to the life, deeds, and accomplishments of Prophet Muhammad.

Sirat al-Mustaqim (A): Literally, "the right path" or "the path pursued by righteous Muslims."

Sufis: The term *sufi* is derived from early Muslim ascetics and pious mystics who wore simple clothes made out of *suf* (coarse wool). *Sufis* became lax in their observance of the *shariah* and devoted their lives to meditation and proselytization. They emphasize the spirit, rather than the literal interpretation of the Qur'an and the *sunnah*, and a search for eternal truth and goodness.

Sufism: That body of Islamic beliefs and practices which tends to promote a mystical communion between Muslims and God. See *sufis.*

Sultan: The title of some Muslim monarchs.

Sultanate: The office of and territory ruled by a sultan.

Sunnah (A): In Islam it is understood as Prophet Muhammad's "trodden path," "way," "custom," or "tradition." The *sunnah* comprising Prophet Muhammad's sayings and deeds complements the Qur'an as the major source of Islamic faith and practice.

Sunni (A): Refers to the majority sect of Islam (approximately 75 to 80 percent of the Muslim world) as well as to the member of that sect. Sunnis follow the *sunnah*, or "the way, the path or the road shown by Prophet Muhammad." However, Shi'ahs follow the *sunnah*, too. See *sunnah, madhabs*, and *fiqh*.

Surah (A): Literally, a "step up or gate." In Islam the term is used exclusively for each of the 114 chapters of the Qur'an, each comprising a "series" of revelations.

Tabarruk (A): Literally, "that which brings a blessing." In Islam, it refers to food, flowers, and the like offered at a saint's shrine.

Tabligh (A): Islamic missionary activity and proselytization directed at Muslims and non-Muslims.

Tafsir: The commentary, explanation, and interpretation of Qur'anic verses and chapters.

Taghut (P): A pre-Islamic idol at Makkah; therefore, its literal meaning is a "false god." Figuratively, it refers to all those individuals and governments that have been corrupted by power. Ayatollah Khomeini often referred to the *shah* of Iran as a *taghuti*.

Tajdid (A): Literally, "revival" or "renewal"; a Revolutionary Islamic movement that calls for a return to the Qur'an and *sunnah* and to the Islamic piety and purity practiced in the classical period of Islamic history, and a rejection of all legislation, customs, and traditions after the Khulafah-i-Rashidin.

Takbir (A): Praising god by saying "Allahu Akbar" (God is the Greatest).

Talib (pl. tulaba or taliban): A student in an Islamic *madrassah*. See *Madrassah*; Taliban.

Taliban: Generally, students or graduates of a *madrassah*. Specifically, the Revolutionary Islamist Afghan regime (made up of Pashtuns) that ruled Afghanistan from 1996 till the end of December 2001.

Taqdir (A): Literally, "destiny," "predestination," or "fate."

Taqiyyah (A): From the Arabic word *waga*, which means "to safeguard" or "to protect oneself," this is the concealment of one's religious beliefs and avoidance of some external religious rituals to avoid imminent harm. Though permitted in Islam, Shi'ahs have had to resort to dissimulation far more often because Sunnis have dominated the Muslim world for most of Islamic history.

Taqlid (A): "Following without inquiry"; in Islam, it means "legal conformity"; Sunni Traditionalist Islamists require rigid and unquestioning adherence to the legal rulings of one or more of the Sunni schools of jurisprudence compiled during Islam's medieval period. See *Fiqh*.

Taqveeat-ul-Iman (U): From an Arabic root, the term literally means "strengthening of the faith."

Taqwa (A): Literally, "fear of God" or "piety." Since God is omnipresent and is aware of our innermost thoughts, it refers not only to doing good deeds but also to avoiding evil thoughts.

Tariqah (A): The term refers to the path or method of mysticism and spiritualism promoted by *sufi* teachers and to the social groups (like *sufi* brotherhoods) formed by followers of such *sufi* teachers.

Tatbiq (A): Accommodation, harmonization, and integration.

Tawaaf (A): The ritual of going around a shrine. Often used for going around the Ka'abah seven times during the *hajj* and *umrah*.

Tawba (A): Repentance; asking forgiveness for one's sins and transgressions and making a commitment to follow the "true" path.

Tawhid (A): In Islam it signifies the unity and oneness of God and His sovereignty. This is the most important tenet of Islam.

Taziyah (A): In Islam, Shi'ahs commemorate the martyrdom of Imam Hussein on the tenth of Muharram by conducting mourning processions with replicas of tombs (made of paper, wood, or metal) of the martyrs of Karbala. Some Sunnis also lead *taziyah* processions.

Theocracy: A country ruled by religious leaders. In a theocracy, there is no separation of church/mosque and state or religion and politics. Iran is the classic example of an Islamic theocratic state, based on the *shariah* and run by Shi'ah clerics. The state's full power is used to assure mass compliance with a particular set of religious doctrines. See *shariah*.

Traditionalist Islamists: Conservative Muslims—often from the ranks of the *ulama*—who prefer to maintain the Islamic laws, customs, and traditions practiced in the classical and medieval periods of Islamic history. Though often apolitical, passive, and status quo oriented, these scholarly minded custodians of Islam do get involved in politics when they perceive Islam and/or the *ummah* to be in imminent danger.

Ulama/ulema **(A):** Learned scholars of Islamic theology and jurisprudence.

Ummah (A): In Islam it refers to the "brotherhood of believers (Muslims)" at the local, national, regional, or global level.

Ummayyads: Descendants of Ummayya within the Quraysh tribe. They were one of the most influential families at the time of Muhammad and established the first hereditary caliphate in 661 CE.

Ummi **(A):** Literally, 'uneducated' or 'unlettered.' Muhammad is referred to in the Qur'an as al-Nabi al-Ummi (the unlettered Prophet). This simply means that he did not attend any school and receive formal education in reading, writing, and arithmetic. However, being an intelligent, curious, and reflective person, he learned much from the numerous people he came into contact with throughout his life.

Umrah: The pilgrimage to Makkah and Madinah undertaken by a Muslim at any time other than during the *hajj* period. See *hajj*.

Urs **(A):** The graveside celebration of the death anniversary of a saint. The popular belief is that the saint goes and meets God upon his or her death.

Ushr **(A):** In Islam a 10 percent voluntary tax is expected from farmers owning irrigated farmland. The levy is payable in money or kind by each landholder to the poor or to charitable institutions.

Ustad **(U):** Literally, "teacher" or "instructor."

Usul **(A):** Literally, "source," "foundation," or "fundamentals." In the Islamic context, it applies to the fundamentals of Islam. The four *usul* of Islam are the Qur'an, *sunnah*, *ijma*, and *qiyas*. Some *ulama* include *ijtihad* as a fifth *usul*.

Usul al-Fiqh (A): Literally, "principles," "roots," "sources," or "foundations" of Islamic jurisprudence.

Usuli (A): From the root *usul* (principles of jurisprudence). A Twelver Shi'ah movement that became influential in Iran at the end of the eighteenth century. In contrast to the Akhbari school, the Usuli school advocated greater speculative reasoning in the principles of theology and Islamic law.

Uthman ibn Affan: A wealthy Makkan merchant in the Quraysh tribe, among the first converts to Islam, Prophet Muhammad's son-in-law, and the third caliph of Islam (r. 644–656 CE).

Velayat-i-Faqih (P): Literally, "Guardianship" or "Government of the Islamic Jurist." Ayatollah Ruhollah Khomeini's idea that a devout, learned, and just Islamic jurist ought to be the supreme guardian of the Islamic state during the absence of the awaited twelfth *imam*. In Iran, Khomeini was the Velayat-i-Faqih for much of the 1980s.

Wa' Alaykum as-Salaam **(A):** Literally, "peace be upon/with you too." When a Muslim greets another Muslim with "*as-salaamu alaykum*," the response should be "*wa' alaykum as salaam*."

Wahhabis: Followers of Muhammad ibn Abd al-Wahhab (1703–1792 CE). Wahhabis belong to the Hanbali school of Islamic jurisprudence and are concentrated in contemporary Saudi Arabia and Qatar, where the royal families in both kingdoms have adopted and propagated Wahhabism. Wahhabis initially disliked the term assigned to them by Westerners, claiming that the term Wahhabi implied that they venerated Muhammad ibn Abd al-Wahhab; in actuality, though, they venerated no one but God. They prefer to be known as *al-Muwahhidun*, which literally means "monotheists" or "unitarians." The term "monotheists," though, encompassed both Muslims and many non-Muslims, while the term "unitarians" had strong Christian overtones. Thus, for want of a more appropriate term and because the term "Wahhabis" had been popularized, they grudgingly came to accept it. Wahhabis are Revolutionary Islamists who revert back to the *Qur'an* and *sunnah* to establish an Islamic state on the *shariah* and classical Islamic principles; draw on Taqi al-Din ibn Taimiyyah's puritanical writings; are critical of the Traditionalist *ulama* for failing to be competent, dynamic, and assertive standard-bearers of the Islamic faith and *ummah*; live an ascetic and pious life; condemn ornamentation, music, dancing, and singing; denounce all accretions that have crept into Islam since the classical era; and engage in a perpetual *jihad* as their principal means of winning converts and redirecting "wayward" Muslims to what they considered "the righteous path."

Wahy **(A):** Literally, "revelation"; in Islam, God revealed the Qur'an to Muhammad over a twenty-two-year period (610–632 CE).

Wahid: Literally, "the one." In Islam, it often refers to the absolute "oneness" of God and to the uncompromising monotheism of the Islamic faith.

Wahy **(A):** Revelation or inspiration from God given to chosen men and women.

Wajib **(A):** Literally, that which is "obligatory," "mandatory," "incumbent," or "binding."

Wali **(A):** In Islam, it denotes a learned *pir, sufi,* cleric, or saint who enjoys God's favor and consequently possesses significant powers. In Islamic law, the *wali* is the guardian or legal representative of an individual. It is also one to whom a ruler delegates authority. Shi'ahs believe that Prophet Muhammad made Ali the *wali* or *imam* over the *ummah*, a point disputed by all Sunnis.

Waqf **(pl. *auqaf*):** An Arabic term for an Islamic endowment (usually of landed property) established for pious charitable purposes. See *auqaf*.

Wasi **(A):** Literally, "legatee," "appointed guardian," or "executor of a will." In Islam, a *wasi* is the vice regent of Prophet Muhammad; in popular Islam, he is a holy man.

Watan **(A):** Literally, "homeland" or "nation"; a concept borrowed from Western nationalism.

Wisaya **(A):** Literally, the appointment or designation of someone to assume specified responsibilities. Among Shi'ahs the term refers to Prophet Muhammad's designation of Ali as his successor as the religiopolitical leader of the entire Muslim world.

Wudhu: The Islamic practice of washing the face, hands, arms, and feet with clean water to achieve a ritually pure state before standing in front of God in prayer.

Yaum al-Akhira **(A):** Literally, "the Day of Judgment." The Qur'an clearly informs Muslims that the world will come to an end someday. On that Day of Judgment, the dead will be resurrected to be judged by an all-knowing, totally just, and immensely merciful God. Righteous human beings who have done good deeds in this world will be rewarded with an eternal life of happiness in Heaven/Paradise, while those human beings who have refused to follow God's guidance and done evil deeds in this world will be sent to Hell to suffer.

Yaum-ul-Jumah **(A):** Literally, the "Day of Assembly." In Islam, it refers to the "assembly" or "congregation" of the *ummah* on Fridays, when Muslims have been recommended to perform their midday prayers along with their coreligionists at the nearest mosque or Islamic community center.

Yazid ibn Mu'awiya: The son of Mu'awiya and the second Ummayad ruler (r. 680–683 CE). He is notorious in Islamic history because he was responsible for the deaths of Imam Hussein and seventy-one of his male relatives and followers on the battlefield of Karbala.

Zakat (A): The fourth pillar of Islam, in which Muslims are enjoined by their faith to donate 2.5 percent of their wealth to the poor or to charitable institutions.

Zamindar: A wealthy and powerful landlord who owns large tracts of land and has many peasants working on his farmland.

Zawiya (A): In North Africa it is a small room in a mosque or in a saint's shrine where members of a tribe or a *sufi* order gather and engage in religious discussions. It may also comprise a building complex that includes a mosque, a *madrassah*, and living quarters.

Zina: Muslims guilty of fornication (premarital sex and adultery) according to the *shariah*.

Zionism: The Jewish nationalist movement advocating the migration of Jews from all over the world to Palestine. Theodor Herzl, an Austrian Jewish journalist, was primarily responsible for launching the Zionist movement with the publication of his pamphlet entitled *Der Judenstaat (The Jewish State)* in 1896 and with his establishment of the World Zionist Organization (WZO) in Basel, Switzerland, in 1897. The WZO was instrumental in establishing the sovereign Jewish state of Israel in Palestine on May 14, 1948.

Ziyarat (A): The visit or pilgrimage that Muslims make to the grave, tomb, mausoleum, or shrine of a venerated Muslim.

Selected Bibliography

Articles

Abbott, Freeland K. "Maulana Maududi on Quranic Interpretation." *The Muslim World*, Vol. 48, No. 1. January 1958.
———. "Pakistan's New Marriage Law: A Reflection of Quranic Interpretation." *Asian Survey*, Vol. I. 1962.
———. "The Decline of the Moghul Empire and Shah Waliullah." *The Muslim World*, Vol. 55, No. 2. April 1965.
———. "The Jama'at-i-Islami of Pakistan." *Middle East Journal*, Vol. 11. 1957.
Abdulla, Ahmed. "Causes of Muslim Decline, XII." *Dawn* [Karachi]. December 12, 1975.
Abdullah, Aslam. "When Is Muslim Might Right?" *Arabia*, No. 26. October 1983.
Abiva, Hoseyin. "The Islamic Revival in the Soviet Union and Its Implications." *The Message International*, Vol. 15, No. 5. October 1991.
Abrahamian, Ervand. "Ali Shariati: Ideology of the Iranian Revolution." *MERIP Reports*, Vol. 12, No. 1. January 1982.
Abu Amr, Ziad. "Hamas: A Historical and Political Background." *Journal of Palestine Studies*, Vol. 88. Summer 1993.
AbuSulayman, Abdul Hamid A. "The Quran and Sunnah on Violence, Armed Struggle, and the Political Process." *American Journal of Islamic Social Sciences*, Vol. 8, No. 2. 1991.
Adams, C. C. "The Sanusis." *The Muslim World*, Vol. 36, No. 1. January 1946.
Adams, Charles J. "The Ideology of Mawlana Mawdudi." In Donald Eugene Smith, ed., *South Asian Politics and Religion*. Princeton, N.J.: Princeton University Press. 1966.
El-Affendi, Abdel Wahab. "Martyrdom, Godhead and Heresy." *Arabia*, Vol. 4, No. 43. March 1985.
Agha, Hussein, and Robert Malley. "Camp David: The Tragedy of Errors." *New York Review of Books*. August 9, 2001.
Ahmad, Aziz. "Cultural and Intellectual Trends in Pakistan." *Middle East Journal*, Vol. 19. 1965.

———. "Maududi and Orthodox Fundamentalists in Pakistan," *Middle East Journal*, Vol. 21. 1967.

———. "Sayyid Ahmad Khan, Jamal al-Din Al-Afghani, and Muslim India." *Studia Islamica*, Vol. 13. 1960.

———. "Islam and the New World Order." *Middle East Affairs Journal*, Vol. 1, No. 3. Spring/Summer 1993.

Ahmad, Khwaja Harris. "The Concept and Principals of Quaranic Justice." *The Law Journal* [Pakistan], Vol. 40, No. 1. 1978.

Ahmad, Manzooruddin. "The Classical Muslim State." *Islamic Studies* [Karachi], Vol. 1, No. 3. September 1962.

———. "The Political Role of the Ulema." *Journal of Islamic Studies* [Islamabad]. 1962.

Ahmad, Mumtaz. "Islamic Revival in Pakistan." In Cyriac Pullapilly, ed., *Islam in the Contemporary World*. Notre Dame, Ind.: Cross Roads Books. 1980.

———. "Facing Up To Change: The Muslim Alternatives." *Arabia*, No. 25. September 1983.

———. "Islamic Fundamentalism in South Asia: The Jamaat-i-Islami and the Tablighi Jamaat of South Asia." In Martin E. Marty and R. Scott Appleby, eds., *Fundamentalisms Observed*, Vol. 1. Chicago: The University of Chicago Press. 1991.

Ahmad, Rashid (Jullundhri). "Pan-Islamism and Pakistan: Afghani and Nasser." *Scrutiny*, Vol. 1, No. 2. July–December 1975.

Ahmed, Rafiuddin. "Redefining Muslim Identity in South Asia: The Transformation of Jamaat-i-Islami." In Martin E. Marty and R. Scott Appleby, eds., *Accounting for Fundamentalism: The Dynamic Character of Movements*, Vol. 4. Chicago: The University of Chicago Press. 1994.

Ahmed, Ziauddin. "Socio-Economic Values of Islam and Their Significance and Resurgence to the Present Day World." *Islamic Studies*, Vol. 10. 1971.

Ahsan, Manazir. "Mawlana Mawdudi's Defense of Sunnah." *Arabia*, No. 26. October 1983.

Ajami, Fouad. "The Sentry's Solitude." *Foreign Affairs*. November–December 2001.

Akhavi, Shahrough. "Shariati's Social Thought." In Nikki R. Keddie, ed., *Roots of Revolution: An Interpretive History of Modern Iran*. New Haven, Conn.: Yale University Press. 1981.

———. "The Dialectic in Contemporary Egyptian Social Thought: The Scripturalist and Modernist Discourses of Sayyid Qutb and Hasan Hanafi." *International Journal of Middle East Studies*, Vol. 29, No. 3. August 1997.

al-Alwani, Taha J. "Taqlid and Ijtihad." *American Journal of Islamic Social Sciences*, Vol. 8, No. 1. Spring 1991.

———. "The Crisis of Fiqh and the Methodology of Ijtihad." *American Journal of Islamic Social Sciences*, Vol. 8, No. 2. Summer 1991.

———. "Taqlid and the Stagnation of the Muslim Mind." *American Journal of Islamic Social Sciences*, Vol. 8, No. 3. 1991.

———. "Taqlid and Ijtihad." *American Journal of Islamic Social Sciences*, Vol. 9, No. 2, Summer 1992.

———. "The Scope of Taqlid." *American Journal of Islamic Social Sciences*, Vol. 9, No. 3. Fall 1992.

———. "Missing Dimensions in Contemporary Islamic Movements." *American Journal of Islamic Social Sciences*, Vol. 12, No. 2. Summer 1995.

Allen, Ernest. "Religious Heterodoxy and Nationalist Tradition: The Continuing Evolution of the Nation of Islam." *Black Scholar*, Vol. 26, Nos. 3–4, Fall–Winter 1996.

Alnasrawi, Abbas. "Collective Bargaining Power in OPEC." *Journal of World Trade Law*. 1973.

———. "Arab Oil and the Industrial Economies: The Paradox of Oil Dependency." *Arab Studies Quarterly*, Vol. 1, No. 1. Winter 1979.

Altman, I. "Islamic Movements in Egypt." *Jerusalem Quarterly*, Vol. 10. 1979.

Al-Alwani, Taha J. "Taqlid and the Stagnation of the Muslim Mind." *The American Journal of Islamic Social Sciences*, Vol. 8, No. 3. 1991.

Aly, Abd al Monein Said, and Manfred W. Wenner. "Modern Islam Reform Movements: The Muslim Brotherhood in Contemporary Egypt." *Middle East Journal*, Vol. 36, No. 3. Summer 1982.

Amin, Osman. "Some Aspects of Religious Reform in the Muslim Middle East." In Carl Leiden, ed., *The Conflict of Traditionalism and Modernism in the Muslim Middle East*. Austin, Tex.: University of Texas Press. 1966.

Anderson, Raymond H. "Ayatollah Ruhollah Khomeini, 89, Relentless Founder of the Islamic Republic." *New York Times*. June 5, 1989.

Ansari, Javed. "Themes in Islamic Revivalism." *Arabia*, No. 24. August 1983.

Ansari, Zafar Ishaq. "Aspects of Black Muslim Theology." *Studia Islamica*, Vol. 53, 1981.

———. "W. D. Muhammad: The Making of a 'Black Muslim' Leader (1933–1961)." *American Journal of Islamic Social Sciences*, Vol. 2, No. 2. Summer 1985.

Appleby, R. Scott, and Martin E. Marty. "Fundamentalism's Many Faces." *Foreign Policy*, January–February 2002.

Arshad, I. A. "Mujadid's Revivalist Movement." In Sardar Ali Ahmad Khan, ed., *The Naqshbadis*. Sharaqpur Sharif, Pakistan: Darul Muballeghin Hazra. 1982.

Artz, Lee Wigle, and Mark A. Pollock. "Limiting the Options: Anti-Arab Images in the U.S. Media Coverage of the Persian Gulf Crisis." In Yahya R. Kamalipour, ed., *The U.S. Media and the Middle East: Image and Perception*. Westport, Conn.: Praeger. 1997.

Aruri, N. "Nationalism and Religion in the Arab World: Allies or Enemies." *Muslim World*, Vol. 67. 1977.

Asaria, Iqbal. "Media Proves Mightier than the Sword and Penetrates Defenses." *Crescent International*, Vol. 11, No. 4. May 1–15, 1982.

Ashraf, Ali. "The Challenge of Modernization and the Response in Turkey and India." *Islam and the Modern Age*, Vol. 12, No. 3. August 1981.

Auda, G. "The Islamic Movement and Resource Mobilization in Egypt: A Political Culture Perspective." In L. Diamond, ed., *Political Culture and Democracy in Developing Countries*. Boulder, Colo: Lynne Rienner.

Ayoob, Mohammad. "Two Faces of Political Islam: Iran and Pakistan Compared." *Asian Survey*, Vol. 19, No. 6. June 1979.

Ayubi, Nazih N. M. "The Political Revival of Islam: The Case of Egypt." *International Journal of Middle East Studies*, Vol. 12. 1980.

———. "The Politics of Militant Islamic Movements in the Middle East." *Journal of International Affairs*, Vol. 36, No. 2. Fall–Winter 1982–83.

Aziz, Ahmad. "Sayyid Ahmad Khan, Jamal al-Din Al-Afghani, and Muslim India." *Studia Islamica*, Vol. 13. 1960.

Badeau, John S. "Islam and the Modern Middle East." *Foreign Affairs*, No. 38. 1958.

Bahadur, Kalim. "The Jamaat-i-Islami of Pakistan: Ideology and Political Action." *International Studies* [India], Vol. 14. January 1975.

Bailey, Clinton. "Lebanon's Shi'is after the 1982 War." In Martin Kramer, ed., *Shi'ism, Resistance, and Revolution*. Boulder, Colo.: Westview Press. 1987.

Balta, Paul. "The Boiling Islamic World: A False Religiosity Fuels Fundamentalist Violence." *World Press Review*. February 1980.

Bandeau, John S. "The Arab Role in Islamic Culture." In B. Winder, ed., *The Genius of Arab Civilization: Source of Renaissance.* New edition. London: Europe Publishing. 1983.

Bari, Muhammad Abdul. "The Politics of Sayyid Ahmad Barelwi." *Islamic Culture,* Vol. 31, No. 2. April 1957.

Barry, John, and Roger Charles. "Sea of Lies." *Newsweek.* July 13, 1992.

Barzin, Saeed. "Consitutionalism and Democracy in the Religious Ideology of Medhi Bazargan." *British Journal of Middle Eastern Studies,* Vol. 21, No. 1. 1994.

Batatu, Hanna. "Iraq's Underground Shi'ah Movements: Characteristics, Causes and Prospects." *Middle East Journal,* Vol. 35, No. 4. Autumn 1981.

Baxter, Craig. "Restructuring the Pakistan Political System." In Shahid Javed Burki and Craig Baxter, ed., *Pakistan under the Military: Eleven Years of Zia-Ul-Haq.* Boulder, Colo.: Westview Press. 1991.

Bayat-Philipp, Mangol. "Shi'ism in Contemporary Iranian Politics: The Case of Ali Shariati." In Elie Kedourie and Sylvia G. Haim, eds., *Towards a Modern Iran: Studies in Thought, Politics, and Society.* London: Frank Cass. 1980.

Beeley, B. "Islam as a Global Force." In A. McGrew and P. Lewis, eds., *Global Politics: Globalization and the Nation State.* Oxford: Polity Press. 1992.

Beeman, William. "Khomeini's Call to the Faithful Strikes Fear in the Arab World." *Philadelphia Inquirer.* May 29, 1992.

Benomar, Jamal. "The Monarchy, the Islamist Movement and Religious Discourse in Morocco." *Third World Quarterly,* Vol. 10, No. 2. April 1988.

Berger, Morroe. "The Black Muslims." *Horizons,* Vol. 6, No. 1. Winter 1964.

Bianchi, R. "Islam and Democracy in Egypt." *Current History,* Vol. 93. February 1989.

Bill, James A. "Class Analysis and the Dialectics of Modernization in Middle East." *International Journal of Middle East Studies,* No. 3. 1972.

———. "Power and Religion in Revolutionary Iran." *Middle East Journal,* Vol. 36, No. 1. Winter 1982.

———. "Resurgent Islam in the Persian Gulf." *Foreign Affairs,* Vol. 63, No. 1. Fall 1984.

———. "The Shah, The Ayatollah, and The U.S." *Headline Series,* No. 285. New York: Foreign Policy Association. June 1988.

Binder, Leonard. "Pakistan and Modern Islamic Nationalist Theory." *Middle East Journal,* Vol. 12. 1958.

———. "Problems of Islamic Political Thought in the Light of Recent Developments in Pakistan." *Journal of Politics,* Vol. 20, No. 4. November 1958.

———. "The Proofs of Islam: Religion and Politics in Iran." In George Makdisi, ed., *Arabic and Islamic Studies, in Honor of Hamilton Gibb.* Leiden, The Netherlands: E. J. Brill. 1965.

Bishara, Azmy. "Palestine in the New Order." *Middle East Report,* Vol. 22, No. 2. March–April 1992.

Blank, Jonah. "Kashmir: Fundamentalism Takes Root." *Foreign Affairs.* November–December 1999.

Blum, Patrick. "Islamic Revival Fuels Maghreb Discontent." *Middle East Economic Digest,* Vol. 24, No. 9. February 29, 1980.

Booth, Newell S. "The Historical and the Non-Historical in Islam." *The Muslim World,* Vol. 60, No. 2. April 1970.

Border, William. "Bhutto in Crackdown on Critics Orders Martial Law for Three Cities." *New York Times.* April 22, 1977.

Borthwick, B. "Religion and Politics in Israel and Egypt." *Middle East Journal,* Vol. 33. 1979.

Braibanti, Ralph. "Political Development: A Contextual Nonlinear Perspective." *Politikon*, Vol. 3. October 1976.

———. "The Recovery of Islamic Identity in Global Perspective." In Bruce Lawrence, ed., *The Rose and the Rock: Mystical and Rational Elements in the Intellectual History of South Asian Islam*. Durham, N.C.: Carolina Academic Press. 1979.

Brett, Michael. "Islam in the Maghreb: The Problem of Modernization." *Magreb*, Review 3. 1978.

Brohi, A. K. "Islam and Other Secular and Religious Ideologies." *The Muslim* [Pakistan]. January 12, 13, and 14, 1981.

Brown, Leon Carl. "The Role of Islam in Modern North Africa." In Leon Carl Brown, ed., *State and Society in Independent North Africa*. Washington, D.C.: Middle East Institute. 1966.

———. "The June 1967 War: A Turning Point?" In Yehuda Lukas and Abdalla M. Battah, eds., *The Arab-Israeli Conflict: Two Decades of Change*. Boulder, Colo.: Westview Press. 1988.

Bruce, James. "Arab Veterans of the Afghan War." *Jane's Intelligence Review*, Vol. 7, No. 4. April 1995.

Budiansky, Stephen. "Democracy's Detours: Holding Elections Does Not Guarantee That Freedom Will Follow." *U.S. News and World Report*. January 27, 1992.

Burns, E. Bradford. "The Modernization of Underdevelopment: El Salvador, 1858–1931." *The Journal of Developing Areas*, Vol. 18. April 1984.

Butt, Gerald. "Iran and Syria Curb Hizbullah Attacks, but Group Gains." *Christian Science Monitor*. February 25, 1992.

Carrol, Lucy. "Nizam-i-Islam: Process and Conflicts in Pakistan's Programme of Islamisation, with Special Reference to the Position of Women." *Journal of Commonwealth and Comparative Politics*, No. 20. 1982.

Chandra, Satish. "History Writing in Pakistan and the Two Nation Theory." *South Asian Studies*, Vol. 2, No. 1. January 1967.

Cherif-Chergui, Abderrahman. "Justice and Equality in Islam." *The Month*, Vol. 13, No. 2. February 1980.

Chiriyankandath, J. "The Politics of Religious Identity: A Comparison of Hindu Nationalism and Sudanese Islamism." *Journal of Commonwealth and Comparative Politics*, Vol. 32, No. 1.

Chowdhury, Anwar. "State and Politics in Islam." *The Muslim*. September 28, 1983.

Cienski, Jan, and Jeff Trimble. "See No Evil: Unnoticed, A Civil War Rages in Tajikistan." *U.S. News and World Report*. February 1, 1993.

Claiborne, William. "Hollywood's Mideast Policy." *Washington Post*. July 14, 1986.

Cobban, Helena. "The PLO and the Intifada." In Robert O. Freedman, ed., *The Intifada: Its Impact on Israel, the Arab World, and the Superpowers*. Miami: Florida International University Press. 1991.

———. "When Arabs Face an Identity Crisis." *Christian Science Monitor*. May 20, 1980.

Coleman, James S. "The Developmental Syndrome: Differentiation-Equality-Capacity." In Leonard Binder, James S. Coleman, Joseph LaPalombara, Lucien W. Pye, Sidney Verba, and Myron Weiner, eds., *Crises and Sequences in Political Development*. Princeton, N.J.: Princeton University Press. 1971.

Cooke, Kieran. "State Ideology Helps Push Indonesian Muslims Out of Politics." *Christian Science Monitor*. January 7, 1985.

Crossette, Barbara. "Muslims Storm U.S. Mission in Pakistan." *New York Times*. February 13, 1989.

Cox, Harvey. "Understanding Islam: No More Holy Wars." *Atlantic Monthly*. January 1981.

Dar, B. A. "Wali Allah: His Life and Times." *Iqbal Review*, Vol. 6, No. 3. October 1965.

Davies, James C. "Satisfaction and Revolution." In David H. Everson and Joann Popard Paine, eds., *An Introduction to Systematic Political Science*. Homewood, Ill.: Dorsey Press. 1973.

Dawn, C. Ernest. "Islam in the Modern Age." *Middle East Journal*. 1965.

Dekmejian, Richard H. "Islamic Revival and the Arab-Israel Conflict." *New Outlook*, Vol. 23. April 1980.

———. "Islamic Revival in the Middle East and North Africa." *Current History*, No. 456. April 1980.

———. "The Anatomy of Islamic Revival: Legitimacy Crisis, Ethnic Conflict and the Search for Islamic Alternatives." *Middle East Journal*, Vol. 34, No. 1. Winter 1980.

Dekmejian, Richard H. and Margaret J. Wyszomirski. "Charismatic Leadership in Islam: The Mahdi of the Sudan." *Comparative Studies in Society and History*, Vol. 14. 1972.

Deming, Angus, Scott Sullivan, and Jane Whitmore. "The Khomeini Enigma." *Newsweek*. December 31, 1979.

Dessouki, Ali E. Hillal. "Arab Intellectuals and al-Nakba: The Search for Fundamentalism." *Middle Eastern Studies*, Vol. 9. 1973.

———. "The Resurgence of Islamic Organization in Egypt: An Interpretation." In Alexander S. Cudsi and Ali E. Hillal Dessouki, eds., *Islam and Power in the Contemporary Muslim World*. Baltimore: Johns Hopkins University Press. 1981.

Deutsch, Karl. "Social Mobilization and Political Development." *American Political Science Review*, Vol. 55. September 1961.

Dil, Shaheen F. "The Myth of Islamic Resurgence in South Asia." *Current History*, No. 456. April 1980.

———. "The Myth of Islamic Resurgence in South Asia." *Current History*, No. 456. April 1980.

Divine, Donna Robinson. "Islamic Culture and Political Practice in British Mandated Palestine, 1918–1948." *Review of Politics*, Vol. 45, No. 1. January 1983.

Al-Djani, Ahmad Sidqi. "The Relationship between Arab Nationalism and Islam." *Current World Leaders: Biography and News/Speeches and Reports*, Vol. 26, No. 8–9. September 1983.

Dorman, William A., and Ehsan Omeed. "Reporting Iran the Shah's Way." *Columbia Press Review*. January–February 1979.

Dorman, William A., and Mansour Farhang. "Nobody Lost Iran." *Politics Today*. May–June 1979.

Dunn, Michael Collins. "Fundamentalism in Egypt." *Middle East Policy*, Vol. 2. 1993.

Dupree, Louis. "Islam: Design for Political Stability." *Christian Science Monitor*. February 15, 1980.

Edens, D. G. "The Anatomy of the Saudi Revolution." *International Journal of Middle East Studies*, Vol. 5. 1974.

Efty, Alex. "Khomeini Aimed His 'Verses' Attack to Stop Liberal Trends." *Birmingham News*. February 26, 1989.

Emajuddin, Ahmed, and D. R. A. Nazneen. "Islam in Bangladesh: Revivalism or Power Politics?" *Asian Survey*, Vol. 30, No. 8. August 1990.

Enayat, Hamid. "The Resurgence of Islam: The Background." *History Today*, Vol. 30. 1980.

Entman, Robert M. "Framing U.S. Coverage of International News: Contrasts in Narratives of the KAL and Iran Air Incidents." *Journal of Communication*, Vol. 41, No. 4. Autumn 1991.

Entelis, J. "Ideological Change and an Emerging Counter-Culture in Tunisia." *Journal of Modern Asian Studies*, Vol. 12. 1974.

El-Fadl, Khaled Abou. "The Place of Tolerance in Islam." *Boston Review.* December 2001–January 2002.

Fakhry, Majid. "The Search for Cultural Identity in Islam: Fundamentalism and Occidentalism." *Cultures*, Vol. 4. 1977.

Fandy, Mamoun. "The Tensions behind the Violence in Egypt." *Middle East Policy*, Vol. 2. 1993.

Farhang, Mansour. "Resisting the Pharaohs: Ali Shariati on Oppression." *Race and Class*, Vol. 21, No. 1. Summer 1979.

Faruki, Kemal A. "Pakistan: Islamic Government and Society." In John Esposito, ed., *Islam in Asia: Religion, Politics, and Society.* New York: Oxford University Press. 1987.

al-Faruqi, Ismail Raji. "Islam and Christianity: Diatribe or Dialogue." *Journal of Ecumenical Studies*, Vol. 5, No. 1. 1968.

———. "Islam and Christianity: Problems and Perspectives." In James P. Cotter, ed., *The Word in the Third World.* Washington, D.C.: Corpus Books. 1968.

———. "The Role of Islam in Global Interreligious Dependence." In Warren Lewis, ed., *Towards a Global Congress of the World's Religions.* Barrytown, N.Y.: Unification Theological Seminary. 1980.

Faruqi, Zia-ul-. "Orthodoxy and Heterodoxy in Muslim India." *Islam and the Modern Age*, Vol. 9, No. 4. November 1978; Vol. 10, No. 1. February 1979.

Fekrat, M. Ali. "Stress in the Islamic World." *Journal of South Asian and Middle Eastern Studies*, Vol. 4, No. 3. Spring 1981.

Feldman, Herbert. "Pakistan—1973." *Asian Survey*, Vol. 16, No. 2. Feburary 1974.

———. "Pakistan in 1974." *Asian Survey.* February 1975.

Ferdows, Adele. "Shariati and Khomeini on Women." In Nikki R. Keddie and Eric Hoogland, eds., *The Iranian Revolution and the Islamic Republic: Proceedings of a Conference.* Washington, D.C.: Middle East Institute, in cooperation with Woodrow Wilson International Center for Scholars. 1982.

Firestone, Reuven. "Conceptions of Holy War in the Scriptures of Judaism and Islam." *Journal of Religious Ethics*, Vol. 24, No. 1. Spring 1996.

Fischer, Michael M. J. "Islam and the Revolt of the Petite Bourgeoisie." *Daedalus*, Vol. 111. Winter 1982.

Fisk, Robert. "Anti-Soviet Warrior Puts His Army on the Road to Peace: The Saudi Businessman Who Recruited Mujahideen Now Uses them for Large Scale Building Projects in Sudan." *The Independent* [U.K.]. December 6, 1993.

Foote, Donna. "At Stake: The Freedom to Imagine." *Newsweek.* February 27, 1989.

Ford, Peter. "Israel and Hizbullah Trade Artillery Fire in Retaliatory Attacks." *Christian Science Monitor.* February 18, 1992.

Friedman, Thomas. "Islamic Militants: Religion Is a Focus for Opposition to Mideast Regimes." *New York Times.* October 8, 1981.

Fukuyama, Francis. "The End of History?" *The National Interest.* Summer 1989. Reprinted in John T. Rourke, ed., *Taking Sides*, 4th ed. Guilford, Conn.: Dushkin. 1992.

Gage, Nicholas. "Stern Symbol of Opposition to the Shah: Ruhollah Khomeini." *New York Times.* December 11, 1978.

———. "The Unknown Ayatullah Khomeini: The Portrait of the Islamic Mystic at the Center of the Revolution." *Time.* July 16, 1979.

Gellner, Ernest. "A Pendulum Swing Theory of Islam." *The Philosophical Forum*, Vol. 2, No. 2. Winter 1970–71.

————. "The Muslim Reformation." *The New Republic.* November 22, 1982.

Ghannoushi, Rachid. "What We Need Is a Realistic Fundamentalism." *Arabia.* October 1986.

————. "The Battle against Islam." *Middle East Affairs Journal*, Vol. 1, No. 2. Winter 1993.

Ghayur, Mohammad Arif, and Hussain Asaf. "The Religio-Political Parties (JI, JUI, JUP): Role of the Ulema in Pakistan's Politics." Paper presented at the New England Conference, Association for Asian Studies, University of Connecticut, Storrs, Conn., October 20–21, 1979.

Gibb, H. A. R. "An Interpretation on Islamic History." *Journal of World History*, Vol. 1. 1953.

————. "Structure of Religious Thought in Islam." *The Muslim World*, Vol. 38. Article reprinted in S. J. Shaw and W. R. Polk, eds., *Studies on the Civilization of Islam.* Boston: Beacon Press. 1962.

Godsell, Geoffrey. "From Libya to Indonesia, the Muslim Belt's Crisis Points are on Display—An Analysis." *Christian Science Monitor.* December 1979.

Gomaa, Ahmed M. "Islamic Fundamentalism in Egypt during the 1930s and 1970s: Comparative Notes." In G. R. Warburg and U. M. Kupferschmidt, eds., *Islam, Nationalism and Radicalism in Egypt and Sudan.* New York: Praeger. 1983.

Gomez, Michael A. "Muslims in Early America." *Journal of Southern History*, Vol. 60, No. 4. November 1994.

Gran, P. "Political Economy as a Paradigm for the Study of Islamic History." *International Journal of Middle East Studies*, Vol. 11. July 1980.

Grew, Raymond. "The Crises and Their Sequences." In Raymond Grew, ed., *Crises of Political Development in Europe and the United States.* Princeton, N.J.: Princeton University Press. 1978.

Griffith, William E. "The Revival of Islamic Fundamentalism: The Case of Iran." *International Security*, Vol. 4. 1979.

El-Guindi, Fadwa. "Religious Revival and Islamic Survival in Egypt." *International Insight*, Vol. 1, No. 2. 1980.

————. "Veiling Infitah with Muslim Ethic: Egypt's Contemporary Islamic Movement." *Social Problems*, Vol. 28. April 1981.

————. "Is There an Islamic Alternative? The Case of Egypt's Contemporary Islamic Movement." *International Insight*, Vol. 1, No. 6. July–August 1981.

————. "The Killing of Sadat and After: A Current Assessment of Egypt's Islamic Movement." *Middle East Insight*, Vol. 2. January–February 1982.

Guiney, Errell. "The Power and the Peril: Growing Solidarity Centered on Anti-Americanism." *World Press Review.* February 1980.

Gunn, G. "Radical Islam in Southeast Asia." *Journal of Contemporary Asia*, Vol. 16. 1986.

Gwertzman, Bernard. "An Anxious Washington Studies the Fever in Islam." *New York Times.* December 9, 1979.

Hadar, Leon. "What Green Peril." *Foreign Affairs*, Vol. 72, No. 3. Spring 1993.

Haddad, Yvonne Yazbeck. "The Arab-Israeli Wars, Nasserism, and the Affirmation of Islamic Identity." In John L. Esposito, ed., *Islam and Development: Religion and Sociopolitical Change.* Syracuse, N.Y.: Syracuse University Press. 1980.

————. "Sayyid Qutb: Ideologue of Islamic Revival." In John L. Esposito, ed., *Voices of Resurgent Islam.* New York: Oxford University Press. 1983.

————. "The Quranic Justification for an Islamic Revolution: The Views of Sayyid Qutb." *Middle East Journal*, Vol. 38, No. 1. January 1983.

————. "Muslim Revivalist Thought in the Arab World: An Overview." *The Muslim World*, Vol. 76, No. 3–4. 1986.

————. "Islamic 'Awakening' in Egypt." *Arab Studies Quarterly*, Vol. 9, No. 3. 1987.

————. "Current Arab Paradigms for an Islamic Future." In Tobin Siebers, ed., *Religion and the Authority of the Past*. Ann Arbor: University of Michigan Press. 1993.

————. "Operation Desert Shield/Desert Storm: The Islamist Perspective." In Phyllis Bennis and Michel Moushabeck, eds., *Beyond the Storm: A Gulf Crisis Reader*. New York: Interlink Books. 1991.

————. "The 'New Enemy'? Islam and Islamists after the Cold War." In Phyllis Bennis and Michel Moushabeck, eds., *Altered States: A Reader in the New World Order*. New York: Olive Branch Press. 1993.

Halasa, Malu. *Elijah Muhammad*. New York: Chelsea House Publications. 1990.

Halliday, Fred. "Iran Chooses." *The Nation*. February 9, 1980.

————. "The Fractured Umma: Islamist Movements, Social Upheaval and the Gulf War." *The Oxford International Review*. Summer 1991.

Halpern, Manfred. "Toward Further Modernization of the Study of New Nations." *World Politics*, Vol. 17. October 1964.

Hanafi, Hassan. "The Relevance of the Islamic Alternative in Egypt." *Arab Studies Quarterly*, Vol. 4, Nos. 1–2. Spring 1982.

Hardar, Leon T. "What Green Peril?" In John T. Rourke, ed., *Taking Sides: Clashing Views on Controversial Issues in World Politics*. 5th ed. Guilford, Conn.: Dushkin Publishing Group. 1994.

Hardy, Peter. "Traditional Muslim Views of the Nature of Politics." In C. H. Phillips, ed., *Politics and Society in India*. London: George Allen and Unwin. 1963.

Harley, Richard M. "Islam Is Not Reactionary, Experts Say." *Christian Science Monitor*. March 27, 1979.

Hart, Jeffrey. "Three Approaches to the Measurement of Power in International Relations." *International Organization*, Vol. 30, No. 2. Spring 1976.

Hasan al-Masumi, M. S. "An Appreciation of Shah Waliyullah Al-Muhaddith Ad-Dihlawi," *Islamic Culture*, Vol. 22, No. 4. October 1947.

Hashmi, Sohail. "Is There an Islamic Ethic of Humanitarian Intervention?" *Ethics and International Affairs*, Vol. 7. 1993.

Hassan, Riffat. "Messianism and Islam." *Journal of Ecumenical Studies*, Vol. 22, No. 2. Spring 1985.

————. "The Basis for a Hindu-Muslim Dialogue and Steps in That Direction from a Muslim Perspective." In Leonard Swidler, ed., *Religious Liberty and Human Rights in Nations and in Religions*. New York: Hippocrene Books. 1986.

Hecht, Richard, and Roger Friedland. "The Bodies of Nations: A Comparative Study of Religious Violence in Jerusalem and Ayodhya." *History of Religion*. November 1998.

Heeger, Gerald A. "Politics in the Post Military State: Some Reflections on the Pakistani Experience." *World Politics*, Vol. 29, No. 2. January 1977.

————. "Socialism in Pakistan." In Helen Desfosses and Jacques Levesque, eds., *Socialism in the Third World*. New York: Praeger. 1974.

Helms, Christine Moss. "The Ikhwan: Badu Answer the Wahhabi 'Call to Unity.'" In Christine Moss Helms, eds., *The Cohesion of Saudi Arabia: Evolution of Political Identity*. Baltimore: Johns Hopkins University Press. 1981.

Hermida, Alfred. "Algeria: Fundamentalists Sweep to Near Victory." *Middle East International*. January 10, 1992.

Hippler, Jochen. "The Islamic Threat and Western Foreign Policy." In Jochen Hippler and Andreas Leug, eds., *The Next Threat: Western Perceptions of Islam*. London: Pluto Press. 1995.

Hiro, Dilip. "Islamist Strengths and Weaknesses in Central Asia." *Middle East International.* February 5, 1993.

Hodgkin, Thomas. "The Revolutionary Tradition in Islam." *Race and Class,* Vol. 21, No. 3. Winter 1980.

Hodgson, Marshall G. S. "The Role of Islam in World History." *International Journal of Middle Eastern Studies,* Vol. 1, No. 2. April 1970.

Hodson, H. V. "The New Third Force: A Global Rival of Communism and Democracy." *World Press Review.* June 1979.

Hopwood, Derek. "A Pattern of Revival Movements in Islam?" *Islamic Quarterly,* Vol. 15, No. 4. October–December 1971.

Hughes, John. "Authors, Death Threats, and Islam." *Christian Science Monitor.* February 22, 1989.

Humphreys, Steven. "Islam and Political Values in Saudi Arabia, Egypt and Syria." In Michael Curtis, ed., *Religion and Politics in the Middle East.* Boulder, Colo.: Westview Press. 1981.

———. "The Contemporary Resurgence in the Context of Modern Islam." In A. E. H. Dessouki, ed., *Islamic Resurgence in the Arab World.* New York: Praeger. 1982.

Hunter, Thomas B. "Terror in the Philippines." *Journal of Counterterrorism and Security,* Vol. 6, No. 4. May 2000.

Huntington, Samuel P. "Political Development and Political Decay." *World Politics,* Vol. 17. 1965.

———. "The Change to Change: Modernization, Development and Politics." *Comparative Politics,* No. 3. April 1971.

Huntington, Samuel P., and Jorge I Dominguez. "Political Development." In Fred Greenstein and Nelson Polsby, eds., *Handbook of Political Science: Macropolitical Theory,* Vol. 3. Boston: Addison-Wesley Publishing Co. 1975.

Huntington, Samuel P. "The Coming Clash of Civilizations." *Foreign Affairs,* Vol. 72, No. 3. Summer 1993.

———. "Islamic Civilization Will Clash with Western Civilization." In Paul A. Winters, ed., *Islam: Opposing Viewpoints.* Reprinted from *Foreign Affairs* (Summer 1993), where it originally appeared as "The Clash of Civilizations?"

Hurewitz, J. C. "The Persian Gulf: After Iran's Revolution." *Headline Series.* Monograph No. 244. April 1979.

Husain, Ahred. "A Myth of Legislative Supremacy in Pakistan, 1947–51." *Journal of History and Political Science,* Vol. 1. 1971–72.

Husain, Asaf. "Ethnicity, National Identity and Praetorianism: The Case of Pakistan." *Asian Survey,* Vol. 16, No. 10. October 1976.

Husain, Mir Zohair. "The Politics of Islam in Pakistan." In Santosh C. Saha and Thomas K. Carr, eds., *Religious Fundamentalism in Developing Countries.* Westport, Conn.: Greenwood Press. 2001.

———. "The Ideologization of Islam: Meaning, Manifestations and Causes." In A. Jerichow and J. Maek Simonsen, eds., *Islam in a Changing World: Europe and the Middle East.* Richmond, Surrey, United Kingdom: Curzon Press. 1997.

———. "4 Faces of Islam Fuel the Religion's Revival." *Orlando Sentinel.* February 12, 1995.

———. "Islam in Pakistan under Bhutto and Zia-ul-Haq." In Hussin Mutalib and Taj ul-Islam Hashmi, eds., *Islam, Muslims and the Modern State: Case Studies of Muslims in Thirteen Countries.* London: Macmillan; New York: St. Martin's Press. 1994.

———. "A Typology of Islamic Revivalists." In Sheikh R. Ali, ed., *The Third World at the Crossroads.* New York: Praeger. 1989.

————, "The Prototypical Muslim Pragmatist and Unconventional Islamic Revivalist: Muhammad Ali Jinnah (1875–1949)." *Journal of the Pakistan Historical Society*, Vol. 36, Part 4. October 1988.

————. "Muslim Modernists: The Torch-Bearers of Progressive Islam." *Islamic Quarterly*, Vol. 31, No. 3. 1987.

————. "Major Differences between American and Pakistani Ways of Life." *Asian Review*, Vol. 8, No. 1. Fall 1987.

————. "Ayatollah Ruhollah al-Musavi al-Khomeini." *The Search: Journal for Arab and Islamic Studies*, Vol. 7. Winter 1986.

————. "Hassan al-Banna: Founder of the Ikhwan al-Muslimin." *Islam and the Modern Age*, Vol. 17, No. 4. November 1986.

————. "Muhammad Abduh: The Pre-Eminent Muslim Modernist of Egypt." *Hamdard Islamicus*, Vol. 9, No. 3. Autumn 1986.

————. "Shah Waliullah Al-Dihlawi: The Indian Subcontinent's Most Revered Scholar." *Journal of Religious Studies*, Vol. 14, No. 2. Autumn 1986.

————. "Iqbal on the Islamic Agenda." *Journal of the Institute of Muslim Minority Affairs*, Vol. 7, No. 2. July 1986.

————. "Maulana Sayyid Abul A'la Maududi: Founder of the Fundamentalist Jammat-e-Islami." *South Asia: Journal of South Asian Studies*, Vol. 9, No. 1. June 1986.

————. "Maulana 'Abd al-Bari Farangi Mahalli: Scholar and Political Activist." *Pakistan Journal of History and Culture*, Vol. 7, No. 1. January–June 1986.

Hyman, Anthony. "The Forces at Work in Militant Islam." *The Round Table*, No. 278. April 1980.

Ibrahim, Anwar. "The Need for Civilizational Dialogue." *Occasional Papers Series*. Center for Muslim-Christian Understanding. Georgetown University, Washington, D.C. 1995.

Ibrahim, Saad Eddin. "Anatomy of Egypt's Militant Islamic Groups: Methodological Note and Preliminary Findings." *International Journal of Middle East Studies*, Vol. 12, No. 4. December 1980.

————. "Egypt's Islamic Militants." *MERIP Reports*, No. 103. February 1982.

————. "An Islamic Alternative in Egypt: The Muslim Brotherhood and Sadat." *Arab Studies Quarterly*, Vol. 4, Nos. 1–2. Spring 1982.

Ibrahim, Youssef M. "Khomeini Assails Western Response to Rushdie Affair." *New York Times*. February 22, 1989.

Ishaque, Khalid M. "The Islamic Approach to Economic Activity and Development." *Pakistan Economist*. July 2, 1977.

Ismael, J. S., and T. Y. Ismael. "Social Change in Islamic Society: The Political Thought of Ayatollah Khomeini." *Social Problems*, Vol. 27, No. 5. June 1980.

Israeli, Raphael. "Islam in Egypt under Nasir and Sadat: Some Comparative Notes." In Metin Heper and Raphael Israel, eds., *Islam and Politics in the Modern East*. New York: St. Martin's Press. 1984.

————. "The New Wave of Islam." *International Journal*, Vol. 34, No. 3. 1979.

Jahan, Rounaq. "Elite in Crisis." *Orbis*, Vol. 17. Summer 1973.

Jansen, Godfrey. "Moslems and the Modern World." *The Economist*. January 3, 1981.

Jurgensmeyer, Mark. "The New Religious State." *Comparative Politics*, Vol. 27, No. 4. July 1995.

Kalaam, Abul. "Muslim Remain Communist Serfs." *The Message International*, Vol. 15, No. 5. October 1991.

Kamm, Henry. "Striking Similarities to Situation in Iran Causing Concern to Indonesian Regime." *New York Times*. June 3, 1979.

Karadia, Chhotu. "Zia's Last Gamble." *India Today*, Vol. 1, No. 9. April 16–31, 1979.

Kaslow, Amy, and George D. Moffet, III. "Pakistan Seeks Influential Role in Central Asia." *Christian Science Monitor*. November 25, 1992.

Kaushik, Surendra Nath. "Aftermath of the March 1977 General Elections in Pakistan." *South Asian Studies*, Vol. 13, No. 1. January–July 1978.

Kaye, David. "Struggling with Independence: Central Asian Politics in the Post-Soviet World." *Middle East Insight*, Vol. 8, No. 6. July–October 1992.

Kaylor, Robert. "Moslem Militants Take Aim at Southeast Asia." *U.S. News and World Report*. March 11, 1985.

Kechichian, Joseph A. "Islamic Revivalism and Change in Saudi Arabia." *Muslim World*, Vol. 80. January 1990.

Keddie, Nikki R. "Intellectuals in the Modern Middle East: A Brief Historical Consideration." *Daedalus*, Vol. 44. Summer 1972.

———. "Iran: Change in Islam; Islam and Change." *International Journal of Middle East Studies*, Vol. 11. 1980.

———. "The Revolt of Islam and Its Roots." In Dankwart A. Rustow and Kenneth Paul Erickson, eds., *Comparative Political Dynamics*. New York: HarperCollins. 1991.

———. "The Revolt of Islam, 1700 to 1993: Comparative Considerations and Relation to Imperialism." *Comparative Studies in Society and History*, Vol. 36, No. 3. July 1994.

Kedourie, Elie. "What's Baathism Anyway?" *Wall Street Journal*. October 17, 1990.

Khan, Muhammad A. Muqtedar. "Sovereignty in Modernity and Islam." *East West Review*. Summer 1995.

———. "Tribalism: The Historical Nemesis of Islam." *The Message*. March 1996.

———. "Dialogue of Civilizations?" *The Diplomat*. June 1997.

———. Islam and an Ethical Tradition of International Relations." *Islam and Christian-Muslim Relations*, Vol. 8, No. 2. Summer 1997.

Khundmiri, S. Alam. "A Critical Examination of Islamic Traditionalism." *Islam and the Modern Age*, Vol. 2, No. 2. May 1971.

Knauerhase, Ramon. "The Oil Producing Middle East States." *Current History*, Vol. 76, No. 443. January 1979.

Kohan, John. "Five New Nations Ask Who Are We?" *Time*. April 27, 1992.

Koven, Ronald. "He Sees Answers to Iran's Plight in the Koran." *Philadelphia Inquirer*. November 15, 1979.

Kramer, Martin. "The Ideals of an Islamic Order." *The Washington Quarterly*, Vol. 3, No. 1. Winter 1980.

———. "Political Islam." *The Washington Papers*, Vol. 8, No. 73. 1980.

———. "Islam vs. Democracy." *Commentary*. January 1993.

Kung, Hans. "Christianity and World Religions: The Dialogue with Islam as One Model." *The Muslim World*, Vol. 77, No. 2. April 1987.

Kuttab, Daoud. "Emotions Take Over." *Middle East International*, No. 382. August 31, 1990.

———. "Forgotten Intifada." *Middle East International*, No. 383. September 14, 1990.

———. "The Palestinian Economy and the Gulf Crisis." *Middle East International*, No. 383. September 14, 1990.

———. "Worries about the Intifada." *Middle East International*, No. 402. June 14, 1991.

La Franchi, Howard. "Algeria's Leadership Chooses Head of Ruling Council." *Christian Science Monitor*. January 16, 1992.

Lamb, David. "Islamic Fundamentalism: A Growing Force in the Mideast." *Current World Leaders: Biography and New/Speeches and Reports*, Vol. 26, No. 8–9. September 1983.

———. "Islamic Revival Grows, But Stays Largely Benign." *Philadelphia Inquirer*. February 19, 1984, part I.

———. "Muslim Faithful Worldwide Preparing for Annual Pilgrimage to Mecca." *Los Angeles Times*. August 19, 1984.

Lambton, Ann K. S. "A Nineteenth Century View of Jihad." *Studia Islamica*, Vol. 32. 1970.

Lapidus, Ira M. "The Separation of State and Religion in the Development of Early Islamic Society." *International Journal of Middle East Studies*, Vol. 6, No. 4. 1975.

LaPorte, Robert. "Pakistan in 1972: Picking Up the Pieces." *Asian Survey*, Vol. 13, No. 2. February 1973.

———. "Regionalism and Political Opposition in Pakistan: Some Observations of the Bhutto Period." *Asian Thought and Society*, Vol. 1. September 1976.

———. "Succession in Pakistan: Continuity and Change in a Garrison State." *Asian Survey*, Vol. 9. November 1969.

———. "The Leadership Crisis in Pakistan." *Asian Thought and Society*, Vol. 2. September 1977.

Laroui, Abdallah. *The Crisis of the Arab Intellectual: Traditionalism or Hitoricism?* Translated by Diarmid Cammell. Berkeley and Los Angeles: University of California Press. 1976.

Lazarus-Yafeh, Hava. "Contemporary Fundamentalism—Judaism, Christianity, Islam." *Jerusalem Quarterly*, No. 47. Summer 1988.

Legrain, Jean-Francois. "A Defining Moment: Palestinian Islamic Fundamentalism." In James P. Piscatori, ed., *Islamic Fundamentalism and the Gulf Crisis*. Chicago: Fundamentalism Project, American Academy of Arts and Sciences. 1991.

———. "The Islamic Movement and the Intifada." In Jamal R. Nassar and Roger Heacock, eds., *Intifada: Palestine at the Crossroads*. New York: Praeger. 1990.

Lekhi, M. V. "Islamic State Controversy in Pakistan." *Political Science Review*, Vol. 6. 1967.

Lenczowski, George. "The Oil-Producing Countries." In Raymond Vernon, ed., *The Oil Crisis*. New York: W. W. Norton. 1976.

Lerner, Daniel. "Toward a Communication Theory of Modernization." In Lucien W. Pye, ed., *Communications and Political Development*. Princeton, N.J.: Princeton University Press. 1964.

Lerner, Eran. "Mawdudi's Concept of Islam." *Middle Eastern Studies*, Vol. 17, No. 4. October 1981.

Lesch, Ann Mosely. "Anatomy of an Uprising: The Palestinian Intifada." In Peter F. Krogh and Mary C. McDavid, eds., *Palestinians under Occupation: Prospects for the Future*. Washington, D.C.: Georgetown University Press. 1989.

Lewis, Bernard. "Islamic Concepts of Revolution." In P. J. Vatikiotis, ed., *Revolution in the Middle East*. London: Oxford University Press. 1972.

———. "The Return of Islam." *Commentary*, Vol. 61, No. 1. January 1976.

———. "The Roots of Muslim Rage." *Atlantic Monthly*. September 1990.

———. "Islam and Democracy." *Atlantic Monthly*. February 1993.

Lewis, Flora. "Moslem Leaders Watching Revival Warily." *New York Times*. December 31, 1979.

Liebman, Charles S. "Extremism as a Religious Norm." *Journal for the Scientific Study of Religion*, Vol. 22. Spring 1983.

Longley, Clifford. "Islam's Problems in the West." *The Round Table*, No. 279. July 1980.

Low, Helen, and Howe Low. "Focus on the Fourth World." In *The U.S. and World Development: Agenda for Action 1975*. New York: Praeger. 1975.

Lowrie, Arthur. "The Campaign against Islam and American Foreign Policy." *Middle East Policy*, Vol. 4, No. 1–2. September 1995.

Lughod, Ibrahim Abu. "Retreat from the Secular Path? Islamic Dilemmas of Arab Politics." *Review of Politics*, Vol. 28. October 1966.

Mady, Abu el-Ela. "Violent Groups Connected to Islam: The Historical Roots, Theological Foundations and Future." International Center for Country Studies. Cairo, March 1998, Arabic monograph.

Magd, A. Kamal Abul. "New Spirit of Awakening Engulfing the Islamic World." *Arabia*, No. 29. January 1984.

Magnus, Ralph H. "Afghanistan in 1996." *Asian Survey*, Vol. 37, No. 2. February 1997.

Malik, Hafeez. "Islamic Political Parties and Mass Politicization." *Islam and the Modern Age*, Vol. 3, No. 2. May 1972.

———. "Islamic Theory of International Relations." *Journal of South Asia and Middle Eastern Studies*, Vol. 2, No. 3. Spring 1979.

Mallison, W. Thomas and Sally V. Mallison. "The Right of Return." *Journal of Palestine Studies*, Vol. 9, No. 125. Spring 1980.

Mamiya, Lawrence H. "From Black Muslim to Bilalian: The Evolution of a Movement." *Journal for the Scientific Study of Religion*, Vol. 21, No. 2. June 1992.

Marquand, Robert. "Seriously Tinkering with 1,000 Years of Tradition." *Christian Science Monitor*. February 12, 1996.

———. "The Hurricane That Swirls over the Head Scarf." *Christian Science Monitor*. February 12, 1996.

Marshall, Susan E. "Islamic Revival in the Maghreb: The Utility of Tradition for Modernizing Elites." *Studies in Comparative International Development*, Vol. 16, No. 2. Summer 1979.

———. "Paradoxes of Change: Culture Crisis, Islamic Revival, and the Reactivation of Patriarchy." *Journal of Asian and African Studies*, Vol. 19. January 1984.

Martin, Richard C. "Religious Violence in Islam: Towards an Understanding of the Discourse on Jihad in Modern Egypt." In Paul Wilkinson and A. M. Stewart, eds., *Contemporary Research on Terrorism*. Aberdeen, UK: Aberdeen University Press, 1987.

Masland, Tom. "Fire on the Border." *Newsweek*. August 9, 1993.

Matin-Asghari, Afshin. "Abdolkarim Soroush and the Secularization of Islamic Thought in Iran." *Iranian Studies*, Vol. 30, Nos. 1–2. 1997.

May, L. S. "Dr. Muhammad Iqbal: Islam and Muslim Nationhood." Paper read at Conference on Pakistan at the Asia Society, New York. June 2, 1979.

Mazrui, Ali A. "The Resurgence of Islam and the Decline of Communism: What Is the Connection?" In *Futures*. London, UK: Buttersworth. 1991.

———. "Islamic and Western Values." *Foreign Affairs*, Vol. 76, No. 5. September–October 1997.

McNamara, Robert S. "The Population Problem." *Foreign Affairs*. Summer 1984.

Medhurst, K. "Religion and Politics: A Typology." *Scottish Journal of Religious Studies*, Vol. 2, No. 2. 1981.

von der Mehden, Fred R. "The Political and Social Challenge of the Islamic Revival in Malaysia and Indonesia." *Muslim World*, Vol. 76. July–October 1986.

Miles, W. "Political Para-Theology: Rethinking Religion, Politics, and Democracy." *Third World Quarterly*, Vol. 7, No. 3. 1996.

Miller, Judith. "The Challenge of Radical Islam." *Foreign Affairs*, Vol. 72, No. 2. Spring 1993.

———. "Faces of Fundamentalism." *Foreign Affairs*, Vol. 73, No. 6. November–December 1994.

Millward, William G. "Aspects of Modernism in Shi'ah Islam." *Studia Islamica*, Vol. 37. 1973.

Moghadam, Val. "Women, Work, and Ideology in the Islamic Republic [of Iran]." *International Journal of Middle East Studies*, Vol. 20. 1980.

Mohammed, Jan. "Introducing Islamic Laws in Pakistan, I." *Dawn*. July, 15, 1983.

Monshipouri, Mahmood. "The Islamic World's Reaction to Satanic Verses: Cultural Relativism Revisited." *Journal of Third World Studies*, Vol. 3, No. 1. Spring 1991.

Monshipouri, Mahmood, and Christopher G. Kukla. "Islam, Democracy and Human Rights: The Continuing Debate in the West." *Middle East Policy*, Vol. 3. 1994.

Moore, R. J. "Jinnah and the Pakistan Demand." *Modern Asian Studies*, Vol. 17, No. 4. 1983.

Moorsteen, Richard. "Action Proposal: OPEC Can Wait—We Can't." *Foreign Policy*, Vol. 18. Spring 1975.

Morris, Joe Alex. "Across the Muslim World, A New Militancy Spreads." *Philadelphia Inquirer*. December 3, 1978.

Mortimer, Robert. "Islam and Multi-Party Politics in Algeria." *Middle East Journal*, Vol. 45, No. 4. Autumn 1991.

Moruzzi, Norma Claire. "A Problem with Headscarves: Contemporary Complexities of Political and Social Identity." *Political Theory*, Vol. 22. 1994.

Mujiburrahman. "Islam and Politics in Indonesia: The Political Thought of Abdurrahman Wahid." *Journal of Islam and Christian-Muslim Relations*. Vol. 10, No. 3. 1999.

Murphy, Caryle. "Islam's Crescent of Change." *Washington Post, National Weekly Edition*. May 25–31, 1992.

Muslih, Muhammad, and Augustus Norton. "The Need for Arab Democracy." *Foreign Policy*. Summer 1991.

Muthalib, Hussin. "Confusion on Islam's Role in Malaysia." *Arabia*, No. 21. May 1983.

Muzzafar, Chandra. "Islamic Resurgence: A Global View." In Taufik Abdullah and Sharon Siddique, eds., *Islam and Society in Southeast Asia*. Singapore: Institute of Southeast Asian Studies. 1987.

Naby, Eden. "The Concept of Jihad in Opposition to Communist Rule: Turkestan and Afghanistan." *Studies in Comparative Communism*, Vol. 19, No. 3–4. Autumn–Winter 1986.

———. "Islam within the Afghan Resistance." *Third World Quarterly*, Vol. 10, No. 2. April 1988.

Nagata, Judith. "Religious Ideology and Social Change: The Islamic Revival in Malaysia." *Pacific Affairs*, Vol. 53, No. 3. 1980.

An-Na'im, Abdullahi Ahmed. "Islamic Law, International Relations, and Human Rights: Challenges and Response." *Cornell International Law Journal*, Vol. 20, No. 2. 1987.

Nait-Belkacem, Mouloud Kassim. "The Concept of Social Justice in Islam." In Altaf Gauhar, ed., *The Challenge of Islam*. London: Islamic Council of Europe. 1978.

Nash, Manning. "Fundamentalist Islam: Reservoir for Turbulence." *Journal of Asian and African Studies*, Vol. 19. Spring 1984.

Naumkin, Vitaly. "Islam in the States of the Former USSR." *Annals of the American Academy of Political and Social Science*, No. 524. November 1992.

Nawaz, M. K. "Some Aspects of Modernization in Islamic Law." In Carl Leiden, ed., *The Conflict of Traditionalism and Modernism in the Muslim Middle East*. Austin: University of Texas Press. 1966.

Nayang, Sulayman S. "Islam in the United States: A Review of Sources." *Journal of the Institute of Minority Affairs*, Vol. 3, No. 1. 1982.

Nelan, Bruce W. "What's Peace Got to Do with It?" *Time*. August 9, 1993.

Nizami, Khaliq Ahmad. "Naqshbandi Influence on Mughal Rulers and Politics." *Islamic Culture*, Vol. 39, No. 1. January 1965.

———. "Shah Wali-Ullah Dehlavi and Indian Politics in the 18th Century." *Islamic Culture*, Vol. 25. January, April, July, and October 1951.

———. "Socio-Religious Movements in Indian Islam (1763–1898)." *Islamic Culture*, Vol. 44, No. 3. July 1970.

Noakes, Greg. "Muslims and the American Press." In Yvonne Yazbeck Haddad and John L. Esposito, eds., *Muslims in the Americanization Path?* Oxford: Oxford University Press. 2000.

Noorani, A. G. "Human Rights in Islam." *Illustrated Weekly of India*. May 3, 1981.

Nortman, Dorothy. *U.N. Reports on Population/Family Planning*, No. 2. September 1976.

Norton, Augustus Richard. "U.S. and the Middle East: Elusive Quest for Peace." *Great Decisions 2002*. New York: Foreign Policy Association. 2002.

Nye, Joseph S., and Robert O. Keohane. "Transnational Relations and World Politics: An Introduction." *International Organization*, Vol. 25. 1971.

Olcott, Martha Brill. "Soviet Central Asia: Does Moscow Fear Iranian Influence?" In John L. Esposito, ed., *The Iranian Revolution: Its Global Impact*. Miami: Florida International University Press. 1990.

Onaran, Yalman. "Transition Proves Hard for Ex-Soviet Republics." *Christian Science Monitor*. November 18, 1992.

Orme, William. "In West Bank, Water Is as Touchy as Land." *New York Times*. July 15, 2000.

Osman, Fathi. "Suni and Shia in the Contemporary World." *Arabia*, No. 12. August 1982.

———. "The Life and Works of Abu al-A'la al-Mawdudi." *Arabia*, Vol. 4, No. 40. December 1984.

———. "Ayatullah Khomeini: A Genuine 'Alim-Leader' in the Contemporary World." *The Minaret*, Vol. 10, No. 3. Summer 1989.

Palmer, Norman D. "Changing Patterns of Politics in Pakistan: An Overview." In Mazooruddin Ahmad, ed., *Contemporary Pakistan: Politics, Economy and Society*. Durham: North Carolina Academic Press. 1980.

Paul, Jim. "Insurrection at Mecca." *MERIP Reports*, No. 91. October 1980.

Pasha, Mustapha Kamal. "Muslim Militancy and Self-Reliance—1, 2, 3," *The Muslim* [Karachi]. April 18–20, 1982.

Pfaff, Richard H. "Technicism vs. Traditionalism: The Developmental Dialectic in the Middle East." In Carl Leiden, ed., *The Conflict of Traditionalism and Modernism in the Muslim Middle East*. Austin: University of Texas Press. 1966.

Pipes, Daniel. "This World is Political! The Islamic Revival of the Seventies." *Orbis*, Vol. 24, No. 1. Spring 1980.

———. "Fundamentalist Muslims." *Foreign Affairs*. Summer 1986.

———. "The Muslims Are Coming! The Muslims Are Coming!" *National Review*. November 19, 1990.

Piscatori, James P. "Ideological Politics in Saudi Arabia." In James P. Piscatori, ed., *Islam and the Political Process*. Cambridge: Cambridge University Press. 1983.

Poruban, Steven. "Special Report: OPEC's Evolving Role: Analysts Discuss OPEC's Role." *Oil and Gas Journal*, Vol. 99, No. 28. July 9, 2001.

Qureishi, M. Naeem. "The Ulama of British India and the Hijrat of 1920." *Modern Asian Studies*, Vol. 13, No. 1. 1979.

Rahbar, Muhammad Daud. "Shah Wali Ullah and Ijtihad." *The Muslim World*, Vol. 45, No. 4. October 1955.

Rahman, Fazlur. "Currents of Religious Thought in Pakistan." *Islamic Studies*, Vol. 7, No. 1. March 1968.

———. "Islam and the New Constitution of Pakistan." *Journal of African and Asian Studies*, Vol. 8. 1973.

———. "Islam: Legacy and Contemporary Challenge." *Islamic Studies*, Vol. 19. Winter 1980.

———. "Islamic Modernism: Its Scope, Method and Alternative." *Journal of Middle East Studies*, Vol. 1. 1970.

———. "The Thinker of Crisis: Shah Waliy Ullah." *Pakistan Quarterly*, Vol. 6, No. 2. Summer 1956.

Rana, Mohammed. "The Concept of State in Islam." *The Law Journal* (Pakistan), Vol. 40, No. 1. 1978.

Randal, Jonathan C. "Bani-Sadr: Advocate of Iranian Independence." *Washington Post*. November 26, 1979.

Rapoport, David C. "Comparing Militant Fundamentalist Movements and Groups." In Martin Marty and Scott Appleby, eds., *Fundamentalisms and the State*. Chicago: University of Chicago Press. 1993.

Rashid, Ahmed. "The Taliban: Exporting Extremism." *Foreign Affairs*, Vol. 78. November–December 1999.

Rashiduzzaman, M. "Islam, Muslim Identity and Nationalism in Bangladesh." *Journal of South Asian and Middle Eastern Studies*, Vol. 28. Fall 1994.

Rehman, Hamood-ur-. "The Concept of Justice in Islam." *Pakistan Administration*, Vol. 16, No. 2. July–December 1979.

Rekhess, Elie. "The Iranian Impact on the Islamic Jihad Movement in the Gaza Strip." In David Menashri, ed., *The Iranian Revolution and the Muslim World*. Boulder, Colo.: Westview Press. 1990.

Richter, William L. "Pakistan." In Mohammed Ayoob, ed., *The Politics of Islamic Reassertion*. New York: St. Martin's Press. 1981.

———. "Pakistan under Zia." *Current History*, Vol. 76. April 1979.

———. "Pakistan: Impasse, Islamic Revolution, and Impending Crisis." *Asian Thought and Society*, Vol. 4, No. 10. April 1979.

———. "Persistent Praetorianism: Pakistan's Third Martial Law Regime." *Pacific Affairs*, Vol. 51, No. 3. Fall 1978.

———. "The Political Dynamics of Islamic Resurgence in Pakistan." *Asian Survey*, Vol. 19, No. 6. June 1979.

Robbins, Thomas. "Religious Movements and Violence: A Friendly Critique of the Interpretative Approach." *Nova Religio: The Journal of Alternative and Emergent Religions*, Vol. 1, No. 1. Fall 1997.

Roberson, B. A. "Islam and Europe: An Enigma or a Myth?" *Middle East Journal*, Vol. 48, No. 2. Spring 1994.

Roberts, Hugh. "Radical Islamism and the Dilemma of Algerian Nationalism: The Embattled Arians of Algiers." *Third World Quarterly*, Vol. 10, No. 2. April 1988.

Robinson, Francis. "Studies of Islam." *Modern Asian Studies*, Vol. 12, No. 1. 1979.

———. "Islam and Muslim Separatism." In David Taylor and Malcolm Yapp, ed., *Political Identity in South Asia*. London: Curzon Press. 1979.

———. "The Veneration of Teachers in Islam by their Pupils: Its Modern Significance." *History Today*, Vol. 30. March 1980.

———. "The Ulama of Farangi Mahall and Their Adab." In Barbara Daly Metcalf, ed., *Moral Conduct and Authority: The Place of Adab in South Asian Islam*. Berkeley and Los Angeles, Calif.: University of California Press. 1984.

Roleau, Eric. "Who Killed Sadat?" *MERIP Reports*, No. 103. February 1982.

Rubin, Uri. "The Ka'ba: Aspects of Its Ritual Functions and Position in Pre-Islamic and Early Islamic Times." *Jerusalem Studies in Arabic and Islam*, Vol. 8. 1986.

Sachedina, Abdulaziz Abdulhussein. "Ali Shariati: Ideologue of the Iranian Revolution." In John Esposito, ed., *Voices of Resurgent Islam*. Oxford: Oxford University Press. 1983.

———. "Activist Shi'ism in Iran, Iraq, and Lebanon." In Martin E. Marty and R. Scott Appleby, eds., *Fundamentalisms Observed*. Chicago: University of Chicago Press. 1991.

Said, Edward W. "Islam Rising." *Columbia Journalism Review*. March–April 1980.

———. "Islam through Western Eyes." *The Nation*. April 26, 1980.

———. "Inside Islam." *Harpers*. January 1981.

———. "The Clash of Ignorance." *The Nation*. October 22, 2001.

Said, Hakim Mohammed. "Enforcement of Islamic Law in Pakistan." *Hamdard Islamicus*, Vol. 2, No. 2. Summer 1979.

Salame, G. "Islam and the West." *Foreign Policy*. Spring 1993.

Saleem, Elie. "Nationalism and Islam." *Muslim World*, Vol. 52. 1962.

Sardar, Ziauddin. "The Science of Islam: The Controversy over a 'Moral Science.'" *World Press Review*. February 1980.

———. "The Greatest Gathering of Mankind." *Inquiry*, Vol. 1, No. 4. September 1984.

Sareen, Rajendra. "Political Scene in Pakistan." *Institute for Defense Studies Analysis Journal*, Vol. 13, No. 2. October–December 1980.

Satloff, Robert. "Islam in the Palestinian Uprising." *Washington Institute for Near East Policy*. October 1988.

Sayeed, Khalid Bin. "Religion and Nation-Building in Pakistan." *Middle East Journal*, Vol. 17. 1963.

———. "The Jamaat-e-Islami Movement in Pakistan." *Pacific Affairs*, Vol. 30. March 1957.

Sayigh, Yezid. "Arafat and the Anatomy of a Revolt." *Surival*. Autumn 2001.

Schwartz, Tony. "Apparent Victor in Iran's Voting: Abolhassan Bani-Sadr." *New York Times*. January 28, 1980.

Sciolino, Elaine. "Iran's Durable Revolution." *Foreign Affairs*, Vol. 61, No. 4. 1983.

Scott, Paul. "Sacred Battles: Questions for Martin E. Marty." *New York Times Magazine*. September 30, 2001.

Shah, Mowahid H. "Modernity Is Not What Muslims Resent." *Christian Science Monitor*. January 22, 1980.

Shahi, Agha. "Roots of Islamic Reassertion." *The Muslim* (Karachi). July 1984.

Shahin, Emad Eldin Ali. "The Restitution of Islam: A Comparative Study of the Islamic Movements in Contemporary Tunisia and Morocco." Ph.D. dissertation, Johns Hopkins University. 1980.

Sharabi, Hisham. "Islam and Modernization in the Arab World." *Journal of International Affairs*, Vol. 19, No. 1. 1965.

Shepherd, William E. "Fundamentalism: Christian and Islamic." *Religion*, Vol. 17. October 1987.

———. "Islam and Ideology: Towards a Typology." *International Journal of Middle Eastern Studies*, Vol. 19. October 1987.

Sherani, Rais-ud-Din Khan. "Muhammad: The Greatest Law-Giver and an Epitome of Justice and Compassion." *Hamdard Islamicus*, Vol. 12, No. 4. Winter 1989.

Shupe, A. "The Stubborn Persistence of Religion in the Global Arena." In E. Sahliyeh, ed., *Religious Resurgence and Politics in the Contemporary World*. Albany: State University of New York Press. 1996.

Siddiqi, Mohammad Suleman. "The Concept of Hudud and Its Significance." In Anwar Moazzam, ed., *Islam and the Contemporary Muslim World*. New Delhi: Light and Life Publishers. 1981.

Siddique, Sharon. "Conceptualizing Contemporary Islam: Religion or Ideology?" *Annual Review of the Social Sciences and Summary of Religion*, Vol. 5, Summer 1981.

Siegman, Henry. "The State and the Individual in Sunni Islam." *The Muslim World*, Vol. 56, No. 1. January 1964.

Singhal, D. P. "The New Constitution of Pakistan." *Asian Survey*, Vol. 2. August 1962.

Sivan, Emmanuel. "How Fares Islam?" *Jerusalem Quarterly*, Vol. 13. Fall 1979.

———. "The Two Faces of Islamic Fundamentalism," *Jerusalem Quarterly*, Vol. 27. Spring 1983.

———. "Sunni Radicalism in the Middle East and the Iranian Revolution." *International Journal of Middle East Studies*, Vol. 21. 1989.

———. "The Islamic Resurgence: Civil Society Strikes Back." *Journal of Contemporary History* (London), Vol. 25. 1990.

Skocpol, Theda. "Rentier State and Shi'a Islam in the Iranian Revolution." *Theory and Society*, Vol. 11. 1982.

Slater, Jerome. "What Went Wrong? The Collapse of the Israeli-Palestinian Peace Process." *Political Science Quarterly*. Summer 2001.

Smith, Donald Eugene. "Emerging Patterns of Religion and Politics." In Donald Eugene Smith, ed., *South Asian Politics and Religion*. Princeton, N.J.: Princenton University Press. 1966.

———. "Secularization in Bangladesh." *World View*. April 1973.

———. "The Politics of Islamic Resurgence." *Almanac*, Vol. 27, No. 6. September 30, 1980.

Springborg, Robert. "Islamic Revivalism in the Middle East." *Current Affairs Bulletin*, Vol. 56, No. 1. June 1979.

———. "On the Rise and Fall of Arab Isms." *Australian Outlook*, Vol. 31, No. 1. April 1977.

———. "The Politics of Resurgent Islam in Egypt, Syria, and Iraq." In Mohammed Ayoob, ed., *The Politics of Islamic Reassertion*. New York: St. Martin's Press. 1981.

Stephens, Robert. "Gift of God and Scourge of the Shah." *The Observer*. January 21, 1979.

Struck, Doug, et al. "Borderless Network of Terror." *Washington Post*. September 22, 2001.

Sundaram, Jomo Kwame, and Ahmed Shabery Cheek. "The Politics of Malaysia's Islamic Resurgence." *Third World Quarterly*, Vol. 10, No. 2. April 1988

Szliowicz, Joseph A. "The Embargo and U.S. Foreign Policy." In Joseph A. Szliowicz and Bard E. O'Neil, eds., *The Energy Crisis and the U.S. Foreign Policy*. New York: Praeger. 1975.

Tabatabai, Shanin. "Women in Islam." *Islamic Revolution*, No. 1. 1979.

Takle, J. "Islam in Bengal." *The Muslim World*, Vol. 4, No. 1. January 1914.

Taraki, Lisa. "The Islamic Resistance Movement in the Palestinian Uprising." *Middle East Report*, Vol. 19, No. 1. January–February 1989.

Tastemain, Catherine and Peter Coles. "Can a Culture Stop AIDS in Its Tracks?" *New Scientist* (London), Vol. 139, No. 1890. September 11, 1993.

Tefft, Sheila. "Muslims Debate Rushdie Uproar." *Christian Science Monitor*. February 27, 1989.

Tehranian, Majid. "Iran: Communication Alienation and Revolution." *Monthly Public Opinion Survey*, Vol. 24, No. 67. March–April 1979.

Telhami, Shibley. "Defeating Terror: Confront Supply and Demand." *Middle East Insight*, Vol. 16. November–December 2001.

Temko, Ned. "Behind Islamic Ferment Is Anger over Lowly Status." *Christian Science Monitor*. December 18, 1979.

Tibi, Bassam. "The Worldview of Sunni Arab Fundamentalists: Attitudes toward Modern Science and Technology." In Martin E. Marty and R. Scott Appleby, eds., *Fundamentalisms and Society: Reclaiming the Sciences, the Family and Education.* Chicago: University of Chicago Press. 1993.

Tinnin, David B. "The Saudis Awaken to Their Vulnerability." *Fortune.* March 10, 1980.

Tritton, A. S. "The Speech of God." In *Studia Islamica,* Vol. 33. 1971.

Turabi, Hasan. "Principles of Governance, Freedom, and Responsibility in Islam." *American Journal of Islamic Social Science,* Vol. 4, No. 1. 1987.

Vatin, Jean-Claude. "Popular Puritanism versus State Reformism: Islam in Algeria." In James Piscatori, ed., *Islam in the Political Process.* Cambridge: Cambridge University Press. 1983.

Venter, Al. "America's Nemesis: Usama bin Laden." *Jane's Intelligence Review.* October 1, 1998.

Voll, John Obert. "The Sudanese Mahdi: Frontier Fundamentalist." *International Journal of Middle East Studies,* Vol. 10, No. 2. May 1979.

———. "The Islamic Past and the Present Resurgence." *Current History,* Vol. 456. April 1980.

———. "Fundamentalism in the Sunni Arab World." In M. Marty and R. Scott Appleby, eds., *Fundamentalisms Observed.* Chicago: University of Chicago Press. 1991.

———. "Islam as a Special World-System." *Journal of World History,* Vol. 5, No. 2. Fall 1994.

Wafi, Ali Abdel Wahid. "Human Rights in Islam." *Islamic Quarterly,* Vol. 11, Nos. 1–2. January–June 1967.

Waines, David. "Through a Veil Darkly: The Study of Women in Muslim Societies." *Comparative Studies in Society and History,* Vol. 24. October 1982.

Waldman, Marilyn Robinson. "Tradition as a Modality of Change: Islamic Examples." *History of Religions,* Vol. 25. May 1986.

———. "Reflections on Islamic Traditions, Woman and Family." In Earl H. Waugh et al., eds., *Muslim Families in North America.* Edmonton: University of Alberta Press. 1991.

Washington, Vernon Loeb. "Terrorism Entrepreneur Unifies Groups Financially, Politically." *Washington Post.* August 23, 1998.

Waterbury, John. "Eqypt: Islam and Social Change." In Philip H. Stoddard, David C. Cuthell, and Margaret W. Sullivan, eds., *Change and the Muslim World.* Syracuse: Syracuse University Press. 1981.

Watson, Russel. "Across the Line, Israel Hits Hizbullah." *Newsweek.* March 2, 1992.

———. "A Satanic Fury." *Newsweek.* February 27, 1989.

Watt, Montgomery. "Islam and the West." In Denis MacEoin and Ahmed al-Shahi, eds., *Islam in the Modern World.* London: Croom Helm. 1983.

Weiner, Myron. "Political Participation: Crisis of the Political Process." In Leonard Binder et al., eds., *Crises and Sequences in Political Development.* Princeton, N.J.: Princeton University Press. 1971.

Weiss, Anita M. "The Historical Debate on Islam and the State in South Asia." In Anita M. Weiss, ed., *Islamic Reassertion in Pakistan: The Application of Islamic Laws in a Modern State.* Syracuse: Syracuse University Press. 1971.

Westwood, Andrew F. "The Problems of Westernization in Modern Iran." *Middle East Journal,* Vol. 2. January 1948.

Willis, John Ralph. "Jihad fi Sabil Allah: Its Doctrinal Basis in Islam and Some Aspects of Its Evolution in Nineteenth-Century West Africa." *Journal of African History,* Vol. 8, No. 3. 1967.

Woollacott, Martin. "Coming to Power: Theocracy Envelopes New Urban Masses." *World Press Review.* February 1980.

————. "The Mosque's Role in the Third Revolution." *The Guardian.* December 3, 1979.

————. "World of Islam" (Special Report). *Time.* April 16, 1979.

Wright, Robin. "Iran's Greatest Political Challenge." *World Policy Journal*, Vol. 14, No. 2. 1997.

————. "Islam, Democracy and the West." *Foreign Affairs.* Summer 1992.

Wright, Theodore P. "A Typology of South Asian Muslims: A Taxonomic Exercise." In Dietmar Rothermund, ed., *Islam in Southern Asian: A Survey of Current Research.* Wiesbaden, Germany: Franz Steiner Verlag. 1975.

Yasin, Muhammad. "Mujadid Alif-i-Sani." In Sardar Ali Ahmad Khan, ed., *The Naqshbandis.* Sharaqpur Sharif, Pakistan: Darul Muballeghin Hazrat. 1982.

Young, Oran. "Interdependence in World Politics." *International Journal*, Vol. 24. Autumn 1969.

Yousef, Ahmed, et al. "Islam and the West on the Eve of the Third Millennium." *Middle East Journal*, Vol. 3, No. 3–4. Summer–Fall 1997.

Zogby, James J. "The Strategic Peace Initiative Package: A New Approach to Israeli-Palestinian Peace." *American Arab Affairs*, No. 35. Winter 1990–1991.

Zubaida, Sami. "Human Rights and Cultural Difference: Middle Eastern Perspectives." In *New Perspectives on Turkey*, No. 10. Fall 1994.

Books

Abbott, Freeland K. *Islam and Pakistan.* Ithaca, N.Y.: Cornell University Press, 1968.

Abdalati, Hammudah. *Islam in Focus.* Indianapolis: American Trust Publications, 1975.

Abdelnasser, Walid Mahmoud. *The Islamic Movement in Egypt: Perceptions of International Relations, 1967–81.* London: Kegan Paul, 1994.

Abdo, Genevieve. *No God but God: Egypt and the Triumph of Islam.* New York: Oxford University Press, 2000.

Abduh, Muhammad. *The Theology of Unity.* Translated by Ishaq Musaad and Kenneth Cragg. London: Allen and Unwin, 1966.

Abdul-Khaliq, Salim. *The Untold Story of Blacks in Islam.* Hampton, Va.: U.B. & U.S. Communication Systems, 1994.

Abdullah, T. and S. Siddique, eds. *Islam and Society in Southeast Asia.* Singapore: Institute of Southeast Asian Studies, 1986.

Abedi, Mehdi, and Gary Tegenhausen, eds. *Jihad and Shahadat: Struggle and Martyrdom in Islam.* Houston, Tex.: Institute of Research and Islamic Studies, 1986.

Abrahamian, Ervand. *Iran between Two Revolutions.* Princeton, N.J.: Princeton University Press, 1982

————. *Khomeinism: Essays on the Islamic Republic.* Berkeley and Los Angeles: University of California Press, 1993.

Abu-Amr, Ziad. *Islamic Fundamentalism in the West Bank and Gaza: Muslim Brotherhood and Islamic Jihad.* Bloomington: Indiana University Press, 1994.

Abu-Bakr, Muhammad. *Islam's Black Legacy: Some Leading Figures.* Denver: Purple Dawn Books, 1993.

Abu-Laghod, Ibrahim, ed. *The Transformation of Palestine.* Evanston, Ill.: Northwestern University Press, 1987.

Abu-Rabi, Ibrahim M. *Intellectual Origins of Islamic Resurgence in the Modern Arab World.* Albany: State University of New York Press, 1996.

AbuSulayman, Abdul Hamid A. *The Islamic Theory of International Relations: New Directions for Islamic Methodology and Thought.* Herndon, Va.: International Institute for Islamic Thought, 1987.

————. *Towards an Islamic Theory of International Relations.* Herndon, VA: International Institute of Islamic Thought, 1993.

————. *A Crisis in the Muslim Mind.* Herndon, VA: International Institute of Islamic Thought, 1993.

Abul-Husn, Latif. *The Lebanese Conflict: Looking Inward.* Boulder, Colo.: Lynne Rienner, 1998.

AbulJobain, Ahmad. *Islam under Siege: Radical Islamic Terrorism or Political Islam?* Annandale, Va.: United Association for Studies and Research Inc., Occasional Papers Series No. 1, June 1993.

Aburish, Said K. *The House of Saud.* New York: St. Martin's/Griffin, 1996.

————. *Arafat: From Defender to Dictator.* London: Bloomsbury, 1998.

Adams, Charles C. *Islam and Modernism in Egypt: A Study of the Modern Reform Movement Inaugurated by Muhammad Abduh.* New York: Russell & Russell, 1933. Reprinted 1993.

Adams, Michael. *More Honoured in the Breach than the Observance: Human Rights and the Israeli Occupation.* Paris: International Committee for Palestinian Human Rights, 1979.

El-Affendi, Abdelwahab. *Who Needs an Islamic State?* London: Grey Seal, 1991.

————. *Turabi's Revolution: Islam and Power in Sudan.* London: Grey Seal, 1991.

Afkhami, Mahnaz and Erika Friedl, eds. *In the Eye of the Storm: Women in Post-Revolutionary Islam.* Syracuse: Syracuse University Press, 1994.

Ahmad, Akhtaruddin. *Nationalism or Islam: Indo-Pakistan Episode.* New York: Vintage Press, 1982.

Ahmad, Aziz. *Islamic Culture in the Indian Environment.* London: Oxford University Press, 1964.

————. *Islamic Modernism in India and Pakistan 1857–1964.* London: Oxford University Press, 1967.

Ahmad, Hisham H. *Hamas: From Religious Salvation to Political Transformation.* Jerusalem: Palestinian Academic Society for the Study of International Affairs, 1994.

Ahmad, Iftikhar. *Pakistan General Elections, 1970.* Lahore: South Asian Institute, Punjab University, 1976.

Ahmad, Jalal Ali. *Gharbzadagi* (Weststruckness), translated by Ahmad Alizadeh and John Green. Lexington, Ky: Mazda, 1982.

Ahmad, Khurshid. *The Religion of Islam.* Lahore, Pakistan: Islamic Publications, 1967.

————. *Islam and the West.* Lahore, Pakistan: Islamic Publications Ltd., 1979.

Ahmad, Kurshid, and Zafar Ishaq Ansari, eds. *Islamic Perspectives: Studies in Honour of Maulana Sayyid Abul A'la Mawdudi.* Leicester, England: Islamic Foundation, 1979.

Ahmad, Manzooruddin. *Pakistan: The Emerging Islamic State.* Karachi, Pakistan: Allies Book Corporation, 1966.

Ahmad, Riaz, ed. *Iqbal's Letters to Quaid-i-Azam.* Lahore, Pakistan: Friends Educational Service, 1976.

Ahmed, Akbar S. *Discovering Islam: Making Sense of Muslim History and Society.* London: Routledge, 1988.

————. *Postmodernism and Islam: Predicament and Promise.* London: Routledge, 1992.

————. *Living Islam: From Samarkand to Stornoway.* New York: Facts on File, 1994.

Ahmed, Akbar S. and Hastings Donnan. *Islam, Globalization, and Postmodernity.* New York: Routledge, 1994

Ahmed, Akbar S., *Islam Today: A Short Introduction to the Muslim World.* New York: I. B. Tauris, 1999.

Ahmed, Eqbal. *Islam: Politics and the State: The Pakistan Experience.* London: Zed Books, 1985.

Ahmed, Leila. *Women and Gender in Islam: Historical Roots of a Modern Debate*. New Haven: Yale University Press, 1992.

Ahmed, Rafiuddin. *The Bengal Muslims, 1871–1906*. 2nd ed. Delhi: Oxford University Press, 1988.

Ahmed, S. R. *Maulana Maudoodi and the Islamic State*. Lahore, Pakistan: People's Publishing House, 1976.

al-Ahsan, Abdallah. *The Organization of the Islamic Conference: An Introduction to an Islamic Political Institution*. Herndon, Va.: International Institute of Islamic Thought, 1988.

Ahsan, Syed Ali, ed. *Islam in the Modern World: Proceedings of an International Seminar*. Karachi: Pakistan Committee Congress for Cultural Freedom, 1964.

Ajami, Fouad. *The Vanished Imam: Musa al-Sadr and the Shi'a of Lebanon*. Ithaca, N.Y.: Cornell University Press, 1986.

———. Fouad. *The Arab Predicament: Arab Political Thought and Practice since 1967*. New York: Cambridge University Press, 1981. Rev. ed. 1992.

Akhavi, Sharough. *Religion and Politics in Contemporary Iran: Clergy-State Relations in the Pahlavi Period*. Albany: State University of New York Press, 1980.

Akhtar, Rafiq, ed. *Pakistan Year Book*. Karachi, Pakistan: East-West Publishing, 1974.

Akhtar, Shabbir. *Be Careful with Muhammad! The Salman Rushdie Affair*. London: Bellew, 1989.

———. *A Faith for All Seasons: Islam and the Challenge of the Modern World*. Chicago: Ivan R. Dee, 1990.

Al-Ahmad, Jalal. *Gharbzadeghi (Westoxification)*. Islamic Students Association of Europe, U.S., and Canada, 1979.

Algar, Hamid. *Religion and State in Iran, 1785–1906: The Role of the Ulama in Qajar Period*. Berkeley and Los Angeles: University of California Press, 1969.

———. *The Roots of the Islamic Revolution*. Markham, Ontario: The Open Press, 1983.

———, trans. *Islam and Revolution: Writings and Declarations of Imam Khomeini*. Berkeley, Calif.: Mizan Press, 1981.

Algosaibi, Ghazi. *The Gulf Crisis: An Attempt to Understand*. London: Kegan Paul International, 1993.

Ali, Abdullah Yusuf. *The Meaning of the Holy Quran*. New Edition, with Revised Translation and Commentary. Beltsville, Md.: Amana, 1989.

Ali, Ameer. *The Spirit of Islam: A History of the Evolution and Ideals of Islam, with a Life of the Prophet*. Rev. ed. London: Christopher's Ltd., 1922.

Ali, Michael Nazir. *Islam: A Christian Perspective*. Exeter, England: Paternoster Press. 1983.

Allana, G., ed. *Pakistan Movement: Historic Documents*. Karachi, Pakistan: Department of International Relations, University of Karachi, 1968.

Allworth, Edward, ed. *Muslim Communities Reemerge: Historical Perspectives on Nationality, Politics, and Opposition in the Former Soviet Union and Yugoslavia*. Durham, N.C.: Duke University Press, 1994.

Alnasrawi, Abbas. *OPEC in a Changing World Economy*. Baltimore: John Hopkins University Press, 1985.

Altorki, Soraya. *Women in Saudi Arabia: Ideology and Behavior among the Elite*. New York: Columbia University Press, 1986.

Ahmad, Khurshid. *Economic Development in an Islamic Framework*. Leicester: The Islamic Foundation, 1979.

El-Amin, Mustafa. *The Religion of Islam and the Nation of Islam: What Is the Difference?* Newark, N.J.: El-Amin Productions, 1991.

Andersen, Roy R., Robert F. Seibert, and Jon G. Wagner. *Politics and Change in the Middle East: Sources of Conflict and Accommodation.* 3rd ed. Englewood Cliffs, N.J.: Prentice Hall, 1982, 1990.

Antoun, Richard T., and Mary Elaine Hegland, eds. *Religious Resurgence: Contemporary Cases in Islam, Christianity, and Judaism.* Syracuse, N.Y.: Syracuse University Press, 1987.

Anwar, Zainah. *Islamic Revivalism in Malaysia: Dakwah among the Students.* Petaling Jaya, Malaysia: Pelanduk Publications, 1987.

Anway, Carol. *Daughters of Another Path.* Lee's Summit, Mo.: Yawna Publications, 1995.

Appignanesi, Lisa, and Sara Maitland. eds. *The Rushdie File.* Syracuse, N.Y.: Syracuse University Press, 1990.

Appleby, R. Scott, ed. *Spokesman for the Despised: Fundamentalist Leaders of the Middle East.* Chicago: University of Chicago Press, 1997.

Apter, David. *The Politics of Modernization.* Chicago: University of Chicago Press, 1965.

Arberry, Arthur J. *An Introduction to the History of Sufism.* London: Longman, 1942.

———. *The Koran Interpreted.* Oxford: Oxford University Press, 1964.

———. *Sufism: An Account of Mystics of Islam.* New York: Harper Torchbooks, 1970.

Arjomand, Said Amir. *The Shadow of God and the Hidden Imam.* Chicago: University of Chicago Press, 1984.

———. ed. *From Nationalism to Revolutionary Islam.* Albany: State University of New York Press, 1984.

———. *The Turban for the Crown: The Islamic Revolution in Iran.* New York: Oxford University Press, 1988.

———, ed. *Political Dimensions of Religion.* Albany: State University of New York Press, 1993.

Armstrong, Karen. *Muhammad: A Biography of the Prophet.* San Francisco: Harper San Francisco, 1993.

———. *Jerusalem: One City, Three Faiths.* New York: Knopf, 1996.

———. *Islam: A Short History.* New York: Modern Library, 2000.

———. *The Battle for God.* New York: Knopf, 2000.

Arnold, T. W. *The Preaching of Islam.* 2nd ed. London: Constable, 1913.

Aruri, Naseer. *Middle East Crucible: Studies on the Arab-Israeli War of 1973.* Wilmette, Ill.: Medina University Press International, 1975.

———. *The Obstruction of Peace: The U.S., Israel and the Palestinians.* Monroe, Maine: Common Courage Press, 1996.

Asad, Muhammad. *The Principles of State and Government in Islam.* 1961. Reprint, Gibralter: Dar al-Andalus, 1980.

Ashraf, Mujib. *Muslim Attitudes towards British Rule and Western Culture in India in the First Half of the Nineteenth Century.* Delhi: Idarah-i-Adabiyat-i-Delhi, 1982.

Aswad, Barbara, and Barbara Bilge. *Family and Gender among American Muslims: Issues Facing Middle Eastern Immigrants and Their Descendants.* Philadelphia: Temple University Press, 1996.

Averill, Lloyd J. *Religious Right, Religious Wrong: A Critique of the Fundamentalist Phenomenon.* New York: Pilgrim Press, 1989.

Axelgard, Frederick W., *A New Iraq? The Gulf War and Implications for U.S. Policy.* Washington, D.C.: Center for Strategic and International Studies, 1988.

Ayoob, Mohammed, ed. *The Politics of Islamic Reassertion.* New York: St. Martin's Press, 1981.

———. *The Middle East in World Politics.* New York: St. Martin's Press, 1981.

Ayoub, Mahmoud. *The Quran and Its Interpreters.* Albany: State University of New York Press, 1984.

Ayubi, Nazih. *Political Islam: Religion and Politics in the Arab World.* London: Routledge, 1991.

―――. *Overstating the Arab State: Politics and Society in the Middle East.* London: Tauris, 1995.

Azam, Ikram. *Pakistan and Nationalities Notion.* Lahore, Pakistan: Amir Publications, 1980.

Azari, Farah. *Women of Iran: The Conflict with Fundamentalist Islam.* London: Ithaca Press, 1983.

al-Azmeh, Aziz. *Islams and Modernities.* London: Verso, 1993.

Azzam, A. R. *The Eternal Message of Muhammad.* Translated by Caesar Farah. Cambridge: Cambridge University Press, 1992.

Azzam, S., ed. *The Muslim World and the Future Economic Order.* London: Islamic Council of Europe, 1979.

Bacharach, Jere L. *A Middle East Handbook.* Seattle: University of Washington Press, 1984.

Badawi, M. A. Zaki. *The Reformers of Egypt.* London: Croom Helm, 1978.

Bahadur, Kalim. *The Jama'at-i-Islami of Pakistan: Political Thought and Political Action.* New Delhi: Chetna Publications, 1977.

Baig, M. R. *The Muslim Dilemma in India.* New Delhi: Vikas Publishing House, 1974.

Baker, Raymond William. *Sadat and After: Struggles for Egypt's Political Soul.* Cambridge, Mass.: Harvard University Press, 1990.

Bakhash, Shaul. *The Reign of the Ayatollahs: Iran and the Islamic Revolution.* New York: Basic Books, 1984. Rev. ed., 1990.

Ball, George. *Error and Betrayal in Lebanon: An Analysis of Israel's Invasion of Lebanon and the Implications for U.S.-Israeli Relations.* Washington, D.C.: Foundation for Middle East Peace, 1984.

Baldick, J. *Mystical Islam: An Introduction to Sufism.* New York: New York University Press, 1989.

Barber, Benjamin R., and Andrea Schultz. *Jihad vs. McWorld: How Globalism and Tribalism Are Reshaping the World.* New York: Ballantine Books, 1996.

Barboza, Steven, ed. *American Jihad: Islam after Malcolm X.* New York: Doubleday, 1994.

Barney, Gerald O. *Global 2000.* Arlington, Va.: Seven Locks Press, 1991.

Barr, James. *Fundamentalism.* Philadelphia: Westminster Press, 1978.

―――. *Beyond Fundamentalism.* Philadelphia: Westminster Press, 1984.

Barton, Greg and Greg Fealy, eds. *Nahdatul Ulama: Traditional Islam and Modernity in Indonesia.* Monash, Australia: Monash Asia Institute, 1996.

Beattie, Kirk J. *Egypt during the Nasser Years: Ideology, Politics, and Civil Society.* Boulder, Colo.: Westview Press, 1994.

Beck, Lois and Nikki Keddie, eds. *Women in the Muslim World.* Cambridge, Mass.: Harvard University Press, 1978.

Beinin, Joel and Joe Stork. ed. *Political Islam: Essays from Middle East Report.* Berkeley and Los Angeles: University of California Press, 1997.

Bellah, Robert, ed. *Religion and Progress in Modern Asia.* New York: The Free Press, 1965.

Belt, Don. *The World of Islam.* Washington, D.C.: National Geographic, 2001.

Benard, Cheryl and Zalmay Khalilzad. *The Government of God—Iran's Islamic Republic.* New York: Columbia University Press, 1984.

Bendinar, Elmer. *The Rise and Fall of Paradise: When Arabs and Jews Built a Kingdom in Spain.* New York: Barnes & Noble, 1983.

Bennigsen, Alexandre, and Chantal Lemercier-Quelguejay. *Islam in Russia.* New York: Praeger, 1967.

Bennigsen, Alexandre, and S. Enders Wimbush. *Muslim National Communism in the So-viet Union*. Chicago: University of Chicago Press, 1979.

Bennis, Phyllis. *Calling the Shots: How Washington Dominates Today's U.N.* Northampton, Mass.: Olive Branch Press/Interlink, 1990.

Bennis, Phillis, and Neal Cassidy. *From Stones to Statehood: The Palestinian Uprising*. Northampton, Mass.: Olive Branch Press/Interlink, 1990.

Bennis, Phillis, and Michel Moushabeck, eds. *Beyond the Storm: A Gulf Crisis Reader*. New York: Olive Branch Press, 1991.

Benvenisti, Mero, and Thomas L. Friedman. *Intimate Enemies: Jews and Arabs in a Shared Land*. Berkeley and Los Angeles: University of California Press, 1995.

Bergen, Peter L. *Holy War, Inc.: Inside the Secret World of Osama bin Laden*. New York: The Free Press, 2001.

Berger, Morroe. *Islam in Egypt: Social and Political Aspects of Popular Religion*. Cambridge: Cambridge University Press, 1970.

Berger, Peter L., ed. *The Desecularization of the World: Resurgent Religion and World Politics*. Washington, D.C.: Ethics and Public Policy Center, 1999.

Berks, Niyazi. *The Development of Secularization in Turkey*. Montreal: McGill University Press, 1964.

Beynon, E. D. *Master Fard Muhammad: "Detroit History."* Newport News, Va.: United Brothers and United Sisters Communications Systems, 1990.

Bhutto, Zulfikar Ali. *Thoughts on Some Aspects of Islam*. Lahore, Pakistan: Ashraf Publishers, 1976.

Bill, James A., and Robert L. Hardgrave. *Comparative Politics: The Quest for Theory*. Columbus, Ohio: Charles E. Merill, 1973.

Bill, James A., and Carl Leiden. *The Middle East: Politics and Power*. Boston: Little, Brown, [1974], 1984.

Bill, James A. *The Eagle and the Lion*. New Haven, Conn.: Yale University Press, 1988.

Bill, James A., and Robert Springborg. *Politics in the Middle East*. 6th ed. New York: Addison-Wesley, 2002.

Billington, James H. *Fire in the Minds of Men: Origins of the Revolutionary Faith*. New York: Basic Books, 1980.

Binder, Leonard. *Religion and Politics in Pakistan*. Berkeley and Los Angeles: University of California Press, 1961.

———, ed. *Crises and Sequences in Political Development*. Princeton, N.J.: Princeton University Press, 1971.

Binder, Leonard, et al. *Crises and Sequences in Political Development*. Princeton, N.J.: Princeton University Press, 1971.

Binder, Leonard. *The Ideological Revolution in the Middle East*. 2nd ed. New York: Robert E. Krieger, 1979.

———. *Revolution in Iran*. New York: Middle East Review, Special Studies No. 1, 1980.

———. *Islamic Liberalism: A Critique of Development Ideologies*. Chicago: University of Chicago Press, 1988.

Birnbaum, Ervin. *Some Theoretical and Practical Aspects of the Islamic State of Pakistan*. Karachi: Pakistan Historical Society, 1956.

Black, Cyril Edwin. *The Dynamics of Modernization*. New York: Harper and Row, 1966.

Blyden, Edward Wilmot. *Christianity, Islam and the Negro Race*. San Francisco: First African Arabian Press, 1992.

Bodansky, Yossef. *Target America and the West: Terrorism Today*. New York: SPI Books, 1993.

———. *Bin Laden: The Man Who Declared War on America*. Rosville, Calif.: Forum Press, 1999.

Boisard, Marcel. *Humanism in Islam*. Indianapolis: American Trust Publications, 1979.

Bonnie, Michael E., and Nikki R. Keddie, ed. *Modern Iran: The Dialectics of Continuity and Change*. Albany, N.Y.: State University of New York Press, 1981.

Boroujerdi, Mehrzad. *Iranian Intellectuals and the West: The Tormented Triumph of Nativism*. Syracuse, N.Y.: Syracuse University Press, 1996.

Borthwick, Bruce Maynard. *Comparative Politics of the Middle East: An Introduction*. Englewood Cliffs, N.J.: Prentice-Hall, 1980.

Boulares, Habib. *Islam: The Fear and the Hope*. London: Zed Books, 1990.

Boullata, Issa J. *Trends and Issues in Contemporary Arab Thought*. Albany: State University of New York Press, 1990.

Boutros-Ghali, Boutros. *Egypt's Road to Jerusalem*. New York: Random House, 1997.

Bowker, John. *What Muslims Believe*. Oxford: Oneworld Publications, 1998.

Bozdag, Ismet. *The 3rd Idea the World Is Waiting For: Socio-Economic Model of Islam*. Karachi, Pakistan: National Book Foundation, 1979.

Bradsher, Henry S. *Afghan Communism and Soviet Intervention*. Karachi, Pakistan: Oxford University Press, 1999.

Braibanti, Ralph, and T. T. Spengler. *Traditions, Values and Socio-Economic Development*. Durham, N.C.: Duke University Press, 1961.

————. *The Nature and Structure of the Islamic World*. Chicago: International Strategy and Policy Institute, 1995.

Brasswell, Jr., George W. *Islam*. Nashville: Broadman & Holman, 1996.

————. *What You Need to Know about Islam & Muslims*. Nashville: Broadman & Holman, 2000.

Bresheeth, Haim, and Nira Yuval-Davis, eds. *The Gulf War and the New World Order*. London: Zed Books, 1991.

Brett, Michael, ed. *Northern Africa, Islam and Modernization*. London: Cass, 1973.

Brice, William, ed. *An Historical Atlas of Islam*. 2nd ed. Leiden, The Netherlands: E. J. Brill, 1954.

Brittain, Victoria. ed. *The Gulf between Us*. London: Virago, 1991.

Brohi, A. K. *Islam in the Modern World*. 2nd ed. Lahore, Pakistan: Publishers United, 1975.

Bromley, Simon. *Rethinking Middle East Politics: State Formation and Development*. Cambridge: Polity Press, 1994.

Brooks, Geraldine. *Nine Parts of Desire: The Hidden World of Islamic Women*. New York: Anchor Books, 1995.

Brown, Lester. *World without Borders*. New York: Vintage Books, 1972.

Brown, Robert McAfee. *Religion and Violence*. 2nd ed. Philadelphia: Westminster Press, 1987.

Brynen, Rex. *Sanctuary and Survival: The PLO in Lebanon*. Boulder, Colo.: Westview Press, 1990.

————, Bahgat Korany, and Paul Noble. *Political Liberalization and Democratization in the Arab World*. Vol. 1. Boulder, Colo.: Lynne Rienner, 1995.

Bucaille, Maruice. *The Bible, the Quran and Science*. Indianapolis: North American Trust Publication, 1978.

Buchan, John. *The Greenmantle*. Hertfordshire, England: Wordsworth Classics, 1994.

Bukhari, Muhammad. *Imam Bukhari's Book of Muslim Morals and Manners*. Translated by Yusuf Talal DeLorenzo. Alexandria, Egypt: Al-Saadawi Publications, 1997.

Bukhari, Muhammad ibn Ismail al-Bukhari. *Sahih Al-Bukhari*. Translated by Muhammad Muhsin Khan. Al-Medina al-Munawara: Islamic University, 1974.

Bulliet, Richard, et al., eds. *Encyclopedia of the Modern Middle East*. 4 Vols. New York: Macmillan, 1996.

Burns, E. Bradford. *Latin America: A Concise Interpretive History*. 5th ed. Englewood Cliffs, N.J.: Prentice-Hall, 1990.

Burns, E. Bradford. *The Poverty of Progress: Latin America in the Nineteenth-Century*. Berkeley and Los Angeles: University of California Press, 1983.

Burton, John. *An Introduction to the Hadith*. Edinburgh: Edinburgh University Press, 1994.

Butterfield, Herbert. *Christianity and History*. New York: Charles Scribner's Sons, 1949.

Caldarola, Carlo, ed. *Religions and Societies: Asia and the Middle East*. The Hague: Mouton, 1982.

Candland, Christopher. *The Spirit of Violence: An Annotated Bibliography on Religious Violence*. New York: Harry Frank Guggenheim Foundation, 1993.

Caplan, Lionel, ed. *Studies in Religious Fundamentalism*. Albany: State University of New York Press, 1987.

Carey, Roane. *The New Intifada: Resisting Israel's Apartheid*. London and New York: Verso, 2001.

Cate, Curtis, ed. *Afghanistan: The Terrible Decade, 1978–1988*. New York: American Foundation for Resistance International, 1988.

Chandra, M. *Islamic Resurgence in Malaya*. Petaling Jaya, Malaysia: Penerbit Fajr Bakti, 1987.

Chaudhry, Kiren Aziz. *The Price of Wealth: Economies and Institutions in the Middle East*. Ithaca, N.Y.: Cornell University Press, 1997.

Chomsky, Noam. *The Fateful Triangle: The United States, Israel and the Palestinians*. Boston: South End Press, 1993.

Chopra, Pran, ed. *Role of the Indian Muslims in the Struggle for Freedom*. New Delhi: Light and Life Publishers, 1979.

Choueiri, Youssef M. *Islamic Fundamentalism*. Boston: Twayne Publishers, 1994.

Cigar, Norman. *Genocide in Bosnia: The Policy of "Ethnic Cleansing."* College Station: Texas A & M University Press, 1995.

Clegg, Claude A, III. *An Original Man: The Life and Times of Elijah Muhammad*. New York: St. Martin's Press, 1997.

Cleveland, William L. *History of the Modern Middle East*. 2nd ed. Boulder, Colo.: Westview Press, 2000.

Cogley, John. *Religion in a Secular Age*. New York: Frederick A. Praeger, 1968.

Cohen, Marc. *Under Crescent and Cross*. Princeton, N.J.: Princeton University Press, 1994.

Cole, Juan R. I., and Nikki R. Keddie, eds. *Shi'ism and Social Protest*. New Haven, Conn.: Yale University Press, 1986.

Connelly, Philip, and Robert Perlman. *The Politics of Scarcity: Resource Conflicts in International Relations*. London: Oxford University Press, 1975.

Cook, M. A. *Muhammad*. Oxford: Oxford University Press, 1983.

Cooley, John. *Payback: America's Long War in the Middle East*. Washington, D.C.: Brassey's, 1991.

———. *Unholy Wars: Afghanistan, America and International Terrorism*. London: Sterling Press, 2001.

Cooper, Mahmoud, and Nettler Cooper. *Islam and Modernity: Muslim Intellectuals Respond*. London: I. B. Tauris, 1998.

Cordesman, Anthony H. *Saudi Arabia: Guarding the Desert Kingdom*. Boulder, Colo.: Westview Press, 1997.

Cordovez, Diego, and Selig S. Harrison. *Out of Afghanistan*. London: Oxford University Press, 1995.

Coulson, Noel J. *Islamic Surveys: A History of Islamic Law*. Edinburgh: Edinburgh University Press, 1964.

Cragg, Kenneth. *The Mind of the Qur'an: Chapters in Reflection*. London: Allen and Unwin, 1973.

———. *The House of Islam*. Belmont, Calif.: Wadsworth, 1975.

Cragg, Kenneth, and Marston Speight. *Islam from Within: Anthology of a Religion*. Belmont, Calif.: Wadsworth, 1980.

Cragg, Kenneth. *Muhammad and the Christian*. London: Darton, Longman and Todd, 1984.

———. *Jesus and the Muslim: An Exploration*. London: Allen and Unwin, 1985.

———. *The Pen and the Faith*. London: Allen and Unwin, 1985.

———. *Readings in the Qur'an*. London: Collins, 1988.

———. *The Call of the Minaret*. 3rd ed. Oxford: Oneworld, 2000.

Crenshaw, Martha, and John Pimlott, eds. *Encyclopedia of World Terrorism*. Armonk, N.Y.: Sharpe Reference, 1997.

Crone, P. and M. Hinds. *God's Caliph: Religious Authority in the First Centuries of Islam*. Cambridge: Cambridge University Press, 1986.

Crow, Ralph, et al., eds. *Arab Nonviolent Political Struggle in the Middle East*. Boulder, Colo.: Lynne Rienner, 1990.

Cudsi, Alexander S., and Ali E. Hillal Dessouki, eds. *Islam and Power*. Baltimore: Johns Hopkins University Press, 1981.

Curtis, Michael, ed. *Religion and Politics in the Middle East*. Boulder, Colo.: Westview Press, 1981.

Curtis, Richard H. *A Changing Image: American Perceptions of the Arab-Israeli Dispute*. Washington, D.C.: American Educational Trust, 1982.

———. *Stealth PACs: How Israel's American Lobby Seeks to Control U.S. Middle East Policy*. Washington, D.C.: American Educational Trust, 1990.

Dabashi, Hamid. *Theology of Discontent: The Ideological Foundations of the Islamic Revolution in Iran*. New York: New York University Press, 1993.

Daniel, Norman. *Islam and the West: The Making of an Image*. Edinburgh: Edinburgh University Press, 1960.

———. *Islam, Europe and Empire*. Edinburgh: Edinburgh University Press, 1966.

Dar, Bashir Ahmed. *Why Pakistan?* Lahore, Pakistan: New Era Publications, 1950.

———. *Religious Thought of Sayyid Ahmad Khan*. Lahore, Pakistan: Shaikh Muhammad Ashraf, 1957.

Darwish, Adeed, ed. *Islam in Foreign Policy*. Cambridge: Cambridge University Press, 1983.

David, Ron. *Arabs and Israel for Beginners*. Enfield, England: Airlift Books, 1993.

Davies, James Chowning, ed. *When Men Revolt and Why: A Reader in Political Violence and Revolution*. New York: The Free Press, 1971.

Davis, Joyce. M. *Between Jihad and Salaam: Profiles in Islam*. New York: St. Martin's Press, 1997.

Dawisha, Adeed, ed. *Islam in Foreign Policy*. Cambridge: Cambridge University Press, 1983.

Dawood, N. J., trans. *The Koran*. 4th ed. Baltimore: Penguin Books, 1974.

Dekmejian, R. Hrair. *Egypt under Nasser: A Study in Political Dynamics*. Albany: State University of New York Press, 1971.

———. *Islam in Revolution: Fundamentalism in the Arab World*. Syracuse, N.Y.: Syracuse University Press, 1985.

Denny, Frederick M. *An Introduction to Islam*. New York: Macmillan, 1985.

————. *Islam and the Muslim Community*. San Francisco: Harper and Row, 1987.

Dessouki, Ali E. Hillal, and Alexandre S. Cudsi. *Islam and Power*. Baltimore: Johns Hopkins University Press, 1981.

————, ed. *Islamic Resurgence in the Arab World*. New York: Praeger, 1982.

Deutsch, Karl. W., Jorge I. Dominguez, and Hugh Heclo. *Comparative Government: Politics of Industrialized and Developing Nations*. Boston: Houghton Mifflin. 1982.

Diamond, L., ed. *Political Culture and Democracy in Developing Countries*. Boulder, Colo.: Lynne Rienner, 1993.

Diller, Daniel C., ed. *The Middle East*. 7th ed. Washington, D.C.: Congressional Quarterly, 1990.

Djait, Hichem. *Europe and Islam*. Berkeley and Los Angeles: University of California Press, 1985.

Doi, Abdur Rahman I. *Shari'ah: The Islamic Law*. London: Taha Publishers, 1984.

Donaldson, Dwight M. *The Shi'ite Religion*. London: Luzac, 1933.

Donohue, John L., and John L. Esposito, eds. *Islam in Transition: Muslim Perspectives*. New York: Oxford University Press, 1982.

Donzel, E. Van. *Islamic Desk Reference* (Compiled from *The Encyclopaedia of Islam*). New York: E. J. Brill, 1994.

Doran, Charles F., and Stephen W. Buck. *The Gulf, Energy and Global Security*. Boulder, Colo.: Lynne Rienner, 1991.

Dorman, W. A., and Mansour Farhang. *The U.S. Press and Iran: Foreign Policy and the Journalism of Deference*. Berkeley and Los Angeles: University of California Press, 1987.

Dorraj, Manochehr. *From Zarathustra to Khomeini: Populism and Dissent in Iran*. Boulder, Colo: Lynn Rienner, 1990.

Downing, J., A. Mohammadi, and A. Sreberny-Mohammadi. *Questioning the Media: A Critical Introduction*. Newbury Park, Calif.: Sage, 1990.

Dunn, Michael Collins. *Islamism and Secularism in North Africa*. Washington, D.C.: Center for Contemporary Arab Studies, Georgetown University, 1994.

Dunnigan, James F., and Austin Bay. *A Quick & Dirty Guide to War: Briefings on Present and Potential Wars*. Rev. ed. New York: William Morrow/Quill, 1991.

Dupree, Louis. *Afghanistan*. New Delhi: Rama Publishers, 1994.

Dwyer, Daisy Hilse, ed. *Law and Islam in the Middle East*. New York: Bergin & Garvey, 1990.

Dwyer, James, David Kocieniewski, Deidre Murphy, and Peg Tyre. *Two Seconds under the World: Terror Comes to America—The Conspiracy behind the World Trade Center Bombing*. New York: Crown, 1994.

Eaton, Charles Le Gai. *Islam and the Destiny of Man*. Cambridge: Islamic Texts Society, 1994.

Eaton, Richard M. *Islamic History as Global History*. Washington, D.C.: American Historical Association, 1990.

Edward, David L. *Religion and Change*. New York: Harper and Row, 1969.

Ehteshami, Anoushiravan. *After Khomeini: The Iranian Second Republic*. London: Routledge, 1994.

Eickelman, Dale F., ed. *Pilgrimage, Migration and Religious Imagination*. Berkeley and Los Angeles: University of California Press, 1990.

Eickelman, Dale F., and James Piscatori. *Muslim Politics*. Princeton, N.J.: Princeton University Press, 1996.

Eickelman, Dale F. *The Middle East and Central Asia: An Anthropological Approach*. 3rd ed. Upper Saddle River, N.J.: Prentice-Hall, 1998.

Eisenberg, Laura Zittrain, and Neil Caplan. *Negotiating Arab-Israeli Peace: Patterns, Problems, Possibilities*. Bloomington: Indiana University Press, 1998.

Eisenstadt, S. N., ed. *Post Traditional Societies*. New York: Norton, 1972.

Elias, Jamal. *Islam*. Upper Saddle River, N.J.: Prentice-Hall, 1999.

Ellis, Kail C., ed. *The Vatican, Islam and the Middle East*. Syracuse, N.Y.: Syracuse University Press, 1987.

Emerick, Yahiya. *The Complete Idiot's Guide to Understanding Islam*. Indianapolis: Alpha Books, 2002.

Enayat, Hamid. *Modern Islamic Political Thought*. Austin: University of Texas Press, 1980.

Endress, Gerard. *An Introduction to Islam*. Translated by Carole Hillenbrand. New York: Columbia University Press, 1988.

Engineer, Asghar Ali. *The Islamic State*. New Delhi: Vikas Publishing House, 1980.

———. ed. *Islam in South and Southeast Asia*. Delhi: Ajanta, 1983.

Esack, Farid. *Quran, Liberation, and Pluralism*. Oxford: Oneworld Publications, 1997.

Esfandiari, Haleh. *Reconstructed Lives: Women and Iran's Islamic Revolution*. Baltimore: Johns Hopkins University Press, 1991.

Esposito, John L., ed. *Islam in Asia: Religion, Politics, and Society*. New York: Oxford University Press, 1978.

———. *Islam and Development: Religion and Sociopolitical Change*. Syracuse, New York: Syracuse University Press, 1980.

———. *Women in Muslim Family Law*. Syracuse, N.Y.: Syracuse University Press, 1982.

———, ed. *Voices of Resurgent Islam*. New York: Oxford University Press, 1983.

———, ed. *The Iranian Revolution: Its Global Impact*. Miami: Florida International University Press, 1990.

———, ed. *The Oxford Encyclopedia of the Modern Islamic World*. 4 Vols. New York: Oxford University Press, 1995.

Esposito, John L., and John O. Voll. *Islam and Democracy*. New York: Oxford University Press, 1996.

Esposito, John L. *Political Islam: Revolution, Radicalism, or Reform?* Boulder, Colo.: Lynne Rienner, 1997.

———. *Islam and Politics*. 4th ed. Syracuse, N.Y.: Syracuse University Press, 1998.

———. *Islam: The Straight Path*. 4th ed. New York: Oxford University Press, 1984, 1998.

———. *The Islamic Threat: Myth or Reality?* 3rd ed. New York: Oxford University Press, 1999.

———, ed. *The Oxford History of Islam*. New York: Oxford University Press, 1999.

Esposito, John L., and John Voll. *Makers of Contemporary Islam*. New York: Oxford University Press, 2001.

Evans-Pritchard, E. E. *The Sanusi of Cyrenaica*. Oxford: Clarendon Press, 1949.

Ewans, Martin. *Afghanistan: A Short History of Its People and Politics*. New York: HarperCollins, 2002.

Faaland, J., and J. R. Parkinson. *The Political Economy of Development*. New York: St. Martin's Press, 1986.

Fakhry, Majid. *Ethical Theories in Islam*. Leiden, The Netherlands: E. J. Brill, 1991.

Fandy, Mamoun. *Saudi Arabia and the Politics of Dissent*. New York: St. Martin's Press, 1999.

Farah, Caesar. *Islam: Beliefs and Observances*. 6th ed. New York: Barron's Educational Series, 2000.

Farah, Tawfic E. *Pan-Arabism: The Continuing Debate*. Boulder, Colo.: Westview Press, 1987.

Farhang, Mansour. *U.S. Imperialism: The Spanish-American War to the Iranian Revolution*. Boston: South End Press, 1981.

Faruki, Kemal A. *Islam Today and Tomorrow*. Karachi: Pakistan Publishing House, 1974.

―――. *The Constitutional and Legal Role of the Ulema*. Karachi, Pakistan: Ma'aref Ltd., 1979.

Al-Faruqi, Isma'il Raji. *Islam*. Niles, Ill: Argus, 1979.

―――. *Sources of Islamic Thought: Three Epistles on Tawhid by Muhammad ibn Abd al-Wahhab*. Indianapolis: American Trust Publications, 1980.

Al-Faruqi, Isma'il Raji, and A. H. AbuSulayman. *The Islamization of Knowledge: General Principles and Workplan*. Herndon, Va.: International Institute of Islamic Thought, 1981.

Al-Faruqi, Isma'il Raji. *Islamization of Knowledge*. Herndon, Va.: International Institute of Islamic Thought, 1982.

―――. *Tawhid: Its Implications for Thought and Life*. Herndon, Va.: International Institute of Islamic Thought, 1982.

―――., ed. *Essays in Islamic and Comparative Studies, Islamic Thought and Culture, Trialogue of the Abrahamic Faiths*. Herndon, Va.: International Institute of Islamic Thought, 1982.

Al-Faruqi, Isma'il Raji, and Lois Lami Al-Faruqi. *The Cultural Atlas of Islam*. New York: Macmillan, 1986.

Faruqi, M. I. *Jama'at-e-Islami in Pakistan*. Lahore, Pakistan: Secretary, Information Bureau of Jama'at-e-Islami, 1957.

Faruqi, Ziya ul Hasan. *The Deoband School and the Demand for Pakistan*. Bombay: Asia Publishing House, 1963.

Fernea, Elizabeth Warnock, and Basima Qattan Bezirgan, eds. *Middle Eastern Muslim Women Speak*. Austin: University of Texas Press, 1977.

Fernea, Elizabeth Warnock, ed. *Women and the Family in the Middle East*. Austin: University of Texas Press, 1985.

―――. *In Search of Islamic Feminism*. New York: Doubleday, 1998.

Firestone, Reuven. *Jihad: The Origin of Holy War in Islam*. New York: Oxford University Press, 1999.

Fischer, Michael M. J. *Iran: From Religious Dispute to Revolution*. Cambridge, Mass.: Harvard University Press, 1980.

Fischer, Michael M. J., and M. Abedi. *Debating Muslims: Cultural Dialogues in Post-Modernity and Tradition*. Madison: University of Wisconsin Press, 1990.

Fisk, Robert. *Pity the Nation: The Abduction of Lebanon*. New York: Atheneum, 1990.

Folkertsma, Marvin J., Jr. *Ideology and Leadership*. Englewood Cliffs, N.J.: Prentice-Hall. 1988.

Foster, Richard H., and Robert V. Edington. *Viewing International Relations and World Politics*. Englewood Cliffs, N.J.: Prentice-Hall. 1985.

Frangi, Abdallah. *The PLO and Palestine*. Translated by Paul Knight. London: Zed Books, 1983.

Freedman, Lawrence, and Efraim Karsh. *The Gulf Conflict, 1990–1991: Diplomacy and War in the New World Order*. London: Faber and Faber, 1993.

Freedman, Robert O. *The Middle East after the Israeli Invasion of Lebanon*. Syracuse, N.Y.: Syracuse University Press, 1985.

―――, ed. *The Intifada: Its Impact on Israel, the Arab World, and the Superpowers*. Miami: Florida International University Press, 1991.

Friedlander, J. *The Middle East: The Image and Reality*. Berkeley and Los Angeles: University of California Press, 1980.

Friedman, Isiah. *Palestine: A Twice-Promised Land?* New Brunswick, N.J.: Transaction Publishers, 2000.

Friedman, Robert I. *Sheik Abdel Rahman, the World Trade Center Bombing and the CIA.* Westfield, N.J.: Open Media, 1993.

Friedman, Thomas L. *From Beirut to Jerusalem.* 2nd ed. New York: Anchor Books, 1995.

———. *The Lexus and the Olive Tree: Understanding Globalization.* New York: Farrar, Straus and Giroux, 1999.

Friedmann, Yohanan. *Shaykh Ahmad Sirhindi: An Outline of His Thought and the Study of His Life in the Eyes of Posterity.* Montreal: McGill-Queen's University Press, 1971.

Fromkin, David. *A Peace to End All Peace: Creating the Modern Middle East.* New York: Henry Holt, 1989; reprint 2000.

Frye, Richard N. *Islam and the West.* The Hague: Mouton, 1957.

Fukuyama, Francis. *The End of History and the Last Man.* London: Penguin, 1992.

Fyzee, Asaf A. *Outlines of Muhammadan Law.* 2nd ed. London: Oxford University Press.

———. *A Modern Approach to Islam.* Bombay: Asia Publishing House, 1963.

Gall, Carlotta, and Thomas de Waal. *Chechnya: Calamity in the Caucasus.* New York: New York University Press, 1998.

Gankovsky, Y. U., and Moskalenko, V. N. *The Three Constitutions of Pakistan.* Lahore, Pakistan: People's Publishing House, 1978.

Gardell, Mattias. *In the Name of Elijah Muhammad: Louis Farrakhan and the Nation of Islam.* Durham, N.C.: Duke University Press, 1996.

Gardezi, Hassan, and Jamil Rashid, eds. *Pakistan: The Roots of Dictatorship.* London: Zed Books, 1983.

Garnham, David, and Mark Tessler, eds. *Democracy, War, and Peace in the Middle East.* Bloomington: Indiana University Press, 1995.

Gates, Robert M. *From the Shadows.* New York: Touchstone, 1997.

Gauhar, Altaf, ed. *The Challenge of Islam.* London: Islamic Council of Europe, 1978.

Gause, F. Gregory, III. *Oil Monarchies: Domestic and Security Challenges in the Arab Gulf States.* New York: Council on Foreign Relations Press, 1994.

Gee, John R. *Unequal Conflict: The Palestinians and Israel.* Northampton, Mass.: Olive Branch Press/Interlink, 1998.

Geertz, Clifford. *Islam Observed: Religious Development in Morocco and Indonesia.* Chicago: University of Chicago Press, 1968.

Gellner, Ernest. *Muslim Society.* Cambridge: Cambridge University Press, 1981.

———. *Postmodernism, Reason and Religion.* London and New York: Routledge, 1992.

Genieve, Abdo. *No God but God: Egypt and the Triumph of Islam.* New York: Oxford University Press, 2000.

George, T. *Revolt in Mindanao.* Kuala Lumpur: Oxford University Press, 1980.

Germanus, Julius. *Modern Movements in the World of Islam.* Lahore, Pakistan: Al Baruni, 1978.

Gerner, Deborah J. *One Land, Two Peoples: The Conflict over Palestine.* 2nd ed. Boulder, Colo.: Westview Press, 1994.

Ghadbian, Najib. *Democratization and the Islamist Challenge in the Arab World.* Boulder, Colo.: Westview Press, 1997.

Ghanea-Bassiri, Kambiz. *Competing Visions of Islam in the United States: A Study of Los Angeles.* Westport, Conn.: Greenwood Press, 1997.

Ghareeb, E., ed. *Split Vision: The Portrayal of Arabs in the American Media.* Washington, D.C.: American-Arab Affairs Council, 1983.

Al-Ghazali, Sheikh Muhammad. *Journey through the Quran.* London: Dar Al-Taqwa, 1998.

Gibb, Hamilton A. R. *Modern Trends in Islam.* Chicago: University of Chicago Press, 1947.

Gibb, Hamilton A. R., and Harold Bowen. *Islamic Society and the West.* Vol. 1, Part II. London: Oxford University Press, 1957.

Gibb, Hamilton A. R., *Mohammedanism: An Historical Survey*. London: Oxford University Press, 1970.

Gibb, Hamilton A. R., and J. H. Kramers. *The Shorter Encyclopedia of Islam*. Leiden, The Netherlands: E. J. Brill, 1974.

Gilani, Riaz-ul-Hasan. *The Reconstruction of Legal Thought in Islam*. Rev. and Enlarged ed. Lahore, Pakistan: Idara Tarjuman al-Quran, 1977.

Gilbert, Martin. *The Routledge Atlas of the Arab-Israeli Conflict*. London: Routledge, 1996.

Gilles, Kel. *Allah in the West: Islamic Movements in America and Europe*. Stanford, Calif.: Stanford University Press, 1997.

Gilmour, David. *Dispossessed: The Ordeal of the Palestinians*. London: Sedgwick and Jackson, 1980.

Gilsenan, Michael. *Recognizing Islam: Religion and Society in the Modern Arab World*. 2nd ed. New York: I. B. Tauris, 2000.

Girardet, Edward, ed. *Afghanistan*. Geneva, Switzerland: Crosslines, 1998.

Gittings, John, ed. *Beyond the Gulf War: The Middle East and the New World Order*. London: Catholic Institute of International Relations, 1991.

Gladney, Dru C. *Muslim Chinese: Ethnic Nationalism in the People's Republic*. Cambridge, Mass.: Harvard University Press, 1994.

Gledhill, Ahan. *Pakistan: The Developments of Its Laws and Constitution*. London: Stevens & Sons, 1957.

Gohari, M. J. *The Taliban's Ascent to Power*. New York: Oxford University Press, 2001.

Goldberg, Ellis, Resat Kasaba, and Joel S. Migdal, eds. *Rules and Rights in the Middle East: Democracy, Law, and Society*. Seattle: University of Washington Press, 1993.

Goldschmidt, Arthur, Jr. *A Concise History of the Middle East*. 7th ed. Boulder, Colo.: Westview Press, 2002.

Goldziher, Ignaz. *Introduction to Islamic Theology and Law*. Translated by Andras and Ruth Hamori. Princeton, N.J.: Princeton University Press, 1981.

Goodson, Larry P. *Afghanistan's Endless War: State Failure, Regional Politics and the Rise of the Taliban*. Seattle: University of Washington Press, 2001.

Goodwin, Jan. *Price of Honor*. New York: Plume, 1995.

Gopinath, Meenakshi. *Pakistan in Transition: Political Development and Rise to Power of the Pakistan's People's Party*. New Delhi: Manohar Book Service, 1975.

Gordon, Joel S. *Nasser's Blessed Movement: Egypt's Free Officers and the July Revolution*. New York: Columbia University Press, 1997.

Gowers, Andrew, and Tony Walker. *Behind the Myth: Yasser Arafat and the Palestinian Revolution*. Northampton, Mass.: Olive Branch Press/Interlink, 1991.

Gowing, P., ed. *Understanding Islam and Muslims in the Philippines*. Quezon City: New Day, 1988.

Gran, Peter. *Islamic Roots of Capitalism: Egypt, 1760–1840*. Austin: University of Texas Press, 1979.

Greenberg, B. S., ed. *Desert Storm and the Mass Media*. Cresskill, N.J.: Hampton Press, 1993.

Gresh, Alain, and Vidal Dominique. *An A to Z of the Middle East*. London: Zed Books, 1990.

Grew, Raymond, ed. *Crises of Political Development in Europe and the United States*. Princeton, N.J.: Princeton University Press, 1978.

Griffin, Michael. *Reaping the Whirlwind: The Taliban Movement in Afghanistan*. Sterling, Va.: Pluto Press, 2001.

Grimwood-Jones, Diana. *The Middle East and Islam: A Bibliographical Introduction*. Zug, Switzerland: Inter Documentation, 1979.

Grunebaum, Gustav von. *Medieval Islam.* 2nd ed. Chicago: University of Chicago Press, 1954.

———. *Unity and Variety in Muslim Civilization.* Chicago: Chicago University Press, 1956.

———. *Modern Islam.* Westport, Conn.: Greenwood Press, 1962.

Guazzone, Laura, ed. *The Islamist Dilemma: The Political Role of Islamist Movements in the Contemporary Arab World.* Reading, Mass.: Ithaca Press, 1995.

———, ed. *The Middle East in Global Change: The Politics and Economics of Interdependence versus Fragmentation.* New York: St. Martin's Press, 1997.

Gurr, Ted. *Why Men Rebel.* Princeton, N.J.: Princeton University Press, 1970.

Habib, John S. *Ibn Saud's Warriors of Islam: The Ikhwan of Najd and Their Role in the Creation of the Saudi Kingdom.* Leiden, The Netherlands: E. J. Brill, 1978.

Haddad, Yvonne Yazbeck. *Contemporary Islam and the Challenge of History.* Albany: State University of New York Press, 1982.

Haddad, Yvonne Yazbeck, Byran Haines, and Ellison Findly, eds. *The Islamic Impact.* Syracuse, New York: University Press, 1984.

Haddad, Yvonne Yazbeck, and E. Findly, eds. *Women, Religion and Social Change.* Albany: State University of New York, 1985.

Haddad, Yvonne Yazbeck. *A Century of Islam in America.* Washington, D.C.: Middle East Institute, 1986.

Haddad, Yvonne Yazbeck, and Adair Lummis. *Islamic Values in the United States: A Comparative Study.* New York: Oxford University Press, 1987.

Haddad, Yvonne Yazbeck. *The Muslims of America.* New York: Oxford University Press, 1991.

Haddad, Yvonne Yazbeck, and Jane Smith I. *Muslim Communities in North America.* New York: State University of New York Press, 1994.

Haddad, Yvonne Yazbeck et al., eds. *Christian-Muslim Encounters.* Gainesville: University Press of Florida, 1995.

Haddad, Yvonne Yazbeck, and John Esposito, eds. *Islam, Gender and Social Change.* New York: Oxford University Press, 1998.

———. *Muslims on the Americanization Path?* Oxford: Oxford University Press, 2000.

Hague, Rod, and Martin Harrop. *Political Science: A Comparative Introduction.* 3rd ed. New York: Palgrave/St. Martin's Press, 2001.

Hale, Sondra. *Gender Politics in Sudan.* Boulder, Colo.: Westview Press, 1996.

Haleem, Harfiya Abdel et al., eds. *The Crescent and the Cross: Muslim and Christian Approaches to War and Peace.* New York: St. Martin's Press, 1998.

Halliday, Fred, and Hamza Alavi, eds. *State and Ideology in the Middle East and Pakistan.* London: Macmillan, 1988.

Halliday, Fred. *Islam and the Myth of Confrontation: Religion and Politics in the Middle East.* New York: I. B. Tauris, 1996.

———. *Nation and Religion in the Middle East.* London: Saqi Books, 2000.

Halm, Heinz. *Shi'a Islam: From Religion to Revolution.* Translated from the German by Allison Brown. Princeton, N.J.: Marcus Wiener Publishers, 1997.

Halpern, Manfred. *The Politics of Social Change in the Middle East and North Africa.* Princeton, N.J.: Princeton University Press, 1963.

Hamidullah, Muhammad. *The Muslim Conduct of State.* 5th ed. Lahore, Pakistan: Shaikh Mohd Ashraf, 1963.

———. *Introduction to Islam.* 5th ed. Enlarged. Chicago: Kazi Publications, 1981.

Hanafi, Hassan. *Islam in the Modern World.* 2 Vols. Cairo: Anglo-Egyptian Bookshop, 1995.

Haneef, Suzanne. *What Everyone Should Know about Islam and Muslims.* Chicago: Kazi Publications, 1979.

Haq, Mahmudul. *Muhammad Abduh: A Study of Modern Thinkers of Egypt.* Aligarh, India: Institute of Islamic Studies, Aligarh Muslim University, 1978.

Haq, Moinul. *Islamic Thought and Movements in the Subcontinent: 711–1947.* Karachi, Pakistan: Pakistan Historical Society, 1979.

Hardy, Peter. *The Muslims of British India.* Cambridge: Cambridge University Press, 1972.

Hardy, Roger. *Arabia after the Storm: Internal Stability of the Gulf Arab States.* London: Royal Institute of International Affairs, 1992.

Harik, Iliya, and Dennis J. Sullivan, eds. *Privatization and Liberalization in the Middle East.* Bloomington: Indiana University Press, 1992.

Harrison, Lawrence E., and Samuel P. Huntington, eds. *Culture Matters: How Values Shape Human Progress.* New York: Basic Books, 2001.

Hart, Alan. *Arafat: A Political Biography.* Bloomington: Indiana University Press, 1989.

Hasan, Asthma Gull. *American Muslims: The New Generation.* New York: Continuum, 2000.

Hasan, M., and A. Waheed. *An Introduction of the Study of Islam: 1001 Questions and Answers.* Karachi, Pakistan: Ferozsons, Ltd., no date.

Hassan, Masud-ul-. *Life of Iqbal.* 2 Vols. Lahore, Pakistan: Ferozsons Ltd., 1978.

Hassan, M. K. *Muslim Intellectual Responses to "New Order" Modernization in Indonesia.* Kuala Lumpur: Dewan Bahasa Pustaka, 1980.

Hathout, Hassan. *Reading the Muslim Mind.* Los Angeles: Minaret Publishing House, 1995.

Haynes, Jeff. *Religion in Third World Politics.* Boulder, Colo.: Lynne Rienner, 1994.

———. *Religion in Global Politics.* New York: Longman, 1998.

Hefner, Robert W., ed. *Islam in an Era of Nation-States: Politics and Religious Renewal in Muslim Southeast Asia.* Honolulu: University of Hawaii Press, 1997.

———. *Civil Islam.* Princeton: Princeton University Press, 2000.

Heikel, Mohammed. *The Road to Ramadan.* New York: Quadrangle, 1975.

———. *The Return of the Ayatollah: The Iranian Revolution from Mossadeq to Khomeini.* London: Andre Deutsch, 1981.

———. *Autumn of Fury: The Assassination of Sadat.* London: Andre Deutsch, 1983.

Held, Colbert C. *Middle Eastern Patterns: Places, Peoples, and Politics.* 3rd ed. Boulder, Colo.: Westview Press, 2000.

Helms, Christine Moss. *The Cohesion of Saudi Arabia: Evolution of Political Identity.* Baltimore: Johns Hopkins University Press, 1981.

Heper, Metin, and Raphael Israeli. *Islam and Politics in the Modern Middle East.* New York: St. Martin's Press, 1984.

Hinebusch, Raymond, Jr. *Egyptian Politics under Sadat.* 2nd ed. Boulder, Colo.: Lynne Rienner, 1988.

Hippler, Jochen, and Andreas Leug, eds. *The Next Threat: Western Perceptions of Islam.* London: Pluto Press, 1995.

Hiro, Dilip. *Iran under the Ayatollah.* London: Routledge and Kegan Paul, 1985.

———. *Holy Wars: The Rise of Islamic Fundamentalism.* New York: Routledge, 1989.

———. *Sharing the Promised Land.* London: Hodder, 1997.

Hirst, David. *Sadat.* London: Faber & Faber, 1981.

Hirst, David, and Irene Beeson. *The Gun and the Olive Branch: The Roots of Violence in the Middle East.* 2nd ed. London: Faber and Faber, 1984.

Hitti, Philip. *Makers of Arab History.* New York: Harper and Row, 1968.

Hodgson, Marshall S. G. *The Venture of Islam*. 3 Vols. Chicago: University of Chicago Press, 1974.

Hoffman, Bruce. *"Holy Terror": The Implications of Terrorism Motivated by a Religious Imperative*. Santa Monica, Calif.: Rand Corporation, 1993.

Hoge, James F, Jr. et al., eds. *How Did This Happen? Terrorism and the New War*. New York: Public Affairs Reports/Council on Foreign Relations, 2001.

Holt, P. M. *The Mahdist State in the Sudan*. Oxford: Oxford University Press, 1971.

———, K. S. Ann, and Bernard Lewis, eds. *The Cambridge History of Islam*. 4 Vols. New York: Cambridge University Press, 1977.

Hooker, M. B., ed. *Islam in Southeast Asia*. Leiden, The Netherlands: E. J. Brill, 1983.

Hopkirk, Peter. *The Great Game: The Struggle for Empire in Central Asia*. New York: Kodansha, 1992.

Hourani, Albert. *Arabic Thought in the Liberal Age, 1798–1939*. 2nd ed. London: Oxford University Press, 1979. Reprint 1983.

———. *Islam in European Thought*. Cambridge: Cambridge University Press, 1991.

———. *A History of the Arab Peoples*. Cambridge, Mass: Belknap Press of Harvard University Press, 1991.

Howard, Lawrence, ed. *Terrorism: Roots, Impact, Response*. New York: Praeger, 1992.

Huband, Mark. *Warriors of the Prophet: The Struggle for Islam*. Boulder, Colo.: Westview Press, 1998.

Hudson, Michael C. *Arab Politics: The Search for Legitimacy*. New Haven, Conn.: Yale University Press, 1977.

Hudson, Michael C., and R. Wolfe, eds. *The American Media and the Arabs*. Washington, D.C.: Georgetown University Press, 1980.

Hughes, William, ed. *Western Civilization: Pre-History through the Reformation*. Vol. 1. 4th ed. Guilford, Conn.: Dushkin, 1987.

Humphreys, R. Stephen. *Islamic History: A Framework for Inquiry*. Princeton, N.J.: Princeton University Press, 1991.

Hunter, Shireen T. *OPEC and the Third World: Politics of Aid*. Bloomington: Indiana University Press, 1984.

———, ed. *The Politics of Islamic Revivalism: Diversity and Unity*. Bloomington: Indiana University Press, 1988.

———. *Iran and the World: Continuity in a Revolutionary Decade*. Bloomington: Indiana University Press, 1990.

———. *Iran after Khomeini*. New York: Praeger/CSIS, 1992.

———. *The Transcaucasus in Transition: Nation-Building and Conflict*. Washington, D.C.: CSIS, 1994.

———. *Turkey at the Crossroads: Islamic Past or European Future?* Brussels: Center for European Policy Studies (CEPS) Paper No. 61, 1995.

———. *The Algerian Crisis: Origins, Evolution and Lessons for the Maghreb and Europe*. Brussels: Center for European Policy Studies (CEPS) Paper No. 63, 1996.

Hunter, W. W. *The Indian Musalmans*. Delhi: Comrade Publishers, 1945.

Huntington, Samuel P. *Political Order in Changing Societies*. New Haven, Conn.: Yale University Press, 1968.

———. *The Clash of Civilizations and the Remaking of World Order*. New York: Simon and Schuster, 1996.

Hurewitz, J. C. *The Persian Gulf: After Iran's Revolution*. New York: Foreign Policy Association's Headline Series No. 244, April 1979.

Husain, Akbar. *The Revolution in Iran*. East Sussex, England: Wayland Publishers, 1986.

Husain, Asaf. *Islamic Movements in Egypt, Iran and Pakistan: An Annotated Bibliography.* London: Mansell, 1983.

————. *Political Perspectives on the Muslim World.* New York: St. Martin's Press, 1984.

Husain, Mir Zohair. *Global Islamic Politics.* New York: HarperCollins College, 1995.

Husaini, Ishak Musa. *The Brethren: The Greatest Modern Islamic Movements.* Beirut, Lebanon: Khayat College Book Cooperative, 1956.

Hussain, Asad, et al. *Muslims in America: Opportunities and Challenges.* Chicago: International Strategy and Policy Institute, 1996.

Hussain, Riaz. *The Politics of Iqbal: A Study of His Political Thoughts and Actions.* Lahore, Pakistan: Islamic Book Services, 1977.

Hussein, Asaf. *Islamic Iran: Revolution and Counterrevolution.* New York: St. Martin's Press, 1985.

Ibrahim, Anwar. *The Asian Renaissance.* Singapore: Times Books International, 1996.

Ibrahim, Ibrahim. *Arab Resources: The Transformation of Society.* London: Croom Helm, 1983.

Ibrahim, Saad Eddin. *The New Arab Social Order: A Study of the Social Impact of Oil Wealth.* Boulder, Colo.: Westview Press, 1982.

————. *Egypt, Islam and Democracy: Twelve Critical Essays.* Cairo, Egypt: American University of Cairo Press, 1996.

Ignatieff, Michael. *The Warrior's Honor: Ethnic War and the Modern Conscience.* New York: Holt, 1998.

Ikram, S. M. *Muslim Civilization in India.* New York: Columbia University Press, 1964.

————. *Modern Muslim India and the Birth of Pakistan (1858–1951).* Lahore, Pakistan: Sheikh Mohammad Ashraf, 1965.

Iqbal, Allama Muhammad. *The Reconstruction of Religious Thought in Islam.* Lahore, Pakistan: Shaikh Ashraf Publishers, 1962. Reprinted 1983.

————, ed. *Letters of Iqbal to Jinnah.* Lahore, Pakistan: Sheikh Mohammad Ashraf Publishers, 1942.

Iqbal, Javid. *Ideology of Pakistan.* Karachi, Pakistan: Ferozsons, 1971.

Irfani, Suroosh. *Revolutionary Islam in Iran: Popular Liberation or Religious Dictatorship?* London: Zed Books, 1983.

Isby, David. *War in a Distant Country: Afghanistan, Invasion and Resistance.* London: Arms and Armour Press, 1989.

Ibn-Ishaq, Muhammad. *The Life of Muhammad (Sirat al-Nabi).* Calcutta: Oxford University Press, 1978.

Israeli, Raphael, ed. *The Crescent in the East: Islam in Asia Major.* London: Curzon Press, 1983.

Israeli, Raphael, and Anthony H. Johns, ed. *Islam in Asia,* Vol. 2. *Southeast and East Asia.* Boulder, Colo.: Westview Press, 1984.

Israeli, Raphael. *Man of Defiance: A Political Biography of Anwar Sadat.* Totown, N.J.: Barnes & Noble, 1985.

Izutsu, Toshihiko. *Ethico-Religious Concepts in the Quran.* Montreal: McGill University Press, 1966.

————. *God and Man in the Koran: Semantics of the Koranic Weltanschauung.* New York: Arno Press, 1980.

Jaber, Hala. *Hezbollah: Born with a Vengeance.* New York: Columbia University Press, 1997.

Jafri, S. Hussain M. *Origins and Early Development of Shi'ah Islam.* London and New York: Longman, 1979.

Jameelah, Maryam. *Islam and Modernism.* Lahore, Pakistan: Mohammad Yusuf Khan, 1971.

————. *Who is Maudoodi?* Lahore, Pakistan: Mohammad Yusuf Khan Publishers, 1973.

————. *Islam in Theory and Practice.* Lahore, Pakistan: Mohammad Yusuf Khan, 1976.

————. *Islam and Modern Man.* Lahore, Pakistan: Mohammad Yusuf Khan, 1976.

————. *Islam and the Muslim Woman Today.* Lahore, Pakistan: Mohammad Yusuf Khan, 1976.

————. *Westernization versus Muslims.* Lahore, Pakistan: Mohammad Yusuf Khan, 1978.

————. *Islam and Western Society.* New Delhi: Adam Publishers, 1982.

————. *Memoirs of Childhood (1945–1962): The Story of One Western Convert's Quest for the Truth.* Lahore, Pakistan: Mohammad Yusuf Khan, 1982.

————. *At Home in Pakistan (1962–89).* Lahore, Pakistan: Mohammad Yusuf Khan, 1990.

Jankowski, James, ed. *Rethinking Nationalism in the Arab Middle East.* New York: Columbia University Press, 1997.

Jansen, G. H. *Militant Islam.* New York: Harper, 1979.

Jansen, Johannes J. G. *The Neglected Duty: The Creed of Sadat's Assassins and Islamic Resurgence in the Middle East.* New York: Macmillan, 1986.

Jeffery, Arthur. *Islam: Muhammad and His Religion.* New York: Library of Liberal Arts, 1958.

————. *A Reader on Islam.* The Hague, The Netherlands: Mouton, 1962.

Johnson, Nels. *Islam and the Politics of Meaning in Palestinian Nationalism.* London: Kegan Paul, 1982.

Jones, Walter S. *The Logic of International Relations.* 8th ed. New York: Longman, 1997.

Juergensmeyer, Mark, ed. *Violence and the Sacred in the Modern World.* London: Frank Cass, 1992.

————. *The New Cold War? Religious Nationalism Confronts the Secular State.* Berkeley and Los Angeles: University of California Press, 1993.

————. *Terror in the Mind of God: The Global Rise of Religious Violence.* Berkeley and Los Angeles: University of California Press, 2000.

Kamali, Muhammad Hashim. *Principles of Islamic Jurisprudence.* 2nd ed. Cambridge: Islamic Tests Society, 1991.

————. *Freedom of Expression in Islam.* Kuala Lumpur: Berita, 1994. Revised ed. Cambridge: Islamic Texts Society, 1997.

Kamalipour, Yahya R., and H. Mowlana. *Mass Media in the Middle East: A Comprehensive Handbook.* Westport, Conn.: Greenwood Press, 1994.

Kamalipour, Yahya R., ed. *The U.S. Media and the Middle East: Image and Perception.* Westport, Conn.: Praeger, 1997.

Kaplan, Robert D. *Soldiers of God: With the Mujahidin in Afghanistan.* Boston: Houghton Mifflin, 1990.

Karsh, Efraim, and Inari Rautsi. *Saddam Hussein: A Political Biography.* London: Brassey, 1991.

Katouzian, Homa. *Musaddiq and the Struggle for Power in Iran.* London: I. B. Tauris, 1990.

Kaufman, Burton I. *The Arab Middle East and the United States: Inter-Arab Rivalry and Superpower Diplomacy.* New York: Twayne Publishers, 1996.

Kayyali, A. W., ed. *Zionism, Imperialism, and Racism.* London: Croom Helm, 1979.

Kazemi, Farhad, ed. *The Iranian Revolution in Perspective.* Special edition of *Iranian Studies,* Vol. 13, Nos. 1–4, 1980.

Keddie, Nikki R., ed. *Scholars, Saints and Sufis: Muslim Religious Institutions in the Middle East since 1500.* Berkeley and Los Angeles: University of California Press, 1972.

————. *Sayyid Jamal al-Din "al-Afghani": A Political Biography.* Berkeley and Los Angeles: University of California Press, 1972.

Keddie, Nikki R., and Yann Richard. *Roots of Revolution: An Interpretive History of Modern Iran.* New Haven, Conn.: Yale University Press, 1981.

Keddie, Nikki R. *An Islamic Response to Imperialism: Political and Religious Writings of Sayyid Jamal al-Din "al-Afghani."* 2nd ed. Berkeley and Los Angeles: University of California Press, 1983.

———, ed. *Religion and Politics in Iran: Shi'ism from Quietism to Revolution.* New Haven, Conn.: Yale University Press, 1983.

Keddie, Nikki R., and Beth Baron, ed. *Women in Middle Eastern History.* New Haven, Conn.: Yale University Press, 1991.

Keddie, Nikki R. *Iran and the Muslim World.* London: Macmillan, 1995.

Kedourie, Elie. *Democracy and Arab Political Culture.* Washington, D.C.: Washington Institute for Near East Policy, 1992.

Kellner, Douglas. *The Persian Gulf T.V. War.* Boulder, Colo.: Westview Press, 1992.

Kelsay, John, and James Turner Johnson, eds. *Cross, Crescent and Sword: The Justification and Limitation of War in Western and Islamic Tradition.* New York: Greenwood Press, 1991.

———. *Islam and War: A Study in Comparative Ethics.* Louisville, Ky.: Westminster/John Knox Press, 1993.

Kennedy, Hugh. *The Prophet and the Age of the Caliphates: The Islamic Near East from the Sixth to the Eleventh Centuries.* London: Routledge, 1986.

Kepel, Gilles. *Muslim Extremism in Egypt: The Prophet and Pharaoh.* Translated by John Rothschild. Berkeley and Los Angeles: University of California Press, 1985.

———. *The Revenge of God: The Resurgence of Islam, Christianity and Judaism in the Modern World.* Translated by Alan Braley. University Park: Pennsylvania State University Press, 1994.

Kerr, Malcolm H. *Islamic Reform: The Political and Legal Theories of Mohammad Abduh and Rashid Rida.* Berkeley and Los Angeles: University of California Press, 1972.

Kettani, M. Ali. *In Muslim Minorities in the World Today.* London: Mansell, 1986.

Khadduri, Majid. *War and Peace in the Law of Islam.* Baltimore: Johns Hopkins University Press, 1955.

———. *The Islamic Law of Nations: Shaybani's Siya.* Baltimore: Johns Hopkins University Press, 1966.

———. *Political Trends in the Arab World.* Baltimore: Johns Hopkins Press, 1970.

———. *The Islamic Conception of Justice.* Baltimore: Johns Hopkins University Press, 1984.

Khadeer, Mohammad Abdul. *Ijma and Legislation in Islam.* Secunder abad, India: Shivaji Press, 1974.

Khalid, Jeraj. *Party Ki Tanzim-e-Nau (The Party's New Organization).* Lahore, Pakistan: S. N. A. Rizvi, 1974.

Khalidi, Rashid et al., eds. *The Origins of Arab Nationalism.* New York: Columbia University Press, 1991.

Khalidi, Rashid. *Palestinian Identity: The Construction of Modern National Consciousness.* New York: Columbia University Press, 1997.

Khalidi, Walid. *Conflict and Violence in Lebanon.* Cambridge: Harvard University Press, 1979.

al-Khalil, Samir. *The Republic of Fear.* London: Hutchinson/Radius Press, 1991.

Khan, Maulana Wahiduddin. *An Islamic Treasury of Virtues.* New Delhi: Goodword Books, 1999.

Khan, Muhammad Muhsin. *The Translation of the Meanings of Sahih Al-Bukhari.* Ankara, Turkey: Crescent Publishing House, 1976.

Khan, Muinuddin Ahmad. *History of the Faraidi Movement in Bengal (1818–1906).* Karachi, Pakistan: Pakistan Historical Society, 1965.

———. *Muslim Struggle for Freedom in Bengal: From Plassey to Pakistan, 1757–1947.* 2nd ed. Dacca, Bangladesh: Islamic Foundation Bangladesh, 1982.

Khan, Sardar Ali Ahmad, ed. *The Naqshbadis.* Sharaqpur Sharif, Pakistan: Darul Muballeghin Hazra, 1982.

Khatami, Muhammad. *Hope and Challenge: The Iranian President Speaks.* Binghamton, N.Y.: Institute of Global Cultural Studies, Binghamton University, 1997.

Khazen, Jihad B. *The Sadat Assassination: Background and Implications.* Monograph, Georgetown University's Center for Contemporary Arab Studies, Washington, D.C. November 1981.

Khomeini, Ayatollah Ruhollah. *Islamic Government.* Translated by the Joint Publications Research Service. New York: Manor Books, 1979.

———. *Islam and Revolution: Writings and Declarations of Imam Khomeini.* Translated and annotated by Hamid Algar. Berkeley, Calif.: Mizan Press, 1981.

Khouri, Fred J. *The Arab Israeli Dilemma.* 3rd ed. Syracuse, N.Y.: Syracuse University Press, 1985.

Khuri, Fuad. *Imams and Emirs: State, Religion and Sects in Islam.* London: Saqi Books, 1990.

Kimmerling, Baruch, and Joel Migdal. *The Palestinians: The Making of a People.* Cambridge, Mass.: Harvard University Press, 1994.

Kincross, Lord. *Ataturk.* London: Weidenfeld & Nicolson; New York: William Morrow, 1965.

Kipper, Judith, and Harold H. Saunders, eds. *The Middle East in Global Perspective.* Boulder, Colo.: Westview Press, 1991.

Kister, M. J. *Studies in Jahiliyya and Early Islam.* London: Variorum Reprints, 1980.

Klass, Rosanna, ed. *Afghanistan: The Great Game Revisited.* New York: Freedom House Press, 1987. Rev. ed. 1990.

Klausner Clara L. *A Concise History of the Arab-Israeli Conflict.* 3rd ed. Paramus, N.J.: Prentice-Hall, 1997.

Korbani, Agnes. *The Political Dictionary of Modern Middle East.* New York: University Press of America, 1995.

Kostiner, Joseph. *The Making of Saudi Arabia, 1916–1936: From Chieftaincy to Monarchical State.* New York: Oxford University Press, 1993.

Kotb, Sayed. *Social Justice in Islam.* Translated by John B. Hardie. Washington, D.C.: American Council of Learned Societies, 1953.

Kozlowski, Gregory C. *The Concise History of Islam and the Origin of Its Empires.* Acton, Mass.: Copley Publishing Group, 1991.

Kramer, Martin. *Political Islam.* The Washington Papers, Vol. 8, No. 73. Beverly Hills & London: Sage Publications, 1980.

———. *Islam Assembled.* New York: Columbia University Press, 1986.

———, ed. *Shi'ism, Resistance and Revolution.* Boulder, Colo.: Westview Press, 1987.

———. *Hezbollah's Vision of the West.* The Washington Institute Policy Papers, No. 16. Washington Institute for Near East Policy, 1989.

Kritzeck, James. *Sons of Abraham: Jews, Christians, and Moslems.* Baltimore: Helicon, 1965.

Krough, Peter F., and Mary C. McDavid, eds. *Palestinians under Occupation: Prospects for the Future.* Washington, D.C.: Georgetown University Press, 1989.

Kubbah, Abdul. *OPEC: Past and Present.* Vienna, Austria: Retro Economic Research Center, 1974.

Kumar, Satish. *The New Pakistan*. New Delhi: Vikas Publishing House, 1978.

Kurian, George Thomas. *Encyclopedia of the Third World*. 3rd ed. New York: Facts on File, 1987.

Lapidus, Ira. *A History of Islamic Societies*. New York: Cambridge University Press, 1988.

Lipman, Jonathan N. *Familiar Strangers: A History of Muslims in Northwest China*. Seattle: University of Washington Press, 1998.

Lacouture, Jean. *Nasser*. Translated by Daniel Hofstadter. New York: Knopf, 1973.

Lambton, Ann K. S. *State and Government in Medieval Islam*. Oxford: Oxford University Press, 1981.

Landau, J. *The Politics of Pan-Islam*. London: Clarendon Press, 1990.

Lapidus, Ira M. *Contemporary Islamic Movements in Historical Perspective*. Papers in International Affairs, No. 18. Berkeley: Institute of International Affairs, University of California, 1983.

———. *A History of Islamic Societies*. Cambridge: Cambridge University Press, 1988.

Laqueur, Walter. *Confrontation: The Middle East and World Politics*. New York: Quadrangle/New York Times Book Co., 1974.

Lacquer, Walter, and Barry Rubin, eds. *The Israel-Arab Reader: A Documentary History of the Middle East Conflict*. 6th ed. New York: Penguin Books, 2001.

Lassner, Jacob. *Islamic Revolution and Historical Memory*. American Oriental Series, Vol. 66. New Haven: American Oriental Society, 1986.

Lasswell, Harold, and Abraham Kaplan. *Power and Society*. New Haven, Conn.: Yale University Press, 1950.

Lateef, Khalid S. *The Holy Quran's Condemnation of the Racist and Un-Islamic Ideology of "The Lessons" of W. D. Fard and the Teachings of Minister Louis Farrakhan's "Nation of Islam."* Wheatley Heights, N.Y.: Americans for Justice and Positive Change, no date.

Lavan, Spencer. *The Ahmadiyah Movement: A History and Perspective*. Delhi: Manohar Book Service, 1974.

Lawrence, Bruce B. "Religion, Ideology, and Revolution: The Case of Post-1979 Iran." In L. D. Kliever, ed., *The Terrible Meek*. New York: Paragon Press, 1987.

Lawrence, Bruce B., ed. *The Rose and the Rock: Mystical and Rational Elements in the Intellectual History of South Asian Islam*. Durham, N.C.: Duke University Press, 1979.

———. *Defenders of God: The Fundamentalist Revolt against the Modern Age*. Columbia, S.C.: University of South Carolina Press, 1995.

———. *Shattering the Myth: Islam beyond Violence*. Princeton, N.J.: Princeton University Press, 1998.

Lederman, J. *Battlelines: The American Media and the Intifada*. New York: Henry Holt, 1992.

Lee, Martha F. *History of the Nation of Islam*. Lewiston, N.Y.: Edwin Mellon Press, 1988.

———. *The Nation of Islam: An American Millenarian Movement*. Syracuse, N.Y.: Syracuse University Press, 1996.

Lee, Robert D. *Overcoming Tradition and Modernity: The Search for Islamic Authenticity*. Boulder, Colo.: Westview Press, 1997.

Leiden, Carl, ed. *The Conflict of Traditionalism and Modernism in the Muslim Middle East*. Austin: University of Texas Press, 1966.

Leila, Ahmad. *Women and Gender in Islam: Historical Roots of a Modern Debate*. New Haven, Conn.: Yale University Press, 1992.

Lemberger, Mathew (Lazar). *The Question and Answer Guide to Judaism and Islam*. 2nd ed. Hollywood, Fl.: Lazar Publications, 1999.

Lenczowski, George. *The Middle East in World Affairs*. 4th ed. Ithaca: Cornell University Press, 1980.

———. *American Presidents and the Middle East*. Durham, N.C.: Duke University Press, 1990.

Lerner, Daniel. *The Passing of Traditional Society: Modernizing the Middle East*. Glencoe, Ill.: The Free Press, 1958.

Lesch, David W. *The Middle East and the United States: A Historical and Political Reassessment*. Boulder, Colo.: Westview Press, 1966.

Levtzion, Nehemia, and John O. Voll, eds. *Eighteenth-Century Renewal and Reform in Islam*. Syracuse, N.Y.: Syracuse University Press, 1987.

Lewis, Bernard, et al. *World of Islam: Faith, People, Culture*. London: Thames & Hudson, 1991.

———. *Arabs in History*. New York: Oxford University Press, 1993.

———. *The Middle East and the West*. New York: Harper and Row, 1970.

———. *The Political Language of Islam*. Chicago: University of Chicago Press, 1988.

———. *Islam and the West*. New York: Oxford University Press, 1994.

———. *The Shaping of the Modern Middle East*. New York: Oxford University Press, 1994.

———. *Cultures in Conflict: Christians, Muslims, and Jews in the Age of Discovery*. New York: Oxford University Press, 1996.

———. *The Middle East: A Brief History of the Last 2000 Years*. New York: Simon and Schuster, 1997.

Lewis, Bernard, et al., eds. *Islam, Judaism, and Christianity: Theological and Historical Affiliations*. New York: Markus Wiener, 1998.

Lewis, Bernard. *The Multiple Identities of the Middle East*. New York: Schocken Books, 2001.

———. *Middle East Mosaic: Fragments of Life, Letters, and History*. New York: Random House, 2001.

———. *Islam in History: Ideas, People, and Events in the Middle East*. New York: Open Court, 2001.

———. *What Went Wrong: Western Impact and Middle Eastern Response*. New York: Oxford University Press, 2001.

Lewis, Philip. *Islamic Britain: Religion, Politics, and Identity among British Muslims*. London: Tauris, 1994.

Lewisohn, Leonard. *The Heritage of Sufism*. Vols. 1–3. Oxford: Oneworld, 1999.

Lewy, Guenter. *Religion and Revolution*. New York: Oxford University Press, 1974.

Lincoln, Bruce, ed. *Religion, Rebellion, Revolution: An Interdisciplinary and Cross-Cultural Collection of Essays*. New York: St. Martin's Press, 1985.

———. *Death, War and Sacrifice: Studies in Ideology and Practice*. Chicago: University of Chicago Press, 1991.

Lincoln, C. Eric. *The Black Muslims in America*. Queens, N.Y.: Kayode Publications, 1991.

Lippman, Thomas W. *Understanding Islam: An Introduction to the Muslim World*. New York: Mentor Books, 1982.

———. *Islam: Politics and Religion in the Muslim World*. New York: Foreign Policy Association's Headline Series No. 258, March–April 1982.

———. *The Middle East: 2000 Years of History from the Rise of Christianity to the Present Day*. London: Weidenfeld & Nicolson, 1995.

———. *The Multiple Identities of the Middle East*. New York: Schocken Books, 2001.

———. *Egypt after Nasser: Sadat, Peace and the Mirage of Prosperity*. New York: Paragon House, 1989.

Lings, Martin. *Muhammad: His Life Based on the Earliest Sources*. London: Unwin Paperbacks, 1986.

Little, D. P. *Essays on Islamic Civilization*. Leiden, The Netherlands: E. J. Brill, 1976.

Lockman, Zachary, and Beinin, Joel, eds. *Intifada: The Palestinian Uprising against Israeli Occupation*. Boston: South End Press, 1989.

Lohbeck, Kurt. *Holy War, Unholy Victory: Eyewitness to the CIA's Secret War in Afghanistan*. Washington, D.C.: Regnery Gateway, 1993.

Lomax, Louis E. *When the Word Is Given: A Report on Elijah Muhammad, Malcolm X, and the Black Muslim World*. Westport, Conn.: Greenwood Press, 1979.

Lowrie, Arthur L., ed. *Islam, Democracy, the State and the West: A Roundtable with Dr. Hasan Turabi*. Tampa, Fla.: World and Islam Studies Enterprise, 1993.

Lukas, Yehuda, and Abdalla M. Battah, eds. *The Arab-Israeli Conflict: Two Decades of Change*. Boulder, Colo.: Westview Press, 1988.

Maalouf, Amin. *The Crusades through Arab Eyes*. Translated by Jon Rothschild. New York: Schocken Books, 1984.

Mabro, J. *Veiled Half-Truths: Western Travellers' Perceptions of Middle Eastern Women*. New York: I. B. Tauris, 1991.

Mackey, Sandra. *The Saudis: Inside the Desert Kingdom*. New York: NAL/Dutton, 1990.

———. *The Iranians: Persia, Islam, and the Soul of a Nation*. New York: Dutton, 1996.

Macridis, Roy C. *Contemporary Ideologies*. 5th ed. New York: HarperCollins, 1992.

Maddy-Weitzmann, Bruce, and Efraim Inbar, eds. *Religious Radicalism in the Greater Middle East*. London: Frank Cass, 1997.

Maddy-Weitzmann, Bruce et al., eds. *Middle East Contemporary Survey*. Vol. 21. Boulder, Colo.: Westview Press, 2000.

Madelung, Wilfred. *The Succession to Muhammad*. New York: Cambridge University Press, 1997.

Magnus, Ralph H., and Eden Naby. *Afghanistan: Mullah, Marx and Mujahid*. New Delhi: HarperCollins, 1998.

Mahmud, Safdar, and Javaid Zafar. *Founders of Pakistan*. Lahore, Pakistan: Sheikh Muhammad Ashraf, 1968.

Mahmud, Y. Zahid. *The Meaning of the Quran*. 5th ed. Beirut: Dar al-Choura, 1980.

Main, Shakir. *Secularization of Muslim Behavior*. Calcutta: Minerva Associates, 1974.

Makdisi, George, ed. *Arab and Islamic Studies in Honour of H. A. R. Gibb*. Cambridge: Harvard University Press, 1965.

Makiya, Kenan. *Cruelty and Silence: War, Tyranny, Uprising and the Arab World*. New York: Norton, 1993.

Makovsky, David. *Making Peace with the PLO: The Rabin Government's Road to the Oslo Accord*. Boulder, Colo.: Westview Press, 1996.

Malcolm, Noel. *Bosnia: A Short History*. New York: New York University Press, 1994.

Malik, Hafeez. *Muslim Nationalism in India and Pakistan*. Washington, D.C.: Public Affairs Press, 1963.

———. *Sir Sayyid Ahmad Khan and Muslim Modernism in India and Pakistan*. New York: Columbia University Press, 1980.

Malik, Jamal. *Colonizing Islam: Dissolution of Traditional Institutions in Pakistan*. New Delhi: Manohar, 1996.

Malik, Zahid, ed. *Pakistan after 1971*. Rawalpindi: Pakistan National Center, 1974.

Man, W. Che. *Muslim Separatism: The Moros of Southern Philippines and the Malays of Southern Thailand*. Quezon City: Ateneo de Manila University Press, 1990.

Maqsood, Ruqaiyyah Waris. *A Basic Dictionary of Islam*. New Delhi: Goodword Books, 1998.

Mardin, Serif, ed. *Cultural Transitions in the Middle East*. New York: Brill, 1994.

Marr, P., and W. Lewis, eds. *Riding the Tiger: The Middle East Challenge after the Cold War*. Boulder, Colo.: Westview Press, 1993.

Marsden, Peter. *The Taliban: War, Religion and the New Order in Afghanistan*. New York: Zed Books, 1998.

Marsh, Clifton E. *From Black Muslims to Muslims: The Transition from Separation to Islam, 1930–1980*. Metuchen, N.J.: Scarecrow Press, 1984.

Martin, B. G. *Muslim Brotherhoods in Nineteenth-Century Africa*. Cambridge: Cambridge University Press, 1976.

Martin, Richard, ed. *Approaches to Islam in Religious Studies*. Tucson: University of Arizona Press, 1985.

Martin, Richard C. *Islamic Studies: A History of Religion's Approach*, 2nd ed. Upper Saddle River, N.J.: Prentice-Hall, 1996.

Marty, Martin E., and R. Scott Appleby, eds. *Fundamentalisms Observed*. The Fundamentalism Project. Vol. 1. Chicago: The University of Chicago Press, 1991.

———. *The Glory and the Power: The Fundamentalist Challenge to the Modern World*. Boston: Beacon Press, 1992.

———, eds. *Fundamentalisms and Society: Reclaiming the Sciences, the Family, and Education*. The Fundamentalism Project. Vol. 2. Chicago: University of Chicago Press, 1993.

———, eds. *Fundamentalisms and the State: Remaking Politics, Economies, and Militance*. The Fundamentalism Project. Vol. 3. Chicago: University of Chicago Press, 1993.

———, eds. *Accounting for Fundamentalisms: The Dynamic Character of Movements*. The Fundamentalism Project. Vol. 4. Chicago: University of Chicago Press, 1994.

———, eds. *Fundamentalisms Comprehended*. The Fundamentalism Project. Vol. 5. Chicago: University of Chicago Press, 1995.

Mashoor, S. M. H. *Muslim Heroes of the Twentieth Century*. Lahore, Pakistan: Sheikh Muhammad Ashraf, 1978.

Matar, N. I. *Islam for Beginners*. New York: Writers & Readers, 1992.

Mathews, Ken. *The Gulf Conflict and International Relations*. London: Routledge, 1993.

Matinuddin, Kamal. *The Taliban Phenomenon, Afghanistan 1994–1997*. New York: Oxford Pakistan Paperbacks, 1999.

Maududi, Maulana Abul A'la. *Musalman aur Maujuda Siyasi Kashmakash (Muslims and the Present Political Conflict)*. Pathankot, India: Dar-ul-Islam, 1938

———. *Nationalism in India*. 2nd ed. Malihabad, India: Maktaba-i-Jamaat-i Islami [Hind], 1948.

———. *Islamic Law and Its Interpretation in Pakistan*. Lahore, Pakistan: Islamic Publications, 1960.

———. *First Principles of the Islamic State*. Lahore, Pakistan: Islamic Publications, 1960.

———. *Political Theory of Islam*. Lahore, Pakistan: Islamic Publications, 1960.

———. *Rights of Non-Muslims in Islamic State*. Translated and edited by Khurshid Ahmad. Lahore, Pakistan: Islamic Publications, 1961.

———. *Musalman aur Maujuda Siyai Kashmaksh (Muslims and the Present Political Conflict)*. Vol. 3. 6th ed. Lahore, Pakistan: Islamic Publications, 1973.

———. *Fundamentals of Islam*. Lahore, Pakistan: Islamic Publications, 1975.

———. *Human Rights in Islam*. Leicester, England: Islamic Foundation, 1976.

———. *A Short History of the Revivalist Movement in Islam*. 3rd ed. Lahore, Pakistan: Islamic Publications, 1976.

———. *Islamic Law and Constitution*. Karachi, Pakistan: Jamaat-e-Islami Publications, 1955. 3rd ed. 1977.

Mayer, Ann Elizabeth. *Islam and Human Rights: Tradition and Politics*. Boulder, Colo.: Westview Press, 1999.

Mazarr, M. J., D. M. Snider, and J. A. Blackwell, Jr. *Desert Storm: The Gulf War and What We Learned*. Boulder, Colo.: Westview Press, 1993.

Mazrui, Ali. *The Satanic Verses or a Satanic Novel? The Moral Dilemmas of the Rushdie Affair*. Greenpoint, N.Y.: Committee of Muslim Scholars and Leaders of North America, 1989.

McCloud, Aminah Beverly. *African-American Islam*. New York: Routledge, 1995.

McDonough, Sheila. *Muslim Ethics and Modernity*. Waterloo, Ontario: Wilfred Laurier University Press, 1984.

McDowall, David. *Palestine and Israel: The Uprising and Beyond*. Berkeley and Los Angeles: University of California Press, 1989.

McGowan, Daniel, and Marc H. Ellis, eds. *Remembering Deir Yassin: The Future of Israel and Palestine*. Northampton, Mass.: Olive Branch Press/Interlink, 1998.

McLaughlin, Leslie. *Ibn Saud: Founder of a Kingdom*. New York: St. Martin's Press, 1993.

von der Mehden, Fred R. *Religion and Nationalism in Southeast Asia*. Madison: University of Wisconsin Press, 1963.

———. *Two Worlds of Islam: Interaction between Southeast Asia and the Middle East*. Gainesville: University Press of Florida, 1993.

Mehr, Ghulam Rasul. *Sayyid Ahmad Shahid*. Lahore, Pakistan: Katib Manzil, 1956.

Meland, Bernard E. *The Secularization of Modern Cultures*. New York: Oxford University Press, 1966.

Mernissi, Fatima. *Beyond the Veil: Male-Female Dynamics in a Modern Muslim Society*. New York: John Wiley and Sons, 1975.

———. *The Veil and the Male Elite*. Boston: Addison-Wesley, 1991.

———. *Islam and Democracy: Fear of the Modern World*. Reading, Mass.: Addison-Wesley, 1992.

Metcalf, Barbara Daly. *Islamic Revival in British India, 1860–1900*. Princeton, N.J.: Princeton University Press, 1982.

Mews, S., ed. *Religion and Politics: A World Guide*. Harlow, England: Longman, 1989.

Michalak, Laurence. *Cruel and Unusual: Negative Images of Arabs in American Popular Culture*. 3rd ed. Washington, D.C.: American-Arab Anti-Discrimination Committee (ADC), Issue Paper No. 15, 1988.

Milani, Mohsen M. *The Making of Iran's Islamic Revolution*. Boulder, Colo.: Westview Press, 1988.

Miller, Judith. *God Has Ninety-Nine Names: Reporting from a Militant Middle East*. New York: Simon and Schuster, 1997.

Minault, Gail. *The Khilafat Movement: Religious Symbolism and Political Mobilization in India*. New York: Columbia University Press, 1983.

Mir, Mustansir. *Dictionary of Quranic Terms and Concepts*. New York: Garland, 1987.

Mirsky, Yehudah, and Matt Ahrens. *Democracy in the Middle East: Defining the Challenge*. Washington, D.C.: Washington Institute for Near East Policy, 1993.

Misztal, B., and A. Shupe, eds. *Religion and Politics in Comparative Perspective: Revival of Religious Fundamentalism in East and West*. Westport, Conn.: Praeger, 1992.

Mitchell, Richard P. *The Society of the Muslim Brothers*. London: Oxford University Press, 1969. Reprinted 1993.

Moazzam, Anwar, ed. *Islam and the Contemporary Muslim World*. New Delhi: Light and Life Publishers, 1981.

Moin, Baqer. *Khomeini: The Life of the Ayatollah*. London: I. B. Tauris, 1999.

Momen, Moojan. *An Introduction to Shi'ite Islam: The History and Doctrines of Twelver Shi'ism*. New Haven, Conn.: Yale University Press, 1985.

Moosa, Matti. *Extremist Shiites*. Syracuse, N.Y.: Syracuse University Press, 1988.

Morgan, Kenneth W. *Islam—The Straight Path: Islam Interpreted by Muslims*. New York: Ronald Press Company, 1958.

Morris, Benny. *The Birth of the Palestinian Refugee Problem*. New York and Cambridge: Cambridge University Press, 1987.

———. *1948 and After: Israel and the Palestinians*. New York: Oxford University Press, 1990.

———. *Righteous Victims: A History of Zionist-Arab Conflict, 1881–1999*. New York: Knopf, 1999.

Mortimer, Edward. *Faith and Power: The Politics of Islam*. New York: Random House, 1982.

Moss, Joyce, and George Wilson. *Peoples of the World: The Middle East and North Africa*. Detroit: Gale Research, 1992.

Mostyn, Trevor, and Albert Hourani, eds. *The Cambridge Encyclopedia of the Middle East and North Africa*. New York: Cambridge University Press. 1988.

Moten, Abdul Rashid. *Political Science: An Islamic Perspective*. London: Macmillan, 1982.

Mottahedeh, Roy. *The Mantle of the Prophet*. New York: Simon and Schuster, 1985.

Moussalli, Ashad S. *Radical Islamic Fundamentalism: The Ideology and Political Discourse of Sayyid Qutb*. Beirut: American University of Beirut, 1992.

Mowlana, Hamid, George Gerbner, and Herbert I. Schiller, eds. *Triumph of the Image: The Media's War in the Persian Gulf—A Global Perspective*. Boulder, Colo.: Westview Press, 1992.

Moyser, G., ed. *Religion and Politics in the Modern World*. London: Routledge.

Mufti, Malek. *Sovereign Creations: Pan-Arabism and Politics*. Ithaca, N.Y.: Cornell University Press, 1996.

Munson, Henry, Jr. *Islam and Revolution in the Middle East*. New Haven, Conn.: Yale University Press, 1988.

Murata, Sachiko, and Schittick Murata. *The Vision of Islam*. London: I. B. Tauris, 1996.

Murphy, Thomas Patrick, ed. *The Holy War*. Columbus: Ohio State University Press, 1976.

Muslih, Muhammad Y. *The Origins of Palestinian Nationalism*. New York: Columbia University Press, 1988.

Muslih, Muhammad Y., and Augustus Richard Norton. *Political Tides in the Arab World*. New York: Foreign Policy Association, 1991.

Mutahhari, Ayatullah Murtaza. *Fundamentals of Islamic Thought: God, Man, and the Universe*. Translated by R. Campbell. Berkeley, Calif.: Mizan Press, 1985

———. *Jihad: The Holy War of Islam and Its Legitimacy in the Quran*. Translated by Mohammad Salman Tawheedi. Albany, Calif.: Moslem Student Association [Persian Speaking Group], no date.

Mutalib, Hussin, and Taj ul-Islam Hashmi, eds. *Islam, Muslims and the Modern State: Case Studies of Muslims in Thirteen Countries*. New York: St. Martin's Press, 1994.

Muztar, A. D. *Shah Waliullah: A Saint-Scholar of Muslim India*. Islamabad, Pakistan: National Commission on Historical and Cultural Research, 1979.

Mylroie, Laurie. *Study of Revenge: Saddam Hussein's Unfinished War against America*. Washington, D.C.: AEI Press, 2000.

An-Naim, Abdullahi Ahmed. *Towards an Islamic Reformation: Civil Liberties, Human Rights, and International Law*. Syracuse, N.Y.: Syracuse University Press, 1990.

Naim, C. M., ed. *Iqbal, Jinnah and Pakistan: The Vision and the Reality*. Syracuse, N.Y.: Syracuse University Press, 1979.

Naipal, V. S. *Among the Believers: An Islamic Journey*. New York: Vintage Books, 1981.

———. *Beyond Belief: Islamic Excursions among the Converted Peoples*. New York: Vintage Books, 1998.

Naff, Thomas, ed. *Paths to the Middle East: Ten Scholars Look Back*. Albany: State University of New York Press, 1993.

Nagata, Judith. *The Reflowering of Malaysian Islam: Modern Religious Radicals and Their Roots*. Vancouver: University of British Columbia Press, 1984.

An-Na'im, Abdullahi Ahmed. *Toward an Islamic Reformation: Civil Liberties, Human Rights, and International Law*. Syracuse, N.Y.: Syracuse University Press, 1990.

Nakhleh, Issa. *Encyclopedia of the Palestine Problem*. Vols. 1 and 2. New York: Intercontinental Books, 1991.

Nardin, Terry, ed. *The Ethics of War and Peace: Religious and Secular Perspectives*. Ethikon Series in Comparative Ethics, Vol. 1. Princeton, N.J.: Princeton University Press, 1996.

Nardo, Don. *The Persian Gulf War*. San Diego: Lucent Books, 1991.

Nashat, Guity, ed. *Women and Revolution in Iran*. Boulder, Colo.: Westview Press, 1983.

Nasr, Kameel B. *Arab and Israeli Terrorism: The Causes and Effect of Political Violence, 1936–1993*. Jefferson, N.C.: McFarland, 1997.

Nasr, Seyyed Hossein. *Islamic Life and Thought*. Albany: State University of New York Press, 1981.

———. *Muhammad: Man of Allah*. London: Muhammadi Trust, 1982.

———. *Traditional Islam in the Modern World*. London: Kegan Paul, 1987.

———, ed. *Islamic Spirituality: Manifestations*. London: SCM, 1991.

Nasr, Seyyed Vali Reza. *The Vanguard of Islamic Revolution: The Jama'at-i-Islami of Pakistan*. Berkeley and Los Angeles: University of California Press, 1994.

Nassar, Jamal R., and Roger Heacock, eds. *Intifada: Palestine at the Crossroads*. New York: Praeger, 1990.

Nasser, Gamal Abdel. *Egypt's Liberation: The Philosophy of the Revolution*. Washington, D.C.: Public Affairs Press, 1955.

Nayang, Sulayman. *Islam, Christianity, and African Identity*. Brattleboro, Vt.: Amana Books, 1984.

———. *Islam in the United States of America*. New York: ABC International Group, 1999.

Neff, Donald. *Fallen Pillars: U.S. Policy toward Palestine and Israel since 1945*. Washington, D.C.: Institute of Palestine Studies, 1995.

Nettler, Ronald L. *Past Trials and Present Tribulations: A Muslim Fundamentalist's View of the Jews*. New York: Pergamon Press, 1987.

Newman, K. J. *Essays on the Constitution of Pakistan*. Dacca, Bangladesh: Pakistan Cooperative Book Society, 1956.

Niblock, Tim, and Emma Murphy, eds. *Economic and Political Liberalization in the Middle East*. London: British Academic Press, 1993.

Nielsen, Jorgen. *Muslims in Western Europe*. 2nd ed. Edinburgh: Edinburgh University Press, 1995.

———, ed. *The Christian-Muslim Frontier: Chaos, Clash or Dialogue?* London: I. B. Tauris, 1998.

Nigosian, Soloman. *Islam: The Way of Submission*. New York: Crucible Press, 1987.

Nima, Ramy. *The Wrath of Allah: Islamic Revolution and Reaction in Iran*. London: Pluto Press, 1983.

Noer, Deliar. *The Modernist Muslim Movement in Indonesia, 1900–1942*. New York: Oxford University Press, 1973.

Nonneman, Gerd, Tim Niblock, and Bogdan Szajkowski, eds. *Muslim Communities in the New Europe*. Berkshire, England: Ithaca Press, 1996.

Norton, Augustus Richard. *Amal and the Shi'a: Struggle for the Soul of Lebanon*. Austin: University of Texas Press, 1987.

Norton, Augustus Richard, and M.H. Greenberg, eds. *The International Relations of the PLO*. Carbondale: University of Southern Illinois Press, 1989.

Norton, Augustus Richard, ed. *Civil Society in the Middle East*. Leiden, The Netherlands: E. J. Brill, 1995.

Olesen, Asta. *Islam and Politics in Afghanistan*. Nordic Institute of Asian Studies, Monograph Series No. 67. Richmond, Surrey, England: Curzon Press, 1995.

Omri, Syed Jalal-ud-Din. *Woman and Islam*. Lahore, Pakistan: Islamic Publications, August 1990.

O'Neil, Bard E., ed. *The Energy Crisis and U.S. Foreign Policy*. New York: Praeger, 1975.

Owen, Roger. *State, Power and Politics in the Making of the Modern Middle East*. London: Routledge, 1992.

Palmer, Monte, and William R. Thompson. *The Comparative Analysis of Politics*. Itasca, Ill.: F. E. Peacock, 1978.

Palmer, Monte. *The Politics of the Middle East*. Itasca, Ill.: F. E. Peacock, 2002.

Parenti, Michael. *Make-Believe Media: The Politics of Entertainment*. New York: St. Martin's Press, 1992.

Partner, Peter. *God of Battles: Holy Wars of Christianity and Islam*. Princeton, N.J.: Princeton University Press, 1998.

Peleg, Ian, ed. *The Middle East Peace Process: Interdisciplinary Perspectives*. Albany: State University of New York Press, 1998.

Peretz, Don, Richard U. Moench, and Safia K. Mohsen. *Islam: Legacy of the Past, Challenge of the Future*. New York: North River Press, 1984.

Peretz, Don. *The Middle East Today*. 5th ed. New York: Praeger, 1988.

Perry, Glenn E. *The Middle East: Fourteen Islamic Centuries*. Englewood Cliffs, N.J.: Prentice-Hall, 1983. 2nd ed. 1992.

Peters, Francis E. *Allah's Commonwealth*. New York: Simon and Schuster, 1973.

———. *Children of Abraham: Judaism, Christianity, Islam*. Princeton, N.J.: Princeton University Press, 1982.

———. *Islam: The Religious and Political Life of a World Community*. New York: Praeger, 1984.

———. *Judaism, Christianity, and Islam*. Vols. 1–3. Princeton, N.J.: Princeton University Press, 1990.

———. *Muhammad and the Origins of Islam*. Albany: State University of New York Press, 1994.

Peters, Rudolf. *Islam and Colonialism: The Doctrine of Jihad in Modern History*. The Hague: Mouton, 1979.

———. *Jihad in Classical and Modern Islam*. Princeton, N.J.: Marcus Weiner, 1996.

Phipps, William E. *Muhammad and Jesus*. New York: Continuum, 1996.

Picard, P. G. *Media Portrayals of Terrorism: Functions and Meaning of News Coverage*. Ames: Iowa State University Press, 1993.

Pickthall, Mohammad Marmaduke. *The Meaning of the Glorious Koran*. New York: Mentor Books, 1953.

Pipes, Daniel. *In the Path of God: Islam and Political Power*. New York: Basic Books, 1983.

———. *The Rushdie Affair: The Novel, the Ayatollah, and the West*. New York: Birch Lane Press, 1990.

Pipes, Daniel, and Adam Garfinkle, eds. *Friendly Tyrants: An American Dilemma*. New York: St. Martin's Press, 1991.

Piscatori, James P., ed. *Islam in the Political Process*. Cambridge: Cambridge University Press, 1983.

———. *Islam in a World of Nation-States*. Cambridge: Cambridge University Press, 1986.

————, ed. *Islamic Fundamentalisms and the Gulf Crisis*. Chicago: University of Chicago Press, 1992.

Poliakov, Sergei P., ed. *Everyday Islam*. Armonk, N.Y.: M. E. Sharpe. 1992.

Polmar, Norman, ed. *CNN War in the Gulf*. Atlanta: Turner Publishing, 1991.

Poston, Larry. *Islamic Da'wah in the West: Muslim Missionary Activity and the Dynamics of Conversion to Islam*. New York: Oxford University Press, 1992.

Poullada, Leon B. *The Islamic State of Pakistan*. M.A. thesis, South Asian Studies Department, University of Pennsylvania, June 1952.

Pullapilly, Cyriac, ed. *Islam in the Contemporary World*. Notre Dame, Ind.: Cross Roads Books, 1980.

Pye, Lucien W. *Politics, Personality and Nation-Building: Burma's Search for Identity*. New Haven, Conn.: Yale University Press, 1962.

————. *Communications and Political Development*. Princeton, N.J.: Princeton University Press, 1964.

————. *Aspects of Political Development*. Boston: Little, Brown, 1966.

Al-Qaradawi, Yusef. *Islamic Awakening between Rejection and Extremism*. 2nd ed. Indianapolis: American Trust Publication and the International Institute of Islamic Thought, 1990.

Quandt, William B. *Saudi Arabia in the 1980s: Foreign Policy, Security, and Oil*. Washington, D.C.: Brookings Institution, 1981.

Quandt, William B., and Michael H. Armacost. *Peace Process: American Diplomacy and the Arab-Israeli Conflict since 1967*. Rev. ed. Berkeley and Los Angeles: University of California Press, 2001.

Qureshi, Ishtiaq Husain. *Ulema in Politics*. Karachi, Pakistan: Ma'aref Publishers, 1972.

————. *The Muslim Community of the Indo-Pakistan Subcontinent (610–1947): A Brief Historical Analysis*. 2nd ed. Karachi, Pakistan: Ma'aref Publishers, 1977.

————. *Perspectives of Islam and Pakistan*. Karachi, Pakistan: Ma'aref Publishers, 1978.

Qutb, Sayyid. *This Religion of Islam*. Translated by Islamdust. Palo Alto, Calif.: A-Manar Press, 1967

————. *In the Shade of the Quran*. Translated by M. Adil Salahi and Ashur A. Shamis. London: MWH Publishers, 1979.

————. *Milestones* [also *Signposts or Signposts on the Road*]. Indianapolis: American Trust Publications, 1990.

————. *The Islamic Concept and Its Characteristics*. Indianapolis: American Trust Publications, 1991.

————. *Islam and Universal Peace*. Indianapolis: American Trust Publications, 1993.

Ragab, Ibrahim A., and Charles K. Wilber, eds. *Religious Values and Development*. New York: Pergamon Press, 1980.

Rahman, Fazlur. *Islam*. 2nd ed. Chicago: University of Chicago Press, 1979.

————. *Major Themes of the Quran*. Minneapolis: Bibliotheca Islamica, 1980.

————. *Islam and Modernity: Transformation of an Intellectual Tradition*. Chicago: University of Chicago Press, 1982.

Rahnema, Ali, ed. *Pioneers of Islamic Revival*. London: Zed Books, 1994.

Raitt, Jill. *Islam in the Modern World: 1983 Paine Lectures in Religion*. Columbia: University of Missouri Press, 1983.

Rajaee, Farhang, ed. *The Iran-Iraq War: The Politics of Aggression*. Gainesville: University of Florida Press, 1993.

Ralph, Philip Lee, Robert E. Lerner, Standish Meacham, and Edward McNall Burns. *World Civilizations: Their History and Their Culture*. Vol. 2. 8th ed. New York: Norton, 1991.

Ramzani, R. K. *Revolutionary Iran*. Baltimore: Johns Hopkins University Press, 1986.

Randal, Jonathan C. *Going All the Way: Christian Warlords, Israeli Adventurers, and the War in Lebanon*. New York: Viking, 1983.

Rapoport, David C., and Yonah Alexander, eds. *The Morality of Terrorism: Religious and Secular Justifications*. New York: Pergamon Press, 1982.

Rashad, Adib. *Elijah Muhammad and the Theological Foundation of the Nation of Islam*. Newport News, Va.: United Brothers and United Sisters Communications Systems, 1994.

Rashad, Ahmad. *Hamas: Palestinian Politics with an Islamic Hue*. United Association for Studies and Research, Washington, D.C., December 1993.

Rasheed, Mian Abdul. *Islam in Indo-Pakistan Subcontinent: An Analytical Study of the Islamic Movements*. Lahore, Pakistan: National Book Foundation, 1977.

Rashid, Ahmed. *The Taliban, Islam, Oil and the New Great Game in Central Asia*. New York: I. B. Tauris, 2000.

Rashiduzzaman, M. *Pakistan: A Study of Government and Politics*. Dacca, Bangladesh: Ideal Library, 1967.

Razia-akter Banu, U. A. B. *Islam in Bangladesh*. New York: E. J. Brill, 1992.

Reeve, Simon. *The New Jackals*. Boston: Northeastern University Press, 1999.

Regan, Geoffrey. *Israel and the Arabs*. Cambridge: Cambridge University Press, 1984.

Reich, Bernard, ed. *Political Leaders of the Contemporary Middle East and North Africa: A Biographical Dictionary*. New York: Greenwood Press, 1991.

Renshon, Stanley A., ed. *The Political Psychology of the Gulf War: Leaders, Publics, and the Process of Conflict*. Pittsburgh: University of Pittsburgh Press, 1993.

Richards, Alan, and John Waterbury. *A Political Economy of the Middle East*. 2nd ed. New York: Westview Press, 1996.

Riesebrodt, Martin. *Pious Passion: The Emergence of Modern Fundamentalism in the United States and Iran*. Berkeley and Los Angeles: University of California Press, 1990.

Rippin, Andrew. *Muslims*. London: Routledge, 2000.

———. *Islamic Reassertion: A Socio-Political Study*. Lahore, Pakistan: Progressive Publishers, 1981.

Roberts, D. S. *Islam: A Concise Introduction*. San Francisco: Harper and Row, 1981.

Robinson, Francis. *Separatism among Indian Muslims: The Politics of the United Provinces' Muslims 1860–1923*. Cambridge: Cambridge University Press, 1974.

———. *Atlas of the Islamic World since 1500*. New York: Facts on File, 1982.

Robinson, Glenn E. *Building a Palestinian State: The Incomplete Revolution*. Bloomington: Indiana University Press, 1997.

Rodinson, Maxime. *Israel: A Colonial Settler State?* New York: Monad Press, 1973.

———. *Islam and Capitalism*. Translated by Brian Pearce. 2nd ed. Austin: University of Texas Press, 1978.

———. *Israel and the Arabs*. Harmondsworth, England: Penguin, 1982.

———. *Cult, Ghetto and State: The Persistence of the Jewish Question*. New York: Saqi Books, 1983.

———. *Europe and the Mystique of Islam*. Seattle: University of Washington Press, 1987.

———. *Europe and the Mystique of Islam*. Seattle: University of Washington Press, 1991.

———. *Muhammad*. Translated by Anne Carter. 2nd English-language ed. Harmondsworth, England: Penguin, 1996.

Rosenthal, E. I. J. *Political Thought in Medieval Islam*. Cambridge: Cambridge University Press, 1958.

———. *Islam in the Modern National State*. Cambridge: Cambridge University Press, 1965.

Roy, Olivier. *Islam and Resistance in Afghanistan*. New York: Cambridge University Press, 1986.

———. *The Failure of Political Islam*. Translated by Carol Volk. Cambridge, Mass.: Harvard University Press, 1994.

———. *Afghanistan: From Holy War to Civil War*. Princeton, N.J.: Darwin Press, 1995.

Rubin, Barnett R. *The Fragmentation of Afghanistan: State Formation and Collapse in the International System*. New Haven, Conn.: Yale University Press, 1995.

———. *The Search for Peace in Afghanistan: From Buffer State to Failed State*. New Haven, Conn.: Yale University Press, 1996.

Rubin, Barry. *Paved with Good Intentions: The American Experience in Iran*. New York: Oxford University Press, 1980.

Rubinstein, Alvin Z., ed., *The Arab-Israeli Conflict: Perspectives*. New York: Praeger, 1988.

Rudolph, Susanne Hoeber, and James Piscatori, eds. *Transnational Religion and Fading States*. Boulder, Colo.: Westview Press, 1997.

Rushie, Salman. *The Satanic Verses*. London: Viking, 1988.

Russet, Bruce and Harvey Starr. *World Politics: The Menu for Choice*. New York: W. H. Freeman, 1992.

Ruthven, Malise. *A Satanic Affair: Salman Rushdie and the Rage of Islam*. London: Chatto and Windus, 1990.

———. *Islam in the World*. 2nd ed. New York: Oxford University Press, 2000.

Rywkin, Michael. *Moscow's Muslim Challenge: Soviet Central Asia*. Rev. ed. Armonk, N.Y.: M. E. Sharpe, 1990.

Sabbagh, Suha, ed. *Arab Women: Between Defiance and Restraint*. Northampton, Mass.: Olive Branch Press/Interlink, 1996.

el-Saadawi, Nawal. *The Hidden Face of Eve: Women in the Arab World*. Boston: Beacon Press, 1982.

Sachedina, Abdulaziz Abdulhussein. *Islamic Messianism: The Idea of the Mahdi in Twelver Shi'ism*. Albany: State University of New York Press, 1981.

———. *The Just Ruler in Shi'ite Islam: The Comprehensive Authority of the Jurist in Imamite Jurisprudence*. New York: Oxford University Press, 1988.

el-Sadat, Anwar. *Revolt on the Nile*. London: Allan Wingate; New York: John Day, 1957.

Sadri, Mahmoud, and Ahmad Sadri, trans. and ed. *Reason, Freedom, and Democracy in Islam: Essential Writings of Abdolkarim Saroush*. New York: Oxford University Press, 2000.

Saha, Santosh C., and Thomas K. Carr, ed. *Religious Fundamentalism in Developing Countries*. Westport, Conn.: Greenwood Press, 2001.

Sahliyeh, Emile. *In Search of Leadership: West Bank Politics since 1967*. Washington, D.C.: Brookings Institution, 1988.

———, ed. *Religious Resurgence and Politics in the Contemporary World*. Albany: State University of New York Press, 1990.

Said, Edward W. *Orientalism: Western Conceptions of the Orient*. New York: Vintage Books, 1978.

———. *The Question of Palestine*. London: Routledge and Kegan Paul, 1980.

———. *Covering Islam: How the Media and the Experts Determine How We See the Rest of the World*. New York: Pantheon Books, 1981.

Said, Edward W. and Christopher Hitchens. *Blaming the Victims: Spurious Scholarship and the Palestinian Question*. London and New York: Verso, 1988.

Said Edward W. *Culture and Imperialism*. New York: Knopf, 1993.

———. *The Politics of Dispossession: The Struggle for Palestinian Self-Determination, 1969–1994*. New York: Pantheon Books, 1994.

———. *Peace and Its Discontents*. New York: Vintage Books, 1996.

———. *The End of the Peace Process: Oslo and After*. Updated Edition. New York: Vintage Books, 2001.

Saikal, Amin, and William Maley. *Regime Change in Afghanistan*. Boulder, Colo.: Westview Press, 1991.

Salame, Ghassan. *Democracy without Democrats: The Renewal of Politics in the Muslim World*. London: I. B. Tauris, 1994.

Salem, Paul. *Bitter Legacy: Ideology and Politics in the Arab World*. Syracuse, N.Y.: Syracuse University Press, 1994.

Sardar, Ziauddin. *The Future of Muslim Civilization*. London: Croom Helm, 1979.

———. *The Shape of Things to Come*. London: Mansell, 1985.

Sardar, Ziaddin, and Zafar Abbas Malik. *Introducing Muhammad*. New York: Totem Books, 1994.

Sarkar, Jagdish Narayan. *Islam in Bengal: Thirteenth to Nineteenth Century*. Calcutta: Ratna Prakashan, 1972.

Saulat, Sarvat. *Maulana Maududi*. Karachi, Pakistan: International Islamic Publishers, 1979.

Savir, Uri. *The Process: 1,100 Days That Changed the Middle East*. New York: Random House, 1998.

Sayeed, Khalid Bin. *Western Dominance and Political Islam: Challenge and Response*. Albany: State University of New York Press, 1995.

Sayigh, Yazid. *Armed Struggle and the Search for State: The Palestine National Movement, 1949–1993*. Oxford: Clarendon Press, 1997.

Schacht, Joseph. *An Introduction to Islamic Law*. Oxford: Clarendon Press, 1964.

———. ed. *The Legacy of Islam*. Oxford: Oxford University Press, 1979.

Schimmel, Annemarie. *And Muhammad Is His Messenger*. Chapel Hill, N.C.: University of North Carolina, 1985.

———. *My Soul Is a Woman: The Feminine in Islam*. New York: Continuum, 1997.

Schultheis, Rob. *Night Letters: Inside Wartime Afghanistan*. New York: Crown, 1992.

Schulze, Reinhard. *A Modern History of the Islamic World*. London: I. B. Tauris, 1999.

Schulzinger, Robert D. *American Diplomacy in the Twentieth Century*. Oxford: Oxford University Press, 1984.

Schuon, Frithjof. *Understanding Islam*. Bloomington, Ind.: World Wisdom Books, 1994.

Sela, Avraham. *Political Encyclopedia of the Middle East*. New York: Continuum, 1999.

Sell, Edward. *The Faith of Islam*. London, 1920. 4th ed., Wilmington, Del.: Scholarly Resources, 1976.

Sells, Michael A. *The Bridge Betrayed: Religion and Genocide in Bosnia*. Berkeley and Los Angeles: University of California Press, 1996.

Shaban, M. A. *Islamic History: A New Interpretation*. Part 2. Cambridge: Cambridge University Press, 1976.

Shadid, Anthony. *Legacy of the Prophet: Despots, Democrats, and the New Politics of Islam*. Boulder, Colo.: Westview Press, 2001.

Shaheen, Jack G. *The T.V. Arab*. Bowling Green, Ohio: Popular Press, 1984.

———. *Reel Bad Arabs: How Hollywood Vilifies a People*. New York: Olive Branch Press, 2001.

Shahin, Emad Eldin. *Political Ascent: Contemporary Islamic Movements in North Africa*. Boulder, Colo.: Westview Press, 1997.

Sharabi, Hisham. *Palestine and Israel: The Lethal Dilemma*. New York: Pegasus Press, 1969.

———. *Arab Intellectuals and the West: The Formative Years, 1875–1914*. Baltimore: Johns Hopkins Press, 1970.

———. *Neo-Patriarchy: A Theory of Distorted Change in Arab Society.* New York: Oxford University Press, 1988.

———, ed. *The Next Arab Decade: Alternative Futures.* Boulder, Colo.: Westview Press, 1991.

Shariati, Ali. *The Islamic View of Man.* Translated by A. A. Rasti. Bedford, Ohio: Free Islamic Literatures, 1978.

———. *Hajj.* 2nd ed. Translated by Ali A. Behzadnia and Najla Denny. Houston: Free Islamic Literatures, 1978.

———. *On the Sociology of Islam.* Translated by Hamid Algar. Berkeley and Los Angeles: University of California Press, 1979.

———. *We and Iqbal.* Tehran, Iran: Husainiyeh Irshad, 1979.

———. *Marxism and Other Western Fallacies: An Islamic Critique.* Translated by R. Campbell. Berkeley, Calif.: Mizan Press, 1980.

———. *Man and Islam.* Translated by Fatollah Marjani. Houston: Free Islamic Literatures, 1981.

Shayegan, Darius. *Cultural Schizophrenia.* London: Saqi Books, 1992.

Shimoni, Yaacov. *Political Dictionary of the Arab World.* New York: Macmillan, 1987.

Shipler, David K. *Arab and Jew: Wounded Spirits in a Promised Land.* New York: Times Books, 1986.

Sick, Gary G. *All Fall Down: America's Tragic Encounter with Iran.* New York: Random House, 1985.

Sick, Gary G., and Lawrence G. Potter, eds. *The Persian Gulf at the Millennium.* New York: St. Martin's Press, 1997.

Sidahmed, Abdel Salam. *Politics and Islam in Contemporary Sudan.* New York: St. Martin's Press, 1996.

Siddiqui, Kalim, et al. *The Islamic Revolution: Achievements, Obstacles and Goals.* Toronto: Crescent International, 1980.

Siddiqui, Kalim. *Issues in the Islamic Movement.* London: The Open Press. 3 Vols.: 1 (1980–81), 2 (1981–82), and 3 (1982–83).

Siddiqui, M. A. Majeed. *Pakistan: The Islamic State.* Lahore, Pakistan: Islamic Publications, 1947.

Sifry, Micah L., and Christopher Cerf, eds. *The Gulf War Reader.* New York: Random House, 1991.

Silk, Mark. *Spiritual Politics: Religion and Politics since World War II.* New York: Simon and Schuster, 1988.

Silverburg, Sanford R. *Middle East Bibliography.* Metuchen, N.J.: Scarecrow Press, 1992.

Simpson, John. *Inside Iran.* New York: St. Martin's Press, 1988.

Singh, N. K., ed. *Encyclopedia of the Holy Quran.* Vols. 1–5. Delhi: Global Vision, 2000.

Sivan, Emmanuel. *Radical Islam: Medieval Theology and Modern Politics.* New Haven, Conn.: Yale University Press, 1985.

Sivan, Emmanuel, and Menachem Friedman, ed. *Religious Radicalism and Politics in the Middle East.* Albany: State University of New York, 1990.

Skeet, Ian. *OPEC: Twenty-Five Years of Prices and Politics.* New York: Cambridge University Press, 1991.

Slater, R., B. Schutz, and S. Dorr, eds. *Global Transformation and the Third World.* Boulder, Colo: Lynne Rienner, 1993.

Smith, Charles D. *Palestine and the Arab-Israeli Conflict.* 2nd ed. New York: St. Martin's Press, 1992. 4th ed., 2000.

Smith, Donald Eugene, ed. *South Asian Politics and Religion.* Princeton, N.J.: Princeton University Press, 1966.

————. *Religion and Political Development*. Boston: Little, Brown, 1970.

————, ed. *Religion and Political Modernization*. New Haven, Conn.: Yale University, 1974.

————, ed. *Religion, Politics, and Social Change in the Third World: A Sourcebook*. New York: The Free Press, 1971.

Smith, Jane I. *Islam in America*. New York: Columbia University Press, 2000.

Smith, Wilfred Cantwell. *Modern Islam in India*. Lahore, Pakistan: Mohammad Ashraf, 1963.

————. *Pakistan as an Islamic State*. Lahore, Pakistan: Sheikh Mohammad Ashraf, 1972.

————. *Islam in Modern History*. Princeton, N.J.: Princeton University Press, 1957.

Sondermann, Fred A., David S. McLellan, and William C. Olson. *The Theory and Practice of International Relations*. 5th ed. Englewood Cliffs, N.J.: Prentice-Hall, 1979.

Sonn, Tamara. *Between Quran and Crown: The Challenge of Political Legitimacy in the Arab World*. Boulder, Colo.: Westview Press, 1990.

————. *Islam and the Question of Minorities*. Atlanta: Scholars Press, 1996.

Soroush, Abdolkarim. *Debating Religion and Politics in Iran: The Political Thought of Abdolkarim Soroush*. New York: Council on Foreign Relations, 1996.

Sourdel, Dominque. *Medieval Islam*. Translated by Montgomery Watt. London: Routledge and Kegan Paul, 1983.

Springborg, Robert. *Mubarak's Egypt: Fragmentation of the Political Order*. Boulder, Colo.: Westview Press, 1989.

Stivens, Maila, ed. *Why Gender Matters in Southeast Asian Politics*. Clayton, Australia: Center of Southeast Asian Studies, 1991.

Stoddard, Philip H., David C. Cuthell, and Margaret W. Sullivan, eds. *Change and the Muslim World*. Syracuse, N.Y.: Syracuse University Press, 1981.

Stowasser, Barbara Freyer. *The Islamic Impulse*. Washington, D.C.: Center for Contemporary Arab Studies, 1987.

————. *Women in the Quran, Traditions, and Interpretation*. New York: Oxford University Press, 1994.

Strayer, Robert W., Edwin Hirshman, Robert B. Marks, and Robert J. Smith. *The Making of the Modern World: Connected Histories, Divergent Paths (1500 to the Present)*. New York: St. Martin's Press, 1989.

Suleiman, M. W. *The Arabs in the Mind of America*. Brattleboro, Vt.: Amana Books, 1988.

Swartz, Merlin L., ed. *Studies on Islam*. Oxford: Oxford University Press, 1981.

Sweetman, Windrow. *Islam and Christian Theology: A Study of the Interpretation of Theological Ideas in the Two Religions*. London: Butterworth Press, 1955.

Syed, Anwar Hussain. *Pakistan: Islam, Politics and National Solidarity*. New York: Praeger, 1982.

Szliowicz, Joseph A., and Bard E. O'Neil. *The Energy Crisis and U.S. Foreign Policy*. New York: Praeger, 1975.

Al-Tabataba'i, Muhammad H. *Shi'ite Islam*. 2nd ed. Albany: State University of New York Press, 1975.

Tabatabai, Hossein Moderressi. *An Introduction to Shi'i Law: A Bibliographical Study*. London: Ithaca Press, 1984.

Taha, Mahmoud Mohamed. *The Second Message of Islam*. Syracuse, N.Y.: Syracuse University Press, 1987.

Talbot, Strobe, and Nayan Chanda, eds. *The Age of Terror: America and the World after September 11*. New York: Basic Books, 2002.

Tambiah, Stanley. *Leveling Crowds: Ethnonationalist Conflicts and Collective Violence in South Asia*. Berkeley and Los Angeles: University of California Press, 1996.

Taylor, Alan R. *The Islamic Question in the Middle East*. Boulder, Colo.: Westview Press, 1988.

Terry, J. J. *Mistaken Identity: Arab Stereotypes in Popular Writing*. Washington, D.C.: American-Arab Affairs Council, 1985.

Tessler, Mark A. *A History of the Israeli-Palestinian Conflict*. Bloomington: Indiana University Press, 1994.

Thompson, Henry. *World Religions in War and Peace*. Jefferson, N.C.: McFarland, 1988.

Thompson, Jack, and R. D. Reischauer, eds. *Modernization of the Arab World*. Princeton, N.J.: C. Van Nostrand, 1966.

Thornton, Thomas Perry, ed. *Anti-Americanism: Origins and Context*. The Annals of the American Academy of Political and Social Science, Vol. 497, May 1988.

Tibi, Bassam. *Arab Nationalism: A Critical Enquiry*. Translated and edited by Marion Farouk-Sluglett and Peter Sluglett. New York: St. Martin's Press, 1981.

———. *The Crisis of Modern Islam: A Preindustrial Culture in the Scientific and Technological Age*. Salt Lake City: Utah University Press, 1988

———. *Islam and the Cultural Accomodation of Social Change*. Translated by C. Krojzl. Boulder, Colo.: Westview Press, 1990.

———. *Conflict and War in the Middle East, 1967–1991*. London: Macmillan, 1993.

———. *Arab Nationalism: Between Islam and the Nation-State*. 3rd ed. New York: St. Martin's Press, 1997.

———. *The Challenge of Fundamentalism: Political Islam and the New World Disorder*. Berkeley and Los Angeles: University of California Press, 1998.

Titus, Murray T. *Islam in India and Pakistan: A Religious History of Islam in India and Pakistan*. Calcutta: YMCA Publishing House, 1959.

Toprak, Binnaz. *Islam and Political Development in Turkey*. Leiden, The Netherlands: E. J. Brill, 1981.

Toropov, Brandon, and Father Luke Buckles. *The Complete Idiot's Guide to the World's Religions*. New York: Alpha Books, 1997.

Timingham, J. Spencer. *The Sufi Orders in Islam*. Oxford: Clarendon Press, 1971.

Titus, Murray. *Islam in India and Pakistan*. Calcutta: YMCA Publishing House, 1959.

Todaro, Michael P. *Economic Development in the Third World*. New York: Longman, 1989.

Tripp, Charles, and Roger Owen. *Egypt under Mubarak*. London: Routledge, 1989.

Tritton, A. S. *Islam: Beliefs and Practices*. 2nd ed. London: Hutchinson, 1954.

Troll, Christian. *Sayyid Ahmad Khan: A Reinterpretation of Muslim Theology*. New Delhi: Vikas, 1978.

Tropp, Sylvia L., ed. *Millennial Dreams in Action: Essays in Comparative Study*. The Hague: Mouton, 1962.

Tuma, Elias. *Economic and Political Change in the Middle East*. Palo Alto, Calif.: Pacific Books, 1987.

Turabi, Hasan. *Women in Islam and Muslim Society*. Translated by London: Milestone, 1991.

Turner, Richard Brent. *Islam in the African-American Experience*. Bloomington: Indiana University Press, 1997.

Turner, Bryan. *Weber and Islam*. London: Routledge and Kegan Paul, 1974.

Udovitch, A. L., ed. *The Islamic Middle East, 700–1900: Studies in Economic and Social History*. Princeton, N.J.: Darwin Press, 1981.

Urban, Mark. *War in Afghanistan*. London: Macmillan, 1988.

Usher, Graham. *Palestine in Crisis: The Struggle for Peace and Political Independence after Oslo*. Rev. ed. London: Pluto Press, 1997.

Vahid, Syed Abdul. *Studies in Iqbal*. Lahore, Pakistan: Sheikh Muhammad Ashraf, 1967.

Van Ess, Joseph, and Hans Kung. *Christianity and World Religions*. New York: Doubleday, 1986.

Vatikiotis, P. J. *The Modern History of Egypt*. New York: Praeger, 1969.

———, ed. *Revolution in the Middle East and Other Case Studies*. London: George Allen and Unwin, 1972.

———. *Nasser and His Generation*. New York: St. Martin's Press, 1979.

———. *Arab and Regional Politics in the Middle East*. New York: St. Martin's Press, 1984.

Vaux, K. L. *Ethics and the Gulf War: Religion, Rhetoric, and Righteousness*. Boulder, Colo.: Westview Press, 1992.

Vaziri, Mostafa. *The Emergence of Islam: Prophecy, Imamate, and Messianism in Perspective*. New York: Paragon House, 1992.

Vernon, Raymond. ed. *The Oil Crisis*. New York: Norton, 1976.

Volkan, Vamik D., and Norman Itzkowitz. *The Immortal Ataturk: A Psychobiography*. Chicago: University of Chicago Press, 1984.

Voll, John Obert, ed. *Sudan, State and Society in Crisis*. Bloomington: Indiana University Press, 1991.

———. *Islam: Continuity and Change in the Modern World*. Syracuse, N.Y.: Syracuse University Press, 1994.

Voltaire. *The Portable Voltaire*. Edited by Ben Ray Redman. New York: Viking, 1961.

Waines, David. *An Introduction to Islam*. New York: Cambridge University Press, 1995.

Walther, Wiebke. *Women in Islam: From Medieval to Modern Times*. 2nd ed. New York: Marcus Wiener, 1993.

Walzer, Michael. *Just and Unjust Wars*. New York: Basic Books, 1977.

Warburg, Gabriel R., and Uri M. Kupferschmidt. *Islam, Nationalism, and Radicalism in Egypt and the Sudan*. New York: Praeger, 1983.

Waterbury, John. *The Egypt of Nasser and Sadat: The Political Economy of Two Regimes*. Princeton, N.J.: Princeton University Press, 1983.

Watherby, Joseph N. *The Middle East and North Africa: A Political Primer*. New York: Longman, 2002.

Watt, William Montgomery. *Islamic Political Thought: The Basic Concepts*. Edinburgh: Edinburgh University Press, 1968.

———. *Muhammad in Medina*. Oxford: Clarendon Press, 1968.

———. *The Influence of Islam on Medieval Europe*. Edinburgh: Edinburgh University Press, 1972.

———. *The Formative Period of Islamic Thought*. New York: Columbia University Press, 1973.

———. *Muhammad: Prophet and Statesman*. New York: Oxford University Press, 1974.

———. *The Majesty That Was Islam*. London: Sidgwick and Jackson, 1974.

———. *What Is Islam?* 2nd ed. London: Longman Group, 1979.

———. *Muslim-Christian Encounters: Perceptions and Misperceptions*. New York: Routledge, 1991.

Waugh, Earle H., Baha Abu-Lanbn, and Regula B. Qureshi, eds. *The Muslim Community in North America*. Edmonton: University of Alberta, 1983.

Waxman, C. I. *The End of Ideology Debate*. New York: Frank and Wagnals, 1968.

Weiss, Walter M. *Islam: An Illustrated Historical Overview*. New York: Barron's, 2000.

Westerlund, David, ed. *Questioning the Secular State: The Worldwide Resurgence of Religion in Politics*. London: Hurst, 1996.

Weaver, Mary Anne. *A Portrait of Egypt: A Journey through the World of Militant Islam*. New York: Farrar, Straus & Giroux, 1999.

Wedeen, Lisa. *Ambiguities of Domination*. Chicago: University of Chicago Press, 1999.

Weekes, Richard V. *Muslim Peoples: A World Ethnographic Survey*. Westport, Conn.: Greenwood Press, 1984.

Weiner, Myron, ed. *Modernization: The Dynamics of Growth*. New York: Basic Books, 1966.

Weiss, Anita M., ed. *Islamic Reassertion in Pakistan: The Application of Islamic Laws in a Modern State*. Syracuse, N.Y.: Syracuse University Press, 1986.

Weissman, Steve, and Herbert Krosney. *The Islamic Bomb: The Nuclear Threat to Israel and the Middle East*. New York: Times Books, 1981.

Welch, Claude E., ed. *Political Modernization: A Reader in Comparative Political Change*. Belmont, Calif.: Wadsworth, 1967.

Weldon, E. C., trans. *The Politics of Aristotle*. New York: Macmillan, 1905.

Wendell, Charles, trans. *Five Tracts of Hasan al-Banna (1906–1949)*. Berkeley and Los Angeles: University of California Press, 1978.

Westerlund, D., ed. *Questioning the Secular State: The Worldwide Resurgence of Religion in Politics*. London: Hurst, 1996.

Wheatcroft, Andrew. *The World Atlas of Revolutions*. New York: Simon and Schuster, 1983.

Williams, John Alden., ed. *Themes of Islamic Civilization*. Berkeley and Los Angeles: University of California, 1971.

———. *The World of Islam*. Austin: University of Texas Press, 1994.

Wilhelm, Dietl. *Holy War*. Translated by Martha Humphreys. New York: Macmillan, 1976.

Willis, Michael. *The Islamist Challenge in Algeria: A Political History*. Reading, England: Ithaca Press, 1996.

Wilson, Samuel Graham. *Modern Movements among Muslims*. New York: Fleming H. Revell, 1976.

Wingate, F. R. *Mahdism and the Egyptian Sudan*. 2nd ed. London: Frank Cass, 1968.

Winter, Herbert, and Thomas Bellows. *People and Politics*. New York: John Wiley, 1977.

Winter, Paul A. *Islam: Opposing Viewpoints*. San Diego: Greenhaven Press, 1995.

Wismar, Adolph L. *A Study in Tolerance as Practiced by Muhammad and His Immediate Successors*. New York: Columbia University Press, 1927. Reprinted AMS Press, New York, 1966.

Wolpert, Stanley. *Roots of Confrontation in South Asia: Afghanistan, Pakistan, India and the Superpowers*. Oxford: Oxford University Press, 1982.

Woodward, Peter. *Nasser*. London: Longman's, 1992.

Wormser, Richard. *American Islam: Growing Up Muslim in America*. New York: Walker, 1994.

Wright, Robin. *In the Name of God: The Khomeini Decade*. New York: Simon & Schuster, 1989.

———. *The Last Great Revolution: Turmoil and Transformation*. New York: Knopf, 2000.

———. *Sacred Rage: The Wrath of Militant Islam*. New York: Simon & Schuster, 2001.

Yamani, Ahmad Zaki. *Islamic Law and Contemporary Issues*. Jidda: Saudi Publishing House, 1988.

Yousaf, Mohammad, and Mark Adkin. *The Bear Trap: Afghanistan's Untold Story*. Lahore, Pakistan: Jang Publisher's Press, 1993.

Youssef, Michel. *Revolt against Modernity: Muslim Zealots and the West*. Leiden, The Netherlands: E. G. Brill, 1985.

Zakaria, Rafiq. *The Struggle within Islam: The Conflict between Religion and Politics*. New York: Penguin, 1988.

———. *Muhammad and the Quran*. New York: Penguin, 1991.

Zangeneh, Hamid, ed. *Islam, Iran and World Stability*. New York: St. Martin's Press, 1994.

Zepp, Ira G., Jr. *A Muslim Primer: Beginner's Guide to Islam*. 2nd ed. Fayetteville: University of Arkansas Press, 2000.

Ziadeh, Nicola A. *Sanusiyah: A Study of Revivalist Movement in Islam*. Leiden, The Netherlands: E. G. Brill, 1958.

Ziring, Lawrence. *The Middle East: A Political Dictionary*. Santa Barbara, Calif.: ABC-CLIO, 1992.

Zubaida, Sami. *Islam, the People and the State: Essays on Political Ideas and Movements in the Middle East*. London: I. B. Tauris, 1993.

Zureik, Elias. *The Palestinians in Israel: A Study in Internal Colonialism*. London: Routledge and Kegan Paul, 1978.

Internet Sites

Chapter One: An Overview of Islam

www.arches.uga.edu/~godlas/Islamwomen.html

Site on Islam and women's rights. Articles by scholars and journalists. Links.

www.mwlusa.org/welcome.html

Muslim Women's League. Nonprofit Muslim organization working for women's status as "free, equal, and vital contributors to society." Position papers and essays. Forum.

www.maryams.net

Muslim women and their religion. Biographies of Muslim women, links, information, articles, discussion forums, information on groups concerned with Muslim women's issues.

www.unn.ac.uk/societies/islamic/about/women/

Current issues and opinions with emphasis on the status of women in Islam.

www.harunyahya.com

Site to "promote and publicize the works of Harun Yahya, a prominent Muslim Turkish thinker and author."

www.islamzine.com/women/

Women's rights and position in Islam, articles and papers by scholars, quotations from the *hadith*.

www.muslimobserver.com/

News and information of the Muslim world and events.

www.islam.com

Comprehensive information on Islam. Discussion forums, links to other Islamic sites, on-line store selling Islamic books and tapes.

www.islam.org

Current news and analysis of events related to the Islamic world. Discussion boards, video and audio Streams and Webcasts, business sites, Islamic books and tapes, information, and links.

www.islamonline.net

Current events, discussion boards, health and science news, directories, cyber counsellor, links, and general information.

www.islamicmedia.com

On-line store for Islamic books and tapes for adults and children addressing many topics. Tapes of various Islamic speakers on different topics; *eid* information and celebration materials.

www.jannah.org

Translation of the Qur'an; links to other Muslim groups and personal home pages. Youth page, articles on Islam, resources, forums, statements by prominent scholars.

www.soundvision.com

Islamic tapes and books, newsletter, articles, links, and discussion forums for adults and youth.

www.usc.edu/dept/MSA/quran/The Noble Qur'an

Introduction to and translations of the Qur'an with an introduction to each chapter and explanations.

www.beconvinced.com

Information on Islam, questions and answers, audio and video files; many topics and links.

www.emamreza.net

Site on Islamic history and worldwide organizations.

www.al-shia.com

Site on Islamic history with viewpoints and articles from the Shi'ah Islamic school of thought.

www.islamicinterlink.com/subject/quran.html

Information on and translations of the Qur'an with interpretations and articles.

www.iio.org/

Islamic Information Office of Hawaii. News of events related to Islam, local news, forums.

http://usinfo.state.gov/usa/islam

U.S. Department of State site on Islam.

www.iiu.edu.my

International Islamic University Web site in Malaysia. Goal is to combine Islamic values with modern education.

www.islamicedfoundation.com/

Islamic Foundation of North America. Islamic books, curriculum development, aid for orphans, scholarships.

www.cie.org

> Council on Islamic Education. Nonprofit educational development organization for grades K–12.

www.posttool.com/cisna

> Council of Islamic Schools in North America. Accreditation of Islamic schools. Links and services.

Interfaith   All of these sites promote understanding and peace between people of different faiths.

http://www.interfaith-center.org/ (International Interfaith Centers)

http://www.mdx.ac.uk/www/religion/cifd.htm (Center for Interfaith Dialogue)

http://www.interfaith.org.uk/ (The interfaith network)

http://www.cpwr.org/ (Council for a Parliament of World's Religions)

http://www.uri.org/index.htm (United Religious Initiatives)

http://www.worldfaiths.org/ (World Congress of Faiths)

http://www.multifaithnet.org/ (Multi Faith Net)

http://www.interfaith-metrodc.org/ (Interfaith Conference; Washington DC)

http://www.al-muslim.org/

http://www.ibn.net

http://www.twf.org

http://www.musalman.com

http://www.eurasianet.org/resource/regional/reading.html

http://re-xs.ucsm.ac.uk/cupboard/filing/info/religions/muslim.htm

http://azerilink.homestead.com/islamgeneral.html

http://www.geocities.com/Athens/Olympus/5352/sufism.htm

http://www.ubfellowship.org/archive/readers/601_islam.htm

http://www.wsu.edu:8080/~dee/ISLAM/CONTENTS.HTM

http://www.religioustolerance.org/islam.htm

http://loki.stockton.edu/~gilmorew/consorti/1gnear.htm

http://www.nmhschool.org/tthornton/Middle%20East%20History%20Database/overview_of_islam.htm

http://www.afghan-network.net/Islam/

http://www.al-islam.org/beliefs/spirituality/suffism.html

http://www.digiserve.com/mystic/Muslim/

http://isfahan.anglia.ac.uk/glossary/sufi/sufism1.html

http://www.qss.org/articles/sufism/toc.html

http://www.sufismjournal.org/

http://www.arches.uga.edu/~godlas/Sufism.html
http://www.ias.org/featured.html
http://www.understanding-islam.com/
http://www.nimatullahi.org/us/WIS/WIS1.html
http://www.sufism.org/society/articles/women.html

Comparing Religions

http://www.onereligion.net/
http://jews-for-allah.org/
http://www.islam101.com/religions/christ_islam.html
http://www.islam101.com/religions/
http://www.religioustolerance.org/comp_isl_chr.htm
http://www.usc.edu/dept/MSA/fundamentals/pillars/fasting/tajuddin/fast_72.html
http://www.geocities.com/WestHollywood/Park/6443/Comparison/
http://eawc.evansville.edu/ispage.htm
http://www.geocities.com/Athens/Agora/6526/ICmenu.html
http://www.jamaat.net/deedat.htm
http://dianedew.com/islam.htm
http://www.abcog.org/islam.htm
http://www.islamfortoday.com/akbar01.htm
http://home.wlu.edu/~marksr/Rel105.htm
http://www.thetruereligion.org/islam.htm
http://www.tulane.edu/~MECCA/islam/islam_explained.html
http://www.sultan.org/#women
http://www.teenoutreach.com/beliefs/islam/
http://www.bbc.co.uk/worldservice/africa/features/storyofafrica/6chapter5.html
http://www.mrdowling.com/605westr.html
http://www.analyzeislam.com/women/womeninislamjudaismandchristianity.htm
http://members.aol.com/AlHaqq4u/

Islam and Politics

http://www.witness-pioneer.org/vil/Articles/politics/default.htm

Status of Women in Three Religions

http://answering-islam.org/Women/inislam.html
http://answering-islam.org/Women/place.html

http://www.beconvinced.com/WOMENINDEX.htm

http://www.greatbooks.org/library/religions/islam/women/index.html

http://www.islamzine.com/women/

http://www.islamicity.com/mosque/w_islam/intro.htm

http://www.geocities.com/Athens/Academy/7368/w_comparison_full2.htm#_Toc 335566668

http://sultan.org/articles/women.html

http://www.usc.edu/dept/MSA/humanrelations/womeninislam/

http://www.submission.org/women-comp.html

http://jews-for-allah.org/women-Judaism-and-Islam/

Other

http://www.pbs.org/empires/islam/profilesmuhammed.html

http://www.lexicorient.com/e.o

http://ourworld.compuserve.com/homepages/ABewley/tafsir.html

http://www.al-islam.org/quran/

http://www.iiu.edu.my/deed/quran/in_the_shade_of_quran/index.html

http://aolsearch.aol.com/dirsearch.adp?knf=1&query=hadeeth

http://www.islamic-paths.org

http://www.bayynat.org.lb/

http://www.arabmedia.com/

http://www.aaiusa.org/

http://www.adc.org/

http://www.cair-net.org/

http://www.alhewar.com/

http://www.shia.org

http://www.Karbala.com

http://www.shia.org/Sahifa/index.htm

http://www.ummah.net/ildl/

http://www.wic.org/bio/bbhutto.htm

http://europe.cnn.com/resources/newsmakers/world/asia/bhutto.html

http://www.oneworld.org/owe/news/owns/hz2_en.htm

http://www.asiaweek.com/asiaweek/96/0906/nat5.html

http://www.defencejournal.com/2001/october/hasina.htm

http://www.storyofpakistan.com/person.asp?perid=P024

http://www.ppp.org.pk/biography.html

http://www.benazir-bhutto.net/default.asp

http://www.medea.be/en/index029.htm
http://perso.wanadoo.fr/jeanpierre.gadbois/ministrefemme.htm
http://www.biu.ac.il/SOC/besa/meria/journal/1999/issue1/jv3n1a6.html
http://www.virtualbangladesh.com/biography/khaleda.html
http://www.un.int/bangladesh/gen/pm-bio.htm
http://gos.sbc.edu/w/zia.html
http://csf.colorado.edu/bcas/sample/megawati.htm
http://www.hebatindo.com/infopages/mega_eng.htm
http://www.flakmag.com/opinion/megawati.html
http://www.bglatzer.de/aga/funda.htm

Chapter Two: Islamism and Islamic Revivals

http://www.ummah.org.uk/ikhwan/
http://atheism.about.com/library/islam/blfaq_islam_jamaat1.htm
http://www.jamaat.org/
http://www.jamaat.org/news/pr052001.html
http://www.bglatzer.de/aga/funda.htm
http://www.pbs.org/wgbh/pages/frontline/shows/binladen/who/alqaeda.html
http://web.nps.navy.mil/~library/tgp/qaida.htm
http://www.satp.org/satporgtp/usa/Al_Queda.htm
http://cns.miis.edu/research/wtc01/alqaida.htm
http://www.time.com/time/nation/article/0,8599,182746,00.html
http://www.terrorismfiles.org/organisations/al_qaida.html

Chapter Three: Revolutionary Islamists

http://www.csis.org/features/nyterror_hunter.htm
http://www.cacianalyst.org/
http://www.saag.org/papers4/paper372.html
http://www.heritage.org/library/categories/forpol/bg1060.html
http://www.ict.org.il/articles/articledet.cfm?articleid=397
http://www.etehadchap.com/Islam.html
http://www.msnbc.com/news/639273.asp
http://www.msnbc.com/news/643005.asp
http://atheism.about.com/library/islam/blfaq_islam_wahhab.htm?terms=
Muhammad+ibn+Abdel+al+Wahhab
http://atheism.about.com/library/islam/blfaq_islam_mahdi.htm

http://atheism.about.com/library/islam/blfaq_islam_qutb.htm
http://atheism.about.com/library/islam/blfaq_islam_jamaat1.htm
http://philtar.ucsm.ac.uk/encyclopedia/islam/sufi/sanusi.html
http://africanhistory.about.com/library/glossary/bldef-muslim_brotherhood.htm
http://lexicorient.com/e.o/abdu_l-wahhab.htm

Chapter Four: Traditionalist Islamists

http://www.sunnah.org/articles/Imam_raza_ahmed_khan.htm
http://www.rediff.com/news/1998/jan/21maha.htm
http://www.milligazette.com/Archives/01072001/28.htm
http://www.milligazette.com/Archives/01072001/28.htm
http://www.al-islam.org/beliefs/practices/taqlid.html
http://www.al-shia.com/html/eng/books/taqlid_meaning_and_reality/taqlid-meaning-and-reality.htm
http://www.people.virginia.edu/~aas/article/article5.htm
http://65.193.50.117/index.php?ln=eng&ds=qa&lv=browse&QR=7216&misc=&offset=0&sort=d
http://www.al-islam.org/begin/intro/rahim.html
http://www.hf.uib.no/smi/paj/vikor.html
http://www.ummah.org.uk/khoei/shia/author.htm

Chapter Five: Modernist Islamists

http://www.en.monde-diplomatique.fr/1996/11/women
http://archives.star.arabia.com/991021/JO7.html
http://news.bbc.co.uk/hi/english/events/indonesia/profiles/newsid_351000/351421.stm
http://www.und.ac.za/und/indic/archives/crime/issue11/islam4.htm
http://leguin.haylaz.org/from-emancipation-to-liberation.html
http://www.icna.org/tm/greatmuslim3.htm
http://www2.jaring.my/just/Islamic_State_Farish.htm
http://www.foreignaffairs.org/articles/Ajami1101.html
http://www.en.monde-diplomatique.fr/1999/09/16islam
http://www.washington-report.org/backissues/0993/9309057.htm
http://www.foreignpolicy.com/issue_novdec_2001/takeyh.html
http://www.muslimedia.com/archives/book99/synthesbk.htm
http://www.islam21.net/pages/keyissues/key1-13.htm
http://www.geocities.com/Athens/Cyprus/8613/index.html

http://www.hf.uib.no/smi/paj/vikor.html

http://www.cqpress.com/context/articles/epr_muhammadabduh.html

http://www.encyclopedia.com/articlesnew/32332.html

http://lexicorient.com/m.s/egypt/azhar.htm

http://www.cis-ca.org/voices/a/afghni.htm

Chapter Six: Failure of Muslim Secularists in Postcolonial Muslim States

http://lexicorient.com/cgi-bin/eo-direct.pl?erbakan.htm

Chapter Seven: Islamic Politics in the Arab-Israeli Conflict

http://www.ict.org.il/arab_isr/frame.htm

The ICT (Interdisciplinary Center), Herzliya, Israel, provides information on terrorist organizations, terror attacks, and the Palestinian-Israeli peace process.

http://www.time.com/time/europe/timetrails/israel/

Time Europe magazine's summary of the Arab-Israeli Conflict.

http://www.middleeastbooks.com/html/books/b-arabisraeli.html

AET Book Club provides searches for books on the Arab-Israeli conflict through author's name or book title.

http://www.school.discovery.com/homeworkhelp/worldbook/atozhistory/a/027260.html

Discoveryschool.com's elementary summary of the Arab-Israeli conflict.

http://www.mepc.org/journal/0103_gazitandabington.htm

Middle East Policy Council's Web site providing journal articles and archives of Arab-Iraeli conflict.

http://www.washingtoninstitute.org/pubs/battlsum.htm

The Washington Institute for Near East Policy provides articles, book excerpts, and policy information.

http://www.assr.org/vlibrary/peace

Arab Social Science Research Web site; includes links to international, Arab, and Israeli resources.

http://www.birzeit.edu/links/

Birzeit University; provides Palestinian Web links to business, advocacy, travel, education, research, and many more topics.

http://www.arts.mcgill.ca/MEPP/meppnet.html

Web site providing various links to Palestinian-Israeli resources and issues.

http://www.historyguy.com/arab-israeli_war_links.html

> Collection of many Web links that discuss the Arab-Israeli conflict in various ways.

http://www.wbz-net.org/islinks.htm

> Collection of many Web links that discuss Israeli resources and issues.

Palestine and Israel

http://www.masada2000.org/historical.html

http://www.dean.usma.edu/history/dhistorymaps/Arab-Israel%20Pages/aitoc.htm

http://www.regiments.org/milhist/mideast/israel.htm

http://www.cactus48.com/truth.html

http://www.mideastweb.org/biblio.htm

http://www.globalissues.org/Geopolitics/MiddleEast/Palestine.asp

http://www.incore.ulst.ac.uk/cds/countries/israel.html

http://www.ariga.com/peacewatch/iscyber.htm

http://www.wafa.pna.net/EngText/IndexE.htm

http://www.oneworld.net/specialreports/palestine/

http://members.tripod.co.uk/alquds/kataib.htm

http://www.adl.org/Israel/advocacy/gl_jihad.asp

http://www.military.com/Resources/ResourceFileView?file=HAMAS-Organization.htm

Arab and Israeli Wars

http://www.mfa.gov.il/mfa/go.asp?MFAH00us0

http://www.historyguy.com/arab_israeli_wars.html

http://www.historyguy.com/suez_war_1956.html

http://www.factmonster.com/ce6/history/A0804479.html

http://www.palestinehistory.com/war.htm

http://www.science.co.il/Arab-Israeli-conflict.asp

http://ebooks.whsmithonline.co.uk/htmldata/ency.asp?mainpage=HTTP://EBOOKS.WHSMITHONLINE.CO.UK/ENCYCLOPEDIA/12/M0002912.HTM

Gaza

http://www.palestinehistory.com/gaza.htm

http://www.gazanews.com/

http://www.gaza.net/pages/History/

http://www.wikipedia.com/wiki/Gaza_Strip/History

Hamas

http://www.needham.mec.edu/NPS_Web_docs/High_School/cur/kane97/P1/alcg/ALCGp1.html

http://www.pallinks.com/history/

http://home.talkcity.com/YosemiteDr/mole333/history.html

http://www.cdn-friends-icej.ca/isreport/hamas.html

Hezbollah

http://www.mg.co.za/mg/books/nov97/10nov-hezbollah.html

http://www.military.com/Resources/ResourceFileView?file=Hezbollah-History.htm

http://www.historyguy.com/new_and_recent_conflicts.html

http://www.adl.org/Israel/advocacy/gl_hezbollah.asp

Oslo Accords

http://almashriq.hiof.no/general/300/320/327/oslo.html

http://www.wisdom.weizmann.ac.il/~hand/Oslo.html

http://www.palestinecenter.org/palestine/osloaccords.html

http://www.earlham.edu/~pols/17Fall96/walkejo/homepage.html

http://www.washingtoninstitute.org/media/latimes.htm

http://www.claremont.org/precepts/277.cfm

http://www.us-israel.org/jsource/Peace/treatytoc.html

Wye River Accords

http://www.mideastweb.org/mewye.htm

http://www.jonathanpollard.org/wye.htm

http://www.loga.org/WyeLttr.htm

http://www.twf.org/News/Y1998/19981117-WyeNotPeace.html

http://www.likud.nl/viol.html

http://www.nad-plo.org/eye/moments.html

Arab-Israel Peace Summits

http://english.peopledaily.com.cn/200010/16/eng20001016_52759.html

http://www.csmonitor.com/durable/1997/11/14/intl/intl.3.html

http://www.la.utexas.edu/chenry/aip/archive/debriefing96/0028.html

http://www.washingtoninstitute.org/watch/Peacewatch/peacewatch1997/134.htm

Camp David Peace Treaty

http://www.usembassy-israel.org.il/publish/peace/peace1.htm
http://www.mideastweb.org/history.htm
http://www.usembassy-israel.org.il/publish/peace/peaindex.htm
http://www.us-israel.org/jsource/Peace/egtoc.html
http://www.arabicnews.com/ansub/Daily/Day/990309/1999030908.html
http://www.jewishgates.org/history/modhis/cdavid.stm

Palestinians

http://davenet.userland.com/2001/09/14/palestinians
http://www.ifc.org/camena/wbgaza.htm
http://www.usip.org/pubs/PW/1296/profile.html
http://www.palestine-net.com/
http://www.ptimes.com/
http://www.birzeit.edu/links/
http://www.palestinechronicle.com/
http://www.palestine-info.com/
http://www.arab.net/palestine/palestine_contents.html
http://www.visit-palestine.com/

Chapter Eight: OPEC, OAPEC, and the OIC: Institutionalizing Pan-Islamism

http://www.opec.org
http://www.opec.com
http://www.eia.doe.gov/emeu/cabs/opec.html
http://www.opecnews.com/
http://www.opecfund.org/
http://www.infoplease.com/ce6/history/A0836844.html
http://www.oic-oci.org/
http://www.irna.com/oic/oicabout.htm
http://www.forisb.org/oic.html
http://www.oapecorg.org/
http://www.iet.com/Projects/HPKB/Web-mirror/OAPEC_EST_FCT/est_fct.html
http://www.washington-report.org/backissues/091784/840917004.html
http://www.arab.de/arabinfo/opec.htm
www.sesrtcic.org

Chapter Nine: The Islamic Revolution in Iran

http://memory.loc.gov/frd/cs/irtoc.html

http://www.time.com/time/daily/special/iran/

http://www.islamic-studies.org/Historical%20grounds.htm

http://www.newschool.edu/centers/socres/vol67/issue672.htm

http://www.macalester.edu/courses/russ64/pdf/daneshvarev.pdf

http://www.irvl.net/

http://globetrotter.berkeley.edu/Islam/iranB.html

http://www.bbc.co.uk/persian/revolution/biogs.html

http://news.bbc.co.uk/hi/english/world/middle_east/country_profiles/newsid_790000/790877.stm

http://www.merip.org/mer/mer212/mer212.html

http://www.ifes.org/eguide/country/iran.htm

http://www.washingtoninstitute.org/pubs/menaexec.htm

Chapter Ten: Afghanistan: One Nation, Divisible

http://web.nps.navy.mil/~library/tgp/qaida.htm

U.S. Department of State summary of the terrorist group al-Qaeda.

http://web.nps.navy.mil/~library/tgp/hua.htm

U.S. Department of State summary of the terrorist group Harakat ul-Mujahidin.

http://web.nps.navy.mil/~library/tgp/algama.htm

U.S. Department of State summary of the terrorist group Gama'a al-Islamiyya.

http://cns.miis.edu/research/wtc01/algamaa.htm

Center for Nonproliferation Studies profile of the terrorist group Gama'a al-Islamiyya.

http://web.nps.navy.mil/~library/tgp/asc.htm

U.S. State Department summary of the terrorist group Abu Sayyaf.

http://web.nps.navy.mil/~library/tgp/jihad.htm

U.S. State Department summary of the terrorist group Al-Jihad.

http://www.oic-oci.org/

The Organization of the Islamic Conference (OIC) is an intergovernmental organization grouping fifty-seven states that have decided to pool their resources together, combine their efforts, and speak with one voice to safeguard the interest and ensure the progress and well-being of their peoples and those of other Muslims in the world over.

http://lexicorient.com/cgi-bin/eo-direct.pl?osama_b_laden.htm

Encyclopaedia of the Orient's summary of al-Qaeda leader Osama bin Laden.

http://lexicorient.com/cgi-bin/eo-direct.pl?qaida.htm

Encyclopaedia of the Orient's summary of the terrorist organization al-Qaeda.

http://www.cia.gov/cia/publications/factbook/geos/af.html

Central Intelligence Agency (CIA) summary information on Afghanistan.

http://www.pcpafg.org/Organizations/undp/

United Nation's Development Program P.E.A.C.E., rebuilding Afghanistan's urban centers, promoting food security and sustainable agriculture, and helping disabled Afghans.

http://devdata.worldbank.org/external/dgprofile.asp?RMDK=82662&SMDK= 1&W=0

World Bank's population, environment, economic, technology, and development statistics for Afghanistan.

http://www.lib.berkeley.edu/SSEAL/SouthAsia/afghan_US.html

University of California at Berkeley's collection of Web site links dealing with Afghanistan, the Taliban, Osama bin Laden, Afghan government statements, Afghan opposition groups, and more.

Chapter Eleven: Perceiving Islam: The Causes and Consequences of Islamophobia in the Western Media

http://www.csis.org/europe/frm990412.html

http://www.ing.org/about_us.htm

http://www.brook.edu/views/op-ed/telhami/19991119.htm

http://free.freespeech.org/manushi/98/islam.html

http://usembassy.state.gov/islamabad/wwwh0005.html

http://www.coloradocollege.edu/dept/PS/Finley/PS425/reading/Huntington1.html

http://www.jochen-hippler.de/Aufsatze/Islam__the_Media__Perceptions/ islam__the_media__perceptions.html

http://www.time.com/time/asia/news/column/0,9754,178470,00.html

http://www.canadianislamiccongress.com/media2001/

http://www.runnymedetrust.org/meb/islamophobia/nature.html

http://www.runnymedetrust.org/meb/islamophobia/Religion_and_belief.html

http://www.runnymedetrust.org/meb/islamophobia/Web_bib.html

http://news.bbc.co.uk/hi/english/uk_politics/newsid_1570000/1570106.stm

http://atheism.about.com/library/weekly/aa101701a.htm?PM=n30102501a

http://www.cbsnews.com/now/story/0,1597,314278-412,00.html

http://www.nytimes.com/books/99/04/18/specials/rushdie-verses.html
http://www.nytimes.com/books/99/04/18/specials/rushdie-bombthreats.html
http://www.nytimes.com/books/99/04/18/specials/rushdie-khomeini.html
http://www.nytimes.com/books/99/04/18/specials/rushdie-qualifies.html
http://www.nytimes.com/books/99/04/18/specials/rushdie-cleric.html
http://www.nytimes.com/books/99/04/18/specials/rushdie-mend.html
http://www.nytimes.com/books/99/04/18/specials/rushdie-rally.html
http://news6.thdo.bbc.co.uk/hi/english/world/newsid_56000/56353.stm
http://www.nytimes.com/books/99/04/18/specials/rushdie-visa.html
http://www.nytimes.com/books/99/04/18/specials/rushdie-drops.html
http://www.nytimes.com/books/99/04/18/specials/rushdie-newmoves.html
http://www.hvk.org/
http://www.cpj.org/Briefings/2001/aljazeera_oct01.html
http://www.meib.org/articles/0006_me2.htm

Islamic Politics in Pakistan

http://www.islamabad.net/offsites.htm
http://regional.searchbeat.com/pakistan.htm
http://news.bbc.co.uk/hi/english/world/south_asia/
http://paknews.com/copy_right.html
http://www.europeaninternet.com/pakistan/news/webnews.php3

Kashmir

http://www.kashmir-information.com/index.html
http://www.economywatch.com/stateprofiles/jammuandkashmir/websites.htm
http://paknews.com/kashmir/kashmir.php
http://www.krrc.org/links-Kashmiri%20Websites.htm
http://hammer.prohosting.com/~kanger/link.html
http://asia.cnn.com/2001/WORLD/asiapcf/south/07/04/kashmir.timeline/

Other Sites on Pakistan

http://www.pak.gov.pk/
    Official Web site of Pakistan.
http://www.cia.gov/cia/publications/factbook/geos/pk.html
    CIA summary information of Pakistan.

http://www.un.org.pk/

United Nations in Pakistan provides information on the worldwide community's contribution to developing Pakistan.

http://news.bbc.co.uk/hi/english/world/south_asia/country_profiles/newsid_1157000/1157960.stm

British Broadcasting Company (BBC) profile of Pakistan.

http://www.asianamerican.net/pakistan.html

Asian American Net provides Web links to news sources in Pakistan, societal information, cultural information, government information, financial institutions information, and American media resources that focus on Pakistan and much more.

http://www.pakistanvoice.com/main.htm

News of and about Pakistan.

http://inic.utexas.edu/asnic/countries/pakistan/

University of Texas at Austin provides Web links dealing with various aspects of Pakistan (government, culture, media, and religion).

http://web.nps.navy.mil/~library/tgp/hua.htm

U.S. State Department summary of the terrorist group Harakat ul-Mujahidin.

http://web.nps.navy.mil/~library/tgp/jamat.htm

U.S. State Department summary of the terrorist group Jami'at ul-Fuqra.

http://cns.miis.edu/research/wtc01/algamaa.htm

Center for Nonproliferation Studies profile of the terrorist group Gama'a al-Islamiyya.

Index